PENGUIN BOOK

THE PENGUIN HISTORY
GENERAL EDITOR: DAVID

THE STRUGGLE FOR MASTERY

David Carpenter is a Professor of Medieval History at King's College,
London.

THE PENGUIN HISTORY OF BRITAIN
Published or forthcoming

DAVID CARPENTER

The Struggle for Mastery

BRITAIN 1066–1284

PENGUIN BOOKS

PENGUIN BOOKS

Published by the Penguin Group
Penguin Books Ltd, 80 Strand, London WC2R ORL, England
Penguin Group (USA), Inc., 375 Hudson Street, New York, New York 10014, USA
Penguin Books Australia Ltd, 250 Camberwell Road,
Camberwell, Victoria 3124, Australia
Penguin Books Canada Ltd, 10 Alcorn Avenue, Toronto, Ontario, Canada M4V 3B2
Penguin Books India (P) Ltd, 11 Community Centre,
Panchsheel Park, New Delhi – 110 017, India
Penguin Group (NZ), cnr Airborne and Rosedale Roads, Albany,
Auckland 1310, New Zealand
Penguin Books (South Africa) (Pty) Ltd, 24 Sturdee Avenue,
Rosebank 2196, South Africa

Penguin Books Ltd, Registered Offices: 80 Strand, London WC2R ORL, England

www.penguin.com

First published by Allen Lane 2003
Published in Penguin Books 2004
1

Printed in England by Clays Ltd, St Ives plc

Contents

CONTENTS

List of Maps and Genealogical Tables

MAPS
(pp. xiii–xxi)

GENEALOGICAL TABLES
(pp. 531–40)

A mid-thirteenth-century map of Great Britain by Matthew Paris
(British Library)

Preface

From the Norman Conquest of England to the English Conquest of Wales is the narrative span covered by this book. The one began with Duke William of Normandy's landing in 1066, the other concluded with Edward I's Statute in 1284 which laid down the future government of Wales. At first sight it seems a very Anglo-centric period. The Normans master England and gradually become English. The English then master Wales before proceeding, at the end of the thirteenth century, very nearly to master Scotland as well. But this is only part of the story. After 1066 English monarchs gave far higher priority to their continental lands than they did to the intensification of their overlordship over Britain. This left plenty of space for the ambitions of the kings of Scotland and the Welsh rulers. 'The Struggle for Mastery' in the book's title is the struggle not for a single mastery of Britain but for different masteries within it. The kings of Scotland aspired to bring much of northern England into their realm and for a while managed to do so. In other directions they expanded their power more permanently, thus creating the territorial extent of modern Scotland. The Welsh rulers strove both to recover areas lost to Norman conquerors, and assert dominion over one another. The princes of Gwynedd in the thirteenth century fashioned a principality of Wales in which they subjected all the native rulers to their authority. It was only in the last quarter of the thirteenth century that these separate masteries were swept away and replaced briefly by a single English mastery of Britain.

The book begins with two thematic chapters about the peoples and economies of Britain, the former dealing with questions of national identity. There are also two later thematic chapters, one about society, and the other about the church and religion. Between and around these chapters, the spine of the book is provided by a political and governmental narrative, beginning with chapter 3. Some readers attracted by 'the story' may prefer to begin there. The narrative offered is very much British in its form. Wales and Scotland appear for their own sake, not just when relevant to England. Sometimes their histories are treated in separate chapters, notably chapters 3 and 16, and sometimes integrated within chapters which also deal with the affairs of England. The plan throughout, rather than dividing the book into long separate sections about England, Scotland and Wales, has been to interlink their histories, showing how they were connected and how they moved together. The book also covers the English intervention in Ireland in the 1170s, and the interaction thereafter of English and Irish politics. Within the chapters which also deal with English affairs, asterisks show where sections on Wales, Scotland and Ireland begin. Asterisks are also used to indicate changes of subject matter within sections on England. Readers wishing to pursue separate themes will be able to do so with the help of the index.

British history in this period was the reverse of being self-contained. This book also reflects on how its course was influenced in new and fundamental ways by continental connections and developments, the theme of R. W. Southern's classic essay 'England's first entry into Europe'. England, Scotland and Wales were all, in varying degrees, affected by the papal government of the church, the new international religious orders, the learning of the European Schools, the business of the crusade, and the castles, cavalry and chivalry of the Frankish nobility. Britain was also linked to the continent as never before by the way the ruling dynasty in England down to 1204 also ruled Normandy and after 1154 Anjou and Acquitaine as well. One consequence in England was the development of uniquely powerful institutions of government to keep the peace in the king's absence and raise money to support his continental policies, a system which itself created an equally unique critique of that government, culminating in Magna Carta. If there is a watershed in British history during this period it was also provided by a continental event, the English king's loss of Normandy and Anjou in 1204, which for the first time since 1066 confined him largely to England. As a consequence, he was able to devote far more time than before to the matter of Britain. The eventual conquest of Wales later in the thirteenth century was the result.

The book is based partly on my own reading of the primary sources and partly on the secondary literature. The amount of work produced by historians in recent years has been truly remarkable. It has invigorated the 'old' history of the period, the history of politics and the constitution, law and government, church and state, about which scholars have written since the days of Stubbs and Maitland in the nineteenth century. It has also opened up a series of 'new' histories, examining the theory and practice of queenship, the position of women, the commercialization of the economy, the predicament of the Jews (expelled from England in 1290), the standard of living of the peasantry, the emergence of the gentry, the changing structures of magnate power, the transition 'from memory to written record', the nature of national identity and the relations between England and the rest of Britain. The work of historians underlies what is said on every page. Because my debt is so large, to have recorded it in detail would have made an already long book impossibly longer. In the Bibliography I have, therefore, given a broad indication of the primary sources and then made suggestions for further reading. A full account of the secondary sources will be found under my name on the King's College London History Department's web site: www.kcl.ac.uk/history.

I am most grateful to Richard Huscroft and Janet Nelson for reading and commenting on parts of the book. The whole of it was read in draft by David Bates, Margaret Howell and John Maddicott. Their criticisms and suggestions have been immensely helpful and I am greatly in their debt. Quite apart from reading the book, Margaret Howell has given constant support and wise advice on all kinds of points of detail. I have received help from many academic colleagues who have answered questions, assisted on points of detail, debated matters of controversy, and sent me copies of their works in advance of publication. I would like to thank in particular Jim Bolton, Paul Brand, Dauvit Broun, Michael Clanchy, David Crook, Anne Duggan, Richard Eales, Charles Insley, Rees Davies, John Gillingham, Derek Keene, Paul Latimer, Samantha Letters, Chris Lewis, Phillipp Schofield, Beverley Smith, Keith Stringer, Nicholas Vincent, Anne Williams, Bjørn Weiler, and Patrick Wormald. I have learnt much from my doctoral students at King's College London and have often made use of their work. Over the years I have been lucky in studying the period with a long line of able and industrious undergraduates and they too have contributed a great deal to the book.

David Cannadine, the general editor of the series, encouraged me with his enthusiasm and made important comments on an early draft. At Penguin, the patience, cheerfulness and understanding of Simon Winder, the commissioning editor, have supported me throughout.

I would like to thank the library staff of my own College, King's College London, as well as the staff of the Institute of Historical Research, the University of London Library, the London Library and the Public Record Office. I am grateful to my colleagues in the History Department at King's for shouldering extra burdens while I was on leave in 1995–6 and again in 1999–2000 when my Special Subject was not running.

My greatest debt is to Jane, Katie and James, who have had to live with a husband and father increasingly preoccupied by 'the book'. All three have given staunch support. Without them I might have begun this book but I would never have finished it.

For the paperback edition of the book I have taken the opportunity to correct a number of errors present in the hardback version.

King's College London
January 2003

1. The counties of England

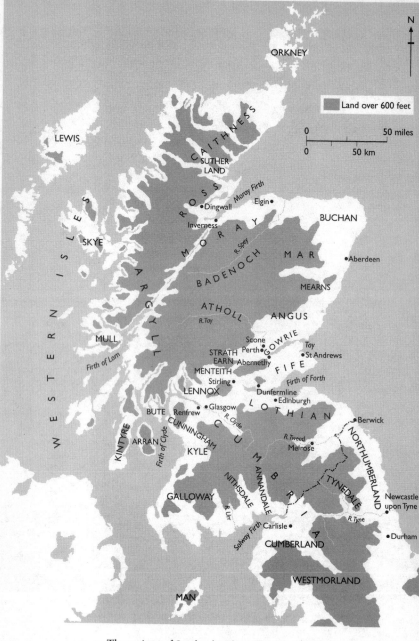

2. The regions of Scotland and northern England

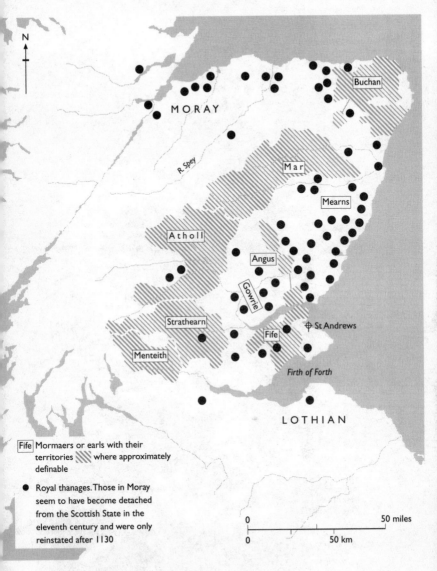

N

Buchan

MORAY

R. Spey

Mar

Mearns

Atholl

Angus

Gowrie

Strathearn

Fife   ⊕ St Andrews

Menteith

Firth of Forth

LOTHIAN

Fife Mormaers or earls with their
      territories ///// where approximately
      definable

● Royal thanages. Those in Moray
   seem to have become detached
   from the Scottish State in the
   eleventh century and were only
   reinstated after 1130

0 _____ 50 miles

0 _____ 50 km

3. The structure of the early Scottish state.
(Based on the map in Alexander Grant's essay in *The Medieval State*,
ed. J. R. Maddicott and D. M. Palliser (Hambledon, 2000), p. 59.)

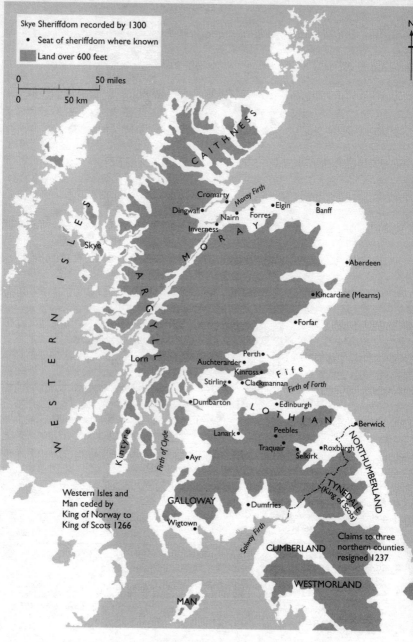

Skye Sheriffdom recorded by 1300
• Seat of sheriffdom where known
     Land over 600 feet

0   50 miles
0   50 km

N

CAITHNESS

WESTERN ISLES

Skye

Cromarty
Dingwall•   •Elgin   •Banff
     Nairn Forres
Inverness

Moray Firth

M O R A Y

A R G Y L L

•Aberdeen

Lorn

•Kincardine (Mearns)

•Forfar

Perth•
Auchterarder•
Kinross•   F i f e
Stirling• •Clackmannan
                 Firth of Forth

•Dumbarton

L O T H I A N
•Edinburgh
                    •Berwick
Lanark•   Peebles•
Firth of Clyde   Traquair• •Roxburgh   NORTHUMBERLAND
                        Selkirk•
Kintyre
•Ayr   TYNEDALE
                             (King of Scots)

Western Isles and
Man ceded by
King of Norway to
King of Scots 1266

GALLOWAY
             •Dumfries
Wigtown•   Claims to three
                                 northern counties
              Solway Firth   resigned 1237
                    CUMBERLAND

                    WESTMORLAND

MAN

4. Royal Scotland: expansion and administrative change

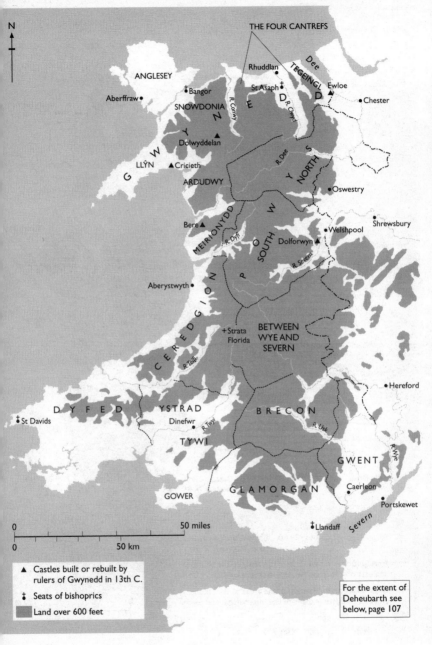

For the extent of Deheubarth see below, page 107

▲ Castles built or rebuilt by rulers of Gwynedd in 13th C.

‡ Seats of bishoprics

Land over 600 feet

5. The regions and political divisions of Wales

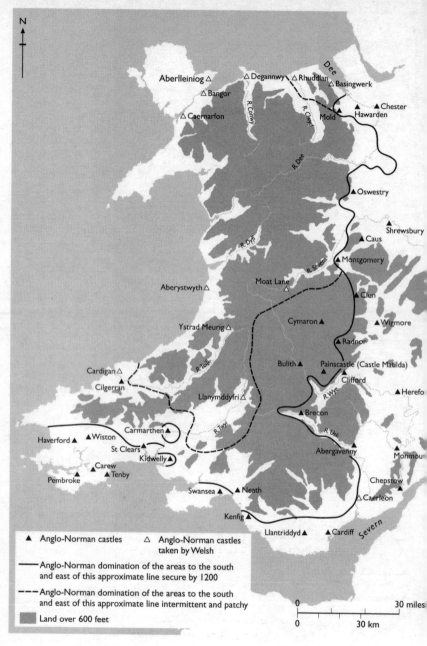

N

Aberlleiniog △   △ Degannwy   △ Rhuddlan
                                        △ Basingwerk
△ Bangor   ▲ Mold Hawarden ▲ Chester
△ Caernarfon

R. Conwy   R. Clwyd   Dee

R. Dee

▲ Oswestry

R. Dyfi   ▲ Shrewsbury
                              ▲ Caus
                    R. Severn   ▲ Montgomery

Aberystwyth △   Moat Lane △   ▲ Clun

Ystrad Meurig △   Cymaron ▲   ▲ Wigmore

                                        ▲ Radnor
Cardigan △   Bulith ▲   Painscastle (Castle Matilda) ▲
Cilgerran ▲   ▲ Clifford
R. Teifi   Llanymddyfri △   R. Wye   ▲ Herefo

Carmarthen ▲   ▲ Brecon
Haverford ▲ ▲ Wiston   R. Twi   R. Usk
St Clears ▲   ▲ Abergavenny
        Kidwelly ▲   Monmou
Carew ▲ ▲ Tenby   Chepstow
Pembroke ▲   △ Caerleon
        Swansea ▲ ▲ Neath
        Kenfig ▲   Severn
        Llantriddyd ▲   ▲ Cardiff

▲ Anglo-Norman castles   △ Anglo-Norman castles
                            taken by Welsh

——— Anglo-Norman domination of the areas to the south
     and east of this approximate line secure by 1200

- - - Anglo-Norman domination of the areas to the south
     and east of this approximate line intermittent and patchy

    Land over 600 feet

0   30 miles
0   30 km

6. Wales by *c.* 1200: the ebb and flow of Anglo-Norman power.
(Based on the map in R. R. Davies, *Conquest, Coexistence and Change: Wales
1063–1415* (Clarendon Press, Oxford; University of Wales Press, 1987), p. 38.)

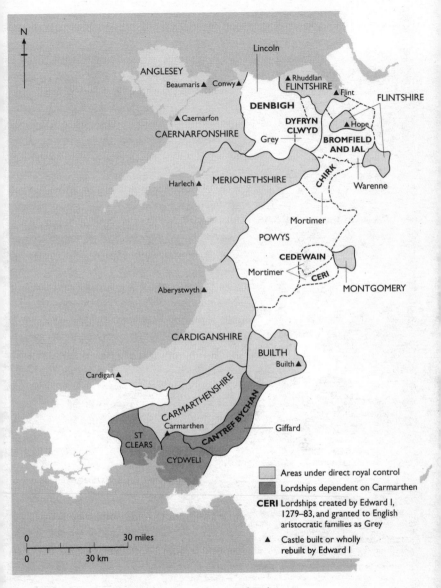

7. The Edwardian settlement of Wales, 1277–95.
(Based on the map in R. R. Davies, op. cit., p. 362.)

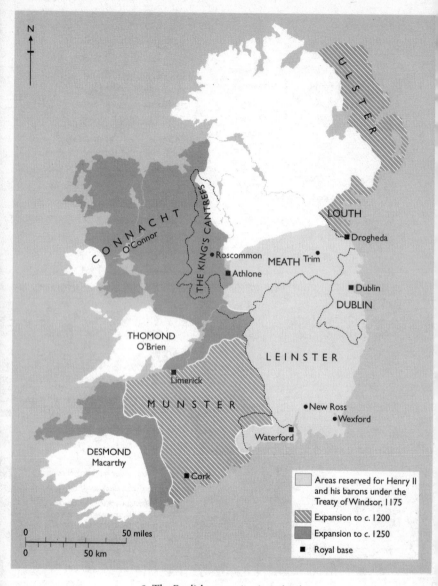

N

CONNACHT
O'Connor

THE KING'S CANTREFS

Roscommon
Athlone

MEATH Trim

ULSTER

LOUTH
Drogheda

Dublin

DUBLIN

THOMOND
O'Brien

Limerick

MUNSTER

LEINSTER

New Ross
Wexford

Waterford

DESMOND
Macarthy

Cork

Areas reserved for Henry II
and his barons under the
Treaty of Windsor, 1175

Expansion to c. 1200

Expansion to c. 1250

■ Royal base

0   50 miles
0   50 km

8. The English expansion in Ireland
(Based on the map in Robin Frame's chapter in *Short Oxford History of the British Isles: The Twelfth and Thirteenth Centuries*, ed. B. F. Harvey (Oxford, 2001), p. 39.)

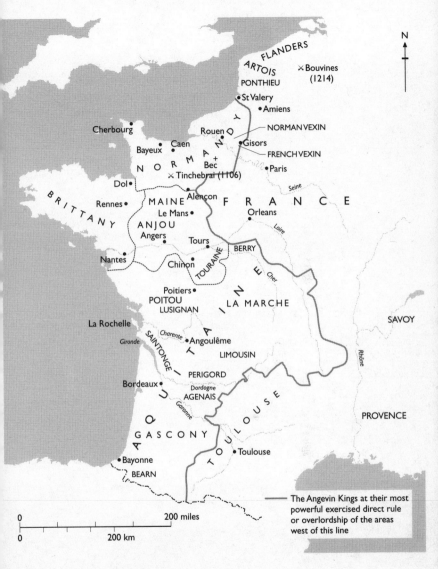

N

FLANDERS
ARTOIS
×Bouvines
(1214)
PONTHIEU
•St Valery
•Amiens
Cherbourg•
Rouen NORMAN VEXIN
•Caen •Gisors
Bayeux N O R M A N D Y FRENCH VEXIN
+Bec •Paris
×Tinchebrai (1106)
Dol• Alençon Seine
Rennes• MAINE F R A N C E
BRITTANY Le Mans• Orleans•
ANJOU Loire
Angers• Tours• BERRY
Nantes• Chinon• TOURAINE Cher
Poitiers• A
POITOU Q LA MARCHE
LUSIGNAN U SAVOY
La Rochelle Charente I
Gironde •Angoulême T
SAINTONGE LIMOUSIN Rhône
A
PERIGORD I
Bordeaux• N
Dordogne AGENAIS PROVENCE
Garonne TOULOUSE
G A S C O N Y
•Bayonne •Toulouse
BEARN

—— The Angevin Kings at their most
powerful exercised direct rule
or overlordship of the areas
west of this line

0   200 miles
0   200 km

9. The continental possessions of the English kings after 1066.

Money, Technical Terms, and Names of People and Places

MONEY

The coinage and divisions of money are explained below, page 40.

TECHNICAL TERMS

Most technical terms (like 'farm' and 'relief') are explained when they first appear; the place can be found through the index.

NAMES OF PEOPLE AND PLACES

In the case of toponymic surnames I have usually given the modern form of the places concerned, with 'of' if the place is in Britain and 'de' if the place is in France. However, I have not allowed this to override conventional usage, so Hubert de Burgh, Waleran of Meulan and William de Mowbray, not Hubert of Burgh, Waleran de Meulan and William de Montbray (Montbray in Normandy).

Following the conventions of the series, I have used anglicized forms of Irish personal names.

In the case of the regions, rivers and places of Wales, I have generally used Welsh forms where they are easily recognizable (so Ceredigion, Tywi, Dinefwr) and English ones where they are very well established (for example Brecon, Usk, Carmarthen). Alternative English and Welsh forms (Brecon, Brycheiniog) are given in the index.

I have used 'the Western Isles' to embrace all the islands off the west coast of Scotland from Arran in the south to Lewis in the north, including both the Inner and Outer Hebrides.

I

The Peoples of Britain

Britain as a geographical entity was a familiar concept to medieval writers. The Venerable Bede had begun his *Ecclesiastical History of the English People* with a detailed description of the island and this, suitably revised, was used by two famous (though very different) twelfth-century historians, Henry of Huntingdon and Geoffrey of Monmouth, to preface their own works. In the thirteenth century, the historian and artist Matthew Paris, a monk of St Albans abbey, drew several maps of Britain, the best of them illustrated at the beginning of this book. Bede's Britain had been populated by *gentes* or *nationes*, two terms, used interchangeably, which can best be translated as 'peoples' or 'nations'. That such groupings were fundamental to political and social organization was accepted without question for thus it had been in the book gigantically more influential than any other, the Bible itself. In 1066 there were three principal peoples in Britain: the English, the Welsh and the Scots.

By far the most numerous of these peoples were the English, the descendants of the Angles and Saxons who had arrived in the fifth and sixth centuries and had gradually established political control over a large part of Britain. Their success had been at the expense of the Britons, the original inhabitants of the island (hence its name), but the Britons survived under their own rulers in the area to the west of the great dike built in the eighth century by King Offa. By the English they were called 'the Welsh' (Latin, *Wallenses*), which meant 'borderers', hence the use of Wales (*Wallia*) for the area they ruled. In the north of Britain there were various peoples, of whom the most important were described in Gaelic as *Albanaig* ('the men of Alba') and in Latin as *Scotti*, hence Scots, and hence also *Scocia* or Scotland. Scotland's extent was much smaller than it is today. Indeed in the twelfth century the term was sometimes used simply for the area between the Forth, the Spey and the central highlands, the core of the realm ruled by the king of Scots. Those in the regions outside that core, as we shall see, even if they acknowledged in some way the king's authority, were not Scots or in Scotland at all.

The peoples of Britain in 1066 were subject to diverse political systems. There was one Welsh people but it was ruled by many kings. There was one king of Scots, but he ruled several peoples. Only the English (apart from those subject to the king of Scots beyond the Tweed) had a single king exclusively their own. All this was soon to change. Between 1066 and the end of the thirteenth century a profound reshaping took place in the identities of the peoples of Britain. The Norman Conquest made England a realm of two peoples, the dominant Norman and the defeated English, yet by the early thirteenth century those two peoples had moulded into one and everyone, whatever their descent, was English. Likewise the various peoples subject to the king of Scots all came to be Scottish, this despite the introduction of a new nobility of Anglo-Norman descent. No comparable remoulding affected the Welsh, for they remained unmixed with any other people, but these years still witnessed important changes in their identity and status.

Peoples or nations, it is often rightly said, are the product of their members' belief that they exist, and in our period the English, the Scots and the Welsh certainly existed in that sense. Of course, divisions of class, career and education can always cut across the horizontal ties that bind a people together. A medieval prelate would doubtless have defined his nationality very differently from a peasant. Some individuals would have been unable or unwilling to define it at all. Likewise ties of region can on occasion seem far more important than those of nation: 'I am of the people of the men of Norfolk and it is proper that I defend my native land,' wrote one twelfth-century monk. Yet horizontal ties of nationality are perfectly capable of existing alongside other loyalties. In this period they worked to give a sense of a shared nationhood to more than simply a small elite. Such ties could include a common history, government and language together with laws and customs; the last three were mentioned by Bernard, bishop of St Davids around 1140, when he affirmed that 'the people' of Wales formed a distinct 'nation'. Faced with external threats, real or imagined, a sense of national identity became a powerful political force in this period amongst the Welsh, the Scots and the English.

*   *   *

There was certainly a strong and pervasive sense of national identity amongst the English before 1066. 'It was hateful to almost all of them to fight against men of their own people, for there was little else that was worth anything apart from Englishmen on either side,' wrote the Anglo-Saxon chronicler about the near civil war of 1052. He was speaking at the very least for churchmen, the high aristocracy and also the 5,000 or so thegns, the country gentry who formed the backbone of English local society. The idea of a single English people, 'Angelcynn', had a long history. It had been popularized by Bede's *Ecclesiastical History of the English People* and strengthened by a single language and a vernacular literature. It had been inculcated by King Alfred and his successors both to defend England from Danish attack and unify the country under their rule. And it had then been solidified by the structures of royal government: a single coinage, a common oath of allegiance to the king, the 'king of the English', and units of local administration, the shires, which embraced the length and breadth of the country.

This identity was shattered by the Norman Conquest. The English bishops, abbots, aristocracy and a large proportion of the county thegns were swept away, leaving the English simply as monks, peasants, minor gentry and townsmen. Into the key positions came Normans and others from across the Channel bringing their own language and customs. The division of the peoples in England was now proclaimed in the king's writs and charters which were addressed to his subjects both 'French and English'.

The process by which the division cleaved by the Conquest was healed and the inhabitants of England became once more universally English has been much debated by historians. One view is that it was largely complete by 1150; another, perhaps more correct, that it embraced the whole of the twelfth century. The process required both the Normans to see themselves as English and those of Anglo-Saxon descent to accept them as such. For the latter, the wounds of the Conquest remained open well into the twelfth century. In the 1120s, the great historian William of Malmesbury, a monk of Malmesbury abbey and a product of a mixed marriage, could still write that 'England is become the residence of foreigners and the property of strangers'. That the native population at this time retained its own identity is shown by the circle of townsmen, minor gentry and hermits, men of old English stock and proud of it, who surrounded the English holy woman, Christina of Markyate. Language remained a divisive factor. Sometime after 1125 Brictric, the priest at Haselbury in Somerset, complained of having to remain silent before the bishop and archdeacon because he knew no French. Reactions to the trauma of the Conquest took various forms. English monks in the two generations after 1066 sought both to explain the events in terms of punishment for sin, yet also, in the very brevity of their accounts, to avoid the painful memory altogether. Another reaction was defiance. Sometime in the twelfth century a monk of Ely wrote a *Life* of the resistance hero Hereward the Wake, a *Life* which defended the English from allegations of inferiority both by denigrating the Normans and extolling Hereward's martial expertise and chivalrous conduct. The *Life*, however, ended with Hereward's reconciliation with King William. The implication was that the English should not rebel but find an honoured place in the new state. There are, indeed, indications that English attitudes were softening. Between 1125 and 1132 another great historian of mixed parentage, Archdeacon Henry of Huntingdon, wrote of the Normans in much the same tone as William of Malmesbury. Yet later when he came to narrate the defeat of the Scots at the battle of the Standard in 1138, he seems to have regarded the victors, whom he calls 'the barons of England, the most famous Normans', as also in some way English. By the 1160s Ailred, the great Cistercian abbot of Rievaulx, a man entirely of old English stock, could declare that the two nations had now been joined together to form once again a single English people. The lead here, so Ailred thought, had been taken by the dynasty itself thanks to Henry I's marriage in 1100 to a descendant of the old English kings, the daughter of King Malcolm and Queen Margaret of Scotland.

Up to a point this was probably wishful thinking. Whether the great barons in the 1160s regarded themselves as wholeheartedly English may be doubted. But Ailred's remarks none the less do reflect important changes. Powerful forces were moving those of Norman descent in the direction of an English identity, beginning with the smaller landholders and ending with great barons and the royal house.

The Conquest had placed perhaps 8,000 Normans throughout the shires of England. Some had single properties of small size. Others had one or several substantial manors and formed the cream of a new country gentry. However, very few, even of the latter (as a study of twelfth-century Warwickshire and Leicestershire has shown), had any land in Normandy. The lives of such men were largely confined to

England, and to an England where they were in daily contact with 'Anglo-Saxons', not merely as lords of peasants, but as colleagues of Anglo-Saxon freemen and minor gentry with whom they worked running the hundred and the shire, the basic units of local government. This was the environment *The Dialogue of the Exchequer* (a book about the running of that office) was thinking about when it declared in 1178 that 'nowadays, when English and Normans live together and marry and give in marriage to each other, the nations are so mixed that it can scarcely be decided (I mean in the case of freemen) who is of English birth and who Norman'.

The way Normans at this level became English reflected contemporary views about the shaping of nationality. One key element here, as the *Dialogue* implied, was 'blood' or descent. Thus William of Malmesbury declared that he drew his blood from both the Norman and the English people (*gens*). Intermarriage therefore had indeed the power to mix up the races, making the offspring, in terms of blood, partly English and partly Norman. That was not the same as making them wholly English of course, but other ideas about identity helped the move in that direction. Blood or descent could be superseded by place of activity, upbringing and birth. Very soon after the Conquest, anyone whose working base was England might call themselves English. Even Lanfranc, whom William the Conqueror made archbishop of Canterbury, styled himself in one of his letters a 'new Englishman' and later referred to 'we English', although by birth he was a Lombard. Closely related to this were ideas about upbringing. In the 1150s, the *Book of Ely* (a chronicle/cartulary produced at Ely abbey) defined a thoroughgoing Norman as one of Norman parentage (that is blood) and also of 'education' in Normandy. The implication was that a person of Norman blood but English 'education' would lose something of his *Normanitas*, would in effect become partly English. Another related factor was place of birth. That too could affect nationality, so much so that an Englishman was defined in 1258 as someone 'born of the kingdom of England'. Hence also the constant demand in the thirteenth century for the king's councillors to be *naturales* – men 'native born'. This Englishness acquired by place of birth, upbringing, and work, if maintained from one generation to the next, could become Englishness by blood or descent. Gerald of Wales (1146–1223), churchman, scholar, royal clerk and prolific writer, described himself as 'by original line' three-quarters English and Norman and a quarter Welsh. The

Englishness here could only have come from the anglicization of his forebears in the way described, for they had no Anglo-Saxon blood in their veins.

Clearly, therefore, place of birth, education and activity combined with intermarriage were all making Norman families based in England English. Of course, it was one thing to be simply labelled 'English', another to feel English in a positive, wholehearted way. That too, however, was happening in the first half of the twelfth century, particularly through a growing interest in England's history. A knowledge of the Anglo-Saxon past had been kept alive after the Conquest in the great monasteries, in part to help maintain their ancient rights. In the twelfth century both William of Malmesbury's *History of the English Kings* and Henry of Huntingdon's *History of the English* were widely circulated amongst religious houses, thus making their Norman-descended heads and patrons familiar with England's story. This was the background to Gaimar's remarkable *History of the English*, written around 1140, and intended specifically for a secular audience of Norman descent, hence its French verse form. It told the story of England from the Anglo-Saxon invasions through to the reign of William Rufus, celebrating the deeds of the English kings. Here then was encouragement to adopt the English past as one's own; hence the crusading knight, Richard de Argentan, commissioned a painting of the martyrdom of King Edmund for a chapel in Damietta, an episode of which Gaimar gave a gripping and lurid description. Gaimar also extolled the exploits of Hereward the Wake. Thus if Hereward, in the *Life* written at Ely, was used to give the English back their self-respect, here in Gaimar he made the English respectable to the Normans. Closely associated with an enthusiasm for history was an attachment to England's 'native soil', to the 'churches, cities, castles, rivers, meadows, woods and fields which are appraised most highly amongst the delights of all realms', as Matthew Paris put it. Thus several copies of Gaimar's *History* concluded with a Topography (written in the 1150s) giving a detailed description of England's roads, counties and bishoprics. From the late eleventh century, lords of Norman descent had themselves been adding to England's 'delights', increasingly preferring to found or endow monasteries in England rather than enrich houses on the continent, a clear sign of shifting loyalties.

The move towards an English identity was strong but it was more sluggish in the higher levels of society than lower down the social scale. Among the baronage there was much less intermarriage and thus Norman descent was not obscured in the way mentioned by the *Dialogue*. There were also much stronger connections with Normandy. Although diminishing during the twelfth century, the number of nobles with lands in both the kingdom and the duchy remained significant (see below, p. 269). Such men probably crossed back and forth over the Channel, like their king. Some were born in the duchy with all the consequences which followed for their sense of identity. As late as the 1220s, the Englishness of William II, earl of Pembroke, was thought by himself and others to have been diluted by his birth on the family estates in Normandy. Twelfth-century noblewomen did not hurry across the Channel so that their children could play for England! The barons of England formed a small but immensely influential group who were naturally aped and courted. Even those who no longer had lands in the duchy had powerful incentives to keep alive their own *Normanitas* and pause before identifying entirely with England. After all, they served a king who down to 1204 spent at least half his time on the continent and certainly did not regard himself as English: 'You English are too timid,' remarked Richard I. The baronage were also well aware of the contrasting fortunes of the Norman and English peoples. The former had been gloriously successful. Before the battle of the Standard in 1138, Henry of Huntingdon imagined the army being encouraged by reminders of how the Norman people (*gens*) had conquered in France, England, Italy and the Holy Land. Likewise in the 1150s Richard de Lucy, Henry II's chief minister, a man largely based in England, could still (when it suited him) talk of the glorious exploits of 'we Normans' in conquering England. The English, by contrast, for all Hereward's exploits, were a defeated people, punished by the Conquest for their sins, and, according to some hostile caricatures, reduced to peasants. Far from marking a new start, Henry I's English marriage was thus ridiculed in some Norman quarters. The one point on identity even the sober *Dialogue of the Exchequer* had been sure about was that unfree peasants were English. Indeed, the regular imposition of the *murdrum* fine on local communities kept alive the equation 'English' equals 'unfree peasant' until the end of the thirteenth century (see below, pp. 102, 413). The lampoon of Gerald of Wales, in an anti-English mood in the 1200s, thus hit home: 'The English are the most worthless of all peoples under heaven, for they have been subdued by the Normans and reduced by the law to perpetual slavery.'

Not surprisingly, therefore, a hesitation over adopting English identity is still powerfully reflected in Jordan Fantosme's account of the victory over the Scots in 1174, written very much for the baronial elite. While the victory was no longer portrayed as a Norman triumph as in 1138, no effort was made to celebrate it as an English one either. Indeed, the only Englishman to appear *eo nomine* was one of Anglo-Saxon descent, Cospatric son of Horm, old and grey-haired, who rather tamely surrendered Appleby to the Scots. Members of the baronial elite were perfectly able to take an interest in England without necessarily acknowledging that they were English. Thus the Topography added to Gaimar's *History* in the 1150s specifically referred to 'we French'. Uncertainty about identity is also reflected in labels applied by contemporary historians. While most spoke of the English conquering Ireland in the 1170s, the dean of St Paul's, Ralph of Diss, could still write of a famous victory over the Welsh as late as 1198 as a victory of the French. Perhaps increasingly in the twelfth century members of the baronial elite, in so far as they thought of the matter, regarded themselves as having a kind of dual nationality. They were Norman and proud of it in terms of their ultimate descent, but English in varying degrees, depending on whether they still had estates in Normandy, in terms of place of birth and activity. Some writers made brave efforts to describe the resulting mix. As early as 1130 a Norman monk of Lewes wrote of the 'Norman-English' (*Normanangli*). Henry of Huntingdon himself, while he thought of the 1138 army as in some ways English, also described it as made up of 'the people (*gens*) of the Normans and the English'. In another formulation he called its leaders 'the barons of England, the most famous Normans', probably there getting closest to how they thought of themselves. The term 'Anglo-Norman' often used by modern historians does perhaps best describe England's baronial elite in the twelfth century.

The final loss of Normandy in 1204 was thus of great importance. 'The barons of England' lost their lands across the Channel. Henceforth they would be born, brought up and based exclusively in England. So would the king. Families might still retain memories of their Norman ancestry, but the logic of embracing an entirely English identity was now overwhelming. Fittingly King John (1199–1216) was the first king to drop altogether the 'French and English' form of address in his documents. His subjects were now all English.

Underlying these changes was another important phenomenon which gradually strengthened the development of an English identity in the twelfth and thirteenth centuries. This was the revival of the English language. Linguistic divisions were still important in separating English from Normans after 1125, as we have seen. Indeed they were still socially divisive in the thirteenth century. The great bulk of the population, the peasantry of Anglo-Saxon descent, spoke only English. French on the other hand remained, as the knight Walter of Bibbesworth put it around 1250, the language 'that any gentleman should know', being used both for polite conversation and for politics and business. Yet the use of English was gradually moving upwards, ultimately creating a bilingual gentry and nobility. For those of Norman descent living and working in close proximity to the English, speaking the language must have been as necessary as it was natural. The knightly lord of Clopton in Northamptonshire, William de Grauntcourt, according to a family history written in the thirteenth century, 'was called William of Clopton by inferiors, since it was easier to have an English name in their own language rather than a Norman one'. The family's consequent replacement of 'Grauntcourt' with 'Clopton' may well reflect a change in the everyday language it spoke. English was certainly spoken in the household of one Suffolk knight in the 1190s for it was in English, indeed in the local Suffolk dialect, that a spirit (according to one story) made known its presence. By the mid thirteenth century there seems little doubt that even the highest aristocracy could speak English. Henry III's brother, Richard, earl of Cornwall, certainly did so. So indeed did Edward I.

There is also evidence that French was losing ground as a naturally acquired mother tongue and was having to be formally taught (in the same way as Latin). Walter of Bibbesworth's comment quoted above came in a treatise he wrote to help Denise de Montchensy teach her children French. Yet Denise was the wife of a great magnate of Norman descent. The fact that the history of England written by Robert of Gloucester around 1300 was in English verse suggests that this was the most natural spoken language of high knightly families like that of Bassingbourn which formed part of the audience. This was the future. Of the many copies made after 1300 of the history of England called The Brut (after Brutus, Britain's eponymous founder) there are 30 in French and Latin and 168 in English. Since much of the Brut was based on Gaimar, it was in the English language that the latter's English history became best known, a powerful combination. By 1300 there was a growing sense that English unified the people in a way French, for all its status, did not. 'These gentlemen use French, but every English person knows English' ran lines in the poem *Arthour and Merlin*. In 1295 Edward I, galvanizing the nation for war, proclaimed that the French wished to destroy the English tongue. Here the English language was being used as synonymous with the English people in a way that would have been impossible even a hundred years before.

Under Edward's leadership in 1295 king and nation stood at one in resisting a foreign threat, just as they had under Alfred. Kingship after 1066 had indeed continued to play a vital part in shaping national identity. Yet it did so in a new way. A sense of community and identity was now not merely shaped by and for the king, as it was in both Scotland and Capetian France. It was also shaped in opposition to him. The twelfth-century kings continued, in Anglo-Saxon mode, to give the nation a real and positive sense of unity under the crown, notably by the formation of the common law. The title they adopted was unambiguous: 'king of the English'. Yet while royal government gave with one hand, it took away with the other, imposing huge financial burdens on the nation in an effort to sustain its continental possessions. The extraordinary power and sophistication of central government in England became matched by an equally remarkable and unique critique of that government from below. Opposition to royal exactions dated back to before 1066, but it was now voiced on an entirely new scale, and out of common grievances came a new national solidarity, this time formed in opposition to the crown. In 1215 everyone was to take an oath to support the enforcement of Magna Carta, thus forming 'the community of the land', a community formed for no other purpose than to take action against the king. In 1258 likewise 'the community of England' swore to support the revolution of that year which reduced the king to a cipher. In all this there was one further factor which did more than anything else to string and solidify through society a sense of universal Englishness. This was the growing belief that the English were a people under threat, under threat from the foreigners introduced into the country by the king himself. In the early thirteenth century all the king's subjects were once again English. But the kings continued to employ officials and give patronage to ministers and favourites who came from overseas, thus offering their native subjects not merely oppression, but oppression at the hands of foreigners. The very survival of the English people was in danger, or so it was proclaimed. More than anything else it was this threat, reaching a climax in the 1260s, which bound the English together, appealing to churchmen, peasants, knights and barons alike. Gilbert de Clare, earl of Gloucester's demand in 1265 that office be confined to Englishmen would have seemed ludicrous to his kinsmen 150 years earlier, lords of Orbec and Bienfaite in Normandy, and not English themselves. It was only with Edward I (1272–1307) that king and kingdom were once more at one.

* * *

Just as English national identity was refashioned in this period so was that of the Scots. In the first half of the twelfth century the racial mix within the king of Scotland's realm had become even more complex. This was thanks to the way King David (1124–53) had introduced a new 'French' nobility, as it was called, into his kingdom, one of Norman or Anglo-Norman descent. There was also, as we have mentioned, a sense in which the Scots themselves were simply the inhabitants of the core of the kingdom between the Forth, the Spey and the central highlands. Thus David could refer in a charter to 'the worthy men of Moray and Scotland', clearly seeing a distinction between the two. Likewise a topographical survey as late as 1200 mentioned 'the mountains which divide Scotland from Argyll'. Place names in Argyll like 'the hill of Scot' suggest that it was not as Scots that the indigenous inhabitants saw themselves. The same was true of the men of the largely Norse province of Caithness in the far north, of the 'Galwegians' or men of Galloway, the 'English' in Lothian (the area between the Tweed and the Forth), and the 'Cumbrians', who inhabited the old British kingdom of Cumbria running south from the Clyde to the southern edge of the Lake District. Galwegians, Cumbrians, English and French, as well as Scots, were all sometimes addressed by name in David's charters. By the end of the thirteenth century, all this had changed. The people in the king's realm were described as Scots and Scotland was the whole area acknowledging the king's authority, broadly the area of modern Scotland.

Exiguous evidence makes this process hard to chart. As late as 1216, the chronicle of Melrose abbey (situated in the heart of Lothian) viewed the Scots as barbaric aliens, 'devils rather than soldiers'. The attitude was much the same in 1235 – certain Scots, 'knaves rather than knights', being accused of pillaging the churches of Galloway. Yet in the section of the chronicle covering the years 1265–6 (transcribed between 1285 and 1291 though perhaps composed earlier) the attitude is different. Guy de Balliol, who died fighting for Simon de Montfort at Evesham, clearly a man of Norman descent, was now described as a 'valiant Scottish knight'. Likewise the achievements of the abbot, Reginald of Roxburgh in Lothian, were said to be unequalled by other 'children of the Scots'. Clearly by this time it was as Scots that the men of Lothian thought of themselves. This was in line with the universal Scottishness asserted by the Guardians of the realm after King Alexander III's death in 1286. The seal made for the government of the kingdom bore on one side the legend 'the seal of Scotland appointed for the government of the kingdom' and on the other 'St Andrew be the leader and compatriot of the Scots'. The assertions of the Guardians show that those of Anglo-Norman descent among the political elite now regarded themselves unequivocally as Scots. How well those assertions played in Caithness, Sutherland, Argyll, and Galloway is less clear, but probably there too a sense of Scottishness was becoming preponderant. A declaration in 1284 about the royal succession was agreed by the earls of Sutherland and Orkney, as well as three rulers from Argyll and the Isles. All were described (with many others) as 'barons of the realm of Scotland'. Later in 1320, the most famous of all statements of the independence of the Scots, the Declaration of Arbroath, was made in the name, amongst others, of the earl of Sutherland and the earl of Caithness and Orkney, as well as 'the freeholders and the whole community of the realm of Scotland'.

How then had the meaning of the 'Scots' and 'Scotland' become all embracing in this way? It had nothing to do with a common language. While the king's court probably spoke French, the use of English was steadily advancing in the lowland towns at the expense of Gaelic, spreading from Perth in a narrow coastal strip up the east coast and round towards Banff and Elgin. That, of course, merely accentuated the differences with the Gaelic-speaking highlanders, a division made much of by the chronicler Fordun, writing in the fourteenth century. The introduction of the Anglo-Normans had also been divisive. One of the best early thirteenth-century English chronicles (which survives in a copy made at Barnwell abbey in Cambridge) commented that the 'modern' kings of Scotland appeared as 'French in race, manners, language and culture'. They only maintained Frenchmen (meaning Anglo-Normans) in their entourages, and had reduced the Scots to servitude. All this, however, was only part of the story. Members of the native Scottish nobility were themselves becoming 'Frenchified', thus making their race far more joinable. (For further discussion see below, pp. 330–31, 424.) At the same time the Anglo-Normans, in important ways, accepted aspects of Scottish 'culture'. It was not simply one-way traffic, giving but not receiving. One aspect of this was the cult of St Andrew. It was Andrew, the brother of St Peter, who, it was believed, had converted the Scots to Christianity. The cult was vigorously developed by the bishop of St Andrews, the self-styled 'bishop of the Scots', with a success seen both in the Guardians' seal and the Declaration of Arbroath which told how Christ wished Andrew 'to protect [the Scots] as their patron for ever'. Accounts of Scottish origins, moreover, by 'Frenchified' Scots probably close to the ruling elite suggest that the latter not merely saw itself as Scots, but Scots in a way congenial to the native population. The accounts showed an acceptance of the Scottish people's Celtic roots, stressing that Ireland was its divinely ordained homeland, having been settled by the Scots, descendants of Gaythelos, a Greek prince, and his wife Scota before they had arrived in Albion, as Britain was then called. The stone on which the Scottish kings were inaugurated at Scone had come from Ireland's royal site of Tara.

According to the Declaration of Arbroath, if Robert Bruce was not prepared to continue the fight for independence (which of course he was), 'we would make king some other man who was able to defend us'. The implication was that the Scottish people had an existence separate from its kings. Yet the reality was different. It was above all the kings who had refashioned the people in the years after 1100. They had introduced the Anglo-Normans and had asserted (in varying degrees) royal authority in Moray, Sutherland, Caithness, Argyll, Galloway, Man and the Western Isles, thereby expanding the effective boundaries of the kingdom and with it of Scotland itself. The title the kings bore from the early twelfth century onwards, modelled on that of the English kings, was emphatically 'king of the Scots'. The indication that all the king's subjects were Scots became unambiguous once William the Lion (1165–1214) addressed his charters simply to 'all his upstanding men of all his land', abandoning altogether the occasional 'to all his men . . . French, English, Scots and Galwegians'. It was likewise King Malcolm about 1161 who used for the first time the expression 'the kingdom of Scotland' in a context which shows that Scotland included Lothian as well as the land north of the Forth. The impact of this royal rhetoric can be seen in increasing numbers of private charters from the 1170s onwards, covering transactions in Lothian, Galloway, and elsewhere, which speak of 'the kingdom of Scotland' or 'the kingdom of the Scots'. Scotland had grown as the kingdom had grown and the Scots were simply all those who were subject to the authority of the king. The king's role in refashioning national identity was thus significantly different from that in England. Whereas the English were bonded, in part at least, by their opposition to the crown, the Scots, enjoying a monarchy far less intrusive and exacting, were bonded at its behest and in its support.

*   *   *

In Wales there was no integration of peoples as there had been in England and Scotland. The Welsh absorbed no one. The Normans arrived in Wales as conquerors, yet they never became integrated within the existing Welsh kingdoms, becoming Welsh in the process. Instead they carved out their own polities, subjecting the native Welsh in the areas they conquered and leaving them under their own rulers in the areas they did not. The crucial difference here lay in the political constitution of the host nation. Both in England and Scotland the newcomers were installed within a single polity and soon felt part of it. That was impossible in Wales, where a whole series of disparate political units constantly changed shape through warfare and family settlement. With no large political unit to subdue and in which they could ultimately be assimilated, the Normans conquered piecemeal and set up their own political units in the form of the marcher baronies. (Much the same happened in Ireland.) The Normans quickly married into Welsh noble families, but the descendants of such unions (like Gerald of Wales) felt at most ambivalent about their nationality. By descent they might be partly Welsh, but brought up in the marcher baronies and with many contacts with the wider Anglo-Norman realm, this Welshness by descent could never be completed by Welshness through 'education'. The upbringing and active life of such men, as Gerald of Wales observed in his own case, remained very much with the English.

*   *   *

Significant changes had therefore taken place in the make-up of the peoples of Britain, or at least of the English and the Scots, in the two centuries after the Norman Conquest. At the same time, partly as a result, there had been equally significant shifts in English attitudes, or the attitudes of writers in England, towards the Welsh, the Scots and also to the Irish. In the twelfth century such writers had begun for the first time to express contempt for the other peoples of the British Isles, regarding them as barbarians and justifying conquests (notably in Ireland) in the light of a civilizing mission. As John Gillingham has put it, this period seems to witness 'the beginnings of English imperialism'. Such attitudes first appear with William of Malmesbury in the 1120s – the Welsh, 'all that barbarianage'; they are later found in the *Gesta Stephani* ('The Deeds of Stephen'), written in the 1150s, where the Welsh are described as a 'barbarous people' of 'untamed savagery'. Likewise towards the end of the century William of Newburgh thought the Scots were 'a barbarous nation', while Gerald of Wales described the Irish as 'so barbarous, they cannot be said to have any culture'. Ralph of Diss thus saw Henry II's invasion of Ireland in 1171 as very much a civilizing mission, bringing law and order to a people hitherto untamed by 'public power'.

At the root of these attitudes were major contrasts between the economy and society of England and those of the rest of Britain (discussed in the next chapter). Gerald of Wales described the frugal diet of the Welsh, based more on meat than bread, and the skimpy clothes worn even by the rulers. Walter Espec (in a speech put into his mouth by Ailred of Rievaulx) ridiculed 'the worthless Scot with half bare buttocks'. King John in Ireland in 1210 laughed at the badly dressed kings riding without saddles on poor horses. These contrasts had existed before 1066 but they were accentuated by the Norman Conquest and rendered far more noticeable. Thus English ecclesiastics, now brought within the mainstream of continental reform, looked increasingly askance at the divorce and concubinage common in Wales, and in Ireland where it was alleged men exchanged wives like horses. And likewise there was an increasing contrast in the area of political conduct. After the Conquest, again in line with continental practice, political murders, executions and mutilations had virtually ceased in England. In Wales, on the other hand, disputes over succession continued to lead to 'the most frightful disturbances . . . people being murdered, brothers killing each other, and even putting each other's eyes out', as Gerald of Wales described it. It was the same in Ireland where one reason why the Irish submitted to Henry II's 'peace', according to Ralph of Diss, was because they lamented the way their fathers had so often been killed by mutual slaughter. Warfare in England came to resemble that on the continent, where the aim was to capture and ransom rather than kill a noble opponent. Celtic customs were very different. As Gerald of Wales observed: 'The French ransom soldiers; the Irish and Welsh butcher them and decapitate them.' Even more fundamental, the Welsh and the Scots took slaves. This was why the Scottish invasion of 1138 was such a profound shock for it revealed the appalling face of war as slave hunt. As one Hexham chronicle put it:

Old men and women were either beheaded with swords or stuck with spears like pigs destined for the table . . . Young men and women, all who seemed fit for work, were bound and driven away into slavery. When some of the girls dropped to the ground exhausted by the pace of the slave-drivers, they were left to die where they fell.

Not surprisingly the invasion of 1138 seems to have been crucial in establishing the reputation of the Scots and Galwegians as barbarians.

*   *   *

Racial stereotypes are often obstinately difficult to shift and it is natural to think those appearing in the twelfth century would be no exception. Henceforth the view of the Scots and the Welsh as barbarians would be entrenched, a development of fundamental importance for the future of Britain. Yet in fact nothing like that happened. One of the most significant features of British history in the thirteenth century is the way such hostile opinions were replaced by others far more positive.

There was, in fact, nothing very deep rooted about the new critique of the Celtic peoples. Resulting from perceived differences between England and the rest of Britain, it was perfectly capable of moderating in the light of new information. Indeed some of the accusations of barbarism were qualified almost as soon as they appeared. Thus Ailred wrote that thanks to the policies of David, king of Scots, 'the whole barbarity of that nation was softened'. The *Gesta Stephani* noted how Richard fitz Gilbert de Clare had brought such peace and prosperity to his part of Wales that 'it might very easily have been thought a second England'. Most striking of all were the changing opinions of Henry II's clerk, the historian Roger of Howden. When he described the invasions of England in 1173–4, he seems to have agreed with William of Newburgh's view that the Scots were 'bloodthirsty barbarians'. But later, when his diplomatic work for Henry II gave him a closer knowledge of Scottish affairs, he began to sympathize with the demands of the Scottish church and kingdom for independence. Of imperialistic attitudes to the Scots (or the Welsh) there is no trace.

By the mid thirteenth century a more sympathetic approach to the Welsh and the Scots was much in evidence. Matthew Paris in his *Chronica Majora* wrote a voluminous history of the years 1235 to 1259 (in a modern printed edition it takes up 1,700 pages). He inherited from his predecessor at St Albans, Roger of Wendover, an intense hostility to continental aliens introduced by the king into England. Had he likewise imbibed twelfth-century attitudes to the Scots and the Welsh, it would certainly be apparent. Yet there is little sign that this was the case. In 1244 King Alexander of Scotland mustered a large army to invade England, yet for Paris this awoke no memories of the brutal invasions of the twelfth century, which had done so much to turn the English against the Scots. The army was led by Alexander, 'good, just, pious, bountiful, and loved by everyone, both the English and his own subjects'. The large numbers of foot soldiers (put at between 60,000 to 100,000), far from being a bare-buttocked, bloodthirsty rabble, were 'all unanimously confessed and consoled by preachers, fearing not to die since they were about to fight justly for their country'. Three years later Paris reported that no one could understand why the pope wished to send a legate to Scotland 'since the Catholic faith flourished there uncontaminated and the peace of clergy and people was absolutely firm'. It could only have been, he concluded, because of greed for the wealth of 'the Scots'. Far from supporting Henry III's intervention in Scottish affairs in the 1250s, Paris reported how the 'indigenous and native born men' were indignant at the way aliens (that is English) were promoted over them. The expulsion of the latter thus meant 'the magnates of Scotland could control the reins of the kingdom more freely and safely'.

When it came to Wales, Paris commended the famous native scholar Thomas Wallensis for returning home as bishop of St Davids, observing that such love for one's native land was absolutely natural. When the Welsh rose against English rule in the 1250s, his attitude was the same as to events in Scotland.

Their cause seemed just, even to their enemies. And this especially comforted them that they fought constantly in the fashion of the Trojans from whom they were descended for their ancient laws and liberties. O miserable English, crushed by aliens and with their ancient liberties extinguished, draw a lesson from the example of the Welsh.

Here then it is the Welsh who are to educate the English. The last thing Paris wrote about the Welsh just before his death in 1259 was to lament the king's rejection of terms which would have allowed them to live 'in peace, tranquillity and liberty'.

Paris, therefore, had no feeling that England should exert a hegemony over the rest of Britain. On the contrary, he believed that the Welsh and the Scots should enjoy peace and independence free from English interference. In taking these views, he was not out on a limb. For the Tewkesbury chronicler in the 1250s Llywelyn ap Gruffudd, the future prince of Wales, was fighting vigorously to preserve his 'paternal liberties'. The Dunstable annalist thought the revolt had been provoked by the attempt to subject the Welsh to English law. Despite the propaganda of Edward I, several chroniclers took a remarkably measured view of his eventual conquest of Wales in the 1270s and 1280s. Thus the Dunstable annalist gave a full list of the grievances which had provoked the Welsh 'to stand together for their laws'.

Up to a point Paris's own views were shaped by his political agenda. The Welsh and the Scots were standing against an English king whom he regarded as both oppressive and incompetent, just as the English needed to do. It was when it suited this critique that the Welsh became momentarily 'the dregs of mankind' – the king could not defeat even these unworthy enemies. But there was more to it than that for Paris's positive attitudes were also founded on good information about Wales and Scotland. St Albans had a daughter house in the north at Tyne-mouth, and its prior was active in Anglo-Scottish affairs, supplying Paris with several important documents. Paris knew Wales well through Richard, bishop of Bangor who, as a result of a series of local quarrels, resided at St Albans between 1248 and 1256. Essentially what had transformed the English attitude to the Scots and the Welsh was that the twelfth-century view of them as barbarians no longer seemed to correspond with reality.

This was partly the result of developments in economic and ecclesiastical organization which will be discussed in chapters 2 and 14. Also important was the transformation in the identity of the Scottish people. In 1150 the Scots were only one of several peoples within King David's realm. English historians were well aware of the fact. When they spoke about the atrocities of 1138 they were clear that the blame lay with the Scots, that is Gaelic speakers from north of the Forth, and with the even more bloodthirsty Galwegians. They did not blame King David himself, who was a perfect Anglo-Norman gentleman, nor his Anglo-Norman followers, who were as civilized as anyone on the other side. A hundred or so years later the descendants of those Anglo-Normans were themselves being called Scots. Where the latter in 1138 were bare-buttocked highlanders, in 1265 they included the knight Guy de Balliol who died a hero's death at Evesham. It was ridiculous to call *him* a barbarian. The same was true of members of the native nobility, who had become as 'French' (to use the term of the Barnwell annalist) as their Anglo-Norman colleagues. Under pressure of the Edwardian wars, the old lampoons reappeared. One ballad on the battle of Dunbar in 1298 described the Scots as a 'barbarous, brutal and foolish people'. But this was manifestly to attack one group of Scotsmen, not the people as a whole, a point made clear by the ballad's further description of the Scots as 'a kilted rabble'. That was not how the Scottish nobility appeared in battle. Indeed, in 1244 Matthew Paris commented favourably on the quality of the thousand-strong Scottish cavalry.

In the event, the Scottish army of 1244 never went into action, a fact which points to the wider context which permitted the development of favourable views of the Scots, namely the long period of unbroken Anglo-Scottish peace between 1217 and 1296. This gave plenty of time for the atrocities of 1138 and (on a smaller scale) 1173–4 to be forgotten. The invasion of 1216 by comparison was a tame affair, reflecting the fact that the Scots had long since given up war as slave hunt. Paris's view of the Scottish foot soldiers in the army of 1244, as we have seen, was not as a kilted bloodthirsty rabble. Apart from being properly confessed, they were 'ready for action and effectively equipped with axes, lances and bows'.

*   *   *

The Welsh, unlike the Scots, did not rise in the world through absorbing a new Anglo-Norman nobility. Indeed, Gerald of Wales alleged that by accepting the very designations 'the Welsh' and 'Wales' in the twelfth century, the Britons (as they previously called themselves) had actually been diminished since they had adopted the labels given them by the English. This, however, did the Welsh less than justice. 'Wales' and 'the Welsh', *Wallia* and *Wallenses* were respectively English and Latin words. They were not taken into the Welsh language itself. In their own tongue the Welsh replaced 'Britons' (*Brytanyeit*) with a word of their own, *Cymry*, one which evoked both the community of their people (it meant 'compatriots') and its long history, for it had been used as a word of self-description since the seventh century.

It was indeed through the discovery, or more exactly the invention of their history, that the Welsh went up in the world in this period, in the process becoming far less easy targets of condescension and abuse. This was thanks to one of the most famous books ever written, namely Geoffrey of Monmouth's *History of the Kings of Britain*, which came out a little before 1139. Geoffrey was a Welshman and one of his purposes was to give respectability to his race, faced with the growing perception that they were barbarians. Henry of Huntingdon had argued that it was a knowledge of history which distinguished rational men from brutes, and Geoffrey's fertile imagination, with little more to go on than what could be gleaned from Bede and vague tales about Arthur, supplied the Welsh with a glorious one. He told how Brutus, grandson of the Trojan Aeneas, had conquered the island of Albion and named it Britain after himself. He and his successors had founded towns, made laws and were manifestly highly civilized. Their line had culminated in Arthur, greatest of all warrior kings, who had driven out the Saxons, conquered the Scots, Picts and Irish, subdued Gaul and defeated the Romans. Ultimately, of course, 'the power of the Britons came to an end . . . and the Angles began to reign', yet Arthur had gone to the isle of Avalon to be cured of his wounds, and Merlin had promised that one day the Britons would rule again.

Of course, it was perfectly possible to enjoy Geoffrey's enthralling tale without imbibing its Welsh message. Ultimately the English adopted Arthur for themselves. Yet the message did go home, inspiring the Welsh and impressing those in England. 'Openly they [the Welsh] go about saying that in the end they will have it all. By means of Arthur, they will get [Britain] back,' declared the author of the description of England at the end of Gaimar's *History*. The Welsh revival in the second half of the twelfth century seemed directly related to a new sense of origin. As Gerald of Wales put it, 'Our British people, now known by the false name Welsh, is, like the Romans, sprung from Trojan blood, and defending its freedom against both Saxons and Normans, has shaken the yoke of slavery from its back.' Likewise in the mid thirteenth century Matthew Paris included references to Brutus and Merlin in his map of Wales, and spoke, as we have seen, of the Welsh fighting for their freedom 'in the manner of the Trojans from whom they were descended'.

Attitudes were also changed by an increasing accommodation between the peoples in Wales, one comparable to that taking place in Scotland, although in this case it did not lead to any merger. The Norman barons admired the 'innate nobility' of the Welsh rulers, and married their daughters, sometimes giving Welsh names to both male and female offspring. Gerald of Wales himself was descended from the marriage between Nest, daughter of Rhys ap Tewdwr, and Gerald of Windsor, Henry I's castellan of Pembroke. The Norman barons had also been less bothered than clerical commentators by the charges of barbarism, and indeed had briefly indulged in taking slaves themselves. They also imbibed more positive aspects of Welsh culture, notably the devotion to St David and other native saints. 'St David' indeed was one of their battle-cries as they conquered Ireland. The native rulers, for their part, quickly adopted castles, armour and cavalry. In 1257 Matthew Paris was highly impressed by the Welsh cavalry, the riders in two large contingents being 'finely armed', and the horses themselves protected with metal. Thus the English and the Welsh had more and more in common. In 1188, during a pleasant day in Hereford culminating in a stroll round the bishop's garden, the Lord Rhys, the ruler of Deheubarth, and members of the great baronial house of Clare paid compliments to the 'high birth' of each other's families, amidst much good-natured banter. The banter itself implied that war might at any time break out again, but that did not alter – indeed it enhanced – the respect in which the two groups held each other, which was also why occasional atrocities seemed so shocking and like a breach of trust.

Welsh warfare itself was coming into line with best 'modern' practice. A letter from the king's camp at Deganwy in 1245 makes no complaints about its barbarism. On the contrary, it criticized the English for plundering the Cistercian abbey of Aberconwy, and felt the Welsh were thus quite justified in killing the culprits. Even so the Welsh, in correct chivalric manner, while dispatching the ordinary soldiers had taken the knights alive, intending to imprison them (doubtless for ransom), only changing their minds when some of their own nobles were killed by the English. Welsh politics too had become less violent, largely through contact with the English. The prince of Wales, Llywelyn ap Gruffudd, imprisoned rather than killed or mutilated his brothers, dangerous rivals though they were. In the end, by a telling irony, the youngest, Dafydd, having caused trouble for over twenty years, was finally executed by Edward I. (For further discussion see below, pp. 428–9.)

When the chronicler Thomas Wykes, writing after the Edwardian Conquest, described the Welsh as a 'savage people' who lived on meat and milk and did not eat bread, his remarks might have applied to the lower classes, but hardly to the rulers for whom wheat was grown and bread baked daily (as Gerald of Wales's own remarks suggest). English writers when describing Welsh nobles, far from making suggestions of savagery, praised them in much the same terms as they did members of their own elite. Thus one of the Welsh nobles killed in the fighting of 1245 was described in the letter quoted above as 'a young man most elegant and *strenuus*', the last a word hard to translate but with connotations of both martial strength and chivalric behaviour. According to Matthew Paris, Gruffudd of Bromfield (a ruler of northern Powys) was Welsh by nation, *gens* and language, and also 'noble, *strenuus* and powerful'. Likewise Llywelyn ap Gruffudd, prince of Wales, for the Dunstable annalist was 'a most handsome man and *strenuus* in war'. Llywelyn was acknowledged by the English to bear a coat of arms, indeed one which was a modified version of the royal arms of England, this the result of his grandfather's marriage to King John's illegitimate daughter.

The positive light in which the English nobility regarded their Welsh counterparts also emerges in the late thirteenth-century 'Legend of Fulk fitz Waryn', a work of fact, fiction and romance which narrates the exploits of the Shropshire knight Fulk fitz Waryn and his ancestors. Here a Welsh ruler might appear sporting a coat of arms, fighting valiantly with his retinue alongside a baronial ally, spending time as a youth at the king of England's court, marrying a royal or baronial wife, and even having contacts with the king of France. These men all passed as members of the same chivalric society.

*　　*　　*

There was another factor which served to moderate English attitudes to the Welsh and the Scots. While the latter had risen in the world, the 'barons of England, the most famous Normans' (as Henry of Huntingdon had called them), had in a way gone down in it – gone down, that is, by becoming English. Around 1280 the Earl Warenne, according to one story, recalled how his ancestors had conquered the land with Duke William, and produced a rusty sword to prove it. But there was no escaping the fact, as we have seen, that Warenne too was now a member of the very people his ancestors had reduced to servitude, however glorious its previous history. The problem of how to view the Conquest is evident in the ambivalent accounts offered both by Matthew Paris and subsequent historians. Should one celebrate William's victory, or sympathize with the oppressed English? The barons of England in the thirteenth century could no longer have the same unalloyed confidence in their pedigree as 'the most famous Normans' of a hundred years before. It was correspondingly less easy to view the other peoples of Britain with contempt.

This view had also been moderated by changes in the barbarian league table. For William of Malmesbury, in the early twelfth century France was the home of civilization. A hundred years later it was also the home of less attractive things. For during the invasion of Louis, eldest son of the king of France, in 1216 appalling atrocities were perpetrated by his followers, 'barbarous aliens' as the Waverley annalist called them. 'The routiers and other wicked plunderers from the kingdom of France set villages alight, did not spare churches or cemeteries, took and despoiled all kinds of men, and by harsh and hitherto unheard-of bodily tortures, compelled them to pay the heaviest ransoms,' wrote Roger of Wendover. This 'great tyranny' was long remembered. Matthew Paris's standard of barbarism was not that set by the Scots or the Welsh but by Louis's Frenchmen: 'even Louis never brought such sordid and violent followers to England as [the king's son, the future Edward I] nourished in his household,' he remarked.

From the political standpoint, these changing ideas in England about the other peoples of Britain point to a conclusion of cardinal importance. The ground for the eventual conquest of Wales and attack on Scotland at the end of the thirteenth century was not laid by long-standing and intensifying English hostility to the Welsh and the Scots. Quite the reverse. The harsh and pejorative opinions of the Welsh and Scots expressed by the English in the twelfth century had largely vanished a hundred years later, changing with changing reality. The English attitude to the Irish, on the other hand, remained unchanged precisely because the Irish rulers seemed much as they had been in the twelfth century, killing opponents and not improving their marital practices. The sketch of Ireland offered to the historian Froissart in the 1390s by one of Richard II's esquires (who had spent time there in captivity) was still of a land without towns, ransoms, stirrups, proper armour and decent saddles. Its kings knew nothing of courtly behaviour, and had to have a crash course in English ways before they could be knighted by Richard II.

There was also no sense in which the emergence of these new identities had rung down nationalistic blinds, making the peoples of Britain more separate as they became more similar. Instead there were numerous contacts which crossed both race and border. The number of Welshmen called *Sais*, a Welsh designation meaning Englishman, multiplied in the thirteenth century even in areas subject to native rulers, which reflected extensive contact with the English, often including marriage to an Englishwoman. At the highest level the number of mixed marriages increased. If these never prevented conflict, their tendency was certainly to sedate it. In 1262 the marcher baron, James of Audley, was asked by the king to ensure the loyalty of Gruffudd of Bromfield, Gruffudd being his brother-in-law. Llywelyn the Great himself described the English baron Ralph Mortimer, who had married his daughter Gwladus, as 'his dearest son', while Roger Mortimer, fruit of the union, both made an alliance with his cousin, Llywelyn ap Gruffudd, the Prince of Wales, and included his coat of arms in a heraldic roll which he commissioned. Meanwhile in the north of Britain there was a substantial cross-border nobility, constantly replenished by marriage, which held lands both in England and Scotland (see below, p. 425). Such men probably thought of themselves as Anglo-Scottish, much as the cross-Channel elite of the twelfth century were Anglo-Norman.

Nor did the reshaping of national identities in the two centuries after the Conquest sever Britain from the rest of Europe, however intense and significant English hostility to foreigners was at times in the thirteenth century. In origin the aristocratic culture, which came in varying degrees to embrace the whole of Britain, was very much that exported from France – France in the wide sense of the French royal lands and the surrounding principalities. Hence in a most telling passage the Barnwell annalist said that in culture the king of Scotland and his nobles were French. He did not say they were English, although it was directly from England that the culture came. The two fundamentals of aristocratic life, the castle and the cavalry knight, had both been brought from France by the Normans, as they had brought chivalric modes of warfare and politics. France in the twelfth century was the home of troubadours and tournaments, and it was in tournaments across France, not in Britain, that William Marshal, the future earl of Pembroke and regent of England, made his name in the 1170s and 1180s as 'the greatest knight in the world'. The loss of Normandy in 1204 made the barons of England finally English but did not confine them to Britain. Richard de Clare, earl of Gloucester, and the heir to the throne, the future Edward I, both frequented the European tournament circuit in the 1250s and 1260s. Earlier a Scottish noble, Duncan, earl of Dunbar, had died in 1248 on the crusade of Louis IX, the king of France who was later canonized. The foreign friends and relatives whom Henry III established in England in the mid thirteenth century kept alive something of the internationalism of the old Anglo-Norman baronage. Thus Meath in Ireland and Ludlow in Wales eventually passed through marriage to Geoffrey de Joinville, lord of Vaucouleurs in Champagne, and younger brother of Jean de Joinville, who had also crusaded with Louis and had later written a life of the Saint. Geoffrey was summoned to the armies of the king of France, crusaded with the future Edward I of England and ended his days in the house of Dominican friars at Trim in Ireland.

Matthew Paris's map of Britain itself had a wider context for it was almost certainly drawn from Britain as it appeared on a map of the world, rather like the *Mappa Mundi* preserved in Hereford cathedral, which has Jerusalem at its centre. In the Hereford map Britain is placed on the world's outer rim, yet it still appears large and impressive. It was in many ways a wealthy island, as the next chapter will show.

2

The Economies of Britain

Between 1066 and 1284 the economies of Britain were transformed. The population at least doubled. A large acreage of new land was brought under the plough. The commercial sector also expanded with the money supply spiralling, and a new infrastructure of towns, markets and fairs growing up. These changes embraced Wales and Scotland as well as England, serving to reduce the contrasts between the different parts of Britain. In the triforium of Westminster Abbey the sculptured head of a craftsman, smiling, assured, naturalistic, humane, seems to sum up this expansionary, self-confident age. Yet below in the chapel of St Faith is another head, with pinched cheeks and sunken eyes, its mouth open as though crying out in pain. This was also an age when a large proportion of the peasant population lived at the level of bare subsistence. In years of bad harvest there was starvation. According to one view the situation was getting worse as the rising population began to outrun the ability of the land to support it. For many peasants there was no 'merrie England'.

The English economy dominated the rest of Britain. England covers 57 per cent of Britain's land mass as against Scotland's 34 per cent and Wales's 8 per cent. England was also mile for mile much richer, a reflection of the far higher proportion of good fertile land as opposed to upland pasture, moor and mountain. Whereas roughly 13 per cent of England's land mass stands at over 600 feet, the respective figures for Wales and Scotland are 42 per cent and 48 per cent. In the assessment of ecclesiastical wealth made for a papal tax in 1291–2, the only figures covering the whole of Britain for this period, the average valuation per square mile in England was £4.04, in Scotland £1.34 and in Wales £0.90. The grand total for Scotland was just short of a fifth of England's; that of Wales was only a twenty-eighth. The English economy was not only the largest. It is possible to know much more about it. Domesday Book, the Hundred Roll survey of 1279, numerous private charters, and a growing body of manorial accounts from the thirteenth century provide sources uniquely rich, if frustratingly patchy.

The picture Domesday Book gives of England in 1086 is of a society overwhelmingly rural. It records some 270,000 heads of rural households, nearly all of them peasants, that is broadly people who lived by working on the land. Against that there were between five and ten thousand lords and some 25,000 heads of urban households, the latter an estimate by historians because Domesday Book gives uneven information about the town population. Domesday placed much of the rural population in units of lordly exploitation which it called manors, although these varied in size and structure. In a broad swathe across the midlands and the south (excluding Kent) large numbers were what historians call 'classical', that is to say they were coterminous with a single 'nucleated' village. Indeed the twelfth-century chronicler Orderic Vitalis wrote that in common speech the words 'manor' and 'village' were interchangeable. Thus at Willingham in Cambridgeshire the bishop of Ely's manor consisted of the whole village and its surrounding arable and meadow lands, embracing in all some 900 acres. Much of the land the bishop had kept in his own hands as his home-farm or demesne. The rest of the arable with a share in the common meadows was held by his peasants: twelve villeins, and eight cottagers. Later evidence (Domesday itself never gives the size of peasant holdings or the terms on which they were held) shows that the villeins each held half a 'yardland' (around fifteen acres). The cottagers probably had under five acres. Both groups had to supply two days' labour a week on the bishop's demesne and further work at harvest time. In 1086, taking all of Domesday England, villeins made up 41 per cent of peasant tenants, most probably holding either a whole yardland or a half, while cottagers accounted for another 32 per cent. The obligation to provide labour was probably heavy and widespread, but peasants could also pay rents both in money and kind. At Willingham there was only one slave but some manors had many more, so that they made up roughly 10 per cent of the rural population. There was one other key feature of the manorial system, namely that both the lord's demesne and the land of each individual peasant was distributed in equal proportions between either two or three great open fields which lay around the village. At Willingham there were three fields and in 1251 the lord had roughly a hundred acres in each. The lands of each peasant were probably divided evenly between the three fields in the same way. This was the normal pattern. As a consequence everyone had to follow the same agricultural regime, accepting, for example, that one field each year should lie fallow (the usual practice), hence such manors were said to have 'common fields', and hence the need for a manorial court to organize the running of the manor.

There were manors of the Willingham type throughout England, although as inheritances were divided and the population increased it was quite usual for there to be more than one manor in a village. In Kent, East Anglia, Lincolnshire and Yorkshire, however, a rather different form of structure was common. This was one composed of a lordly centre, often a nucleated village, linked to a series of outlying hamlets whose peasants gave renders in kind and money to the centre, rather than extensive labour services, the renders often being more important in the lord's income than the direct produce from any central demesne. Such peasants were often called 'sokemen', the subordinate hamlets being part of the 'soke' or jurisdiction of the centre. Attached to the five carucates of land (about 600 acres) at William de Warenne's great base at Conisbrough in Yorkshire were a further eighty-six carucates held by sokemen in twenty-eight subordinate hamlets. In Domesday Book sokemen and other freemen made up roughly 14 per cent of England's peasant population.

In this society there were therefore gaping disparities in wealth. Even a lord of a single manor had far more wealth and power than a villein, let alone a cottager. And great lords had many manors: Willingham was one of fifty held by the bishop of Ely across six counties. His estates in Domesday Book were valued at an annual £484 – 318 pennies a day, when one penny a day was the wage (when he could find work) of a twelfth-century labourer.

Taken as a whole the Scottish and Welsh economies were very different from the English. This was largely the result of the much higher proportion of high ground which made pastoral farming far more important than arable. As a sixteenth-century writer remarked, Scotland was always 'more gevin to store of bestiall than ony production of cornys'. Gerald of Wales in the 1190s made the same point about Wales: 'the greater part of the land is laid down to pasturage; little is cultivated'. Another consequence of this largely pastoral economy was that settlements were often small and scattered. According to Gerald, the Welsh lived a solitary life in huts on the edge of woods rather than communally in villages. He would probably have said much the same about the Scots.

This contrast between England and the rest of Britain should not, however, be overdrawn. Even at the start of our period there was probably extensive corn production, if mostly of oats (more suitable than wheat for poorish land) both in the coastal lowlands of Wales and in the lowlands of eastern Scotland south and north of Forth. Gerald of Wales himself described Welsh ploughing, which was of a peculiar nature. The driver of the oxen walked in front but facing backwards, so that he often fell and was run over. Although there is little sign of manorial structures, a point to which we will return, there was certainly the equivalent both in Wales and Scotland of the soke-type estates found in parts of England. In Wales, historians are increasingly detecting nucleated villages which apparently pre-date the Norman Conquest. In Dyfed, these had the strips of the peasant bondmen arranged round them in radial fashion. In Gwynedd considerable progress has been made in tracing the sites of *llys* and *maerdref* complexes. *Llys* means 'court', that is the residential and judicial centre of the local ruler. The *maerdref* was the associated village in which the peasant bondman lived. These Welsh villages were not subject to fully formed manorial institutions; the strips of the peasant bondmen, whether scattered or radial, seem to have been run individually, rather than as part of some common field system. Since, however, the bondmen gave renders in kind and also had to labour on the land of the lord, the two systems were not that dissimilar.

If there were features in common between the English rural economy and that of Scotland and Wales, that was much less so when it came to towns, commerce and coinage, at least if the comparison is with England south of York. North of that city, apart perhaps from a market and urban beginnings at Durham, there were no towns in 1066 either in England or Scotland. There is scant evidence of English money circulating north of the border; in any case, York was the northernmost English mint. The Scottish kings did not mint coins before 1136. A contemporary *Life* of Queen Margaret of Scotland, who died in 1093, tells how she encouraged merchants to come to Scotland by land and sea with precious wares, hitherto unknown, which hardly suggests a high level of pre-existing commerce. As late as the 1140s King David, Margaret's son, expressed doubts as to whether ships were likely to arrive at Perth 'for the sake of trade'. In Wales there were no towns before the Normans and little evidence of money. The economy depended on barter and plunder, with a trade (to Ireland) in one of the most valuable items of that plunder: slaves. Plundered slaves were also important in Scotland, hence the appalling impact of the Scottish invasion of the north in 1138. (See above, p. 16.)

In England things were very different. 'And one coinage is to be current throughout all the king's dominion, and no man is to refuse it,' thundered King Edgar (959–75). The assertion of a royal monopoly over the coinage, and the minting of plentiful and high-quality silver coins to sustain it, was one of the greatest achievements of the Anglo-Saxon kings. In the last years before the Conquest, a quarter of the coinage was minted in London. All the coins bore the king's head on one side, and all the dies for striking this image were manufactured in London before being distributed to the regional mints. Of the latter there were between sixty and seventy, making it possible for the king in a single simultaneous exercise to replace one type of coin by another throughout the country, a practice to which surviving coin hoards bear testimony.

Most of these mints were situated in what the Domesday clerks called boroughs: all told they gave the name (or that of city) to some 112 places in England while listing thirty-nine more as having markets. The clerks were not using 'borough' in any technical sense. They simply meant a place where a significant number of the inhabitants lived from non-agricultural pursuits, that is from trade and manufacture. It is equally clear, however, that these boroughs differed from the country-side legally and administratively. There was already burgage tenure, which meant that townsmen held their property in return for money rents and enjoyed freedom to alienate it. Boroughs had their own courts (mentioned in Anglo-Saxon law codes) and could owe the king an annual 'farm' (that is a payment) separate from that of the rest of the county. Domesday provides no surveys for London and Winchester, and its information is incomplete elsewhere. One can only offer a guess at the total number of townspeople in 1086 – one already mentioned is 25,000 heads of households, which would make with their families an urban population of, say, 120,000. Around thirty places perhaps had populations of between 1,000 and 5,000 inhabitants, with only York, Lincoln, Norwich, Winchester and London exceeding that figure. London's population may have been around 25,000. It was already divided into wards, each under an alderman.

Most of the small towns were involved in local trade, which will be discussed in more detail later, but trade was also international. Around the year 1000 merchants from Normandy, Ponthieu, Flanders and the Rhineland were active in London. Of these the Flemings were already the most important, shipping England's chief export, wool, to Flanders for its burgeoning cloth industry. Tin was also exported, while imports included wine, cloth and spices. Some part of the trade at least was in English hands. According to one legal tract, the rights of a merchant were enhanced if he crossed the sea three times (and some are known to have reached Pavia). In 1066 England with its currency, cornfields, sheep and towns was a wealthy country; indeed it was a wealth about which William the Conqueror's chaplain, William of Poitiers, waxed lyrical. Hence the Norman Conquest, and what a good investment that proved to be. Over the next 250 years England's resources increased several times over. Just when the expansion began is hard to discover, but it certainly predated the Conquest. Norwich, it has been estimated, covered fifty acres in 900 and 200 in 1066. It is much easier to describe the features of the expansion, which embraced much of western Europe, than it is to detect its underlying causes, though these included the opening up of new European supplies of silver, the absence of plague and, more tentatively, a slightly warmer climate than that prevalent before 900.

At the heart of the expansion in England lay a rise in population, although this is the subject of much debate. Domesday Book, as we have seen, recorded some 270,000 heads of rural households, but what, to arrive at a total number, should be the multiplier for their families – 3.5 or, as most historians now seem to think, between 4.5 and 5? And how accurate are estimates of the urban population and how many people have to be added in for unnamed under-tenants, bailiffs, monks, priests, household retainers and castle garrisons, as well as for the people of Northumberland of which there was no survey? Depending on the answers to these questions the population can be put as low as 1.1 million and as high as 2.5 million. Recent considerations of the subject have arrived at a population of around 2 million, a figure which currently commands fairly wide acceptance.

In the 200 years after 1086 the evidence for a significant rise in the population is abundant. Willingham's tenants in 1086 (including the slave) numbered 23. A survey of the manor in 1251 put the number at 79, a 3.4 times increase. At Martham in east Norfolk there were 74 tenants in 1086, 107 around the middle of the twelfth century and 376 in 1292, a fivefold increase. At Taunton (here getting away simply from tenants) the adult male population rose from 612 to 1,448 between the years 1209 and 1311. Expansion was not universal, however, for it depended very much on local conditions, to which we will return. Between 1086 and 1279 the population of six villages in the Warwickshire hundred of Stoneleigh rose by a factor of 3.6 and eight new settlements appeared. But in the adjoining hundred of Kineton the population hardly rose at all. Unfortunately the Hundred Roll survey from which the 1279 figures come survives (sometimes in fragmentary form) for only six counties, namely Warwickshire, Oxfordshire, Bedfordshire, Buckinghamshire, Cambridgeshire and Huntingdonshire. Arriving at overall figures for the population increase is therefore a highly speculative exercise. One approach has been to work back from the 1,386,196 males and females over fourteen revealed by the poll tax of 1377. Allowing for evasion, paupers and children, this could, on one estimate, convert into a population of 2.5 to 3 million. Allowing then for a 40–50 per cent death rate in the plagues in and after 1348, the population might have been between 5 and 6 million on the eve of the Black Death, having already, in one view, been reduced from its 1300 peak by the terrible famines of 1315 to 1317.

There is, however, clearly much that is speculative about a proposed 5 to 6 million population for 1300, and in recent years some historians have suggested a markedly lower total. B. M. S. Campbell, in particular, while accepting a figure of around 2 million for 1086, has argued that England in 1300 could not have supported a population much in excess of 4 to 4.25 million. Yet while this view is based on a detailed consideration of land use and yields both in 1300 and 1086, it is admittedly provisional and subject to revision. The evidence from individual properties, when viewed as a whole, may well point to a rather higher rate of increase between 1086 and 1300 than that envisaged by Campbell. A population level in 1300 of 5 or even 5.5 million retains powerful advocates. In the current state of research, all we can say is that the population at the very least roughly doubled between 1086 and 1300, rising from around 2 to 4 million plus. A higher rate of increase and a larger total in 1300 is by no means out of the question.

Whatever the precise rate of growth, the rising population was the engine driving forward the economy in these centuries. Food was not imported in any significant quantities; fundamentally England had to feed itself. Hence the stimulus to production. More peasants necessitated greater peasant production, both for food and rent. More peasant mouths to feed also encouraged lords to increase their own production, for – and this is a crucial fact – a large and growing proportion of the peasantry were certainly not self-sufficient. They, like the increasing numbers of townspeople, needed to buy food, a rising demand from which lords, seeking more opulent lifestyles, could profit by increasing their own production and thus their marketable surpluses.

Food, but of what type? The countess of Leicester's accounts in 1265 show her household consuming bread (always a staple), fish (300 herrings from stores one Friday), meat (oxen, pigs, sheep, kids, calves and hens), and dairy products (cheese, milk, and hundreds of eggs a day), all washed down with ale and wine. Lower down the social scale, wine disappears and the supply of meat diminishes. An elite peasant yardlander at Bishop's Cleeve in Worcestershire, where peasant budgets have been reconstructed by Christopher Dyer, had perhaps a pig for bacon, a couple of cows for cheese, around thirty sheep (primarily for the sale of their wool) and draught oxen. But the far more numerous cottagers probably had no more than a solitary cow. Indeed, nearly 50 per cent of the tenants on some bishopric of Winchester manors in the thirteenth century possessed no animals at all. Fundamentally (although this would not be the case in largely pastoral areas) the great bulk of the peasantry lived off bread and pottage, a kind of porridge made from oats and pulses; bread was by far the largest component in the diet of harvest workers at Sedgeford in Norfolk in 1256. Considerable efforts were certainly made in this period to improve animal husbandry. At Rimpton in Somerset, new farm buildings, better feeding and a professional bailiff improved the fertility and survival rates of the lord's cattle and pigs, and maintained those of sheep at an impressive level. But all the evidence suggests that the primary need was for corn production; that was where life and profit lay. Indeed, in calorific terms (according to one calculation) corn accounted for 93 per cent of agricultural output.

Throughout this period, therefore, gargantuan efforts were made by both lords and peasants (it is often difficult to distinguish between their efforts) to bring new land under the plough. North of Trent in 1086 lay a great deal of under-utilized land, partly through Yorkshire's depopulation after its ravaging by William the Conqueror. Even in the heavily manorialized midlands and the south there were swathes of waste and woodland between villages which could be taken in, a 'drive to the margins' which ultimately created a sea of arable with the fields of one village hard up against those of the next. Very large inroads were also made into the royal forest, which around 1200 covered a third of the country. The abbot of Peterborough, his knights and free tenants created 450–600 acres of new arable in the soke of Peterborough in the first quarter of the thirteenth century. Twelfth-century clearances in the soke had already spawned the new village of Paston and the attendant hamlets of Dogsthorpe and Cathwaite, an indication (and there are many others) that colonization involved the foundation of new settlements as well as the expansion of old ones. The greatest enterprises, however, involved drainage – of the Somerset levels, of the Essex marshes, of Romney marsh in Kent and above all the East Anglian fens. In Lincolnshire the men of the Holland district reclaimed over 100 square miles from the sea and converted it, in the words of the Crowland chronicler, into 'good and fertile arable'.

The landscape of England was being transformed, yet the end result can nowhere near have doubled, let alone tripled, the area under cultivation. The need to sustain, and the desire to profit from, the rising population also inspired efforts to cultivate the land more efficiently. This is related to the whole question of how lords ran their estates.

At the time of Domesday Book many of the new Norman knights were probably keeping their manors in hand and seeking to reorganize and expand the demesnes or home-farms within them. Great lords, on the other hand, while treating some of their property in that way, seem more generally to have followed a policy of leasing out both whole manors and parts of the home-farm sections of the manors they kept in hand. In the second half of the twelfth century, this pattern began to change as great lords increasingly shifted out of leases. In 1176 all Peterborough abbey's manors were leased; by 1210 all were in hand. This process of resumption began on big ecclesiastical estates like Peterborough's and was probably inspired by worries over the permanent loss of property through leases becoming hereditary. It was also believed that in-hand manors could yield much more profit than those let out on ancient leases. One of Bury St Edmunds' manors, Tilney in the Norfolk fenland, had formerly been leased at £4 a year. By resuming it in the 1180s Abbot Samson increased the revenue to an annual £20 to £25. Probably here and elsewhere the property had gained in value as it gained in population. Meanwhile, another factor came into play in the early thirteenth century which encouraged lords both to take manors in hand and expand their home-farms. This was an economic event of overarching importance, one which was also central to politics and royal finance, namely the great inflation.

Although evidence is limited, prices in the twelfth century seem to have been fairly stable. Those of wheat, by far the most important saleable commodity, moved upwards in the ten years either side of 1180, but in the 1190s fell back to their old levels. Then in the four or five years from 1200 prices rocketed. Although this was followed by some falling back, the old levels were never recovered and prices remained at at least twice their twelfth-century level, ultimately, in the last quarter of the thirteenth century, averaging between three and four times as much. Prices of other items, like oxen, followed comparable trends. The reasons for the inflation, which was an English, not a continental phenomenon, have been much debated. One hypothesis has explained it in terms of a flow of silver into the country to pay for English wool, but it is difficult to see how this could account for a sudden rise in prices around 1200. Another suggestion is that in the early 1200s numerous hoarders of coin suddenly decided to spend their money and save less than before, the inflation again being monetary but the money coming from a different source. The hoarders acted in this way, it is said, because they had lost confidence in a currency much debased by clipping and general wear since the last major recoinage in 1180 (hence the need for King John's recoinage in 1205). Coin hoarders, however, are not the kind of people who need to eat more bread. They would have spent their money on goods other than corn, and would that have released such a quantity of coin as to create a general rise in prices? By far the most likely cause of the inflation, at least when it came to the price of wheat, the commodity which dominated the market, was that given at the time by Ralph, abbot of the Cistercian monastery of Coggeshall in Essex. He blamed the very high prices in 1205, which he contrasted with those in the time of Henry II, on the freezing weather which had destroyed the harvest. Chroniclers also commented on the bad weather of 1201. Almost certainly it was a succession of poor harvests which drove up corn prices, with perhaps the release of hoarded coins affecting those of other commodities. The subsequent failure to resume earlier price levels may well have been due to longer-term factors, namely the influx of silver, which certainly fuelled a large increase in the money supply from the 1180s, and the demands of a rising population outrunning the supply of corn.

Whatever the cause, while inflation did not begin the move to take manors in hand, for that had begun earlier, it certainly consolidated the trend and with it the related move to develop the demesne or home-farming side of activities. This did not mean that rents were unimportant. In the thirteenth century, some lords (like the archbishop of Canterbury) continued to lease individual manors. Once a manor was in hand, lords were keen to raise the rents paid by free and unfree tenants. They also increased their income through commuting rent owed in labour to rent paid in cash, in the process often imposing heavier burdens on the peasantry. On some estates, lords still received more money from rents than from selling corn on the market. Nor was the market the destination for all produce, that coming from manors near a lord's principal residence often being consumed rather than sold. None the less, for all these qualifications the thirteenth century does stand apart as an age where lords directly exploited their manors and made money by selling the produce on the market, thus profiting from the high prices produced by inflation. To have as large a surplus as possible to sell, the lords strove to expand and consolidate the home-farm portions of their manors through purchase and exchange, a process well documented in numerous charters. In farming more efficiently they were aided by a growing army of professional estate stewards, some of whom wrote treatises on estate management, the most famous being Walter of Henley's *Husbandry*, a veritable 'good dung guide'.

Just how far yields per acre were increased as a result of this expertise and activity is hard to know. A comparison with those at the time of Domesday Book is simply unavailable. Figures from lordly demesnes in the thirteenth century are often not encouraging. On the estates of the bishop of Winchester yields of wheat remained around eight to twelve bushels per acre (a bushel is thirty-six litres), where on modern farms they are in the seventies. The yields from barley and oats actually declined. Perhaps the Winchester administrators, having greatly expanded the area of the demesne arable and with it the bishop's income, felt no pressure to farm it more intensively. Elsewhere in the country attitudes were different. In parts of fertile eastern Norfolk yields were three times those of the Winchester estates, thanks to intense use of labour and flexible cropping which virtually eliminated fallow. Although in lowland England there was no general shift from a two- to a three-field rotational system, thus reducing the amount of land lying fallow, the distinction between the two systems became blurred as portions of fallow fields were kept in cultivation. Whether peasant productivity equalled or exceeded that of lords is impossible to say as there are no figures. The need to cultivate increasingly marginal lands and the soil exhaustion due to lack of manure – a lack, as at Holland in Lincolnshire, arising from new arable eating into meadow and pasture – may have particularly affected peasant agriculture. On the other hand, with yields literally a matter of life and death peasants must surely have farmed with absolute commitment. There was plenty of labour to weed and to spread what dung there was. Indeed in eastern Norfolk the ratio of labour to land on peasant holdings was some six times that on demesnes.

Part and parcel of these developments in farming was an accentuation of regional specialisms. There were areas of intensive arable production like East Anglia; various balances between production of corn for the market and for personal consumption in the common fields of the midlands and the south; in the south-west, as at Rimpton, corn production was combined with quite extensive sheep rearing; and of course sheep and other cattle were the speciality of the pastoral uplands, where the Cistercian monasteries, founded in the twelfth century, entered the sheep business on a large scale. Sheep indeed were everywhere, kept both by prosperous peasants and great lords. If the rising population was the main engine behind the expansion, the Flemish cloth industry's demand for wool provided a powerful auxiliary motor. England already boasted many sheep at the time of Domesday Book, and thereafter their numbers multiplied. The contribution to cash income varied but was rarely insignificant: on three great ecclesiastical estates at the end of the thirteenth century it amounted to between 11 per cent and 35 per cent, the rest coming from corn sales, rents and various rights of jurisdiction. By this time England had probably 10 million sheep. Here too the countryside had been transformed.

* * *

There is virtually no statistical evidence from which to compute the populations of Wales and Scotland. The population of Wales around 1300 has been hazarded at 300,000 and of Scotland at 1 million, largely by reference to a likely 5 to 6 million in England, which itself, as we have seen, is open to debate. However, there can be no doubt that the Welsh and Scottish populations substantially increased. Indeed Gerald of Wales specifically commented on the rise in that of Wales in the twelfth century, the only contemporary ever to refer to the subject of population increase.

In Wales, growth was related to other changes in the economy. These were partly the result of the Norman conquest of much of the southern lowlands from Gwent through to Dyfed, which began soon after 1066 (see below, p. 110). To protect their lands the Norman lords built castles, and to exploit them they set up manors very similar to those in England, the first time, as we have seen, such institutions had appeared in Wales. As a consequence there was a considerable increase both in cereal production and the number of nucleated villages. Some of the sites developed were probably new, others (like Carew, just east of Pembroke) were very old. The peasants on whom the working of the new manors depended were both native Welsh and, in substantial numbers, Anglo-Saxons introduced from England. The balance between the two peoples varied, something reflected in the way personal and field names shifted from English to Welsh between the east and west of coastal Gwent. In parts of Dyfed lived a different people altogether because in the early twelfth century Henry I opened the area up for Flemings, who had been displaced from their native land by flooding and over-population. These men may well have been recruited and settled by professional agents acting for lords, hence the way in which some of the new villages (Templeton is an example) seem to have been formally planned with plots set in rows beside a street. Throughout the conquered south there is plenty of evidence of expansion. Around the castle at Carew two new settlements grew up, Carew Newton and Carew Cheriton. In the wetlands of coastal Gwent, the Norman lords seem to have laboured to re-colonize and rehabilitate areas which the Romans had once reclaimed from the sea, rebuilding the sea wall in the process.

There were also new and expanding settlements in native Wales. By the end of the thirteenth century Llysdulas (Dulas) in northern Anglesey had thrown up a series of subsidiary farms and hamlets. At Aberffraw, further south, by tradition the principal seat of the rulers of Gwynedd, the *llys* boasted an impressive complex of buildings while the *maerdref* had spawned four outlying hamlets. Some of the *llys/maerdref* complexes in the thirteenth century, like the manors in the marcher lordships in the south, were linked to substantial demesne farms, with the culti-vation relying on the services of the peasant 'bondmen' in the *maerdref*. At both Aberffraw and nearby Rhosyr there were over 600 acres of land in hand, and at nearby Llan-faes thirteen carucates were valued at £20 10s. a year. Tax records from the end of the thirteenth century show that at Aberffraw wheat was grown extensively, indeed the balance between wheat and oats was better than in some parts of Oxfordshire.

In Scotland there was also a substantial increase in the arable area through inroads into forest, wasteland and moor, although most of the exiguous evidence is confined to the south-east between the Tweed and the Mounth. There the process is reflected in the name Aithmuir ('oat moor') in Perthshire. Further north at Arbuthnott in Mearns, sometime before 1206, a lord seems to have removed peasant pastoralists and ploughed up their lands. Scottish lords still derived far more income from rents than from demesne farming, judging from evidence both from the earldom of Fife and the monasteries of Lothian in the 1290s, but some great abbeys did have extensive demesnes: at Swinton that of Coldingham priory extended to around 500 acres.

Despite these developments, the wealth of Wales and to a lesser extent of Scotland remained in flocks and herds. Properties with sub-stantial arable were usually attached to pastures running back up into the hills. Here the wool trade brought important developments. Welsh wool was not of the highest quality, but the Cistercian abbey of Strata Florida was already exporting it in the early thirteenth century. Scottish monasteries became involved with sheep on the grandest scale. In the late thirteenth century Melrose abbey, another Cistercian house, could provide fifty sacks of wool a year for Italian merchants, which implies a flock of over 12,000 sheep.

*　　*　　*

Changes to the rural economy were inseparable from those in the commercial sector which were nothing less than revolutionary. A developing network of markets, fairs and towns, together with their associated trade and manufacture, provided lords with goods to buy and centres where they could sell their produce in order to make the money to do so. The ability to procure thus stimulated the effort to produce. Peasants too used markets. They sold corn to raise money for their rents. They also bought corn on which to live if they were not self-sufficient, and other items if they were. A peasant yardlander might have an annual surplus of around £2 to spend. None of this would have been possible without money itself.

The only coin in Britain for nearly all this period was the silver penny, of which there were twelve in a shilling, 240 in a pound, and 160 in a mark (two thirds of a pound). Shillings, marks and pounds were simply terms of account. There were no coins of those values. Large sums of money had to be transported in barrels full of thousands of pennies. In England there were recoinages involving significant changes in design in 1158, 1180, 1247 and 1279, with the previous types being demonetized. A large number of regional mints were involved in such recoinages but at other times most minting in the thirteenth century was concentrated at London and Canterbury, much of it to change coin brought in by foreign merchants. The money supply in this period is necessarily a speculative subject. Down to 1205 it has to be deduced from coin hoards; thereafter, more reliably, on mint records. The increase in the supply was certainly stupendous, and was supported by an influx of silver to pay for English and Scottish wool. According to the estimates of Nicholas Mayhew, in England in 1086 there were £37,500, or 9 million pennies, in circulation, 4½d. per head if the population stood at 2 million. In 1300 the circulation was £900,000, or 216 million pennies, 54d. a head for a population of 4 million, and 36d. per head for a population of 6 million. There was therefore a twenty-four-fold increase in the money supply between 1086 and 1300, most of it taking place after 1180 when there were perhaps £100,000, or 24 million pennies, in circulation. When allowance is made for inflation, which would reduce the real value of money in 1300 by a factor of three or four as compared with 1086, the change is both less spectacular and more significant. Even a penny was a valuable coin – a day's wages for a labourer. Although it could be cut into halves and quarters (in 1279 Edward I at last minted halfpennies and farthings) there was no way, throughout this period, one could simply go into a tavern and buy a drink. At that level it remained a barter (or credit) economy. The diminishing value of money, however, and its greater supply must have monetized and debarterized a whole range of trans-actions, in the process stimulating production and exchange. The increasing money supply also enabled the velocity of money, that is the speed with which it circulated, to slow down. Money had to work less hard. This facilitated commerce because it meant cash balances could be built up and purchases take place immediately rather than one transaction having to wait upon another.

There was one other factor which worked in the same direction, namely the increasing use of credit, much of it provided by the Jews. William the Conqueror had brought Jews from Rouen and established them in London, the first known settlement in England. By 1159 there were communities in at least nine other towns. The Jews probably acted, as they had in Rouen, both as moneylenders and dealers in coin, plate and bullion, doing good business changing into English money the silver that flowed into the country to pay for the export of wool. Under Henry II (1154–89) the Jews began to concentrate primarily on moneylending, and became England's main source of credit. The opportunity had been created both by Henry II reducing the number of mints and moneyers, thus removing one traditional source of credit, and by the disappearance of the great Christian financiers (like William Cade) from whom Henry and many others borrowed money early in his reign. Perhaps such men were discouraged by the increasing hostility of the church to open usury and the king's threat that its practitioners, on death, would forfeit their property to the crown, as apparently Cade did. The Jews were ideally placed to fill the gap. As tightly-knit communities with connections throughout England and the continent, they easily formed business partnerships. They also enjoyed both the king's protection and help in collecting their debts. Since in law the Jews were regarded as crown property, Henry II quickly realized that he did not have to take loans from them; that would be like taking loans from himself. He could simply tax them instead, but for there to be anything to tax he and his successors naturally ensured that money borrowed from the Jews was indeed repaid.

The total number of Jews remained small, probably fewer than 5,000, but by 1190 there were significant communities in seventeen towns, and smaller settlements in many others. The majority of loans were of small amounts advanced to townsmen and free tenants of minor importance in the immediate vicinity of the towns. But most of the money (for the individual amounts were much larger) was loaned to great lay and ecclesiastical lords. Cade, who died around 1166, had lent at least £5,000 to clients, including some of the most important men of the realm. The greatest of his Jewish successors, Aaron of Lincoln (and most Jewish wealth was in the hands of a few plutocrats), was owed on his death in 1186 some £18,466, a sum not far short of the annual revenue of the crown. Religion and usury made the Jews deeply unpopular, but until their wealth was destroyed in the second half of the thirteenth century they were a vital lubricant to the economy and adjunct to the money supply.

Intimately related to the expansion of that supply was an entirely new infrastructure of markets, fairs and boroughs. Within that structure, speed and range of contact for both lord and peasant were increased by the greater use of horse as opposed to ox haulage, arguably a revolution in transport. Markets and fairs were usually established and run by lords with the aim of profiting from tolls paid by traders. Markets were held weekly on a specified day. Most had a largely local function, being a forum for buying and selling corn and other wares from the surrounding fields and villages. Others, however, like Henley, an entrepôt for supplies for London, were also involved in inter-regional trade. Fairs, which were held for longer periods though usually only once a year, also served inter-regional functions, particularly as centres for trade in livestock. At the top of the scale in the thirteenth century were half a dozen great international fairs, held at Winchester, Northampton, Stamford, St Ives, Boston and King's Lynn.

Taking the whole period from 900 to 1516, around 1,550 markets and 2,060 fairs are known to have existed in England. Of these, only 13 per cent and 3 per cent respectively can be discerned before 1199. In the next century a revolution appears to have taken place. Between 1199 and 1272 the king licensed the establishment of some 770 markets and 920 fairs, 47 per cent of the total number. Up to a point these figures are misleading. Some of the new institutions had an earlier existence, the licence being simply a precaution now that the king was insisting on his right to sanction new establishments. Market and commercial growth early in the twelfth century is certainly reflected in Winchester fair, whose permitted duration increased from three days in 1096 to sixteen in 1155. Yet there is little doubt that the majority of the markets and fairs licensed in the thirteenth century were genuinely new. The statement, common in inquiries into episodes of violence and sudden death, that 'he recovered from his wound and went to markets and taverns as usual' shows just how much the market had entered the fabric of everyday life.

Some new markets never really got going, others grew quickly into boroughs, or (like Stratford-upon-Avon in 1196) were planned as part and parcel of new boroughs from the start. The proliferation of towns was indeed another cardinal feature of the expanding economy. M. W. Beresford has listed 172 towns established in the medieval period, of which eighty-eight belong to the years from 1154 to 1250. The initiative was again that of the lords (including the king), and many new boroughs were established beside castles or ecclesiastical institutions. With an existing population to supply, and usually on a strategic site, they were ideal situations for craftsmen and traders. The north in 1066 had been virtually an urban desert. By 1150 seven boroughs had appeared, including Newcastle upon Tyne, Durham, Berwick and Carlisle. The years 1150 to 1199 saw another fifteen. Even more spectacular was the growth of east-coast towns on the back of the wool trade and fishing (Kingston upon Hull, Boston, King's Lynn, Yarmouth). Yet the expansion equally embraced settled inland areas. By 1348 twenty-seven new towns had appeared in Oxfordshire and Gloucestershire to add to the original Domesday six.

As new towns were founded, old ones grew in size. The growth was both extensive, so that Bristol rebuilt its walls to take in the new settled areas, and intensive, so that frontages in Winchester's High Street averaged as little as eight feet in width. Estimates of town populations are as chancy as those of the population as a whole and indeed can slide up and down in relation to them. By 1300, at the bottom of the scale, there were perhaps 550 market towns with an average population of 750. At the top of the scale, leaving aside London, were around twenty towns with populations of over 5,000 and four more (Norwich, Bristol, York and Winchester) with over 10,000. This was small beer compared with northern Italy where there were as many as thirty-five towns of at least 100,000 inhabitants. Yet it was still a great change from the situation in 1086 when only 111 boroughs were mentioned in the Domesday Book and only four towns, not including London, had putative populations of over 5,000. One calculation gives the towns between 6 and 7.5 per cent of the total population in 1086, and between 10 and 15 per cent in 1300. The urban sector had thus grown more quickly than the economy as a whole.

This period was equally important for the consolidation of London's position as 'the queen of the whole kingdom', to quote the *Gesta Stephani* written in the 1150s. Situated in a low river basin, sheltered by the friendly surrounding hills of Blackheath, Brockley, Richmond and Hampstead, location had long ago made it England's pre-eminent town. Its place on the eastern side of the country opened it to merchants from continental Europe. The great river enabled those merchants to unload (before seeking refreshment at the famous cookhouse), not at some Channel port, but already well inland. And the bridge, the most seaward over the river, meant that from London one could move north and south, as well as west along the Thames itself, which was navigable as far as Lechlade in Gloucestershire. What was new in this period was London's emergence as the political and governmental capital. The might of kingship at the Tower (keeping in check the unruly Londoners), the majesty of kingship at Westminster (symbolized by the Confessor's abbey and Rufus's great palace hall), meant that already in 1170s William fitz Stephen could describe London as 'the seat of the monarchy of England'. The move around this time of the exchequer and treasury from the old capital, Winchester, to Westminster confirmed the change, as did the emergence from the 1190s of the court of common bench, hived off from the exchequer, which became the central law court of the kingdom. These factors, together with the end of the cross-Channel state in 1204, and the king's devotion to Edward the Confessor, ensured that Henry III spent more time at Westminster than any previous king.

London's population has been estimated at around 25,000 in 1086 and 40,000 in 1200. Thereafter the city may have grown more slowly than some provincial towns, especially those on the east coast, which were more favoured by wool merchants. But with changing trading conditions at the end of the thirteenth century, London quickly recovered. By 1334 it had five times the assessed wealth of its nearest rival, Bristol. Its population around 1300 can be variously estimated at between 60,000 and 100,000, half the size of Paris, perhaps, but still one of the great European cities. London in the early fourteenth century had 354 taverns and 140 parish and other churches. Here indeed one could recover from wounds and 'go to markets and taverns as usual'.

Growth in the size of towns was accompanied by important developments in the structure of their government largely under licence, that is by charter of the king, a phenomenon discussed later (see below, p. 392). Town growth naturally had an impact on the countryside, for a start by recruiting from its population, a process reflected in the famous rule found already in the customs of Newcastle upon Tyne, *c.* 1135, that peasants who spent a year and a day in a borough would thenceforth be free to remain there. Most towns drew the bulk of their population from within a twenty-mile hinterland, but London reached out to between twenty and forty miles. Towns, of course, required food as well as people, and this stimulated agricultural production. The feeding of London generated intensive cultivation of fruit and vegetables in the immediate vicinity and pulled in corn from counties as far distant as Oxfordshire, with Henley and a ring of other market towns acting as local depots. In return, townsmen supplied the countryside (and also, of course, themselves) with a range of goods, the dominant occupations in most places being trade and manufacture related to food, drink, clothes, shoes and metal.

Most trade and manufacture was simply for local needs, but some towns gained a national reputation for their wares. 'Herring of Yarmouth, plaice of Winchelsea, merling of Rye, cod of Grimsby' ran one thirteenth-century doggerel about places and their associations. (It also included the prostitutes of Charing, soon to be Charing Cross.) Herrings in particular, salted and with no sell-by date (hence in the countess of Leicester's stores), were widely distributed. The doggerel also tripped through 'scarlet of Lincoln, hauberge of Stamford, blanket of Blythe, burne of Beverley, russet of Colchester', enumerating some famous cloths and their places of manufacture. Cloth manufacture was an expensive and many-staged business which often came under the control of the dyers at the end of the process. The towns, however, faced stiff competition from imports, especially from Flanders, and from work in the countryside, of which more later. It was in the countryside too that England's extractive industries were situated. Here too there was significant growth.

'Marble of Corfe', 'iron of Gloucester', 'tin of Cornwall' all featured in the doggerel. The first, from the Isle of Purbeck, was just one of many building stones quarried in England from which (with some imports) the great castles and churches of the period were built. Gloucester's iron (for horseshoes, wheel rims and so forth) came from the ore mined and forged in the Forest of Dean, which accounted for a fifth or a sixth of the country's total output. The number of bloomeries throughout the kingdom increased perhaps fivefold between 1086 and 1300 with production reaching 1,000 tons a year. Cornwall's tin, judging from a remark by Henry of Huntingdon, was marketed at Exeter in the early twelfth century, as it probably had been for centuries. In the 1150s fifty to sixty-five tons a year were mined, rising to over 600 in 1214, although production may then have levelled out.

England exported tin, as it did cloth and grain. But one export stood out above all others: wool, largely for the Flemish cloth industry, though it also went elsewhere, notably to the Rhineland. Hard evidence for the volume of exports only comes after 1275 with the introduction of customs duties, but exports had almost certainly multiplied several times over in the previous 200 years. By the early fourteenth century they averaged some 35,000 sacks a year, each sack being the product of roughly 200 to 250 fleeces. With additions for the home market, this is the basis for the calculation that England had 10 million sheep. Much of the wool was paid for in silver, so that the dramatic expansion of the money supply is a rough measure of the expansion of wool exports. But of course England also imported, if largely for the wealthy: building stone (especially from Caen in Normandy), fine cloths, silks, and spices (the countess of Leicester had cinnamon in her sauces). Merchants of Norway supplied Geoffrey de Buketon with goat skins, chests full of miniver and fifty-seven ox-hides. Yet just as there was one pre-eminent export, so there was one pre-eminent import: wine, the aristocracy's principal beverage. In the twelfth century the great bulk of wine drunk in England came from Anjou and Poitou. The loss of these provinces in 1203 and 1224 was the making of Gascony and the start of England's love affair with claret. In the 1300s (according to surviving records) exports from Bordeaux had reached 100,000 tonnes a year (double the amount exported in 1956) and a quarter of this went to England, being unloaded at Bristol, Portsmouth and Southampton.

A great deal of England's trade was in the hands of foreign merchants from Norway, the Rhineland, and above all from Flanders. In the second half of the thirteenth century Italian merchants too came to play a large part in the business of wool exports. But the same period also sees the emergence of some great English merchants; many prominent London citizens were heavily engaged in both exporting wool and importing wine. In 1273 English merchants were licensed to export 8,100 sacks of wool. Between 1331 and 1335 their exports averaged annually 24,000 sacks. In 1303 Edward I summoned together merchants from forty-two towns. An English merchant class was emerging.

*　　*　　*

The commercial revolution in Wales and Scotland was even more striking than in England given that it started from a much lower base, with no towns and little currency. The crucial change in Wales took place in the thirteenth century, hence the extraordinary contrast between the 10,000 cows, forty warhorses and sixty chasers which Llywelyn the Great of Gwynedd promised King John in 1211 (clearly he had little money), and the £9,166 (or perhaps £12,500) which his grandson actually paid Henry III between 1267 and 1271. Coins were not minted by the Welsh rulers, who were doubtless fearful of the king of England's likely response. Rather the rise in the money supply resulted from English coins coming across the border, doubtless reflecting the sharp rise in the money supply in England itself. By the 1300s there were around eighty places in Wales with urban characteristics. Most prominent were the towns founded by the Normans in the south, in a sweep from Chepstow round to Pembroke. Cardiff, Carmarthen and Haverford, with populations significantly more than a thousand, were the largest towns in Wales. There were also urban developments in the native principalities; Welshpool in southern Powys, with its trade across the English border, was the largest town. In Gwynedd there were burgesses at Nefyn, while Llanfaes (in Anglesey) had a twice-yearly fair and a port. Wales imported cloth and salt, and in years of bad harvest was dependent on English corn. From Llanfaes wool and hides were exported to Scotland and Ireland. There were certainly native merchants because the agreement between the Welsh and Scottish rulers in 1258 made provision for those of both sides. Continental merchants made their appearance too, for both Italians and Flemings dealt in Welsh wool.

For all these changes, the commercial sector in Wales remained small. That was not the case in Scotland, richer as it was, and facing continental Europe. Rough calculations from coin hoard evidence in Scotland suggest the following expansion of the money supply:

Date	Value of pennies in circulation
mid twelfth century	£12,500–20,800
1247–51	£50–60,000
1278–84	£130,000–£180,000+

Even if the threefold increase between 1247 and 1284 needs scaling down, the growth in Scotland between these dates was still probably larger than that in England in the same period. Indeed, according to one possible calculation, in the 1280s there were more coins in circulation *per capita* north of the border than there were south of it. The great majority of the coins in question were English, but Scottish coins made a contribution, for King David had minted them in his own name from 1136 and his successors followed his example. Central to this remarkable expansion were wool exports, which reached perhaps 20 per cent of those of England. Italian and Fleming merchants established bases in Berwick, as did fifteen religious houses which supplied much of the wool. It was the Berwick mint, significantly, which produced by far the largest part of Scotland's own coin; the next most important for the recoinage of 1250 were the mints at Perth and Edinburgh.

Perth, Edinburgh, Berwick. Scotland had also gained an urban infrastructure. By 1300 there were around fifty burghs. Of these, Berwick and Roxburgh appear before 1124, Edinburgh, Dunfermline, Stirling and Perth are mentioned between 1124 and 1130, while the first datable reference to Glasgow is with the dedication of its cathedral in 1136. Glasgow was very much an ecclesiastical burgh, its lord the bishop. St Andrews likewise was episcopal. The great majority of the important burghs, however, were established at royal centres: both Edinburgh and Stirling sheltered at the foot of ancient rock fortresses. King David (1124–53), with his upbringing in England, saw such towns as a way of making money (they were one of his few sources of cash income) and encouraged them by conferring the kind of privileges coveted by boroughs in England. Certainly that was the practice of later kings, the customs of Newcastle upon Tyne being particularly imitated. Thus the Scottish burgesses gained freedom of tolls, control over their courts and responsibility for paying their monetary dues to the king. There were also merchant guilds, nineteen being known by 1300. The majority of Scottish burghs served the same kinds of local functions as those in England. Where they gained a wider importance it was thanks again to location. Ayr imported corn from Ireland. Aberdeen (with fish exports reaching Cologne and Flanders) was the centre for the whole hinterland beyond the Mounth. Perth, which grew in area roughly fourfold between the 1120s and the fourteenth century, was on the Tay at a point where it was navigable, fordable and also (by the early thirteenth century) bridgeable. Berwick-on-Tweed was the port of entry from England, receiving herrings and corn from King's Lynn, while exporting wool. Those exports were not all in the hands of foreign merchants. By the 1290s the Scots had their own quarters in Bruges and a stretch of canal was named after them: 'Schottendyc'.

*　　*　　*

During this period there had, therefore, been considerable expansion in the English economy. Estimates of gross domestic product (GDP) are, of course, extremely hazardous but Campbell, assuming a population increase between 1086 and 1300 of 2 million to 4.25 million, suggests a growth of real GDP (adjusted for inflation) of some 130 to 150 per cent. Mayhew, on the basis of a population rise from 2.25 million to 6 million, puts the increase at over fourfold. The expansion also embraced Wales and Scotland, as we have seen. Indeed, square mile for square mile, the diocese of St Andrews in the 1290s was almost as wealthy as that of Winchester. There had also been important changes in the form of this wealth: far more of it was in money. Hence in many parts of Britain the commutation into money of rents previously paid in labour and kind; hence too the evident cash resources of Llywelyn prince of Wales, Alexander III of Scotland and Edward I of England. Without the expansion of the money supply Edward could never have raised some £661,400 in lay and clerical taxation between 1290 and 1307.

The period also saw striking increases in the cash resources of the great lords. The wealth of the Scottish church, when assessed for taxation, seems roughly to have doubled over the thirteenth century. In England the net income of the bishop of Ely rose as follows:

1086	£484
1171–2	£920
1256–7	£1,930
1298–9	£2,550

The 2.7-fold increase here between the 1170s and the 1290s would probably be a broad average for many ecclesiastical estates. It is more difficult to get figures for the laity but groups of estates studied by Sidney Painter yielded a median baronial income of £115 a year between 1160 and 1220, and £339 for the years 1260 to 1320, the respective averages being £202 and £668. Most of the English earls in the mid thirteenth century had incomes of between £2,000 and £3,000 a year. In Scotland the annual income of the earl of Fife in the 1290s was £500 less than those of the English earls, but still significant.

This rise in income, made possible by the growing population and by inflation, was also driven by lords themselves, from the king downwards. Quite apart from the ravenous demands of warfare, they wanted extra money to impress in finer clothes, to reward followers with cash rather than land, to live and worship in more splendid buildings, and to eat and drink with more abundance and refinement. Contemporaries noticed the changes. The chronicler Orderic Vitalis wrote of the new cathedrals, monastic buildings and village churches which were built during the peace of Henry I. Likewise the Life of Gruffudd ap Cynan (d. 1137) spoke of the prosperity of Gwynedd in his time: people began to live off the fruits of the earth, and limewashed churches glittered 'like the firmament of the stars'. The result of Queen Margaret's labours in Scotland (according to her *Life*) was a novel variety of dress among the Scots, and a new splendour and refinement at court. The biography of William Marshal, earl of Pembroke, noted that in the 1160s even a king's son rode with his cloak rolled up behind his saddle. Now (in the 1220s) a mere esquire had a baggage animal: 'The world was not then so proud as it is on our days.' On his hunting expeditions in the 1260s and 1270s Llywelyn as prince of Wales had 500 followers, 200 more, it was said, than his grandfather, Llywelyn the Great.

Standards of living had been rising before 1066, but the Conquest arguably boosted the aristocratic demand for cash and raised expectations of the kind of lifestyle that cash was to fund. To a much greater degree than before the attitudes of the nobility were shaped by the religious, military and chivalric ethos of the continent, a natural development, since it was from the continent that the new nobility had come. Nobles needed revenue in cash rather than in kind because that was the form in which it could easily be shipped home, but they also wanted to spend their money in a continental way in England. Although there was a precedent in Edward the Confessor's Westminter Abbey, William of Malmesbury was surely right to think that the Conquest spurred on the construction of new abbeys and cathedrals as well as parish churches. It also brought to England an entirely new form of fortified residence, administrative centre and status symbol: the castle. There were over 500 of them by 1100. While pressed peasant labour could throw up the early mottes, the stone keeps and fine timber halls which followed needed money and lots of it. William of Malmesbury again contrasted the 'mean and despicable houses' of the Anglo-Saxons with the 'noble and splendid mansions' of the Normans and the French, a contrast well illustrated by the way in which the Anglo-Saxon residence at Goltho in Lincolnshire was rebuilt on far grander lines after 1066. It was rebuilt indeed several times because lords, lay and ecclesiastical, were never content. Churches, castles and manor houses were constantly refashioned. And around lordly residences the landscape too was transformed by the creation of hunting parks for the excitement of the chase, the pleaure of the venison and the prestige of the jurisdiction. Between 1227 and 1258 the king granted no less than 630 charters of 'free warren' allowing lords to set up such private parks.

That the nobility had progressively more cash in this period and embraced a more opulent lifestyle seems clear. Yet one must be careful about claiming too much. The fivefold increase in income enjoyed by the bishops of Ely between 1086 and 1298–9 becomes less impressive when adjusted for a three- to fourfold increase in prices in the intervening period. For the same reason, the £661,400 levied by Edward I in taxation over and above his ordinary revenues between 1290 and 1307 was hardly worth more in real terms than the £214,500 raised from taxation to pay off the Danes between 1002 and 1018. This may not be a fair comparison. The sums for 1002 to 1018, even if the figures from the Anglo-Saxon Chronicle can be believed, were effectively squeezed from the kingdom by invading armies. A better marker might be the £24,000 which was certainly Henry I's revenue in 1130, but this sum too in real terms Edward rarely bettered on any regular basis, even with the heavy taxation of the last years of his reign. If, moreover, one takes into account the increase in GDP between 1100 and 1300, then Edward I was taking a significantly smaller share of GDP than Henry I.

*　　*　　*

To understand why this was so takes us back to the condition of the peasantry. Here the period after 1066 saw important changes, the first being the end of slavery in England and of both slavery and the slave trade in Wales and Scotland. The trade was gradually killed off by ecclesiastical censure during the course of the twelfth century. Slavery itself gave way to changing economic conditions, though the process is really only traceable in England. In England, Domesday Book mentioned some 28,000 slaves. If, as seems likely, some had families they may have accounted for anything up to 10 per cent of the rural population. Slaves worked to their lord's orders (men were often ploughmen and women dairymaids), and could be punished by death or mutilation. Some lived in the manor house complex, others (probably the great majority) in the village. A hundred years later, when the king's lawyers were defining status, they made no mention of slaves at all.

The population was either free or unfree, and the latter, while restricted in many ways, were certainly not punishable by their lords in life or limb as slaves had been. 'The bodies and members of serfs belong only to the king,' declared the king's judges in 1244. Apart from that difference, some lords in the thirteenth century (as at Cuxham in Oxfordshire) maintained labourers, living in the manor house complex, whose position seems comparable to that of earlier slaves. But these were but the remnants of a much larger group whose numbers had been in decline long before the snapshot in Domesday Book. This was why twelfth-century lawyers could ignore and in effect abolish the category. The decline was not primarily because of the teaching of the church. The church certainly forbade the trade, and regarded the manumission of slaves as an act of piety, but it accepted the continuance of the institution: there were slaves on its own estates. Rather the reason for the decline was economic. Slaves were more trouble than they were worth, largely because, with no land of their own, the lord had to support them. In the relatively stable economic conditions in the tenth century, and then again after Cnut's conquest, lords probably deemed it easier and more profitable to grant land to slaves in return for labour services and rents, integrating them, therefore, into the rest of the peasantry, something which also happened in Wales and Scotland. The Normans, keen on money rent because they were absentees and with land in abundance on which to settle slaves, probably took this view even more strongly.

The disappearance of slavery meant that a larger proportion of the rural population had land, and no one was at his lord's mercy in matters of life or limb. Other changes, however, were less favourable. Domesday Book shows that between 1066 and 1087 many counties saw a sharp fall in the number of sokemen and free peasants. Probably they had been turned into villeins, an alteration which meant a loss of status, for they were now obliged for the first time to perform significant labour services. The change may well have been brought about as new Norman lords reorganized their manors, creating home-farms worked by peasant labour.

A century after the Conquest another reduction in the status of the peasantry was being introduced. The king's lawyers, with far more precision than ever before, began to define exactly who was unfree. As a result, by 1200 a sharp line had been drawn dividing the free and the unfree in England. 'The villeins', to use what was now the technical term for the unfree, were all those who held land in return for labour services. The consequences of unfreedom were likewise codified for the first time. A lord could sell his villeins with their land 'like oxen and cows', and exact 'merchet' from them, a payment for a daughter's marriage. He could also tax his villeins and increase their rent and labour services at will. As *Bracton*, a law book of the 1220s, put it, villeins did not know in the evening what they would have to do next morning. However unreasonable the lord's conduct, the villein had no legal redress in the courts of the king. Those courts were closed to him for any matter concerned with land and the terms of its tenure.

The occasion for the change was almost certainly the introduction of new legal procedures in the 1160s and 1170s, which enabled plaintiffs to bring civil actions against their lords (see below, p. 242). By specifying that those plaintiffs had to be free, and by establishing the labour service test for unfreedom, the judges made the procedures unavailable to a large part of the peasantry. The wider social and economic background gave such a ruling particular importance, for this was the very moment when lords were increasingly taking their manors in hand and embracing demesne farming, making the ability to control and discipline the peasant workforce all the more important.

Just how far these changes really worsened the lot of the peasantry has been questioned by historians. A significant proportion of peasants remained free – the sokemen who had survived in eastern England, and the numerous peasants on many manors who had always held their land by rent. By the late thirteenth century the unfree represented at most 60 per cent of the peasantry. The distinction between free and unfree was also blurred, though not removed, by the movement to commute labour services into money, either permanently or on an *ad hoc* basis. In general, by the end of the thirteenth century heavy weekly work was probably exacted from only a third of the unfree peasantry. It was still exacted at Cuxham, but at Willingham roughly half that owed was sometimes commuted. Parallel changes were also taking place in Scotland, and in Wales where many peasants in the *maerdref* in which the *ilys* was situated no longer provided labour for the cultivation of the lord's demesne. In England, moreover, the peasants who were deemed legally unfree were hardly deprived of benefits they or their ancestors had once enjoyed; few can ever have brought legal actions against their lords. In practice those performing labour services had long been regarded as bound to the manor and very much their lord's property. The Norman kings issued writs helping lords recover 'fugitive' peasants, and an imitative procedure was introduced by King David in Scotland where indeed 'fugitive' became a generic term for peasant. Although the English definitions of unfreedom were never introduced in the rest of Britain, the peasants in Scotland, and in Wales where they were aptly named 'bondmen', were certainly no better off.

It has also been argued that in thirteenth-century conditions there were even some positive advantages in being unfree. A freeman, especially if taking land on a new lease, was exposed to the full force of market conditions, which given the shortage of land could dictate very high rents. Villeins, on the other hand, whatever the legal theory, were sometimes protected from radical changes in their conditions by the force of manorial custom, a custom enshrined in the procedures of the manorial court. Walter of Henley in his *Husbandry* advised that the level of fines imposed by the court should be determined by a peasant's 'peers', in other words not by the lord's will, and records show this was often indeed the case.

These qualifications, however, go only so far. There are numerous examples of landholders great and small (like the queen's uncle Peter of Savoy or the knightly lords of Rycote in Oxfordshire) imposing heavier burdens on their villeins in the thirteenth century. Such lords frequently justified their actions on the grounds that their tenants were indeed unfree and so had no protection against greater burdens. Clearly they were determined to exploit their legal rights, whatever manorial custom. Many peasants, moreover, wanted the benefits of freedom – rents rather than labour services, and access to the king's courts; large numbers bought their freedom in the century, and (alleging that they were free or specially privileged) initiated court cases against their lords to try and keep down the level of their rents and services. The courage and resource displayed by peasant communities in pursuing such actions over decades is one of the most inspiring and significant features of the thirteenth century.

If the legal position of many peasants deteriorated, what of their standard of living? This brings us to the most fundamental fact about the great expansion of the twelfth and thirteenth centuries, indeed about Britain itself: while the economy expanded it did little or nothing to improve the living standards of the peasantry. The growth in GDP was real but of course it had to be divided among a growing population. Outside the noble elite, the achievement between 1086 and 1300 was at best to sustain more people at the same standard of living. For a large proportion of the peasantry, that level was the lowest possible compatible with sustaining life. In the occasional years of really bad harvest, life was not sustained for there was starvation. With these statements probably most historians would agree. More controversial, as we shall see, is the argument that far from simply failing to improve, the peasant lot actually worsened as the population began to outrun the ability of the land to support it.

For Wales and Scotland, lack of evidence makes these issues difficult to probe in any depth. In both there were numerous peasants with very small amounts of arable land. At the end of the thirteenth century one can see such men both in Meirionydd and in Berwickshire. Such peasants might also have flocks and herds in the hills but not ones of any great size if the evidence from Gwynedd is anything to go by. There, records from the 1290s suggest that the average tax-paying farmer and his family enjoyed but a bare subsistence. Alongside them were many others too poor to pay tax at all. In all of this there were close parallels with the situation in England. There the starting-point for any investigation of living standards is to ask how much land a peasant family (of 4.5 units) needed for bare subsistence. Of course this varied greatly but a plausible estimate for a typical open-field manor has put the figure at between ten and thirteen acres, depending on whether the rotation was between two fields or three. Now in E. A. Kosminsky's samples from the Hundred Rolls, 26 per cent of the free and unfree peasantry had half-yardland holdings and thus achieved this minimum. Another 24 per cent had holdings of a whole yardland, that is between twenty-four and thirty acres, and apparently lived well above subsistence levels, at least if they had only one family to support. Sometimes peasants, exploiting village land markets, were able to build up more substantial holdings. A few indeed, like the Knivetons of Derbyshire, ultimately ascended into the knightly class. Yet if one half of the peasantry were in reasonable circumstances, Kosminsky's figures reveal that the other half, some 46 per cent, were smallholders, usually holding well under ten acres of land. Surveys of manors from beyond the Hundred Roll area reveal a similar pattern. Outside the intensively cultivated areas of East Anglia such people cannot have supported themselves from their arable land. Their prospects seem grim.

Of course, they cannot have been fatally grim because then such people could not have survived, as manifestly they did. Clearly they had other sources of income apart from their arable land, though these sources differed according to region. At Willingham, for example, the numerous smallholders revealed in the survey of 1251 could place pigs, cattle and above all sheep in the three great common meadows created by reclamation from the fens. Likewise the forest of Arden could be exploited by the rising population of Stoneleigh hundred, as could Windsor forest by the many smallholders at Pyrton in Surrey. There was also in varying degrees the possibility of rural employment. It is noticeable how many of a small group of villein litigants at Beach-ampton (Bucks.) in 1286 had occupational surnames: Smith, Iron-monger, Carter, Marshal. One indeed had become a university professor, Master Henry of Beachampton. Most villages had brewers (who were often women), and there was employment at mills. Important too was the wide spread of the rural cloth industry. The initial prep-aration process, the washing, combing and spinning, was very labour intensive, accounting perhaps for between 45 and 70 per cent of total manufacturing costs. Here the countryside, with an abundance of cheap labour and streams suitable for driving fulling mills, had obvious advantages. In order to survive many smallholders must also have been wage labourers, perhaps needing (according to a calculation from Bishop's Cleeve) 130 days' work a year at 1½d. a day to achieve sufficiency. There certainly was work available. Even at Cuxham where the lord (Merton College, Oxford, by the second half of the thirteenth century) exacted labour services in full and where there was a permanent staff of demesne labourers, around 1,000 days of paid work were still required – enough to give 130 days' pay for seven of the thirteen smallholders in the village. Where labour services were commuted, lords would have required more labour. Peasants holding substantial holdings of thirty acres and upwards might also be employers.

The exploitation of woodland and meadow, and income derived from crafts and labour, were all ways in which smallholders might obtain sufficiency, but it must often have been sufficiency of the barest kind. The most deprived peasants were probably those in the open-field manors in the midlands and the south, where the villages were like islands in seas of arable and there was little meadow and forest left to be exploited. Here and elsewhere employment in village crafts cannot have helped more than a minority. The problem with relying on wages came in years of bad harvest. If a labourer was paid in kind, as some were, then he was protected. But the many paid in cash, who needed it to buy corn or bread, were in a dangerous situation; there was no way their wages would respond to a sudden surge in prices consequent on harvest failure, and indeed wages (with labour abundant) had not kept pace with the general path of inflation. The only recourse was to find more work, and that may have been impossible.

In years of bad harvest, therefore, there was famine. The failure of the harvest of 1257 meant that by the early summer of 1258 the price of wheat was two and a half times what it had been in 1254–5. In the manor of North Waltham the bishop of Winchester gave relief to sixty 'poor tenants', 27 per cent of the smallholders with fewer than ten acres of land. The prevalence and utility of this kind of succour is hard to judge, as is the extent to which suffering within a village was alleviated by family or communal action (see below, p. 414). It is clear, however, that such remedies were often inadequate. In 1258 so many people wandering about searching for food died from starvation that the government relaxed the rules about the identification of bodies. Matthew Paris described the situation:

Such great famine and mortality prevailed in the country, that a measure of wheat rose to fifteen shillings and more . . . The dead lay about, swollen and rotting, on dunghills, and in the dirt of the streets, and there was scarcely any one to bury them; nor did the people dare or wish to receive the dead into their houses for fear of contagion.

The year 1258 was far from unique. On several occasions in the 1270s the price of wheat approached or exceeded the 1258 figure. In years of bad harvest and high prices smallholders were often forced to raise money by selling land, thereby undermining their position further. A great deal of thirteenth-century crime (and there was a widely held belief that it was increasing) was committed by 'unknown' vagabonds and malefactors, men quite probably forced out of village communities by these conditions. The chattels of identified criminals were nearly always pathetically small; many had no chattels at all. Life expectancy was short. For the peasants of the bishop of Winchester there was a crude annual death rate in the thirteenth century of seventy to seventy-five per thousand, as opposed to twelve per thousand in post-war England and Wales. In the second half of the thirteenth century, even the more substantial tenants amongst the Winchester peasantry had a life expectancy of only twenty-four years on reaching the age of twenty. For the smallholders it was probably far shorter.

The situation in the thirteenth century could be bad; was it getting worse? That certainly has been argued by historians, partly at least on the basis that a population which grew from 2 million to 5 or 6 million between 1086 and 1300 must have been outrunning the ability of the land to support it, especially if peasant productivity was affected by soil exhaustion. Campbell, by contrast, arguing for a population increase of only 2–2.25 million to 4–4.25 million, shows how much the same standard of living could have been sustained through the creation of new arable land and some small rise in productivity. Even if, however, the sustainable ceiling was indeed around 4.25 million, there is nothing in Campbell's model which precludes the population having been pressed up hard against it, leaving a growing proportion of the peasantry living at bare subsistence levels and falling into danger in years of bad harvest.

There is indeed some evidence of this happening, most notably in the proliferation of smallholdings in areas where sources of income outside the arable had long been restricted. At Cuxham in Oxfordshire the process of wood clearance was complete by 1086. Meadow and pasture were very limited. None the less the tenant population rose from eleven to twenty-one between 1086 and 1279. But whereas the number of smallholders tripled from four to thirteen, those with half-yardland holdings increased by only one. Although some of the smallholders were subsequently given half-yardland holdings, these were on poorish land, much of it today rough grazing. Of course the smallholders were also wage labourers, but it is hard to avoid the conclusion that the villagers as a whole were worse off in 1279 than they had been in 1086. The same expansion in the number of smallholders can be seen on numerous other properties. In general they made up 33 per cent of the peasant population in Domesday Book and 46 per cent in Kosminsky's sample from the Hundred Rolls. Indeed the 1279 survey may make things look better than they were, since many half- and whole-yardland holdings probably supported extended family groups, formal divisions being prevented by the lord's desire to preserve the integrity of holdings. Where division was possible there is sometimes striking evidence for the proliferation of smallholdings: at Martham in Norfolk 1,066 acres were held by 107 tenants in the mid twelfth century and by 376 in 1292.

The growth in the population between the eleventh and thirteenth centuries was in large part a growth in the ranks of peasant smallholders, the latter therefore forming, as we have seen, a larger proportion of the population in 1300 than they had in 1086. Although alternative sources of income increased, they are unlikely to have offset the deterioration in living standards this implies. Lords still profited from the rents of the new smallholders. The king, save as a landholder himself, hardly profited at all. Roughly 60 per cent of the peasant population in the late thirteenth century were deemed too poor to pay taxation. That remarkable and chilling fact more than anything else puts the great expansion of the twelfth and thirteenth centuries into perspective. It is certainly the reason why the GDP could increase without commensurate benefit to the crown.

＊　　　＊　　　＊

The economic transformation in these years was none the less very real and had been dependent upon developments on the continent, notably the growth of the Flemish cloth industry which fed on British wool and paid for much of it in silver, hence the explosion of the money supply. More generally, the rise in the population, the clearance of land, the growth of towns and the proliferation of coinage were all phenomena common to much of Europe. They were related to that process of expansion and homogenization which is the theme of Robert Bartlett's book *The Making of Europe* – the expansion, that is, of a Franco-Latin Christian core, exporting as it went much the same military, social and ecclesiastical institutions. It was from France, as we mentioned in the last chapter (and will show more fully in the next), that castles and cavalry came to Britain through the agency of the Normans. Likewise it was from France and Italy that Britain received in the twelfth and thirteenth centuries both new religious orders and the structures of papal government of the church. These too helped to homogenize England, Wales and Scotland, and incorporate them into Europe.

One scene encapsulates something of this incorporation. It is 1188 in a remote valley in the uplands of central Wales. Gathered there are the Lord Rhys, ruler of Deheubarth, and his sons. They are dressed in the Welsh manner, indeed one son has his legs and feet left bare. Yet the scene is also very European. The group is close to the abbey of Strata Florida, whose monks by 1212 were exporting their wool overseas from English ports. The abbey itself is part of the great international Cistercian order in which every house has the same constitution and is subject to central control. Although founded by a lord of Norman descent, Robert fitz Stephen, Strata Florida has been embraced whole-heartedly by the Lord Rhys, and will become the mausoleum for many of his family. It is a substantial church, 200 feet long, and soon will have a remarkable round-arched, roll moulded western doorway, flanked by an elegant lancet window. Rhys and his party are being addressed by a group of high-powered ecclesiastics. One is Gerald of Wales, partly of native descent, yet shaped very much by his studies in Paris and his work in the Anglo-Norman world. Another, the leader, is the archbishop of Canterbury. He is the envoy of the pope and his mission, following the fall of Jerusalem in 1187, is to preach the crusade.

Within a few years of this peaceful scene, Rhys was attacking the Anglo-Norman lordships in south Wales. In 1212, a few months after licensing its exports, King John ordered Strata Florida to be destroyed for helping his Welsh enemies. Such conflict had its roots in the way the Normans had conquered important areas of Wales in the years after 1066. In many parts of Europe as the Franco-Latin centre expanded so it created tensions, both because of the very different cultures into which it cut, and because the cutting edge was so often violent. The response, in varying degrees, was resistance, submission and conform-ity. It was a response which differed across Britain, in part because the Normans came to Wales as conquerors and to Scotland by invitation of the king. In England itself they did not meet a culture 'inferior' to their own, save in one crucial area, that of military technology. Thanks to their military might the Normans would soon change the face of Britain.

3

The Norman Conquest of England, 1066–87

Edward the Confessor, last king of the ancient Wessex line, died on 5 January 1066. Next day he was buried in the new abbey he had built at Westminster and Harold was crowned in his stead, scenes graphically depicted on the Bayeux Tapestry. Earl over Wessex, brother-in-law to the Confessor, Harold had dominated England since the death of his father, Earl Godwin, in 1053. The Confessor had no children and had in his last feeble days designated Harold as his successor. The great men gathered at Westminster sanctioned the choice and both archbishops probably officiated at the coronation. Tall, strong, clever and courageous, Harold had long planned this take-over. He was mighty in arms: in 1063 in a campaign by land and sea he had crushed Gruffudd ap Llywelyn, 'king over all the Welsh', and laid his head before the Confessor. He was also a clever politician: in 1065 he had condoned, if not encouraged, the northern rebellion against his brother Tostig, earl in Northumbria since 1055, and had thereby removed a rival, conciliated the north and made alliance with the only family whose wealth remotely approached his own, that of Edwin, earl in Mercia, and his brother Morcar, who succeeded Tostig as earl in the north.

Having gained the throne, Harold could be both optimistic and anxious. He had succeeded to a state of great power, or at least of potential power. Yet his title to the throne was open to challenge, notably from Duke William of Normandy, and Harold himself had seen at first hand the cavalry and the castles which made the Norman military machine superior to the Anglo-Saxon.

During the tenth century, the Confessor's forebears had moved out from their Wessex base and brought under their rule the areas in East Anglia, the midlands and the north seized and settled by the Danes after 865, for the first time unifying England under a single king. The subsequent Danish conquest under King Cnut (1016–35) had shaken up the English aristocracy, bringing new families to the fore (like the Godwins), but had not replaced it with Scandinavians. On the death of Cnut's son Harthacanut in 1042, leaving no direct heirs, the old Wessex dynasty had been peacefully restored with Edward the Confessor returning from exile in Normandy. The Anglo-Saxon state had three pillars: a pervasive sense of Englishness which held king and people together, something already discussed (above, p. 3); a kingship high in status and strong in administrative structures; and a church, gentry and nobility integrated within the king's government of the realm.

The ideal of the king as a great warrior was a constant throughout the medieval period. Even the Venerable Bede wrote with admiration of how King Aethelrith of Northumbria, 'ambitious for glory', had conquered more territories from the Britons than any other ruler. Yet Anglo-Saxon kingship also glittered as Christian and civilian. The *ordo* for the 973 coronation of Edgar, shot through with Carolingian influences, formed the basis for all later ceremonies. The king was crowned and anointed with holy oil just as the prophet Samuel had anointed King Saul and King David. He was thus chosen by God, imbued with the blessings of the Holy Spirit, and elevated above all his subjects. Hence it was crowned and enthroned that the Confessor was depicted on his seal. The oath the king took at his coronation stressed his duty to maintain peace and dispense justice. In the late Anglo-Saxon period he was taking increasing steps to do so. In the past the king had not so much punished crime as regulated the compensation payments its victims or their families were to receive from the perpetrators, the role of the courts being to oversee such settlements. Now, alongside this system, the king started to isolate a group of major crimes, namely homicide, robbery, serious theft, rape, arson and treason, which he, and only he, had the right and duty to try and punish, the punishment often being death by hanging. Such offences constituted breaches of the king's 'peace', which by 1066 probably extended throughout the country. This itself was related to the oath of loyalty to the king taken by all adult males, which included a pledge not to be thieves or receivers of thieves. Peasants probably swore this oath when they entered the tithings (as they were later called), the associations of ten adult males whose members stood surety for each other's good behaviour. In later practice (and quite probably before 1066) the tithing's failure to arrest a delinquent member resulted in an amercement, a monetary penalty imposed by the king for an offence.

The old English kings had also developed an administrative structure which enabled them to run this peacekeeping system and also to exact their revenues, always the twin purposes of local government. They thought of England as a series of counties, making their announcements to the officials and men of Northamptonshire, Oxfordshire, and so on. The counties were the essential building blocks of the kingdom, and indeed survived unchanged in shape until 1974. By the year 1000 there were thirty-two of them. Some, like Kent and Essex, were ancient kingdoms, others in the midlands were probably created by the Wessex kings as they expanded their rule in the tenth century. Each county was subdivided into hundreds, of which there were over 600 in the thirteenth century. Both counties and hundreds had courts, the former meeting, at least according to legislation, twice a year, the latter once every four weeks. These courts were central to maintaining the peace and settling civil disputes over property. If they were very much 'popular' courts run by the leaders of local society doubtless in very different ways, they were also presided over, as we shall see, by royally appointed officials.

The king's revenues came in part from his lands, which were scattered through most of the country, the proceeds in cash or kind being worth some £6,000 per annum in 1066, according to the figures in Domesday Book. These sums were either paid into the treasury at Winchester or given to the king directly (and if in kind, consumed) when he was in residence in the locality. More remarkable was England's land tax, a tax with Carolingian parallels but now unique in Europe. It depended on a territorial division called the hide or carucate, which varied considerably in size but was often around 120 acres. Each hide had to contribute so many shillings to the tax (the rate could be varied), with the king expecting a lump sum from each hundred depending on the number of hides within it. If the figures from the Anglo-Saxon Chronicle can be believed (a debated point), early in the eleventh century the geld, as this tax was called, had raised vast sums to pay off the Danes, the £72,000 taken by King Cnut in 1018 being the largest. Equally impressive is the possibility that regular annual gelds between 1012 and 1051 raised up to £14,000 a year to support the king's fleet and army. Underpinning this taxation and the economy more generally was the superb coinage, universal, exclusive, of high quality, and controlled centrally by the king (see above, p. 30).

To run this system the king appointed local officials of whom the most important were the sheriff and the earl. It was often to them as the governors of the shire that the king addressed his orders and pronouncements. The sheriff was the official who did the day-to-day work of collecting the king's revenues and executing his orders. If there was no earl in the county, as often there was not, the sheriff was directly answerable to the king. The number of earls varied, as did their powers and the counties over which they presided. Often an earl would head a group of shires, and with the sheriffs in some sense as his deputies, command their military forces and preside over their courts. Both earl and sheriff were present in the Herefordshire county court during an important case in Cnut's time.

There were various ways in which kings sought to proclaim their will and enforce their decisions in the localities, thus solving the problem of government at a distance. The royal court was both the centre and the cementer of the realm. As it travelled the country the local nobility came in to discuss their affairs with ministers, king and queen, the latter (her role is discussed later) often being at the heart of court ceremonial. In fact the royal itinerary, though imperfectly known, was still largely confined to the midlands and the south. But if the king did not visit all his realm, he brought the realm to him in great assemblies or 'witans' where legislation was promulgated and important decisions taken. The king could also send his envoys into the localities. Present at the meeting of the Herefordshire county court referred to above was Tofi the Proud, there 'on the king's business'. As his ultimate 'muscle', there was a body of troops attached to the royal household and supported by the allotment of land and by pay. Some of these were thegns, others of Scandinavian origin were described as 'housecarls', a name sometimes given to the body as a whole. Apart from forming the nucleus of armies, these men watched over the king's interests in the shires and if necessary put down trouble, for example punishing the non-payment of taxation in brutal fashion.

In granting favours and issuing orders kings also utilized written communication. Indeed they were doing so with increasing efficiency, gradually embodying grants not in the elaborate and wordy 'diploma' but in a far more concise and standard form document, namely the 'writ' (*brevis*), essentially a letter authenticated by the king's seal being attached to it. Where diplomas and writs made concessions to ecclesiastical institutions they were often written by the beneficiaries themselves, but there is considerable evidence that the king relied on his own clerks, however few in number, to write his orders to local officials. In the last years of his reign the Confessor certainly had a chancellor, the official who can be seen later keeping the king's seal and presiding over his writing office. The train was already starting for its thirteenth-century destination where the chancery controlled the whole government of England through issuing thousands of documents a year, all derived in form from the sealed writ of the Anglo-Saxons.

None of this structure of government, of course, was sustainable without military force. At the heart of the king's armies were the troops of the royal household just described. They were supplemented through a system (set out most fully in Domesday Book for Berkshire) in which every five hides of land had to provide one warrior for the army or one sailor for the fleet, a great lord thus supplying a contingent in accordance with the hidage of his estate. The Old English kings could certainly raise armies of very substantial size, as the ability to fight three battles in 1066 shows. There was, however, one key feature about these forces. They seem to have been composed of foot soldiers, not combined foot and cavalry. At Hastings the English fought exclusively on foot, just as they had at the battle of Maldon in 991. In 1051 the reason for an English defeat in Wales, according to the twelfth-century chronicler John of Worcester, was because they had been ordered to fight on horseback 'contrary to their custom'. There was also one other key feature of the English military system. England had walled towns but, as the chronicler Orderic Vitalis pointed out, lacked the kind of fortifications 'called castles by the French'. There is little to suggest Orderic was wrong in this judgement. Excavations have revealed only one pre-Conquest castle in the sense of a significantly fortified residence. This is at Goltho in Lincolnshire, and there the pre-1066 earthworks were later supplemented by a much stronger Norman motte-and-bailey castle. One qualification for being a thegn, according to an early eleventh-century document, was to have an enclosure with a gate-house, but there is nothing in the historical narrative (about the crisis of 1051–2 for example) to suggest that such residences had much military value. The importance of these features of the English military system, which certainly set it apart from that developing on the continent, the events of 1066 were to show.

If there was a question mark over English military practices, there was none over the way the church, aristocracy and gentry were part and parcel of royal England. The church indeed had helped to unify England in the first place. By 1066 there were twelve English bishoprics,

Durham being subject to the metropolitan authority of the archbishop-ric of York and the rest to the authority of the archbishopric of Canter-bury. There were also some forty-five monastic houses (including eight nunneries), the richest, like the episcopal sees, being very wealthy. It was clearly vital for kings to control an institution which held some 26 per cent of England's land, and they certainly did so, appointing the bishops and abbots and ensuring that church land owed military service as part of the five-hide system. That the monasteries existed at all was thanks to King Edgar (959–75), for he had sponsored the reforms which saw their foundation or re-foundation. They prayed daily for the king and queen and were mostly situated within the monarchy's midlands and southern bases. The bishop was often addressed with the sheriff and the earl in the king's pronouncements and attended the county court, ecclesiastical pleas (see below, p. 101) being heard there or in the court of the hundred.

The thegns were the county gentry of Anglo-Saxon England, vital for the governing of the shires. They gave judgements in the county courts; they were addressed along with royal officials in the king's writs – 'all my thegns of Somerset', 'all my thegns of Berkshire'; and it was they who served in royal armies under the five-hide system. There were perhaps four or five thousand thegns spread through the counties. In theory the minimum qualification to achieve the status included having the residence with gate and enclosure mentioned above together with five hides of land, the equivalent of a medium-sized manor. Some thegns were specially attached to the king, 'king's thegns'; others were in the service of great lords.

Lordship too was central to the workings of government and society. The king relied on great lords to bring contingents to the army, give counsel at witans, and hold office as earls. Domesday Book shows that there were ninety or so lords on the eve of the Conquest with wealth substantially larger than the ordinary county thegns and above them there were three great families who combined their own lands with the tenure of earldoms, namely the families of Seward, of the brothers Edwin and Morcar, and above all of Harold himself. There was always a danger, of course, of such men becoming over-mighty, but in general lordly power before 1066 seems to have been less disruptive of the state than in some areas of the continent. This was due both to the absence of castles and to the limited competence of lords in the areas of justice and law and order. Lords before and after 1066 were certainly developing manorial courts but the latter's purpose was essentially to discipline the peasant workforce and ensure the smooth running of the manor. At a higher level, although at least 100 hundreds in 1066 seem to have been dominated by great lords, lay and ecclesiastical, the king never appears to have formally relinquished control of their courts. Even if he had, provided he reserved the royal monopoly over the serious crimes mentioned above it would only have meant conceding jurisdiction over cases of minor crime and disorder. It was certainly only that which was involved in the grants the king did make of 'sake and soke, toll, team and infangenthief', the most important right here being 'infangenthief' (often later seen attached to manorial courts) which involved having a gallows on which to hang petty thieves taken red-handed on the lord's property.

The structures of Anglo-Saxon monarchy might be strong, yet individual kings weak, as a result of personal inability and political circumstance. Weakness in a king could also have an effect on structure. The Confessor reduced the number of hides on which some hundreds paid geld and (in 1051) abolished the highly unpopular annual army geld altogether. It is difficult to think that the Confessor was other than dangerously threatened by Harold's family whose lands in 1065 were £2,000 a year more valuable than his own. Harold, as earl throughout the counties of Wessex, had been encroaching on royal lands and absorbing them into those of his family. He had also recruited numerous sworn followers. Yet these problems vanished with Harold's accession. The over-mighty earl became the king. In combining his family lands with those of the crown he was far more powerful than his predecessor. Apart from a doubt over its military structure, Harold's difficulties lay not with the state he inherited but with his political position. His alliance with Edwin and Morcar was fragile, despite his marriage to their sister. His brother Tostig in exile plotted revenge. Nothing could give Harold the prestige of the ancient House of Wessex. His own father, Godwin, who had made the family fortunes through service to King Cnut, came from a Sussex family of merely local importance. Harold's succession had depended on brushing aside a clear representative of the Wessex dynasty, Edgar Atheling, who at some stage had perhaps received the title 'Atheling', meaning throne-worthy, from the Confessor himself. A great-grandson of King Aethelred (971–1016), and grandson of the heroic Edmund Ironside, Edgar was a teenager born in exile, and kept landless in England, doubtless through Harold's influence. Another claimant, William, duke of Normandy, was a very different proposition.

*   *   *

The basis of Duke William's claim was that he had been made heir to the throne by the Confessor himself back in 1051. This was probably true enough and was part of the latter's abortive attempt to throw off the Godwins. Edward naturally looked to Normandy. His mother, Emma, was the daughter of Duke Richard I, the Conqueror's great-grandfather. Edward himself had spent the period of Danish rule as an exile at the Norman court and it was with Duke William's support that he had returned in 1042 to secure the English throne. The Normans also alleged that Harold had taken an oath to accept William's succession. Again true enough, though probably the oath had been forced from him in 1064 or 1065 as the price of release after he had fallen into Duke William's hands during an ill-fated diplomatic mission.

The precise merits of William's claim, however, were beside the point. The first part of the Bayeux Tapestry opens and closes with a magnificent picture of Edward the Confessor, huge and imposing, crowned and enthroned. Against him William, holding court as duke of Normandy, bare-headed like everyone else, seems small and insignificant. William had every incentive to reach out for the wealth of England and the manna of a crown. He certainly had the resources to do so. In 911 the Frankish Carolingian king, Charles the Simple, had granted Rouen and its surrounding area to the Viking leader Rollo and his followers. This was the origin of Normandy. In the next century Rollo's descendants, frequently using the title Duke, established their rule within Normandy's historic frontiers. Although Viking settlement had probably been quite extensive, the newcomers ultimately lost their connection with Scandinavia and became essentially French in language, politics and social structure.

For the power of the Norman nobility the years between c. 1025 and c. 1050 were critical. The flaccid rule of Duke Robert (1027–35) was followed by the long minority of his son William, the future Conqueror. Only seven or eight on his accession, he was the fruit of an unconsecrated union between Robert and the daughter of a Falaise tanner. The great nobles, many probably descended from long-established families, gained control of both ducal lands and local office, notably that of the vicomte, the duke's chief local agent. They also increased the number and geographical spread of the men who owed them allegiance, in the process rewarding followers with 'benefices' or 'fees' in land, and asserting lordship over 'allodial land' which families had previously held freely from no lord at all. The nobility likewise seized monastic lands and challenged what had previously been a ducal monopoly by themselves founding numerous monasteries, which protected the souls of the patron family and proclaimed its status. This was a period of violence and instability which spawned nobles – ambitious, aggrieved, unrewarded – who sought outlets beyond the duchy's frontiers. Thus Normans began to arrive as fighters in southern Italy where they ultimately established their own kingdom. It was the same dynamism which established the Normans in England.

Put like this the Normans appear as a uniquely expansionist, martial and chosen race, and that is how they appear in the marvelling pages of one of the greatest of all medieval chroniclers, Orderic Vitalis (1075–c. 1141). He was born in England of a French father and English mother but became a monk at one of those 'noble' monasteries in Normandy, St-Evroult. In fact, however, Norman militancy and expansion were inseparable from a much wider aristocratic diaspora which was Frankish rather than specifically Norman. The nobles of Anjou were just as aggressive as those in Normandy and knights from many parts of France took part in the conquest of southern Italy, as indeed they did of England. Also common to many parts of Europe, it has been suggested, were changes in family structures which help to explain this aristocratic conduct. These involved large kin groups, which had shared property widely on the death of one of their members, narrowing into lineages in which the patrimonial land passed intact to the eldest son. The validity of this hypothesis has been much debated. The evidence is treacherous and may, on one view, reveal less a general trend than a favouring of the direct male line in particular situations. In Normandy, however, the development of lineages does seem to be reflected in the appearance, from the 1040s, of toponymic surnames like Beaumont and Montgomery, the result, it can be argued, of a single line retaining and thus becoming attached to its core properties. If land was concentrated in fewer hands than before it would explain how the nobility gained resources to build castles, found monasteries and extend its lordship over men. It would also help to explain the pressure to expand and conquer, for this solved the problem of younger sons, the custom becoming – perhaps the result of the conquest of England – for acquisitions to go to them, leaving the patrimony intact to descend by primogeniture.

Whether or not this was an exceptionally violent age throughout much of Europe has also been debated. On one view, the impression that it was is simply the result of better documentation. There was certainly nothing new about the military preoccupations of the aristocracy. Many of the ingredients of knighthood can be found in the ninth century. Yet the fact that the Normans did indeed concentrate on and define their status through the practice of arms remains of overwhelming importance. With the rest of the Franks, they favoured above all heavy cavalry, like the contingent pictured on the Bayeux Tapestry charging into Brittany to attack Dinan. A 'knight' might simply be a cavalry soldier equipped by a lord. But because the armour and the horse could only be afforded by an elite, the term was also used increasingly as an honorific title to a rank, with initiation ceremonies like that depicted on the tapestry where William 'gives arms' to Harold. In one vital respect, moreover, the nobility in this period did gain an entirely new means of wielding power, ultimately violent power. This was the castle. The encastellation of Europe between the tenth and the thirteenth centuries was indeed 'a development of quite fundamental military and political importance' (Robert Bartlett). In Normandy, although the evidence is fragmentary, the aristocratic elite seem to have been building castles from the 1030s. Just how second nature it had become to construct such buildings is illustrated by the castle thrown up at Hastings as soon as the Normans arrived in England, another scene depicted in the tapestry.

The Norman nobles were central to the Conquest, but only because William had brought them under control, reviving ducal authority in Normandy after its collapse during his minority. In 1047, in alliance with Henry I, king of France (1031–60), he won a great victory over his domestic foes at the battle of Val-ès-Dunes, and then, in the next decade, turned and beat off the assaults of King Henry and his ally Count Geoffrey of Anjou. William maintained a tight hold over appointments to bishoprics and presided over a series of reforming councils which enhanced the authority of bishops within their dioceses. He also won the favour of the pope and obtained a banner signifying the latter's approval for the conquest of England. To counter the spread of aristocratic power, he went some way towards establishing a tenurial hierarchy in which nobles, lay and ecclesiastical, did him homage and held their land from him in return for military service, if unspecified in extent. William also prevented the castellans from effectively destroying the public structures of local government inherited from the Carolingians by taking over for themselves the maintenance of law and order. He asserted the right to control private castles and he built castles of his own; the one at Caen, between the two great monasteries founded by himself and his wife, still seems to hinge the city.

By the 1060s the duchy was dominated, under the duke, by a small and tested group of around a dozen nobles, most from long-established families and as a group far more unified than their equivalents in England. Where Harold had quarrelled disastrously with Tostig, William's half-brothers, Robert, count of Mortain, and Odo, bishop of Bayeux, were among his leading lieutenants. Individually the great men of Normandy were very different, Count Robert stolid and reliable, Odo voluble and boastful. It was Odo who commissioned the tapestry, still at Bayeux, which tells the story of the Conquest. But they were all, as William of Malmesbury put it, 'inured to war'. The duke was absolutely equipped to be their leader. Bursting with confidence, he could make and take jokes, and accept and reject advice. Above all, he too was a warrior. 'It was a sight at once both delightful and terrible to see him managing his horse, girt with sword, his shield gleaming, his helmet and his lance alike menacing,' wrote his chaplain, William of Poitiers. Stout (a very different physical type from Harold), but always leading from the front, William was a brilliant and ruthless exponent of the lightning cavalry expeditions, the siege operations and the burning and pillaging which were the business of war. And it was above all through warfare, external warfare, that William canalized the energies of his men. Here he was helped by events across his frontiers, which freed him from external threat. In 1060 both King Henry of France and Count Geoffrey of Anjou died. Anjou entered a period of weak rule and civil war. The new king of France was a minor, in the custody of Baldwin, count of Flanders, whose daughter William had married, thereby securing an important ally to the north. In 1062 William invaded Maine and wrested it from the count of Anjou. In 1064 or 1065 he led a punitive expedition into Brittany. It was this drive, expertise and organization which was now to be felt in England.

* * *

With promise of great rewards, William raised an army, in part mercenary, from Normandy and other parts of France. And then he was lucky. Hostile winds, so William of Poitiers states, highly unusual in the Channel at that time of year, kept him from crossing while Harold's army guarded the coast, and then shifted to release him when the army had departed to deal with a crisis in the north. Tostig had thrown in his lot with the king of Norway, Harold Hardrada, who nourished his own claims to the throne, and in September they sailed up the Ouse to York and mauled the forces of Edwin and Morcar at the battle of Fulford Gate. By this time Harold was already hurrying north and on 25 September he surprised and killed both Tostig and Hardrada at Stamford Bridge. Two days later, on the evening of Wednesday, 27 September, the Norman army embarked at St-Valéry-sur-Somme in Ponthieu (whose count was William's vassal), and next morning landed at Pevensey in England.

William also made his own luck. His military administration had kept his forces in being during the long wait. Some of Harold's, by contrast, had departed through lack of supplies even before the invasion of Hardrada. William's strategy once ashore was equally clever. He refused to be drawn inland, away from his lines of communication. Instead he made Hastings his base, built a castle there, and ravaged the surrounding countryside, much of it Harold's ancestral land. 'Here a house is burnt' ran the caption on the Bayeux Tapestry above a picture of a pathetic woman with child in hand fleeing as her home is fired. William's tactic was to provoke Harold into coming to him and Harold duly obliged. Perhaps he felt his political position would not brook delay; perhaps he was over-confident and sought to repeat his success at Stamford Bridge. Either way, instead of harrying William's army and blockading the Channel with his fleet, he hastened south to do battle without Edwin and Morcar – without half his army, according to the chronicler John of Worcester (writing between 1124 and 1140).

That battle was joined at nine in the morning of 14 October, six miles north-west of Hastings. Harold had formed up his army on foot in a solid shield wall occupying the plateau, about a quarter of a mile broad and half a mile deep, overlooking a little valley. William had thus to drive his cavalry and infantry up a steepish hill merely to reach the English lines. Soon a contingent of Breton foot in William's army gave way, and the rumour spread that Duke William was dead. This was the climax of the battle and William was its equal. The tapestry shows him raising his helmet to reveal his face, a necessarily static picture whereas the actual event was fast-moving, William galloping down his lines to inspire his men. Throughout the battle he had far more command and control than Harold who, wedged in his shield wall, was invisible within a few feet of his standard. There is here a wider point. The English, as we have seen, had no cavalry. It was a fatal deficiency. Once the Bretons had given way and panic had spread through the Norman ranks, the moment had come for a cavalry charge down the hill to sweep all before it; as it was, the English charged on foot and were cut off by Norman cavalry. So little indeed did the Normans fear such foot charges that they twice feigned retreat in order to repeat the cutting-off tactic. So Hastings became a killing match and the Normans had more effective means of killing: horsemen, and also archers. The lack of English archers is one of the puzzles of the battle. Only one English bowman is shown on the tapestry, the consequence perhaps of the haste with which the army had been assembled. By contrast the shields and bodies of the English bristle with Norman arrows. As the day wore on, and the English numbers dwindled, the Norman cavalry established themselves on the plateau and broke into the shield wall. They killed Harold's brothers Gyrth and Leofwine, then Harold's immediate bodyguard, and then at last, as the shadows of the autumn evening lengthened, they cornered Harold himself, already wounded by an arrow in the head, and struck him down.

Only part of the English forces had been engaged at Hastings, and in London Archbishops Stigand and Ealdred, Earls Edwin and Morcar and the townsmen rejected William's demands for submission and nominated Edgar Atheling, who was with them, as king. Early in December, William began a long circular march round the city burning and pillaging as he went. Edgar was as powerless to resist him as he had been earlier to resist Harold. When William reached Wallingford, Stigand came to him and swore allegiance; he was followed at Berkhampstead by Archbishop Ealdred, Bishop Wulfstan of Worcester, and Edgar himself, as well as by Edwin and Morcar, with citizens of London and many others. On Christmas Day, 1066 William was crowned king in Westminster Abbey.

William's triumph was due to more than luck and superior tactics. It also reflected significant differences between the Norman and English polities, as we have seen. In England the Normans certainly did not meet a state inferior to their own. Quite the reverse. The duke's role in the maintenance of law and order in the duchy, though significant, was less pervasive than that of the king in England. The duke had no chancellor, no writs, no seal, and no geld tax. He minted a greatly inferior coinage. Yet William conquered, as Cnut had done earlier in the century. The state which the English created but could not defend: there is some truth in that aphorism. In terms of armour, martial values and military effectiveness there was little, in some ways, to choose between the English and the Normans, which was why Hastings was such a long battle. The five-hide system, on paper at least, was a more clearly defined and established method of raising armies than any in place in Normandy. Where the Normans had the edge was not in the way the armies were recruited, but in what they produced. In a conflict like Hastings the simple truth was that a force which could fight on horse as well as foot was superior to one which could only do the latter. Given the amount of training mounted warfare takes, English society was, in that respect, less militarized than Norman. On both sides of his seal as king of England, the Confessor showed himself enthroned. William, on the seal he made once he became king, was enthroned on one side but on the other appeared as a mounted knight. Nothing sums up better this vital contrast between the Norman and the English polities.

There was another significant difference, as we have seen. Orderic Vitalis did not merely mention the absence of English castles. He also affirmed that this was why 'the English, in spite of their courage and love of fighting, could only put up a weak defence against their enemies'. Fundamentally, when it came to defences the English had fallen between two stools. The defences of royal and magnate residences were too small to allow any effective resistance to the Normans. Those of the towns were too large to do so. According to a document of the early tenth century ('The Burghal Hidage'), 27,000 men were needed just to defend the boroughs of Wessex, numbers impossibly large in a time of dislocation like 1066 when so many men were already called up in the armies. And there was here a double bind. Just as the absence of castles enabled the Normans to seize England, so it was by building huge numbers, over 500 by the year 1100 according to one plausible estimate, that they secured their rule. The castles of the Conquest, built both by king and lords, took a variety of forms. In London the great stone keep begun by the Conqueror, now called the White Tower, is ninety feet high, has walls over thirteen feet thick, and still looks a mighty building even against the present London skyline. Elsewhere structures were simpler. Some were just ditches and banked enclosures topped with palisades (called by historians 'ring works'). Others, indeed the great majority, were of the motte-and-bailey type, as at Berkhampstead. The motte was a great earthen mound protected by a ditch and topped with a stockade and a wooden keep, the adjoining bailey an enclosure protected by earthen ramparts, topped again with a stockade, and surrounded by an outer ditch. Such structures could be built speedily and defended by small numbers of knights, yet they were quite sufficient to dominate their strategic environment; that, not the protection of the local population, was of course their purpose. Utterly novel, standing high above town and village, road and river, the castle as both symbol and sanction lay at the heart of the Conquest.

Cavalry and castles were integral to the intensely competitive military and political environment in France, where small principalities – Anjou, Maine, Brittany, Normandy, the French kingdom – were engaged in constant fast-moving warfare across great plains and open frontiers. England was very different. Since Cnut's accession in 1016 it had suffered neither invasion nor civil war. Harold had triumphed in Wales, but this was not cavalry territory. There had been no need to develop either cavalry or castles. The English state had been too successful for its own good.

*   *   *

William's success in 1066 cannot be explained entirely in military terms. Following his initial victories the English had accepted him as king. After all, he proclaimed himself the Confessor's designated heir and took the same coronation oaths as his Anglo-Saxon predecessors. When he returned to Normandy in March 1067, he left as regents his brother Bishop Odo and his friend since childhood, William fitz Osbern, but he also retained many English sheriffs and recognized and appointed English earls. In the next few years William, faced with a series of rebellions, was utterly to destroy this Anglo-Norman co-operation.

There was immediate discontent at the taxation and the castles which were a concomitant of Norman rule. The Anglo-Saxon Chronicle commented at once on the breach of William's coronation oath to rule his people well. Worst of all, as Orderic Vitalis later put it, was 'the anger at the loss of patrimonies and the death of kinsmen and fellow countrymen'. From the start, as a writ to the abbot of Bury St Edmunds shows, William demanded the lands of all who 'stood in battle against me and were slain', including the lands of Harold and his brothers. From William's point of view, these dispossessions were justified on the grounds that Harold was a perjured usurper (in Domesday Book he was not even given the title of king). They were also utterly necessary both to grip the kingdom and, as with taxation, reward those who had fought for his victory and in the case of the Norman monasteries had prayed for it. Yet the dispossessions sent shock waves through English society. They destroyed Harold's house which had dominated England for a generation and disinherited the families of the other fallen. Thoroughly alarmed, large numbers of English landholders flocked to William or his deputies hoping to secure or recover their lands. Some were lucky, like Azo the steward of the Confessor who found William at Windsor, but many had to offer money. 'The people bought their lands,' grumbled the Anglo-Saxon chronicler.

Trouble began before William returned to England in December 1067. In the new year he had to march into the West Country, where he besieged and took Exeter and built a castle in the town. Then he drove on into Cornwall where he ultimately established his half-brother Robert, count of Mortain. The coronation of William's wife Matilda in May 1068 was the last of the great Anglo-Norman occasions. Earl Edwin found himself threatened locally by Roger of Montgomery's earldom in Shropshire and challenged at court by 'greedy Normans', as Orderic put it, who opposed his prospective marriage to William's sister. Between 1068 and 1070 he was joined in rebellion by Earls Morcar, Waltheof and Gospatric, whom the Conqueror himself had placed over Northumbria. Most dangerous of all, Edgar Atheling, with succour and support from King Malcolm of Scotland, now revived his claims to the throne. In his first response, in 1068, William marched north, building castles as he went at Warwick (where Edwin and Morcar surrendered), on the rock at Nottingham, and at York. Early in 1069, however, the Atheling attacked York and was chosen king by his supporters. So William went north again and gave York a second castle. It was not enough. In the autumn of 1069 a great fleet sent by Sven Esthrison, king of Denmark (1047–76), a nephew of King Cnut, entered the Humber, and joined up with the Atheling. On 21 September they defeated and captured William's sheriff of York and seized the city. Meanwhile Exeter and Shrewsbury (the seat of Roger of Montgomery's new earldom) were also attacked.

This was the crisis of William's reign and he knew it. He ignored a rebellion which threatened his conquest of Maine, and acted in England with a combination of energy, brutality and conciliation. Leaving Bishop Geoffrey of Coutances to deal with the trouble in the west, he again marched north and on Christmas Day, 1069 wore his crown, especially dispatched from Winchester, in the ruins of York Minster, a symbolic riposte to the pretensions of the Atheling. He then marched to the Tees, ravaging the country as he went. The Danes were bought off, the Atheling retired to Scotland, and Gospatric and Waltheof admitted defeat, retaining their earldoms. But William was not finished. He led his troops on an extraordinary winter march across the Pennines, fell upon the Shrewsbury rebels, built castles at Chester and Stafford, ravaged the surrounding areas, and was back at Winchester in time for Easter (April 1070). By this time his forces in Yorkshire had reduced much of it to a wasteland.

Historians have sometimes been sceptical about the extent of 'the harrying of the north' but the evidence is terribly powerful and consistent. William 'went northwards with all his army that he could collect and utterly ravaged and laid waste that shire [Yorkshire],' wrote the Anglo-Saxon chronicler. Sixteen years after the event Domesday Book still recorded 33 per cent of Yorkshire 'waste' and another 16 per cent as virtually without resources. The sheer scale of the waste, amounting to 80 per cent of that recorded in Domesday, can scarcely be explained by clerks simply writing off areas for which they had no information, as has been suggested. Columns of refugees, young and old, women and children, fleeing the famine caused by 'the devastation', reached as far south as Evesham, where they died of weakness even as they ate the food provided by the abbot. Simeon of Durham, writing in the early twelfth century but with local knowledge, likewise spoke of the great famine; the exodus of refugees; the decaying corpses and 'the land deprived of anyone to cultivate it, reduced for nine years to an extensive solitude. . . . There was no village inhabited between York and Durham.' The Conqueror's knights were masters of the ravage and they rose to the appalling challenge. Small parties of them, moving rapidly from village to village, could easily have accomplished the destruction in the months between Christmas and Easter. They were helped by the winter season. The corn for both eating and sowing was in the barns. By setting them ablaze the food for two years was effectively destroyed. The last word is with Orderic Vitalis, who was born in 1075 and grew up in Shropshire till he was ten:

My narrative has frequently had occasion to praise William, but for this act which condemned the innocent and the guilty alike to die by slow starvation I cannot commend him. For when I think of helpless children, young men in the prime of life, and hoary grey-beards perishing alike of hunger I am so moved to pity that I would rather lament the griefs and sufferings of the wretched people than make a vain attempt to flatter the perpetrator of such infamy.

William's northern campaign almost ended English resistance, but not quite. Edwin and Morcar had been kept out of the upheavals of 1069–70, but in 1071 they escaped from court. Edwin was soon trapped and killed; but Morcar fled to the Isle of Ely where he joined up with an adventurous Lincolnshire thegn, Hereward (Hereward the Wake of later legend). King William invested the isle and in October 1071 Morcar surrendered, ending his life as a prisoner. Hereward escaped. His further exploits inspired poets but did not threaten Norman rule. The Conquest itself was over. In 1074 the Atheling recognized as much; he left Scotland and became a pensioner at William's court. Lacking a real sense of dynasty and destiny, his later role was as a captain of Norman and Scottish armies, not as a candidate for the throne. William of Malmesbury provides a last glimpse of him in the 1120s, aged and obscure, living quietly in the country.

*   *   *

The Normans had come to exploit the peasantry, not replace them. The overwhelming bulk of the English population thus remained in place after the Conquest, if battened down by more exacting lords. The latter, often absentees, strove to get their income in cash rather than in kind, a desire for money which accelerated the end of slavery. Reorganization of manors also led to a substantial decline in the numbers of sokemen and free peasants (see above p. 52). Peasants laboured on the new castles and fled or starved to death when a Norman army burnt its way through the countryside. Towns too suffered. Much of York was wrecked in the great rebellions of 1069–70 while elsewhere houses were pulled down to make way for the new castles and cathedrals. There was some immigration. At York, 145 properties once held by Anglo-Scandinavians were taken over by Frenchmen. There were French quarters too at Norwich and Northampton. But probably the great bulk of the town populations remained English.

If peasants and townsmen remained in place, a huge swathe of English landowners was dispossessed, including virtually all the aristocracy. It was that, more than anything else, which secured the Conquest so absolutely. This disappropriation had begun after Hastings and increased in pace with every rebellion. The result can be seen in Domesday Book which surveyed England both in 1066 and 1086. Only four Englishmen, Edward of Salisbury, Gospatric son of Arnkell, Thorkell of Warwick and Colswein of Lincoln, remained as major landholders. Gone were Harold's family and those of the other English earls, gone were all ninety or so of the lords who had possessed land worth £40 a year or more, and gone too, at least in the record, were perhaps fifteen or twenty thousand smaller English landholders. Many of the latter were very small fry indeed, which shows how devastatingly low the blades of disappropriation had been set. Others, perhaps four or five thousand of them, were thegns, who, as we have seen, formed the country gentry of Anglo-Saxon England. In many counties page after page of Domesday Book, manor after manor, reveals hardly a single Anglo-Saxon lord. 'Henry de Ferrers holds Kingston [in Berkshire]. Ralph holds it from him. Stanchil held it in the time of King Edward' runs a typical entry, where the 1066 lord Stanchil has been replaced by the great Norman baron Henry de Ferrers, who has in turn granted the manor to his knight, Ralph de Bacquepuis. Just occasionally the survival of wills and charters shows what all this meant for a particular English family. For more than a generation prior to 1066 a spread of lands in Lincolnshire had supported Ulf, son of Tope, and his kinsmen. 'They acted in concert, endowed their favourite monastery (Peterborough), transacted business together, attested each other's charters and lent each other a helping hand in troubled times' (Robin Fleming). Within half a decade of the Conquest this family network was no more. Ulf, son of Tope, had departed for the Holy Land, never to return, and the family's lands were split between five Norman lords. Where families did survive it was often in much reduced circumstances. In Cambridgeshire, Almaer, lord of Bourn, was reduced from an estate of twenty-two hides to one of fewer than four.

William's Conquest had thus turned out very differently from that of Cnut, who, as William of Malmesbury shrewdly noted, restored their lands unimpaired to the conquered. Cnut had rewarded his followers with money rather than with land. The Conqueror chose land, perhaps inevitably given Norman expectations, and thus set off the

vicious cycle of rebellion and deprivation which ended with the elimination of so many English landholders. Malmesbury was a monk, writing
in the 1120s, half Norman and half English. He believed that the sins
of the English explained the Conquest. Yet he could still write about it
with great bitterness. Hastings was 'a fatal day', 'a melancholy havoc
of our dear country', making it 'the residence of foreigners and the
property of strangers'.

The Conquest was, therefore, devastating, but large numbers of
Englishmen did survive at levels above the peasantry. Almaer of Bourn
was not alone. When a great Norman baron, a Henry de Ferrers or
Ilbert de Lacy, swept into an area to take possession of the estates
granted him by the Conqueror, he was met by dozens of Englishmen
promising faithful service and seeking to obtain or retain land. Some
were lucky and, like Aelfwine, tenant of the Ferrers at Brailsford in
Derbyshire, were predecessors of major gentry families of the twelfth
and thirteenth centuries. Indeed around ten of Henry de Ferrers's
twenty-five tenants in Derbyshire had English-sounding names and the
proportion was even higher on the Lacy estates in Yorkshire. Further
evidence of English survival is provided by the lists of king's thegns at
the end of every county section of Domesday Book. Most held just a
few hides of land, but they were also probably local officials – huntsmen,
foresters, sheriff's bailiffs – and thus significant. Domesday Book may
also conceal a whole class of English sub-tenants and officials because
it rarely reveals who were the lessees or bailiffs of the manors held by
the Norman lords. Thaxted, the most valuable Essex manor of Richard
de Clare, was leased to an Englishman. He may well have been one of
many. For running the hundred, the basic unit of local administration,
the English remained vitally important. Indeed they provided nearly
half the jurors drawn from the Cambridgeshire hundreds who gave
evidence to the Domesday commissioners. Much later history – the bid
made by Norman kings for English support, the survival of the English
language – becomes understandable against that background. At the
level of the county and the hundred, unless there was to be constant
disturbance, Normans and English had to work together. Gradually a
new nationality and local society formed to replace the old.

In that formation a significant role was played by women. After the
Conquest the Normans had no place for the male kin of the killed and
dispossessed. Women, or at least women of a certain status and place
in the life cycle, were a different matter. Marriage to the widow or

daughter of a thegn might help secure possession of his lands. It was to escape such a fate, or worse, that English women after the Conquest fled to monasteries. But many such marriages did take place, like that between Robert d'Oilly and Ealdgyth, daughter of Wigod of Wallingford. Of course, the whole purpose of such matches was to divert property away from English kin. But Ealdgyth and the rest cannot have suddenly disowned their Englishness. They passed it on to their children and thus took a first step in bridging the divide of the Conquest.

*   *   *

The church, with some struggle, by and large kept its lands intact before and after the Conquest, holding some 26 per cent of Domesday England. Beyond these possessions, however, virtually all the land of England had come into the king's hands, and Domesday Book shows what he did with it, illuminating both the resources of the crown and the structure of the new aristocracy. The first and most striking fact is the amount of land William kept for himself: in all some £12,600 worth, 17 per cent of Domesday England. These royal lands, giving a presence in nearly every shire, were double in value those held by the Confessor. Whereas before 1066 the leading nobles had roughly 16 per cent more land than the king, afterwards it was exactly the reverse. William was thus far more powerful than the Confessor, though that would have been true for Harold too had he remained on the throne.

Apart from his own possessions and those of the church, William had redistributed the great bulk of the land of England to his followers from Normandy and elsewhere in France. The most important land-holders in each county were listed individually at the start of each county section of Domesday Book and came to be called tenants-in-chief of the crown, a 'baron' being simply a major tenant-in-chief. In the twelfth century there were between 150 and 200 of the latter. Domesday shows that these tenants-in-chief had themselves granted to their own tenants, in varying amounts, roughly 45 per cent of their land in terms of value. We have seen how Henry de Ferrers gave Kingston in Berkshire to Ralph de Bacquepuis. On the Clare estates, 40 per cent of the land in terms of value was held by around fifty tenants. Similar 'sub-enfeoffments' were made by the new Norman bishops and abbots on their church estates. The reasons for such grants were various. One was to win friends and influence people, hence some of the tenants were very great men, barons themselves or major tenants of other barons. Another reason was to reward followers, so that many tenants of the Clares and the Ferrers were, like Ralph de Bacquepuis (Bacquepuis near Evreux), their tenants or neighbours in Normandy.

The structures of power which resulted from these landed endowments can be analysed in different ways. Where tenants-in-chief had granted manors to tenants, it was generally the latter who enjoyed the revenues. Yet tenants-in-chief still expected service and support from their tenants and continued to have rights over their lands, as will be seen. Thus in assessing their power it is not irrelevant to add the value of tenanted land to that they kept in their own hands, that is 'in demesne'. Below is an analysis made along these lines, based on the pioneering work of W. J. Corbett published in the 1920s:

Tenants-in-chief, 1086: value of lands in demesne and tenanted

A	£650–£3,240	10
B	£400–£650	10
C	£200–£400	24
D	£100–£200	36
E	£15–£100	200+

Calculated like this the concentration of wealth at the top of the scale is remarkable, for the barons from class A commanded between a quarter and a fifth of Domesday England. Since they were all close associates of the Conqueror, and included his brothers, this explains much of the hold he established over the country.

A rather different picture, however, emerges if one makes a survey of the landed wealth of tenants as well as tenants-in-chief, and does it in terms simply of the land held in demesne. This both hugely increases the numbers of people surveyed and reduces the separation between the great barons and the rest. An analysis along these lines by J. J. N. Palmer shows that 34 per cent of secular wealth (apart from the lands of the king) was in the hands of 940 landholders with lands valued at between £5 and £45 a year. Another 11 per cent was possessed by 1,720 landholders with lands worth between £1 and £5 a year. Below this there were some 3,470 men with lands valued at less than a £1 a year. All told, the analysis reveals over 6,200 landholders. If a proportion of these were English it was a comparatively small one. Having made some estimate of the numbers in Essex, Norfolk and Suffolk (counties excluded from his analysis), Palmer puts the total of Norman landholders (Norman here meaning loosely everyone from France) at over 8,000.

These findings are immensely significant because they explain the grip which the Normans gained on England and the power of local society in later centuries against both great lords and the king. Even if some of these lesser Normans had other sources of income (for example as professional knights) and were largely absentees, the great majority were almost certainly resident on their estates in England. These were the men who were the first to speak the language and intermarry with the native English. That half the personnel of the Cambridgeshire hundred juries were Norman, some holders of substantial properties, others with only tiny holdings, is as significant as the fact that half were English. Nothing shows more clearly how involved the Normans had become from the start in running local affairs in England. The more substantial families with lands worth £5 and upwards came to form the cream of a new gentry class, the county society of the knights coming to replace the county society of the thegns. Their establishment in England was often reflected in place names. Thus the Bacquepuis's Kingston became Kingston Bagpuize, showing very clearly how this family from the Evreçin had taken root in Berkshire.

In terms of their physical configuration, the lands of individual barons, both demense and tenanted, were often spread over many shires while having a core in one or more particular regions (see below, pp. 404-5). Since such estates were usually built up from the possessions of many dispossessed Englishmen, they were as a whole new creations. A common pattern was for a baron to receive a large proportion of the lands of a few great English nobles together with the properties of numerous smaller fry. Of the Clare lands in Surrey, 40 per cent in terms of value derived from three major 'ancestors' (as previous owners of significance were called), while the other 60 per cent came from seventeen men, only three of whom contributed more than one property. Many of the large antecessorial grants took place soon after the Conquest, while the lands of the lesser individuals were swept up later in disappropriations following the rebellions. In all this William showed a keen strategic eye. Outside the Welsh borders, he never gave all the lands in a shire to a single baron, but he was quite prepared to create smaller blocs of power in order to hold down particular areas. In the north, Henry de Ferrers gained nearly all the land within Derbyshire's Appletree wapentake, while Ilbert de Lacy received nearly all that in

Skyrack wapentake in Yorkshire. (A wapentake was the equivalent of a hundred.) In Sussex, William accepted the ancient divisions into rapes, but completely ignored earlier tenurial patterns when he concentrated the land within them under single lords. There was a similar concentration of Clare holdings around their great castle at Tonbridge in Kent.

Politics and family history were always reshaping the contours of great estates, if at a slower pace than in the Conquest period. In the long run, what was more significant was the transformation in the terms on which land itself was held. After the Conquest, the king and nobility, it can be argued, came to form a new kind of tenurial hierarchy. This hierarchy, together with castles and cavalry, lies at the heart of 'feudalism' as defined by many English historians, who thus eschew the much broader definitions, including in effect the whole of medieval society, adopted by continental colleagues. The introduction of feudalism to England is a complex and controversial subject; it may be helpful to describe the structures as they can be seen in place after 1066 before going back to consider how far they were comparable with what had existed in Anglo-Saxon England and how far they were significantly different.

Domesday Book makes clear, for example in its entry for Shropshire, that the great lay and ecclesiastical landholders listed at the start of each county section 'held' their land from the king. Such men came to be called 'tenants-in-chief'. In 1086 they had probably all performed an act of homage in which they knelt before William, placed their hands between his and swore allegiance for the land they held from him. The land was usuually called a *feodum*, that is a 'fee' or 'fief': hence 'feudalism'. The ceremony of homage was solemn and consequential. Breach of the oath was treason and involved the forfeiture of the fief. In return for its tenure, the Conqueror required each tenant to provide contingents of knights either for the royal army when it was called out or to guard royal castles, the individual quotas (on the evidence of a survey in 1166) ranging from fifty or sixty knights down to a handful. William's imposition of such service is described in the twelfth century by Orderic Vitalis and the chroniclers of Abingdon and Ely. If the survey of 1166 does indeed reflect the quotas he determined, as is not unlikely, then the tenants-in-chief as a whole owed some 5,000 knights. Although tenure of this kind came to be called tenure by 'knight service', actual military service represented only one part of its value. There were also, probably from the start, what historians have sometimes called 'the feudal incidents'. When a tenant-in-chief died his heir had to make a money payment to the king to inherit the fee, a payment later described as a 'relief' when considered reasonable in size and a 'fine' when arbitrary and exorbitant. If the heir was a minor, which was often the case given the prevalence of early death, the wardship of the lands and the revenues from them passed to the king. The king also contolled the marriages of the widows of tenants-in-chief; and he controlled too those of heirs and heiresses when they were his wards. Although it was quickly accepted that the fees were hereditary, the king retained power to influence their descent, especially where there was no direct male heir, and he used this power to raise up those who were in favour and pull down those who were not. Ultimately, in default of heirs the fee would 'escheat', that is return to the king, although this was comparatively rare. What feudalism gave the king was thus military service, money, sources of patronage (in the marriages of widows and – best of all – of heiresses), and also social and political control. There was in addition the ecclesiastical equivalent of wardships, since after the death of bishops and abbots the king received the revenues from the lands they had held in chief until a successor was appointed.

Henry I's coronation charter of 1100 suggests that the feudal structure just described was in place and that relations between the tenants-in-chief and their own tenants had developed on similar lines. The former expected their own tenants to supply quotas of knights which would help them provide the service owed to the king as well as military support at other times, for example rebellion. Very broadly tenants of a single property might owe a single knight, and so on in increasing numbers. A baron, just like the king, through inheritance payments, wardships and the bestowal of marriages gained sources of revenue, patronage and social control. His ability to discipline his tenants and to forge them into a real community was, potentially at least, facilitated by the 'honourial court' as it is sometimes called by historians. This was a court held by the baron and attended by his tenants by knight service, a court which had jurisdiction, amongst other things, over disputes concerning the tenure of the fees and the services due from them. The 'fee' or 'honour' (the words at this level were used interchangeably) which the baronial tenant-in-chief held from the king and which would pass to his heir was thus composed of his tenants and their lands as well as the lands he had kept in hand, 'in demesne'.

The feudal structures in England after the Conquest were not imported intact from Normandy. There both the duke and individual lords had been extending their lordship over allodial lands, but the process was far from complete and the rights and service were probably often undefined. Nor did the structures have any general parallel in England before 1066. England was an 'old' country with diverse forms of lordship and land tenure. There certainly were tenants holding land in forms comparable with those found after the Conquest (for example, some of the lessees of the bishop of Worcester). Lords also tried to assert lordship over family land, much as they did in Normandy. But Anglo-Saxon wills and charters, together with Domesday Book which throws much light on conditions before the Conquest, suggest there was still a great deal of allodial land held from no one at all. Those with such land might well have sworn fealty to a great lord or in a special way have been in the service of the king, but they were not their tenants. The circumstances of the Conquest meant a complete new start, bringing all secular land into the hands of the king. He gave it out again to men he made his tenants, and likewise made tenants of the bishops and abbots. That was how all land came to be held from the king. The king's position, unique in Europe, at the head of a tenurial hierarchy with all its attendant rights and revenues, stemmed from these unique events.

Of course, a new form of tenurial hierarchy is still perfectly compatible with kings and lords before 1066 having enjoyed in some respects equivalent powers. When it came to the raising of armies, the contrast between the two systems certainly seems of little moment. The core of royal armies was always provided by household forces, the thegns and housecarls before 1066 and the household knights thereafter. Beyond that, although in neither case is there real evidence for the size of the forces produced in actual practice, the system in which lords owed so many warriors according to the hidage of their estates seems just as good as one in which they owed a number of knights (unrelated to hidage) as determined by the Conqueror.

In other ways too kings and lords before 1066 exercised powers comparable with those of their post-Conquest successors. Land was certainly forfeited for breach of faith. Indeed it was forfeited to the king for any failure to turn up when summoned to the army. Both king and lords had large numbers of followers in their special allegiance, and on the death of such men they could demand a 'heriot' from their families, a death duty rather than the later feudal payment to inherit, but probably just as valuable.

Yet despite these similarities, the change brought by the Conquest was still momentous. The fact was that kings and lords before 1066 wielded much less power over their men than their post-Conquest successors. Since there was often no tenurial content to lordship, they lacked the same ability to manipulate the descent of land and take possession of it when heirs were under-age; there are no pre-1066 references to wardships. By the same token they also had less power over the marriages of women, and therefore significantly fewer resources of patronage, something discussed more fully in a moment. The king's exploitation of his new feudal rights was absolutely central to the workings of politics and society in the century and a half after the Conquest. It could be a major cause of friction between the king and his baronage as the concessions in the early clauses of both the Coronation Charter of 1100 and Magna Carta in 1215 show. At the level of the baron and his tenants the honour and its court were also new. If lords before 1066 sometimes had rights of soke or jurisdiction over extended areas it is difficult to see how this was equivalent, let alone the origin (as has sometimes been suggested), of later honourial jurisdiction because the key to the latter was the kind of feudal tenure which simply did not exist in any general way before the Conquest. There has been debate about the importance of the honours after 1066. They were never self-contained and autonomous institutions since from the start there were tenants who held from several honours or were tenants-in-chief themselves. Honours also had very different histories and came in various shapes and sizes. Yet when all these qualifications have been made, in the century after the Conquest and for many years thereafter honours formed an essential element in magnate power. (For further discussion, see below, pp. 404–7.)

Associated with the introduction of feudalism were wider changes in the structure of the family. England too saw the transition from the extended to the linear family, which, as we have noted, has been detected taking place rather earlier elsewhere in Europe. Neither the speed nor the extent of the change should be exaggerated. The numbers of kin amongst whom property was usually divided seems to have been narrowing before the Conquest, with a bias in favour of direct male heirs at the expense of brothers, nephews, sisters, widows and others. After 1066, eldest sons did not in fact get everything. Fathers could still make provision for younger offspring from acquisitions and sometimes from patrimonial lands, and they also continued to provide for widows and daughters. None the less, the Normans, with stronger notions of patrimony and primogeniture than those current in pre-Conquest England, arguably shut the door more firmly on the wider kin, and created a greater expectation that the key properties, including the principal castle, would go to the eldest son. A change in practice is reflected in the absence of toponymic surnames before 1066 and their development thereafter. Likewise there is a remarkable alteration in the nature of wills: those before 1066 went into great detail, allotting land to various members of the kin, while those after 1100 say nothing at all about land and concentrate on distributing the movable property. There was indeed no need to say anything because, unless previous provision had been made, the descent of the patrimony by the rules of primogeniture was simply accepted.

It is difficult to generalize about how these changes in lordship and family structure affected the position of noblewomen, partly because the evidence bearing on the descent of property through women is tenuous, partly because politics, status and life cycle could make female experiences far more diverse than those of men. Anglo-Saxon wills show widows and daughters receiving property, and widows also disposing of it, apparently as they wished. In a case in the Herefordshire county court a woman (presumably widowed) actually announced that she would grant nothing to her son. Yet after the Conquest too women could hold property. The Coronation Charter of Henry I in 1100 laid down that widows were to receive both their dower and 'marriage portion'. The former was land assigned by the husband on marriage for his wife's support after his death. (In the law book *Glanvill* of *c.* 1189 it was specified as a third of the husband's estates unless a smaller amount was stipulated.) The latter was land given with the bride by her own family. The Charter also shows that women could inherit land. Indeed in the law of the twelfth and thirteenth centuries there was nothing to prevent a widow alienating her inheritance, so in theory the Herefordshire episode could have been replicated after 1066. If the development of primogeniture after the Conquest meant that daughters were less likely to get a share of the inheritance, they were by the same token more likely to scoop the lot if they had no brothers.

If all this suggests that women, before and after 1066, enjoyed independent power as landholders, the impression may be misleading. In the Herefordshire case, the woman is not named and the whole transaction was probably masterminded by its chief beneficiary, the great thegn Thurkill the White. After the Conquest, when widows alienated land, they usually did do so with the consent of their heirs. In any case few twelfth-century widows remained so for very long, pressure to marry again being intense. In all marriages, in twelfth- and thirteenth-century law the husband had total control over his wife's property.

The Conquest did, however, bring changes especially when it came to the control exercised by king and lords over marriage. Women before 1066 were certainly forced into marriage, as the charter issued by King Cnut (perhaps at his coronation) shows. But after 1066 the new tenurial rights of lordship gave the king and lords tighter controls in this area, as the greater precision of Henry's Charter compared with Cnut's demonstrates. As it was, the attempts at regulation in the former were unavailing. Henry did not keep the promise not to force widows of tenants-in-chief to marry. He did not relinquish the right to find husbands for the heiresses of deceased tenants-in-chief, promising only to arrange such marriages after having taken counsel from his barons. Since such heiresses would be wards in the king's hands until they married and only then able to inherit, he was well placed to stand his ground. He also had every incentive to do so because the gift of a wealthy wife was by far the easiest way to enrich both his close family and rising ministers. There were also plenty of heiresses about. Fifty-four of the 189 honours in existence in 1166 passed into the female line at least once after 1086. The king's ability to conjure up heiresses was also enhanced by the relative fluidity of female (and male) inheritance rights. A woman could, for example, be made more eligible at the expense of an unfavoured brother by giving her a large marriage portion. Later the opportunities for manipulation became all the greater when the practice developed (perhaps influenced by a decree of Henry I around 1130) that in default of sons the inheritance was to be divided equally amongst all the daughters, instead of the eldest, like an eldest son, getting everything. This both increased the pot of patronage available to the king and allowed him, despite the supposed equality of division, to chop up the respective portions according to the pecking order of the prospective husbands. As for widows, a second husband in the law as defined later in the century would control his wife's dower from her first marriage, together with her inheritance and marriage portion, as long as she lived. The dower would then pass back to the heir of the first husband, the inheritance and marriage portion to the heir of the wife – one and the same person if the first marriage had produced offspring but not otherwise. However, if the second marriage produced a child, the husband could continue to keep the marriage portion and inheritance for the length of his own life, before they passed back to any child of the first marriage. Complex! The interpretation and implementation of such rules gave plenty of room for royal interference. The resulting disputes were the stuff of politics.

*　　*　　*

King William thus introduced a new 'feudal' aristocracy to England, yet he established it within the framework of the Anglo-Saxon state. Here there were deep continuities before and after 1066, and also significant changes.

For William his coronation, which followed closely the old Anglo-Saxon order of service, had immense significance. From a duke he was now a king and he made sure no one forgot it. Surrounded by his bishops, barons and knights he wore his crown three times each year, at Christmas, Easter and Whitsun, rites based on German imperial practice and probably introduced into England in the 1050s but now made much grander, judging from the awe-struck description in the Anglo-Saxon Chronicle. Likewise William continued the *Laudes Regiae*, the great ceremonial hymns invoking God's aid for the king and the whole Christian community: 'Victory and long life to the most serene William, crowned by God, great and pacific king,' chanted the choirs. 'Behold I see God,' cried one of William's jesters, like so many jesters getting at a truth. Such rituals were a constant reminder that the king was the Lord's anointed, ruling with his blessing and protection. They were of immeasurable importance in securing service and stilling revolt.

The basic structures of Anglo-Saxon government, superior in many ways to those in Normandy, William gratefully took over: the counties and hundreds with their courts; the sheriffs; the pervasive royal peace with its specially reserved royal pleas; the geld; the coinage; the chancellor and the sealed writ. The nerve centre of William's government, the royal household, was similar to the Confessor's. Here were the chamberlains receiving, storing and spending the money for his day-to-day expenses, here some of the household knights (others might be away trouble-shooting on special missions), here his chancellor heading the clerks of the chapel who sang the daily services and wrote documents, here the kitchen staff providing food and drink, and the grooms looking after the dogs, horses and stables. Around the household the wider court was gathered, with its councillors, some of whom were great barons, lay and ecclesiastical, others men of much lower status; and around the court William regularly assembled the nobility in great councils, similar to the pre-1066 witan, to witness his wearing of the crown and discuss affairs of the realm, for example the making of Domesday Book.

Yet Norman rule was also significantly different from that of the Confessor and his Wessex predecessors. In the first place, after 1072 William was largely an absentee. Of the 170 months remaining of his reign he spent around 130 in France, returning to England on only four occasions. This was no passing phase. Absentee kings continued to spend at best half their time in England until the loss of Normandy in 1204. This was not simply because the continent was home; rather, as William of Malmesbury shrewdly appreciated, Normandy with its long open frontiers was far less secure than England and needed constant minding. In the purely personal sense these kings must, therefore, have been less 'hands-on' and interventionist than their Anglo-Saxon predecessors, though perhaps not less than Cnut who was also king of Denmark. But this absenteeism solidified rather than sapped royal government since it engendered structures both to maintain peace and extract money in the king's absence, money which was above all needed across the Channel. Malmesbury indeed compared England and Normandy to two sisters joined at the waist, the healthy one supporting the other, who is terminally diseased.

By far the most important of William's regents was Bishop Odo, who had authority to act independently in the king's name. At other times, Archbishop Lanfranc, or a small group of magnates headed by Lanfranc, received the king's orders, but William also wrote direct to sheriffs and other local officials when he was abroad. Many such orders were reactions to complaints and petitions. Already the trek across the Channel to the real centre of power had begun. 'Do this so that I quickly hear the truth of the matter by your letter,' one writ to Lanfranc concluded. However far away he might be, England was always under that stern exacting oversight.

As the exchange between William and Lanfranc suggests, the exigencies of the cross-Channel state significantly increased the role of written orders in government. William took over Regenbald, the Confessor's chancellor, and with him the sealed writ, which soon came to be written in Latin rather than English. William issued large numbers of writs in favour of abbeys and bishoprics confirming their rights and properties. Here he was frequently being reactive, the initiative coming from the beneficiary who not surprisingly (as before 1066) often wrote the document. The chancellor's task was just to check the draft by the beneficiary, supply standard writ formulas and affix the king's seal to the finished copy. But William was also proactive. Writs were issued to summon armies, and give orders to local officials. Had more of these survived in the original, we would probably detect the hands of a small group of clerks at court writing for the king, although in fact only one has been identified.

One particularly important use of the writ was to command local courts to hear law cases. Although employed for that purpose before 1066, such orders multiplied thereafter as the Conquest produced numerous disputes over the tenure of land. William also sent Lanfranc, Odo of Bayeux and the bishop of Coutances into the county courts to hear such pleas. If all this enhanced the role of the king in local affairs, so did changes in the structures of government. One innovation, derived apparently from Normandy, lay in the way William began to subject parts of England (the New Forest for a start) to a type of royal forest law which was later to be a major source of both income and unpopularity. Another change related to the earls because, as compared with 1065, the number of counties subject to their authority was greatly reduced. William set up earls in Kent and the Welsh borders, who guarded the frontiers very much as the counts did the frontiers of Normandy. But these frontier earls were the only ones William had. There would be no over-mighty officials in his England, any more, in all probability, than there would have been in Harold's.

This limited use of earldoms meant that William established a direct relationship with the sheriff, who was no longer the earl's deputy and was more powerful as a result. Even more important was the way the king's castles, planted in the county towns, became the military and administrative bases for royal government in the shires, housing the sheriff's office, the mint, and the county court over which the sheriff presided. Secure in the castle and keeping troops there to enforce his will outside it, the sheriff could afford to be far more unpopular, and thus more ruthless in the king's interests (and his own), than before. 'Art thou called Urse? Have thou God's curse,' Archbishop Ealdred thundered at Urse d'Abetot, sheriff of Worcestershire. The sheriffs were powerful but William was determined to control them. He ordered the regents to summon them together and forbid seizures of property from the church. He moved them frequently from one sheriffdom to another and more often appointed 'new men', owing everything to him, than he did great barons; he was doubtless aware of how the equivalent office in Normandy, that of the 'viscount', had fallen into the hands of magnates, some of whom had been notably disloyal in the great crisis of 1046-7. William was not going to have a repeat performance in England.

The Anglo-Saxon coinage was far superior to the Norman and William naturally continued it, but he standardized the weight of the coin and increased the annual money payments made by the mints. The symbolic importance of the coinage remained. Circulating everywhere, seen by everyone, it was the most visual demonstration possible of the unity of the realm under the king. Although the evidence is fragmentary, William probably levied the geld annually, usually at 2s. a hide (producing perhaps £2,500) but occasionally at higher rates. The 6s. a hide in 1084 provoked cries of protest from the Anglo-Saxon chronicler. If William never equalled the sums raised by geld early in the century, assuming the figures can be believed, that was because he levied it at lower rates (that in 1018 was possibly 20s.), and exempted the demesne manors of his barons (though not the peasant lands within them) from payment. Yet these early gelds had in effect been harried out of the kingdom by invading armies. The more regular army geld levied between 1012 and 1051 had itself proved unsustainable. Up to a point William may actually have revived a tax which was falling into decay. He certainly needed the money to pay the mercenaries who had helped make and sustain the Conquest, but his noble followers he had rewarded with land. That being the case, it made sense to reduce the tax liability of his barons on their main reward, especially when the exemptions could be reversed, as some of them were after 1087. How right William was to choose land rather than money. His followers, unlike those of Cnut, had come to stay.

Much of this makes kingship seem more powerful and pervasive after the Conquest, especially when one adds in the new 'feudal' package of powers. But this is only part of the story. The baronial fees or honours introduced new structures of magnate power, cutting into and across the counties and hundreds of Anglo-Saxon England, destroying the monopoly of their courts and raising the question of whether the allegiance of under-tenants belonged to the baron or the king. Before 1066 the only private court had been that of the manor. Afterwards, while the upheavals of the Conquest doubtless brought business into the courts of shire and hundred, it is difficult to think that they were not weakened by the loss of land pleas to the honourial court, as also of ecclesiastical pleas to the courts of the church. At the centre of honourial power, moreover, was something completely new: the private castle. If the royal castle enhanced the king's local position, so did the private castle that of the baron. Of the 500 or so castles in England around 1100 perhaps two-thirds were in private hands. The castle was thus not confined to a small elite as it had been in Normandy. It was common to all barons and many major under-tenants. What had begun as an instrument of conquest, continued as an instrument of lordship. In the castle, the lord held his honourial court, feasted his friends and followers, and generally displayed his wealth and status – hence the elaborately decorated entrance to the great stone keep at Castle Rising in Norfolk built by Earl William II d'Albini after 1138. There was nothing in any of this necessarily threatening to the king. William I had probably ordered the building of castles by his followers in order to secure the country. He and his successors depended on strong loyalist barons. But if barons were ever to be disloyal, the Conquest has certainly placed new weapons in their hands with which to resist the crown.

*   *   *

In 1066 William had wanted to postpone his coronation until his wife, Matilda, then holding the fort back in Normandy, could be crowned with him. In the event he went ahead without her, but Matilda's eventual coronation in May 1068 was still a magnificent affair. Queens, therefore, were important and, as the ceremony of crowning and anointing showed, they held a formal office. Matilda had her own set of regalia, which may have included such symbols of authority as the orb and sceptre. Certainly Henry I's queen, Edith Matilda, appears with both on her seal. All this had probably been equally true before 1066. If the framework of queenship altered after the Conquest, its basic structures did not. Matilda's ceremony in 1068 was similar to those performed for Emma, queen of both Aethelred and Cnut, and Edith, queen of the Confessor. All these queens gained lustre through the growing cult of the Virgin Mary, who was depicted as a mother and increasingly as a crowned queen, the Queen of Heaven. She appears as both in a Winchester prayer book of Emma's time.

Matilda's status did not derive solely from her marriage and her office. It also, in common with other queens, came from her own family. As her tombstone proudly proclaimed, she was the daughter of a count of Flanders and the granddaughter of a French king (Robert the Pious). She was of far higher status than William himself, hence his anxiety to be crowned with her in 1066, and the manner in which a form of the *Laudes Regiae*, introduced for her coronation, applauded king and queen in almost parallel terms. Cnut, trying to establish a new dynasty, had felt the same need of linkage to his wife: the coronation *ordo* of 1017, after his marriage to Emma, widow of the previous king and daughter of a duke of Normandy, described her as *consors imperii*, a sharer in his rule.

Anglo-Saxon precedent and practice also meant that as queen Matilda enjoyed her own resources. Some of these probably came, as they certainly did under Edith, from a share in the financial offers made to the king for favours, a payment later called 'queen's gold'. More important was land. Before 1066 certain individual estates were traditionally used to provide for the queen, although they were neither drawn on exclusively nor uniformly. Since the queen as widow seems to have kept the lands she held as queen, a new clutch had to be found for her successor. But the fact that queens did have lands which they could expect to keep after the king's death gave them their own income and a measure of independence. The Conqueror himself allowed Edith to keep her extensive possessions until her death in 1075, and did not then pass them to Matilda. But he found Matilda other lands worth around £500 a year, most of them coming from the estate of the fallen thegn Beorhtric. From these Matilda was able to endow monasteries and, like Emma and Edith, support her own household, rewarding her chamberlains, for example, with grants of land. This household was separate from that of the king when Matilda and William were apart, but merged more or less with his when they were together.

At their coronation queens, unlike kings, took no oath of office. Was there none the less a conception of what they should so? Before and after 1066, they sometimes appear in charge of the royal treasure but perhaps this was more the result of particular crises, or of activity as the king's deputy, than of any role they were generally allotted. Queens certainly were expected to feature prominently in court ceremonial. Indeed they could mastermind it, at least if we can believe the *Life of Edward the Confessor* which has Edith, who commissioned the work, both encouraging her unworldly husband to put on royal finery and arraying him in it. Whether Matilda did the same for the Conqueror may be doubted but she was often at court, judging from the large number of royal documents she witnessed, something which itself reflects her status. The coronation ceremony indicated that queens should be fruitful, the prayers linking them with the biblical women, Sarah, Rebecca and Rachel, who produced the line of David. The influence that queens established over their sons (sometimes through controlling their upbringing) could indeed lead to important political roles both as queens and queen-mothers. According to the coronation prayers, the queen was also to imitate the biblical example of Esther and persuade the king to act with mercy. Intercession was not, of course, an exclusively queenly prerogative, but that of the queen did have a special moral force, as well as the unique advantages provided by proximity to the king not merely at court but in the bedchamber. Nor was there really any clear line between pleading from a sense of mercy and pleading from a sense of politics.

All of this, of course, amounted to the queen influencing the men who pulled the levers of power, while not pulling them herself. And the men did not have to listen. When Matilda interceded with William for Robert, her eldest son, she got nowhere. When, testimony both to her spirit and resources, she dispatched money to him despite William's prohibition, he ordered one of her servants to be blinded. The queen was not in any sense a joint ruler of the kingdom. Indeed, neither the *consors imperii* of the 1017 coronation nor the queen's place in the 1068 *Laudes* were generally adopted. Emma, in the first depiction of an English queen, might stand beneath the Virgin opposite Cnut, but he was crowned, she was merely veiled. There had to be a king. There was no permanent need for a queen. William did not remarry after Matilda's death in 1083. His successor, William Rufus, did not marry at all. Scotland had no queen between 1130–31 and 1186. Nor was queenly status itself unalterable. It depended on life cycle, as the king's did not. If her husband's death did not 'de-queen' her, it certainly diluted her status, particularly if the new king married and created another queen.

For all these limitations, the queen was unquestionably in a position of potential influence and, in effect, of power. What she actually achieved depended on a whole range of variables including political circumstance, personal ambition, and the particular relationship with the king. In one way, queens after 1066 did have potentially more scope than before. Cnut had governed several realms, yet there is (perhaps surprisingly) virtually no evidence that he ever made Emma his regent. William was different. He made Matilda regent on several occasions both in Normandy and in England. In England she was sought out by those with grievances and presided over important law cases in the counties. She was the first in a series of formidable post-Conquest queens given opportunities by the exigencies of the cross-Channel state.

*　　*　　*

The church was central to royal power both before and after the Conquest, and William was no less determined to control and exploit it than his predecessors had been before 1066. Kings also swore at their coronations to protect the church, which at the very least meant maintaining its properties. It also implied they should be supporters of reform. The struggle for reform envelops the whole period covered by this book and constantly impinges on the course of politics. The reform movement had begun outside the papacy but in the pontificate of Leo IX (1048–54) was taken over by it. The ultimate aim was to ensure that the church worked with enthusiasm and devotion for the spiritual welfare of its flock. Monks were to devote themselves to the round of divine service and pray for the salvation of the faithful. Priests and bishops were, as Pope Gregory VII (1073–85) put it, to be 'pastors of souls'. For this to be achieved, certain abuses had to be eradicated. One was clerical marriage, which snared priests in the world and threatened to make their offices hereditary. Another was pluralism, the holding of more than one benefice, behind which there was often simony, the buying and selling of ecclesiastical office. If the church was to be rid of these abuses, a necessary condition was clear lines of authority. Bishops needed to be able to rule their dioceses and archbishops (metropolitans) their provinces. Above all, the ultimate authority of the pope in matters of doctrine, law and discipline needed to be recognized in theory and exercised in practice. To that end the great mass of canon law – passages from the Bible, the pronouncements of popes and the decrees of councils – was edited and arranged so as to lay bare the basis of papal power.

For the future of royal power the implications of reform were explosive in England as elsewhere. Was the pope to exercise a direct authority over churchmen? Was the church to be freed from control by the king? To break the royal hold over ecclesiastical appointments, in particular, seemed essential to reformers, given that such appointments implied the king had some kind of spiritual authority, and resulted in totally unsuitable royal clerks gaining high office. How could *they* be instruments of reform? But such a fissure seemed utterly unreasonable to the king, given the wide lands held by bishops and abbots, for which, apart from anything else, they owed military service. Until the last years of William's reign, however, there was little to presage any fundamental conflict, thanks in large measure to William's relationship with the man who replaced the discredited Stigand as archbishop of Canterbury in 1070: Lanfranc.

From Pavia, born around 1010, Lanfranc had studied arts in the Italian Schools, and had gained an easy mastery of its fundamental method: the deployment of evidence in support of argument. He had gone to Normandy to teach and then, around 1042, had entered the impecunious infant monastery at Bec. There, in novel fashion, he used the methodology of the arts to study the Bible, and made his school internationally famous in the process. Having defused an early quarrel with Duke William through a joke ('I would go into exile more quickly if you gave me a better horse'), in 1063 Lanfranc became abbot of the new ducal monastery of St-Étienne at Caen, a resounding vote of confidence. From there the move to Canterbury was a natural one. Lanfranc was far more than a dry and cloistered academic. He had a good head for business and had masterminded building operations at Bec. He tempered sternness with humility, and had a brisk, humane common sense: 'Whatever death overtakes the just man his soul will be in peace,' he declared, quoting scripture. Here was the man who could act as archbishop and also as regent. Lanfranc believed wholeheartedly in reform yet he also thought that 'the practice of Christianity' could only be established through good kings. Hence he entreated God to grant William a long life, for William *was* a good king. Indeed with the archbishop of Rouen, he had presided since 1049 over reforming councils in Normandy.

'In order to confirm his power in the kingdom he had acquired,' as the chronicler John of Worcester put it, William replaced the English bishops and abbots. By the end of the reign there were only three important native prelates. Yet in establishing his power, reform of the church was almost as important as the change in personnel, although that was far from the only motive for it. William complained that church laws before 1066 contravened the 'precepts of the holy canons', and the English themselves, if William of Malmesbury is at all representative, came to believe him. Thus the Normans could regard the Conquest as a divinely sanctioned mission (the pope after all had given his approval) and the English could accept it as a punishment for their sins. The propaganda had at least some basis in fact. True, Wulfstan of Worcester, the only English bishop remaining in 1087, was a model of erudition, eloquence, practical piety and unostentatious austerities. English bishops attended the great papal reforming council in 1049 and avoided the schismatic Stigand. Yet there had been no reforming synods in England before 1066, and no parallel to Lanfranc's school at Bec and the duchy's other vibrant monasteries. The pre-Conquest church under the other-worldly Confessor and the all too worldly Stigand was very different from that after 1066, driven forward by William and Lanfranc.

Not all Lanfranc's work was successful or well judged. His attempt to assert Canterbury's primacy over the whole of Britain and more particularly over the archbishopric of York was motivated by the passionate concern with Canterbury's rights. But it lacked precedent, sucked his successors into a quagmire, and actually weakened rather than strengthened church discipline and the unity of the kingdom. Indeed it became impossible in later centuries, thanks to disputes over status, for the two archbishops to appear in each other's presence. Lanfranc, however, was sensitive to English conditions. He came to revere some of the Anglo-Saxon saints and accepted the uniquely English institution (found at Canterbury itself) of cathedral clergy organized as monks rather than as chapters of canons. But there was still much to do. Between 1070 and 1076 five councils were held which promulgated statutes for the reform of the church; the first two were presided over by papal legates. A sensibly cautious start was made in eliminating clerical marriage – a more radical approach in Normandy led to the stoning of the archbishop of Rouen. Much attention was given to increasing the authority of the bishop within his diocese and improving its administration. Several cathedrals were moved to more populous centres: Dorchester on Thames to Lincoln (1072), Selsey to Chichester (1075), Sherborne to Salisbury (1078) and Elmham ultimately to Norwich (1094). Dioceses seem to have been formally divided into territorial archdeaconries and then subdivided (sometimes using old Anglo-Saxon minister divisions) into deaneries. Archdeacons may have existed before 1066 but they were now more able, along with the rural deans, to 'scrutinise the character of [the local clerics] and their competence as priests', as Lanfranc put it, describing his own activities.

The parish priesthood was the lowest rung of the church, yet the most important. Here significant changes were taking place, both for good and ill. Characteristic of Anglo-Saxon England had been large territorial areas served by priests based in minsters. Occasionally, as at Farnham and Chertsey in Surrey, these survived, in whole or in part, to form later parishes. But for the most part, before and after 1066 such jurisdictions were being undermined as individual lords founded new churches, an activity itself related to the breaking-up of great estates and the formation of manors and nucleated villages. The pace may well have quickened after the Conquest for William of Malmesbury speaks of churches rising in every village. Thus the new Norman lords of manors marked their arrival in the country and God's sanction for it. By 1086 in Surrey 60 to 70 per cent of later parish churches had already begun their life; the actual formation of the new parish boundaries was largely complete here and elsewhere by 1200, a process as central to the shaping of England as it is hard to trace.

Another way William and his followers thanked God for their victory and indirectly tied kingdom and duchy together was by giving land in England to their family monasteries back home. Around thirty continental houses, most of them in Normandy, received land in England. Fécamp's endowment was worth £200 a year. But the Normans also thanked God and proclaimed their arrival by founding monasteries in England, around thirty-four of them by 1087, just over half being daughters of continental houses. Battle, William's own foundation, was placed symbolically on the very site of his victory. Other houses like the Warenne foundation at Lewes in Sussex, a daughter house of Cluny, marched side by side with the baronial castle. The Normans also began to endow pre-1066 English houses, indeed by the end of the century such grants were on a far greater scale than those made to the continental monasteries. The major English houses, of course, acquired continental abbots. Some of the latter, like Thurstan at Glastonbury, quarrelled violently with their English monks, but all of them (and the same was true of the Norman bishops) had one decisive advantage over their English predecessors: they were far more successful, as the contrasting fortunes of Abingdon under English and Norman abbots shows, in recovering and retaining property, hence the church's success in broadly maintaining its estates over the Conquest period. In general, William of Malmesbury was right to think that monastic life flourished under the Normans. Lanfranc himself drew up a series of constitutions to govern the life of the monks at Christ Church, Canterbury and these were adopted by at least twelve other monasteries. Many of the new abbots were men of exemplary sense and piety, and they attracted recruits. The monks at Gloucester rose from ten to 100 under Serlo, abbot from 1072 to 1104. The Normans were also great builders. The massive, cold stone columns of their new abbeys and cathedrals seem almost with the aid of God and man to be treading down Norman rule into English soil.

Lanfranc's reforms depended absolutely on the support of the king, and none more so than one of the most important of these. Churchmen before 1066 had been aware that there was a category of offences committed by the laity but related to 'the rule of souls' (blasphemy and adultery, for example) which should come within the jurisdiction of the church; so should disputes over wills and burials. But the bishop or his deputy had none the less heard such cases in secular tribunals, usually in the hundred court. To Lanfranc this seemed a scandalous breach of canon law, and William agreed. 'I order and by my royal authority command' ran the consequent royal ordinance, which banned the practice, laying down that henceforth such cases were to be heard in a place decided by the bishop. Indeed, if necessary they were to be brought there 'by the force and justice of the king and the sheriff'. There could be no clearer indication of William's support for the church, even though the competence of his own courts was diminished. Although in practice there was no sudden or clear-cut break with the past, the ordinance facilitated the development of separate ecclesiastical courts, over which, for most routine cases, the archdeacon and rural dean presided.

Under Lanfranc and William, therefore, the English church, as archbishop Anselm later put it, was like a plough drawn by two well-matched oxen. If the pope was formally the driver, he followed where they led. The pope had been useful in getting rid of some English prelates and sanctioning through his legate some early reforms. William and Lanfranc were meticulous in showing proper respect, but essentially it was 'we'll call you, don't call us'. The relationship changed with

Gregory VII (1073–85) who was determined to make the papal headship of the church a reality. As his quarrel with the Emperor Henry IV deepened and the latter set up his own anti-pope, Clement III, so William's attitude became increasingly ambivalent. Gregory complained that William was preventing Lanfranc and other bishops visiting the Holy See. But Lanfranc's loyalties were with William. He explained that while England ('our island') had not abandoned Gregory for Clement it might decide to do so. After Gregory's death in 1085 William and Lanfranc hesitated to recognize his successor. This, however, was only the beginning of the story. In the long term William and Lanfranc's pick-and-choose attitude to the papacy was to prove unsustainable.

*   *   *

After the suppression of Edwin and Morcar in 1071, English attacks on individual Normans continued, something which William sought to counter by introducing the 'murder' fine. It had to be paid by the hundred or the village in which a murder took place if it could not apprehend the murderer or prove the victim was English. But any general resistance was at an end. The rebellion of 1075 illustrated as much. It was joined rather weakly by Waltheof, the last surviving English earl, who had followed Gospatric in Northumberland and also apparently presided over Northamptonshire and Huntingdonshire. The leaders, however, were two young continental nobles, one at least irritated by the way the king's sheriffs were challenging his local power. Since equivalent tensions had sometimes surfaced before 1066, normal politics had been resumed. The revolt was quickly put down. Waltheof was executed, Earl Ralph of Norfolk fled to his estates in Brittany and Earl Roger of Hereford (son of the ultra-loyalist William fitz Osbern, as Lanfranc never ceased to remind him) was imprisoned for life. There he flung the fine robes sent him by the Conqueror on the fire, a furious and futile gesture which sums up the rebellion. The Conqueror had demonstrated his mastery and he was to do so again even more dramatically in 1082. Faced by the vaulting ambition of his half-brother, Bishop Odo, for whom Kent, the regency and the Bayeux Tapestry seemed not enough, William hurried across the Channel and had him tried and imprisoned.

William juggled his problems in England with those across the Channel where, as we have seen, he spent most of his time. In Normandy the brief respite which had permitted the Conquest had ended and he was on the defensive. He faced a count of Flanders, Robert the Frisian, who was a sworn enemy, a count of Anjou, Fulk Rechin, who aimed to recover Maine, and a king of France, Philip I (1060–1108), who had gained hold of the French Vexin in 1077 and so was able to prowl along the Norman frontier. All of them were ready to exploit William's quarrels with his son Robert who, approaching twenty-five in 1077, coveted a good deal more power than his sceptical father would accord him. There was also one final challenge to William's rule in England: an invasion planned by King Cnut of Denmark in alliance with the king of Norway and the count of Flanders. William levied a heavy geld and then in 1085 came over with a large paid army. But it was not needed. The Danes quarrelled among themselves and eventually in July 1086 Cnut was murdered. For England this was a decisive moment. The kings of Denmark had made their last bid for the throne.

'Having found out for a fact . . . that his enemies could not carry out their expedition,' as the Anglo-Saxon chronicler put it, William decided to survey his winnings. At his Christmas court of 1085 he 'had much thought and very deep discussion with his council about this country – how it was occupied or with what sort of people'. The result was the great survey of England embodied in the two volumes of Domesday Book. (The name, signifying the final and definitive nature of the testimony, was in use by 1179.) Domesday mentions 13,418 places and contains 2 million words. 'Not one ox, cow or pig was left out,' grumbled the Anglo-Saxon chronicler. To carry out the survey England was divided into at least seven circuits each with its own commissioners. They had some existing material to help them, for example lists of geld liabilities and of dues from royal manors, but the great bulk of the information probably derived from written returns about their properties presented by the tenants-in-chief. This material was then co-ordinated with the evidence presented by local juries at sessions of the hundred courts. The survey's rapid completion, quite probably by August 1086, testified to the strength of pre-1066 governmental structures and William's ability to exploit them.

Studies of Domesday are full of friendly controversy. One ingenious suggestion (by David Roffe) is that William commissioned the survey but not the book, the latter being the brainchild in the 1090s of William Rufus's chief minister, Ranulf Flambard. But a Worcester chronicler of the early twelfth century states that the Conqueror ordered that everything be written in a book, and the returns would certainly have been useless unless edited. As for the purpose of the whole exercise, one view is that William wanted information to enable a reassessment of the geld. But there is no indication that the geld *was* generally reassessed, nor does Domesday Book itself highlight the information which would have been relevant. If the Conqueror wished to increase his revenue from the geld, it could be done much more simply by altering the rate at which it was levied, and reducing the number of exemptions. The form of the book suggests the principal aim was rather different: the king wanted information about his own properties and those of his tenants. Domesday arranges its information county by county. At the start of each section there is a survey of the county town and a statement of the customs of the shire. Then follow the estates of the landholders one after another, listed hundred by hundred and then manor by manor. The first landholder is always the king. The survey thus provided William with detailed information about his own lands, including assessments of their potential value. His harshness as a landlord is referred to explicitly by the Anglo-Saxon chronicler and he was now ideally placed to demand more from his reeves and lessees. Any efficient landholder taking over a new estate would have it surveyed; for William, Domesday Book was such a survey on a gigantic scale. William was equally determined to know about the estates of his tenants. The list of their names at the start of each county section made it easy to find the page where the entry for each began. In 1085 William had parked out his army, brought to meet the Danish threat, on the lands of his barons, hence perhaps his immediate desire for more information about their possessions. But the broader background was the gigantic turnover in landholding which had taken place since the Conquest. For all William's attempts to control it through written orders and special officials, some barons had just helped themselves, and there was no record of the final results. Domesday provided just that. Now, when William wanted to seize estates after a tenant's forfeiture or death, he knew what to take. If he kept those estates in his own hands during an ecclesiastical vacancy, or through wardship or escheat, then he could exploit them as effectively as any land of his own. Domesday Book was therefore very much about exploiting the king's feudal rights and revenues.

Why then did the magnates themselves co-operate in the making of the survey? The answer is that Domesday Book provided them with something approaching a written title to their lands, if not a definitive one. This was why it recorded the name of the Anglo-Saxon holder of the land in 1066. That was completely irrelevant to the exploitation of the estate, but it was very relevant indeed if (as was so often the case) land was claimed by a Norman lord as the successor of an English 'ancestor'. Of course what precisely an 'ancestor' had held often gave rise to disputes, and the Domesday commissioners were far too busy to determine all of them. Nevertheless the whole process provided an opportunity to ventilate claims which the king issued writs ordering local courts to settle.

In the generation after its construction, and probably for longer, Domesday was central to the exploitation of the king's lands and his feudal rights and revenues. Almost at once, moreover, William responded to something else the survey had been designed to reveal: the names of the under-tenants enfeoffed by the tenants-in-chief. Would these men be loyal to the king or simply to their overlords? William, with characteristic precision, provided an answer. He could not demand homage from the under-tenants because they did not hold land from him. But he could demand an oath of fealty. In August 1086 he summoned to Salisbury 'all the landholding men of any account that were over all England *whosoever men they were*' (my italics) and made them swear just such an oath. Domesday Book thus revealed the dual polity which had emerged out of the unitary Anglo-Saxon state. On the one hand there were the pre-1066 counties and hundreds giving the king a direct relationship with all his subjects, particularly through maintenance of his peace. On the other, within this old framework, were the new structures of feudalism.

After the Oath of Salisbury, William returned to Normandy and within a year lay buried in his great abbey at Caen. 'I was brought up in arms from childhood,' he groaned on his deathbed, according to Orderic Vitalis. This martial, stern, demanding, jovial, pious, intelligent and farseeing man had transformed the face of Europe.

4

Wales, Scotland and the Normans, 1058–94

According to his obituary in the Anglo-Saxon Chronicle, King William subdued both Wales and Scotland and would have conquered Ireland too had he lived a few more years. The comment reflected the aura of William's power but not the reality of his policies, which were more defensive than aggressive. This was chiefly because of the limited value of Celtic Britain and William's higher priorities elsewhere. It was also because of the nature of William's kingship. Lanfranc, on becoming archbishop of Canterbury, investigated the ancient rights of his see and argued he was 'primate of all Britain'. William, on the other hand, rarely toyed with the British imperial titles sometimes adopted by the Anglo-Saxon kings. Instead he proclaimed himself simply 'king of the English', a kingship which at most carried claims to tribute from the Welsh rulers and a loose overlordship over the king of Scots. William inherited no lands from the Confessor in Wales or Scotland and gained none from the forfeitures after the Conquest. He used Harold's estates in Herefordshire to set up a frontier lordship for William fitz Osbern. It was not William but his Norman barons who were to transform the face of Wales, gripping it within a generation far more fundamentally than had the Anglo-Saxons in many centuries. No similar transformation in this early period took place in Scotland. Indeed in the north it was the king of Scots who was the aggressor, not the Normans.

*   *   *

In its entry for 1069 the *Brut*, the principal native chronicle for the whole period covered by this book, implied that Wales was divided into three political entities: Gwynedd, Powys and Deheubarth. Gwynedd was the whole of north-west Wales from the estuary of the Dee to the estuary of the Dyfi. Powys was north-east Wales from the Dee to around the upper valley of the Severn. Deheubarth meant broadly the whole of south Wales, Wales that is to the south of the Dyfi estuary and the Wye, although it came later to mean simply those parts of south-west Wales which had escaped Norman rule. Gwynedd and Powys were far more coherent politically than Deheubarth but all three were liable to division between rival rulers. This was facilitated by the way they were made up of a series of smaller administrative regions called cantrefs and commotes, the latter sometimes being subdivisions of the former. There were five commotes, for example, within Gwynedd's western cantrefs of Llŷn, Ardudwy and Meirionydd. Cantrefs and commotes could themselves form parts of larger units. In Deheubarth, the latter included Ceredigion, Dyfed, Ystrad Tywi, and Glamorgan, the last with kings of its own. All these regions appear as separate entities again and again in the *Brut*. In Gwynedd the four cantrefs between the Conwy and the Dee gave the name 'the Four Cantrefs' to the whole area.

There has been much debate about the origins of the cantrefs and commotes. Had they grown up almost as separate kingdoms so that their holders enjoyed near kingly rights and status, or had they been created from above by kings who decided – at least in theory – the authority their lords enjoyed? Whichever was the case, cantrefs and commotes were both centres of lordship, with dues paid to a central court, and focuses of community; hence the ease with which Gwynedd, Powys and Deheubarth could be broken up, and the 'hostile heart' engendered by the round of plundering warfare between men of different regions.

Underlying many of these features were the basic facts of geography. Nearly all the divisions mentioned above had their own geographical logic, very often drawn by rivers. A single political entity embracing them all had none. The great mountains which dominated Wales prevented any easy journey across the country. In the north, Gwynedd itself was divided naturally by the river Conwy. Viewed from the eastern side of its estuary on the great rock of Deganwy, the menacing mountains of Snowdonia to the west, running sheer into the sea, still seem to guard an almost impenetrable land. In the south-west, Ceredigion centred on the narrow coastal plain between the rivers Dyfi and Teifi. In the south the major divisions all had their own characteristics: the lowlands of Dyfed with the great ecclesiastical centre of St Davids; Ystrad Tywi, the heart of the kingdom of Deheubarth, with its mountainous cantrefs of Mawr and Bychan severed by the deep-grooved Tywi; Glamorgan, cut through by rivers, with lowlands in the south, uplands in the north, and then to the east the rich pastures of Gwent. Acting as a hinge between north and south Wales, there was a mountainous region described as 'between the Wye and the Severn'. The upper valleys of these two great rivers provided avenues eastwards into England and westwards through to south-west Wales. The strategic importance of this area led to constant battles for its control.

Given this geography it was not surprising that Wales was subject to a multiplicity of competing rulers. Before his defeat by Harold in 1063, Gruffudd ap Llywelyn had brought all Wales under his rule but it was a brief and unique achievement. A single language, a native law and a common descent from the ancient Britons and so, as legend had it, from Brutus and the Trojans made the Welsh think of themselves as a separate and distinctive people. But there were conflicting ideas about how or indeed whether this needed to be expressed politically. 'They obstinately and proudly refuse to submit to one ruler,' commented Gerald of Wales towards the end of the twelfth century. Welsh law books of that time and later might begin with a vision of a united Wales basking in the rule of the tenth-century King Hywel the Good, but they actually dealt with a Wales in which there was a plurality of kingdoms. (See below, p. 228.) Whether Welsh law also enforced division by stipulating that kingdoms should be apportioned among the sons of a ruler is more questionable. Such partition was certainly the law and custom with ordinary patrimonies, but with kingdoms the laws envisaged a single heir, the *edling*, designated by the ruler. Just who the *edling* should be, however, was less clear. Throne-worthiness was not confined to the sons, let alone the eldest son, of the previous king; therefore the potential existed for disputes over the succession, in the course of which kingdoms *were* divided up, so much so that, whatever the precise law, the practice became regarded as almost customary. Claims and feuds were also encouraged (as Gerald of Wales observed) by the practice of fostering out sons to different noble families and by the intense pride in lineage – Rhys ap Tewdwr ap Cadell ap Einon ap Owain ap Hywel Dda, ran one genealogy.

Conflict was also fostered by the nature of Welsh kingship. The *Brut* frequently used the word *brenin* which in Latin was translated as *rex*, that is 'king'. Yet there was not one of Henry II's knights (it was later said) who did not regard himself as worth a Welsh king. The latter were very different from those of England and not just because of their puny resources. They went through, as far as is known, no coronation or inauguration ceremony; and they had a much smaller role in the maintenance of law and order, which was largely a communal responsibility. To a far greater extent than their English counterparts they were simply warrior chiefs, their aim to secure 'vast spoil and return home eminently worthy' as Gruffudd ap Llywelyn did after his campaign of 1055.

The nature of this warfare and the politics which went with it was extremely violent, sometimes exultantly so. 'Amidst that [battle] Trahaearn was stabbed in his bowels until he was on the ground breathing his last, chewing with his teeth the fresh herbs. Then Gwcharki the Irishman made bacon of him as of a pig.' So the *Life* of Gruffudd ap Cynan celebrated the death of his rival, Trahaearn ap Caradog, at the battle of Mynydd Carn in 1081. Having won this victory Gruffudd marched to Powys where, according to the *Life*, 'he straightaway displayed his cruelty in the manner of a victor'. 'He destroyed and killed its people, burned its houses and took its women and maidens captive . . . He destroyed the land completely.' Two things separated this kind of politics and warfare from that evolving in the Anglo-Norman world (discussed more fully below, pp. 126–7). One was the slaying of noble rivals. Between 1069 and 1081 no less than eleven Welsh princes fell in the violence. A minister of Henry I (1100–1135), in a later period of strife, arranged a truce 'out of love of the land for he knew they were all killing one another'. The second difference was the seizure of women and children to be kept or traded as slaves, something encouraged by the absence of castles in which to keep prisoners and of money with which to ransom them. Thus the ruler Iorwerth ap Bleddyn was allowed to promise Henry I £300 of silver 'in whatever form he could, horses, oxen and other things'.

At the heart of the violence between 1069 and 1081 were the conflicts within the kin of Gruffudd ap Llywelyn, king over all the Welsh, who was murdered by his men in 1063 following his defeat by Harold. 'After innumerable victories . . . he was now laid in the waste valleys,' lamented the *Brut*. At last in 1081, after the great victory at Mynydd Carn, Rhys ap Tewdwr established himself in Deheubarth, 'the kingdom of the south', while his ally Gruffudd ap Cynan, grandson of a king of Gwynedd, bid for supremacy in the north. These events had not been played out in a vacuum. The whole of the west coast of Wales was very much within the orbit of Irish and Scandinavian politics. Gruffudd ap Cynan's father had fled to Ireland where he married the daughter of Olaf, the Danish king of Dublin, Gruffudd himself being the fruit of the union. Gwcharki who made bacon of Trahaearn was only one of many Irishmen who swelled the armies of the Welsh rulers. To the east, on the other hand, Wales was accessible to England. Before the Conquest there had been English settlement as far west as Rhuddlan in the north. In the south, Harold had established a hunting lodge at Portskewet in Gwent although this was soon burnt down by the Welsh. The Normans would not be so easily removed. Their hand was already apparent at the battle of Mynydd Carn for King Caradog of Glamorgan, killed there alongside Trahaearn, had been a client of King William. The purpose of William's solitary expedition to Wales in 1081 was to secure a similar submission from Caradog's supplanter, Rhys ap Tewdr. Meanwhile within a year of his victory at Mynydd Carn, Gruffudd ap Cynan found himself a prisoner of Earl Hugh of Chester, who was determined to establish is own supremacy in the north. 'That was the first plague and fierce advent of the Normans to the land of Gwynedd,' groaned Gruffudd's *Life*.

The Normans had reached Wales very soon after their arrival in England. Within three years of Hastings William had established William fitz Osbern, Roger of Montgomery and Hugh of Avranches as earls with great power in the border counties of Herefordshire, Shropshire and Cheshire respectively. This was a strategy to protect the frontier from Welsh incursions. But it could also serve as the base for Norman advance. In the south William fitz Osbern established a castle at Chepstow at the mouth of the Wye and another castle higher up the river at Monmouth, and began the advance into Gwent. By 1086 there was a Norman castle at Caerleon on the Usk, and its lord held considerable lands west of the river. William also established Clifford castle four square in the upper valley of the Wye, and this could support the Norman advance (gathering pace in the 1090s) towards Brecon and Builth. Fitz Osbern's death in 1071 and the rebellion of his son Roger in 1075 inevitably slowed the pace of advance, the Conqueror being content to hold the line through the sheriff of Herefordshire and receive tribute from the Welsh rulers. Domesday Book shows that paid by Rhys ap Tewdwr was an annual £40. Having secured Rhys's submission William's 1081 expedition metamorphosed into a pilgrimage to St Davids. Until his final demise in 1093, Rhys's problems were less with the Normans than with his Welsh rivals whom he defeated and killed (after a period of exile in Ireland) in 1088 and 1091.

All this was to change in April 1093 when Rhys was killed by the Normans edging into Brecon. Cadwgan ap Bleddyn of Powys then immediately plundered Ceredigion and Dyfed and departed. Two months later the Normans overran the same areas and stayed. Arnulf, Roger of Montgomery's son, now established the first castle at Pembroke, one never afterwards taken by the Welsh. South-west Wales, 'which was not in their power before that', as the *Brut* put it, thus came under Norman rule. Rhys's death must likewise have facilitated Bernard of Neufmarché's conquest of Brecon and further south Robert fitz Hamon's of southern Glamorgan, for which Cardiff castle was the base. The Normans also moved into upper Gwent, the base here being the castle at Abergavenny.

Further north, after 1066, Roger of Montgomery's position in Shropshire had actually been more dominant than that of fitz Osbern's in Herefordshire because he was given all the non-ecclesiastical land in the shire. He parcelled much of it out, in solid strategic blocks, to his followers, who built their own mottes, like that of the Corbets at Caus and the Says at Clun. Roger himself established the first castle of Montgomery, named after his home in Normandy, just as Caus was named after the pays de Caux. Montgomery was a hinge on which Norman and subsequently English control of Wales turned. It stood just to the west of Offa's Dyke, at the point where the Severn plunges into the mountains of central Wales, to connect via narrow passes with the Dyfi valley. Thence the way was opened to Aberystwyth and the whole of south-west Wales. Doubtless this was the route (protected by eight mottes built down the Severn valley) the Normans took when they advanced into Ceredigion and Dyfed.

It was north Wales which saw the most spectacular and ultimately the most illusory of these early Norman advances. In Cheshire Earl Hugh had received a concentration of lands much like Roger of Montgomery's in Shropshire. From there his nephew, Robert, had advanced probably in the 1070s to establish a castle at Rhuddlan, by this means controlling the valley of the Clwyd. The seizure of Gruffudd ap Cynan after his victory at Mynydd Carn was clearly designed to eliminate any challenge from that quarter. By the time of Domesday Book the Normans had pushed on to the Conwy above which Robert had probably completed his castle of Deganwy. By sea as by land, that was the base for the conquest of the rich corn lands of Anglesey together with most of the rest of Gwynedd, the hold consolidated by castles which in their skilful siting (one was at Caernarfon) foreshadowed those of the ultimate Edwardian conquest in the thirteenth century.

With Anglesey, Gwynedd and the rest of the north held by the castles of Robert of Rhuddlan and Earl Hugh of Chester, and with Ceredigion, Pembroke, Glamorgan and Gwent being secured in the west and south, it looked as though all of Wales would soon fall to Norman rule. Yet it was not to be. On 3 July 1093, Robert of Rhuddlan was killed in a skirmish by his Welsh foes, led – at least according to Orderic – by Gruffudd ap Cynan. Next year, in the words of the *Brut*, the Welsh 'being unable to bear the tyranny and injustice of the French, threw off their rule'. In the north, Gruffudd ap Cynan and Cadwgan ap Bleddyn of Powys destroyed the Norman castles in Gwynedd and slaughtered a relief expedition. In the south, helped by the death of Roger of Montgomery in July 1094, the new castles in Ceredigion and Dyfed, with the exception of Pembroke, were destroyed in risings. The Normans ultimately held on to most of the coastal lowlands of south Wales but their control of Gwynedd was never fully restored, the greatest reverse they suffered in all their conquests in Britain.

The changes wrought by the Normans remained profound. In the areas which came and remained under their sway, notably the southern lowlands, the native rulers were either eliminated or subjected and eclipsed. At a lower level, some Welshmen became peasants within the manors established by the Normans, being interspersed with English immigrants. In Dyfed in the early twelfth century substantial numbers of Flemings were also introduced (see above, p. 38). Alongside these new manors there were settlements which remained Welsh, some populated by freemen and some by bondmen, both groups now giving their services and renders to their new lords. There was a tendency for these 'Welshries', as they came to be called, to be pushed onto less fertile land, hence the profound difference which developed between south and north Glamorgan, lowlands and uplands, one Anglo-Norman and the other Welsh. Yet the transformation in Wales, dramatic though it was, proved less awesome than that in England. The English aristocracy was destroyed after 1066; the Welsh was not. Substantial parts of Wales, if shifting in size, remained under native rulers. In the thirteenth century, the descendants of Gruffudd ap Cynan, Cadwgan ap Bleddyn and Rhys ap Tewdwr still held sway in Gwynedd, Powys and regions of the south.

The Norman conquest of Wales was thus permanent yet incomplete. For the incompleteness there was, of course, one paramount reason, as Gerald of Wales pointed out. Wales was formidably defended by its mountains, woods and rivers. The political fragmentation caused by this geography in fact served Wales well. There could be no Welsh Hastings, no overthrow of the kingdom in a single battle. Wales would have to be conquered piecemeal, with armies, fleets and castle-building all co-ordinated. That, as Gerald noted, would take the 'diligent and constant purpose' of the king for at least a year. William, given his scale of priorities, could not give that amount of time. Nor could his successors in the 200 years after 1066. It followed, therefore, that the conquest of Wales remained a baronial, not a royal, enterprise. Yet the barons too had rival preoccupations. William fitz Osbern died fighting for William in Flanders; his son was disinherited after rebellion in England; the Montgomerys had wide lands in France. Moreover once the most fertile parts of Wales, the southern lowlands, had been absorbed, the incentive to 'go on' lessened. On a day-to-day basis, the consolidation and continuation of the conquest of Wales were left to knightly tenants with no more resources than their Welsh opponents.

The Welsh, moreover, were redoubtable opponents. They are 'entirely bred up to the use of arms', commented Gerald of Wales, almost echoing the Conqueror's dying remarks about himself. A great chief (like Hywel ap Goronwy) slept with his sword above his head and his spear at his feet, and wished to die in battle, not in bed. Later evidence shows that Welsh rulers could raise armies of foot several thousand strong, exploiting the obligation on all freemen to perform military service as needed within the kingdom and for a period of six weeks a year outside it. (This at any rate was the obligation as stated in the Welsh law books of the late twelfth and thirteenth centuries.) Alongside such forces was the king's permanent war band, his *teulu*, which was really the central institution of his kingship. Composed of young nobles maintained at court, the *teulu* might be used to eliminate the king's opponents by mutilation or murder, and generally to act as the enforcer of his rule. It formed the core of royal armies, and was doubtless the chief beneficiary of the plunder. Confronted by such lightly armoured, sure-footed warriors, equipped with bows and spears, masters of the sudden ambush and the quick retreat, the armies of the Normans rarely achieved decisive victories. The Welsh, moreover, also learnt from the Normans. They had long bred horses and now learnt to fight on them. They donned mail and built castles. Militarily they thus had the best of both worlds.

The permanence of the Conquest, even if the conquered areas fluctuated, owed everything to the many-sided abilities of the Normans themselves not only in the realms of violence but also of accommodation. In Wales the Normans were the same explosively confident, brutally professional, free-wheeling warriors who had campaigned in Maine and Brittany and had conquered England. In Wales their war joy and greed could be unconfined. They now operated in the March, that is the frontier zone beyond the English kingdom. Instead of receiving their lands from the Conqueror they carved out their own marcher lordships. Instead of being hedged around by the structures of royal government, within their lordships they exercised almost sovereign power. When the powers of the marcher barons were defined in later centuries, they had near total control over justice (hence the king's writ did not run) and enjoyed the right to wage war and build castles. Historians once thought that these powers were either conceded by the king or taken over with the cantrefs and commotes of native Wales. But it was far more fun than that. The Normans in Wales were conquerors, not constitutionalists. Sometimes they exploited existing territorial units, but equally (as in Glamorgan) they often ignored them. With the king's acquiescence, the powers of the marcher lords were taken into their own hands. They were absolutely necessary to conquer and control.

Individual marcher baronies could expand and contract depending on the ebb and flow of conquest. Some remained small like Clun (held directly from the king after the forfeiture of the Montgomery family). Others like Pembroke and Glamorgan came to be considered as the equivalent of English shires. Central to the survival of all of them was the castle; no less than 300 pre-1215 sites have been identified in Wales. Castles were centres of aggressive lordship and bastions of safety in times of retreat. They were also intended to be psychologically crushing: Carew was built on top of ancient earthworks and overlooked a cross commemorating a former ruler of Deheubarth. Many began as simple motte-and-bailey structures topped with wood but usually at some point wood was replaced by stone. Sometimes stone was used from the start. Again and again in the narrative of the *Brut*, the Welsh risings swept over everything else only to break against the great stone keeps. Nothing marks the distinction between English and Norman methods more clearly than the contrast between Harold's palace at Portskewet, so easily burnt down in 1065, and fitz Osbern's massive keep at Chepstow, never afterwards taken by the Welsh. Of course, masonry is nothing without the men to man it, and here too the Normans had an answer. Many of the major castles were centres of what historians have called 'castleries' where the lord's tenants held their land in return for providing a garrison for the castle's defence. At Clun, for example, the building of the castle in the 1090s was quickly followed by the enfeoffment in the surrounding area of tenants who owed a total of seven knights for 'castle guard', the rest of the garrison probably coming from paid troops.

There was also a 'spiritual' side to the Norman conquest of Wales, as there was to that of England. The Welsh *clas* ('community') churches, with their hereditary clergy, unregulated in behaviour, seemed scandalous to these church-militant Normans. They used the lands of such institutions to found new houses (nineteen were established between 1070 and 1150) and endow existing monasteries in England and Normandy. In one evocative passage, Orderic Vitalis described the peaceful scene in the chapter house of his monastery, St Evroult, when Robert of Rhuddlan confirmed his gifts in England and Wales to the house. In another passage Orderic gave a graphic picture of Robert's violent death under the towering cliffs of the Great Orme, just north of Conwy, as he rushed forward on foot to confront his foes; two scenes which encapsulate the gallantry, piety and ranging activity of these Norman conquerors.

The Normans were self-confident in their prowess and in their piety, but they were not blindly arrogant. They were quite ready to learn from the Welsh and adapt to conditions, even coming in the early days to see the possibilities of the slave trade. The Welsh long remembered with grudging respect how Earl Hugh of Chester paid off some Scandinavian mercenaries not with young men and women but with toothless hags. Given the Welsh terrain, the Normans soon saw the value of lightly armoured cavalry, and some tenants (for example in the lordship of Oswestry) held their lands in return for providing it. The Normans also recruited foot soldiers, sometimes in large numbers, here drawing on the Welsh who remained within their lordships. The Normans too got the best of both worlds. At a higher level, they were very ready to make alliances with the Welsh rulers, indeed there were Normans fighting for King Caradog at the battle of Mynydd Carn. There was nothing socially demeaning about such contacts. Just as they came to venerate Welsh saints like Dogmael and David, so the Normans also respected the status of the Welsh rulers. Thus Caradog rubbed shoulders with Norman barons at the consecration of St Mary's church at Monmouth. Later in the 1120s Gruffudd, the son of Rhys ap Tewdwr, though now virtually landless, might still ride in company with two great marcher barons and be complimented on his 'innate nobility'. By this time intermarriage between Welsh and Norman noble families was commonplace. Once it was clear that the Welsh rulers were not going to be destroyed like their equivalents in England, the Normans, if they were to profit from their gains, had just as much interest in peace as they had in war. If violence brought the Normans their possessions in Wales, it was often accommodation which enabled them to keep and exploit those gains.

Of course, it takes two to accommodate and the Welsh proved willing partners. That was another important reason for their survival. King Caradog and Rhys ap Tewdwr were the first in a long line of Welsh rulers who tried by a policy of submission and alliance to limit Norman attacks, while gaining Norman support in their struggles for mastery over their native rivals. The Normans were far more, however, than simply new ingredients in old politics. Their advent was traumatic. 'Why have the blind fates not let us die? . . . O [Wales] you are afflicted and dying,' cried a despairing poet in the 1090s. The whole pattern of life had changed for ever. The Welsh within the marcher baronies faced new and exigent foreign lords. The Welsh rulers now played out their old politics as part of a much greater and more dangerous game, one in which, challenged by the marcher barons and the English king, they strove to retain what they held and recover what they had lost. The game only ended with the final conquest of Wales by Edward I.

*   *   *

In 1040 Macbeth (of Shakespeare's play) killed Duncan, king of Scots, and seized his throne. It was not till 1058 that Duncan's son Malcolm, after a period of exile in England, was effectively restored, thus inaugurating one of the most significant reigns in Scottish history. Two fundamental points need to be made about Malcolm's kingship. The first is that he ruled an area far smaller than Scotland today. The second is that the Scots were only one of several peoples who inhabited the north of Britain. The history of the north during the period covered by this book is essentially that of Malcolm's descendants expanding the area of their rule, both by conquest and accommodation, thus creating the boundaries of modern Scotland and a single people of the Scots.

The line of King Malcolm had been founded in the mid ninth century by a king of Scots, Kenneth MacAlpin, who had established himself east of the highlands between the firths of Forth and Moray. That this area was the original heart of the Scottish kingdom is suggested by the way the thanages, the basic units of royal administration in the localities (discussed later), were concentrated within it. It is also suggested by the use of the terms Scotland and the Scots. These are English forms of the Latin *Scocia* and *Scotti* which were themselves the equivalents of the Gaelic *Alba* and *Albanaig*. Now when we first have evidence of geographical meanings in the twelfth century, 'Scotland' could still stand for broadly this same area between the firths of Forth and Moray (see above, p. 11). The only difference, for reasons we will mention, was that the use excluded Moray itself, the area running westwards from the river Spey, although it possessed a significant number of thanages and had almost certainly been part of the original kingdom.

The limited extent of early Scotland is easily explained. There was a substantial Norse population in the far north in Caithness. Lothian, running south from the Forth to the Tweed, was largely inhabited by English. In the west, the Galwegians (the men of Galloway) and the Cumbrians (Cumbria extending from the Clyde to the southern edge of the Lake District) had their own identities, ones which owed much to the Norse Gaelic culture of Ireland. The rulers of Caithness, Argyll and Galloway were all striving to increase their power: Galloway itself, as a single political entity, was the creation of Fergus in the 1120s and 1130s. His style 'king of the Galwegians' well reflects his own view of his status. The rulers of Argyll and Galloway looked, not east to Scotland, but west to the Irish Sea, where they struggled for mastery over the Isle of Man and Western Isles with the dynasty – often highly factionalized – established as kings of Man by the great Irish warrior Godred Crovan around 1079. Here, as with Orkney and Shetland, the nominal overlord, formally recognized from 1098, was not the king of Scots at all, but the king of Norway.

The MacAlpins were certainly not content with this situation. Their claims to wider authority are reflected in the way 'Scotland' was also used in a second, larger, sense to mean the whole area north of the firths of Clyde and Forth. This 'larger' Scotland still excluded Lothian and Cumbria, but it was here that the kings made some of their early advances. Between around 960 (when Edinburgh was a royal base) and 1018 they had taken hold of Lothian, placing the south-east border on the Tweed. They had also gradually asserted dominion over Cumbria, ultimately after 1018 using it as an appanage for the heir to the throne. But there were also setbacks. In 1054 Cumbria south of the Solway seems to have fallen to Siward, Earl of Northumbria. Even worse, a division was opening within the original kingdom through conflict with Moray. Moray had been the power base of Macbeth (himself a member of the MacAlpin dynasty) and after his demise, as we will see, a kinsman continued to rule there. The growing fissure explains why in the next century Moray was not part of Scotland at all in the narrow use of the term referred to earlier.

In the assertion of royal power, one important factor made for continuity and stability. Although there might be dispute over who should be king of Scots, the kingship itself was not usually divided. The severance with Moray was the exception which proved the rule. Already therefore there was a fundamental contrast with the multiple kingship prevalent in Wales. The MacAlpin kings, while they were not anointed, enjoyed a much higher status than their Welsh counterparts, being almost certainly inaugurated with ceremony at Scone. The king had also, as Alexander Grant has shown, a local organization which enabled him to exploit his resources. The latter were essentially derived from the royal lands, which were organized into shires or what were later called 'thanages' after the official, the thane, who ran them. A thanage, of which seventy-one are known, normally embraced one or two parishes (or what were to become parishes), with the thane collecting renders in kind from the dependent settlements at the estate centre. Although their existence has always to be deduced from later evidence, the great majority of the thanages probably existed at the time of Malcolm's accession, being largely situated between the Firths of Forth and Moray. Within the area of the thanages the king did not hold all the land, for there were many lords with their own estates. There were also superior officials, who took the proceeds of land attached to their offices, and held the title 'mormaer', or 'earl'. (The titles were interchangeable, with the latter eventually becoming general.) However, the earldoms within the core of the kingdom, Fife, Gowrie, Angus and Mearns, were hedged around and honeycombed by the thanages. Gowrie, indeed, was in the king's hands. The thanages thus formed the heart of royal Scotland. Round them was a ring of provinces: Menteith, Strathearn, Athol, Mar and Buchan, in which, unlike the inner-core earldoms, there were no thanages at all. These too were under mormaers or earls who were certainly subject to the king in a way the rulers of Galloway, Argyll and Caithness were not. But with their offices becoming hereditary and without thanages to contend with, they also enjoyed a large measure of independence. This distinction between the inner core of the kingdom formed by the thanages and the outer ring by earldoms was to be fundamental to the history of Scotland throughout our period (see Map 3).

Within the kingdom serious crime was settled by compensation, as in England, but without being an offence against the king: there was no king's peace covering the whole realm. The hereditary legal official, the 'brithem', played an important part in both arranging compensation and settling disputes over land. The king, as far as the evidence goes, made no use of writing and minted no coins. Yet in context the MacAlpin monarchs were powerful and successful rulers. It is highly likely that they had more wealth than all the mormaers put together, partly because the lands of the latter were generally in the uplands. Even within the earldoms a general system of military service obtained, similar to the five-hide system in England, with (at least in theory) a specified number of men coming from each ploughgate or its Gaelic equivalent, the 'davoch'. An important task of the mormaers was to lead out this 'common army' from their provinces, an army which fought on foot and could be large and ferocious. The kingdom as a whole was liable to tax, namely 'cain', comparable to the geld, though paid in kind and raising unknown amounts. The royal estates themselves seem impressively organized. They provided 'conveth', a food render designed to support the royal household. This was organized so as to allow the kings literally to eat their way round the kingdom, in the process doing much to impress royal authority within the core of this small but manageable realm. All this reflected another fundamental difference from Wales, for the Scottish lowlands were sufficiently large, coherent and central, as the lowlands of Wales were not, to encourage the development of a powerful single kingship which would eventually greatly expand its territorial authority.

After ascending the throne in 1058 King Malcolm was indeed eager to expand his power, but should he attempt to do so to the north or to the south? His first marriage to the widow of Thorfinn, earl of Orkney might help him reassert authority in Moray and lay claim to over-lordship further north. In 1078 he crushed Macbeth's step-grandson, Malsnechtai, who ruled in Moray, seizing his treasures and cattle. But the victory seems short-lived for in 1085 the Ulster annals recorded the 'happy death' of Malsnechtai 'king of Moray', and the history of the area is then obscure for over forty years. Essentially Malcolm looked south. The recovery of Cumbria south of the Solway was a major ambition and there were also rich pickings to be had across the Tweed border. An English king based in the south before 1066, and thereafter a Norman one who was often overseas, together with the general chaos of the Conquest, all encouraged Malcolm to chance his arm. He was to lead no fewer than five southern expeditions, being remembered at Durham as 'a man of the greatest ferocity and bestial character, who ravaged Northumbria miserably with frequent invasions'. In these invasions he was to set a pattern followed by Scottish kings for over 150 years.

The first incursion was in 1061. While Tostig, Siward's successor, was absent in Rome, Malcolm marched into Northumbria and then probably crossed to the west to recover control of Cumbria south of the Solway. This southern orientation was confirmed by Malcolm's second marriage. In 1068 he welcomed to his court Edgar Atheling and other English exiles. Some two years later he married Margaret, Edgar's sister and granddaughter of Edmund Ironside, thus uniting himself with the ancient line of Wessex kings. Margaret was significantly to influence her husband's policies and to found a line of Scottish kings.

In 1070, in the aftermath of Edgar Atheling's abortive invasion of England, but after King William himself had disbanded his forces, Malcolm went south again. He consolidated his hold over southern Cumbria and then ravaged Teesdale. It was this invasion (and perhaps also the marriage to Margaret) which provoked William's one inter-vention in Scotland when in 1072 he marched to Abernethy. Malcolm 'gave hostages and was his man', as the Anglo-Saxon chronicler put it, but he did not remain quiet for long. In 1079, having triumphed in Moray, and with William back in Normandy, he harried Northumbria as far south as the Tyne. William responded by sending his son Robert north. He penetrated as far as Falkirk, secured Malcolm's renewed submission, and on his way back began the building of a new castle on the Tyne, the beginnings of that great northern city.

The castle was formidable yet it was also a recognition of Malcolm's power, for it stood not on the Tweed but on the Tyne, some seventy miles further south. As the northern chronicler Simeon of Durham complained, the way remained open for Scottish incursions, hence the need for the castle built at Norham on Tweed in the 1120s. Equally important, indeed related, was the fact that by 1086 the enfeoffments of Norman barons had gone no further north than Mitford, some fourteen miles beyond Newcastle. This highlights the greatest of all the contrasts between Wales and Scotland. There was never any equivalent in the north of the Welsh marcher baronies; there were no Norman lords aggressively pushing into the frontier zones and planting out their castles beyond the Tweed or the Solway. On the contrary the pressure was often from the other side.

Malcolm's fourth invasion came after the Conqueror's death in 1091. With Edgar Atheling once more at his court and William Rufus away in Normandy, he penetrated almost to Durham. Later in the year both Rufus and Robert marched north and Malcolm yet again submitted. But the real response came in the following year, when Rufus assembled a large army, expelled Malcolm's client ruler from Cumbria south of the Solway, and established a castle and town at Carlisle. For Malcolm this was a devastating blow. He was deprived of the great territorial gain of his career and, with Carlisle stopping one end, his access to the primary east–west route through the valleys of the Irthing and the south Tyne. In 1092 Malcolm went south to see Rufus at Gloucester, and was told his status was simply that of an English baron. Not surprisingly, the next year he launched his fifth and last invasion. He was trapped by Earl Robert de Mowbray in Northumbria and killed, together with Edward, his eldest son. Queen Margaret, already ailing, died when she received the news.

Malcolm's invasions of England, until the last, were superbly timed. Their motives were mixed. Doubtless he hoped to extend his authority over an area south of the Tweed on a permanent footing, just as he tried to do south of the Solway, but he lacked the technology either to acquire the one or retain the other. No castles were built by Malcolm. The invasions were still immensely worthwhile if only for booty, partly in the form of slaves. The Durham source quoted earlier tells of 'the very many men and women led away as captives'. Queen Margaret herself tried to purchase the freedom of English slaves she found in Scotland. Yet paradoxically she was also one cause of the invasions.

Margaret, thanks to her Wessex descent, was a queen of high status, something Malcolm acknowledged by naming their first four sons after Anglo-Saxon kings. The children themselves enhanced Margaret's role because she controlled their education and was inevitably involved in what were, as we shall see, the complex politics of the succession. A Life of Margaret, written within a few years of her death almost certainly by her former confessor, Turgot, the prior of Durham (1087–1107), affords a unique glimpse of the personal chemistry between husband and wife, on which so much queenly power depended. Malcolm honoured his wife as more educated and in religious matters more fervent and informed than himself. He gazed at her books which he could not read and jestingly threatened her with punishment when she took his money to give to the poor. Margaret's fabled piety was perhaps the product of her early upbringing in the only recently converted Hungary, whence she had arrived at the Confessor's court in 1057. She heard several Masses a day, read and re-read the Psalter, and filled the palace with paupers. She was also concerned with the more general reform of the church.

Margaret venerated some of the Scottish hermits but it seems certain that the church in general needed reform. There had been no wave of monastic revival in the tenth century or later, as there had been in England and Normandy, and apart from a few earlier survivals the nearest approach to monasteries were communities of Culdees ('vassals of God'), established from Ireland in the ninth century and now largely regarded as the private domains of noble families. As for local churches, these were often grouped together, in a way comparable to the Anglo-Saxon minsters, under Culdee communities and communities of other clerics. But the ministry provided, judging from Margaret's legislation, was often lax. Bishoprics certainly existed, but long vacancies were apparently customary and neither the numbers of bishoprics nor the diocesan boundaries seem very fixed.

The scope of Margaret's reforms was limited. The abuses condemned by the councils over which she and her husband presided (neglect of the Sabbath and improper celebration of the Mass, for example) were to be condemned again when Turgot became bishop of St Andrews. Margaret certainly built a 'noble church at Dunfermline' to house a Benedictine priory – the first regular Benedictine monastery in Scotland

– but this was not followed by a monastic revival. Margaret's daughters had to be sent for their education to Romsey abbey in England; and there was no prospect of Margaret and Malcolm working hand-in-hand with a great bishop as William did with Lanfranc in England. St Andrews was probably recognized as the senior Scottish bishopric, but it had no metropolitan authority, and in any case Fothad, who held the see between 1059 and 1093, was no reformer.

There was a political dimension to such reforms as there were because they fitted well with the agenda of southern conquest. In 1072 Lanfranc adopted the title of 'primate of all Britain' but accepted the authority of the archbishop of York over Durham and northwards 'to the ultimate limits of Scotland'. Later Scottish kings were determined to maintain the independence of the Scottish church from the pretensions of York and Canterbury, yet there is no sign that this was the agenda of Malcolm and Margaret. Indeed, Margaret sought Lanfranc's help in founding Dunfermline. Malcolm expected to expand southwards, not to defend himself from any southern threat. Both his violence and Margaret's reforms might, in different ways, encourage the English to accept his rule. So might their adoration of St Cuthbert at Durham. Malcolm laid the foundation stone of the new cathedral there in 1093 and secured the convent's prayers in perpetuity for himself and his wife.

Both reform and invasion were related to another consideration, one which dominated the later stages of Malcolm's reign: the question of the succession. Although the Scots of the MacAlpin realm had long had a single king, and probably sometimes a successor designated in advance (the 'tanaise'), succession was not by primogeniture. Rather (until 1005) the throne had gone to the member of the royal house who had seemed most suitable or been most powerful. Malcolm II's succession by his grandson Duncan in 1034 was the first example of the throne's passage in the direct male line since the mid ninth century. And then Duncan had soon been overthrown by Macbeth. There were now several potential challengers for the succession: Malcolm's brother Donald Bàn, for example, or an even more likely candidate, Duncan, the son of his first marriage, who had been dispatched to King William as a hostage in 1072 but was still inconveniently alive at the Norman court. Malcolm himself was absolutely determined to be followed by Edward, Margaret's eldest son, thus grafting the MacAlpin line on to that of the Wessex kings. But Margaret was unpopular. At the councils she had to argue down opposition and this was not helped by her lack of Gaelic;

Malcolm himself had to act as her translator. It was absolutely vital therefore to enhance the prestige and power of the new dynasty. The reform of the church, it was hoped, would win the favour of God, if not of man. The southern wars might also contribute to this end – Margaret may have regretted the slaves, but she needed the wealth and the prestige which the expeditions brought. In some remarkable passages Turgot's *Life* makes it clear that at court Margaret was the mistress of ceremonial, striving to make 'the magnificence of royal honour much more magnificent for the king'. Had she seen Queen Edith (after whom she named her eldest daughter) do much the same at the court of the Confessor? Margaret thus adorned herself 'in costly elegance as befitted a queen'. She decorated the palace with silken cloths, made native courtiers dress in coloured robes, introduced gold and silver vessels to the table, and 'instituted more ceremonious service of the king' so that henceforth he rode and walked surrounded by a large retinue. Malcolm certainly had a strong sense of his kingly authority and insisted his subjects swear an oath of allegiance to him. When Turgot refused to do so he was prevented from setting up a monastery at Melrose.

In the end it was all worth it, for the line of Malcolm and Margaret did indeed survive in Scotland. Through the marriage of their daughter to Henry I it became established in England too.

5

Britain and the Anglo-Norman Realm,
1087–1135

King William's deathbed dispositions, whatever his earlier intentions, accorded with developing customary law in Normandy which distinguished between patrimony, which must go intact to the eldest son, and acquisitions, which a father could dispose of as he wished. Robert became Duke of Normandy and the Conqueror's second son, William Rufus, king of England. Henry, the third son, received only money. The quarrels between the Conqueror's children, grandchildren and their noble followers dominated Anglo-Norman politics down to 1154, had constant repercussions in Wales and Scotland, and did much to shape and re-shape the political face of Britain. This chapter covers the history of Britain during the reigns of William Rufus (1087–1100) and Henry I (1100–1135).

*   *   *

English politics in the years after 1087 were enacted within an Anglo-Norman framework, one which involved far more than simply an old play acted out on a larger stage. The central struggle of the Conqueror's descendants to defy the division of 1087, oust their rivals in England or Normandy, and thus unite the Anglo-Norman realm, was entirely new. So were the complications which ensued for the nobility, especially when they held lands on both sides of the Channel. Not everyone, to be sure, was in this position. There were major Norman landholders after the Conquest, like the count of Evreux, who held little or no land in England. And politics, particularly in border areas (like the Norman Vexin), had their own momentum distinct from those of the wider realm. Yet the fact remains that large numbers of influential men did have extensive cross-Channel holdings. That was ultimately true of eight of the ten barons closest to the Conqueror at the end of his reign.

When England and Normandy came under separate and contending rulers, as was frequently the case after 1087, the position of such men became intolerable. 'How can one serve two masters?' the cry went up again and again. Cross-Channel barons had to commit treason to one ruler or the other, and for that the normal penalty was disinheritance. As the barons complained in 1088, according to Orderic, 'If we serve Robert, Duke of Normandy as we ought we will offend his brother William, who will then strip us of our great revenues and mighty honours in England. Again if we obey King William dutifully, Duke Robert will confiscate our inherited estates in Normandy.' The situation was equally fraught for the ruler, who sought to prevent the succession of disloyal heirs and the marriage of women to 'enemies' (as Henry I put it in his Coronation Charter of 1100). Nor was the problem solved when the lands of a Conquest baron were divided between sons in England and Normandy, which usually (though not invariably) happened in accordance with the distinction between patrimony and acquisitions. Such separations were rarely final and clear-cut. For instance, a baron disinherited for disloyalty in England might find safety with his kin across the Channel and support for the recovery of his lands. Families did not forget, and cherished claims to lost lands down the generations.

One reaction of the nobility to these circumstances was to strive for good relations between the rival rulers. 'A few attentive to their own advantage for they had possessions in both countries were mediators of peace,' noted William of Malmesbury of the civil war of 1088. Another was to work for the triumph of one party over the other, thus ending the conflict of interest. 'Then let us make Duke Robert ruler over England and Normandy to preserve the union of the two realms' (Orderic) was the majority decision in 1088 – not that the majority got its way.

Politics thus gained a new intensity after the Conquest, and yet they were also less bloody. In the great Anglo-Norman and English battles between 1106 and 1264, as in the more general ravaging warfare, very few nobles were ever killed. The immediate reason, as Orderic stressed, was the protection of armour, but ultimately any knight could be surrounded and disarmed. The key point was that when this moment came he simply surrendered and was taken off for ransom. The institution of ransom was, therefore, absolutely central to the failsafe warfare enjoyed by the nobility in this period. Indeed the whole aim in battle was to capture, not to kill, a noble opponent. There was here a wider context because politics too, not just warfare, was largely bloodless. It is a remarkable fact (and one quite contrary to usual perceptions of the Middle Ages) that between Waltheof's demise in 1076 and Gaveston's in 1312 not a single English earl, and indeed hardly a single baron, was executed (or murdered) in England for political reasons. Rufus and Henry I mutilated a few of their enemies but such corporal punishments too were on the way out. The usual penalty for treason was disinheritance and imprisonment. This was not because of any lack of theory. Treason, in the sense of breach of faith to one's lord, was very old, could cover a wide range of offences, and might certainly be punishable by death. It was simply that in this period the death penalty was not exacted.

These basic conditions of warfare and politics were already becoming established in Normandy before 1066. In England, political killings persisted (the last took place at court in 1064) and there had been no softening of the view that the penalty for treason should be death. Thus Waltheof's execution in 1076 was, wrote Orderic, according to 'the law of England' while 'the laws of the Normans' stipulated imprisonment and forfeiture. Nobles were also killed in English warfare, in part because until 1016 it had been in conflict with another people, the Danes, and the whole future of the dynasty had been at stake. In Normandy, on the other hand, warfare both foreign and domestic was between high-status nobles of similar outlook and background, very often sharing kith and kin. It ebbed and flowed across open frontiers and around castles, with victory and defeat unpredictable, and usually nothing utterly fundamental at stake. Of course, when the Normans engaged in all-out warfare against another people, as they did in 1066, they too killed with a will. But normally it seemed natural to spare noble enemies. Orderic specifically mentions how family ties kept down casualties in battle. This type of politics was reinforced and confirmed by the special circumstances created by the Anglo-Norman realm. What was the point in executing rebels in England if that just antagonized their kin in Normandy? Thus in 1095 Rufus, as Orderic observed, treated the rebels mercifully 'out of respect for their exalted kinfolk who might have sought vengeance in Normandy'.

After 1066, therefore, English politics and warfare were embraced by those of Normandy and France and followed their conventions. It was the latter which created the conditions for the development of chivalry, that code of values which so profoundly influenced the attitudes of the aristocracy in this period. What distinguished chivalry from earlier codes was principally 'courtesy', a 'courtesy' manifested most strikingly in the civilized treatment of one's opponent. It was that comfortable context which made the practice of the other chivalric virtues – loyalty, largesse, and above all valour – so much more enjoyable; enjoyable, that is, for the nobility. Chivalry was very much a code which governed their conduct towards each other; it had nothing to do with how they treated townsmen and peasants. Knights might not kill each other in warfare. They killed everybody else.

*   *   *

Physically the sons of the Conqueror were much alike: short, stocky, and barrel-chested, though Robert was the stoutest and shortest, hence his nickname 'Curthose' ('Short-stockings'), while Rufus had blond hair, a florid complexion and a red beard. Henry's hair was black. All three were bred to war, though for Rufus it was a passion, for Henry a business. On the face of it the future seemed to belong most probably to Robert. His right to Normandy was unchallenged and, as eldest son, he had some claim to England. Yet Robert was ultimately swept aside by his brothers, both in Normandy and in England, and no wonder. He was eloquent, plausible and chivalrous, yet at the same time he was lazy, prodigal and utterly without judgement. Rufus was totally different. Ecclesiastical writers treated him with horror, the result of his public pillage of the church and the murky dissipation of his private life. In fact he was probably heterosexual but with the court at night deliberately unlit it was easy to think otherwise. Rufus, however, was no spendthrift playboy. William of Malmesbury shrewdly noted the adroitly controlled contrast between his private and public face; the *intus* and the *extus*. At table with his intimates, Rufus was affable, relaxed, and self-mocking; in public assemblies he was intimidating, with glaring eyes (of different colours) and a ferocious voice, that was all the more frightening for becoming slightly halting when he was angry. Rufus's sharp intelligence could slice through to the political heart of any question. His boundless energy contrasted with Robert's torpor, and his expansive self-confidence with Henry's doubts and fears. Above all, as Malmesbury recognized, Rufus was ambitious, he was greedy for power and fame. His deeds of personal gallantry, his 'mighty plans' and his 'courtesy' (he offered a place in his household to a knight who had unhorsed him) became legendary. To later secular writers (most notably Gaimar, in his *History of the English*, written around 1140) he seemed the epitome of the heroic, chivalric king. His success was phenomenal. He secured Normandy, conquered Maine, expanded England's frontiers northwards, and asserted his supremacy over Scotland. Only Wales, thanks to these and other preoccupations which included a tumultuous quarrel with Archbishop Anselm, escaped his power.

None of this seemed likely at the start of the reign. Almost at once Rufus faced a rebellion designed to set Robert on the throne, the aim being to place England and Normandy under one ruler. The leader was Rufus's uncle, Odo of Bayeux, who had been released on the Conqueror's death. His capture and that of Rochester castle in the summer of 1088 brought the revolt to an end. The anarchy in Normandy and Robert's loss of Maine now gave Rufus ample opportunity to turn aggressor. In January 1091 he arrived in the duchy with a large army and forced Robert both to cede him significant territory and expel Edgar Atheling, still a potential focus for intrigue. Edgar, however, went to the court of his brother-in-law, King Malcolm, and in May 1091, with Rufus still in Normandy, the two invaded the north. (See p. 121.) Rufus's reaction came in two stages. An expedition to the Forth in 1091 forced Malcolm's submission; an expedition to the Solway in 1092 led to the foundation of Carlisle. Rufus and Carlisle: the two should always march together as the best measure of this king's ambition and achievement. Since 1061 Cumbria south of the Solway had probably been King Malcolm's. But now the foundation of Carlisle with its castle superbly sited on a bluff between the rivers Caldew and Eden brought it clearly within the English kingdom and opened the way for further advance. Carlisle was a far more aggressive statement than Newcastle upon Tyne, which merely retained what had long been in the realm.

These and other plans, however, were soon hampered by Rufus's quarrel with the church. In March 1093 he fell dangerously ill and, in the hope either of survival or salvation, filled the see of Canterbury, scandalously vacant since Lanfranc's death in 1089, with Anselm, the abbot of Bec. Anselm, an Italian like Lanfranc, was sixty years old and had been a monk of Bec for thirty-three years. He was famous for his piety, intellectual brilliance and theological writings. He warned that his appointment meant shackling a raging bull to an old and feeble sheep. But Anselm was no sheep; a wiry mule with a forceful kick would have been a better analogy. Like Lanfranc, Anselm was determined to defend Canterbury's rights and properties, many of which had been lost or damaged during the vacancy. He burned too with the desire to hold Lanfrancian-style councils for the reform of the church. But two things were different. The first was that Rufus was not like his father. He had absolutely no interest in the church save as a source of profit. The second was that Anselm, younger than Lanfranc and from a more uncompromising reform generation, was not prepared to qualify obedience to the pope for the sake of peace and royal power in England.

Rufus recovered, although he never thanked Anselm for it, and in the next month decisive events occured in Wales. The killing of Rhys ap Tewdr in April 1093, recognized by the Conqueror as ruler in the south, allowed Arnulf, Roger of Montgomery's son, to establish himself at Pembroke. It also facilitated Bernard of Neufmarché's conquest of Brecon and Robert fitz Hamon's of southern Glamorgan (see above, p. 111). With Gwynedd in the north encastellated by Robert of Rhuddlan and Earl Hugh of Chester, it looked as though the whole of Wales was coming under Norman rule. But at once there was a contrary sign. On 3 July, in a skirmish under the cliffs of the Great Orme, Robert of Rhuddlan was killed by (or so Orderic believed) the native claimant to Gwynedd, Gruffudd ap Cynan. For the moment, however, Rufus was busy with the affairs of Scotland. In August 1093, he asserted that his barons could sit in judgement on King Malcolm, a novel claim which implied the Scottish king had merely baronial status. The result, as we have seen, was Malcolm's last invasion of England and his death together with that of his eldest son Edward at the hands of Earl Robert of Mowbray, a pardoned rebel of 1088. With Queen Margaret's death a few days later the tensions created by Malcolm's policies exploded. The English at court were expelled, Malcolm's other sons by Margaret were brushed aside, and the throne was taken by Malcolm's younger brother Donald Bàn. Rufus now seized the chance to make his own man king of Scots. He received the fealty of Duncan, Malcolm's son by his first marriage (long a hostage at the Norman court), and sent him north with an army. Donald Bàn was ousted and Duncan became king. Yet, a measure of Rufus's priorities, he himself crossed to Normandy in March 1094, having first refused Anselm's demand to fill vacant abbeys and sanction the holding of a reforming council.

When Rufus returned at the end of 1094, Britain was in turmoil. That

November Duncan had been killed and Donald Bàn restored. There had also been a general rising in Wales, Roger of Montgomery's death in July 1094 following the killing of Robert of Rhuddlan the year before having cleared the way. The Norman base at Pembroke survived but the other castles in Ceredigion and Dyfed were destroyed, as were the Norman castles in Gwynedd (see above, p. 112).

Rufus was in no position to mount an immediate response. In January 1095 at a council held at Rockingham, his quarrel with Anselm reached a climax. Rufus demanded that the archbishop abandon Pope Urban II, whom Anselm had recognized while abbot of Bec, and like everyone else in England since the Conqueror's time (above, pp. 101–2) await the royal decision over which of two rival popes should be recognized. The king's authority to make this decision was integral, so Rufus asserted, to the rights of the crown. Anselm freely acknowledged the allegiance he owed the king 'in the things that are Caesar's', but denied that this extended to making him abandon the pope. Rather than do that, he declared, he would leave the kingdom. In the event, Rufus, always quick on his feet, decided to accept Urban in the hope that this would bring Anselm's deposition, which it did not. On top of this problem, in the summer of 1095 Rufus faced a baronial revolt. Its aim was to replace him, not with the hapless Robert, but with the Conqueror's nephew, Stephen, count of Aumale. The leader, the tall, dark, unsmiling Earl Robert de Mowbray, perhaps felt his dispatch of King Malcolm had lacked reward. Rufus reacted with confidence. Indeed in October 1095, with Mowbray's castle at Bamburgh under siege, he led an expedition to north Wales. Traditional Welsh tactics were a match for it. Gruffudd ap Cynan laid ambushes and retreated to the hills, thus baffling a general who was used to a very different terrain and had little time to spare.

The revolt, however, was suppressed. Mowbray was imprisoned for life, Earl Hugh of Shrewsbury was fined £3,000, and the count of Eu blinded and castrated. Thereafter Rufus enjoyed almost unbroken triumphs. He maintained peace in England, installed a client king in Scotland, took possession of Normandy, conquered Maine, and dispensed with his awkward archbishop of Canterbury. The real turning-point for all this was Robert's decision to embark on the First Crusade, when in order to raise money he leased Normandy to Rufus for five years in return for £6,666. In September 1096 Rufus took possession of the duchy. This was followed the next year by his second and grander invasion of Wales, this time in the south. The results were unspectacular but Rufus penetrated to St Davids, and stabilized the Norman hold on Pembroke. The campaign led to the final break with Anselm, who was accused of providing substandard knights for the expedition. In November 1097, pouring scorn on the custom that no one could visit Rome without royal permission, he left England to put his case to the pope. 'Go if you must,' laughed Rufus's councillor, the count of Meulan, 'we will get what we want'; and for the rest of the reign Canterbury's revenues flowed into the royal coffers.

By this time William had transformed the situation in Scotland. In October 1097 he sent Edgar Atheling (now an ally) north with an army. It drove Donald Bàn from the kingdom and installed Edgar, Malcolm's eldest surviving son by Queen Margaret, in his place. He was to reign till his death in 1107. The Malcolm–Margaret line had been restored for good. Yet Edgar was not intended to be an independent king like his father. In a charter issued before his installation, he styled himself king of Scots and Lothian by the gift of his lord King William.

Next on Rufus's agenda was the recovery of Maine, which his father had conquered and Robert had lost. By the end of July 1098 this had been achieved, thanks in good part to an extraordinary nobleman whose power stretched across many frontiers and whose military skills were as legendary as his sadism. This was Robert of Bellême, the second surviving son of Roger of Montgomery. Bellême ruled the county of Ponthieu in right of his wife, and held both his father's lands in Normandy and his mother's to the south of the duchy, including Bellême itself. It was in Wales, however, that he received his reward, with important consequences for Gwynedd's independence.

In the summer of 1098 Bellême's brother, Earl Hugh of Shrewsbury, together with Earl Hugh of Chester, made a determined attempt to recover Gwynedd. They penetrated Anglesey and forced both Gruffudd ap Cynan and Cadwgan ap Bleddyn to flee to Ireland. But at this moment a dramatic intervention took place in these western seas, one with an outcome that affected the political shape of both Wales and Scotland.

Magnus Barelegs, king of Norway (grandson of Harold Hardrada), had gathered a great fleet 'to plunder and gain dominion in the west beyond the sea'. He occupied the Shetlands, the Western Isles, and the Isle of Man, his authority over all three (according to Magnus's Saga) being now formally recognized by the king of Scots. Certainly it was not till 1266 that Norway resigned this lordship in the west. Magnus then descended on Anglesey, killed Hugh of Shrewsbury with a lucky shot from his bow, and departed as suddenly as he had come. In the vacuum created by this disaster, both Gruffudd and Cadwgan returned from Ireland. Gruffudd was suffered by the Normans to keep Anglesey and Cadwgan parts of Ceredigion and Powys. The vacuum was confirmed by Rufus's own decisions. Instead of passing Hugh's lands to Arnulf, lord of Pembroke, his brother on the spot, he preferred the absentee Robert of Bellême, a decision determined and vindicated by the situation in Maine, where in the summer of 1099 Bellême's help was needed to put down rebellion. Rufus himself when he heard the news abandoned his hunt in Clarendon forest, galloped to Southampton, crossed to Normandy in the teeth of a storm ('Whoever heard of a king perishing by shipwreck?'), took the horse of a local priest and surrounded by cheering crowds rode off to muster an army with which he soon recovered Le Mans. Next year Rufus held his Whitsun court at Westminster in the great hall which he had built. The massive structure still survives: 240 feet long and 67 feet wide, at the time by far the largest hall in Europe. Yet Rufus's reaction was characteristic: 'It should have been twice as big.'

Rufus's successes depended above all upon money, hence his ability to buy Normandy from his brother. Although there were 'feudal' contingents (like Anselm's) in his armies, he also recruited household knights from all over Europe, and was famous as an open-handed hirer of soldiers. The revenue-raising ability of the administration in England was vital, and here Rufus found a minister of drive and genius in Ranulf Flambard. Flambard had risen from obscure origins to be keeper of the royal seal in the 1080s and ultimately (in 1099) he became bishop of Durham. He was arrogant, abrasive, expansive, jocular, licentious, sharp-tongued and quick-witted, a man after Rufus's heart. His nickname Flambard meant 'incendiary' or 'scorcher'. Contemporaries recognized that Flambard was 'second after the king'. He authorized many writs and (as Orderic makes clear) was in charge of both the dispensation of justice and the exaction of revenue. He may well have developed schemes to make more money from the geld, and certainly it was a heavy geld which raised the money to purchase Normandy. He almost certainly masterminded the exploitation of the king's 'feudal' rights, an exploitation for which, as we have seen, Domesday Book was the central tool. For the first time, to the disgust of reforming churchmen, abbeys and bishoprics were deliberately kept vacant so that the king could enjoy their revenues. Inheritance fines reached such levels that some barons complained they were made to buy back their own land. Wardships and the attendant marriages were exploited by the king not left in the hands of families. As the concessions made by Henry I in his Coronation Charter show, all this was deeply resented.

It is doubtful if any of this worried the king. He had treated rebels with a cunning mixture of punishment and pardon. He had made Robert of Bellême his trusted aide and rewarded other supporters, usually from old baronial families, with earldoms. Henry de Beaumont, for example, became earl of Warwick and William de Warenne earl of Surrey, yet this was at small cost to the crown because such titles (notably in the case of Warenne) were largely honorary. Stories later abounded of what Rufus intended next: he would conquer Poitou; he would build a bridge of boats across the sea and conquer Ireland; he would make himself king of France; he would take Rome itself. The reality was different. On 2 August 1100, having feasted in the morning, Rufus went hunting in the afternoon. He was killed in the New Forest by an arrow shot by Walter Tirel, almost certainly an accident. The body was taken back, blood dripping from the cart, for burial at Winchester.

*　　*　　*

On 5 August 1100, three days after Rufus's death, his younger brother Henry was crowned king of the English. Henry was to conquer Normandy, bring thirty-three years of peace to England, develop its structures of government, reach a settlement of fundamental importance with the papacy, and (as the *Brut* put it) 'subdue under his authority all the island of Britain and its mighty ones'. To Orderic Vitalis he seemed to be the mightiest king ever to sit on the English throne.

Henry was now thirty-two years old. His youthful struggles with his brothers had educated him politically, as Orderic noted. In contrast to the open-handed Robert, he knew the value of money and the importance of bestowing patronage carefully. In contrast to the self-confident Rufus, he was always fearful of treason and the turn of fortune's wheel. Never a risk-taker, Henry preferred, as William of Malmesbury observed, to gain his ends by diplomacy rather than the sword; and he had that rarest of all assets among the successful: he knew when to stop. That characteristic, together with his preoccupations in Normandy (where he spent more than half his time), meant that over Wales and Scotland his aim was more to control than to conquer. The political shape of Britain came to owe much to his restraint. This did not mean that Henry was in any way a mild man. There was no contradiction, as there had been with Rufus, between his public and private face. With little laughter in his household, everything was business. Even his womanizing (so William of Malmesbury thought) was a duty imposed by the desire for children. Henry's bullock body, his bawling voice, his decisive actions, his righteous punishments, his very restraint, were all intimidating.

In gaining the throne Henry was lucky, for Robert was still absent on crusade. When he returned only a month later he took possession of Normandy and at once cast eyes on England. Henry had already moved to gain support. On the day of his coronation, he had issued a Charter which disavowed Rufus's 'oppressions'. Henceforth the king would not exploit ecclesiastical vacancies and would charge heirs a 'just and lawful relief', instead of making them virtually buy back their lands. He would not force widows to marry, and would arrange the marriages of heiresses only after consultation with his barons. Widows too, or other relations, were to have custody of land and children during minorities, which seemed virtually to eliminate the royal right of wardship. Henry thus appeased his barons, but he also sought the loyalty of the undertenants, very much on the lines of the oath of Salisbury (see above, p. 105). The Charter stipulated that the barons were to give like concessions to their own men, and exempted knights from paying geld on their demesne lands. Henry capped all this by sending Ranulf Flambard to the Tower; and by his marriage to Edith, daughter of Margaret and Malcolm of Scotland, who was conveniently in his power at Romsey abbey, he hoped to graft the Norman dynasty onto the old Anglo-Saxon root, and conciliate the kind of Englishmen on whom much of local government depended. Such men had already given Rufus significant support in the crisis of 1088.

As Henry braced himself to meet Robert's challenge, Archbishop Anselm returned to England and exploded a bomb. He refused either to receive the customary investiture of ring and staff from the king or to do him homage; both had been forbidden at the council in Rome the previous year, which he had attended. He had not come back to England, he said, for the king to disobey the pope. The investiture dispute was part of a much wider European struggle which had already led to violent conflict between Pope Gregory VII and the Emperor Henry IV. For the king to invest a bishop or abbot with ring and staff, the spiritual symbols of office, the church argued, implied that he had spiritual jurisdiction, 'a monstrous idea' as Pope Paschal II (1099–1118) put it, tantamount to saying that man had created God. Likewise if ecclesiastics performed homage to the king it showed they were subject to him. All this was part of a wider programme to free the church altogether from secular control and in particular to ensure that rulers had no part in ecclesiastical appointments. Bishops should be chosen by the clergy and people of their diocese, and abbots by their communities: free canonical elections. If on the other hand, as Paschal explained to Henry, kings 'open the door of the church', those chosen would 'not be shepherds but thieves and robbers'.

Henry had an appalling dilemma. He needed Anselm's support against Robert but its price might gravely damage his control over the church. Eadmer, a Canterbury monk and Anselm's biographer, even described Henry, with pardonable exaggeration, as facing 'as it were the loss of half his kingdom'. At one extreme, lay investiture could be defended (as in the works of a writer known as 'Anonymous of York') precisely because the king did have spiritual functions: he was both king and priest, *rex et sacerdos*. A more moderate line was taken by Ivo, bishop of Chartres, who argued that what was being given was nothing spiritual but simply the temporal properties of the prelates which princes had conferred on the church down the ages. Henry himself made his stand partly on custom, 'the usages of my predecessors', which he would not alter, and partly (here moving to the question of homage as well as investiture) on his refusal to tolerate 'anyone in my kingdom who is not my man'.

In the short term an agreement to refer the whole question back to the pope found a way out of this impasse. Anselm married Henry to Edith, now re-named Matilda, and gave essential support, both material and moral, in the ensuing crisis. As in 1088, Robert had the backing of the greatest Anglo-Norman magnates, partly from their desire to unite the two realms. Henry countered in March 1101 by promising the count of Flanders £500 a year in return for bringing a thousand knights to England in the event of invasion or revolt, a classic example of the importance of money and mercenaries. However, Robert's challenge soon evaporated. He reached England in July 1101 and then, to the disgust of his supporters, resigned his claims to the kingdom in return for £2,000 a year and other concessions. Those dispossessed on either side were to be reinstated. In future neither ruler would harbour the other's enemies. The Anglo-Norman realm was to function through a peaceful accord between its rulers. The aspiration was sensible, but foundered on Henry's success in England and Robert's failure in Normandy.

Henry, in fact, soon moved against his brothers' leading supporters, namely Robert of Bellême and Arnulf of Pembroke, the sons of Roger of Montgomery. Unlike Rufus, he did not need Bellême's support to hold down Maine, and in 1102 he struck, besieging Robert's English castles and forcing the brothers back across the Channel with the loss of all their English and Welsh possessions. After the fall of the Bellêmes in 1102, England, as Orderic Vitalis noted, enjoyed peace until the end of Henry's reign. If Henry could dispossess *them*, small wonder 'no one dared rebel or hold a castle against him'. But Henry's peace was not just based on fear. He also strove to create a group of loyalist barons. William de Warenne, earl of Surrey and lord of Lewes and Conisborough, had backed Robert in 1101 and been dispossessed in the next year. Yet he was soon to be a pillar of Henry's regime. Henry also knew how to reward his servants, many from old baronial families – Robert of Meulan, for instance, a leading councillor until his death in 1118, added the honour and earldom of Leicester to his large Norman estates. In the first years of the reign, however, one vital ingredient necessary to peace was absent: Henry did not control Normandy. Those disaffected in England could flee to their cross-Channel estates, and were bound to back Robert in a fresh attempt on England. To the conquest of Normandy, therefore, Henry assigned top priority. That decision had important repercussions on royal authority in Wales, limiting intervention when the opportunities for it were abundant.

Earl Hugh of Chester had died in July 1101, leaving a seven-year-old son, Richard, whose estates thus came into the king's hands, the first example of how the right of wardship could suddenly transform the king's power in Wales. Would Henry now seek to recover the dominion over Gwynedd which Hugh had exercised before the great revolt of 1094? Faced with that prospect, Gruffudd ap Cynan journeyed to King Henry's court for one of the most crucial interviews in Welsh history. He was welcomed by the king, who was looking for allies against the Bellêmes and was conceded much of Gwynedd west of the Conwy. In the years down to 1114, with Henry preoccupied with Normandy, he was able to build up his power east of the river too. Further south, Henry was more hands-on, partly to round off the destruction of the Bellêmes. He kept Shropshire and placed it under a sheriff. He also kept western Dyfed and Pembroke where he made Arnulf's former deputy, Gerald of Windsor, his castellan. In Ceredigion he replaced Cadwgan ap Bleddyn of the Powys dynasty (a client of the Bellêmes) with his brother Iorwerth ap Bleddyn, here showing an early ability to exploit the divisions within the native dynasties. But it was not long before Iorwerth himself was languishing in Henry's prison, having been taken to court and been judged guilty of various offences. From now on, the 'fear of King Henry and his law' was upon the Welsh rulers.

After Henry had secured the kingdom, he allowed Anselm to hold the one great reforming council of his archiepiscopate (at Westminster in 1102). Nine abbots were deposed for simony, and legislation governing the lives of monks and clergy was passed. Yet the impasse over investiture and homage remained. At the end of 1103, with Anselm now in Rome and the pope standing firm, Henry seized the revenues of Canterbury. It took the critical situation in Normandy to break this log-jam. There Henry, or so his apologists claimed, was being urged to rescue the duchy from anarchy. He was only too pleased to comply, but just before he could launch what was his second campaign (in 1105), the pope excommunicated Robert of Meulan, Henry's chief adviser, and raised the prospect of excommunicating Henry himself. It was imperative to reach a settlement and this was achieved just before the climax of Henry's final campaign in 1106. That climax came in the battle joined outside Tinchebrai on 28 September. Robert was captured and spent the last twenty-six years of his life in comfortable confinement in a succession of castles in south-west England. Beating off several later challenges, Henry was to hold England and Normandy together for the rest of his life.

In August 1107, back in England the settlement of the investiture dispute was formally pronounced. Henry promised to give up the practice of investiture for good. Pope Paschal conceded that no one was to be denied consecration because they had done homage to the king. True, this was only until the rain of Anselm's prayers persuaded Henry to renounce homage, but it would have taken an ocean of tears in which Henry was drowning to effect that. Although nothing explicitly was said about it, Henry continued to control appointments (as Anselm acknowledged) so that his chief minister, Roger, became bishop of Salisbury and his chaplain, Thurstan, in 1114 archbishop of York. Henry continued to exploit ecclesiastical vacancies: Canterbury remained unfilled for five years after Anselm's death in 1109, when it passed to a 'safe' man, Ralph, prior of Caen. The verdict of the York historian, Hugh the Chanter, seemed about right: faced by the greatest of all attempts to free the church from secular control, Henry had lost something in royal dignity but little in real power. Henry was not, in any case, a man of outward show, and he had scaled down his father's thrice-yearly crown-wearing ceremonies. He owed his ability to keep control of the church partly to the fact that the episcopal bench was so royalist. Eight of the thirteen bishops in 1097 had been royal clerks, although such men, it should be stressed, could often be conscientious and independent diocesans: Thurstan showed a real pastoral concern and was a tiger in asserting the rights of York. Moreover, where curial bishops remained in secular office, like Roger of Salisbury, they could act as a hinge between church and state. Even the most committed reformers, for example Gilbert Crispin, abbot of Westminster, were uncertain about Anselm's stand. Should he not have remained at home tending his flock? Henry was no Rufus, as his permission for the Westminster council had shown in 1102. And after all, what Anselm himself most wanted was to hold such councils and work generally for the reform of the church. As it was, his practical achievements were far smaller than Lanfranc's save in one area which concerned them both, the assertion of Canterbury's primatial authority over the whole of Britain. Thus Anselm received from Bishop Urban of Llandaff (1107–35) the first (or at least the first known) profession of obedience to Canterbury from a Welsh bishop. Anselm's career had also both reflected and reinforced a tide bringing England into a much closer relationship with the papacy.

Pope Paschal complained that Henry prevented contact with Rome, but if so the prevention was intermittent. In fact during the reign much closer ties were established with the papacy. Of the archbishops and bishops in 1100, only four had visited the pope, each on a single occasion; of those in office in 1135 all save two had done so, some many times over. In 1119, moreover, Pope Calixtus II had himself consecrated Archbishop Thurstan, and next year he freed York explicitly from any obedience to Canterbury. This was directly against Henry's wishes, yet he accepted the verdict. If that was partly because Calixtus promised not to send legates to England without the king's permission (only one presided over a council during the reign), it still represented a considerable assertion of papal authority. Other developments were also changing the face of the church. No fewer than 137 monasteries were established in the reign, of which forty were daughters of continental houses. Henry himself established the great Cluniac abbey at Reading, where he was buried. Most important of all was the arrival of the Cistercians. The first monastery was established at Waverley in Surrey in 1128, followed in 1132 by Rievaulx in Yorkshire, founded by Henry's great minister Walter Espec. Over the next twenty years Cistercian houses covered the land, transforming England's spiritual life and influencing the course of politics.

*   *   *

The outcome of the battle at Tinchebrai reunited the Anglo-Norman realm and for the moment brought peace to Normandy as well as to England. Henry, like some great puppet master, could once more pull the strings in Britain. Soon after 1106, he gave the lordship of Carlisle to Ranulf le Meschin, who had led the van at Tinchebrai, the son of the vicomte of the Bessin. This was to relinquish Rufus's great foundation, but to a loyal vassal and at a time when relations with Scotland were harmonious. King Alexander I (1107–23), who succeeded on his brother Edgar's death, had spent time at Henry's court, and his sister, of course, was Henry's queen. In south Wales, Henry consolidated his hold around Pembroke, in 1108 settling large numbers of Flemings in the area (see above, p. 38). This part of the country long afterwards retained its Flemish character. At the same time Henry founded a royal castle at Carmarthen on a strategic site just above the estuary of the Tywi where it controlled the river which cut through the heart of Ystrad Tywi.

All this was interrupted by an extraordinary act of romantic folly. In 1109 Owain, son of Cadwgan ap Bleddyn of Powys and Ceredigion, seized and seduced Nest, the alluring and eager wife of Gerald of Windsor, Henry's castellan at Pembroke. Since Nest was the daughter of Rhys ap Tewdwr, the king of Deheubarth killed by the Normans in 1093, the marriage (and it does not stand alone) illustrates a growing accommodation between the Welsh and the Normans. So in a sense does the sequel, which shows the Welsh princes still as major players, while accepting that their games were refereed by the king.

The immediate effect of the seizure (graphically described in the *Brut*, which is particularly comprehensive in dealing with this period) was like that of an explosion which sends a flock of birds rising in panic into the air. Cadwgan, Owain's father, filled with the 'fear of King Henry on account of the injury to his officer', hurried to court but nevertheless he was deprived of everything save one township. Henry was then free to give Ceredigion to Gilbert fitz Richard de Clare, one of England's wealthiest magnates: 'You were always asking me for a portion of Wales . . . now go and take possession of it.' Gilbert did just that, establishing castles at Aberystwyth and Cardigan, and enfeoffing his followers, who also established castles. So the Normans for a time recovered Ceredigion, which they had lost after the Welsh resurgence of the 1090s. This was also a major step in Henry's rapprochement with the old baronial families in England and in Normandy, where Gilbert's brother was lord of Orbec and Bienfaite.

Meanwhile Henry's sheriff of Shropshire exploited the segmentation of the Powys family and its violent feuds by enlisting Owain's cousin, Madog ('Do you want to please King Henry?'). Madog indeed seized Owain's and Cadwgan's portions of Powys, and then in 1111 killed both Cadwgan and Cadwgan's brother Iorwerth, whom Henry had released from prison to fight him, for by this time Madog and Henry had fallen out. Yet, after these triumphs, Madog still went to King Henry's court, where he was soon followed by Owain, both clamouring for royal recognition and the support that that would bring. For the moment, truces were arranged, hostages taken and both gained shares in Powys; not long after, however, Owain trapped and blinded Madog.

Henry's moderate response was utterly conditioned by threats far away on the southern frontiers of the Anglo-Norman realm. In August 1111 he left England for Normandy where he remained for nearly two years. His policies in Britain continued to be adjusted in the light of his anxious defence of the duchy. One problem was that he had no clear 'right' to Normandy, which as he said he had simply 'subjugated by battle'. At best, as William of Malmesbury put it, he had 'done wrong' (in deposing Robert) 'to put an end to wrong' (Robert's anarchic rule). Even Henry's partisans, like Orderic, acknowledged that Robert's son, William Clito, born in October 1102, had a good claim to the duchy. Having just escaped Henry's attempt to seize him in 1111, he had fled to the French court and he remained a constant danger until his death in 1128. There were other threats across the frontiers. The count of

Flanders was antagonized by the marriage in 1110 of Henry's daughter Matilda to his enemy the Emperor Henry V. In the same year Fulk V of Anjou had become count of Maine, and he refused to acknowledge Henry's overlordship. And then there was the king of France, Louis VI, 'the Fat' (1108–37). With steady energy and wily ambition, Louis was determined to establish Normandy's status as a fief and to destroy the great castle of Gisors, built by Rufus on the frontier of the Epte, which divided the Norman from the French Vexin. All these external foes were very ready to take up Clito's cause, and tempt from Henry's allegiance those Norman barons who had no stake in England.

The barons with interests spanning the Channel were in a different position. The land they held in England and Wales – land completely in Henry's power – could keep them loyal in Normandy, rather as a plank held down at one end by a great weight will remain in place even if the ground at the other end gives way. Equally vital were the resources and prestige of his English kingship for they were the support behind everything done in Normandy. Orderic was making a practical, not a constitutional, statement when he described Henry as issuing 'royal commands' in the duchy. To emphasize the point Henry in his Norman writs and charters usually styled himself king rather than duke. To the pressures he faced between 1111 and 1113, he reacted with a mixture of pre-emptive strikes, patronage and diplomacy. He seized and imprisoned Robert of Bellême; he established his nephew and eventual successor, Stephen, as count of Mortain in the vulnerable south-west corner of the duchy, also giving him the honours of Lancaster and Eye in England; and above all he engaged his son and heir, William, to Fulk V's daughter Matilda, accepting Fulk's rule in Maine, while Fulk acknowledged Henry's overlordship. There would, then, be no re-conquest of Maine, a restraint very different from the reactions of Rufus, which parallels Henry's earlier decision not to re-conquer Gwynedd.

The stabilization of Normandy had immediate repercussions in Britain on Henry's return there in July 1113. He made David, King Alexander of Scotland's younger brother, an earl, married him to the widowed daughter of Earl Waltheof (see above, p. 102), and gave him custody of her inheritance, which included extensive lands in the midlands, the beginning of a long-term connection between the Scottish royal house and what came to be called the earldom of Huntingdon. Since Alexander was childless and David, who was often at the English court, was his heir, this was a clever way to secure a hold over the future Scottish king. In 1115 Henry at last moved to assert his authority in Wales. Here Gruffudd ap Cynan's expansion of Gwynedd east of Conwy had brought him into conflict with Richard, who had now succeeded his father as earl of Chester. Owain ap Cadwgan (of Nest fame) was likewise struggling with Gilbert fitz Richard for power in Ceredigion. Henry's campaign was the greatest yet mounted in Wales, and anticipated much later strategy in having three armies split between the south, the centre (against Powys) and the north. The writer of the *Brut* feared for the extermination of his race, yet Henry was content when Gruffudd ap Cynan, Owain and other men of Powys submitted and paid tribute. His lesson had certainly gone home. In 1117 when Gruffudd, Nest's brother, the son of Rhys ap Tewdwr, returned from Irish exile and attempted to recover his lands, he got scant support. On Henry's instructions, Gruffudd ap Cynan plotted to seize him; 'Yes!' shouted the Welsh garrison of Carmarthen when asked if they were true to the king, and Owain, having been knighted by Henry in Normandy, joyfully set out to put down the revolt – only to be killed by the forces of Gerald of Windsor in revenge for Nest's abduction.

By this time Henry was once more in Normandy and facing a formidable coalition which had rallied in support of Clito. Again Henry made artful use of patronage, giving William de Warenne the castle of Saint-Saens in the heart of the Warenne family lands, a castle which inevitably would be lost in any Clito victory, having belonged to Clito's faithful guardian Elias. Diplomacy played an important part too with the marriage of Henry's son, William, which finally took place in 1119. And then, on 20 August 1119, Henry decisively defeated King Louis's forces at the battle of Brémule. At its climax William Crispin brought a great blow down on Henry's helmet, only to be felled by Roger fitz Richard – how Henry must have blessed the day he gave Ceredigion to Roger's brother! In 1120 the two kings came to terms. Hitherto Henry had avoided doing homage to the king of France and thus acknowledging explicitly that he held Normandy as a fief. He may well have hoped his authority in the duchy would become more and more regal. But the top priority was to see Clito off. So William, Henry's son, now did homage in return for Normandy (with Gisors included), which indicated Louis had abandoned Clito. Henry still avoided doing homage himself but wanted no more uncertainty about his position. On his new seal, used from 1121 (and perhaps earlier), he firmly styled himself duke of Normandy.

Yet there was to be no absolute certainty. In November 1120 William, heir to the English throne, was drowned in the wreck of the White Ship. Apart from his daughter Matilda, married to the emperor, Henry had no other legitimate children and his re-marriage next year to the daughter of the count of Louvain failed to produce a child. The question of the succession dogged the rest of Henry's reign and exploded in civil war after his death. For the moment, however, Henry's return to England in 1120 had an impact on Wales and Scotland, much as had his return in 1114. In 1121 he led his second expedition to Wales, this time directed just towards Powys. Gruffudd ap Cynan of Gwynedd refused to support the men of Powys, saying he had 'made peace with King Henry', which left the remaining sons of Cadwgan ap Bleddyn and their uncle, Maredudd, no alternative but to submit and pay heavy tributes.

In the next year, 1122, Henry turned his attention to the north, with highly significant results. His concern for the northern border is explained by the pretensions of King Alexander in Scotland, the first sign of much future conflict.

*   *   *

As king of Scotland, Alexander almost certainly acknowledged Henry's overlordship. His childless marriage to one of Henry's illegitimate daughters itself emphasized his subordinate status. It was to perform the military service he owed that he accompanied Henry on his Welsh campaign of 1114. In all probability Alexander's grant to his brother David of southern Lothian, and Cumbria north of the Solway, was also the result of Henrician pressure. That Alexander began to resent this demanding overlordship is strongly suggested by his conduct of ecclesiastical affairs.

In 1109 Alexander had filled the see of St Andrews, vacant since Fothad's death in 1093, with Turgot, prior of Durham and his mother's biographer. During his episcopate which lasted till 1115 Turgot brought the Scottish church into direct contact with the papacy, and tackled the same issues of discipline and morality that had concerned Queen Margaret. The king's connections with the south also explain his establishment of Augustinian canons at Scone, the very heart of the kingdom, for these priests came from Nostell priory in Yorkshire. There were also, in all probability, important developments in episcopal organization. By 1155 the Scottish church was divided into ten dioceses. Some were of long standing, like St Andrews, although they were often left unfilled. Others may well have been founded in the reigns of Alexander and David, his successor. Certainly in or soon after 1115 there were bishops of Moray and Dunkeld. These developments raised in acute form the question: to whom was the Scottish church subject? Here Alexander was determined to overthrow the Canterbury–York agreement of 1072 which, without any consultation with the Scots, as he complained, had placed the Scottish church under the metropolitan authority of the archbishop of York. That had seemed of little moment when King Malcolm's thrusts reached as far south as Durham. It was different now with King Alexander on the defensive. At York, meanwhile, Thurstan was equally determined to uphold his metropolitan authority, which meant consecrating and receiving professions of obedience from all the Scottish bishops. In 1119 Pope Calixtus issued a letter supporting this stance. It was to rebut these pretensions that in 1120 Alexander, seeking a new bishop of St Andrews, turned to the Canterbury monk Eadmer, Anselm's biographer, and manifestly no friend of York. But Eadmer, apart from raising problems over homage and investiture, sought simply to replace York's authority with that of Canterbury. Alexander was firm: 'He would never in his life consent to a Scottish bishop being subject to the archbishop of Canterbury,' Eadmer reported him as saying. This was part of a wider view of his royal authority, which he may well have derived from Henry I in England. As the bishop of Glasgow told Eadmer, Alexander 'wishes in his kingdom to be all things alone; and he will not endure any authority to have the least power in any matter, without his consent'. The logic of all this, in the ecclesiastical field, was that St Andrews should be raised to metropolitan authority, and it was precisely this that King David (doubtless picking up the ball from Alexander) was to seek from the pope in 1124-5, soon after his accession. The political ramifications were clear. As Thurstan said, the demand implied that the king of Scotland was not subject to the king of England, whereas (so he said) the reverse was indeed the case.

Therefore when Henry returned to his kingdom in 1120 he found Alexander showing unwelcome independence. His brother David too, in Cumbria, made sure that John, bishop of Glasgow (1118-47) was consecrated by the pope, not by York. It was no accident that in 1121 Henry permitted (and quite probably instructed) Ranulf Flambard, long rehabilitated as bishop of Durham, to build a castle at Norham on Tweed, thus at last protecting the northern border. Around this time he also established two 'new men', who owed everything to him, in the north: Walter Espec at Wark on Tweed (and Helmsley in Yorkshire), and Eustace fitz John at Alnwick. Meanwhile, in the north-west Henry gained security beyond the border by marrying an illegitimate daughter to Fergus, the ruler in Galloway, and in a move of enormous importance reversed his earlier policy towards Carlisle. Richard, earl of Chester had perished in the White Ship without any direct heirs. Henry allowed the earldom to pass to Ranulf le Meschin, vicomte of the Bessin, but in return he took back into his own hands the lordship of Carlisle which he had granted Ranulf in the 1100s. Royal authority was in this way planted once again on the Solway; by 1130 the region to the south was divided, rather imprecisely, into two administrative districts under royal officials, one described as 'Carlisle' and later in the century as 'Cumberland', the other (much less important) as Westmorland. This was an important moment in the history of the north, and one deeply offensive to the Scottish royal house from whom Carlisle had been taken by Rufus in 1092. In 1122 Henry went north, began the great square keep of Carlisle castle, which still survives, and surrounded the town with a wall, thus protecting its burgesses. He also laid plans for a separate bishopric which would sever the area from the authority of the bishop of Glasgow. This was finally sanctioned by the pope in 1133, by which time Carlisle had its own mint, supported by a silver mine run by the town's burgesses at Alston.

These advances in the north were interrupted in 1123 by the last of the Norman revolts which Henry had to face, again with the aim of making Clito duke. As before, Henry triumphed with a mixture of diplomacy and force. The plans of his son-in-law, the Emperor Henry V, for invasion kept Louis VI quiet. The pope annulled Clito's dangerous marriage to the daughter of Fulk V of Anjou and in return a papal legate, John of Crema, was allowed to hold a council in England. By the time this took place in 1125, Henry's household knights in March 1124 had crushed the rebels at the battle of Bourgthéroulde.

The crisis was over but the door of the succession still swung on its hinges. The death of the emperor in May 1125 gave Henry the opportunity to try and slam it shut. He brought Matilda to England and in the New Year exacted an oath from the great magnates to accept her succession both in England and Normandy. There was an immediate reason for such speed. Louis VI had once more adopted Clito's cause, and in January 1127 he accepted his homage both for Normandy and the French Vexin. There was considerable support for him, even within Henry's court. He seemed the 'natural' heir, at least to Normandy, while there were no precedents in either the kingdom or the duchy for female succession. Later in 1127, therefore, Henry took out further insurance in a move which shaped the whole future of the dynasty. He betrothed Matilda to Geoffrey, the son and heir of Fulk V, count of Anjou. The marriage (finally celebrated in 1128) was a variation on an old theme, for William, Matilda's brother, had married Geoffrey's sister. The aim in both cases was to forge an alliance with the count of Anjou and prevent him supporting rebels in Normandy.

Clito's death in 1128 without direct heirs was thus a great relief, especially as King Louis had just made him count of Flanders. Henry could also be reassured about affairs in Scotland and Wales. At the Christmas court of 1126 David, who had now succeeded his brother Alexander as king of Scots, had both supported Matilda's succession and abandoned his attempt to get metropolitan status for St Andrews. In return Archbishop Thurstan relinquished his own efforts at Rome to subject the Scottish bishops to York's obedience. In south Wales Henry was very much in control. He had established royal bases at both Pembroke and Carmarthen. He had married his trusted minister Miles of Gloucester to the heiress of the lordship of Brecon, and his illegitimate son Robert to the heiress of Glamorgan. Robert had also received Bristol and the earldom of Gloucester. One branch of the Clares was in Ceredigion while another had gained Chepstow and lower Gwent between the Usk and the Wye, the lordship founded by William fitz Osbern.

In north Wales, in the 1120s, Gruffudd ap Cynan's sons, taking up the baton from their father, had pushed Gwynedd eastwards at least to the Clywd, this at the expense both of native rulers and the earl of Chester. But given Gruffudd's loyalty, and the earl's unreliability, that had not bothered Henry. In his extraordinary career, Gruffudd had thus rescued Gwynedd from virtual extinction and made it the dominant force in the north. In the last years before his death in 1137, so his Life recalled, he held great feasts, adorned his land with churches, and brought peace and prosperity to his people. He was also anxious to 'modernize' Gwynedd, especially in ecclesiastical affairs, something which paralleled developments elsewhere in Wales. Before the Normans the Welsh church had bishops but no diocesan structure, either in terms of boundaries or government. In the south, a reflection of Norman influence, territorial dioceses emerged in the first half of the century in part through the disputes between Bishops Urban of Llandaff (1107–34) and Bernard of St Davids (1115–48). Llandaff, embracing forty-six churches, was defined as lying between the Wye and the Tywi. The dispute was also important in putting the Welsh church in close touch with the pope who issued five bulls in relation to it, and in 1132 appointed 'judges delegate' to hear the case back in Britain, one of the earliest examples of such commissions. All this is revealed in *The Book of Llandaff*, which documents the struggle. In the north, the Normans had established Hervé, a Breton, as bishop at Bangor in the 1090s but, appalled by Welsh customs, he soon departed. The decisive moment in establishing a diocese at Bangor came in 1120 when Gruffudd made David bishop; David was of mixed Welsh and Irish ancestry, had studied at Würzburg and been a much-travelled clerk of Henry I. So Gruffudd had placed Bangor under a man familiar with best international practice and in this appointment had also pleased Henry I. If Gruffudd had given birth to modern Gwynedd, Henry had indeed been the midwife.

With south Wales in his own hands or under loyalist magnates and ministers, with north Wales under the trusty Gruffudd ap Cynan, with loyalists enfeoffed in Northumberland, with the king himself at Carlisle, and both the king of Scots and the Welsh rulers frequenting his court, Henry could indeed be called, as Walter Map put it later in the century, 'lord of the whole English island'.

* * *

King Henry's hold of Normandy and control of Britain depended directly on his government of England, which secured much of the revenue on which they were based. That government had also to maintain law and order, thus fulfilling Henry's pledge in his Coronation Charter: 'I establish a firm peace in all my kingdom and I order it henceforth to be kept.' Ministers had to do all this, moreover, in the frequent absences of the king, absences which after the conquest of Normandy in 1106 were clearly to be a permanent feature of his rule. In the event he spent more than half his reign outside England. Henry himself was well qualified to oversee this government. He was the most educated of the brothers and was heard to quip that an unlearned king was like a crowned ass (his only known joke). Orderic observed how he subjected everything to vigilant scrutiny and wished to be cognizant of the affairs of all his servants. Under that watchful eye, in the long Henrician peace an experienced cadre of ministers gave careful attention to detail and made improvements from year to year, in this way developing the structures of a royal government more powerful and intrusive than ever before.

Henry's household, as shown by a 'Constitution' written down soon after his death, consisted of over 150 men, together with fifty more in the hunt, and one solitary woman, the laundress. The basic structure was probably much as under his predecessors, but Henry had introduced one important reform. Under Rufus and at the start of Henry's reign the court had lived in part by plundering the countryside, so much so that the peasantry fled as it approached. In 1108 Henry laid down the penalty of mutilation for anyone guilty of such seizures, 'alleviating the evils which pressed most heavily on the poor', as Eadmer put it. This was probably the origin of the regulations seen in the 'Constitution', which stipulated in great detail how each member of the household was to be supported – by wages, food, drink and candles, all carefully graduated according to position.

The officials of Henry's chamber were responsible for the room in which he lived. They included the bearer of his bed, and his 'ewerer' who filled his bath and dried his clothes after a journey. They also received, stored and spent the king's money; the increasing sums for which they were responsible were reflected in the office of treasurer of the chamber, which appears for the first time in the 1120s. There was also an expansion in the work of the chancellor. Averaged across the reign, forty documents a year survive (in originals or copies) from Henry's chancery and less than twenty from that of Rufus. The level of chancery business (of which the surviving documents are but a tiny fraction) is reflected in the existence of a deputy, the 'master of the writing office', whose wages Henry doubled, and in the gigantic offer of over £3,000 which Geoffrey Rufus, the chancellor in 1130, made to obtain the office.

The 'Constitution' does not mention the branch of the household which gave these written orders punch: the household knights. However, their position and function in Henry's reign have been much studied. Perhaps Henry did not retain as many knights as Rufus but according to Orderic he had several hundreds of them. Drawn both from noble families and from the lower ranks of society, many of them building up traditions of family service in the household, they were expected to be worthy (as Orderic said) of the wages and food which supported them. They might also serve in the hope of recovering lost patrimonies, as Eadmer noted, and gaining new ones. They appear throughout the pages of Orderic as councillors, castellans, and (at Bourgthéroulde) as victors. They were vital to Henry's rule.

The king's household was the most fundamental institution unifying the Anglo-Norman realms. Some of the stewards were based largely in England or Normandy, but the master of the writing office, the treasurer of the chamber, and probably the bulk of the household went back and forth across the Channel. When in England and not pulled by emergencies to Wales or the north, Henry spent most of his time at palaces and palace-castles in the south. According to the number of known documents issued from them, Westminster-London was first in rank with 237, followed by Winchester (127), Woodstock (93) and Windsor (71). Henry thus did not need to travel to rule England and could remain, as far as his itinerary went, very much a Wessex king. To cope with his absences, Henry set up small regency courts or councils in England and in Normandy. In Normandy they were headed for many years by John, bishop of Lisieux; in England until her death in 1118 by Queen Matilda.

Matilda, as the daughter of King Malcolm and Queen Margaret of Scotland, was descended from the line of the Anglo-Saxon kings through her mother. Her initial position cannot have been easy. There had been no queen of England since the death of the Conqueror's wife in 1083. Matilda brought with her no inheritance and was scorned by some Normans for her Anglo-Saxon pedigree. Her change of name from Edith to Matilda, from that of the last pre-Conquest to the first Norman queen, itself reflected sensitivity on the subject. Yet Matilda, clever and co-operative, played a significant part in the first phase of Henry's reign. Henry himself in remembering his mother, Matilda of Flanders, must have had a very positive image of queenship, and he soon gave his own wife a similar kind of landed endowment. So Matilda had her own resources which she exploited, according to William of Malmesbury, with some harshness. If to some of the Norman elite Matilda seemed an alien, her ancestry, in which she was intensely interested, made her very much at one with the mass of Henry's subjects. Poets indeed celebrated her as 'the glory of England', 'sprung from kings on both sides'. Matilda could also draw on another positive image of queenship, indeed she did so quite deliberately, for it was she who commissioned the Life of her mother, Queen Margaret, which showed Margaret playing a very full part in the daily affairs of court and kingdom (see above, p. 124).

Matilda's religious observance certainly echoed that of her mother, for example in her concern for the poor and oppressed. On one occasion she astonished her brother David, the future king of Scots, by washing and kissing the feet of lepers. To David's remark that if Henry found out he would never kiss her again, she retorted that the feet of the eternal king were preferable to the lips of a mortal one. In her patronage of religious houses Matilda stood in the tradition of both her mother and mother-in-law. Just as the one had founded Dunfermline priory and the other Holy Trinity at Caen, so Matilda founded Holy Trinity, Aldgate in London, one of the first Augustinian houses in England, using the revenues of Exeter to do so. Here, as in her endowment of other houses like Abingdon, Matilda's grants were confirmed by her husband, the two acting very much in partnership.

Contemporary comment, for example in the so-called Hyde abbey chronicle, shows that Matilda's religiosity earned her great respect; so, indeed, did her success in providing the king with children. Of course, there was no scope at Henry's court for the kind of role played by Queen Margaret at the court of King Malcolm where she had laboured to bring its ceremonial up to date. Nor was Henry always approachable. On one occasion, faced by a crowd of complaining clergy, Matilda was tearfully sympathetic but apparently too frightened to intervene. Intervene, however, she sometimes did, and effectively. For example, she helped persuade Henry to return Canterbury revenues to Anselm and later to give in marriage Earl Waltheof's daughter to her brother David. She was careful, however, in matters of controversy to take her husband's part. Solicited for help by both Anselm and the pope throughout the investiture dispute, she explained that there could be no settlement which 'diminished the rights of royal majesty'. This loyalty to the king and understanding of his objectives was the key to her appointment as regent when Henry was out of England. The success of Henry's mother in the post had created a precedent, yet it was also one which could be ignored: no similar position was accorded to Henry's second wife, Adela of Louvain. As regent, Matilda issued writs in her own name, heard petitions, and tried law cases in, as she put 'the court of my lord and myself'. She made clear to ministers that she must be consulted and was complimented by the bishop of Norwich for 'administering royal affairs with laudable solicitude'. Matilda's seal, with which she authenticated her writs and charters, showed her standing, a tall imposing figure, holding as symbols of authority an orb in one hand and a sceptre in the other. Here indeed was a woman who could govern a kingdom.

Of the ministers of the king and queen, one was pre-eminent: Roger, bishop of Salisbury (1107–39). A poor priest from the suburbs of Caen, he had, so the story went, impressed Henry by racing through the Mass and had become his chaplain. In England he soon headed both the judicial and financial administration. The large numbers of writs he witnessed and in effect authorized shows that the writing office and central government moved at his command. He worked under Henry when the king was in the kingdom, under Matilda when he was not. After Matilda's death, Roger was left formally in charge and issued writs in his own name. He was in fact 'second under the king', as Henry of Huntingdon put it, and 'justiciar of all England', the title ultimately adopted by his successors, although Roger himself did not use it. In many ways Roger's position was similar to that of Rufus's great minister Ranulf Flambard, and contemporaries described them in similar terms. Yet in approach they were as different as their masters. Rufus's mighty plans and high-cost wars required large sums of money to be raised very quickly; for that purpose Flambard's aggression and fertility were ideal, and his unpopularity the measure of his success. After 1106, Roger operated in calmer waters even with the emergencies in Normandy, and was able to build slowly; for that his bureaucratic mentality (he attended to affairs of state in the morning and those of his bishopric in the afternoon) was ideal. So was his plausible and conciliatory nature. Letters poured in to him begging for justice and favour. His ability to balance the options they posed, gauge the limits of his authority (did the king need to be consulted, was the queen persuadable?), and come up with acceptable solutions made an essential contribution to England's peace.

Central to Roger's power and the control of the king's revenues was the exchequer, where he presided probably from 1110. That greatest of all institutions of central government for the first time emerges into the light. Its task was first to exact or collect the king's annual revenue;

second, to store it and spend it on the king's orders; and third, to audit annually the accounts of those responsible for the revenue's collection. A great book written by Bishop Roger's great nephew, *The Dialogue of the Exchequer*, explains the exchequer's workings in 1178 and they were not fundamentally different in Roger's own day. Each year the exchequer officials, the barons of the exchequer, usually meeting at Winchester, prepared lists of the sums which the sheriffs were to collect and pay in, one half at Easter and one at Michaelmas. The payments were made into the treasury, which was also at Winchester, and by 1130 effectively a branch of the exchequer. By 1178 it was often called the 'lower exchequer' or the 'exchequer of receipt'. At the treasury two chamberlains received the money, kept it and dispensed it on the king's orders, the great bulk often being sent to the king's chamber. The receipts for payments were wooden tallies (one for each individual debt), that is sticks cut down the middle with the payment recorded both in notches and writing on either side. One half was kept by the sheriff, the other by the exchequer. After Michaelmas each year, at stated intervals, the sheriffs and other collectors of revenue came back to the exchequer, or more specifically to the branch later called the 'upper exchequer' or 'exchequer of audit'. There they accounted for the money they had been summoned to pay in at the previous Easter and Michaelmas, the tallies being matched up as proof of payment. If the sheriff had been ordered by the king to pay some of his revenue directly into the chamber or spend some of his revenues locally, for example on the garrisoning of a castle, he now produced the authorizing writ and was credited accordingly. The state of play in respect of each debt was worked out visually with counters on a great chequered cloth, which gave the exchequer its name. Like the tally sticks, this was clearly designed to help those who could not read.

The results of the annual audit were recorded on a great roll (the 'pipe roll', as it was later called), a new one being opened for every year. That for 1130 is the first to survive, and the only one from Henry's reign. It is mightily impressive. Sixteen separate membranes, each around four feet long and a foot wide and made up of two smaller membranes, were written up on both sides. All sixteen were then sewn together at the top so that they could be rolled up into a single roll. The roll of 1130 runs to 161 pages in a modern printed edition, records over 300 writs authorizing expenditure by sheriffs or pardoning debts, and mentions over 2,000 people and places.

If Bishop Roger conceived the exchequer *de novo* he was an administrative genius. Yet even the friendly *Dialogue* does not make that claim, but discusses whether it went back to Anglo-Saxon times or whether it was introduced by the Conqueror and modelled on the exchequer in Normandy. There certainly was a Norman exchequer under Henry I but its origins are as obscure as its English brother's. Probably at least the name exchequer and the chequered cloth method of accounting from which it derived were fairly new in Henry's reign. Although the abacus system on which it was loosely based had been known in England for a long time, there is no reference to the exchequer *eo nomine* before 1110. On the other hand, previous kings can hardly have been without means of recording and auditing their dues. The *Dialogue* mentions that the original name for the exchequer was 'the tallies', which seems to recall a time before the exchequer cloth when wooden tallies may have been used to record debts as well as receipts. The treasury at Winchester existed before the Conquest and it certainly kept records of the farms due from royal estates and lists of hides for the levying of the geld. Both are referred to in Domesday Book. Probably the system of 1130 emerged gradually. The absenteeism of the Norman kings, which made it harder to audit accounts *ad hoc* as the king went round his estates, and accelerated the replacement of revenue in kind from royal manors with revenue in cash, necessitated a central audit and increased the amount of money it had to deal with. The number of debts owed to the king was also increased by new feudal revenues and the increasing impositions made by royal justices in the localities. According to the *Dialogue* the exchequer flourished exceedingly under Bishop Roger's direction, as the rolls showed. It may well be that much of the procedure which existed in 1130 was due to him. Certainly in his time the exchequer was a hugely powerful instrument of government. It was central to the exaction of revenue, the control of local officials, and the web of political control which the king could spin over the country, for nearly everyone of importance owed money to the crown and could be punished or rewarded by varying the rates of repayment.

Where did Henry's revenues come from? In one key area these had actually been declining, since land brought in over £3,000 less in 1130 than it had in 1087, the result of the amount given away in patronage during the intervening period. Nevertheless land in 1130 was still by far the largest component of the total income: £2,600 came from estates which had come into the king's hands through forfeiture and escheat, and £9,900 from the county farms. The latter were fixed sums which the sheriffs had to pay each year, being derived largely from the king's lands in the county, though also from other customary payments (like 'sheriff's aid'), and minor pleas in the county and hundred courts. The exchequer was also working hard to get more money from the farms, having revalued them only a few years before, and in 1129 demanding a £666 increment from eleven shires specially grouped together. The decline in revenue from land provided an incentive to make more money by other means. One of these was the royal forests. In his Coronation Charter Henry had promised to keep the forests as in the time of his father, which implied he would not imitate Rufus's malpractices. Yet Henry had royal forests in twenty-five counties and certainly expanded their bounds, a process Stephen (in 1136) promised to reverse.

Other sources which could be exploited were 'justice' (of which more later) and the king's feudal rights. It was these, of course, which had been opened up by Flambard's shameless energy and Henry in his Coronation Charter had forsworn them – not for long, although not on Flambard's brazen scale. Ecclesiastical vacancies brought in £1,100 in the 1130 roll, and inheritance fines, reliefs, and payments for wardships and marriages another £1,300. A further £5,550 still to be paid hung unpleasantly over baronial heads. With £2,500 coming from the geld (and more pardoned as patronage), Henry's total recorded revenue in 1130 was £24,550 of which £22,900 was paid into the exchequer (barring a small amount going directly to the king's chamber) and the rest expended locally. This sum was only exceeded four times in the reign of Henry II and was more than that raised a hundred years later in 1230, although by then there had been considerable inflation. The total actually demanded (as opposed to paid in and expended) was £66,800, so Henry was also owed a great deal of money; a useful position to be in. He was very rich, and was probably every year generating a considerable surplus; a treasure of fabled size glowed at Winchester.

There were other ways in which Henry kept hold of local government. Like his father and brother he was careful about the creation of earldoms. Henry made Robert, count of Meulan, earl of Leicester in 1107, his brother-in-law David in effect earl of Huntingdon around 1114, and Robert, his own illegitimate son, earl of Gloucester between 1121 and 1123. But these earldoms were different from the border palatinates created after the Conquest, of which only Chester now survived. The new earls had much more limited powers and their counties were essentially run by the sheriff appointed by the king, and responsible at the exchequer for the shire's revenues. Henry was also determined to control the sheriffs, whose performance he had criticized in a writ of 1108. Early in his reign twelve counties were under sheriffs who had been in office at the time of Domesday Book or were the sons of such men. Henry allowed the trusty Miles to follow his father in Gloucester but in general made it very clear the office was not hereditary. He appointed tenants of loyalist barons to some counties (like Nottinghamshire), and over others placed *curiales*, that is men who were high in his service and members of his court. At times he dramatically increased the numbers of the latter so that in 1130 they held no less than eighteen counties.

In 1108 Henry's criticism was that the sheriffs were holding extra sessions of the county and hundred courts to suit their own 'needs', meaning for their own profit. One source of that profit was hearing pleas of the crown. Described at length in *The Laws of King Henry I*, a book on legal procedure written between *c*. 1114 and 1118, these included (as they had since Anglo-Saxon times) homicide, robbery, assault, serious theft, rape and arson. It was vital for the king to control and exploit such business, and Henry developed two ways of doing so more efficiently. One was through the increasing use of an official who had existed before 1100, namely a local justiciar empowered to 'keep the pleas of the crown of the king', which probably involved investigating them, and then prosecuting the offenders in the local courts, taking over all this from the sheriff. Prosecution could also be either by juries drawn from the hundreds or by individuals following a process known as appeal. In 1130 the keeper of the crown pleas in Norfolk and Suffolk promised to make the king a 'profit' of £333, which shows just how much money could be made.

A second development was more significant. This was the practice of sending judges on circuit round the shires to hear crown pleas and whatever civil business was brought before them. These judges were later called 'justices in eyre' ('eyre' meaning visitation) or 'itinerant justices'. Since the leading itinerant justices were *curiales*, they gave the king far tighter control over his pleas than the local justiciars and the sheriffs whom they superseded. It was on the 'itinerant justices' that the administration of royal justice in the shires in the later twelfth and thirteenth centuries was largely to depend. The precise stages between the Conqueror's practice of sending a judge to a shire to hear an important individual plea, on the one hand, and the judges going through several shires to hear all crown pleas, on the other, is difficult to trace in the absence of pipe rolls. In 1096 Flambard may have held a West Country crown pleas circuit. By the 1120s, as the 1130 pipe roll shows, the eyres were certainly in full swing. Richard Basset, for example, had heard pleas in six shires; Geoffrey de Clinton in eighteen; and Ralph Basset (Richard's father) in eleven. In 1124 the Anglo-Saxon Chronicle provides a glimpse of Ralph Basset at work in Leicestershire where he hanged forty-four thieves and mutilated six. Henry's eyres provided an impressive manifestation of royal power, contributing most of the £3,600 owed for pleas in the 1130 pipe roll, and demonstrating that everyone was subject to the king's justice. Even the peasants of the mightiest northern barons were saddled with amercements which had to be paid to the king. A significant by-product of this activity may well have been to diminish yet further, indeed perhaps largely eliminate, the role of local courts in arranging compensation payments like those seen in the Anglo-Saxon law codes for offences to person and property, although these certainly continued unofficially.

Beneath the level of pleas of the crown, Henry had no quarrel with private jurisdiction, whether exercised in the (often overlapping) courts of manor, honour or private hundred. He ordered lords to implement the judgements of their courts (if they didn't, the sheriff would) and restore land to tenants 'justly', which probably indicated that the matter should be decided in a court of law. Quite probably many cases were moving from honourial to shire courts, or coming before the king himself because of default of justice. But Henry was quite prepared to shore up the jurisdiction of particular honourial courts and command tenants to perform the service due to their lords. In his 1108 writ he laid down that pleas over the occupation and division of land between the tenants of the same lord should be heard in the lord's court. (For further discussion of the honour, see below, pp. 403–7.) The 1108 writ also made clear that actions between barons were to come before the king himself. In such cases, in particular, the king could charge large sums for 'justice', £3,500 being offered for judicial favours in the 1130 pipe roll.

There has been much debate among historians about the type of men Henry I employed to run his government. Orderic Vitalis in a famous passage described how Henry 'ennobled men of base stock, who had served him well, raising them, as it were, from the dust'. There was certainly nothing new about kings taking servants from outside the ranks of the baronage. Indeed Hugh of Buckland, named by Orderic as one of Henry's new men, had been a sheriff under Rufus. All kings needed to recruit servants who were dependent on the crown for their fortunes and could be relied upon to be loyal and diligent in its service. The length, stability and administrative developments of Henry's reign may have made such men more conspicuous than before, and also have given them wider opportunities for holding office. Geoffrey de Clinton, for example, was sheriff of Warwickshire, a justice in eyre in numerous counties, chamberlain of the Winchester treasury and a prominent figure at court. The background of some of Henry's servants is obscure, justifying Orderic's remark that they had been 'raised from the dust'. The *Dialogue of the Exchequer* itself referred to Bishop Roger's 'lean poverty'. Others like Clinton and Ralph Basset, who headed Orderic's list of examples, came from families of essentially knightly status holding small amounts of property in England or Normandy, sometimes in both. Western Normandy, where Henry had been based before his accession, was a particularly fertile recruiting ground. There were also ministers who came from more substantial backgrounds, like Miles of Gloucester, son of the Domesday sheriff, and Aubrey de Vere, son of a minor baron. Henry's servants were certainly enriched, as Orderic noted. Clinton by 1130 had added 578 hides of land to his father's single manor at Glympton in Oxfordshire. Walter Espec, Eustace and Payn fitz John, and Nigel d'Albigny (who began as a household knight), as well as Miles of Gloucester, all became great barons through marriages arranged for them by the king. Such men were ruthless acquisitors, disseising tenants within the honours they had acquired and forcing men to grant them land; as a result Nigel d'Albigny was conscience-stricken on his deathbed. This suited the king. The very unpopularity of these ministers made them all the more dependent on his favour. Their loyalty might also be ensured by the large sums of money they could owe him, sometimes as punishment, sometimes through having to pay for favours they received. Together they formed a loyal and ruthless cadre on which Henrician government depended.

The work of the chancery; Bishop Roger and the exchequer; control over the sheriffs; justices in eyre; use of new men: in all these areas Henry built on earlier precedents. In all he probably went beyond them. The resulting structure of government was formidably strong.

Orderic wrote enthusiastically about the new cathedrals, monastic buildings and village churches permitted by Henry's peace, a peace which was both 'law and order' and 'political' in the sense of the absence of civil strife. To the political peace Henry's relations with many of his barons had made a crucial contribution. He had proved adept at exploiting the bonds which could tie nobles to the king: the desire for the status conferred by a place at court; the delight in fighting alongside the king on military campaigns; and the rewards that might come from faithful service. Henry was constantly taking counsel from his barons, both formally in specially summoned large assemblies and informally in his chamber and at the hunt. Orderic remarked on Henry's new men but he also declared that the king had 'won the loyalty of magnates by treating them with generosity and adding to their estates' – of which we have already seen many examples. In particular, just like his father, Henry had sought to make close family pillars of the regime. He had raised up his illegitimate son Robert, his nephew Stephen and his brother-in-law King David. Indeed, in a crucial move in 1125 Stephen had been married to a great heiress, the daughter of the count of Boulogne, gaining the highly strategic county of Boulogne itself and also lands centred on Essex which with the honour of Eye made him the most powerful landholder in south-east England. Meanwhile Stephen's clever and articulate brother Henry had become bishop of Winchester (1129–1171).

One leading Henrician scholar, C. W. Hollister, has argued that Henry left behind a largely harmonious political system, yet this may be to claim too much. While old magnates and new men rubbed shoulders at court, there was tension between them. 'The noblest men in the kingdom grudged [Henry's new men] their distinction because they were of the lowest origins and exceeded in wealth and power those far better born than themselves,' wrote the author of the *Gesta Stephani*. While, moreover, many barons enjoyed the king's favour, significant numbers felt they did not. There was tension, too, over the king's continued exploitation of his feudal rights. Rufus's own exploitation of inheritance payments, wardships and marriages had clearly antagonized many barons, resulting in Henry I's promises in his Coronation Charter, but these promises were not kept. There were also many families burning with the desire to regain lands of which they felt they had been deprived. This situation had not arisen because Henry had denied the principle of hereditary succession; in fact the principle was implicit in many clauses in his Coronation Charter. In practice, of the 193 baronies existing in 1135, 102 (52 per cent) had descended in the male line since 1086. But that still left plenty of room for royal interference through the processes of marriage and forfeiture, interference necessitated by the circumstances of Anglo-Norman politics described at the start of this chapter. Forty-seven baronies (24 per cent) had come into royal hands between 1087 and 1135, mostly through forfeiture, usually to be granted out again to those in the king's favour. Twenty-one (11 per cent) had been gained by new families through the marriage of heiresses. All this created material for dispute. Gilbert de Lacy wanted to recover the honour of Pontefract, which Henry I had taken from his father in 1114 for suspected treason and given ultimately to William Maltravers, a man whose origins are quite obscure. Simon de Senlis wanted the honour of Huntingdon which Henry had given King David on his marriage to Waltheof's daughter, Simon being the son of her first marriage. Payn fitz John, and Roger, son of Miles of Gloucester, disputed possession of the honour of Weobley with the Talbots and another branch of the Lacys. Under Stephen, these and many other 'family history' disputes and claims flooded to the surface and turned the mills of the civil war. The issue was not hereditary succession (which both sides freely conceded) but who should enjoy it.

There was also potential tension between the centralizing ambitions of the crown and the decentralizing ones of the nobility. As Judith Green has remarked, the nobles were both collaborators of the king and his competitors in the pursuit of power, that competition being particularly sharp in the local arena. The aim of an ambitious lord was to assert his rule in the localities by combining his castles and feudal structures with office and privileges received from the king – an earldom with real power, a private hundred, a royal castle, and a sheriffdom held either by himself or one of his men. If the king wanted to reward a great lord and gain a powerful local agent he might well condone such ambitions. Yet there were clearly dangers in doing so, especially if a baron's hold on local office became hereditary. Equally, if the king's immediate priority was cash paid into the exchequer, the last thing he wanted was such great local agents for they aspired to keep much of the king's revenue for themselves. Henry I, as we have seen, combated these centrifugal tendencies, preventing the sheriffdoms becoming hereditary and hesitating to set up palatine earldoms. But the result unfortunately was to leave a body of disgruntled magnates who nursed claims to such possessions, and resented those who held local office. Earl Roger of Warwick clearly detested the way his activities were monitored by the sheriff Geoffrey de Clinton, established at Warwick castle. Earl Ranulf II of Chester (who succeeded *c.* 1129) and his half-brother, William de Roumare, had claims to the castle and sheriffdom of Lincoln, while Geoffrey de Mandeville eyed up the Tower of London and the sheriffdoms of London and Middlesex, and Essex and Hertfordshire, which Henry had taken from his grandfather. When he finally recovered them under Stephen he secured a concession enabling him to exclude the justices in eyre (see below, p. 175). Those outside the regime must also have resented the power of the exchequer which recorded their debts and if ordered to do so exacted them for the crown. The pipe roll of 1130 shows Geoffrey de Mandeville owing £846; Earl Ranulf II of Chester £1,613; his mother Lucy, £646; and Earl Roger of Warwick £218. In all this too there were strains which were to explode after Henry's death.

In the very last years of Henry's reign, problems were also looming on the frontiers. The native rulers in Glamorgan were seething with discontent over Earl Robert of Gloucester's expansionary rule. In Gwynedd, the sons of Gruffudd ap Cynan threatened to be far less accommodating than their venerable father. In 1135 the incursions of the rulers of Powys into Shropshire were making Henry plan a return to Britain. In Scotland, King David owed much to Henry, yet had been thwarted over Carlisle. Henry's wealth and power enabled him to hold all these tensions in check. 'No one dared injure another in his time,' wrote the Anglo-Saxon chronicler. When his successor ran out of money it would be a different story.

And who was that successor to be? Henry, as we have seen, wanted it to be his daughter Matilda, 'the Empress' as she proudly styled herself, being the widow of the Emperor Henry V. The king's intent was strengthened after she had given birth to a son, the future Henry II, in 1133. But her path would not be easy. Quite apart from the fact that she was a woman, there was the question of the role to be played by her husband, Geoffrey, count of Anjou, for whom the Anglo-Norman magnates had no brief. In 1130 Henry had extracted another solemn undertaking to accept his daughter's succession, but he had granted her lands and castles neither in England nor in Normandy, despite Geoffrey's demands for the latter. Therefore she had no power base from which to stake her claim. Nor did Henry crown the Empress, or

THE STRUGGLE FOR MASTERY

associate her in any way with his rule – unlike Baldwin II, king of Jerusalem (1118–31) when he made his daughter Melisende his heir, an example widely known since Melisende's husband was none other than Fulk V of Anjou, Geoffrey's father. Henry, now well into his sixties, would not give way. He wanted no rival. And while he had failed to secure the position of the Empress, he had built up those of both Stephen and Robert, thus laying the foundations for the former's usurpation and the latter's championship of the Empress's cause, the heart of the civil war.

6

Britain Remodelled: King Stephen,
1135–54, King David, 1124–53,
and the Welsh Rulers

When Henry I died on 1 December 1135, Stephen was superbly placed to seize the throne. He was the son of Stephen, count of Blois, and Adela, the Conqueror's daughter, and was thus of illustrious descent. True he was only a younger son (his elder brother Theobald became count of Blois), but the patronage of Henry I had none the less made him the greatest baron in the Anglo-Norman world. On one side of the Channel he held the counties of Mortain and Boulogne, the latter in particular strategic and valuable. In England he was lord of the honours of Lancaster and Eye as well as other lands. His brother Henry was bishop of Winchester. It was in Boulogne that Stephen heard the news of Henry's death, while the Empress, the old king's daughter and chosen successor, was far away in Anjou. He immediately crossed the Channel, won over the Londoners, and then hurried to Winchester where, with the help of Bishop Henry, he secured the late king's mammoth treasure and the crucial support of Bishop Roger of Salisbury, head of the administration. On 22 December Stephen was crowned king in Westminster Abbey. In the words of the old dictum, 'one cannot serve two masters', success in England carried the day in Normandy, where the Empress and Geoffey of Anjou advanced up the well-trodden route from the south as far as Argentan, but got no further. Stephen's Coronation Charter was the briefest of affairs, in sharp contrast to Henry I's tissue of promises, and next year he received confirmation from the pope.

From then on it was steadily downhill. In 1136 royal and baronial power in Wales was shaken by a native revival; in 1139 King David secured much of northern England, while the Empress invaded and thereafter held sway over significant parts of the country. By 1144 Normandy was lost to Geoffrey of Anjou. 'In this king's time there was nothing but disturbance, wickedness and robbery,' declared the

Peterborough chronicler. Some challenge to Stephen's position was always likely. His title, based on election by clergy and people together with papal confirmation, might always seem inferior to that of the Empress, derived from hereditary right. The force of the oath to the Empress continued to prick consciences, despite stories of Henry's deathbed change of mind. Yet Henry's own title to England had been open to challenge, and he had virtually no title to Normandy. Stephen's failure was partly because of the formidable problems he inherited, sketched at the end of the last chapter. It was also because of his character and his mistakes.

'Everyone ought to regard the king as an angry lion,' remarked the chronicler John of Worcester, but no one could see Stephen in that light. As a count he had been famed for his amiability and he continued in the same vein as king. According to the *Gesta Stephani*, the best chronicle of the reign, on occasion he forgot his exalted rank and treated those around him very much as equals The expectation of such behaviour after Henry I's intimidating conduct was one reason for making him king in the first place. 'He was a man of energy but little judgement, active in war, of extraordinary spirit in undertaking any difficult task, lenient to his enemies and easily appeased, courteous to all; though you admired his kindness in promising, still you felt his words lacked truth and his promises fulfilment,' wrote William of Malmesbury in his brilliant sketch of the king.

Stephen's difficulties, culminating in his captivity, created space for one person in particular: his own queen, Matilda. On her marriage she had no expectation of queenship, though she was of impeccable pedigree. Through her father, count Eustace of Boulogne, she was descended from Charlemagne, and through her mother (a daughter of Queen Margaret and King Malcolm of Scotland) from the line of the Wessex kings. Astute, loyal and courageous, and with Boulogne a great heiress (unlike her predecessors since the Conquest), she came to play a major part in diplomacy, politics and warfare. Without her Stephen might not have survived.

At once Stephen faced trouble across his frontiers. On 15 April 1136, Richard fitz Gilbert de Clare of Ceredigion was ambushed and killed by Morgan and Iorwerth, rulers of Gwynllwg in east Glamorgan. They then went on to seize Caerleon and Usk, together with other parts of lowland Gwent, recovering much of the kingdom held by their grandfather King Caradog. The killing itself was a signal for a general

rising led by the dynasties of Gwynedd and Deheubarth. The sons
of Gruffudd ap Cynan from the north, Owain and Cadwaladr, and
Gruffudd ap Rhys and his sons from the south, fell upon Ceredigion,
burned Aberystwyth, defeated a force of Normans and Flemings outside
Cardigan, and then returned home with 'captives, costly raiment and
fair armour', the *Brut* recounts. There was no royal response, even
when in the next year, 1137, the marcher lord and sheriff, Payn fitz
John, was also killed. So later in 1137, in a highly significant shift of
tactics, plunder turned to political control, the rulers of Gwynedd
seizing Ceredigion. Meanwhile the sons of Gruffudd ap Rhys (not at
all set back by Gruffudd's murder) secured much of Dyfed, parts of
Ystrad Tywi and, triumph of triumph, the royal castle of Carmarthen,
with help from the rulers of Gwynedd. What a contrast to the one
miserable commote to which Gruffudd ap Rhys had been reduced in
the 1120s!

Apart from the loss of Gwynedd in the 1090s, these were the most
significant defeats suffered by the Normans in Wales. Miles of Gloucester still held Brecon, Earl Robert of Gloucester Cardiff and parts of
southern Glamorgan, and Gilbert fitz Gilbert de Clare (brother of the
murdered Richard) Chepstow and parts of Gwent. But Stephen had lost
Carmarthen and in effect Pembroke too, for in 1138, powerless to give
it assistance, he had made Gilbert fitz Gilbert earl with virtually royal
rights. Given Stephen's preoccupations elsewhere, his failure to respond
was understandable. For the same reason, Robert of Gloucester, whose
advances in Glamorgan had done much to provoke the trouble, recognized the conquests of Morgan and Iorwerth and added to them, thus
securing valuable allies. But Stephen, unlike Henry I, never had the
opportunity to reassert his authority. Indeed the earl of Chester's
disaffection and Earl Robert's rebellion soon shut him out of Wales.

In the north, Stephen's losses were even more catastrophic. Early in
1136 King David of Scotland, having recently seen off internal rebellion,
moved south and seized Carlisle and Newcastle, the two great royal
bases in the north of England. In the west his aim was to make
good longstanding Scottish claims to Cumbria south of the Solway (or
Cumberland and Westmorland as it was coming to be called). To the
east, ancient claims to Northumbria were given added force by his
marriage to the daughter of Waltheof, Northumbria's last Anglo-Saxon
earl. Stephen responded with more vigour than he was to show in
Wales. With a large mercenary army hired from the treasure of Henry I,

he marched north to Durham and in February 1136 agreed terms. David abandoned his Northumbrian conquests. In return, his son Henry did homage to Stephen, for his father's earldom of Huntingdon, and for Carlisle and southern Cumbria as well. Nominally the latter were still within the English realm; in practice they were now part of the Scottish kingdom. Whether David had ever acknowledged Henry's overlordship of that kingdom is unclear. He certainly never acknowledged Stephen's.

David, however, soon felt he could improve on the 1136 settlement. In 1138, professing support for the Empress, he launched no less than three invasions into England. Stephen marched north to counter the first, but, with tension rising elsewhere in the kingdom, ignored the second, which ravaged the lands of the bishopric of Durham and penetrated as far south as Craven in Yorkshire. The Scots and Galwegians in the armies committed appalling atrocities (tossing babies on the points of their spears, according to one testimony), and drove long columns of naked and fettered women off to prostitution and slavery. All this was but the prelude to the third invasion which began in late July and soon progressed across the Tees into Yorkshire. A sizeable chunk of the northern nobility supported David, but faced with the atrocities, and with his long-held views about the integrity of the English realm, the aged Archbishop Thurstan of York saw resistance as a holy cause. His forces made their stand on 22 August at Northallerton, under the standards of the northern saints (hence the battle of the Standard) and won what seemed a God-given victory.

The battle saved Stephen's throne, but failed to drive David from the north. He retained Carlisle and by November had forced the surrender of Walter Espec's castle at Wark on Tweed. With Eustace fitz John at Alnwick in David's allegiance, Northumbria lay open. So at Durham in the April of 1139 another settlement was brokered by Stephen's queen, Matilda, David's niece and friend. Stephen confirmed David and Henry his son in possession of Carlisle, Cumbria south of the Solway and the earldom of Huntingdon. He then gave way on the main issue, and granted Henry Northumbria between the Tweed and the Tyne, saving the castles of Bamburgh and Newcastle upon Tyne, although these too were soon in Scottish hands. In return, David and Henry promised Stephen their fealty. Stephen had eliminated the danger from the north. In the next year Henry fought for him, while David watched the Empress and Earl Robert struggle in choppy waters until their

victory at Lincoln in 1141 and then hurried south to encumber them
with help. Yet the price was momentous. In practice Northumbria and
southern Cumbria were now part of King David's realm. Would it
indeed expand even further south? After all, Stephen's troubles had
hardly begun.

*   *   *

Fundamentally, Stephen had abandoned Wales and the north because
of anxieties about his English heartland. But here, floated by Henry's
treasure, he had enjoyed initial success. At Easter 1136 he received
the homage of Robert of Gloucester, momentarily impressed by the
mercenary forces which had just confronted King David. This was a
major coup. Robert, illegitimate son of Henry I and thus the Empress's
half-brother, was by far her greatest potential supporter. He was lord
of Glamorgan and had wide lands in Gloucestershire, Wiltshire and the
west country, centered on Bristol and its castle. He also held Bayeux
and Caen in Normandy. Robert was well educated, phlegmatic in
adversity, self-mocking with his intimates, ruthless, stubborn and daring; if he remained on side, Stephen was safe.

Already, however, there were signs of trouble. In April 1136 Stephen
issued a new charter, one far more comprehensive than that vouchsafed
at his coronation. He promised to abandon the areas which Henry I
had taken into the royal forest, extirpate the oppressions of the sheriffs
and deal justly in law cases, all concessions which reflected the unpopularity of Henry's rule. Stephen also promised neither to interfere in
appointments nor exploit vacant bishoprics. On the face of it, royal
control over the church had been abandoned. Stephen was also hit by
a great wave of demands for 'estates, castles, anything which took their
fancy' (as William of Malmesbury put it) from potential supporters,
many of whom, as we have seen, had felt thwarted or disinherited by
Henry. For many the whole point of King Stephen was to look favourably on such petitions. Stephen wisely sought to build up his own party
of supporters, gaining the loyalty of Gilbert de Lacy by restoring his
honour of Pontefract (confiscated by Henry in 1114), something Lacy's
men had facilitated by murdering the 'new man', William Maltravers,
whom Henry I had installed there.

Stephen also added spectacularly to the number of earldoms: in 1135
there were seven; by 1140 at least twenty-two. Some were largely titular.

Others were associated with grants of all the royal castles, lands and forests in the shire, and even the homage of the tenants-in-chief. Stephen hoped that the beneficiaries 'would be bound the more straightly to [his] service', as John of Worcester put it of a later grant, and act as powerful local agents who could stand up to the mounting trouble. To this end, after the battle of the Standard Stephen gave William d'Aumale the earldom of York in order to block further advance from King David. Likewise his installation of Waleran of Meulan in Worcestershire was designed as a counter-weight to Robert of Gloucester. Waleran and his twin brother, Robert, were the sons of Henry I's great minister Robert de Beaumont, earl of Leicester, who died in 1118. Waleran, a fiery, swaggering, jesting soldier, had inherited his father's lands in central Normandy as well as Meulan in the French Vexin. Robert, staid and statesmanlike, a future justiciar of England under Henry II, inherited the English lands with the earldom of Leicester, though he was also through marriage lord of Breteuil in Normandy. The twins also had powerful relations. Earl William de Warenne III was their half-brother, their first cousin was the earl of Warwick, their brother-in-law, Gilbert fitz Gilbert de Clare, earl of Pembroke (through Stephen's grant) and their younger brother, Hugh Poer, castellan and earl of Bedford. It was on the Beaumonts and their kin that much of Stephen's early rule rested both in England and Normandy.

One trouble with all this, as William of Malmesbury noted, was that when Stephen refused patronage on the grounds that the possessions of the crown would be depleted, those who were disappointed resorted to violence. In 1136 Hugh Bigod seized Norwich castle and had to be ejected; Baldwin de Redvers, hoping perhaps for the earldom of Devon, put his men into Exeter and it took a three-month siege throughout the summer to remove them. Given the complex web of competing family claims to land and office, patronage to one man often meant thwarting the claims of another. Bedford castle had to be besieged to get Miles de Beauchamp out and Hugh Poer in. Waleran of Meulan's installation at Worcester antagonized William de Beauchamp who had his own claims to its castle and sheriffdom. No wonder people doubted the worth of some of Stephen's promises.

Stephen's handling of the early troubles also damaged his reputation. He brought the siege of Exeter to an end and conciliated Robert of Gloucester who urged clemency by allowing the garrison to go free. But the lesson was obvious. 'When the traitors understood that he was a mild man and gentle and good and did not exact the full penalties of the law, they perpetrated every enormity,' commented the Peterborough abbey chronicler. Meanwhile, Stephen's one campaign in Normandy in 1137 succeeded in gaining recognition from Louis VI of France, but failed to dislodge Geoffrey of Anjou from Argentan in the south of the duchy. Stephen was also running out of money, as the chronicler William of Newburgh later noted. This shortfall was due to his heavy expenditure on the armies of 1136–7 and the decline in his cash revenues, the latter the inevitable downside of the endowment of earldoms with 'landed estates and revenues which had belonged to the king in his own right', as William of Malmesbury perceptively put it. Waleran of Meulan, indeed, as earl of Worcester, referred specifically to the 'geld of the king which belongs to me' and forest rights 'which before were the king's and afterwards mine'.

As the number of Stephen's mercenaries declined in parallel with his cash resources, so the loyalty of Robert of Gloucester came increasingly into question. If Stephen could not trust him, as clearly was the case, then the best policy was his elimination, just as Henry I had eliminated the Bellêmes. During the Norman campaign of 1137 Stephen attempted just that, but the ambush designed to kill or, more likely, capture Robert miscarried. Stephen disclaimed responsibility, but Robert thenceforth began to plot the Empress's bid for the throne.

The war began in 1138 with a series of co-ordinated actions, partly fuelled by private disputes over land and office. In May, while David ravaged the north, Geoffrey Talbot, alienated by Stephen's preference for Roger, son of Miles of Gloucester's claims to the honour of Weobley, seized Hereford. Then William fitz Alan asserted his supposed rights to the castle and sheriffdom of Shrewsbury by seizing the town. Soon after 22 May Robert of Gloucester in Normandy formally defied Stephen, only for his arrival in England to be delayed for over a year by the initial failure of Geoffrey of Anjou's invasion of the duchy. This should have given Stephen his opportunity to take Bristol, 'almost the richest city in the country', and break Robert's power at its heart, just as Rufus had broken the 1088 rebellion by taking Rochester. He did indeed commence operations but then, in the words of John of Worcester, 'weary of the tedious blockade he went away to besiege the earl's other castles'. It was the greatest mistake of his career. If he could not take Bristol when it was commanded by one of Robert's sons, he would never do so once Robert and the Empress were installed there.

Before that happened in September 1139, Stephen had been further weakened, again partly through his own mistakes, understandable though they were. At the end of 1138, he secured the election of Theobald, abbot of Bec, as the new archbishop of Canterbury, thus rewarding Waleran of Meulan, Bec's patron, for his sterling defence of Normandy. But the appointment alienated the man whose early support had been so critical, Stephen's brother, Bishop Henry of Winchester, who coveted the position for himself. And next year Henry's power was increased when he became papal legate. Within the context of obedience to the pope, Theobald was quite aware of the duty he owed the king, but he was no Stephen man, as later events were to show.

By 1139 Stephen was bracing himself to meet invasion, hence his momentous concessions to King David that April; hence too the extraordinary events of the Oxford council in June. There Stephen suddenly arrested Roger, bishop of Salisbury, and his nephew Alexander, bishop of Lincoln. By this means he rid himself of suspected traitors, gained castles which would have taken months to siege, and destroyed the family's spidery hold over central government which was so much resented by the Beaumonts and other baronial families. The chancery continued to function normally and no bishops joined the Empress before 1141. Altogether an effective *coup de main*. But there were humiliating consequences. According to canon law, ecclesiastics and their properties should be subject to the jurisdiction of the church, not the king, and Stephen had promised as much under his 1136 charter. Bishop Henry himself convoked a legatine council at Winchester and demanded action against his brother. In the event, no action was taken and Bishop Roger died at the end of the year. But Stephen was forced to appear and plead his case. The whole episode reflected the advance in ecclesiastical independence since the trials of Bishop Odo and William of St Calais of Durham in the 1080s, when the idea (which Stephen tried to advance) that the king acted against bishops as barons and not as churchmen had been universally accepted and Lanfranc himself had acted as chief accuser.

On 30 September 1139, only a month after the synod at Winchester, the Empress and Robert of Gloucester landed at Arundel. Robert, apparently with Bishop Henry's acquiescence, rode on to Bristol. Stephen surrounded Arundel only to allow the Empress a safe conduct to join her brother. This was another turning-point in the war, for surely Stephen should have captured the Empress and imprisoned her for life, just as Henry I had imprisoned his brother Robert. As it was, seduced (so Henry of Huntington thought) by 'perfidious' council, he believed it would be much easier to overcome Robert and his sister when they were together in one part of the country – a remarkable testimony to the pathetic quality of his decision-making. In fact, Miles of Gloucester immediately went over to the Empress (who made him earl of Hereford) and the base at Bristol became impregnable. Miles was followed more altruistically, for he was much more vulnerable, by Brian fitz Count, a protégé of King Henry, whose castle at Wallingford thereafter remained the Empress's eastern outpost and a constant thorn in Stephen's side. With castles proliferating, the fighting in 1140 was inconclusive. It took a great battle in 1141 to break the deadlock.

The *bouleversement* of 1141 turned on baronial ambitions of long standing. Ranulf, earl of Chester and his half-brother William de Roumare had long nourished claims to Lincoln since their mother was probably the daughter of a pre-Domesday sheriff. At the end of 1140 through a trick, played by their wives (an intriguing glimpse of noblewomen in politics), they had seized its castle. The following January Stephen marched north to recover it. Up to this point Ranulf had shown scant regard for either side, but now he made terms with Robert of Gloucester. And Robert saw his chance. He marched to Lincoln, placed the disinherited in the van of his army, and on 2 February won a comprehensive victory. Stephen, who had fought to the last, was taken off to captivity at Bristol.

The Empress now moved to enter her own. In April 1141 she was proclaimed by Bishop Henry as 'Lady of England and Normandy', a title which indicated immediate royal authority and heralded an imminent coronation. There was certainly no precedent in England for female succession, but neither contemporary ideas nor practice ruled it out. The Anglo-Norman elite were well aware that Melisende and her husband Fulk of Anjou, Count Geoffrey's father, had succeeded to the kingdom of Jerusalem in 1131. Indeed, on Fulk's death in 1143 Melisende had governed by herself until superseded by her son in 1152. She had earlier successfully resisted Fulk's bid to ignore her, itself an encouraging precedent for those, like Robert of Gloucester, who supported the Empress but had little brief for Geoffrey of Anjou. There were also biblical precedents for female succession (Robert cited the case of the daughters of Zelophehad) and for women as rulers, for example Esther and Judith. And then there were models from classical mythology, for instance the *virago*, the man-woman, and the Amazons, that legendary race of martial women. Both terms were applied to twelfth- and thirteenth-century women in complimentary fashion. To be sure, in these stereotypes women only succeeded by adopting male characteristics. As St Bernard put it in a letter to Melisende, 'although a woman you must act as a man . . . so that all may judge you from your actions to be a king rather than a queen'. Yet he could also be more positive, encouraging her to be a 'strong woman' and a 'great queen'.

The Empress gained control of Oxford and Devizes, received the congratulations of King David (who hurried south), entered London, and made plans for her coronation. It was at this juncture, however, that another woman stood forth in heroic fashion: Stephen's queen, Matilda. With the mercenary captain William of Ypres she held Kent and 'by prayer and price' did all she could to gather an army. This gave comfort to the Londoners who, from the start, had been reluctant to desert King Stephen, both because of their trading links with Boulogne, and his reduction of the farm, the annual payment they rendered to the exchequer. The Empress's entry into the city had been facilitated by the Londoners 'mortal enemy' Geoffrey de Mandeville who controlled the Tower, and whom she quickly confirmed as earl of Essex. But to secure Geoffrey's complete loyalty a further grant of the sheriffdoms and local justiciarships of London and Middlesex (held by his grand-father) was required. That, however, would antagonize the Londoners even more since these very offices had been granted them by Henry I.

This then was a situation which required that mixture of strength and astuteness which Bernard recommended to Melisende and for which Stephen's queen was praised. But the Empress was not astute. 'She alienated nearly all hearts by her intolerable pride,' wrote Henry of Huntingdon. Unlike the affable Stephen, she was haughty and aloof. Unlike the generous Stephen, she believed in being tight with patronage; as she said, one trains a hawk by keeping it hungry. Doubtless she modelled herself on her father, but what was acceptable for a king of immense power was quite unacceptable for a prospective queen in a fragile political situation. Thus the Empress alienated Bishop Henry, in part by refusing to confirm Boulogne to Eustace, Stephen's son and Henry's own nephew. And she infuriated Londoners by replacing Stephen's easy regime by demands for taxation. On 24 June, with the city in tumult, she fled to Oxford. At the end of July she occupied

Winchester, only to be besieged there by Queen Matilda and Geoffrey de Mandeville with a formidable army. On 14 September the Empress fled again, reaching Gloucester strapped to a litter 'like a corpse'. Earl Robert, travelling more slowly to cover her retreat, was captured. On 1 November 1141, in return for his release, Stephen too was freed.

With the release of Stephen and Robert the game resumed, but with Stephen now down more pieces. As soon as he heard of the king's capture, Geoffrey of Anjou invaded Normandy. By this move he weakened Stephen's position in England, for those who deserted in the duchy naturally did so in the kingdom also. In the latter half of 1141 Waleran of Meulan himself went over to the Empress, acting as one of Geoffrey's commanders during the final conquest of Normandy in 1144. In England his defection meant that he now held Worcestershire, where Stephen had installed him with virtually regal powers, in the interests of the Empress. With the latter's authority radiating out from Bristol and Devizes while Stephen was strong in the south-east, the conflict ebbed and flowed along the routes from London to the west, but with neither side able to gain a decisive advantage. In 1142 Stephen took the Empress's eastern headquarters at Oxford, but the Empress herself, disguised in white, escaped on foot across the snow to Wallingford. Next year Stephen was defeated by Earl Robert in a battle at Wilton, and lost control of Sherborne.

Spewed out in the wake of this struggle for the throne were a whole series of dark, swirling vortexes, composed of the private demands and disputes which had confronted Stephen during his brief peace, and now twisted round both candidates with all the intensity of war. Both were forced into auctions to gain support. At the end of 1141 Stephen tried to buy the loyalty of Geoffrey de Mandeville, earl of Essex, by confirming all the Empress had given him in a last belated attempt to keep his loyalty. In 1146 he granted his own honour of Lancaster, as well as Lincoln castle, to the earl of Chester, giving way on that tender point. Yet he continued to suspect both men and resent the way they usurped royal rights. He arrested both at court, Mandeville in 1143, Chester later in 1146, much as he had earlier arrested Bishop Roger. As a result the Tower was regained, and so was Lincoln. Yet Stephen lacked the strength to detain either noble, in contrast to Henry I who imprisoned Robert of Bellême for the rest of his life after seizing him at court in 1112. Mandeville, by the time of his death in September 1144, had devastated the area around Ely and Ramsey, while Chester took his trade elsewhere and secured opulent concessions from the Empress's son, Henry fitz Empress, the future Henry II.

The numerous private disputes were one reason why the conflict was so hard to settle. When a magnate deserted to the Empress, his rival had every incentive to remain with Stephen, or to return to him. Just as Stephen's support for Miles of Gloucester's claim to the honour of Weobley had been a major factor in the rebellion of his rivals, the cousins Gilbert de Lacy and Geoffrey Talbot, so Miles's reconciliation with the Empress led eventually to Gilbert's return to Stephen's side. Likewise King David's relations with the Empress secured Stephen the unshakeable loyalty of the rival claimant to the Waltheof inheritance, Simon de Senlis, who was rewarded from 1141 with David's earldom of Huntingdon. If Robert, earl of Leicester, remained at least nominally on Stephen's side despite the defection of his twin brother Waleran, it was partly because of his dispute with Miles of Gloucester over control of Herefordshire. The brothers kept a foot in both camps, Robert looking after their interests in England and Waleran those in Normandy.

Other factors worked against a military solution. Old castles were strengthened and at least forty new ones (including fifteen siege works) built. Geoffrey of Anjou remained fearful of rebellion in Normandy and never came to England, despite pleas to do so. He sent Henry fitz Empress over on three occasions between 1142 and 1149, but without enough troops to make a decisive breakthrough. Meanwhile the rebellion had reduced Stephen's resources even further, indeed catastrophically so. He continued to control London and the counties of the south and east (Kent, Surrey, Sussex, Essex and East Anglia), where he held most of his private lands from the honours of Eye and Boulogne. Outside these heartlands Stephen's hold was at best intermittent. After 1142 there was a dramatic decline in the number of writs produced by his chancery and most were now issued within sixty miles of London. Even in areas still nominally subject to his control, his authority was often non-existent. In Yorkshire the earl, William d'Aumale, took over both royal and private hundreds and seemed, in the words of William of Newburgh, 'more truly king beyond the Humber than King Stephen'. In a treaty regulating their respective spheres of influence in the midlands, the earls of Chester and Leicester did not refer to the king at all, merely to the 'liege lord', and then they placed limits on service they owed him.

Such magnates were not reluctantly shouldering burdens forced on them by the collapse of central authority. Rather, they often were realizing longstanding ambitions incompatible with Henry I style centralized rule. In the charters he extracted, Geoffrey de Mandeville stipulated that he was to hold the sheriffdoms of London–Middlesex and Essex–Hertfordshire in hereditary right in return for the same annual farms as those given by his grandfather, thus preventing additional payments like those which Henry I had demanded from eleven counties in 1130. Likewise he stipulated that no justices were to enter his sheriffdoms to hold pleas except with his permission, in this way restricting the activities of justices in eyre. He secured the pardon of all his debts, getting the exchequer off his back. Such men might well covet a place at the king's or the Empress's court, but the influence they gained made it all the easier to combine earldoms, sheriffdoms and private hundreds with their own castles and honours to construct, however shakily and temporarily, spheres of power and influence largely outside central control.

The most striking testimony to the decentralization of this period lies in the state of the coinage. Stephen's first coinage had been issued by mints throughout the country from dies produced in London. Stephen's second and third types, which ran between 1145 and 1154, although they maintained their weight were minted only in the south and east. Elsewhere, the Empress issued coins in her own name from Bristol, Cardiff, Oxford and Wareham; so did some great barons, for example Earl Robert of Leicester from Leicester, and Eustace fitz John from York. King David minted coins in the north. There were also some thirty-five coin types minted in Stephen's name but from unauthorized dies, doubtless by magnates nominally loyal but outside his effective control. The royal monopoly of coinage, the greatest achievement of the pre-Conquest kings, had utterly broken down.

What all this meant in financial terms is suggested by the early pipe rolls of Henry II (none survives between 1130 and 1156). Stephen had alienated some £3,000 of royal demesne. He must also have pardoned numerous debts and failed to generate others to replace them: in 1155–6 the money the crown could claim from old debts incurred in previous years (that is under Stephen) was under £500. In 1130 it had been £42,000. In 1130 total cash income was £23,000. In the first two full years of Henry II's reign it averaged £7,032. Stephen's income must have been much smaller. He was cataclysmically less powerful than Henry I.

The weakening of Stephen's authority made it more difficult to control ecclesiastical affairs where developments, becoming apparent before 1135, were already working against him. Papal power was growing as were notions concerning freedom of the church. Both were championed by the new Cistercian order with its charismatic leader, Bernard of Clairvaux. By the end of Stephen's reign, England had fifty Cistercian houses. Bishop Henry of Winchester, however, with whom Stephen was reconciled after 1141, was a Cluniac, and his legatine authority, which had lapsed in 1143, was certainly not going to be renewed by the Cistercian Pope Eugenius III (1145–53). In 1147 the pope consecrated the Cistercian abbot of Fountains, Henry Murdac, as archbishop of York, having deposed Stephen's candidate, his nephew William fitz Herbert – a novel demonstration of papal power. Next year, in best Henrician fashion, Stephen allowed only three bishops to attend the papal council at Lyons, but was defied by Archbishop Theobald who went too, although forbidden to do so. In response to these challenges, Stephen was able to exclude both Theobald and Murdac from their sees, only then to allow both back. With Murdac he established a working relationship; with Theobald he did not. Meanwhile, other elections to abbeys and bishoprics (like Gilbert Foliot's to Hereford in 1148) often went through with little reference to the king; hence in part the reform-minded prelates faced by Henry II.

The chroniclers of this period, all ecclesiastics, were clear that the withering of central authority had led to anarchy in the sense of a breakdown of law and order. Modern historians have been more cautious. Whatever the tensions within Stephen's diminished realm, for example in Kent, for much of the time he maintained reasonable order within it. In Essex, at least after the fall of de Mandeville, he retained control over the forest which covered much of the county, despite promises of deforestation in his charter of 1136. In Suffolk he was able to enforce payment of a £20 amercement on a knight 'for a certain enormity committed in the locality'. The exchequer continued to function and justices went out to hear royal pleas. Chroniclers themselves praised both King David and Earl Robert, in varying degrees, for establishing peace and issuing laws in their dominions. Individual barons certainly exploited the disorder, but they had clear political objectives in the recovery and retention of land, office and rights. They wanted to exercise local rule, not create an anarchy which would destroy their estates and shake the allegiance of their knightly tenants.

Private attempts were made to limit the violence, such as the treaty between the earls of Chester and Leicester, a treaty which itself reveals Leicester's problems in asserting authority over one of his tenants, William de Launay. The chroniclers do not always sing the same tune; that of Peterborough, having given the most lurid of all the descriptions of the anarchy, added that 'during all this evil time' Abbot Martin rebuilt the church, planted vineyards, held great commemoration feasts and generally provided the monks and guests with everything they wanted. According to one calculation 171 religious houses of all types were founded in Stephen's reign, a 50 per cent increase in the number existing in 1135. The thirty-two founded in Yorkshire between 1140 and 1154 suggest the relative stability of the area under the count of Aumale.

Yet there is another side. Religious houses could be founded precisely as acts of atonement. Ailred, as abbot of Revesby south of Lincoln, was eager to accept grants of land from knights, because otherwise how would they be saved 'in times so chaotic with slaughter and harrying'? The treaty between the earls of Chester and Leicester, referred to above, still allowed them to attack specified enemies and each other after fifteen days' notice, while the earl of Chester could use the castle of Mountsorrel in Leicestershire to make war on whoever he liked. There were certainly places and periods of intense violence and destruction, especially at the points between London and the west where Stephen and the Empress confronted each other. This may well explain why an average 32 per cent of the sums demanded for the geld early in the reign of Henry II from Oxfordshire, Berkshire, Wiltshire, Gloucestershire and Worcestershire were pardoned because of 'waste'. In Leicestershire the figure was 51 per cent. Armies did not destroy for destruction's sake. They plundered for supplies and then burnt fields and villages, so that, as Stephen's advisers put it in 1149, 'reduced to the extremity of want, [your enemies] might at last be compelled to surrender'. But the political purpose did not make the result seem any the less appalling. 'You could easily go a whole day's journey and never find anyone occupying a village, nor land tilled . . . Wretched people died of star-vation,' wrote the Peterborough chronicler. Towns were particular targets. Hereford, Worcester, Tewkesbury, Wilton, Winchester, Not-tingham and Lincoln were all sacked. The local chronicler, John of Worcester, gives a graphic account of the assault on his city by a force from Gloucester: the citizens rushing with their possessions into the cathedral; the enemy rabble repulsed at one quarter, breaking in at another; the burning of the north of the town; the seizure of immense quantities of booty, and the sad columns of people strung together in couples 'like hounds' led away to captivity and ransom.

Above all, letters, miracle stories and chronicles all testify to this being the great age of the castellans. 'We suffer as many kings as the castles which burden us,' ran a letter of Gilbert Foliot when abbot of Gloucester in the 1140s. It took the miraculous intervention of St Germanus to protect the area round Selby abbey in Yorkshire from the tyranny of knights based in a nearby castle. 'When the castles were built, they filled them with devils and wicked men' (the Peterborough chronicler). In order to supply such garrisons and assert their local rule, castellans, often with scant allegiance to either side, routinely engaged in imprisonment and torture in order to exact ransoms and *tenserie* (a kind of protection money) from the surrounding population. Some castellans were knights who were escaping the jurisdiction of their lords. William de Launay, for example, from his castle of Ravenstone, was waging his own private plundering war in Leicestershire. And not all the violence was coolly political. These men enjoyed what they did. Robert fitz Hubert, who seized Devizes for a time in 1140, boasted (to the horror of William of Malmesbury) that he had once seen eighty monks burnt to death in a church, and would do the same again and again in England: 'May God never be grateful to me!' Waleran of Meulan boasted after an attack on Tewkesbury 'that he had scarcely ever, in Normandy or in England, accomplished such a burning'. At certain times and in some areas anarchy was very real, and the peasantry, 'the wretched people', were the main sufferers.

There was no point, the chronicler Henry of Huntingdon opined of this period, in recording where the king spent Christmas or Easter, for his treasure had gone and the solemnities at court had wholly evaporated. It was very different in the realm of King David in the north.

*   *   *

The situation in England gave David ample opportunity to build on his earlier success. He consolidated his hold over southern Cumbria and asserted overlordship over northern Lancashire, extending his realm in the west to the Ribble. In the east, according to the northern chronicler William of Newburgh, he ruled in peace as far south as the Tees.

Fuelling the southern expansion, and being fuelled by it, was the transformation David brought about in the government and society of Scotland itself. If never a dashing knight in the Stephen mould, he was plausible and pious, the piety being the result of his mother's upbringing. Around forty when he came to the throne in 1124, he was also experienced and impatiently ambitious. Above all, through his time at the court of his brother-in-law, Henry I, and his tenure of the earldom of Huntingdon, he was steeped in everything Anglo-Norman. He introduced to Scotland Anglo-Norman nobles and structures of government, giving his kingship an altogether new power.

Even before Henry I's death David had made important advances. His own accession meant that Cumbria north of the Solway, with key lands around both Ayr and Lanark, which his brother Alexander I had granted him as an appanage, now came directly under the king. He had also reasserted royal authority in Moray, the region running westwards from the Spey, where there were strong separatist tendencies. In 1130 its ruler, Angus, appears as earl of Moray in Anglo-Norman sources, which was doubtless David's view, but as its king in Irish annals. Angus also had claims to the Scottish throne itself for he was the grandson of Lulach, king briefly in 1058, the son of Macbeth. In 1130, with David away at the English court, Angus sought to make good these claims. He was joined by Malcolm MacHeth, of royal blood according to Orderic Vitalis and perhaps the son of a ruler of Ross, the province to the north-west of Moray, certainly a man of high status and married to a sister of Somerled, lord of Argyll. The upshot was a great Davidian victory. In 1130 Angus was killed, in 1134 Malcolm captured and imprisoned. David now seized control of the fertile coastal plain where Moray's wealth lay. He recovered the royal thanages in the area, abolished the earldom and granted some of its lands to trusted followers. Other lands he retained and these became the base for a string of castles. All this was decisive in at last anchoring Moray into the kingdom.

Meanwhile significant changes were taking place in the structure of government. After the death of his wife (the Conqueror's niece) in 1130–31, leaving a son, David did not re-marry and it was to be over fifty years until the next Scottish queen. There is no sign of a Scottish exchequer, but David's court and household, with its steward, constable, marshal and chamberlain (responsible for keeping and spending the king's money), must have seemed very much like that of Henry I's in miniature, especially when these posts were themselves held by

Anglo-Normans. A chancellor and a seal had both appeared in the reigns of David's brothers. But David almost certainly increased the output of documents, issuing writs (*brieves*) very much on the English model in order to govern his expanding realm. David also maintained a substantial body of household knights, who were Anglo-Norman. One, Alexander de St Martin, was granted ten marks a year from the king's chamber, until his half fee in land was made up to a whole one; an arrangement (probably learnt from Henry I) which shows David's canny use of patronage, his cash resources, and his general wealth.

David's household knights (like Henry's) may also have been employed as sheriffs and castellans in the localities. Sheriffs were ultimately to spread throughout royal Scotland as the king's chief local agents and they appear for the first time under David, being based south of the Forth at Berwick, Roxburgh and Edinburgh, and north of it at Perth. The thanages and the thanes who ran them, collecting the traditional renders in kind due to the king, survived, but they did so within the jurisdiction of the sheriffs. Many sheriffs, though not all, were based in castles, and it was almost certainly David who introduced the castle to Scotland. His local agents had far more power than before; they may also have been more active in holding courts for the settlement of land disputes, and also for the punishment of crime if, as seems likely, the isolation of certain serious crimes as being crown pleas (much as in England) began in David's reign. Related to these developments was another royal official who appears intermittently under David, namely the justiciar (*justitia*), who may have fulfilled a role similar to that of the English local justiciar. David was also active on his own account. He intervened to command the hearing of law cases, and as he travelled the realm heard those of the old and poor sitting at the entrance to his hall.

David's ecclesiastical work was important in 'modernizing' Scotland. His command that 'teinds' (tithes) be paid to local churches was central to the establishment of parishes through endowing the priests and determining boundaries, the latter a necessary condition for deciding which church should receive the teinds. David was also a patron of the religious orders. In the heart of the old kingdom he built the church at Dunfermline, with its great columns reminiscent of Durham, and raised it from a priory to an abbey. He completed the introduction, begun by his brother, of Augustinian canons to serve the cathedral at St Andrews. He founded religious houses in the north and south of his kingdom, well aware of their importance as bases of royal authority. He placed a daughter house of Dunfermline at Urquhart in Moray, while in Lothian he established the highly successful Tironensian monastery at Kelso and the first Cistercian house in Scotland at Melrose. Since the latter was colonized from Rievaulx in Yorkshire, David thereby reduced the significance of the Tweed border.

It was not only for monks that David looked south. By far the most important development in his reign was the establishment of Anglo-Norman nobles in Scotland. This was the point at which the histories of Scotland and Wales fundamentally diverged. In Wales the Normans came as conquerors. They created their own areas of rule, and never integrated within the native kingdoms. In Scotland it was the opposite. The Anglo-Normans came as royal invitees. They became part of the existing kingdom, in the process transforming its structure and ultimately creating a new Scottish race. Many of those introduced, like Hugh de Moreville, were tenants of David's honour of Huntingdon. Others were men he had probably befriended at the royal court, like Henry I's protégé Robert de Bruce, ancestor of the line of kings. Bruce (now Brix) was in western Normandy, Henry I's base before his accession. In Lothian and along the eastern coastal plain between the Forth and the Dee, the grants of land were usually quite small, like the half fee near Haddington given to Alexander de St Martin. In places between the Solway and the Clyde, some large provincial lordships were established. Walter fitz Alan was placed in Renfrew and Kyle, Hugh de Moreville in Cunningham, and Robert de Bruce in Annandale, where he controlled the key route from Cumberland to the north. The aim was to establish men with sufficient power to combat the independent rulers of Galloway and Argyll while at the same time tying the periphery to the centre; for all these men had also places at David's court: Robert de Bruce until 1138 was the leading counsellor, Hugh de Moreville the constable and Walter fitz Alan (ancestor of the Stewarts) the steward. Meanwhile the lands of the earldom of Moray were granted to Freskin, probably a Fleming, the first of a great dynasty, whose tenure of other lands in Lothian prevented him 'going native'. Such great lords in their turn enfeoffed their own followers, so that between 1160 and 1241 one can trace around 100 vassals, tenants and dependants of the fitz Alans, many from their family lands in Shropshire. It was these new lords, great and small, and their descendants who were largely responsible for the encastellation of Scotland. As many as 318 possible motte sites have been revealed, the great majority between the Clyde and the Solway, but also considerable numbers in the east between the Firths of Forth and Moray.

The terms on which David granted land were the 'feudal' ones he knew in England. Although evidence is lacking he probably received homage, demanded inheritance fines, and controlled wardships and marriages. He certainly exacted knight service, and the contingents brought by his barons probably served with the forces of the royal household. At the battle of the Standard, according to John of Worcester, these were 200 strong, a respectable number given that Henry I's household knights at the battle of Bourgthéroulde were only a hundred more. Scottish armies, hitherto largely 'bare-buttocked' foot, as Henry of Huntingdon had called them, were now potentially far more formidable.

David, therefore, as a Scottish chronicler put it, 'wisely taking thought for the future had furnished his kingdom with castles and weaponry'. He had brought his kingdom's military technology into line with that of the rest of western Europe. Just where the land to endow the new aristocracy came from is, in the absence of an equivalent to Domesday Book, one of the unsolved mysteries of Scottish history. The large enfeoffments between the Solway and the Clyde may well have come in part from the lands which David had held before his accession. In Moray the lands of the fallen earl were employed, while between the Forth and Aberdeen earldom lands were also perhaps the key, since the earldom of Gowrie at some unknown time had come into the king's hands, as had some of the lands of the earldoms of Mearns and Angus. But the endowment must also have involved the expropriation of native landholders. David himself acknowledged that others might have just claims to the land he was granting to Walter of Ryedale, near Jedburgh in Lothian.

David was able to contain tensions (which broke out on several occasions under his successors) because much of old Scotland remained in place. The royal thanages of the south and east were neither destroyed by the sheriffdoms nor used to endow the incomers. Just as well, since many native thanes aspired to hold their offices in hereditary right. Around the thanages the 'outer ring' of native earldoms – Menteith, Strathearn, Atholl, Mar and Buchan – were left undisturbed. David seems rarely to have visited those regions or issued writs concerning matters within them. Apart from expanding southwards to take in

Newcastle and Carlisle, his itinerary, although evidence is limited, was largely confined to the area between the Tay, the Clyde and the Tweed, with Scone, Perth, Edinburgh, Stirling and Dunfermline being the most favoured centres. David did not, however, simply ignore the native Scots. If he had, he could scarcely have mobilized 'the common army' so effectively for his southern expeditions. The bishops, outside St Andrews and Glasgow, remained Scottish. One of the earls within the core of the kingdom, Duncan of Fife, became a leading councillor. If there was to be a standard-bearer for the disaffected, the obvious candidate was William fitz Duncan, whose descendants indeed made several bids for the throne. He was the son of David's half-brother Duncan, who had been king briefly in the 1090s. But fitz Duncan's loyalty was totally secured by David's judicious favours. Another potentially dangerous kinsman, Madad, earl of Atholl, David married to a daughter of the earl of Orkney, recognizing their son, Harald Maddadson, as earl of Caithness. It was thus through diplomacy and conciliation that David sought to extend his influence in the far north, and protect his conquest of Moray.

David's expansion southwards made an essential contribution to his ability to transform Scotland. He gained the resources to hold down resentment at home and offset his loss of royal and earldom lands in the great endowment of his followers. The farms of Northumberland and Cumberland alone were worth around £350 a year, judging from later figures. The Cumberland mines at Alston provided the silver for the first coins struck by a Scottish king. These, minted at Carlisle, Newcastle, Edinburgh and Perth, were of a full 22-grain standard, in marked contrast to the debased private issues elsewhere in England. Apart from bringing him an altogether new prestige, which was why he minted at Perth in the heart of the old kingdom, the new coins helped David to pay household knights with money from his chamber. His income was no longer simply in kind. Southern cash and silver were also part and parcel of a much wider commercial expansion in Scotland which produced cash income from the burghs David had established (see above, p. 48).

In striving to consolidate his rule in the south, the new technology was vital. King Malcolm had ravaged and departed. King David built castles and stayed: he constructed, or completed, the great keep at Carlisle and perhaps also built those at Lancaster, Warkworth and Bamburgh. But the old methods could be equally effective The prospect of further barbaric visitations, like those of 1138, was a powerful incentive to accept David's rule, especially when David himself (getting the best of both worlds) seemed so apologetic about it. When Abbot Richard of Hexham came to Carlisle at the end of 1138 to complain, almost before he could open his mouth, David was promising reparations.

David also did all he could to foster cross-border landholding. In 1135 only one of the northern barons held land in Scotland – Robert de Bruce, who combined Annandale with Skelton in north Yorkshire. Quite probably Henry I had forbidden such cross-border holdings on the principle that one cannot serve two masters. Now David installed his constable, Hugh de Moreville, in Westmorland, gave Gilbert de Umfraville, lord of Prudhoe in Northumberland, land in Lothian and Stirlingshire, and, most striking of all, married William fitz Duncan to the heiress of the honours of Egremont in Cumberland and Skipton in Craven, the latter strategically placed astride the east–west pass through the Pennines. David was also 'one of us' and made every effort to demonstrate it. At the end of 1138, having taken Wark, he allowed the garrison to go free with their arms and gave them twenty-four horses: the right chivalric stuff. It was likewise to seem conciliatory that David's son, Henry, acted as earl in Northumberland so that the area seemed less directly subject to Scottish rule.

It was not all plain sailing, however. The failure to make Durham a base (he never controlled its mint) was a serious weakness. In 1141 David had supported the candidacy of his former chancellor, William Cumin, for the bishopric, but this thoroughly alienated the cathedral monks; Cumin never gained possession and was finally removed by the pope in 1144. In 1152 the monks elected as bishop Stephen's nephew, Hugh de Puiset. While few of the northerners had extensive landholdings either in England or in Normandy, their lands in Yorkshire made them hesitate before joining David if they calculated his rule might fail to reach so far south. Thus in 1138 while Eustace fitz John sided with David in order to secure his great lordship of Alnwick in Northumberland, Walter Espec plumped for Stephen, losing Wark on Tweed but keeping Helmsley in Yorkshire with its adjoining monastery at Rievaulx, which he had founded. Robert de Bruce himself, lord of Annandale in Scotland and Skelton in North Yorkshire, was similarly torn and begged David to make peace, much as the Anglo-Norman barons had tried to keep the peace between king and duke. But when there was war he chose Stephen. The solution here in the next generation was a division of the properties between Robert's sons.

Another threat to David's realm in the 1140s was presented by Ranulf, earl of Chester, who was pressing his own claims to Lancaster and still made something of his father's loss of Carlisle. And then there was the Empress's son Henry, the future Henry II, who was gradually assuming the leadership of his cause. Since 1141 David had remained nominally within the Empress's allegiance. But if Henry one day gained the crown, would he accept all David's conquests? In 1149 David tried to solve these problems. He welcomed Henry to Carlisle along with Earl Ranulf and Henry Murdac, whom Stephen was excluding from the archbishopric of York. Ranulf surrendered his claims to Carlisle, and received instead the honour of Lancaster which extended as far south as the Ribble. A swap, but one which left David as Lancaster's overlord. At the same time Henry fitz Empress promised that he would never deprive David's heirs of 'any part of the lands which had passed from England to his dominion', a definitive recognition, or so it seemed, that Northumberland, Cumbria south of the Solway and the honour of Lancaster were now in David's kingdom. After these agreements, the plan was to march to York, install Murdac and then go south to put Henry on the throne. But Stephen acted with his normal decision. He hurried to York himself and the hostile invasion fell apart. In 1151 he came to terms with Murdac, removing the archbishop from David's camp. Yet David, old though he was, was not finished. In the same year he marched south and put William fitz Duncan firmly in possession of Skipton, characteristically giving silver chalices to the churches robbed by the Scots along the way.

David had created a new realm in the north of Britain. To the core of the Scottish kingdom (including Lothian) he had bound or re-bound both Moray and Cumbria north of the Solway. He had then expanded his realm to take in the whole of the far north of England. To secure the future, David had, perhaps as early as 1136, made his son Henry 'king designate', in imitation of Capetian practice. The harmony in which Henry was groomed for kingship, in such stark contrast to the quarrels of the Conqueror and Henry II with their sons, was not the least of David's achievements. And then in 1152 Prince Henry died. David was now nearly seventy. He ordered Duncan, the native earl of Fife (an astute choice), to take Malcolm, Henry's eldest son, around the realm and proclaim him heir. He himself went to Newcastle and persuaded the leading men of Northumberland to accept the over-lordship of Henry's second son, William – ominously having to take hostages as security. Next year David himself, the greatest of all the Scottish kings, died at Carlisle. Malcolm was only twelve. The future of the newly-expanded realm would depend very much on events in England.

*   *   *

The turmoil in England after 1141 also benefited the Welsh rulers. They consolidated the gains made between 1136 and 1138, and advanced beyond them. True, in 1144 Hugh de Mortimer of Wigmore re-established his position in Maelienydd and Elfael in the area between Wye and Severn. In 1147 the pope pronounced against Bishop Bernard's passionate attempt to establish a metropolitan see at St Davids. His successor, like the new bishops of Bangor and Llandaff (in 1139–40), all professed obedience to Canterbury. However, in 1146 the rulers of Deheubarth and Gwynedd combined to see off a formidable effort by Gilbert de Clare, earl of Pembroke and lord of Chepstow, to establish himself at Carmarthen and recover his family's hold over Ceredigion. In 1147, when Gilbert might have renewed the struggle, he was em-broiled in Stephen's quarrel with the earl of Chester. He died in 1148 or 1149, leaving a teenage son, and the pressure was off. In 1150 it was Cadel ap Gruffudd of Deheubarth who rebuilt the castle at Carmarthen 'for the strength and splendour of his kingdom'. Advances were likewise made by Madog ap Maredudd, who held sway in Powys from 1132 to 1160, the greatest of its rulers and a 'firm anchor in a deep sea', as the poet sang. In 1149 Madog moved beyond the border into Shropshire and built a castle at Oswestry, an advance made possible by the enfeeblement of its lord, William fitz Alan, in the civil war. The 'county now called Shropshire once belonged to Powys,' wrote Gerald of Wales. Perhaps it might again.

In the north Owain ap Gruffudd ap Cynan of Gwynedd also moved east. He captured the earl of Chester's castle at Rhuddlan and in 1146 destroyed the castle at Mold, which guarded the pass through the mountains from the Clywd valley to the Cheshire plain. Earl Ranulf's reaction was to seek help from Stephen. But the result was not an expedition to Gwynedd but his arrest at Northampton, whereupon the Welsh invaded Cheshire. Although Owain was driven back, his power now embraced the whole of the Four Cantrefs from the Conwy to the Dee. Ranulf's death in December 1153, leaving a six-year-old son as heir, seemed to make this enlarged Gwynedd secure. But by this time Owain's position had been shaken by family strife: between 1150 and 1152 he imprisoned his son Cynan, drove his brother Cadwaladr into exile, and blinded and castrated a nephew. This turmoil probably explains how the rulers of Deheubarth at this time wrested Ceredigion from Gwynedd, expelling Owain's son Hywel, and securing their conquest with castles. By 1155 three princes dominated Wales: Owain of Gwynedd, Madog of Powys and Rhys ap Gruffudd of Deheubarth. Would they be able to keep their gains in the new world after 1154?

Some of the signs were encouraging. The Welsh had learnt from the Anglo-Normans, and not merely militarily. Stephen had consoled himself after his early disasters, according to the *Gesta Stephani*, with the thought that the Welsh would soon begin slaughtering each other. Yet in fact political conduct in native Wales was beginning to imitate that in the Anglo-Norman realm where murders and political executions were rare. Indeed there were none at all, so far as great nobles were concerned, in the whole of Stephen's reign. Tensions certainly existed within Gwynedd in the 1150s, as elsewhere in Wales, but the blood-letting and competition paled before that of the past. The rulers of Gwynedd and Deheubarth co-operated effectively in the campaigns of 1136–7 and 1146, and again in the 1160s. In Powys the killings within the ruling house earlier in the century cleared the way for the long and stable rule of Madog ap Maredudd. In Deheubarth, the four sons of Gruffudd ap Rhys each held sway in turn. The brothers Morgan and Iorwerth, grandsons of King Caradog, co-operated effectively as they recovered Caerleon and other family lands in Gwent. Their careers illustrate another point. The Welsh were nothing if not pragmatic; if they were enemies of the Anglo-Normans, they were also their allies. Morgan and Iorwerth's early success depended on their agreement with Robert of Gloucester, Morgan even fighting for the earl at the battle of Lincoln. Later Morgan was recognized as a king by Earl Roger of Hereford and (here masquerading as a marcher baron) he was confirmed in possession of 'the honour of Caerleon' by Henry II himself.

In all this the Welsh were fired by an increasingly self-confident patriotism, the product in part of Geoffrey of Monmouth's rediscovery of their history and re-invention of their greatest king – King Arthur himself (see above, p. 20). Caerleon, which King Morgan had recovered, had hosted courts of Arthur. In the north, the biography of Gruffudd ap Cynan saw its hero specifically as another Arthur, 'king of the kings of the isle of Britain'. No wonder an Anglo-Norman survey of Britain in the 1150s lamented how the Welsh 'threaten us . . . openly they go about saying, by means of Arthur they will have [the island] back . . . They will call it Britain again'. All this was very different from the apprehensive mood in which the Scottish court faced the accession of Henry II.

*   *   *

There was nothing inevitable about Henry's emergence, however. In 1147 Stephen had knighted his young and warlike son Eustace. There was therefore a clear potential heir. Meanwhile death had removed the Empress's chief supporters, Miles of Gloucester in 1143, and Earl Robert himself in 1147. Of their sons, Roger, earl of Hereford, played his own hand while William, earl of Gloucester, proved more a knight of the bedchamber than the battlefield. Then in February 1148 the Empress retired to Normandy. Her long, lonely, courageous sojourn at Devizes after 1141, where she had consolidated support by the judicious use of patronage, had been the most impressive part of her career.

None of this exactly cleared the way for Stephen and Eustace. The issue was no longer the succession of the crusty Empress, but of her dynamic and dextrous sixteen-year-old son, the future Henry II. Henry's plans in 1149 had been thwarted by Stephen's swift march to York. But across the Channel, by his father's concession, he had become duke of Normandy, and then in 1152, in a remarkable coup, duke of Aquitaine, this through his momentous marriage to Eleanor of Aquitaine, the divorced wife of Louis VII of France. The match altered the political shape of Europe with results that lasted for 200 years. But in the short term it threw Louis, shocked at his wife's re-marriage, into the arms of Eustace. In 1152 they campaigned together in Normandy, while in England Stephen was able to take Newbury. There, with characteristic humanity and humour, he saved the boy William Marshal, a future regent of England, from being catapulted into the castle when his father refused its surrender, and took him off to play in his tent.

In 1153 Henry arrived in England, but with Normandy's resources depleted by his father's concessions, he brought no overwhelming force. There were stand-offs at Malmesbury (where rain stopped play) and at

Wallingford. The fact was that the magnates were reluctant to fight a decisive battle. They too had suffered from the disorder, which had weakened their hold over some of their knightly tenants. They wanted peace, but not some dominant victor who might retrieve their gains from the crown and threaten their local power. They preferred, as Henry of Huntingdon put it, to keep Stephen and Henry 'in fear of each other' so that 'the royal authority should not be effectively exercised against them'. In these circumstances it was vital for Stephen to secure Eustace's coronation, but this the pope and Archbishop Theobald refused to sanction. Building on a papal ruling of 1143, they were doubtless influenced too by their own clashes with the king. But Theobald equally did not declare for Henry, for that would only have infuriated Eustace and ensured the continuation of the war. Fundamentally the church sat on the fence and waited for a victor.

In the end, a stalemate war could only end in a compromise peace, and the way for that was opened by Eustace's sudden death in August 1153. In terms of conduct and attitudes, Stephen himself had never really made the transition from count to king, and William, his surviving son, was very ready to go back to being a count. A settlement, the Treaty of Winchester, was agreed on 6 November 1153. Henry confirmed William in all Stephen's possessions before 1135, and granted him Norwich castle, all the king's rights in Norfolk and much else besides. Then a dispute which had raged for twenty-four years was settled in a few crisp lines. Stephen made Henry his heir and successor, and granted him the kingdom in hereditary right. Henry on his part accepted Stephen as king for the rest of his life.

But what then of the magnates' disputes with one another, and the royal lands and offices which they had extracted from Stephen, the Empress and indeed from Henry himself? At Winchester it was agreed that the new castles built during the war should be demolished, a necessary condition of peace. It was agreed too, according to the chronicler Robert of Torigny, that 'possessions seized by invaders' should be restored to the 'legitimate possessors' in place under Henry I. This, of course, might prove highly contentious, but no mechanisms were set up to bring it about. In any case what constituted 'invasion' and 'legitimate possession'? Henry probably felt the settlement licensed him to recall all grants of crown property since 1135, but Stephen was not going to act in that spirit. There was no way he would resume the grants to his own supporters. Fundamentally everything was still to play for. The peace threatened a continuation of the war by other means. Henry was not to succeed at once as a mighty conqueror, but at some unknown time in the future with all Stephen's pieces still on the board. This was indeed a magnates' peace.

Stephen enjoyed a brief Indian summer in which he dismantled some of the new castles and issued a coinage once again from mints throughout the country. He died on 25 October 1154. Henry succeeded without difficulty but faced a monumental task in rebuilding royal power.

7

King Henry II, Britain and Ireland, 1154–89

Henry II inherited a very different realm from that seized by Stephen nineteen years earlier. Royal revenue was down by two-thirds; royal lands, together with castles and sheriffdoms, had been granted away, often in hereditary right; earldoms, often with semi-regal powers, had proliferated; control over the church had been shaken; the former royal bastions in south Wales had passed into the hands of barons and native rulers; and the far north of England was now subject to the king of Scots. The picture was much the same in Normandy, where Geoffrey of Anjou had alienated extensive ducal land in his struggle for the duchy and had also (as the price for his support) conceded Gisors and the Norman Vexin to King Louis.

England and Normandy were now part of a much larger political entity which historians often call (without any precise constitutional meaning) 'the Angevin empire'. Its ruling dynasty came from Anjou, Henry having inherited Anjou, with its satellites of Maine and Touraine, from his father. He had also gained the duchy of Aquitaine by his marriage. No Anglo-Angevin or Anglo-Aquitainean nobility ever developed to equal the Anglo-Norman. But the kings of England now had far wider preoccupations than ever before. Might not that militate against any recovery of royal authority in England, leaving it truncated in the north and fragmented into a collection of earldoms? In fact nothing like this happened. Henry restored royal authority in England and fashioned the common law. He subjected Scotland and conquered Ireland. Across the Channel he rebuilt ducal power in Normandy and established his lordship over Brittany.

These extraordinary successes owed everything to Henry himself. He was domineering, passionate, wily and highly intelligent, speaking Latin and French and understanding English. He had a sure grasp of the facts of power: 'No, I can't depose a bishop,' he cried, 'but I can certainly push him out,' making a gesture with his hands at which his courtiers dutifully dissolved into laughter. Henry had an agile, stocky body, a large head and fine face. Often 'crucified with anxiety' over crises in his dominions, in the words of his clerk, Roger of Howden, his speed of movement was legendary: 'The king of England is now in Ireland, now in England, now in Normandy, he seems rather to fly than to go by horse or ship,' exclaimed Louis VII. No wonder Henry relaxed in long days of hunting and preferred sometimes to dine apart. The determination to restore his authority in England and Normandy to the heights achieved under his grandfather, Henry I, was a leitmotiv of Henry's rule. He was equally concerned to preserve law and order. Henry had a strong sense of 'the general care of his subjects given him by God', as the *Dialogue of the Exchequer* put it. Indeed, the duty imposed on him by the Coronation Oath to govern and protect his people was his stated reason for refusing to crusade. But Henry was far more than simply a conservative restorer. Whereas Henry I decided against exploiting potential rights in Maine and north Wales, Henry II pushed his rights to their limits and beyond. In Ireland he conquered where he had no rights at all. Thus to Jordan Fantosme, a clerk of Bishop Henry of Winchester, he seemed the greatest conqueror since Moses, Charlemagne only excepted.

What role was there for the wife of this bully with brains and brawn, that figure of legend and romance, Eleanor of Aquitaine? In terms of personality Eleanor was easily her husband's equal. She was fiery, courageous, resourceful and – so the rumours went – flirtatious: far too hot for the dull, conventional Louis VII to handle. That, and the failure to beget male heirs, was the reason for the divorce (see above, p. 188). She too was physically strong and though a decade older than Henry and subject to numerous pregnancies outlived him by fifteen years. Eleanor had brought her own inheritance to the marriage, the whole of Aquitaine. Henry at once assumed the ducal title but accepted that the duchy remained in some ways Eleanor's rather than his own: he made no mention of it in his will. In Poitou, the northern half of the duchy and the home of her dynasty, Eleanor at times held her own court where she patronized poets (her grandfather had been a famous troubadour) and, so those poets liked to imagine, debated issues of courtly love. Eleanor's dynastic interests in Poitou were central to her politics. In England, her position was in one way significantly different from that of her predecessors since before the Conquest. She was not given substantial lands by Henry, being supported instead, when she was in the country, by *ad hoc* cash payments ('corrodies') from the sheriffs. Since this set a precedent queenship, potentially at least, had been significantly weakened. Yet there was no intention here to diminish Eleanor. Royal land was in short supply and she had her own abundant resources from Aquitaine. Like Matilda, wife of Henry I, Eleanor acted as regent and was far more than a mere figurehead. And then there were Eleanor's children. Four sons and three daughters survived beyond infancy and she played a major part in their upbringing. Through them too she gained a political role.

Eleanor thus had many potential avenues to power, and she was anxious to parade down them. Yet it was only after Henry's death, as queen mother, that she did so in full state. Her role before that depended on the space Henry allowed her, which in the later part of his reign was none at all.

*　　*　　*

'There is nothing left to send to bring the king back to England but the Tower of London.' It was easy to see the joke, recorded by the dean of St Paul's, Ralph of Diss. Henry spent 43 per cent of his reign in Normandy, 20 per cent elsewhere in France (mostly in Anjou, Maine and Touraine) and only 37 per cent in Britain. This was not because Henry undervalued his kingdom. It supplied 'the honour and reverence of the royal name', as Richard of Poitiers put it, and a major part of his revenues. Yet the pressures and the opportunities remained greater across the Channel.

In Normandy Henry quickly restored order and recovered ducal rights, yet he rarely felt secure. In part this was because of a paradox in the political structure he had created. He possessed far wider dominions than his predecessors, but far more than they, he recognized the over-lordship of the king of France. Henry I had never performed personal homage to the French king. Henry II did so on several occasions, the first, as crowned king, in 1156. His motives were pragmatic; in 1156 they were to shut out his brother Geoffrey, who had claims to a share of the Angevin dominions. But the result was that Henry was now restricted by the oath of loyalty he had sworn, and punishable by forfeiture of his fiefs for its breach. Under his son John, that is exactly what happened.

Henry's dominions also lacked defensible frontiers. The great rivers from which their prosperity stemmed all flowed into (and sometimes from) 'enemy territory'. In the north, Henry in 1160 managed to recover Gisors and the Norman Vexin, and thus restore the traditional frontier with the French royal demesne along the Epte, but Louis continued to resent their loss. He was amiable and peace-loving yet knew how to exploit Henry's weaknesses. Henry's reaction to these problems was the reverse of defensive. The counts of Anjou indeed had always been acquisitors, gaining Maine, Touraine and ultimately Normandy. Henry was born in Le Mans and it remained his favourite city. In its outskirts he built the hospital whose ranging, spacious three-aisled hall still reflects his expansive, self-confident character. Buoyed up by his early success in England and Normandy, Henry moved against Toulouse. He could claim the county in right of his wife, for Eleanor was the granddaughter of Count William IV who had died in 1093. Louis himself had tried to assert Eleanor's rights in 1141 with total lack of success. If Henry succeeded he would hold all the south of France. With an army enlarged with men from all his dominions, in 1159 he invaded the province only to duck a direct assault on his overlord, Louis VII, who was standing shoulder to shoulder with Count Raymond in Toulouse itself, a first indication of the importance of the 1156 homage.

The failure of the 1159 campaign, the greatest defeat of his career, changed Henry's attitude to the south of his dominions. In 1170 he betrothed his daughter Eleanor to Alfonso VIII of Castile and apparently promised their descendants possession of Gascony after Eleanor of Aquitaine's death. With its great vineyards the duchy was wealthy, but ducal lands were exiguous and it was not till the late thirteenth century that the customs on wine exported from Bordeaux made the revenues substantial. In Poitou, the northern half of the duchy, authority could be exercised from ducal castles, but there were also powerful noble families (Lusignan, Thouars, Parthenay, and the counts of Angoulême and La Marche) who held their fiefs in virtual independence. Eventually Henry installed his son Richard in Poitou as count with his mother alongside him. Henry's own itinerary largely centred on Normandy, Maine and Anjou. Normandy, in terms of revenues, was by far the most valuable of his continental possessions, and to its east lay the duchy of Brittany. Here Henry remained aggressive. In 1166 he married his second son Geoffrey, then aged seven, to Constance, daughter of

Count Conan IV of Brittany. He then forced Conan into retirement and took possession of the duchy in right of his son and daughter-in-law. He had thus converted the overlordship over Brittany, long claimed by the Norman dukes, into its actual possession. The acquisition was hardly trouble free. Henry campaigned in Brittany in 1167, 1168 and 1173. In 1168 he also put down a revolt in Poitou. These and other continental preoccupations meant that Henry was out of England between 1158 and 1163, and 1166 and 1170. However, Henry had not neglected England. Indeed everything else had depended on his success in rebuilding royal authority there.

*   *   *

Looking back from the perspective of the 1190s, the chronicler William of Newburgh marvelled at the way Henry at the start of his reign had restored unity to a kingdom 'mutilated' by the loss of royal lands and the overrunning of its frontiers. This success revolved around a series of spectacular and high-risk assaults on leading magnates, assaults which deprived them of royal demesnes, counties, castles and earldoms. At the start of his reign Henry I had broken the Bellêmes; Stephen at the start of his had tamely released the garrison of Exeter castle. Henry II knew whose example to follow. In 1155 he marched to the north and destroyed the semi-regal position which William, count of Aumale, had enjoyed in Yorkshire. He then wrested the royal castle of Bridgnorth from Hugh de Mortimer and denied Walter, brother of Roger, earl of Hereford, who had died in October 1155, succession to both the earldom and the royal castles of Gloucester and Hereford – one of several baronial deaths which cleared the way for Henry in these early years. In 1157, having returned from quashing his brother Geoffrey's revolt in Anjou, he forced William, King Stephen's son, to surrender the castles of Norwich, Pevensey, Eye and Lancaster, all this in clear breach of the Treaty of Winchester. In the same year he also made King Malcolm of Scotland surrender Newcastle upon Tyne, Bamburgh and Carlisle and all his possessions in the north of England, thus restoring the old frontier along the Tweed and the Solway, while breaking the promises he had made to King David in 1147. The kingdom was whole once more.

All this was part of a wider policy of resuming royal lands which had been alienated during the civil war. Here the terms of the peace settlement gave Henry some support (see above, p. 189), and he had other arguments ready. In 1157 he furiously rebuked the bishop of Chichester for seeming to challenge the inherited and God-given majesty, dignity and rights of the crown. The concept of the incorporeal crown, to which rights and possessions attached (as opposed to them being attached to the person of an individual king), had come to prominence under Henry I. The 'pleas of the crown' are mentioned in the pipe roll of 1130, its lands and castles in the peace of 1153. At his coronation Henry II quite probably took an additional oath which bound him to maintain and recover the crown's possessions, an undertaking perhaps modelled on a similar promise made by bishops at their consecration with regard to the estates of their churches. Certainly at the start of his reign Henry mounted an inquiry into the lands possessed by his predecessors down to 1135, and commanded those alienated under Stephen (worth at least £3,000) to be surrendered. Charters of Stephen were now considered invalid and even those of the Empress and of Henry himself before his accession deemed subject to review.

Henry in this early period completed the expulsion of foreign mercenaries and the demolition of unlicensed castles which Stephen had begun. He also erased the memory of the baronial coinages by issuing in 1158 a penny with a new cross and crosslet design. Forgoing the revenue from the frequent changes of design customary in the past, he continued to mint this penny down to 1180, a deliberate mark of stability. Henry had also to cope with the numerous private disputes which were the stuff of anarchy and which had generated so much violence and disorder. The peace treaty had promised restoration of their inheritances to those who had lost them to 'invaders' during Stephen's reign, a stipulation which threatened a nightmare scenario of claim and counter-claim (see above, p. 189). In part Henry dealt with the problem through his general measures to maintain law and order, and facilitate litigation over land (this will be discussed later). A series of *ad hoc* settlements also took place, sometimes private, sometimes brokered or imposed by the king. Henry himself gave Weobley to the Lacys, ending the longstanding dispute with the family of Miles of Gloucester. He conceded the earldom of Lincoln to neither of the rival claimants (William de Roumare and Gilbert de Gant) and twisted and turned over the earldom of Huntingdon (claimed by Simon de Senlis and the kings of Scotland). Several of these cases, like that over Lincoln, flared up again in John's reign, amid claims that Henry had acted unjustly and without judgement. The key fact was that Henry's restoration of royal authority made him powerful enough to keep the lid on this simmering pot (excepting the rebellion of 1173–4).

This success was partly because after reasserting royal authority on his accession, Henry did not then relax. Of the castles he acquired in the 1150s he retained thirty, beginning the process which converted 225 baronial and 49 royal castles of 1154 into 179 baronial and 93 royal castles of 1214, a shift in ratio of 5:1 to 2:1. Over the reign as a whole, Henry expended some £21,500 on castle-building, an average of £650 a year. The great square keep at Dover with two lines of curtain walls is his creation. As Allen Brown put it, Henry 'literally dug himself in'. The royal lands which he recovered at the start of his reign he quickly granted as rewards to his own supporters, but thereafter grants of royal demesne virtually ceased, in striking contrast to the methods of Stephen and indeed of Henry I. The value of alienated royal land stood at around £3,000 in 1159 and at much the same sum thirty years later. This was closely linked to a ruthless and retentive attitude to forfeitures and escheats. In the 1180s there were thirteen baronies in the king's hands with lands worth some £2,900 a year.

The danger of much of England falling into the hands of earls wielding near royal powers in the counties was also over. Since Henry created no new earldoms, their numbers steadily declined. According to one calculation there were twenty-four in 1154 and twelve in 1189. Apart from Chester, moreover, earldoms were no longer linked to the possession of a large slice of the king's rights in the county. Most of them were largely titular, as had sometimes been the case in earlier times. The chief local government official was once again the sheriff and here too Henry repeatedly demonstrated his authority. At Michaelmas 1155 the sheriffs of two-thirds of the counties were replaced; in 1162 another sweep covered roughly half the counties; and then in 1170 Henry mounted a major inquiry (the 'Inquest of Sheriffs') into the sheriffs' activities, after which nearly all were sacked. Henry had no objection to the right magnates holding sheriffdoms (they were anyway often *curiales*) but he also employed county knights and, especially after 1170, knights of the royal household, some of whom (like William Brewer and Geoffrey fitz Peter) were beginning spectacular careers in the royal service.

Henry also revived the workings of royal forest law, which had lapsed in many areas during Stephen's reign. Henry's agent here was his chief forester, 'the odious' Alan de Neville. The whole exercise was highly unpopular because forest law was concerned much more with making money than protecting actual hunting, and it ran not merely in the king's own demesne woods but also in woods and lands held by numerous private individuals. Indeed it embraced most of Essex. Offences under the law included waste (created by cutting down trees for timber or firewood), assart (clearances to create new arable land), and purpresture (making of enclosures), all of which were punishable by fines. Consequently those unlucky enough to find their own woods within the royal forest, whether bishops, abbots, barons, knights, or freeholders, were prevented from exploiting them, a restriction all the more vexatious given the pressure on land created by the rising population. There were also offences against the protected beasts of the forest, namely deer and wild boar, and here punishment for the poor might be death or mutilation. All punishments were anyway entirely a matter of the king's will. Forest law as here defined was probably introduced by the Conqueror, but the areas subject to it were evidently expanded by Henry I because Stephen in 1136 promised to abandon his predecessor's afforestations. Whether Henry II simply restored the forest boundaries to their 1135 state or went beyond them became a matter of intense dispute. Certainly by the end of the reign parts of more than twenty counties were subject to forest law. From 1166 onwards Alan de Neville headed visitations of forest judges who heard the offences and imposed penalties, a lucrative and deeply resented exercise.

Restoration of royal authority in the localities was impossible without strong central institutions, something also required by a cross-Channel state, now more far-flung than before. The ultimate centre was, of course, Henry's court and household. Within England its itinerary was largely southern based, much like that of Henry I. Ranked according to the number of surviving writs and charters issued from them, the tally was as follows: Westminster-London (268); Winchester, Clarendon, and the surrounding area (200); Woodstock (103); Northampton (80); Windsor (45), with only Nottingham (51) in the north. Henry did not, therefore, have to travel for the purposes of routine government. It was the constant alarms and excursions which sent him shuttling round his dominions at breakneck speed. When across the Channel he was pursued by a stream of petitioners from England: the abbot of St Albans found him in Normandy, the litigious Richard of

Anstey as far south as Auvillar on the Garonne. The response was an equally constant stream of writs to the English regents, ordering them, among other things, to hear law cases or prevent shrieval oppression.

In the early years, in dealing with such petitions and issuing the writs one minister, always travelling with the king, was central: the chancellor Thomas Becket, a former clerk of Archbishop Theobald, whose flamboyance Henry found amusing and whose energy and ambition he embraced as like his own. The output of Henry's chancery was almost certainly much higher than that of his grandfather Henry I, the total of known documents (of course only a fraction of the whole) averaging 120 a year as against forty in the earlier period. The reign also saw the culmination, or near culmination, of longstanding developments in what the chancery produced, the Anglo-Saxon sealed writ having evolved certainly by 1199 into three distinct types of document, namely charters, writs patent and writs close. The last two in the thirteenth century were equally described as letters patent and letters close. Charters, since they usually conferred rights and properties in perpetuity, were the most solemn documents the chancery issued. They were addressed to all the king's subjects, usually recorded the names of many witnesses and had the seal appended by silken threads. The difference between writs patent and writs close was that the latter were closed, that is folded up, with the seal being broken on opening, while the former were patent or open, the seal being attached to a tongue cut from the bottom of the document. Writs close, usually addressed to a single individual or institution and with a single witness, were used for the mass of routine administrative orders on which government depended, as well as for the writs initiating the comon law legal procedures described later. Writs patent, with a general form of address like charters but usually with a single witness, were used to grant exemptions, make appointments and proclaim a range of government decisions.

Around 1160 the head of the English government in Henry's absence was Queen Eleanor. She was appealed to over the heads of senior officials, and issued written commands (sometimes more effective than theirs) to magnates, sheriffs and the exchequer. Alongside her were two great ministers, Robert, earl of Leicester, and Richard de Lucy, whom contemporaries saw increasingly as holding a formal office, that of 'justiciar of England' or 'chief justiciar of the king'. In fact their position was very similar to that enjoyed by bishop Roger of Salisbury under

Henry I; with Queen Eleanor increasingly overseas they came to act formally as regents in the king's absence, continuing as chief ministers when he was present. At the heart of their power was the exchequer, where they presided, the detailed work being controlled by the treasurer, Richard fitz Nigel, nephew of the great Bishop Roger. His triumphal labours in reviving an office, running in 1154 at a sluggish pace, are reflected in his *Dialogue of the Exchequer* (1178), a book of proud and passionate precision which describes the whole process of the exchequer's work from collecting the money, through to the final audit of the accounts, and its record on the pipe roll.

Lucy and Earl Robert worked together harmoniously until the latter's death in 1168. Lucy, who was no yes-man, continued alone till his resignation ten years later. Richard fitz Nigel held office as treasurer from c. 1159 to 1196. Henry depended absolutely on such loyal, expert and long-serving ministers. Some of them were ecclesiastics (fitz Nigel became bishop of London); others were laymen, very much of the type employed by Henry I. Richard de Lucy himself, whom Henry took on from Stephen, came from a family of knightly status. Geoffrey fitz Peter and William Brewer were both sons of royal foresters. Henry followed the advice of his mother, the old Empress, and trained such men as he would hawks, keeping them eager by keeping them hungry. Lucy never became an earl and had to supplement his grants from the royal demesne, worth an annual £125, with numerous private acquisitions. His chief property at Chipping Ongar came from William, son of King Stephen. If such men lost royal favour, the vultures would gather round.

The transformation of Henry's position is revealed most tellingly in his revenue recorded in the pipe rolls. The average for 1155 to 1157, his two first full years, in cash and authorized expenditure amounted to some £10,300, as against £24,500 in 1130. In the 1160s the annual average rose to £16,700, in the 1170s to £19,200; in the last eight years of his reign it was £23,300. On three occasions the figure for 1130 was exceeded (this in a period of relatively stable prices). There is little question but that England was by far the most valuable of Henry's dominions. In Normandy there had been a similar policy of recovering ducal lands and rights, doubtless masterminded by the Norman ex-chequer. But the one surviving Norman pipe roll for the reign, that for 1180, indicates a revenue equivalent to only £6,750 in English money. Two years later, in his will, Henry distributed 5,000 marks for pious purposes in England, 3,500 marks in Normandy and only 1,000 marks in Anjou. England was the paymaster for the rest of the empire. As early as 1159 it provided some £8,000 for the Toulouse campaign.

In managing his money Henry was an innovator. He was the first king (at least as far as the evidence goes) to use credit on a large scale, borrowing around £12,000 (and possibly much more) from various lenders between 1155 and 1166, and repaying them from local revenues. Over half this sum came from one great financier, the Fleming William Cade, who had probably made his money in the wool trade. Cade died around 1166 and had no Christian successors, partly because of changing attitudes to usury. For a while Henry borrowed money from the Jews until he realized it was much simpler to tax them, thus opening up a new and major source of royal revenue.

Henry's increasing wealth underpinned other policies designed to reassert authority over the baronage. In 1166 he demanded that all his barons send him in writing the names of their tenants and how much knight service each of them owed. Part of the background here was scutage. This was a money payment a baron could make, if the king agreed, instead of providing military service. The rate varied between different scutages but was often a pound for every knight owed. Scutage had existed under the Norman kings although it is only after 1154 that hard evidence survives of its operation. The aim in 1166 was to gain information enabling the tax to be levied, not on the number of knights a baron owed the king as hitherto, but on the total number he was himself owed by his tenants, which, as the inquiry showed, was some- times considerably more. Another aim (which was why Henry wanted to know the names of the under-tenants) was to make sure they had actually sworn allegiance to him – very much the 1086 Oath of Salisbury over again. There was to be no one in Henry's England immune from his authority. In 1170 the Inquest of Sheriffs inquired into the malpractices of baronial as well as royal officials. In 1178 the *Dialogue of the Exchequer* asserted the principle that the king could employ whoever he liked in his service no matter from whom they held their land.

From this point of view Henry's rule seems dangerously abrasive. It certainly spawned the baronial malcontents who joined the rebellion of 1173–4. It also, notably in the working of the forest law, created wider disaffection. Yet there was another side, and indeed without it Henry would never have survived. The new procedures for civil litiga- tion were highly popular with under-tenants (see below, p. 240); and one major concession benefited the realm as a whole. This was abandonment of the geld, the great land tax the Normans had inherited from the Anglo-Saxon kings. The levy of 1161–2 was the last. In the long term the significance of this was potentially immense. Had the tax continued on an annual basis and been levied at gradually higher rates it could have solved the financial problems of English monarchy in the thirteenth century, in which case, since the geld required no consent, parliamentary taxation and parliament itself might never have developed! As it was, Henry decided to forgo the £2,500 a year the tax had raised under Henry I, in this regard quite definitely not returning to the days of his grandfather. To some extent the gap was filled by other measures, notably tallage, a lump sum assessed on cities, boroughs and royal manors (with origins in the reign of Henry I), but this was neither annual nor nationwide.

There was also another side to the king's relations with his barons. Few of them were placed under much financial pressure by the crown. If scutage had sometimes to be paid on the total number of fees, only seven were levied in the reign. Although Henry had nine opportunities to exact a fine or relief for a succession to an earldom, he did so only once. In terms of the financial pressures placed on his barons, Henry's rule was very different from King John's which led to Magna Carta. The barons also benefited from the peace, which enabled them to re-establish a hold over knightly tenants. Indeed the very process of the 1166 inquiry, which forced them to identify and define the services they were owed, did that. At the centre, all Henry's major governmental measures were issued with the 'advice and assent' of the lay and ecclesiastical barons. The barons, as the Constitutions of Clarendon made clear in 1164, gave judgements in law cases before the king. Such men also featured among Henry's principal counsellors. As justiciar, Richard de Lucy shared power not with some Bishop Roger type but with that veteran of the nobility, the worldly-wise Earl Robert of Leicester, his loyalty secured by the restoration of the family fiefs of Breteuil and Pacy in Normandy. Likewise Geoffrey de Mandeville, earl of Essex, having had his castles seized in 1157, ended up as one of Henry's judges. His son, William de Mandeville, was Henry's leading counsellor in later years and was made mightier still by his marriage to Hawisia, heiress of Holderness and Skipton in England and Aumale in Normandy.

Henry, therefore, in reviving royal authority had struck a delicate balance between taking and giving, one which helps to explain the great rebellion of 1173 and why Henry triumphed over it. How would he get on in re-establishing royal authority over the church?

*   *   *

'What miserable traitors have I nourished in my household who let their lord be treated with such shameful contempt by a low-born clerk!' With these anguished words, or ones very like them, Henry II triggered the murder of Thomas Becket in 1170 and bloodily consummated the greatest of all clashes between the medieval church and state.

From the start of his reign Henry was determined to recover the customary rights over the church lost under Stephen. Accordingly he reasserted control over appointments, took the revenues from vacant bishoprics and abbeys, and insisted that barons could not be excommunicated without his consent. He also made clear that contact with Rome required his licence, and berated bishops and abbots when they appealed to papal authority in derogation of royal rights. Yet for long there was no open conflict partly because Theobald, the wily old archbishop of Canterbury, was expert in giving way on some issues to get his way on others: thus his clerk Bartholomew, a learned canon lawyer, became bishop of Exeter with Henry's consent. On Theobald's death in 1162, Henry made Becket his successor. By this time, so Becket believed, Henry was gearing up for a much wider assault on the church. The contrary view was that the assault was provoked by Becket himself. The truth lay somewhere between the two. Certainly Henry wished to place more of the bishoprics under his own men; Becket's appointment was just the start. Probably, too, he meant to assert his authority over clerks accused of serious crimes. Yet he did not envisage a regional church protected from the papacy behind some ring fence, as modern historians have sometimes suggested. In 1163, after all, he allowed all the English bishops to attend the papal council at Tours. Equally Henry had not ready and waiting a list of customs he wished to impose; in 1162 there seemed no need. Becket, Henry's faithful servant, was now to combine the chancellorship with the archbishopric. In so far as Henry wished for tighter control, Becket would achieve it.

Nothing like that happened. Becket at once resigned the chancellorship and plunged into a series of acrimonious disputes with the king, initially over the defence of Canterbury's rights and properties, a defence which was an important sub-text to the whole dispute. All bishops had a sacred trust to protect the possessions of their sees and Becket in standing up for Canterbury's was following in the footsteps of his predecessors. But they, perhaps, might have set about it more diplomatically. Certainly his new primate's behaviour came as a total surprise to Henry. He had worked intimately with Becket for seven years but he had utterly mistaken his man. Henceforth all Becket's passion and energy were to be diverted from the service of the state into the service of the church.

Given Becket's background, this transformation was less surprising than it seemed. A later archbishop of Canterbury, Hubert Walter, who doubled up gleefully as chancellor, had laboured all his life in royal service. Becket had not. Born around 1120, the son of a London merchant, his formative years were spent in the household of Archbishop Theobald from where he had moved to the chancellorship in 1155. In Theobald's service Becket was surrounded by learned clerks, many of them destined like himself for high ecclessiastical office. After an initial degree in arts, these men had often studied theology in the Paris Schools, or canon and civil law in the Schools of Bologna. They had lectured and had gained the coveted title of 'master'. Their learning was intimidating. The canon lawyers revelled in citations from Gratian's 'Concordance of Discordant Canons' or *Decretum* published in Bologna around 1140. The theologians, with their encyclopaedic knowledge of the Bible and its stunning allegorical meanings revealed by the 'Great Gloss' (the commentaries of the Paris theologian Peter Lombard), could punch any untrained opponent out of the ring. And Becket himself was relatively untrained. He had studied arts in Paris and law at Bologna and Auxerre, but had never become a master. A proud man, he stood in awe; the mark left was indelible. The whole dispute with the king is unintelligible outside this wider European background.

On becoming archbishop, Becket thus returned to his roots. Like Theobald he surrounded himself with scholars. One, Herbert of Bosham, abrasive and flamboyant, taught him theology and urged him to fight the good fight. Ultimately, all the new learning in theology and canon law came back to the pope; it asserted his supremacy over secular powers in theory, and intensified his headship of the church in actual practice. The learning of the Schools was indeed very practical. Theology prepared future priests and prelates for a ministry in the world. The image of the good prelate, forthright and incorruptible, influenced

Becket from the start and spurred on his defence of Canterbury's rights. Equally important was the way in which the Schools had sharpened old ideas about the relationship between church and state. For Becket, the clergy formed a separate and distinct body under Christ, subject to its own laws and discipline, and superior to, indeed the 'constituter' of, the secular power. 'Since it is certain that kings receive their power from the church and the church receives hers not from them but from Christ . . . you do not have the power to command bishops to [obey your rules] simply because they are customs,' Becket wrote to Henry on one occasion, getting to the very heart of their quarrel.

At the Council of Woodstock in July 1163 Becket refused Henry's demand that a traditional payment due to the sheriffs from Canterbury lands ('sheriffs aid') should henceforth be made direct to the treasury. By this time Henry was greatly incensed by what he saw as the treachery and ingratitude of his low-born protégé. He now drove matters on with the aim of either subjugating Becket or breaking him, and because he met resistance, the quarrel escalated at an explosive pace. At the Council of Westminster in October 1163 Henry demanded that clerks accused of serious crimes, having been convicted in ecclesiastical courts and stripped of their clerical status, should then be handed over to royal officials for secular punishment in the form of execution or mutilation; this in contrast to being punished merely by what Henry saw as the inadequate spiritual penances imposed by the church, which had no deterrent effect at all. The issue of criminous clerks Henry would probably have tackled in 1158, faced by a particularly notorious clerical crime, had he not been recalled to France by his brother's death. In 1163 there was another *cause célèbre* and the judges warned of a threat to public order. Even Herbert of Bosham later admitted that Henry was moved by zeal for the public peace. The procedure Henry now demanded had probably been customary until eroded under Stephen, but for Becket it was anathema. In spirit if not in letter it challenged the whole concept of the clergy as a separate order. It also conflicted with the best interpretations of canon law and violated scripture, which declared that God would not judge and thus punish twice for the same offence, a passage cited in *Policraticus*, the great work of another of Becket's famous clerks, John of Salisbury. So Becket stood firm and the bishops with him.

Henry immediately raised the stakes and demanded that the bishops observe his 'royal customs'. By the time a council met at Clarendon in

January 1164 these had been formulated in writing: criminous clerks were to be punished as outlined above; tenants-in-chief were not to be excommunicated without royal permission; revenues from vacancies were to flow to the treasury; elections of bishops and abbots were to take place in the king's chapel and thus be subject to royal control. There were also restraints on contact with Rome: ecclesiastics were neither to leave the kingdom nor pursue appeals beyond the arch-bishop's court without royal licence. The Constitutions of Clarendon may well have been, as they claimed, the customs in force under Henry I. But to codify them for the first time threatened a much more exact and exacting regime than in the past, and in an age far less prepared to bear it. Becket rallied the bishops in defiance of the Constitutions, only then in an extraordinary volte-face to give way and accept them.

For Henry this was too little, too late. He was resolved to be rid of his archbishop, who in any case soon made no secret of regretting his submission. So in October 1164 Henry summoned Becket to North-ampton to answer purely secular charges, some related to misappropri-ation of funds while chancellor. Becket refused to resign (the real object of the exercise) and before he could be sentenced to forfeit the lands he held by barony, he had fled. He would not return to England for six years, and then only to meet his death.

At Northampton several bishops had urged Becket to step down, and none had given him much succour. This might seem surprising given that most of the bench were churchmen, not royal administrators. They had close links with the papacy and several had enjoyed distinguished careers in the European Schools. If they felt that the church was under threat, they were just as likely, in terms of training, to resist, as was Becket. Until Northampton, up to a point they had done so. Not one claimed that submission at Clarendon was more than a necessary evil. Yet later in 1164 Gilbert Foliot, bishop of London and a distinguished lawyer, declared that the whole quarrel had arisen over a minor matter which could easily have been settled had Becket displayed 'a discrete moderation'. When angry, Foliot was more pithy: 'He always was a fool and always will be.' The implication was that a concession over criminous clerks, where the king's case had some support in canon law, could have prevented the Constitutions in the first place. In reply Becket (and who knew the king better?) would have urged the impossibility of appeasing Henry. And was not Foliot a man with personal grudges, having aspired to Canterbury himself? Yet at Northampton even the sympathetic Bartholomew of Exeter had declared that the quarrel was personal, not general. Becket should be sacrificed rather than the church. The teaching of the Schools and the ambitions of the king had narrowed the parameters and made conflict more likely, but not inevitable. The missing ingredient had indeed been supplied by Becket himself. Not for nothing did one contemporary dream of him as a prickly hedgehog.

Before and after Becket's departure in 1164 there remained room for manoeuvre. Henry himself, for all his aggression, never advanced exalted theoretical claims for the secular arm. He hinted that he held his power direct from God rather than from the church, but fundamentally he just stood on custom. And then there was the position of the pope. Alexander III (1159–81) was a celebrated canonist. He expressed horror at the Constitutions of Clarendon and absolved Becket from his oath to observe them. Yet he never issued a formal condemnation and frequently prevented Becket from excommunicating his enemies. The problem was that from 1159 through to 1177 Alexander faced a series of anti-popes sponsored by the Emperor Frederick Barbarossa. His first priority was inevitably the freedom of the papacy itself. Perhaps Henry II could not have brought his dominions into Frederick's camp, but he was adept at hinting otherwise. Alexander dared not take the risk. Henry, however, remained under pressure to reach a settlement. He was unable to make episcopal appointments while the conflict lasted and had to endure both Becket's excommunication of Foliot in 1169 and his dalliance with the king of France. Then in 1170 he scored what seemed a colossal victory. That July his eldest son was crowned king of England at Westminster by Roger, archbishop of York (see below, p. 223). The ceremony was a flagrant violation of Becket's rights as archbishop of Canterbury. He was desperate to reach a settlement so that he could reassert his authority and punish the offenders. Henry, on the other hand, hoped a settlement would reconcile Becket to what had happened. Thus he restored the properties of the archbishopric and allowed Becket to return to England. As for the Constitutions of Clarendon, nothing was said, which allowed Becket to think they were dead, and Henry that they were still very much alive. Becket landed on 1 December, having already suspended the bishops involved in the coronation and renewed the excommunication of Foliot. When news of these proceedings reached Henry in Normandy, he let fly the fatal words, and four household knights acted upon them. On 29 December they reached Canterbury, saw Becket in his chamber, and were chased out with shouts of defiance, much to the dismay of the fearful John of Salisbury. An hour or so later, in the gathering dusk, the four found the archbishop again in his cathedral. They probably intended arrest rather than murder, but when Becket resisted, they hacked him to death.

No single event in the central Middle Ages, apart perhaps from the fall of Jerusalem in 1187, so profoundly shocked western Christendom. As the news spread, Henry was hit by great waves of revulsion. The monks of Grandmont near Limoges stopped work on their buildings and sent away the workmen Henry had provided lest they be tainted by the deed. 'The gold of your crown is tarnished and the roses which adorn it have fallen,' lamented a former prior of the monastery. Even before Becket was canonized in March 1173, Henry was forced into concessions, though their precise significance is open to debate. At Avranches in 1172, in return for his own absolution he agreed to abolish the evil customs he had introduced; in practice this meant the end of the Constitutions of Clarendon. They were never cited again as good law, however much some of the individual practices continued. Yet arguably Becket had done no more than destroy the written definitions he himself had provoked. The Constitutions of Clarendon were the consequence of the dispute as much as its cause. There was no equivalent to the conflict elsewhere in Henry's dominions. Four years later, in 1176, Henry freed criminous clerks from secular punishment. If as seems likely such punishment had always been Henry's intention, Becket's victory was here unalloyed. It secured 'benefit of clergy' down to the Reformation, at some cost to law and order. In 1172 Henry had also promised not to impede appeals or visits to the pope. Thereafter large numbers of appeals certainly went to Rome and were usually resolved by judges delegate appointed to hear the cases back in England. The papal decrees on points of law spawned by such cases were brought together in decretal collections, like those compiled by bishops Bartholomew of Exeter and Roger of Worcester, both of whom were very active as judges delegate. When an official collection of Decretals was issued by the papacy in 1234, 180 of the 470 decrees were addressed to England. The kingdom was thus fully within the compass of papal government. Yet it is far from clear that these developments were the result of the Becket dispute. It did not take 1172 to open the floodgates between Rome and England. The flow had been increasing gradually throughout the century. Henry's concession in 1172 (in form at least) meant the end of a licensing system which dated back to the Conqueror, yet outside times of emergency kings had always seen this as a sieve rather than a fence. They had little interest in the great bulk of matters which went to Rome, many involving minor disputes within and between ecclesiastical institutions over rights and jurisdiction. Nor in practice could they stop such business without great difficulty, because the pope was not forcing his justice down people's throats. The demand came from below, from within England itself (as from elsewhere in Europe), and was the product of the attitudinal change wrought by the general movement of reform and the study of canon law and theology.

On occasions when Henry did need to safeguard the rights of the king and kingdom, he still had weapons to hand. He sometimes had papal judges delegate hear their cases in his presence. Under the settlement of 1172 he was allowed to take securities for good behaviour from anyone going to Rome whom he suspected. Cases concerning both advowson (the right to appoint to a church living) and church land held in return for secular services continued, in accordance with the Constitutions, to come before secular courts. Above all, Henry retained control over the areas most vital to him: namely appointments and vacancies. 'I order you to hold a free election but forbid you to elect anyone save Richard [of Ilchester], my clerk.' So Henry allegedly wrote to the electors of Winchester in 1173 about their new bishop, and Ilchester was indeed elected, as around this time were several other royal clerks. If Becket's successors as archbishop, Richard of Dover and Baldwin of Ford, were not king's men, neither caused trouble. In 1176 Henry had also promised not to keep bishoprics and abbeys vacant for more than a year save in cases of urgent necessity, but necessity pressed often, especially when the sees were wealthy: York was vacant from 1181 to 1189.

During the course of the twelfth century the church in England embraced papal government and was transformed in the process. The king's hold in some areas, however, remained strong, and was bitterly criticized by conscientious churchmen. How could a diocese be healthy when it had a bishop absorbed in secular affairs or indeed no bishop at all? But, on the other hand, how could bishops do their work if standing up for ecclesiastical rights led to titanic struggles between church and state? There had to be a middle way, and there was. Richard of Ilchester was twice excommunicated by Becket, yet as bishop of Winchester he acted as a judge delegate and elicited important rulings on legal points for the pope. He also continued in the royal service, yet won the tacit approval of the dean of St Paul's and former Paris Schoolman Ralph of Diss for so doing. The divisions between church and state were rarely as clear-cut as the rhetoric of the Becket dispute suggested. Bishops like Richard of Ilchester created the harmony between church and state in which pastoral work could flourish. There was much of it to do. Late in life one of Becket's former clerks, Gervase of Chichester, lamented the immorality and worldliness of clergy and lay people alike. In response to such problems, in 1175 Archbishop Richard of Dover promulgated important canons at a great provincial council. It was work like this which pointed the way forward for the bishops of the thirteenth century (see below p. 437).

*   *   *

At the start of his reign, King Henry had moved decisively to repair the mutilated state of his kingdom in the north, recovering all that had been lost to King David. For David's grandson, Malcolm IV, who had succeeded to the Scottish throne at the age of twelve in 1153, this was a deep humiliation. He had also to face the internal tensions which the new Davidian state had created. Yet Malcolm emerged triumphant. Rebuffed in the south, he expanded his power west and north, a re-orientation which, continued by his successors, ultimately created a new Scottish kingdom.

For the northern chronicler William of Newburgh, writing in the 1190s, Malcolm seemed chiefly remarkable for his pious chastity, which survived, so it was said, the planting of a virgin in his bed. He also burnt with knightly ambition and impressed Newburgh with his 'royal authority and severity'. But given his youth and his kingdom's internal problems, there was little he could do to resist King Henry. In 1157, he surrendered all David had gained south of the Solway and the Tweed. However, Malcolm remained part of the Anglo-Norman world. His mother was Ada de Warenne, his ministers the Anglo-Norman magnates inherited from his father, notably the steward Walter fitz Alan, and constable Hugh de Moreville. Henry II, as a sop and a control, had granted him his father's old earldom of Huntingdon and also land in Tynedale, the beginnings of an important lordship held by the Scottish kings in that area. It was to cut a dash on the wider stage, and to fulfil his obligations as an English earl, that Malcolm went on the Toulouse expedition of 1159 (see above, p. 194), being knighted by

Henry in the bishop's meadow at Périgueux – some 750 miles from Edinburgh, and a remarkable testimony to the extent and pulling power of the Angevin state.

Henry II remained acutely conscious of his northern frontier, not surprisingly after past events. He retained and rebuilt Wark castle on the Tweed border, and looked on testily as Malcolm invaded Galloway (1160) and married his sisters to continental nobles. In 1163 he made Malcolm come south to Woodstock to renew his homage, though probably just for Huntingdon and Tynedale rather than the Scottish kingdom. At least Malcolm had avoided that. As security for the fidelity he owed, Malcolm handed over his brother David, Henry having initially pressed for castles within Scotland itself.

Malcolm had bowed to King Henry partly because of his internal preoccupations. In 1153, at the start of the reign, he faced a rebellion led by Somerled, ruler of Argyll, and his nephews, the sons of Malcolm MacHeth, who 'perturbed and disquieted Scotland in great part' (as the Holyrood Chronicle recorded). They were joined by 'very many men' and doubtless exploited the resentments against the Anglo-Norman Davidian state. If MacHeth's descent was in some way royal, and his confinement in prison since capture in 1134 suggests as much (see above, p. 179), this may well have been a threat to the throne itself. It was a threat which Malcolm overcame. In 1156 Donald, one of MacHeth's sons, was taken and next year there was a settlement, MacHeth being released and ultimately becoming earl of Ross. Malcolm was lucky, for the interests of the MacHeths' ally, the great Somerled, were essentially elsewhere.

Somerled (in Norse, 'summer warrior') was of Scoto-Norse extraction. In the 1120s and 1130s he recovered his family's position in Argyll, doubtless helped by his alliance with the MacHeths (Malcolm MacHeth had married his sister), and his own marriage to the daughter of Olaf, king of Man, who dominated the Western Isles. The year 1153 had seen the death of two kings, Olaf himself as well as King David. The second might open up chances in Scotland, but it was the first which concerned Somerled more immediately because it threw the western seas into turmoil. There Somerled competed with Godfrey, Olaf's son, and the king of Dublin for mastery in the area, with the nominal overlord, the king of Norway, making only noises off. In fact no Norwegian king intervened directly in the Western Isles between 1098 and 1264. Given the instability in Norway, they were usually powerless to do so.

Essentially in this cold and choppy North Sea world, periphery to the Scottish kingdom, central to the contestants, the rulers of Argyll, Galloway, Dublin, and the Isle of Man fought things out for themselves. In 1156 Somerled defeated Godfrey in a great naval battle and two years later drove him from Man into Norwegian exile. In the words of an Irish annal, he was 'king of the Hebrides and Kintyre'; probably he was king of Man as well.

Malcolm's defeat of the MacHeths was not the end of his problems. When he returned in 1160 from the Toulouse campaign and reached Perth he was confronted by Earl Ferteth of Strathearn and five other earls determined to take him prisoner. The Melrose chronicle states they were 'enraged against the king because he had gone to Toulouse', which suggests native hostility to Malcolm's Anglo-Norman outlook and policies. Threatened by the new Anglo-Norman lordships to his north and east, the conspiracy was joined by the veteran Fergus, 'king of the Galwegians', who, married to an illegitimate daughter of Henry I, had both unified Galloway for the first time and had expanded its frontiers. Having avoided capture, Malcolm, according to the Melrose chronicle, went thrice into Galloway with a large army and subdued his enemies. This was an important moment in the westward expansion of royal authority. Malcolm forced Fergus into retirement and established a royal base at Dumfries on the Nith; he planted his chamberlain, Walter of Berkeley, astride the Urr, the ancient eastern boundary of Galloway, behind which Fergus's sons, Uhtred and Gilbert (never described as more than 'lords'), were pinned. Malcolm could now glare across the Solway at King Henry in Carlisle.

Meanwhile Malcolm established a group of Flemings in Clydesdale and set up a sheriffdom at Lanark (or at least in the records one now appears there). He also increased the lordship of his steward, Walter fitz Alan, ancestor of the Stewarts, around Renfrew, something which proved too much for Somerled. In 1160 he had settled with Malcolm, perhaps acknowledging his overlordship of Argyll. Now in 1164 he gathered 160 ships, teeming with warriors including some from Dublin, and attacked Renfrew itself, only to meet his death there. His achievement survived. Godfrey, son of Olaf, recovered Man, Skye and Lewis but Somerled's descendants (the MacSorleys) long held sway over Argyll, Kintyre and the adjoining islands.

Malcolm also held the line in the ecclesiastical field. The loss of the south made York's claims to metropolitan authority over the Scottish church far less tolerable than in David's heyday, and in 1159–60 Malcolm begged the pope to give such status instead to St Andrews, raising it to an archbishopric. He had no success, but at least, in clear rebuttal of York's pretensions, the pope in 1164 personally consecrated Ingram, Malcolm's chancellor, as bishop of Glasgow, and in the next year authorized the consecration of a new bishop of St Andrews, Malcolm's chaplain, by the Scottish bishops themselves. By this time Malcolm was a sick man, but when he died in December 1165 the dynasty was secure, a tribute to his own work, and also to the structure and balances of the Davidian state. William, Malcolm's brother, succeeded without challenge to a political system which worked.

*   *   *

King Henry had put the clock back in Scotland. He also aimed to do so in Wales, where the native rulers in Stephen's time had made substantial gains at the expense of both the king and the marcher barons. In the 1150s three great rulers held sway in native Wales. In the north Owain had dominated Gwynedd since the death of his heroic father Gruffudd ap Cynan in 1137; in the north-east Madog ap Maredudd had (temporarily) unified Powys, while in the south in Deheubarth, the young Rhys ap Gruffudd was just beginning his illustrious career.

Owain, however, was at odds with Madog from whom he had wrested Iâl in north-west Powys, with Rhys to whom he had lost Ceredigion, and with his own brother Cadwaladr whom he had expelled from Anglesey. Henry was quick to exploit these divisions. He forced Madog to surrender Oswestry, and then in 1157, with Madog in his army, invaded Gwynedd. He had a secure base from which to advance, for the earldom of Chester was in his hands during the minority of the heir (1153–1163). Having survived an ambush in the woods of Coleshill, Henry marched on relentlessly to Rhuddlan, near the mouth of the Clwyd. Owain did homage and resigned Tegeingl, the cantref between the Dee and the Clwyd which he had seized from the earl of Chester. Thus Henry's approach was strikingly different from that of Henry I who had accepted Gwynedd's expansion at the earldom's expense. In the south, Henry had already denied Pembroke to Richard fitz Gilbert de Clare and it remained a royal base throughout the reign, leaving Richard just with Chepstow. Now Rhys ap Gruffudd hastened to court and resigned Carmarthen to the king, Ceredigion to Earl Roger de

Clare, and Cantref Bychan in Ystrad Tywi to Walter de Clifford. Wales was back to where it had been in 1135.

Almost at once Rhys repented and went on the warpath, to be spared retribution by a factor which, as Gerald of Wales observed, saved Wales again and again in this period: the king's continental priorities. In July 1158 Henry's brother Geoffrey died at Nantes. The Loire valley and control of Brittany, or the Tywi valley and control of Deheubarth? There was no contest. Henry crossed the Channel and did not return for over four years. In 1159, as Henry advanced on Toulouse, Rhys besieged Carmarthen, and defeated royal forces with their Gwynedd allies. Next year Madog died, and Powys became divided between four segments of his kin; a decisive moment in its history, for unity was never restored. Henry needed to reassert his authority and in 1163 he returned to Britain. He marched into Rhys's fastness of Cantref Mawr and forced his submission. That July at Woodstock he received the homages of Rhys, Owain Gwynedd and the rulers of Powys.

All this, however, was but a signal for a general rising. In 1164 Rhys ravaged Ceredigion and seized Dinefwr on the Tywi, the 'principal seat' of Deheubarth. Early next year Owain's son Dafydd invaded Tegeingl in an attempt to reverse its loss in 1157. Henrician revenge seemed certain and in July 1165 Owain, Rhys and the rulers of Powys united their forces at Corwen in the Dee valley to meet it. Henry indeed struck hard, marching his army up onto the great range of the Berwyn hills, 2,000 feet above sea-level, only to be driven back by torrential rains. Apart from the Toulouse campaign, it was the greatest defeat of his career. It was also a critical moment for the Welsh rulers, for little would have remained of their independence had Henry descended from the hills and scattered their armies. The fear that Henry would try again the following year prompted a response from Owain which shows a remarkable grasp on his part of the wider European stage. In 1165 those in the know across the Channel had calculated that Henry would not attack the Welsh until he had reached a settlement with King Louis. Owain saw the connection too and wrote on three occasions to the French king, ultimately suggesting that they should co-ordinate military operations. This is the first known occasion on which a Welsh ruler had established contact with a European monarch. In the event Louis was not needed, because a rebellion in Brittany took Henry once more across the Channel in 1166 and he did not return for four years. So in the north Owain was able to consolidate his hold of Tegeingl, turning Rhuddlan into 'the noble castle' where his son entertained Archbishop Baldwin and Gerald of Wales 'most handsomely' in 1188. His ambitions also reached beyond the territorial expansion of Gwynedd to the assertion of dominion over all native Wales. He was doubtless influenced by the way minor rulers had sought the protection of his father, Gruffudd ap Cynan – at least according to Gruffudd's *Life*. Probably there were also memories of Gruffudd ap Llywelyn, king of ales 'from end to end' before his defeat by Harold in 1063. In his first two letters to Louis, Owain described himself as 'king of Wales' and 'king of the Welsh'. In his last letter to Louis, Owain went further still, styling himself not king but 'prince of the Welsh', the first native ruler to use this style. He thus proclaimed both his uniqueness and his independence for in Roman law 'prince' indicated a sovereign ruler, which was why Henry was so angry when he heard about Owain's use of the title. By calling himself 'prince *of the Welsh*' Owain was also, of course, asserting his supremacy over the other native rulers. It was that which Owain's descendants were to achieve in the thirteenth century.

Owain died in 1170 with Gwynedd once more extended to the Dee, and while making claims for a wider hegemony. How those played with the other rulers if they were ever presented to them we do not know – badly, one would think, given their own ambitions and fierce independence. That was always the obstacle to any single overlordship. The *Brut* saw 1165 not as a national movement, but one simply of co-operation: 'All the Welsh united to throw off the rule of the French.' As it was, Owain's sons and the rulers of Powys were soon at each other's throats. The future lay with Rhys ap Gruffudd of Deheubarth, the Lord Rhys (*Yr Arglwydd Rhys*), as he was often described in the *Brut*. In November 1166 he took Cardigan and ended at long last the Clare connection with Ceredigion. He also ousted the Cliffords from Cantref Bychan and wrested Cilgerran and Emlyn in northern Dyfed from William fitz Gerald. This time it was not the continent that saved Rhys, but Ireland.

In 1171 Henry led a great army to Pembroke, whence he sailed for Ireland. This was a decisive moment in Welsh history. Henry's intervention in Ireland made the security of south Wales an absolute necessity. Had he met resistance he would doubtless have achieved it by force. Instead it was achieved by Rhys's immediate submission, a submission so spontaneous and dignified that it immediately won Henry's trust. Next year, as Henry passed through Wales on his way back to Normandy, he made Rhys, in the words of the *Brut*, 'justiciar on his behalf in Deheubarth'. Rhys's policy in 1171 had been masterly, and represented a complete change of tack. He saw he would gain far more from co-operating with King Henry than competing with him. His new position meant the king recognized his conquests and would protect them from attack by royal officials and marcher barons. In return Rhys would ensure that the native rulers of Deheubarth kept the peace, an obligation which, of course, enhanced his own authority. Henceforth if in one role he was Henry's justiciar, in another, as Roger of Howden put it, he was 'king of South Wales'.

＊　　＊　　＊

In the years after 1171 Ireland in significant part was conquered and colonized by the English, or so the invaders were usually called because they came either from England or from England's colonies, the marcher baronies of Wales. This was the beginning of England's baleful attempt to dominate Ireland. The Vikings had attacked and settled in Ireland in the ninth century (Dublin, Wexford and Waterford remained very much Norse towns in the twelfth) but, apart from that, as contemporaries observed, the island had never before been conquered, not even by the Romans. These events, therefore, were both momentous and extraordinary and they were recorded by the victors themselves in two great works of literature, Gerald of Wales's *The Conquest of Ireland* (finished in 1189) and *The Song of Dermot and the Earl*, a celebratory poem dating, in its original form, to soon after 1176.

The English came to Ireland because they were invited by Dermot MacMurrough to help recover his kingdom of Leinster and defeat Rory O'Connor, king of Connacht, his rival for the 'High Kingship'. Ireland was a land of many kings (like earls elsewhere, said *The Song of Dermot*) and there was constant conflict between them for control of the provincial kingdoms and, among the greater kings, for possession of the High Kingship of all Ireland. This was partly because there were no clear rules of succession; kings might have many sons by many wives, all of whom could be considered throne-worthy. It was partly too (though this was changing) because kingship had little institutional content, and hegemonies based on oaths, tribute and military aid easily rose and fell.

MacMurrough's recruits came from the marcher magnates of south

Wales and in particular from a group of men of mixed Welsh and Norman blood, to which Gerald of Wales himself belonged. These were the descendants of Nest, daughter of Rhys ap Tewdr, and the various Normans, including Henry I, with whom she had had relationships. The power of these marcher lords had been severely trimmed by the triumphs of Rhys ap Gruffudd in the south. They were as eager to go as Rhys was to wave them on their way: to that end he actually released from imprisonment Robert fitz Stephen, son of Nest by Stephen, castellan of Cardigan. In May 1169 fitz Stephen arrived in three ships with 30 knights, 60 men at arms and 300 foot archers. He was followed by Raymond le Gros, Maurice fitz Gerald, Meiler fitz Henry (a grandson of Henry I and Nest), and Robert and Philip of Barry, Gerald of Wales's brothers. With such help MacMurrough was astonishingly successful and soon recovered control of much of Leinster. Then a baron of even greater power came to his aid. This was Richard fitz Gilbert, lord of Chepstow in Wales and son of Gilbert fitz Gilbert de Clare, Stephen's earl of Pembroke. His usual nickname 'Strongbow' is not contemporary and gives him an altogether false glamour. Fitz Gilbert was intelligent, circumspect, and highly temptable; as a former supporter of Stephen, Henry had refused to recognize him as an earl, and had deprived him of Pembroke. Fitz Gilbert landed in August 1170 with 200 knights and 1,000 other troops. Waterford was captured at once, and then on 21 September the combined English and MacMurrough forces took Dublin, already recognized as the 'head of the kingdom'.

The most fundamental feature of the invasion now became apparent. The English had not come for pay and plunder on a 'here today, gone tomorrow' basis. They had come for land and meant to stay. 'Whoever shall wish for soil or sod richly shall I enfeoff them,' proclaimed MacMurrough, according to *The Song of Dermot and the Earl*. With this in view he gave fitz Stephen Wexford, and promised Richard fitz Gilbert the hand of his daughter Aife and, with her, succession to the kingdom. When MacMurrough died in May 1171 it seemed that fitz Gilbert might indeed become king of Leinster and perhaps even High King of all Ireland. This was too much for King Henry. He could not possibly have disaffected barons carving out kingdoms for themselves in Ireland. But this was not the only reason for the expedition he now planned. Before it sailed fitz Gilbert, brought to heel by the confiscation of his Welsh and English lands, had already surrendered Dublin, Waterford and Wexford and agreed to hold the rest of Leinster from the king.

The truth was that Henry, as William of Newburgh put it, wanted to have 'the glory of such a famous conquest' and its proceeds for himself.

There was a wider background here. Ireland was the reverse of remote. It had longstanding trading links with Bristol and Chester. Welsh rulers had often gone there in exile. Rumours that kings of England might conquer Ireland had been prevalent since the time of William I. Rufus, according to one story, had boasted of building a bridge of boats across the sea. Such ideas were strengthened by the extraordinary success of Geoffrey of Monmouth's *History of the Kings of Britain*, for Ireland had been conquered with remarkable ease by its hero Arthur. Already in 1155 Henry himself had held a great council at Winchester to discuss the plans for 'the conquest'. Some of the initiative here may have come from Archbishop Theobald, who hoped to re-establish Canterbury's claims to authority over the Irish church: in 1152 its independent diocesan structure had been recognized by the pope. But Henry also saw Ireland as a fitting kingdom either for his younger brother William or, after William's death, for his youngest son, John. The only problem was that he had no clear and convincing right to it. But here Pope Adrian IV came to the rescue. In 1155–6, hoping to further the cause of reform among its church and people, he issued a bull which could at least be interpreted as granting Ireland to Henry II in hereditary right. (The only purported text, however, known as *Laudabiliter*, was probably concocted by Gerald of Wales.)

The idea for conquest was there. The activities of fitz Gilbert and his fellows were the catalysts, as was Henry's desire both to please the pope and vanish after Becket's murder. In October 1171 Henry crossed from Milford Haven to Waterford with (according to Gerald) 500 knights and numerous mounted and foot archers. He gained the peaceful submission of at least fifteen Irish kings, including those of Desmond and Thomond, together with the native archbishops and bishops. The conquest immediately revealed the face of its 'civilizing' mission: a council at Cashel, attended by nearly all the Irish bishops, legislated for lawful marriages and the proper payment of tithes. But it was not all plain sailing. The kings of Meath and Ulster remained defiant, as did Rory O'Connor of Connacht, who declared that he 'ought to be king and lord of Ireland'. For the summer of 1172, therefore, Henry planned a further campaign. The history of Ireland might have been very different had he carried it out and completed the conquest. Instead, learning that papal legates were in Normandy ready to discuss a settlement of his rift with the church, he hastily departed and on 21 May 1172 was reconciled to the church at Avranches. The pope had already rejoiced at events in Ireland, and had issued bulls which seemed to confirm dominion over the island to Henry and his heirs.

Higher priorities meant that Henry never came back to Ireland. Without the immediate catalysts in 1171 he might never have gone there. Yet he often threatened to return, and regarded its affairs as 'great matters' to be closely monitored and controlled. The richest pickings were to be his, not fitz Gilbert's. Before leaving, Henry placed Waterford, Wexford and Dublin with their surrounding territories under his own officials. For the rest he made Leinster and Meath great fiefs to be held for knight service and the other conditions of feudal tenure. The former was to be held by fitz Gilbert and the latter by Hugh de Lacy, lord of Weobley and Ludlow.

Henry's aim was to create a stable and wealthy kingdom for his son John, but he faced problems from both the native kings and English invaders. In 1174, after Henry had pulled fitz Gilbert and others out of Ireland to meet the crisis elsewhere in his dominions, 'all the people of Ireland with one consent rose against the English' (so wrote Gerald of Wales). Meath, which Hugh de Lacy was busy wresting from its native rulers, was a particular centre of the rising. These events encouraged Henry the next year to reach a settlement with the greatest of the native rulers, he who had defied him in 1171: Rory O'Connor. Under the 1175 Treaty of Windsor Rory was to hold Connacht under Henry and, as recognition of his High Kingship, have authority over the rest of Ireland outside the English areas. But the agreement soon collapsed and the English advance continued. In 1177 Henry gave Robert fitz Stephen and Miles de Cogan the opportunity to seize the kingdom of Cork, while Limerick he eventually passed to Philip de Braose. Both were to be fiefs held by knight service but with the towns of Cork and Limerick reserved for the crown. In the same year John de Courcy, granted Ulster by Henry 'if he could conquer it', began his extraordinary career, a career which was to lead to the subjection of the ancient native dynasty and the creation of one of the greatest of the new English lordships. Nothing exemplified more clearly how a fortune could be made in Ireland, because John, a younger son of the Courcys of Stogursey in Somerset, had started his career almost landless. And nothing better demonstrated the importance of English connections: the Courcys had important interests in northern England, particularly in Cumbria, only seventy miles from the Ulster coast, and it was from there that the men who supported John's conquest came, stepping across the sea all the more easily after he had married Affreca, daughter of the king of Man.

Sometimes Henry was incensed by rumours that Hugh de Lacy or John de Courcy was aspiring to create independent kingdoms; hence his joy at de Lacy's murder in 1186. To keep control he sent in commissions of investigation, appointed as viceroy his steward William fitz Audelin, played Lacy off against fitz Gilbert, and in 1173 made the latter prove his worth in Normandy before allowing him back to Ireland. After fitz Gilbert's death in 1176, leaving only infant children, the whole of Leinster came to Henry in wardship, where it remained till the end of the reign. Henry's ensuing Ordinance for the government of Ireland, issued from Oxford in 1177, in its display of colonial mastery and power anticipates Edward I's statute of 1284 after his conquest of Wales.

In 1177 Henry had designated John as king of Ireland. Eight years later in 1185, now nineteen, John arrived. His Norman entourage offended the native nobles by pulling their flowing beards; Hugh de Lacy and John de Courcy, not surprisingly, given the challenge to their own positions, were unco-operative, and John was home in six months, expressing no desire to return even when a crown of peacock's feathers arrived from the pope. Nevertheless the expedition gave fresh impetus to the English settlement, for John's followers received grants in both Louth (Bertram de Verdon and Gilbert Pipard) and Munster (William de Burgh and Theobald Walter), grants which it was up to them to transform into reality by conquest. Meanwhile, structures of government for the areas under the king's direct control were developing very much on English lines. An exchequer was formed at Dublin and the administration placed under a justiciar, while the chief local agent became the sheriff. By the end of Henry's reign the conquest was secure, although, of course, incomplete. It had been well worth it. In the thirteenth century Ireland provided kings of England with revenue and sources of patronage, yet they had to go there only once. The best type of colony.

Fundamentally the struggle for Ireland had been between two very different economic, social and political systems. The Irish had no armour, cavalry or castles and so were extremely vulnerable to invaders who possessed all three. The cavalry forces introduced by Dermot MacMurrough were small, yet again and again they faced his enemies with devastating results as though they were some utterly novel secret weapon, which indeed they were.

> He charged them speedily without any pause
> And the Irish who had no armour
> They scattered themselves
> By sevens and eights, by threes and fours
> So that they did not hold together
> And the earl then slew of these men
> Seven score and ten.

In these words *The Song of Dermot* describes a charge by Richard fitz Gilbert. These were men on the make, with limited prospects at home, 'strong-limbed barons of bold heart', as the *Song* described Miles de Cogan. When the army was held up by the river Shannon outside Limerick, Meiler fitz Henry charged to the front on his white horse, plunged into the water and was carried across to the other side. 'Pass over, knights. Why do you tarry?' he shouted. Who indeed could tarry with such leaders? 'And the earl then slew of these men seven score and ten.' The English also learnt from the Irish. After some debate they soon abandoned the chivalric ways of Anglo-Norman warfare and politics. They killed in battle, murdered prisoners *en masse*, and publicly executed Irish kings, throwing the body of one of them to the dogs.

Having won the battles, it was above all by the castle that the English conquest was, in the words of *The Song of Dermot*, 'well rooted'. That at Trim was the centre of Lacy power in Meath. In Louth, some twenty-three motte and motte-and-bailey castles have been traced. Even more important were the men who built the castles – not just the great lords but the under-tenants whom they introduced. Well might the *Song* triumphantly list the thirty or so vassals who were endowed with 'rich fiefs and fair lands' by fitz Gilbert and Hugh de Lacy. These men, tenants and associates from Normandy, Wales and above all from England, formed manors and introduced peasants to exploit them. Given that they were not great barons, John de Courcy in Ulster and Verdon and Pipard in Louth did not have the same reserves of tenants to draw on, but they were quite able to recruit from England, Courcy as we have seen from the north, Verdon and Pipard from their kinsmen, neighbours and connections in the west midlands and Shropshire. These under-tenants would fight tooth and nail to have and to hold. They formed the backbone of the English conquest of Ireland.

However potent their weaponry, the English with their small numbers would never have survived the dangerous early days in Ireland without the support of Dermot MacMurrough. No wonder native annals stigmatized him as 'the ruin of the Irish'. Yet Dermot's own conduct itself points to another side, which helps to explain both the conquest's success and Irish survival: the Irish, like the Welsh, were quick to accommodate themselves to the new order, the bishops because they genuinely welcomed the reforms, the kings because they had no alternative. But at least Henry made the submissions easy and not unlike those offered to High Kings in the past. He held his court at Christmas 1171 in a palace built of wattles by the Irish kings 'according to the custom of the country'. Native kings, moreover, did not only survive in the unconquered areas. In Leinster fitz Gilbert allowed Dermot's son and nephew to act as 'kings of the Irish of the country'. In Meath, while Donnel O'Melaghlin of the native dynasty was hanged at Trim, his brother Art was left ruling in the west.

Up to a point the conquest was an accident waiting to happen. From the moment that the Normans with their devastating military superiority arrived in Wales, warring Irish kings must have contemplated an appeal to them. Yet the price was high, and only the desperate (like MacMurrough) would pay it. It had to be paid in land because there was no coinage; indeed in fitz Gilbert's case by the offer of a kingdom, an offer which (although this is debated) did violence to Irish custom. Even then it took the narrowing of opportunities in Wales for the offers to be accepted. In fact the conquest was never completed. That was partly because of the techniques of accommodation practised by the Irish kings, but also because the movement ran out of steam. The richest part of Ireland lay in the east and had been taken at the start. If the English kings sometimes hoped for more, they would not go out to get it. John's expedition of 1210 was to discipline the barons, not to eliminate the native rulers. The second generation of baronial conquerors quarrelled among themselves, and sometimes had many interests elsewhere.

Thus the threefold division of Ireland, already apparent under Henry II, remained: the areas under direct royal control, the great fiefs and the surviving native kingdoms. Like the Normans in Wales, the English came to Ireland as piecemeal conquerors. For the most part they retained their own identity and constructed their own distinct polities, in part because there was no single kingdom to conquer; hence the fundamental differences between the histories of Scotland on the one hand and Wales and Ireland on the other.

*　　*　　*

Having restored royal authority in England and Normandy, conquered Ireland and settled the Becket dispute, Henry seemed at the height of his power. Yet he was almost at once engulfed by a massive rebellion which constituted the greatest crisis of his reign, just as his ultimate victory was his greatest triumph. In Britain the result was to confirm Rhys's dominance in south Wales and to destroy Scotland's independence.

The rebellion began within the royal house, the product of Henry's wish to provide for his sons and settle the future government of his dominions. In 1170, with the act which so offended Becket, Henry's eldest son (also named Henry), having done homage to King Louis for Normandy, was crowned king of England in deliberate contrast to Henry I's failure to crown the Empress. In 1172 Richard, Henry's second son, now aged fourteen, was invested with his mother's county of Poitou. Geoffrey, the third son, was through his marriage to be duke of Brittany; John, the youngest, was to be lord of Ireland. Henry envisaged his sons gradually gaining more authority in their dominions and ruling them in harmonious splendour under his supervision. But for the moment the Young King, as his eldest son was called, felt he was simply a 'paid servant', with councillors who were 'more masters than ministers'. His ultimate inheritance also seemed threatened by Henry's scheme to endow John not just with Ireland but with castles in Touraine. In March 1173 he fled from court to join Louis VII, his father-in-law, in Paris.

The Young King was soon joined at Louis's side by his brothers Richard and Geoffrey, dispatched there by none other than their mother, Eleanor of Aquitaine herself. Matilda, the Conqueror's queen, had sent funds to support her son Robert, but this was rebellion on an entirely different scale. Since 1170 Eleanor had been holding her own court in Poitou, and was thus quite able to act against her husband. She had good reason to do so. After John's birth in 1166, she had been replaced by mistresses. She had also seen her rights in Aquitaine flouted, most notably when Henry himself received the homage of the count of Toulouse in 1173.

The explosion within the royal family provided an opportunity for all Henry's internal and external foes. Only Gascony remained relatively quiet. Since the Young King aimed to make himself ruler in Nomandy and England ('Here is the king of England,' proclaimed Louis) he could promise much. Roger of Howden gives separate lists of the Norman and English rebels, but the two revolts were inseparable and several of the great English rebels had extensive lands in the duchy. Their grievances are starkly apparent. Hugh, earl of Chester, for example, had never succeeded to the lands and castles granted to his father by Henry before his accession; Earl William de Ferrers had failed in his claims to the Peverel inheritance of his mother, and had been denied the title earl of Derby; Hugh Bigod, earl of Norfolk, now promised Norwich by the Young King, had been forced to pay £666 to recover his castles of Framlingham and Bungay and had then been threatened by the brand-new royal castle at Orford; Robert, earl of Leicester, had had to pay scutage – unlike his father, the great justiciar – and been amerced £333 for breach of the peace. The great revolt posed difficult choices for the Welsh and the Scots. Hywel ab Iorweth 'while the king was contending beyond the sea', as the *Brut* put it, recovered his castle of Caerleon which Henry had seized in 1171, and plundered around Chepstow. The Lord Rhys of Deheubarth, in contrast, calculated he had most to gain from backing Henry II, to whom of course he owed his overlordship in the south. He sent a son to serve in Normandy, and himself laid siege to Earl Ferrers's castle at Tutbury. In Gwynedd, Dafydd, son of the great Owain, struggling for power both with his brothers and the earl of Chester, made a similar calculation. In Scotland, King William reacted very differently. He checked first with King Henry, who offered nothing, and then threw in his lot with the Young King, who promised Carlisle and the northern counties. There would never be a better chance to restore King David's realm.

Henry met this the greatest crisis of his reign with a combination of calculation and anger, sang-froid and demonic energy. In August 1173 he drove King Louis from Verneuil and then galloped into Brittany where the earl of Chester (who was also viscount of Avranches) surrendered. In England the justiciar Richard de Lucy besieged Leicester and then moved to counter King William's invasion of the north. William took no major castles, but he ravaged Northumbria and reduced it to famine before agreeing a truce. Meanwhile Henry's cause was boosted by the capture of the earl of Leicester (in October, near Bury

St Edmunds) and Queen Eleanor herself, who was making her way to the French court disguised as a man (an all too brief glimpse of her spirit and resource). All this, however, was just round one. In 1174, King William, King Louis and the Young King co-ordinated their operations. In May, William once more invaded the north. Again he took no major castles, but he wasted Cumbria, and Carlisle agreed to surrender if the town could not be relieved by 29 September. In the midlands, William's brother David secured control of the earldom of Huntingdon, made alliance with Earl Ferrers and took Nottingham. Earl Bigod took Norwich. Messenger after messenger pleaded for Henry's return. He crossed the Channel on 8 July in a great storm (declaring that if God wanted him to win through he would be safe enough), made straight for Canterbury and on 12 July did penance at Becket's tomb. Next day God responded, or so it seemed. A northern force surprised King William at Alnwick and took him prisoner. On 26 July, his legs pinioned beneath his horse, he was delivered to an exultant Henry at Northampton.

The capture of King William soon brought the revolt in England to an end. Would Henry now descend on Wales and recover Caerleon? A Welsh seer assured Iorweth otherwise, because a great city across the sea was under siege. He was right. Henry crossed the Channel on 6–7 August with a large force of Welshmen supplied by Rhys. Four days later he entered Rouen in triumph, the besieging forces of Louis, the Young King, and the counts of Flanders and Blois melting away as he approached. Henry then proceeded to Poitou where he received Richard's tearful submission, and by the end of September both the Young King and Geoffrey, with Louis's agreement, had also submitted.

Henry's victory owed much to 'an abundant hoard of money in the royal treasury', as William of Newburgh put it, which he used to hire large numbers of Brabantine mercenaries. And while he had clearly provoked some barons, Howden's list of supporters 'in England' included ten earls, many with important interests in Normandy. Just before the crisis broke, moreover, Henry had been able to insert his men into six bishoprics. By contrast, contemporaries were quick to criticize King William's 'wild rashness', as Jordan Fantosme put it. He had made little impression on Henry's well-prepared northern castles, hampered as he was by his lack of siege engines and hardly helped by the 3,000 or more Scots, 'naked men' according to Jordan, from the kingdom's common army. But at the least the latter's ravaging and brutality demonstrated William's power. The real disappointment was that, apart from Roger de Mowbray, Richard de Moreville and the bishop of Durham, he won little support from the northern nobility, the men whom David had worked so hard to bind to his regime. The fact was that in the north Henry had built well, inserting his men, like Robert de Vaux, the defender of Wark, into northern baronies and making the loyalist Stuteville brothers (enemies of Mowbray) sheriffs of Yorkshire and Northumberland.

One result of the collapse of royal authority during the revolt had been a whole series of encroachments on the royal forest, and these were punished by a forest eyre of Alan de Neville which imposed amercements totalling an exorbitant £12,000 (in 1176–8). But Henry was also merciful. His aim, as Ralph of Diss observed, was to restore peace and harmony as quickly as possible. Queen Eleanor remained in custody, but Henry's sons were soon restored to favour. As for the rebels, not one was executed or even kept in prison. Henry destroyed their castles (the ruins long testified to his victory) but returned their lands. The Welsh loyalists now reaped their reward. In 1174 Henry married his half-sister Emma, an illegitimate daughter of Geoffrey of Anjou, to Dafydd of Gwynedd. According to the *Brut* he 'thanked Rhys much for his fidelity', and called him his 'right loving friend'. Rhys's position as Henry's justiciar over Deheubarth was now doubly secure.

Only Scotland was exempted from this magnanimity. By the Treaty of Falaise in 1174 William was released, but in return for acknowledging that his kingdom was henceforth a fief held from the king of England. Henry was also to receive the homage and fealty of the earls and barons and other men 'of the land of the king'. And all this was to be guaranteed through the surrender by King William of the castles of Roxburgh, Berwick, Jedburgh, Edinburgh and Stirling. Henry had cut his way into the Scottish kingdom and he had done so potentially on a permanent basis, for the agreement was to last in perpetuity. While the Scottish church, under the treaty, was to owe its 'customary' subjection to the church of England, there was no attempt to justify the subjection of the kingdom as 'customary', which suggests indeed that David and his successors had not in fact done homage for it. Henry was quite happy to see this as something new.

The king could now glory in dominions which stretched 'from the last bounds of Scotland to the mountains of the Pyrenees', as William of Newburgh put it. Within the British context, Henry, so Gerald of Wales opined, had conquered Ireland and Scotland and had 'included by his powerful hand in one monarchy the whole island of Britain', something never achieved before, even by the Romans. The reality did not quite measure up to this unificatory rhetoric. Britain was rarely at the top of Henry's agenda, as his failure to return to Ireland and his postponement of Welsh campaigns shows. Nor was Henry's attitude at all consistent. In Ireland he conquered and took the best part of the land under his direct rule. In Wales he became content to assert over-lordship over the native rulers. In Scotland, he wanted a loyal vassal king, but his essential policy was reactive and defensive. In his formative years King David had dominated northern England, and Henry natur-ally dreaded a renewal of the invasions which had brought that about. The events of 1173–4 confirmed his worst fears. The royal and baronial castles in the north had proved no defence. He needed to try something new. The extreme measures, the subjection of the king and his nobles, and the taking of castles within Scotland (first mooted in 1163), were a measure of the threat, not a base for conquest. In fact Henry never garrisoned Stirling in the heart of the Scottish realm, and after William had proved his dependability, in 1186 Henry actually returned Edin-burgh to him. These moves would have been inconceivable had he really planned to expand his authority within Scotland.

After 1174 the situations of the Welsh rulers and King William were very different. The former could build on success, the latter had to come to terms with failure.

*   *   *

In 1188, on his great tour with Archbishop Baldwin to preach the crusade, Gerald of Wales was entertained by the Lord Rhys at Cardigan and by Dafydd ab Owain Gwynedd at Rhuddlan, the former some-times described by contemporaries as 'king of South Wales' and the latter as 'king of the North'. Having thrown back the yoke of its English conquerors, native Wales seemed to Gerald to have 'increased remarkably in population and in strength'. This was a golden age.

In the south, Rhys's power centred on the cantrefs of Mawr and Bychan in Ystrad Tywi with their great pastures and mountain fast-nesses. In the former, above the river Tywi which divided the two cantrefs, lay Dinefwr, 'the royal seat', as Gerald of Wales put it, of the rulers of Deheubarth. Rhys also held sway in Ceredigion and parts of Dyfed, which he had wrested from the Clares, the Geraldines and other marcher barons. Outside these areas, Rhys's authority over the native rulers of the south was loose and unobtrusive, owing much to the ties of kinship that he had in part created: the native rulers between Wye and Severn and in Glamorgan included his sons-in-law, nephews and a cousin. The co-operative nature of his rule is reflected in the earliest of the Welsh law books ('the Cynferth redaction'), which was put together in south Wales during his time. While its allegiance was clearly to the 'lord of Dinefwr', it accorded the symbols of royalty to all the Welsh rulers. (The Welsh jurists who compiled the law books recorded not legislation and official law codes, but their own views of customary rules and practices.)

For a while Rhys also maintained good relations with Henry II, acting dutifully as his justiciar of Deheubarth. In 1175 and 1177 he presented the rulers of the south at Henry's court. In 1179 Henry, for his part, punished Roger Mortimer and his men when they murdered the ruler of Maelienydd. Meanwhile Rhys married sons and daughters into the marcher families and, always courteous and quick-witted, elicited compliments from the Clares over his conquest of Ceredigion: they could not have lost it, they said, to a more 'noble and valiant prince', an exchange which took place over breakfast during a pleasant meeting at Hereford in 1188.

These were the conditions in which Rhys's rule flourished. He increased his cash revenues by changing renders in kind into money, and perhaps sponsored the Welsh law books we have referred to, books which begin by listing the rights of the king. Rhys also won the favour of God, strengthened his hold on Ceredigion, and showed his integration into the wider European world by richly endowing the new Cistercian monastery at Strata Florida. He also affirmed the pre-eminence of Deheubarth by promoting the cult of St David as the premier saint of Wales; it was at St Davids that he himself was buried. At his new castle of Cardigan in 1177 he held the first Eisteddfod. Well might poets, chroniclers and the scribes of his own and later charters trumpet his praises: 'Rhys the Great', 'Rhys the Good', 'rightful prince of South Wales', indeed 'the Unconquered Head of all Wales'.

In the north, Dafydd's power never equalled that of Rhys, for he shared Gwynedd with his nephews and his brother Rhodri. Yet his basic approach was much the same, with his marriage to Henry II's sister, and his alliance forged by 1177 with the earl of Chester. But there was no way such arrangements could bring any permanent stability to Wales. That was partly because both Rhys and Dafydd wished to use their English-derived power against their Welsh neighbours. As Ralph of Diss put it, Dafydd hoped 'to strike terror into the other Welsh as a result of his new affinity', referring here to his marriage to Henry's sister. In 1177 he and the earl of Chester invaded northern Powys. In the same year Rhys secured a grant of Meirionydd, Gwynedd's southernmost district bordering Ceredigion, from Henry II (who thus demonstrated his lordship over all of Wales), only to be repulsed by Dafydd's nephews. Deep fissures could also open up between the Welsh rulers and the marcher barons. William de Braose might have married a daughter to one of Rhys's sons, yet he was also implicated in a terrible massacre in 1177 at Abergavenny after which 'none of the Welsh dared place trust in the French'. For all the compliments bobbing between Rhys and the Clares everyone knew that in Wales the ebb and flow of battle might at any time recommence.

There was also a gradual shift in Rhys's relations with the king, product of a series of minorities among marcher barons which between 1176 and 1184 brought Chepstow, Lower Gwent, Glamorgan and Gower into royal hands. As a result the pressure from the marcher barons was off. But instead Rhys found himself hedged round by royal bases under assertive officials. Urged on by an aggressive brood of sons now reaching manhood, Rhys changed tack. Between 1182 and 1184, while Henry was out of England, he 'devastated the king's land and killed his men' (Roger of Howden). When in 1184 this produced Henry's return, Rhys immediately submitted, but then, Henry's campaign abandoned, he refused to implement promises he had made. In the next few years Rhys, with all his old tactical skill, was testing the ground to see just how far he could go. His aim was to take Gower, Kidwelly and above all Carmarthen, where royal officials controlled traffic on the Tywi and monitored events some fifteen miles away at Dinefwr. It was to be a policy pursued with vigour after Henry's death in 1189.

*   *   *

The Treaty of Falaise left King William in an appallingly dangerous situation. Since he now held his kingdom as a fief from King Henry, it was liable to forfeiture for any act of disloyalty, much as Scotland was ultimately forfeited by John Balliol in the 1290s. At the same time his capture and humiliation released all the tensions within the realm, rather as the succession of the boy king Malcolm had, back in 1153. William's reaction was the reverse of unintelligent and hot-headed. On the contrary his flexible determination saved the monarchy from King Henry and increased its authority over his native subjects.

Henry's overlordship was far from merely nominal. He garrisoned the castles of Edinburgh, Roxburgh and Berwick, and thus virtually excluded William from the richest burghs in the kingdom. As a consequence, William shifted his itinerary and spent a much higher proportion of his time north of the Forth, notably at Perth, Stirling and Forfar. Henry also summoned William to his court. He was there in eight of the fourteen years between 1175 and 1188, as against only two of the seven years up to 1172. The climax to this career as the Angevin dynasty's 'house' king came in 1186 when William married in the royal chapel at Woodstock the bride found for him by King Henry, namely Ermengarde, daughter of the vicomte of Beaumont, a lady of status but few resources. Yet his concurrence paid dividends. Henry made Ermengarde's dowry the castle of Edinburgh. He had also been conciliatory over William's English fiefs. He had never confiscated Tynedale and in 1185 returned the earldom of Huntingdon, allowing William to grant it to his younger brother, David.

In one area the Treaty quickly came to nothing. Its stipulation that the Scottish church should owe its 'customary' subjection to that of England had an immediate background in Malcolm's attempt to secure metropolitan status for St Andrews, thus freeing Scotland from the claims of York. 'Customary', however, was deliberately vague and almost anticipated the upshot, a renewal of the Canterbury–York dispute over where subjection was due. In 1176 Pope Alexander III kicked the whole matter into touch when he ordered the Scottish bishops to acknowledge the authority of neither, and condemned the ecclesiastical clauses of the Treaty outright as a shocking intrusion into church affairs. This was not something Henry much regretted, having learnt the dangers of powerful archbishops. The immediate sequel in Scotland was a long dispute over St Andrews, where William in 1178 tried to force his chaplain, Hugh, into the bishopric in place of the cleric elected by the canons, John the Scot. Both the pope and King Henry intervened. In 1181 William was briefly excommunicated and his kingdom placed under an interdict, but he emerged victorious. He excluded the monk's candidate and on the death of his own in 1188 he succeeded in placing his chancellor in the bishopric. In 1192 the pope issued a celebrated bull (*Cum Universi*) which confirmed and amplified the verdict of 1176. The 'Scottish church', with its nine named bishoprics, was henceforth to be subject directly to the papal see. William had retained his hold over ecclesiastical appointments and severed the Scottish church definitively from that of England.

The list of the Scottish church's bishoprics included neither Argyll, suggesting it was still tenuously connected to the kingdom, nor Galloway, the latter acknowledged to be subject to York. In fact in Galloway, under cover of Henry's overlordship, William had gone far to reassert an authority shaken in the aftermath of the débâcle of 1174. The native rulers, Gilbert and Uhtred, hitherto held west of the ancient frontier of Galloway on the Urr, had then destroyed both the castle of Walter of Berkeley astride the river and Malcolm's castle base at Dumfries, expelling the royal bailiffs from Nithsdale. The number of English settlers like Walter was small. Some had been introduced by Uhtred himself from Cumbria, Uhtred having married the daughter of the lord of Allerdale. Gilbert and Uhtred's father, Fergus, had himself married an illegitimate daughter of Henry I and founded the Premonstratensian house at Soulseat. Galloway was changing. Yet the brothers probably exploited widespread resentment. Even today the motte at Urr (the largest in Scotland), sticking up like a great thumb, seems an awesome intrusion in the landscape. King Henry's anxiety over security in the north inevitably led him to monitor events in Galloway. It was the recruiting ground for violent soldiers, notorious for their atrocities during the Scottish invasions of England. Events in the province impinged on Cumberland and Carlisle. Henry's policy was to use King William to discipline the native rulers, much like the Lord Rhys in Wales. Thus in 1176 William took an army into Galloway and brought Gilbert, who by this time had murdered Uhtred, south to swear fealty to King Henry. When a succession dispute arose following Gilbert's death in 1185, Henry himself marched to Carlisle and made the new ruler, Uhtred's son Roland, agree to stand to right 'in the court of the king of England' for the lands claimed against him by Gilbert's son, who was later compensated with the earldom of Carrick. Roland also swore fealty to Henry and his heirs, this 'by command of the king of Scotland'. Henry was not, therefore, trying to prise Galloway from its tenuous place within the Scottish realm. Indeed, with Henry's acquiescence William rebuilt his castle at Dumfries and saw Walter of Berkeley restored to Urr.

William's harmonious if humiliating relations with King Henry also allowed him to deal with problems in the far north of his realm. There royal Scotland, the Scotland of royal castles, thanages and sheriffdoms, effectively ended with Moray. Beyond that stretched two provinces with extensive Norse settlement, namely Ross, with its great timber resources, and Caithness, whose earl held Orkney and Shetland from the king of Norway. The bishoprics of Ross and Caithness were part of the Scottish church in 1192 but the king of Scotland's overlordship over the provinces was loose indeed. Worse, Ross was now to become the base for a series of intermittent but dangerous challenges to the throne which lasted down to 1230. They were mounted by the Mac-Heths and the MacWilliams, the descendants of Malcolm MacHeth and William fitz Duncan. Malcolm MacHeth (see above, pp. 179, 211) had died as earl of Ross in 1164, after which no successor appears in the earldom, which suggests the district's independence. The family, perhaps in some way throneworthy, had caused trouble since the 1130s. The MacWilliams were certainly 'descended from the ancient line of the Scottish kings', as the Barnwell annalist put it, and had also nothing to do with the dynasty of King Malcolm and Queen Margaret which had introduced the Anglo-Normans. Instead William fitz Duncan was the son of the King Duncan killed in 1094, the son of Malcolm III's first marriage, not his second to Margaret. If William fitz Duncan had been turned by David's patronage into a pillar of the throne (see above, p. 183), his son Donald emerged in the 1180s as its greatest challenger. He enjoyed, according to Howden, considerable support from Scottish earls and barons, and exploited resentment against the Anglo-Norman court. It was while explaining the MacWilliam risings that the Barnwell annalist remarked on how 'the modern kings of Scotland' had reduced the Scots to servitude, counting themselves French and keeping only Frenchmen in their household.

The trouble in the 1180s centred on Ross and Moray, to which Donald may have had a claim through his mother, and was finally ended by the killing of Aed, grandson of MacHeth, in 1186, and of Donald himself in the following year. His death seemed to contemporaries to mark a turning-point between years of disturbance and the 'great peace' that followed. Certainly it was not till 1211–15 that the MacWilliams and MacHeths again caused trouble. In Moray, William built a new castle and burgh at Nairn to control the crossing to Cromarty, and in the 1190s and 1200s he was able to assert his power in Caithness (see below, p. 256). He had therefore triumphed over adversity. In 1188 he led a unified resistance to King Henry's demanded for taxation to support his forthcoming crusade. He was soon to throw off the English yoke altogether.

＊　　＊　　＊

King Henry's power in Britain and elsewhere had depended on the rebuilding of his revenues in England. His reign also saw the foundation of the common law. For that reason more than any other it constituted a watershed in English history. At the heart of the common law lay new procedures for civil litigation which ultimately transformed the nature of kingship, government and society. These have to be placed in the wider context of the structure of courts in Henry's day and his insistent concern with the punishment of crime and the maintenance of order.

Henry II's own court, held in his presence whether in England or overseas, remained the forum for great political cases, notably those between powerful barons, or between a baron and the king. But for less important and more routine cases other courts, no less the king's though not held in his presence, existed. At the centre the chief officials of the exchequer, increasingly sitting at Westminster, did not merely exact and audit the revenue, they also heard civil pleas. They had done that intermittently under Henry I. Now, at least from the late 1170s, they did so on a regular basis. Alongside the exchequer, and carrying a far heavier load of business, were the king's judges sent on visitations (or eyres) around the counties. There had been judicial eyres under Henry I but those of Henry II were far more impressive. Firstly, they were much more frequent. In the 1120s the judges seem to have covered the country gradually. From 1174–5 onwards they travelled the whole of England every other year on average. This was achieved by the regular commissioning of nationwide or 'general' eyres, with the entire kingdom divided into circuits in which separate panels of judges operated simultaneously; this differed from the practice under Henry I where the judges confined their activities at any one time to one particular locality. Secondly, the eyres of Henry II did far more business and in a far more regular and systematized way. This was partly because the eyres as a result of being so frequent were able to take over from sheriffs and local justiciars the hearing of the pleas of the crown, thus giving the king a much tighter control over law and order.

The pleas of the crown, as we have seen, had their origins in Anglo-Saxon times, and included all major offences ('felonies') against persons and property – homicide, robbery, serious theft and assault, arson, rape – pleas now for the first time actually described as 'criminal' as distinct from 'civil': *Glanvill* or *The Treatise on the Laws and Customs of England*, written *c.* 1189 by the legal circle around Ranulf Glanvill, Henry's chief justiciar, divided all pleas into those two categories. In asserting his control over 'the peace', Henry faced one developing problem. This lay in the way that kings since the Conquest had often, as a form of patronage, conceded control of hundreds (and the profits of their courts) to great lords, lay and ecclesiastical, sometimes recognizing a *de facto* situation which had existed before 1066. The jurisdiction of these courts was over small debts, and fights and brawls which did not involve a breach of the king's peace. Such cases of minor disorder might also be heard in the manorial court, with whose jurisdiction there was a great deal of overlap. The Norman kings, like their predecessors before 1066, had also granted lords the right to have private gallows on which to hang thieves caught red-handed, a liberty ('infangenthief') which could be attached to either a manorial or a private hundred court. In a private hundred it might be the lord rather than the sheriff who held every Michaelmas the 'view of frankpledge', which meant checking to see that the peasants were in their tithing groups, a lucrative exercise since the groups could be subject to all kinds of amercements. This was essentially 'magistrate court' jurisdiction, which was why kings were prepared to give it away. Yet it still meant that lords gained powerful social controls over the local population and played a significant part in the maintenance of the peace. Henry was determined to supervise what was going on. A government measure in 1166, the 'Assize of Clarendon', laid down that the sheriffs were to enter all private courts, even if held in castles, to check personally that the peasants were in their tithing groups. At the same time, no one was to prevent sheriffs entering their lands and jurisdictions to arrest those accused or outlawed for serious crime.

All this was part of major drive in 1165–6 designed to 'keep the peace'. Those accused of serious crimes, if caught, were to be tried by the ordeal of water, an old procedure, but now apparently to replace all others. Those convicted were to lose a foot; ten years later, by the assize of Northampton 'for the sake of stern justice' they were to lose a hand as well. Even those acquitted were to leave the kingdom, if they were of ill-fame. The accusations which initiated the procedures were the responsibility of juries composed of twelve knights and freemen from each hundred. Such juries of presentment or accusation can be traced back to Anglo-Saxon times. What seems to have been new in 1166 was the king's insistence that they were to operate throughout the land.

Down to the 1160s, in the absence of itinerant justices the sheriffs and local justiciars heard the pleas of the crown, but they did not always prove very efficient. So in 1166, by the Assize of Clarendon, Henry placed the new procedures under the justices in eyre. Once their visitations became regular in the 1170s the whole work of trying cases of serious crime came to depend on the connection established between the king's judges and the local juries. On it, too, depended the maintenance of royal rights, about which the jurors had also to answer a whole series of questions. What lands, for example, should be in the king's hands through wardship or escheat? All this was crown plea business. The questions (known as the 'Articles of the Eyre') grew in size from one visitation to the next and came to embrace the malpractices of local officials, both royal and baronial. The eyre thus became a powerful weapon in the king's battle to maintain his authority in the localities.

Although much is obscure about how Henry's measures worked in practice, they do seem to have brought about significant changes. The ordeal, instead of being a procedure of last resort, now appears to have replaced other customary methods of arriving at guilt or innocence, such as attempts to establish the facts, and where these were unclear, the swearing of oaths. The usual punishment, however, remained death by hanging. The ordeal might be either by hot iron or by water, in both the idea being that it was God who gave the verdict. In the ordeal by water, those accused were bound and lowered into a pit full of water. If they sank they were innocent, and if they floated, guilty, in the one case being in effect embraced by God and in the other rejected. The procedures were presided over by the ecclesiastical authorities. It was when they were forbidden to participate by the Fourth Lateran Council in 1215 that the ordeal was replaced by trial by jury. Up to that point there was a curious contrast between the rationality of the new procedures for civil litigation introduced by Henry, and the irrationality of the criminal. As for the methods of accusation, the generalization of the juries of presentment seems to have ended prosecution by sheriffs and local justiciars, but prosecution by individuals continued (as intended). Whether in fact the maintenance of law and order was better served by all these measures is unknowable. Statistics from the thirteenth century (see below, p. 483) are not encouraging. What is certain is that the eyres began to raise large sums of money for the king: by the 1240s the proceeds of a nationwide visitation amounted to over £20,000, with judges sending back regular reports about how much they were making. Two-thirds of the proceeds from an eyre came from the crown plea business – from amercements imposed on the juries of presentment for such things as concealment and false presentation, from the *murdrum* fine paid by the hundred (see above, p. 102), and from the chattels of convicted or outlawed criminals, individually small (since most criminals were poor) but collectively lucrative. The kings had long been entitled to the chattels forfeited through crown pleas, but in 1166 Henry made a point of stressing that they were his and subsequently took measures to ensure that he got them.

Financially oppressive, the crown pleas side of the eyre was highly unpopular. The civil side was different, and it was there that the really great leap forward took place. What made the eyres of Henry II decisively different from those of Henry I was that they heard civil pleas on an altogether novel scale. This was thanks to a series of new legal procedures called assizes which brought such pleas before them. These new procedures lay at the heart of the common law. The most important of these new assizes were *mort d'ancestor*: a remedy for a freeman denied succession to his inheritance; and novel disseisin: a remedy for a freeman disseised (that is, dispossessed) of property unjustly and without judgement. Neither of these assizes were concerned (at least in the first instance) with questions of ultimate right to land. Novel disseisin turned on whether the plaintiff had been dispossessed without judgement of a court, not whether he had any right to the property in the first place. This greater question of right was decided by another new procedure, that of the grand assize. (*Mort d'ancestor*, novel disseisin and other similar procedures were called, in contrast, the petty assizes.) *Mort d'ancestor* was introduced in 1176 and the grand assize in 1179. Novel disseisin in its final form may well have come some years later. The key point is that all these assizes were well established by the end of the reign, when their workings were explained by *Glanvill*.

Grand assize was a complex procedure. The petty assizes, by contrast, all ran on straightforward and very similar lines. In novel disseisin, for example, the plaintiff, having suffered disseisin, went or sent a messenger to the king and obtained from the chancery the writ which initiated the action. If the king was overseas, this would be issued by the chief justiciar. The writ was addressed to the sheriff and ordered him to bring a jury of twelve free and law-worthy men before the king's justices on their next visitation to say, having viewed the land, whether the plaintiff had indeed been disseised unjustly and without judgement. The sheriff also returned the writ itself to the justices (hence it was a 'returnable writ') so that they could see, by reading it, what the case was about. On the appointed day the jurors gave their verdict, and if it was for the plaintiff the judges gave judgement in his favour and issued a writ in the king's name ordering the sheriff to put him back in seisin. They also, at least in later practice, awarded damages.

There were, of course, problems here. Sheriffs might be inefficient and juries corrupt. Obtaining the originating writ was clearly more expensive, in terms of time and money, the further one lived from the king's or justiciar's usual itinerary in the south. Yet the new procedures were entirely voluntary. That people throughout the country came to use them in such growing numbers shows how valuable they were. The procedures dealt with issues that were central to a society based on land and over whose possession there was so much dispute. The politics of Stephen's reign had seemed nothing but a universal dispute over seisin and inheritance. Now there was an alternative to the round of violence which might be triggered by self-help. This implies the new legal procedures were significantly better than the old and, with due allowance for lack of evidence, this was indeed the case. Their distinctive features were as follows:

1. There had always been legal actions over disseisin and inheritance, but each of the new actions dealt with a clear and distinctive problem, defined by the question to the jury. Has A disseised B unjustly and without judgement? Did A die possessed of the property 'in fee' and is B his nearest heir? It was thus evident to plaintiffs what the actions were about and which one suited their needs. It was equally clear to juries what they had to decide.

2. There was a new emphasis on speed in reaching a verdict, an emphasis which in *Glanvill*'s account of them ran explicitly through all the assizes, reaching a climax in novel disseisin where the defendant

was not allowed a single essoin, that is excuse for non-attendance, and the jury gave its verdict whether or not he appeared.

3. The verdict was by a jury, the rationality of which *Glanvill* specifically contrasted with trial by battle, the means by which such cases had sometimes been decided in the past.

4. The cases came before the king's judges, as opposed to the county court or the honourial court of a lord, a key advantage if the lord himself had committed the disseisin or had kept the plaintiff out of his inheritance. The king's judges, moreover, now had a far more important role than in the past. Under Henry I those on eyre had merely presided over civil cases, with judgements being given by suitors to, that is those attending, the county courts. Under Henry II the judges gave the judgements themselves after receiving the verdict from the jury. It was the new assizes, excluding the county suitors and relying on the verdict of a small jury selected by the sheriff, which opened up this role. The uniformity of the assizes also invited the judges to formulate standard rules of procedure (*Glanvill* is full of them), which did much to create the common law, something impossible in the past because of the multiplicity of procedures followed by the county courts.

5. Before the new assizes kings from Anglo-Saxon times had issued writs commissioning juries to hear civil cases. But they did so *ad hoc* as acts of favour, perhaps sometimes in return for large sums of money. Now the writs which originated the new assizes were issued routinely and at low prices. Quite probably the 6*d.* per writ, for which there is later evidence, was the usual fee from the start. With a day's wage for a labourer about a penny, that was a sum within the reach of the humblest freeman. More than anything else it was the low cost and routine issue of the writs (called writs *de cursu*, 'of course') which made possible the great expansion in royal justice.

Writs, sheriffs, juries deciding civil actions, and the concepts of seisin, inheritance and right had all existed long before Henry II. Henry I had been determined to supervise the jurisdiction of private courts and, if necessary remove cases from them (see above, p. 157). But hard creative thinking was needed to put all this together to form procedures of such supreme utility. The idea of 'utility' indeed ran throughout Henry II's administration. As the author of the *Dialogue* put it, he wrote of things not theoretical but useful (*non subtilia sed utilia*). Likewise *Glanvill* when discussing the grand assize declared that the judges should always strive to make it 'more useful and equitable' (*utilius et equius*). Utility and equity were closely linked and lay behind many key features of the assizes, including the numerous rules governing procedure and the way judges, on eyre and at the exchequer, were by the end of the reign recording the cases they heard on rolls, the beginnings of the plea rolls.

Essential to the running of Henry's system of law were his judges and in particular a core group of under twenty who served either on several eyres or for long periods at the exchequer, sometimes both. It was these men who must have done the thinking which made the developments possible. Roughly half were clerks and three were university masters. Certainly the development of law under Henry II, like the Becket dispute, is incomprehensible outside the wider developments of European learning. Knowledge of Roman law both sharpened the distinction between right and seisin and provided *Glanvill* with his categories of criminal and civil pleas. The new learning was apparent in the whole drive to categorize and record seen in the writing of *Glanvill* and the introduction of the plea rolls. To this academic knowledge was joined a wealth of practical experience brought by the lay contingent among the judges. Ranulf Glanvill's father was a Suffolk knight who had spent long years attending the local courts. Glanvill himself had held several sheriffdoms (and captured the king of Scots in 1174) before moving to the higher reaches of the royal service and ultimately the justiciarship.

Henry II himself, according to Ralph of Diss, took immense care over the selection of his judges. He may well have participated in their discussions about the new civil procedures. He also showed great skill in settling difficult lawsuits (according to Walter Map), discussed the precise wording of charters with his ministers and devised formulas to get round legal problems. His general concern for peace and justice drove on the developments in both criminal and civil law. According to William of Newburgh, he was 'extremely studious' and a 'fitting minister of God' in punishing malefactors and preserving the public peace. Ralph of Diss saw him as 'the father of the English', 'more and more solicitous of the common health' and 'most intent on exhibiting justice to everybody', precisely what the new assizes did. Well might *Glanvill* describe the grand assize as a 'royal benefit granted to the people'. Henry was certainly well aware that justice was profitable, but that was not a major motive behind the assizes. The small individual sums paid for the writs went to the chancellor; the value of the amercements was significant but not overwhelming.

The assizes did, however, help to enhance royal authority, chiming exactly with Henry's determination, much like his grandfather's to maintain a direct relationship with under-tenants, and assert his authority over private courts and jurisdictions. If a dispute over seisin or inheritance was between tenants of the same lord, or between a tenant and his lord, then the new procedures opened up the king's court for the under-tenants involved, taking the case out of the honourial court of their lords. The king also developed a direct relationship with the under-tenants by using them to staff the juries on which the new procedures depended. Though certainly welcoming the gradual flow of business into his courts, Henry's aim was less to subvert than supervise private jurisdiction. If the action of novel disseisin was aimed particularly at lords who had been disseising their tenants, the implication was that the latter should secure judgements in their courts before doing so. It was likewise to monitor rather than undermine that the legal rule described in *Glanvill* was established, namely that anyone wishing to bring a property action in the court of a lord had to commence his case with a writ from the king, the 'writ of right' ordering the lord to do justice in the case, and declaring that the king would, if he failed to do so.

Glanvill resonates with pride at the procedures it describes, yet it can scarcely have anticipated the sheer scale of their success. On the Wiltshire eyre of 1194, the first eyre for which records survive, there were fourteen actions of novel disseisin and fourteen of *mort d'ancestor*. On the eyre of 1249 there were respectively 105 and 109. And there would have been similar increases in every county. These procedures had proved immensely popular, and they had come to be surrounded by many others which worked on similar lines. As *Glanvill* remarked, 'it is easy to formulate writs to deal with different matters', thus pointing the way forward for the whole future of the common law. That law came to be viewed increasingly as a series of separate procedures each originated by its own 'original' writ. By the time of *Glanvill* there were already fifteen such writs. By 1272 there were over sixty-five.

Absolutely central to the success and significance of the procedures was the range of their appeal, an appeal essentially to sections of society beneath the baronage. The litigants came from the county gentry, from the kind of middling under-tenants who staffed the hundred juries (see below, p. 411), and from the free peasantry. The amounts of land involved were often very small: 60 per cent of identifiable properties in cases on the 1240 Suffolk eyre were under ten acres in extent. More than anything else, the growing number of litigants using royal procedures before royal judges widened the scope, enhanced the utility and ensured the future of royal government. Magna Carta in 1215 condemned much of what Angevin kingship had done, but welcomed the petty assizes of Henry II.

Whatever Henry's intentions, in the long term the effect of the assizes was certainly to weaken a baron's control over his tenants. Although as early as the reign of Henry I the latter had sometimes challenged and escaped the jurisdiction of the honourial court, they could now do so much more easily. *Mort d'ancestor* did not create hereditary succession for under-tenants (many fees had been hereditary since their creation after the Conquest), but it certainly made it more difficult for lords to deny it. Likewise, novel disseisin made lords less ready to discipline their tenants by seizing their land (having to go through a tedious court process or face novel disseisin). The earl of Warwick when he disseised one tenant, Richard of Claverdon, for default of service did take the precaution of getting a judgement of his court first, but Richard still brought and won an action of novel disseisin against him before the eyre at Coventry in 1221, and the earl was amerced £27. That lords resented the interference is shown by the clause in Magna Carta which prevented cases being removed from their courts by the use of a particular writ, *praecipe*. Yet 'feudal' jurisdiction was still important in the thirteenth century, and continued to stand with other pillars of baronial power. (For further discussion, see below, pp. 403-10.) In Henry's reign and those of his sons, what seemed more serious for the barons (or at least those out of favour) was that, when litigating against each other, they were excluded from the benefits of the cheap, regular, standard-form litigation offered by the assizes. This was because as tenants-in-chief they were subject directly to the jurisdiction of the king and had to litigate in his presence. While judgement ought ultimately to be by their 'peers', that is their social equals and thus their fellow barons, there were all kinds of traps the king could spring before a case got that far. This helps to explain a paradox in Henry's reputation. On the one hand he was praised by contemporaries for his zeal for justice, on the other condemned for the way he delayed and sold it. The contrast is between the routine cases involving unimportant men covered by the great bulk of the assizes, and those between great men where 'justice' was really a branch of patronage and where it might indeed be sold or (for good prudential reasons) delayed or denied; hence the way Henry dealt with the disputes arising from Stephen's reign, favouring some barons, disfavouring others. Henry's successors acted in a similar fashion, and were ultimately brought to book by Magna Carta.

If the baronage were prevented from using the new procedures, at least when litigating against each other, so were a proportion of the peasantry. Indeed it was worse than that. One result of the measures was decisively to depress a section of the peasantry's legal status. The rigid dividing line between the free and the unfree (discussed above, p. 53) was very much the product of the new assizes, because the king's judges decided to prevent peasants who performed labour services from using those assizes against their lords. To do so they deemed such men unfree villeins and laid down that the new procedures were only open to the free. For all matters connected with their land and services (though not their lives and limbs) unfree peasants were now legally subject to the jurisdiction of their lords. Intentionally or not, the latter had received a *quid pro quo* for the new assizes being open to their free tenants. For a significant proportion of the population, the common law was not common at all.

This was not something that bothered contemporary commentators on the legal system. Indeed it seemed absolutely right. So did the fact that women, even when free and noble, were certainly not equal under the law (see below, pp. 416–17). In the thirteenth century contemporaries spoke increasingly and without apology of 'the common law', by which they meant the legal procedures common to the whole kingdom both in terms of their form and their general applicability. These 'general' laws and customs of the king's court were the avowed subject of *Glanvill*, not the procedures of other courts (county, hundred and private) for these were, as *Glanvill* said, simply too numerous to write down. The foundations for the common law had been laid in both the Anglo-Saxon period, with the royal monopoly over cases of crime, and in Anglo-Norman times, with the beginnings of the eyre and the general customs of feudal tenure. But it was under Henry II that the structure really came into being.

*　　*　　*

Henry loved his sons and quickly forgave their rebellion. He still wanted, as Ralph of Diss observed, to make them 'lords of great nations' whose peoples they would govern 'with moderation', terrorizing tyrants and destroying enemies. Richard was restored to Aquitaine where he suppressed local revolts, in the process performing extraordinary feats of arms. In Brittany, Geoffrey (after he at last married Constance in 1181) enjoyed considerable independence and presided over important administrative reforms. The Young King went on a joyous round of tournaments and was praised by Henry for his exploits. He was also involved in the government of England and (in 1177) helped make good his father's claims to the great castle of Châteauroux in Berry. In the late 1170s, when he also made a bid for Angoulême, Henry seemed as assertive as ever. As he told the Young King, he had lost nothing of his rights when he ruled alone, and it would be shameful to lose them now when he had sons to rule with him.

Yet in the last decade of his life Henry mellowed. He declared he would no longer appoint prelates for other than spiritual reasons, and made the saintly and courageous Carthusian, Hugh of Avalon, bishop of Lincoln. According to William of Newburgh, he became increasingly sick of war and anxious not to stir it up. Yet peace he did not have. In 1183 friction between himself and the Young King and between the latter and Richard exploded in a violent conflict which was ended only by the Young King's sudden death on 11 June 1183. The death of Geoffrey in 1186, leaving an infant child, Arthur, by his wife Constance as heir to Brittany, meant that of Henry's sons only Richard and John survived. Richard now wanted to be recognized as heir to England, Normandy and Anjou, but Henry, after his experiences with the Young King, would not indulge him – or not unless Richard surrendered Aquitaine to John, which he utterly refused to do.

These problems might have been contained had it not been for the involvement of the king of France. Here Henry found himself faced with a new and dangerous antagonist. Louis VII had died in 1180 and been succeeded by his fifteen-year-old son Philip, one day to be called Augustus. Philip was wily, unscrupulous, and unwaveringly clear about his main objective: to increase his power and diminish that of Henry II and his successors. In the short term he wished to defeat Henry II's challenge in Berry and to recover Gisors and the Norman Vexin. Ultimately, in a reign which lasted until 1223, he was to destroy the Angevin empire altogether. Philip naturally sought to weaken Henry by championing Richard's demands, demands given an added impetus by a new factor which was soon to transform European politics. This was the overwhelming imperative of the crusade.

Henry II's attitude to the crusade had been sympathetic but non-participatory. He sent considerable sums of money to the Holy Land but refused to go there in person, even in 1185 when he was urged to do so by the patriarch of Jerusalem. Two years later these hesitations were swept away by Saladin's crushing victory at the battle of Hattin (3 July 1187) and his capture that October of Jerusalem itself. Henry took the cross, as did Richard and King Philip. Richard, however, was determined to have the succession settled before his departure. When it was not, he defied his father and formally threw in his lot with Philip, who in November 1188 recognized him as heir to the Angevin dominions. In May 1189 the two of them drove Henry from Le Mans (his birthplace) and early in July forced him to agree a humiliating settlement. Henry cursed the traitors who had deserted him (they now included John) and vowed revenge. But the poison from an ulcer was gradually spreading through his body. He retreated to Chinon and died there on 6 July. A few days later he was taken down the river Vienne for burial by the nuns at Fontevraud.

Clerical writers found it easy to explain Henry's tragic end. It was surely God's punishment for his persecution of Becket and his initial refusal to join the crusade. Other groups had their own grievances: peasants excluded from the common law; magnates denied justice (or what they thought was justice); the numerous victims of the forest law. Yet chroniclers like Ralph of Diss, William of Newburgh and Ralph of Coggeshall also expressed immense admiration for the king. Again and again Diss pictured him returning to England having secured peace throughout his dominions, dominions which stretched from the mountains of the Pyrenees to the Breton ocean and from there to the borders of France. 'The whole of human fate seemed to respond to the nod of the king.' Here also was a king with a real sense of care for his kingdom, who had restored its mutilated frontiers, recovered the rights of the crown, restored peace and order and built the common law. His successor was to be very different.

8

Richard the Lionheart, 1189–99, and William the Lion

King Richard I, conqueror of Cyprus, crusader extraordinary (the sobriquet 'Lionheart' was contemporary), spent less than six months of his ten-year reign in England. Yet his crusade and his subsequent wars with the king of France which explain that absence placed the kingdom under novel pressures, which culminated under King John with the rebellion of 1215 and Magna Carta. Richard's reign was equally consequential for the dynasty's wider dominions. Normandy's defences were significantly undermined, foreshadowing its ultimate loss to the king of France in 1204. Scotland, under King William, recovered its independence. William's own sobriquet, 'the Lion', was not contemporary, but it was deserved.

At turns affable and intimidating, depending on his audience, Richard was domineering in the council chamber and supreme in the field of war. A master of logistics, strategy and battlefield tactics, he led from the front, aware of the risks but also of the valuable example. Outside Gisors in 1198, against all advice, he plunged into the fray, unhorsed three knights with a single lance, and then publicized the exploit throughout his dominions. Here then was a 'great and fierce character', as William of Newburgh put it, and he had as his helper an 'incomparable woman', to quote Richard of Devizes, namely the queen mother, Eleanor of Aquitaine. Before his arrival in England, Richard had already sent letters ordering her release from captivity; and although in her mid sixties, instead of retiring to Poitou she had gone on a progress, opening the prisons and receiving oaths of allegiance to her son and herself. Assigned an extensive dower, some of it (like Exeter) traditionally associated with queens, Eleanor was now to play a central role in the diplomacy, politics and government of the Angevin empire, acting at times as virtual regent in England. Although she interceded for John, her youngest son, she was utterly loyal to Richard on whose authority, formal and informal, her power depended.

Richard's accession brought a temporary halt to the conflict with King Philip. The two agreed to crusade together and Richard succeeded to the Angevin dominions without difficulty. On 13 August 1189 he landed in England. On 3 September he was crowned. On 11 December he departed. Throughout the three months, preparations for the crusade overshadowed everything else. For Richard the Mediterranean hardly seemed remote. His sister had married the king of Sicily. The descendants of his great-grandfather, Fulk of Anjou, had been kings of Jerusalem. For someone often prey to a morbid sense of his own sinfulness, the spiritual benefits of the crusade, with the promise of remission of all sins, were compelling. So was the chance to exercise martial talents, as St Bernard had so often said, not against fellow Christians but against the infidels, and at a time when the issue was the very survival of the crusader state and the recovery of Jerusalem itself. (For further discussion of crusading see below, pp. 455–9.)

Richard's commitment to the cause of Christ won him immense respect, nor was he heedless of the security of his dominions. In 1190, before his departure, he toured Aquitaine and protected its southern boundaries by arranging to marry Berengaria, daughter of the king of Navarre. Likewise he took steps to keep in check both King William of Scotland and the Welsh rulers. The five ministers on England's regency council were trustworthy and experienced. Richard secured the loyalty of one of them, William Marshal, by marrying him to the daughter of Richard fitz Gilbert (Strongbow) thus making him a great baron in Ireland, Wales and Normandy. Richard's overriding aim, however, was to gain the resources for his crusade. In England he received money for making men sheriffs and for conceding to heirs and claimants a wide range of lands which Henry II held in hand through wardships and forfeitures. The results were spectacular. The revenue recorded in the pipe roll of 1190 was £31,000, £10,000 more than in 1188. Yet there was also a cost. At the very top of the government Richard's arrangements were shambolic, for the new justiciar, Hugh de Puiset, bishop of Durham, who had been appointed not from 'zeal for justice' but simply for the money he offered, clashed repeatedly with William Longchamp, bishop of Ely, Richard's chancellor and protégé. Instability was also inherent in the extraordinary favours Richard bestowed on his younger brother John, who now demanded recognition as heir to the Angevin dominions. This Richard refused to concede, but he tried to kill discontent with kindness. John was already lord of Ireland and count of Mortain. Richard now married him to Isabella, whose inheritance included the earldom of Gloucester and lordship of Glamorgan. The union had long been planned by Henry II, but it is difficult to believe that Henry would have given John in addition six castles and total control of seven English counties, counties which now simply disappeared from the pipe rolls, the chief records of the exchequer.

William of Newburgh criticized Richard for dismembering his kingdom, and showing a lack of care for its subjects, criticism which shows just how powerful the Henrician model of good kingship had become. Roger of Howden remarked testily how 'everything was for sale, counties, sheriffdoms, castles and manors'. Yet when daring councillors objected that Richard was alienating the possessions of the crown, the king merely laughed, declaring, 'I would sell London if I could find a buyer.' He saw nothing permanent about the concessions and resumed many of them on his return in 1194. In any case, his agenda and situation were different from his father's. Richard was used to the decentralized form of rule in Aquitaine. The kingdom he inherited was wealthy and at peace. Instead of labouring to restore royal rights he could happily give them away to please John and fund the crusade. That crusade moreover was in many ways a triumphant success. 'Many famous and magnificent deeds were done by him in those parts, so that he triumphed in every conflict and freed the greater part of that land from the enemies of Christ.' So said Abbot Ralph of Coggeshall, succinctly summing up the achievement.

Richard arrived in Sicily, on his way to Palestine, in September 1190. He immediately plunged into a quarrel over the dower of his sister Joan, widow of the last Norman king of Sicily, seizing the city of Messina in the process. Then, as part of the settlement, he recognized his nephew Arthur, son of Geoffrey of Brittany, as his heir and agreed he should marry the daughter of Tancred, the new Sicilian ruler. Richard knew this would grievously offend John back home but the funds and support which the agreement gained for the crusade seemed far more important. Having wintered in Sicily, Richard sailed for the east on 10 April 1191. By the end of May he had conquered Cyprus, thus securing a valuable base to support the crusade. On 8 June he joined King Philip at the siege of Acre, before its capture by Saladin the greatest city and port of the old crusading kingdom. He drove the siege forward with a new vigour and on 12 July the city surrendered. Early in August King Philip returned to France to make good his rights to Artois following the count of Flanders's death. Richard knew that Philip might threaten his continental dominions, but he had no intention of returning himself, a telling illustration of the two kings' different priorities. In any case Richard with Philip had always been, as Richard of Devizes put it, like a cat with a hammer tied to its tail.

In the year and two months in which he remained in the east, Richard twice advanced to within twelve miles of Jerusalem, only to retreat because he lacked resources for a lengthy siege. However, he extended the crusading kingdom southwards, notably by taking and fortifying Jaffa, so doing much to ensure the kingdom's survival for another hundred years. He also established his nephew, Henry of Champagne, as ruler in Jerusalem and compensated a rival candidate, Guy de Lusignan, with the gift of Cyprus, which the Lusignans were to rule till 1489. Truly no king of England had ever wielded such power on the European stage. His atrocities and exploits became the stuff of legend: the beheading of some 3,000 prisoners taken at Acre; his decisive charge at the battle of Arsuf; his jumping into the sea and leading his knights ashore to rescue Jaffa; and the silver shackles which he made for the ruler of Cyprus, thus fulfilling his promise not to put him in irons!

Richard sailed from Acre on 9 October 1191. The plots of John and King Philip made his swift return essential. But the journey was a disaster. Weather in the Mediterranean, the enemies along its shores, forced him to travel in disguise through Austria. Outside Vienna on 20 December he was taken prisoner, eventually passing in March 1192 into the hands of the Emperor Henry VI. Henry, a claimant to Sicily through his wife, was trying to wrest the kingdom from Tancred, Richard's ally. For Richard's release he demanded a ransom of £100,000, money he would use to conquer Sicily.

While Richard had been away, his government in England had proved incapable of keeping the peace. The principal victims were the Jews who suffered in 1190 a series of horrific attacks on their lives and properties.

Henry II's sponsorship of the Jews, declared William of Newburgh, had disfigured his rule, here expressing a general opinion made all the sharper by the crusading fervour. There was envy of Jewish wealth, ostentatiously displayed in great townhouses, and while men needed their credit, they loathed the usury which necessarily went with it.

Usury took several forms, all of them having been practised equally by Christian financiers like William Cade. The interest rate might be one or two pence a pound per week, that is 22 per cent or 44 per cent per annum. It could run from the moment the loan was contracted or, as a kind of penalty clause (this more acceptable to the church), from the moment repayment was due. Most loans were short-term and became due after a year. The loans were often secured on land, with the result that a great deal of it came into Jewish hands. Alternatively, those unable to pay often raised the money by selling land to fellow Christians, even to the point of ruin. Most of the loans were of small amounts to men of small estate. But the bulk of the money (and thus the greatest profit) was tied up in significant sums from tens to hundreds of pounds loaned to the great, loaned that is to knights, barons and ecclesiastical institutions; precisely the classes most able to make their resentment felt.

Religious intolerance gave an extra edge to this resentment. The Jews were not merely infidels. They were also the murderers of Christ. The Third Lateran Council in 1179 stressed the dangers of spiritual contamination through contact with them. Throughout Europe violent assaults on Jewish communities were on the increase – at Blois, for example, in May 1171. But it was in England that the powerful and pernicious belief originated that the Jews ritually parodied the murder of Christ by seizing and crucifying small Christian boys; the source of the belief was the alleged murder of a boy, 'little St William', at Norwich in 1144, after which there were further 'martyrdoms' at Gloucester (1168), Bury St Edmunds (1181) and Bristol (1183). On top of all this was the growing fervour over the crusade. By despoiling the Jews, those who had taken the cross could both fund their expeditions and make an early start assaulting the infidel.

By 1189 these waves of antipathy were held back only by the stout banks of Henrician power. Under Richard they gave way. On the day of the coronation the city mob and those gathered in town for the ceremony slaughtered London Jews and plundered and fired their properties. Richard was furious but his punishments for once were inadequate. Next year, with both Justiciar Puiset and Chancellor Longchamp across the Channel, similar outrages occurred at King's Lynn, Norwich, Bury St Edmunds, Stamford and Lincoln. The climax was reached at York. The Jewish community there had been established in the 1170s. By 1189 it numbered around 150 men, women and children and was dominated by two great financiers, Benedict and Josce (the former fatally wounded on the day of the coronation), whose great houses were a source of wonder and envy. There was also a celebrated Jewish scholar, Rabbi Yomtob of Joigny.

The Christian assailants, whose background and circumstances were well analysed by William of Newburgh, were led by local barons and knights heavily in debt to the Jews, often with their lands in pledge. They were joined by crusaders looking for plunder, a fanatical Premonstratensian hermit, and clergy, youths and workmen from the town; the city magnates stood aside, fearing royal reprisal. After the initial attack on their houses, the Jews found safety in the castle, only then to shut out the castellan, not surprisingly since he was Richard Malebisse, a northern baron who was himself heavily in debt. Malebisse mounted an all-out siege and by 16 March, the eve of the Jewish 'great Sabbath', the position in the castle was hopeless. Rabbi Yomtob persuaded his fellows to follow the course sanctioned by long precedent. Fathers cut the throats of their wives and children; Rabbi Yomtob cut the throats of the men, concluding with Josce's and his own. A dissident group, who hoped to live by embracing Christianity, were slaughtered by the Christians as they surrendered. The murderers, combining barbarity with business, then proceeded to the minster where they destroyed the evidence of their indebtedness by burning all the 'bonds', the written records of Jewish loans, which were deposited there.

The massacre sent shock waves through the Jewish communities of Europe and inspired at least three Hebrew elegies. In May 1190 Chancellor Longchamp descended on York to restore order. If he inflicted no corporal penalties, he certainly confiscated the lands of murderers and imposed substantial fines. The Jews eventually returned to the city and formed one of the wealthiest English communities in the thirteenth century. For the Jews as a whole the events of 1189–90 proved but a temporary setback. Attitudes to them were far less immutable than those events implied. Admittedly even the humane and judicious William of Newburgh considered the attacks, at least on property, a judgement of God on the Jews' burgeoning pride. Yet the attackers too, covetous and unauthorized, were evil. Their actual slaughter of the Jews seemed forbidden by the Psalmist: 'Slay them not lest my people forget', a passage made famous by St Bernard which was also quoted by Ralph of Diss in connection with the killings. The Jews, in short, were to be preserved as a reminder of Christ's passion, and also as material for conversion to Christianity. If they were also to live humbly and apart, that was never compatible with their credit activities which continued to be desperately needed. In practice Jews often established reasonable working relationships both with their clients and their neighbours, hence their ability to store bonds in York Minster.

Above all, the Jews survived and flourished because they were generally protected and promoted by the king. The Jews and all their possessions had always belonged to the crown. As Henry II came to realize, the king could levy tax or 'tallage', as it was called, on them at will. Between 1186 and 1194 the total demanded was well over £13,333. The king could also extract money on the death of a Jew for allowing the family to succeed to his property, which was mostly composed of the portfolio of debts. Alternatively, as was done with Aaron of Lincoln, the king could retain the property in his own hands and collect the debts for himself, which meant that numerous Christians ended up making their repayments to the king. The king could also impose large financial penalties for a range of often trumped-up offences. In 1130 the London Jews owed £2,000 for allegedly murdering a sick man. The greater the exploitation, the greater too the pressure on the Christian debtors, so the king was sailing here in dangerous waters politically. But the profits were large and the king had every reason to protect their source. For this reason, a royal castle was always the resort of Jews in time of trouble. It was security as much as business which tied them to the towns.

In the aftermath of the events of 1189–90 the government developed new institutions and procedures both for exploiting and protecting the Jews. A group of officials had been appointed to deal with the numerous debts seized by the king on the death of Aaron of Lincoln. In the 1190s, described formally as 'the justices of the Jews', they and their successors took on a wider role. Sitting with Jews appointed by the king (the chief was called the 'arch-priest') they were responsible for collecting Jewish taxation and the debts owed by Christians which had come into the king's hands. They also ordered the sheriffs to help Jews collect their debts, and provided a less prejudiced forum for Jewish litigation against Christians than that offered by local courts. Essentially a sub-branch of the main exchequer, in the thirteenth century this body became called 'the exchequer of the Jews'. In 1194 the whole process of Jewish money-lending in the localities was also regulated, in part to prevent the kind of destruction of records which had taken place in 1190.

Henceforth the contracting of loans and their repayment was to be confined to six or seven main towns under the oversight of two Christians, two Jews and clerks of the central justices. Each town was to have a chest (an *archa*) where a copy of the bond recording the loan was to be deposited, the other copy being kept by the Jew. All the bonds and repayments were also recorded on separate rolls. These arrangements, with some modifications (the number of towns was soon increased to seventeen), survived until the expulsion of the Jews in 1290.

The Jews had been in the eye of a more general storm stirred up by Richard's absence and arrangements. Having sought to placate John by giving him great power, he had then provoked him by promising the succession to Arthur. It was William Longchamp who had to pick up the pieces. Having finally supplanted Puiset in June 1190 he was now justiciar as well as chancellor. He had also secured a legatine commission from the pope. Longchamp was quick-witted, courageous and completely loyal to Richard. He was also an experienced and innovative administrator. It was he who introduced for the first time to charters and writs a concluding clause, party modelled on papal practice, which gave their date of issue. (Before that only the place of issue had been included.) But Longchamp imitated his master's arrogance and was soon widely stigmatized as a misshapen little monkey of a man, who came from Norman peasant stock and despised English customs – an early sign of national feeling! A virtual civil war in the summer of 1191, when Lincoln castle was defended by its Amazonian lady castellan Nicola de la Haye, was concluded by an agreement between John and the government which read like a treaty between two independent states. Then in September Longchamp arrested Geoffrey, archbishop of York (Henry II's illegitimate son), and was ousted in the ensuing outcry. John was recognized as Richard's heir. The government was taken over by an acceptable Norman, Walter, archbishop of Rouen, a change Richard himself had sanctioned back in February on hearing news of Longchamp's performance.

King Philip's return to France at the end of 1191 brought fresh strains. He had left as Richard's friend and he came back as his enemy. The immediate reason centred on his sister Alice. She had long been intended as Richard's bride and to that end had been brought up at the Angevin court. Philip indeed had agreed to resign his claims to Gisors and the Norman Vexin to their heirs. Henry II, however, had refused to allow the marriage to go ahead. Now it could. Yet Richard married Berengaria instead. There were strategic reasons for that marriage, but they only operated once Alice had been rejected, rejected because she had been Henry II's mistress. Queen Eleanor was so opposed to the match that she herself brought Berengaria out to Richard at Messina. For all the proffered compensation, Philip remained bitterly offended. On Richard's capture in December 1192 he offered Alice to John (whose wife could be divorced) and took his homage for all the continental lands. John falsely proclaimed that Richard was dead and demanded recognition as king of England.

In England, Queen Eleanor held the line. It was in Normandy that the real damage was done, partly because the English government, debilitated by John's endowment and the great sale at the start of the reign, was unable to give its customary help, revenue having fallen back to an annual £11,000 – much the same as at the start of Henry II's reign. In April 1193 Gisors, which Richard had carelessly promised to Philip if he himself died without heirs, was surrendered. 'That famous and mighty castle', as Gerald of Wales put it, with its 700 metres of perimeter walls (the longest in Normandy) and its great motte topped by Henry II's state of the art octagonal keep, visible for miles as a symbol of Angevin power, had guarded the vital frontier defences along the river Epte. Philip could now consolidate his hold over much of Normandy.

In these dire circumstances Richard's release was absolutely imperative. With England making a large though unknown contribution, enough of the £100,000 demanded was raised to secure Richard's freedom on 4 February 1194. 'The devil is unchained,' King Philip warned John. On 14 March the devil landed in England and extinguished the remains of the revolt. Soon afterwards, thanks to Eleanor's intervention, Richard restored John to favour. The condescending attitude to his kid brother ('not a man to win a kingdom') which had governed his policy all along had proved justified, in England at least. The situation in Normandy was not so easily restored.

*   *   *

On the death of Henry II, the Lord Rhys went to war. Richard took notice. After his coronation, he journeyed to Worcester to receive the homage of the minor rulers of south Wales, and sent John, now through his marriage lord of Glamorgan, to raise Rhys's siege of Carmarthen.

Rhys indeed came under safe-conduct to Oxford only to depart in dudgeon when Richard, either standing on his dignity or pressed for time, would not come to meet him. It did not take much to set Rhys and his sons on the warpath, for they had been prospecting its possibilities in the last years of the old king. Rhys now secured both St Clears and Kidwelly on either side of the Tywi, thus cutting off Carmarthen from the sea, and in 1192 moved east and besieged Swansea. His sons, however, were grievously at odds. The intended succession of Gruffudd, the eldest, strong in Ystrad Tywi and usually supported by Rhys Gryg, was challenged by the impulsive and charismatic Maelgwn, 'the man in the world [Gruffudd] most hated' (as the *Brut* put it), who was based in Ceredigion and had the backing of another brother, Hywel Sais. In 1189 Rhys imprisoned Maelgwn, only (in 1194) to be imprisoned by him. Disputes between the brothers broke up the siege of Swansea in 1192. At least there was no blood-letting, but all this contrasted with the co-operation between Rhys and his brothers in the Deheubarth of the 1140s and 1150s.

Rhys also met violent resistance from William de Braose, Gruffudd's father-in-law, who was the royal castellan at Carmarthen and Swansea. In 1191 William took possession of Elfael, the region north of the Wye valley, linking up his own lordships of Radnor, Builth and Brecon. In 1195 he followed this up by taking St Clears, Rhys having already lost Kidwelly. But Rhys was not finished. In 1196 he burnt Carmarthen, and then marched on Elfael where he briefly secured the new Braose fortress at Painscastle – its heroic defence by William's formidable wife Matilda de St-Valéry (later starved to death by King John) led to the English calling the castle thereafter 'Castle Matilda'. Rhys died next year. His magnificent successes had depended on knowing when to co-operate with the English government, and when to exploit its weakness. His son Gruffudd tried to follow in his footsteps, hurrying to seek recognition from Richard's deputies. But he soon found himself ousted by his brother Maelgwn. The continuing quarrels between Rhys's descendants effectively ended Deheubarth's greatness.

With Gwynedd also divided, Gwenwynwyn, ruler of southern Powys (Powys Wenwynwyn, as it came to be called) was able briefly to take centre stage. He supplied the force which enabled Maelgwn to oust Gruffudd from Ceredigion, and in 1198 gathered his Welsh allies to eject William de Braose from Elfael by laying siege to Painscastle. But the situation was now very different from that which existed early in the 1190s. A stable and well-funded government in England was in place under the justiciar Hubert Walter. Gwenwynwyn was utterly defeated and reputedly over 3,000 Welsh were killed. Braose's hold of Elfael was affirmed; Gruffudd, who had helped the English campaign, was restored in Deheubarth (though Maelgwn kept Cardigan); and Gwenwynwyn's dreams of emulating Rhys were shattered for good.

*   *   *

While Rhys waged war on Henry II's death, King William opened negotiations. He was aware that in the great sale in England by far the biggest item in the shop window was a kingdom, the kingdom of Scotland. With Richard in a hurry, a bargain was quickly struck. William gave £6,666 to recover the castles of Berwick and Roxburgh and free his realm from the subjection to England imposed in 1174. No longer would William have to parade as a vassal king at the Angevin court, act as the English monarch's virtual justiciar in Galloway, and stand in danger of forfeiting his kingdom for contumacious conduct. He had freed the realm from 'the heavy yoke of domination and servitude', as the Melrose chronicler later put it.

'But alas the grief, that so great and magnificent an honour should vanish from the English crown for a price not worth naming,' lamented Gerald of Wales. Richard's perspective was different. If he lost a sub-king, he gained money and an ally. During the crisis of 1193–4, King William did not repeat his northern invasion of twenty years before. On the contrary, he contributed to Richard's ransom. He still hoped to recover the northern counties, but by diplomacy rather than by force. In 1194 he peppered Richard with requests and offers and got nowhere. Next year he did better, negotiating a remarkable agreement which might ultimately have brought Northumberland, Cumberland and Westmorland once more within the Scottish realm. For that indeed was what Richard promised if his nephew, Otto of Brunswick, should marry Margaret, William's daughter and heir. Richard thus hoped to instal as king of Scots his protégé Otto, who had grown up at the Angevin court following the exile of his father Henry the Lion, duke of Saxony. The cost would have been dismemberment of the kingdom, but then, as J. C. Holt has remarked, Richard probably viewed the north of England much as he regarded Gascon lordships in the foothills of the Pyrenees.

In fact the marriage never took place and the agreement came to nothing. In 1198 William's son, the future Alexander II, was born. Frustrated if only for the moment (as he hoped) in the south, King William compensated in the north. Here Caithness, with its Norse population and fertile lands adjoining the Pentland Firth, was ruled by Earl Harald Maddadson (1159–1206). He wielded considerable power in Ross, was married to a daughter of Malcolm MacHeth (see above p. 211), and held his earldom of Orkney from the king of Norway. He rarely if ever appeared at the Scottish court: altogether a dangerous man. Constricted by the loss of Shetland in 1195, Harald resented the growing power of the crown and its vassals in Moray and Cromarty. In 1196 he invaded Moray. William responded with three expeditions during 1196 and 1197, destroying Harald's castle at Thurso in the far north of Caithness and replacing him with a rival. The removal was not permanent and in 1202 William, having gone north once again, decided to accept Harald's position as earl in return for a proffered £2,000. But at least he had removed the threat to Moray and asserted some authority over Caithness.

Although troubled in the closing years of his reign down to 1214 by the demands of King John and the resurgence of the MacHeths and MacWilliams (see below p. 277), King William had achieved a remarkable transformation since the débâcle of 1174. He had thrown off English overlordship and expanded his power in the north and west. That success was very much underpinned by the consolidation and development of the governmental and political structure created by King David.

After the recovery of the southern castles in 1185 and 1189, Edinburgh resumed its Davidian place as a pre-eminent royal centre, within an itinerary which continued to revolve around the traditional eastern core of the kingdom. At court, under the chancellor, there was a growing staff of professional clerks (a dozen can be identified over the reign) writing the king's writs and charters which themselves followed the English model. In the 1170s the form king 'by the grace of God', little used in the pevious decade, was permanently adopted. From 1195 dates of issue were included, imitating in part the new practice in England.

William continued the policy of enfeoffing followers with land, usually in return for the service of one or two knights or a serjeant. Forty-one acts of enfeoffment are known, twenty-nine of them north of the Forth, being especially numerous between the Tay and Aberdeen.

The chief beneficiaries, as before, were men of Anglo-Norman descent, as their names show: Giffard, Berkeley, Montfort, Melville, and so on. In this way William secured knight service and castle guard to set beside the foot soldiers of the common army. There was also a development of sheriffdoms so that their putative numbers increased from seventeen to twenty-three during the reign, some reflecting the expansion of royal authority to the north and west. Thus a sheriff appears in Moray in the 1170s, in Galloway in the 1190s, and, around the turn of the century, at Ayr, Nairn and Inverness. There was a growing move to commute the revenue collected by the sheriffs from kind to cash. Cash revenue was also boosted by the foundation of burghs, whose payments to the king were entirely in money. Although the great bulk of the specie was English, William enhanced his prestige and the money supply by minting his own coins, in 1195 introducing a new design based on Henry II's short-cross penny of 1180. Both the growth in the money supply and what William of Newburgh called 'the threat of royal power' were reflected in the ability to raise Richard's £6,666, some of it probably coming from a tax on land, like the geld now abandoned in England.

William also enhanced the king's role in the maintenance of the peace, building on the way David had probably isolated certain major crimes as, in effect, pleas of the crown. In 1197, influenced again by initiatives in England, he ordered everyone in his kingdom to swear to keep the peace. In another measure of unknown date he stipulated that sheriffs should be present in lords' courts to see that justice was done and also by implication to ensure that the crown pleas, specified as murder, rape, plunder and arson be reserved for the court of the king. That court was probably convened by the sheriffs but presided over by justiciars, who travelled their regions to hold pleas. There was one justiciar for Lothian, one for Scotland north of the Forth, and one, at least for a while towards the end of the century, for Galloway. The justiciars also heard civil pleas, partly through the development of the king's appellate jurisdiction which apparently involved the introduction of an equivalent to the English 'writ of right'.

Despite William of Newburgh's comment about the threat of royal power, royal government in Scotland remained much less intrusive and pervasive than in England, and this was true of the 'inner core' sheriffdoms and even more of the 'outer ring' native earldoms and new provincial lordships. There was neither a Scottish exchequer nor any equivalent, as yet, to the common law assizes. A much higher proportion of the sheriffdoms than in England were probably in the hands of magnates. Although William reserved for himself the hearing of crown pleas (or pleas belonging to his 'regality', as he put it) within the Bruce lordship of Annandale, it is far from clear whether that was a general rule, and whether, in any case, it worked in practice. It is unlikely to have applied to the 'outer ring' earldoms, which, as in the past (like the new provincial lordships), seem largely to have been immune from royal visitations, orders and enfeoffments. This lack of pressure was vital in order to retain the loyalty of the new nobility and to sedate the resentments of the old, resentments which fed the MacHeth and MacWilliam risings. Equally important was the continuing accommodation between new and old. Native ecclesiastics acted as ministers and bishops. Patrick of Dunbar and Duncan II of Fife, earls from within the inner core of the kingdom, were important councillors, both acting as justiciars. The Barnwell annalist alleged that William and his court were 'French' in their way of life and that they despised the Scots, but members of the Scottish nobility were becoming 'French' too (see below, p. 424). The ruler of Galloway (the son of Uhtred) was often called 'Roland' rather than the Celtic Lachlan, had a largely Anglo-Norman household, founded the Cistercian monastery at Glenluce, married the daughter and heir of Richard de Moreville, and bore the title justiciar (presumably of Galloway itself). Before his death in 1200, he seemed to be tying the region more firmly into the kingdom. It was a kingdom far more stable politically than that subject to the pressures of Angevin kingship south of the border.

*   *   *

Richard sailed from England on 12 May 1194, never to return. The struggle to recover his continental losses was rightly the supreme priority. England's resources were vital, yet they could be secured from a distance. Richard greeted petitioners crossing the Channel to see him with glares, violent gestures and bullying demands for money. He kept the English government on its toes by sending the abbot of Caen from the Norman exchequer to stamp out the peculations of the sheriffs. When there was delay in executing one abrasive order, he threatened to dispatch his mercenary captain Mercadier. 'You English are too timid,' he declared.

Who would govern England for such a master? Neither Queen Eleanor nor Queen Berengaria. Richard's mother now returned to Poitou; his wife never left the continent. Fortunately, on this occasion getting an appointment absolutely right, Richard found the ideal man: Hubert Walter, an astute politician and a brilliantly inventive administrator. Born around 1140-45, Hubert was the nephew of the chief justiciar Ranulf Glanvill and throughout the 1180s had sat at the exchequer. He was the epitome of those ministers, fertile, precise, self-confident, whose labours were reflected in *Glanvill*, *The Dialogue of the Exchequer*, and the developing forms of the chancery's writs and charters. Hubert had accompanied Richard on crusade and been one of the first to seek him out in captivity. In May 1193 Richard insisted on his election to the archbishopric of Canterbury and in December made him chief justiciar, a post he held till his voluntary retirement in July 1198. The humane and scrupulous Bishop Hugh of Lincoln urged Hubert to lay down the justiciarship and concentrate on his archiepiscopal duties. Yet the church benefited from the combination. If Hubert was ostentatious and testy, he was also accessible (allowing monks to sleep around his bed) and sympathetic, smoothing out Bishop Hugh's own quarrels with Richard, and trying to restrain some of Richard's more arbitrary acts. He also took his ecclesiastical duties seriously, holding reforming councils for the provinces of York and Canterbury.

As justiciar one part of Hubert's task was to maintain peace and dispense justice. He probably had much to do with hiving off from the exchequer in the 1190s a separate court at Westminster for the hearing of civil litigation which came to be known as 'the common bench' and later as the 'court of common pleas'. He was directly responsible for devising the tripartite final concord by which agreements between litigants reached before the king's judges were recorded thrice over, with one copy, the 'foot', being kept by the government for the security of both parties. The attraction of having agreements recorded in this way became another major factor in drawing litigation to the king's courts, indeed such litigation was often initiated with the concord already in mind. No less than 42,000 'feet' survive in the Public Record Office for the period to 1307, their even distribution throughout the country showing there was nothing 'home counties' about the common law: Yorkshire was only just beaten into first place in numbers of 'feet' by the most populous shire, Norfolk. Hubert Walter also tightened up procedures on the criminal side, introducing in 1194 three knights and a clerk in each county who were to hold inquests on dead bodies and keep a record of the pleas of crown the eyre was to hear. This was the origin of the office of the coroner.

A major reason for staging judicial eyres was, of course, to make money and Hubert boasted about the amounts he had raised. But the almost continuous warfare after 1194 was very different from the intermittent campaigns down to 1189, and far more voracious, especially as Richard depended very much on paid mercenaries. Hubert was full of expedients. He made the sheriffs answer for increments worth an annual £700 above the ancient farms of the counties, commissioned the justices in eyre to tallage the royal demesne, tried (without spectacular success) to revive a land tax, and appointed special officials ('escheators') to exploit the lands which had been seized from John's supporters. The years after 1194 have indeed been seen by historians as marking a new stage in the financial exploitation of the kingdom, which eventually led to Magna Carta. Certainly Abbot Ralph of Coggeshall, writing in 1201, affirmed that no king had exacted more from his kingdom than had Richard between 1194 and 1199. The abbot believed that for all his crusading lustre his death was a just judgement of God. In fact Richard's revenue between 1194 and 1198, as recorded on the pipe rolls, averaged some £25,000 a year, little different from that achieved by Henry II in his last years, and failing to parallel the striking increases in Normandy. But this came on top of the tax for Richard's ransom, which at a quarter of everyone's rents and movable property was by far the heaviest levied in medieval England. There was also the problem that a decreasing proportion of royal revenue was being derived from politically acceptable sources like crown lands and escheats. Although Richard had recovered control of some of the lands he had alienated in 1189, by the end of the reign he had given away royal lands worth some £2,000, in striking contrast to Henry II who jealously guarded such assets. As a result Richard had to exploit other more sensitive sources of revenue. In 1198 many widows of tenants-in-chief were made to offer money to stay single or marry whom they wished. The pressures on great barons too were increasing. Henry II's earls, in his thirty-four-year reign, paid some £3,540 into the exchequer. Richard's earls, in his ten years, paid in £11,231. Some of this money was freely offered to purchase land and rights which Henry would not sell. But while Hubert Walter counselled caution, Richard also demanded large sums from his barons to succeed to their inheritances and have 'justice' in law cases. He also inflicted swingeing penalties for offences, £800, for example, being exacted from the northern baron Robert de Ros for allowing a prisoner to escape.

There were already signs of the demands which were finally to surface in Magna Carta. One baron, William of Newmarket, defined a 'reasonable relief' as being £100, just like the Charter. Another, the earl of Norfolk, Roger Bigod, asked that he should only be deprived of property by judgement of his peers, in other words not simply by the 'will' of the king, here again anticipating the Charter. Equally striking was William of Newburgh's comment that Richard had elevated Longchamp, a foreigner of low birth, 'without the counsel and consent of the great men'. The implication that the king's ministers should be natives and chosen by common consent foreshadowed a central constitutional demand of the thirteenth century. The role of great councils during Richard's absence supported such ideas: after Long-champ's fall the new form of government was established 'by the common decision of the king's faithful men'; in 1215 the Charter similarly forbade taxation save with the 'common counsel of the realm'. Politics and government were also opening up to sections of society beyond the great barons. Knights were appointed as coroners and (in 1195) as keepers of the peace. Equally apparent was the importance of London. The refusal of the citizens to support Longchamp in 1191 was crucial to his fall, and they were rewarded by the grant of a *commune*, permission that is to bind themselves together in a sworn association. In 1215 the Charter formed a 'commune of all the land'.

Between his departure from England in 1194 and his death in 1199, Richard was involved in warfare on the continent, interrupted occasionally by truces and one formal peace, that made at Louviers in January 1196. This was a war not of great battles but of attrition, fought by small bodies of troops, and centred round the siege of castles and the ravaging of land. King Philip proved ominously resilient. After facing Richard for nearly five years he still retained Gisors, building a great cylindrical tower at the castle's south-east corner. Yet in this period Richard's outstanding qualities were never more apparent: as a builder of castles, a constructor of alliances, a judge of priorities, a mobilizer of resources, and as a fighting knight. He recovered most of Normandy, re-took Loches on the eastern frontiers of Touraine and reasserted his authority further south by seizing Taillebourg and Angoulême.

To protect Normandy Richard built the great complex of fortifications at Les Andelys, west of Gaillon. Medieval military experts often debated whether to build castles high on hills, or down by rivers. At Les Andelys, Richard did both. He sank a wooden stockade across the Seine, fortified the little island in its middle, joined the island by bridge to a new walled town on the river bank, and then on the great limestone rock above threw up an extraordinary castle, which he called his 'beautiful castle of the rock', or Château Gaillard, his 'impudent castle'. On all this Richard expended some £11,500, more than was spent on his English castles during his entire reign. He could now block Philip's moves down the Seine to Rouen and had a base for the ultimate recovery of Gisors.

Richard's success was also built on diplomacy. With his clear, unsentimental insight, he realized that Normandy was far more valuable than his old bases in the south. So in 1197 he conceded rights and territory in Aquitaine to bring about the marriage of his sister Joan, widow of the king of Sicily, to the count of Toulouse. He thus ended forty years of intermittent warfare and was free, as William of Newburgh put it, 'to return untrammelled to his war with the king of France'. Richard also succeeded in prising from King Philip the counts of Boulogne and Flanders, the latter by an embargo on wool exports on which the Flemish cloth industry depended. With these alliances topped off by the elevation of Richard's nephew Otto to the kingship, not of Scotland, but of the Romans on Henry VI's death in 1197, the final expulsion of King Philip from Normandy seemed but a matter of time.

It was not to be. In 1199 Richard laid siege to the viscount of Limoges's castle of Châluz, seeking to punish him for defecting to King Philip. He was struck by a crossbow bolt, and died on 6 April. There was nothing irresponsible about Richard's last campaign, but it was in Normandy, not the Limousin, that the future of his empire would be decided. Richard was buried beside his father at the abbey of Fontevraud. The effigies, imposing and impassive, erected over their tombs still seem to radiate with the power of the dynasty. That power, however, was about to collapse.

9

The Reign of King John, 1199–1216

On the night of 10 April 1199 Hubert Walter was roused from his sleep in Rouen priory by the news of Richard's death. There were, as he at once observed, two possible candidates for the succession: Richard's youngest brother, John, and Richard's nephew, Arthur. But Arthur, twelve years old, allied to the king of France and brought up in Brittany (to which he was heir through his mother Constance), had few connections with the great Anglo-Norman barons, as one of them, William Marshal (who had flung on his clothes and gone to waken Hubert), pointed out. Thus John's accession in the north went without a hitch. On 25 April he was invested at Rouen with the duchy of Normandy; on 27 May he was crowned king of England at Westminster. It was the start of one of the most disastrous and momentous reigns in history. John was to lose Normandy and Anjou, concede Magna Carta, and die in the midst of a civil war. By then a French prince controlled more than half of England, the king of Scotland was established in Carlisle, and Llywelyn ab Iorwerth of Gwynedd was dominant in Wales, a dominance he retained till his death in 1240.

On his accession John was thirty-three years old, slightly built (though later he grew corpulent), and five foot six and a half inches tall. His body, entombed in Worcester cathedral, is the first of an English king to survive. He had behaved irresponsibly in Ireland in 1185 and had rebelled against his father and his brother. Yet the picture of John as an evil, godless tyrant for whom hell was too good, as the chronicler Matthew Paris put it, was essentially the product of the reign itself and later legend. John had fought loyally and successfully for Richard between 1194 and 1199. In 1199 the jury was still out.

After his coronation John hurried back across the Channel, and with the help of his mother, Queen Eleanor, now well into her seventies, beat back Arthur's challenge in Maine and Anjou. Under the Treaty of

Le Goulet in May 1200, King Philip accepted John's succession to all the Angevin dominions, a major concession since it meant abandoning Arthur and with him the longstanding Capetian ambition to break up the dominions. Arthur was to have only Brittany and to hold it from John as duke of Normandy, not from Philip as king of France. John on his part, however, forswore alliances with both his nephew Otto, recently crowned emperor, and the count of Flanders. He also accepted the loss of the Evreçin, which Philip had overrun on Richard's death. So another deep hole was dug in Normandy's frontier. In England John was lampooned in some circles as 'softsword', yet he was also praised as a peacemaker who understood far better than Richard the burdens imposed by the seven years' war since 1193. When in November 1200 John settled a quarrel with the Cistercians, Ralph of Coggeshall, a monk of the order, erased previous criticisms from his chronicle and wrote of a wise and pious king, touched by the hand of God. Coggeshall's tune was soon to change. Within four years of the Le Goulet treaty the whole edifice of John's continental empire had come crashing to the ground. At one level that was very much the result of his character and the mistakes he made.

In August 1200, having divorced his first wife, John married Isabella, daughter and sole heir of the count of Angoulême. Strategically, in knitting together his southern dominions the match was a masterstroke. But instead of compensating Hugh de Lusignan, the great Poitevin noble to whom Isabella had been engaged, John tried to bully him into submission. Hugh appealed for justice to the king of France, and thus gave Philip his chance. His court in the spring of 1202 sentenced John to forfeit all his continental fiefs. In the ensuing war, John at first triumphed. At Mirebeau in July 1202 he captured Arthur, the Lusignans and all his Poitevin enemies. But he then made another great mistake by antagonizing the great Angevin magnate, William des Roches, the main architect of his success. By the spring of 1203 the defection of William with his allies had given King Philip both Maine and Anjou.

Normandy, however, was the real prize, its revenues greater than the rest of the continental possessions put together. Here the north-east, centre and south-west of the duchy, as Daniel Power has shown, came under different pressures. The south-eastern frontiers had never been threatened by the king of France, but the nobles there (like Robert, count of Sées and Alençon) had close connections with their fellows in Maine and Anjou and were influenced by their conduct. In January

1203 Count Robert breakfasted with John in the morning and defected to Philip in the afternoon, thus prising away the south of the duchy and blocking John's route onwards into Maine. By this time the cruel treatment of the prisoners taken at Mirebeau and ugly rumours about Arthur's fate were staining John's reputation. John took no heed. On 3 April 1203, in a drunken rage, he murdered Arthur at Rouen. Richard had starved to death one of John's partisans, but to murder a great prince in this manner was shocking and unprecedented. Had not Henry I kept his brother Robert all those years in prison? The immediate consequences were again in the south-west, on the frontier with Brittany. Arthur's mother Constance, and her husband, Guy de Thouars, joined Philip and played a large part in disrupting John's hold on eastern Normandy.

It was in the north-east that King Philip could bring most pressure, thanks to his acquisition of the Amienois, his alliance with the count of Ponthieu (married to Richard's discarded Alice), and his possession of Evreux, Gisors and the Norman Vexin. The Norman nobility in these areas, like Hugh de Gournay and the count of Meulan, often held land across the frontiers from the king of France or his vassals, and had no alternative but to flow with the tide. In these circumstances supreme importance attached to maintaining Richard's northern alliances. But John lacked Richard's prestige and was unable to outbid Philip. As a result, in 1201 the warrior count of Boulogne followed the count of Flanders (who was soon to be absent on crusade) into Philip's camp. The Emperor Otto's own troubles in Germany ruled out any succour from that quarter. Philip was free to attack.

Angevin rule was most secure in central Normandy between Caen and Rouen, but it was precisely this area and its towns that had borne the brunt of Richard's mounting exactions. John made matters worse. In August 1202 he appointed a low-born and aggressive seneschal, William le Gros, to run the duchy; he then stationed his mercenaries, under Louvrecaire, not on the frontiers but at Falaise, where they offended Anglo-Norman barons, like the earl of Leicester, and pillaged 'as though they were in an enemy country' (so the *Life of William Marshal* recorded). 'For such things was he hated and betrayed by the barons of the land,' commented a Caen burgess.

Philip began his invasion in the summer of 1203 and in August laid siege to Château Gaillard. John made only one attempt to relieve it. Everywhere, as Ralph of Coggeshall observed, he suspected betrayal.

He had betrayed his father and his brother and expected the same conduct from everyone else. In the end he was right, but partly because his suspicions, so openly displayed, became self-fulfilling. 'He who trusts no one is distrusted by all the world,' commented *The Life of William Marshal*. In the end John's nerve cracked. In December 1203 he slunk back to England, a fugitive in his own land. How different it would have been with Richard! John's aim was to gather resources to return. But he was too late. On 6 March, as he arranged to send his dogs back to Normandy, Château Gaillard fell. On 24 June Rouen surrendered. Normandy was Philip's.

There was more to come. The death of Eleanor of Aquitaine on 1 April 1204 shook John's hold on Poitou and the Touraine. In August 1204 Philip held court in Poitiers, and next year took the great fortresses of Loches and Chinon, the latter long defended by an English hero, Hubert de Burgh. Further south King Alfonso VIII of Castile overran part of Gascony, determined to make good the promise of its possession after Eleanor's death, made to him – or so he claimed – on his marriage to Henry II's daughter. It was not till 1206 that John at last launched an expedition to reverse his losses. He landed at La Rochelle in Poitou, evicted Alfonso's garrisons from Gascony, and then marched north to Angers only to retreat in the face of Philip's army. A truce in October left Philip in control of all the country north of the Loire, as well as Poitiers, and with the allegiance of the Lusignans to the south.

The expedition of 1206 showed the measure of John's task. It was one thing (with limited interference from Philip) to dabble in the shifting allegiances of the barons south of the Loire, and win back the Gascon towns. Indeed he had never lost Bordeaux and Bayonne. It was quite another to recover Normandy. He had neither ports nor, having lost Anjou and Maine, contiguous frontiers from which to invade. Philip held Normandy in a vice, becoming 70 per cent richer thanks to its abundant revenues. He cleared out those he distrusted, comparing them to soiled toilet tissue, and installed his own men in the key castles. Learning from John's mistake, he left Anjou and Maine under William des Roches, but further south he retained Saumur, Chinon, Tours and Poitiers. Just to get near Normandy, John had to advance through hostile territory.

Mean in triumph where Richard had been generous, despairing in disaster where Richard had been supremely confident, an unremarkable fighting knight where Richard had been a legend, John inspired fear and loathing, Richard fear and respect. These were the differences between the loss and retention of the empire. Yet there was also more to it than that. King Philip was a far more formidable opponent in 1200 than he had been in the 1180s. That was partly because of his seizure of Gisors and the Norman Vexin. It was also (though more arguably) because Capetian revenues had been increasing faster than those of the Angevins. The revenue of England had remained comparatively static under Richard; and if Richard in the 1190s had on occasion tripled his revenue from Normandy in comparison with the level in 1180, this was by resorting to loans and tallages that were difficult to sustain. The Capetian increases, on the other hand, were soundly based on administrative reforms and the acquisition of new territory, notably Artois and the Amienois. By the 1200s the resources King Philip had for the war in Normandy were almost certainly larger than those of John. In the financial year 1202/3 (for which a set of accounts survives) 'ordinary' Capetian revenue was some £42,000, while 'extraordinary' levies brought in another £10,000: total, £52,000. These sums enabled Philip to sustain, throughout the year, over 2,300 troops of whom 500 were mounted knights and sergeants, a formidable force. If the loans and tallages found in the Norman pipe roll for 1198 were indeed still in place, then the duchy's annual revenues on the eve of the war totalled some £24,000. The revenue from England between 1199 and 1202 (including an estimate for an 'extraordinary' tax in 1200) averaged almost exactly the same, John having notably failed to expand it in this period. The total for England and Normandy was £48,000 and to it should be added perhaps a thousand or so pounds apiece from Maine, Anjou, Aquitaine and Ireland. But if the combined Angevin total was much the same as the Capetian, it could not be transferred to Normandy by the flick of a switch. Indeed, the revenues from Maine, Anjou and Aquitaine were probably absorbed locally. Only Normandy and England really entered the equation, and the treasure of England had to be transported across the Channel, whereas Capetian resources came from a compact, lucrative royal demesne, adjoining the Norman frontier. The Capetians also had one other advantage. Their revenue rivalled that of the Angevins but provoked far less political discontent, largely because a much higher proportion came in easily and uncontentiously from land. 'The French kings got rich without strain,' in R. W. Southern's classic phrase. Whereas a sense of community and national identity in England developed in opposition to the crown, in France it was exactly the reverse. There was no chance that John's cause would be helped by any kind of Capetian political collapse.

In this period of intensive warfare, John, like Richard, faced the problem of how to mobilize his full military potential. At the heart of royal armies were the household knights. At any one time, John had over a hundred of them supported by money and (more often) by grants of wardships, marriages and escheats. If their numbers seem smaller than the several hundreds sometimes ascribed to Henry I, the comparison may be misleading. John's knights could well have been more heavily equipped. We also know of their numbers from record sources as opposed simply to the statements of chroniclers. Closely linked to the household contingent were the fluctuating mercenary forces under such experts as Mercadier and Louvrecair. And then each individual tenant-in-chief, lay and ecclesiastical, had to provide the king with knights in return for the tenure of their fees. Such feudal service, however, was supposed to last only for forty days, long enough for a foray into Wales or Scotland, but useless for long periods of campaigning on the continent. Indeed some claimed it was not owed for service on the continent at all. There was also the question of just how many knights feudal service could raise. According to the survey of 1166, which perhaps reflects the quotas imposed by the Conqueror, the grand total of knights the tenants-in-chief owed the king was around 5,000. Record evidence from John's reign, however, shows both that his armies were much smaller (he took 800 knights to Ireland in 1210) and that his tenants-in-chief mustered contingents which were only a fraction of their 1166 quotas. Gilbert de Gant went to Ireland with six knights, not the sixty-eight he supposedly owed. The 1166 quotas seem chiefly relevant for the levying of scutage. Had he not campaigned, Gant would certainly have paid on the full sixty-eight knights. (The rate in 1210 was £2 per knight.) To what extent all this represents a dramatic decline in the military obligations of the baronage, and if so when and why it took place, is difficult to say given the lack of hard evidence for the actual size of earlier contingents. There is also once again the question of different levels of equipment. However, that kings from Henry II onwards felt feudal military service was unsatisfactory is clear. To have replaced it altogether with scutage would have weakened their authority, even if the paid forces on whom to spend the money were available. So they attempted reform. Richard and Hubert Walter demanded that the tenants-in-chief as a whole provide 300 knights to serve abroad for a year. John, for his part, kept armies in the field by giving knights 'prests', that is loans of money (often left unpaid), which apparently they felt were more dignified than wages.

It was not easy, therefore, to exploit the military potential of England, and much depended on the general supportiveness of its barons and knights, something itself connected with how far they had a stake of their own in Normandy. Among the county knights at the heart of English local society, that stake was very limited. In the twelfth century only seven of the seventy leading families in Warwickshire and Leicestershire held land in the duchy. There were equally numerous Norman landholders with no base in England: of the thirty-eight Normans known to have deserted John in 1203, only eight had English lands which he could confiscate. Cross-Channel ties had weakened over the century. Few new Norman families were established in England after the immediate post-Conquest period. The number of individuals holding land in both England and Normandy diminished as families split property between branches on either side of the Channel. By 1200 all but one of the seven Warwickshire and Leicestershire families mentioned above had lost their continental possessions. This is not, however, the whole story, for even in 1200 there remained significant numbers of barons who did hold land in both the kingdom and the duchy. Indeed acts of royal patronage could recreate such families: the marriage Richard arranged for William Marshal made him lord of Longueville in Normandy as well as Chepstow in Wales and Leinster in Ireland. Of the 199 Norman tenants-in-chief in 1172, 107 (or their descendants) held lands on both sides of the Channel in 1204. Likewise (and the groups overlapped) some of the greatest members of the English nobility held substantial lands in Normandy: for example the earls of Chester, Leicester, Warenne, Clare, Hereford, Arundel and Pembroke (William Marshal), together with William de Mowbray and Robert de Ros. If these men did not fight with more vigour, it was partly because of John's flaws of character. It was also because until the last moment they hoped for some arrangement whereby they could indeed serve two masters, holding their lands in England from John and those in Normandy from Philip. William Marshal secured such a concession. His subsequent refusal to go on the 1206 campaign shows how right John was to force a choice on everyone else. If barons did homage to King Philip, then they forfeited their English lands and Philip naturally responded with equivalent seizures in Normandy.

The Capetian conquest of Normandy was a turning-point in European history. It made the Capetian kings dominant in western Europe, and ended the cross-Channel Anglo-Norman state. True, even in political terms England did not cease to be part of the 'community of Europe'. It was not till 1259 that John's son formally resigned his claims to Normandy and Anjou, and even then he retained Gascony. Yet the days of the absentee kings were over. Gascony, lacking revenues and great ducal palaces, had never attracted more than infrequent visits before 1204, nor did it afterwards even when its revenues increased. From 1204, in terms of their itineraries kings of England for the first time since 1066 were just that. The fact that John returned to England in 1206 after just six months across the Channel was symptomatic. The mutual seizures of property had also helped to bring the cross-Channel nobility to an end. Henceforth the high aristocracy would be born and hold lands only in England. They could become as English as everyone else. The consequences of these changes for the political structure of Britain would be profound.

* * *

At the start of his reign John had continued to keep Geoffrey fitz Peter in office as justiciar while recalling Hubert Walter to the colours as chancellor. From any role at the centre, however, one person was absent: the queen John had acquired at such cost, Isabella of Angoulême. Since she was only about twelve on her marriage that was inevitable. Subsequently John used her to beget heirs, two sons (the eldest the future Henry III, born in 1207) and three daughters. But despite her magnificent coronation in 1200, he used her for little else. He treated Angoulême as his own and granted Isabella no land in England for her support. Her dower (much of it formerly held by Eleanor of Aquitaine) she was to receive only on his death. Isabella was therefore totally dependent on John's supplies of money and played no discernible part in the politics and government of the reign, despite being, as later evidence shows, a passionate and highly political woman.

Under the fitz Peter/Hubert Walter partnership England enjoyed a 'tranquil peace', according to Gervase of Canterbury, during which Hubert introduced significant changes to the practices of the chancery. Hitherto it had kept only one annual roll, a record of 'fines', that is the money offered to the king for concessions and favours. Now it opened three more rolls to record charters, writs patent, and writs close (see above, p. 199). With another roll, hived off from the close rolls in 1226, to record writs dealing with the expenditure of money, these chancery rolls became a permanent feature of English royal government, transforming the materials available to later historians. The record they provided of concessions and orders meant the king could potentially rule his agents and subjects with novel precision.

This 'tranquil' period came to an end with the loss of Normandy in 1204, a watershed on the road to Magna Carta. John now spent more time in England than any king since 1066, excepting only Stephen. For 'ten furious years' (J. C. Holt) he lashed his court round the country, rarely staying for more than a week in one place. His aim was to amass the treasure to win Normandy back. His need for money was accentuated by the rapid inflation which occurred around the start of his reign (see above, p. 35), with prices more than doubling. A mercenary knight had to be paid 8d. a day under Henry II and 2s. a day under John, a threefold increase, though possibly one influenced by the need for heavier equipment. Income derived from selling agricultural produce on the market rose with the prices and was thus protected, but a far smaller proportion of royal than baronial revenue came in that way. Instead, with the depletion of the royal demesne under Stephen and Richard, kings relied increasingly on other sources of income, sources which bore down directly on individuals, and were far more unpopular than land, whose exploitation only harmed the peasantry.

John's revenues have been investigated by Nick Barratt. Between 1199 and 1202, they averaged around £24,000 a year, much the same as the best figures attained by Richard I and Henry II, and much the same indeed as Henry I's revenue in 1130. Between 1207 and 1212, the average was some £49,000 a year, double the earlier sum. If we make the reasonable assumption that two-thirds of a £44,000 tallage levied on the Jews in 1210 were paid, then the average becomes some £54,000. In real terms, allowing for the inflation, John's revenue between 1207 and 1212 (including the Jewish tallage) was running at roughly 25 per cent a year more than that of Henry I in 1130. And Henry I, of course, was a king of fabled wealth. Probably the years after 1207 saw the greatest level of financial exploitation since the Conquest. None of this takes account of the revenue John got from the church during the Interdict: some £100,000, more than half of which he probably never returned. No wonder that by 1214 John had a treasure of some £130,000.

The new financial policies were signalled in 1204 when John appointed new sheriffs who, building on the precedent of 1194, were expected to raise substantial additional sums above the 'ancient' farms of their counties (see above, pp. 155, 260). As a result, between 1207 and 1212 they owed on average an extra £1,400 per annum to the exchequer. Having less money for themselves, they recouped their losses through a series of illicit extortions. John also exploited the royal forest, mounting forest eyres in 1207 and 1212 which imposed amercements totalling some £11,350, the most oppressive since those of Henry II in the 1170s. In 1210 he demanded a £44,000 tallage from the Jews. A Bristol Jew, according to one story, had a tooth knocked out each day until he paid up. The more normal penalty was the seizure of Jewish assets, with the result that Christian borrowers ended up owing their money to the king. One way or another, pressure on the Jews put pressure on everyone who owed them money, from barons down to peasants. John's most lucrative measure, however, was the great tax (or 'aid') he levied in 1207, with the common consent of the realm, or so he said. The demand was for 13 per cent of the value of everyone's rents and movable property, largely corn and animals. There were precedents for such taxation, notably in the aid for Richard's ransom, but this is the first for which the take is known: a stupendous £60,000, which dwarfed the £2–3,000 raised by scutage. Not surprisingly the tax pointed the way forward for the whole future of English royal finance.

These financial policies affected not just magnates and the church but knights, freemen and peasants, 'the miserable provincials' as the Barnwell annalist called them. But there were also exactions which were borne more directly by the baronage, at least in the first instance. John expanded Richard's policy of charging baronial widows large sums for staying single or marrying whom they wished: there were 149 such fines in the reign, averaging £185, as against sixty-eight averaging £114 between 1189 and 1199. The barons were likewise put under pressure by the increasing incidence of scutage: the product of John's campaigns both on the continent and in the British Isles. Henry II had levied eight scutages in thirty-four years, Richard three in ten years; John levied eleven in sixteen years, and at higher rates than before. John also, like Richard, demanded large sums for 'justice' and succession to inheritances. Between 1199 and 1208 magnate indebtedness to the crown increased by 380 per cent. The rebellion of 1215, as

J. C. Holt has remarked, was indeed a rebellion of the king's debtors.

While John took too much from his subjects in money, he gave back too little in the form of justice. The new procedures for civil litigation, introduced by Henry II, had proved highly popular with the gentry and free tenants (see above, p. 240). By developing them the king could win the support of those sections of society and outflank the great barons. John certainly showed an interest in the routine of justice, yet instead of playing his strongest card he threw it away. Fearful of rival centres of authority during the Interdict, and distrustful of his justiciar, Geoffrey fitz Peter, between 1209 and 1214 he virtually closed down both the common bench at Westminster and the judicial eyres in the counties. Instead, even routine assizes had to be heard by judges who were with the king; impossibly inconvenient for litigants, given John's hectic peregrinations around the country. Barons litigating against each other, meanwhile, continued to be subject to the venal and arbitrary processes determined by the king, rather than the routine procedures of the common law (see above, p. 241).

Sale and denial of justice, as well as financial extortion and arbitrary disseisin, are all illustrated by the interlocking histories of two Yorkshire baronial families, those of Stuteville and Mowbray. The Stuteville lands, forfeited in 1106, had been given by Henry I to his protégé, Nigel d'Aubigny, whose descendants took the name of Mowbray after the centre of their Norman estates. The Stutevilles had subsequently worked their way back into royal favour, and in 1200 William de Stuteville began a legal action to recover his inheritance, offering John £2,000 to receive 'right' in the case. William de Mowbray countered by offering £1,333 'to be treated justly according to the custom of England'. In the event a compromise was arranged in 1201, and Mowbray was not made to pay the money immediately. In 1209 he still owed £1,200. But then, as John tightened the financial screw, matters changed. By 1212 Mowbray had been forced to reduce his obligations by £560, only then to be saddled with another £400 thanks to his Jewish debts being taken into the king's hands. Mowbray's small frame (he was as small as a dwarf) must have seethed with resentment. No wonder he was a leading rebel in 1215. Meanwhile, William de Stuteville had died. His lands had come into royal wardship and been ruthlessly exploited by the king's agent, Brian de Lisle. Eventually in 1205 William's brother, Nicholas de Stuteville, succeeded him, but his payment to enter his inheritance was not the £100 widely claimed as the reasonable figure for a barony but an exorbitant £6,666 (10,000 marks). This time John did not want the money. He wanted the Stuteville castle of Knaresborough and retained it as security for payment. This was regarded by the Stutevilles as arbitrary disseisin 'by will of the king'. No wonder Nicholas joined the rebels.

The Stuteville–Mowbray story reveals another failing of John's rule, namely the narrowing circle of 'ins' and the widening circle of 'outs'. In the end, John lost the Stutevilles as well as the Mowbrays. To be sure, with his cynical political intelligence the king understood well enough the need for the carrot as well as the stick. At the start of his reign he gave William de Ferrers some of the Peverel inheritance and recognized him as earl of Derby (see above, p. 224); henceforth Ferrers remained 'on side'. So did Ferrers's brother-in-law, Ranulf, earl of Chester, after he received the honour of Richmond in 1205. Yet in other cases it all went wrong. John, for example, brought Henry de Bohun in by making him earl of Hereford but then cast him out by seizing Trowbridge, another alleged act of dispossession 'by will'. The growing number of hostages taken from his barons and of fines to recover royal favour were a measure of John's mounting isolation and distrust.

As John's baronial supporters fell away, so it seemed that those who took their place were parvenus and foreigners. At first this was least apparent at the centre. Hubert Walter had died in 1205 but Geoffrey fitz Peter, self-made but courteous and acceptable, whom John created earl of Essex, remained as justiciar until his death in 1213. In the localities it was different. There a set of aggressive royal agents became entrenched in office. Some were not merely 'new men' but also aliens like Engelard de Cigogné, sheriff of Gloucester, from Touraine, and all the more ruthless for their lack of English ties. All kings needed 'new men' in their service, but it was a great mistake to give the impression, as John had also done in Normandy, that such creatures alone had his trust.

Resentment against John's style of government was particularly strong in the north. The financial burdens born by northerners like William de Mowbray and Nicholas de Stuteville created wide circles of antagonism. Mowbray's pledges in 1209 for the repayment of his debts included Eustace de Vesci, Robert de Ros and Roger de Montbegon, all great northern barons and leading rebels in 1215. The royal forest in the north was extensive: the eyres of 1207 and 1212 each demanded more than £1,200 from Yorkshire. Pressure also came from revenue demanded above the county farms; the income for which the sheriff of Yorkshire accounted in 1212 was roughly twice that of 1204 and treble that of 1199. The north was also the home of some of John's most ruthless agents: Brian de Lisle (whose origins are totally obscure) took over at Knaresborough; Philip Mark (from Touraine) became sheriff of Nottingham. Then in 1214 another Tourangeau, Peter de Mauley (rumoured to be Arthur's murderer), was established at Doncaster through marriage. Of course, such tensions were not unique to the north, but they seemed more novel since the northern counties had only gradually, from Henry II's reign onwards, felt the full force of royal government. John indeed came north in every year of his reign bar four – far more frequently than any of his predecessors. The face he showed was minatory. The leading part played by 'the Northerners' in the ultimate rebellion was the result.

While John drove forward the government of England, he also plunged into a great quarrel with the papacy. Hubert Walter's death in July 1205 was followed by a dispute over the election of his successor, with the monks of Canterbury, or a party among them, choosing their sub-prior and then being forced by John to plump instead for John de Grey, an effective bishop of Norwich and a trusted royal agent, later to be justiciar of Ireland. Next year Pope Innocent III quashed both elections, summoned a delegation of the monks of Canterbury to Rome and made them elect Stephen Langton. Langton was an Englishman from a modest Lincolnshire family (Langton is near Wragby). He had spent twenty years in the Schools of Paris, becoming a master both in arts and theology. His lectures on the Bible, disputations and sermons had given him a towering reputation. In 1206 Innocent summoned this academic superstar to join the cardinals at Rome and was impressed by the purity of his life and the wisdom of his counsel. John saw things differently. University professors did not swim into his orbit very often and he did not know this one. The old custom that the king should at least influence the election and consent to its outcome had been flouted. Langton might be English by birth but he had spent twenty years in the Capetian capital. What a contrast to Hubert Walter, steeped in Angevin service before his election and continuing in harness thereafter! There would be no help like that from Langton. His appointment spelt one thing: trouble.

John refused to accept him. His predecessors would have done the same. The result was that in March 1208 an Interdict was imposed on

England and in November 1209 John was excommunicated. Under the terms of the Interdict no church services and offices were to be permitted save the baptism of infants and the confession of the dying. The laity were left without the Mass, and without burial in consecrated ground. 'O what a horrible and miserable spectacle it was to see in every city the sealed doors of the churches, Christians shut out from entry as though they were dogs, the cessation of divine office, the withholding of the sacrament of the body and blood of our Lord, the people no longer flocking to the famous celebrations of saints days, the bodies of the dead not given to burial according to Christian rites, of whom the stink infected the air and the horrible sight filled with horror the minds of the living': these were the comments of Abbot Ralph of Coggeshall on the much shorter Interdict in France in 1200. His feelings about the English Interdict were so extreme that after John's settlement with the pope he excised them from his chronicle.

John, however, was made of sterner stuff. Although he founded the Cistercian abbey at Beaulieu, he was not a pious man: his household accounts are full of offerings to the poor to atone for hunting on feast days or eating meat on Fridays. 'How fat that stag has grown without ever attending Mass,' ran one reported joke. In any case, the Interdict did nothing to affect the basic processes of government. Indeed the church revenues, seized during its course, made a major contribution to John's great mulct of the kingdom.

And yet John found himself under increasing pressure to reach a settlement. The bishops, forced to choose between king and pope, chose the pope. Once John de Grey had gone off to be justiciar of Ireland in 1208, only one bishop, the Tourangeau Peter des Roches, bishop of Winchester, remained by the king. Even those who were former chancery clerks and exchequer officials recognized Langton and went into exile. There could be no more striking testimony to the growth of papal authority over the previous hundred years. Innocent was also lucky in that he could exploit both John's unpopularity in England and his conflict with the king of France. His hints that John might be deposed fell on fertile soil, and John became increasingly nervous, travelling with a large retinue. In 1211 he at last indicated that he would accept Langton, but he still haggled over the amount of compensation due to the church.

*   *   *

After 1204, John had one overriding ambition: to recover his lost continental empire. Yet his involvement in Britain was of an unparalleled intensity, partly because he was now confined there. Like Henry and Richard, he was determined to neutralize any threat from Scotland and also, far more actively than they, to increase his lands and revenues in Ireland and Wales. Baronial politics too assumed a British, rather than Anglo-Norman, mould. When William Marshal and William de Braose fell from favour they did not go to Normandy but to Ireland.

At the start of his reign John had brushed aside King William's renewed claim to the northern counties and thereafter tensions remained not far below the surface. In 1209 they exploded. John suddenly heard of a scheme for one of William's daughters to marry none other than King Philip of France. He immediately marched north and imposed the exigent Treaty of Norham on the Scottish king in August 1209. Under its terms, John received both William's daughters into his custody and agreed to marry one to his eldest son and the other to an English noble. In return for these unpalatable favours, William was made to promise £10,000, of which at least £6,700 was paid. He now no longer had the resources, either diplomatic or financial, to cause John trouble. His situation soon deteriorated further. In 1211 Guthred, son of the Donald Mac William killed in 1187, arrived from Ireland and gained support both in Ross and Moray. William, faltering with age, began to fear for the very succession of his son Alexander, born in August 1198. His fears were shared by Alexander's mother, Ermengarde de Beaumont, the French noblewoman Henry II had married to William in 1187. It was thus Ermengarde, a striking image of a Scottish queen in politics, who helped early in 1212 to negotiate the agreement which brought John to the rescue. With some vague talk of Northumberland as her marriage portion, the latter betrothed his infant daughter Joan to Alexander, made him a knight, and sent him back to Scotland with a force of Brabantine mercenaries. With these, Alexander soon put down Guthred's revolt, Guthred himself being caught and hanged. To the Barnwell annalist it looked as though the Scottish kingdom itself had been formally entrusted to John's care.

*　　*　　*

John's involvement in Scotland was not merely to prevent a French alliance. It was also related to the state of affairs in Ireland. John had been effectively 'lord of Ireland' since his visit in 1185. He enjoyed the status, and retained the title after becoming king. Ireland provided both sources of patronage and money. Year after year a thousand pounds or so were shipped across the sea to swell his English treasure. John's primary policy, in parallel with that in England, was to make those revenues larger, which could be done by gaining more land and exploiting it more effectively. In 1203 he therefore ordered his justiciar to take over the best ports and villages in Connacht, and invest the revenues in building castles, founding more villages and doing everything possible for royal 'profit'. It was likewise with the aim of making money that John in 1207 instituted the first Irish coinage. His lordship did indeed mark a decisive period in Ireland's history. He achieved a large and lasting expansion in the areas under direct royal control, annexed (temporarily) two of the great settler lordships, and established the procedures of English common law.

The political conditions in Ireland facilitated John's forward policies. There was not merely conflict between Irish kings and English lords. The kingly families in the west – the MacCarthys of Desmond, the O'Briens of Thomond, and the O'Connors of Connacht – competed against each other and were themselves divided into rival and often warring segments. The great English lords – the justiciar Meiler fitz Henry, Walter de Lacy in Meath, John de Courcy in Ulster, William Marshal in Leinster (through his marriage to the daughter of Richard fitz Gilbert) – likewise presented no united front. All this was grist to John's manipulative mill. He had no fixed policy towards either the native Irish or the settler lords, and he cosseted or caned them as seemed expedient. This is not to say he saw them in the same light. John had pulled the beards of the Irish rulers when he arrived in 1185, and always regarded them as objects of ridicule. He could maltreat them, moreover, without repercussions outside Ireland, whereas with settler lords he had always to remember the wider stage. Yet just for that reason John could tolerate the independence of the former more readily than he could the latter.

In the 1190s John had made major advances at the expense of both English lords and native kings. In the north his men had pushed Walter de Lacy out of Drogheda, which then (with its castle) developed into a royal base, though one Walter always aspired to recover. In the south-west, the death of Donnell O'Brien, king of Munster in 1194, and the quarrels between his sons, enabled John to gain Limerick. Occupying a highly strategic position at the mouth of the Shannon, it opened up a whole new field of royal power. John's other major gain arose from exploiting the contest for the succession to Connacht, playing off his protégé, William de Burgh, against competing members of the O'Connor family. In 1205 John, discarding William, conceded to Cathal Crovderg two-thirds of Connacht for the customary tribute, and a third (the best) in hereditary right as a barony. Here was a striking example of a native ruler attaining his ends by accommodation. By going baronial, Cathal hoped to ensure the succession of his son Aedh, and also to guarantee his lands from further English attack. In return, after various exchanges, John eventually acquired two cantrefs near Athlone. There in 1210 a great castle was erected above the Shannon. Right in the centre of Ireland, between Meath and Connacht, this long remained a pivotal royal base. John's guarantees were never worth very much, however. On the same day in 1215, he issued one charter granting Connacht to Cathal Crovderg and another to Cathal's rival Richard de Burgh, William's son!

William de Burgh merely fell from favour in the early 1200s. John de Courcy, the conqueror of Ulster, lost everything. In 1201 the chronicler Roger of Howden had placed him in a list of European rulers alongside the pope and the kings of England, France and Germany; not bad for a near landless younger son, but too much for King John. He backed the Lacys in a war which ended with de Courcy's defeat and capture. In 1205 John granted Ulster to Hugh de Lacy. These tensions paled before John's quarrel with William de Braose, which became one of the defining events of the reign. Lord of Bramber in Sussex and wide lordships in Wales, Braose had started as one of John's leading henchmen and been rewarded in 1201 (despite William de Burgh's presence in the area) with a grant of the honour of Limerick. John, however, retained the chief prize, the town of Limerick itself. It was needed, so John's justiciar Meiler fitz Henry insisted, to control the king's lands in Cork and Connacht. So possession of Limerick town became a great bone of contention, and there was yet another. Braose had promised to pay £3,333 at £666 a year for his grant. By 1207 he had managed a mere £468. As trust disintegrated, John began to regret the early favour he had shown Braose including in Wales a hereditary grant of the lordship of Gower. John eventually seized chattels in Wales to enforce payment of the debt. The result was a violent conflict which culminated, during the winter of 1208/9, in Braose's flight to Ireland. There he was welcomed by his son-in-law Walter de Lacy and William Marshal, who had retreated to his Leinster lordship (where he busily developed the port of New Ross) after falling from grace for refusing to join the Poitevin expedition of 1206. In effect, the great barons of Ireland were in rebellion against the king.

In 1209 John marched north to ensure the rebels received no help from Scotland (the occasion for the Treaty of Norham) and then, in the summer of 1210, crossed to Ireland. He came to terms with some of the native kings, but made the mistake of laughing when he saw Cathal Crovderg riding bareback. He then caused further offence by demanding hostages and tribute from both Cathal and Aedh O'Neil, king of Cenel Eoghain in the north, who thereafter remained a thorn in the side of royal government. John, however, could afford to be careless. Flush with money, he had brought over 1,000 foot soldiers and at least 800 knights, probably the largest army ever seen in Ireland, all supported by payments out of the chamber. William de Braose, having returned to Wales, had already tried to submit before John's crossing, but John was determined to show his power. He chased Braose's wife Matilda, together with Walter and Hugh de Lacy, out of Ireland.

Matilda was captured in Galloway and sent to John. She was already celebrated for her efficient household management, her defence of Painscastle in the 1190s (thereafter renamed Castle Matilda), and her fiery refusal to surrender her sons as hostages – 'Arthur's fate reveals what happens to boys in John's custody,' she declared. John's own account of the quarrel shows he regarded husband and wife very much as a team. Once in John's hands, Matilda was made to offer £33,333 merely for the life and limbs of herself and her family. Wretched but courageous, she insisted on seeing her husband, who came under safe conduct and then fled to France (where he died in 1211), leaving Matilda to her fate. When the king's ministers came to her in prison and demanded the first payment of the monstrous sum, they found but £16 and a few pieces of gold. She and her eldest son (married to a daughter of Richard de Clare, earl of Hertford, and already acting as lord of Brecon) were starved to death in the dungeons of Windsor Castle. Stories of the pathetic attitudes in which their bodies were found were soon on every baronial lip. Here again was a shocking and unprecedented crime.

John's expedition, however, had been a triumph. Both in Wales and Ireland the Braose lordships were in his hands. So in Ireland were the

Lacys' Meath and Ulster. In 1212, to control the latter and secure contingents of Galloway's violent soldiery, he granted Ulster (abortively, in the end) to Galloway's lord, Alan fitz Roland. During his 1210 visit, John had also taken major steps to settle the whole governmental structure of Ireland. He wanted to monitor and exploit Ireland yet had no desire to go there, as he once confessed to Gerald of Wales. He relied on sending letters (usually in great batches after the advent of messengers) and summoning the justiciar, head of the government, to court. From 1208 until his death in 1214 the post was held by the ultra-loyal John de Grey, bishop of Norwich, an accomplished administrator who had no personal axe to grind in Ireland – unlike his predecessor, Meiler fitz Henry. Grey built the castle at Athlone and did much to develop law and government. As justiciar he presided over the exchequer which was based in Dublin castle, built in 1204 to control the city and store treasure. The pipe rolls of the Irish exchequer are lost, but a partial copy of that for 1212 suggests procedure was similar to that in England. It shows that the king's lands were grouped under three sheriffs, for Dublin and Drogheda, for Munster (embracing Limerick and Tipperary), and for Waterford and Cork. The Lacy lordships of Meath and Ulster in John's hands were under stewards.

In 1210 John, in a charter which built on initiatives in 1204 and 1207, laid down that English laws and customs were henceforth to be observed in Ireland. The pleas of the crown, which included cases of serious crime, were reserved for hearing by the justiciar or by judges sent to the localities. The justiciar was also empowered to issue the same writs to initiate civil litigation as existed in England. Later in 1210 a register of those writs was sent to Ireland. The English common law had arrived. It operated first and foremost for the English within the king's own lands. But John was more ambitious than that. In 1208 he clamped down on the Marshal's Leinster and de Lacy's Meath by reserving for himself in both the hearing of the pleas of the crown. In Meath he also reserved for himself the issuing of the common law writs. In fact in the thirteenth century, in both Meath (restored to Walter de Lacy in 1215) and Leinster, these restrictions were not upheld. But at least lordship law was the king's law of England, not marcher law as to some extent it was within the great lordships of Wales.

John was equally keen to extend his authority within the native kingdoms. His proclamation about the pleas of the crown in 1207 had been 'to everyone of the whole of Ireland' and such pleas were reserved in the grant of Connacht to Cathal Crovderg in 1215. The implication is that the Irish in the native kingdoms were to be subject to such pleas, as they probably were (although contemporary evidence is non-existent) within the royal lands. Yet John was realistic. As he put it in 1207, his authority ran 'through all our land and power of Ireland'. In practice his power within the native kingdoms was negligible. They escaped the 'blessings' of English law. So, when it came to civil litigation, did the native Irish even within the royal lands. Perhaps that was partly by choice. They preferred their own customs, which royal government made no effort to eliminate. Later they were denied the choice, being deemed unfree and thus excluded. It might have been different had John's aggressive rule continued to subject both the lordships and the native kingdoms to royal 'power'.

＊　　＊　　＊

In Wales, as in Ireland, John exploited chances to increase his terri-tories at the expense of both the native rulers and the English barons. He knew Wales better than any of his predecessors. Having obtained Glamorgan through his first marriage in 1189, he retained it, despite his divorce, until 1214. He imposed his authority on the native rulers with a new sharpness and precision, thus foreshadowing tensions which exploded later in the century. Yet John never dealt with Wales, any more than Ireland, in isolation, something encapsulated in his attitude to an archbishopric of St Davids, plans for which he encouraged or discouraged depending on whether his relations with the archbishop of Canterbury, Hubert Walter, were bad or good, as Gerald of Wales who aimed to be archbishop noted dyspeptically. Again, it was as a reward for easing through his accession that John recognized the claim of William Marshal, hitherto just holding Chepstow, to the earldom and lordship of Pembroke – a major concession, since Pembroke had been in royal hands since Henry II had denied it to the Marshal's father-in-law, Richard fitz Gilbert (see above, p. 217). Against this, John made an early gain through exploiting the divisions between descendants of the Lord Rhys in Deheubarth. In return for confirming his tenure of Emlyn in northern Dyfed, John received from Maelgwn, son of the Lord Rhys, acting 'in hatred of Gruffudd his brother', the cession in perpetuity of Cardigan. This 'lock and stay of all Wales' (as the Brut put it) which the Lord Rhys had finally wrested from the Clares in the 1160s was now for the first time in royal hands, marching with the existing base at Carmarthen. As in Ireland, however, it was rash to trust John's bargains. In 1204 he allowed William Marshal to drive Maelgwn from Emlyn. In the north, John had similarly tried to exploit divisions among the Welsh, but by 1202 Llywelyn ab Iorwerth (the future Llywelyn the Great) had emerged as master of all Gwynedd 'from the Dyfi to the Dee'. So John changed tack and in 1205 gave his illegitimate daughter, Joan, in marriage to Llyelyn. He thus hoped to secure the latter's loyalty, not least as a counterweight to the earl of Chester.

The Welsh rulers submitted to John to gain his support in their fratricidal quarrels and immunity from royal and baronial aggression. The terms of their submissions were set out in a series of charters and other documents, which were themselves then copied onto the new chancery rolls. The relations between the king and the Welsh rulers, recorded in writing apparently for the first time, thus gained a novel exactitude. The Welsh themselves regarded these charters later in the century as marking a new start in their dealings with the English crown. John made it very clear that the rulers in Deheubarth, Gwynedd and Powys held their lands from him in return for homage and service 'against all mortals'. Breach of this faith involved forfeiture. In Llywelyn's case 'the magnates of his land' swore fealty too so that John was asserting authority within Gwynedd itself, an ominous precedent for the future. An agreement of 1202 with Llywelyn also gave the king in some circumstances the right to send his own officials 'into the land of Llywelyn' to hear law cases. The Welsh rulers were becoming trammelled up in the law and bureaucracy of England; ultimately it would strangle them.

After the loss of Normandy in 1204, John visited Wales or the March in every year down to 1211. On William de Braose's fall in 1208 he took possession of the Braose lordships of Radnor, Elfael, Builth, Brecon, Abergavenny and Gower, gaining an altogether new power in Wales. He placed these territories under the Tourangeau, Gerard d'Athée, erstwhile castellan of Loches. Also in 1208 John imprisoned Gwenwynwyn, ruler of southern Powys, and seized his lands. Llywelyn, however, like a beast scavaging its share of the prey, managed to take the western districts of Arwystli and Cyfeiliog for himself, controlling as a result the great east–west pass through central Wales. He went on to drive Maelgwn out of Ceredigion and seize Aberystwyth. John was furious. In 1211, building on his Irish triumph, he invaded Gwynedd with an army which included both Maelgwn and Gwenwynwyn, the latter now back in favour. This was the first royal expedition to Wales since that of Henry II in 1165 and it penetrated to Bangor, further west than any of its predecessors. Llywelyn, with the wisdom he showed throughout his career, sent his wife Joan to beg for terms. They were harsh. John was to have hostages, a large tribute in cattle, and the allegiance of any of Llywelyn's men he wished (the stipulation of 1202 once again). He was also to have in perpetuity the Four Cantrefs between the Conwy and the Dee, and to become heir to the rest of Gwynedd if Llywelyn himself had no heirs by Joan. He thus truncated Gwynedd and, in the future, might have it altogether. Meanwhile in the south John's Norman military captain, Falkes de Bréauté, in a separate expedition from Cardiff advanced into Ceredigion, captured Aberystwyth and built a new castle there for the crown. 'Thus in Ireland, Scotland and Wales there was no one who did not bow to the nod of the king of England, which, as is well known, was the case with none of his predecessors,' wrote the Barnwell annalist.

*   *   *

John, then, seemed triumphant in Britain. He was also moving towards a settlement of the Interdict, and building up the continental allies necessary for the recovery of his empire. In May 1212 he reached an agreement both with Reginald, count of Boulogne and the Emperor Otto, the latter braced to meet the challenge in Germany of the future Emperor Frederick II. John then began to assemble a fleet at Portsmouth only to call the expedition off, probably because he had failed to reach an agreement with the count of Flanders. His fortunes were beginning to spiral inexorably downwards.

Llywelyn, after attending John's 1212 Easter court, had made a bid for freedom. He brought, or so he claimed, 'all the princes of Wales' into a confederation, made an alliance with the king of France (like his grandfather Owain Gwynedd), and seized back the Four Cantrefs, determined to break his enemies' castle-enforced 'yoke of tyranny'. Llywelyn was joined by John's erstwhile ally Maelgwn, who had already destroyed the royal castle at Aberystwyth, and by Gwenwynwyn of southern Powys. John, following Henry II's precedent in 1165, in revenge killed Maelgwn's hostage sons (two died after castration, and one, although only seven, was hanged), and then planned an expedition which would effectively have ended Welsh independence. Over 8,000 labourers were to assemble, a castle-building force double that deployed by the eventual conqueror of Wales, Edward I. But Llywelyn had not been foolhardy; he had been in league with the English barons.

On 16 August 1212 at Nottingham, John suddenly learnt of a baronial plot either to murder him or leave him to his fate during the campaign in Wales. Of the two known conspirators one was the cagey, independent Eustace de Vesci, the lord of Alnwick in Northumberland. The other was Robert fitz Walter, lord of Little Dunmow in Essex and Baynards Castle in London. Something of fitz Walter's valour and connections can be sensed in his silver seal die, now in the British Museum. It shows him in a grim flat-topped helmet, brandishing his sword, and galloping along on a splendidly caparisoned horse, the heraldic devices proclaiming his links with both the Clares and the Quencies. Fitz Walter nursed grievances over debts and thwarted claims to Hertford castle. He also put it about that John had tried to seduce his daughter. Vesci, if a later story can be believed, resented similar attentions to his wife. Both Henry I and Henry II had been promiscuous, but never with political repercussions. In John's case accusations that he tampered with the wives and daughters of his magnates were widespread and not always without foundation. An entry on one of the chancery rolls reveals John apparently joking with his mistress, the wife of Hugh de Neville, over what a night back with Hugh was worth; the answer, a ridiculous 200 chickens. Together with his murders such activities show why hostility to John took on such a personal hue. They do not explain Magna Carta, but they were a major factor in the rebellion which led up to it.

The depth of the 1212 crisis can be measured from John's reaction. He called off the Welsh expedition and marched north to assert his authority, forcing fitz Walter and Vesci to flee to France. He also made a series of concessions 'worthy of remembrance and praise', as the Barnwell annalist puts it, abandoning revenues he was exacting above the county farms, investigating the abuses of the sheriffs and foresters, and promising to relax repayments of money owed to the Jews. Having stabilized his position, however, he did not revive his Welsh expedition because he was facing a much graver threat. By the spring of 1213, in touch with English dissidents and encouraged by papal hints of John's imminent deposition, King Philip was preparing a great invasion to be led by Louis, his eldest son. In May John gathered a large army in Kent to meet the threat. He also realized he must now settle with the pope.

On 13 May 1213 he agreed to receive back Langton, the other exiled bishops, and also Vesci and fitz Walter who had somehow joined their cause to that of the church. Two days later he made both England and Ireland fiefs to be held henceforth from the papacy. In return, he was absolved from excommunication, by Langton himself, on 20 July. The Interdict itself was finally lifted a year later, after compensation had been set in train. John had been forced to accept an archbishop he distrusted – with reason, as things turned out. Yet he probably repaid less than half the £100,000 he had extracted from the church, and now had the pope as his staunchest friend: hence ultimately the survival of his dynasty. God too conferred an immediate reward. On 30 May the earl of Salisbury and the count of Boulogne destroyed the French invasion fleet at Damme and the danger was over.

John could go on the offensive, and it was not in Wales. Having now received the allegiance of the count of Flanders, and with the diplomatic breaches so disastrous in the loss of Normandy finally repaired, John sailed in February 1214 for Poitou, without many of his barons, but with a large treasure and numerous paid knights. The strategy was to split the French forces in two. The Emperor Otto, the counts of Flanders and Boulogne, and the earl of Salisbury attacked from the north and John from the south. In June he advanced beyond Angers; only then, confronted by a large French army and deserted by his Poitevin allies, was he forced to retreat. By 9 July he was back at La Rochelle. On 27 July his northern allies were comprehensively defeated by King Philip at the battle of Bouvines. Bouvines deservedly ranks among the world's decisive battles. In Germany it undermined Otto and set up Frederick II. In Normandy it ended the chance of Angevin recovery. In Europe it made King Philip supreme. In England it shattered John's authority and paved the way for Magna Carta.

John had left a kingdom seething with discontent, which had mounted during his absence. This was partly due to the extraordinary man he had left behind as justiciar, Peter des Roches, bishop of Winchester. Peter, from the Touraine, was a skilled administrator and a military expert (he later fought at the battle of Lincoln) who had risen in John's service and had been the only bishop not to desert him during the Interdict.

> The warrior of Winchester, up at the exchequer
> Sharp at accounting, slack at the scripture,

ran one lampoon (in Michael Clanchy's rendering). Regarded as an abrasive foreigner by many barons, and certainly very different from his cautious predecessors, Peter strove to raise the scutage John demanded from those who had not come on the 1214 expedition, only to find that in Yorkshire in particular resistance made that impossible. On John's return in October 1214, 'the Northerners', as they are called in many sources, emerged as a distinct body, leading the resistance. They included, at this early stage, Eustace de Vesci, William de Mowbray and Roger de Montbegon (another baron heavily in debt to the crown), who had all refused to go on the 1214 campaign. They sent envoys to the pope and by early 1215 had forced John into negotiations, demanding at the very least that he confirm the Coronation Charter of Henry I. There had been, therefore, a decisive change in objectives since the plot to murder the king in 1212. The aim now was not to eliminate him but to bind him to conditions. This was not because he seemed any more trustworthy or salubrious. It was just that murder or deposition, especially when there was no obvious replacement, seemed harder to contemplate now that John, instead of being excommunicated, was a favourite son of the church.

John played for time, and postponed consideration of these matters to a council due to meet at Oxford at the end of April 1215. Yet his position continued to weaken. Offers to Llywelyn and Maelgwn did not prevent them combining with the barons. The pope remained supportive but he was distant, and Langton refused to excommunicate the dissidents. To be sure, in November 1214 John had tried to buy Langton's support and that of the church in general by issuing a charter which promised free and speedy canonical elections to abbeys and bishoprics. But this was less momentous than it seemed. John still hoped that his candidates would be elected; he could still, under the terms of the charter, refuse his assent to elections, in which case he would retain the vacancy revenues until a successor was appointed. Langton therefore increasingly played the role, not of a supporter of the king, but of a mediator between the two sides and one largely in sympathy with baronial aims.

The opposition barons did not come to the Oxford council at the end of April. Instead they mustered in arms at Stamford in Lincolnshire and on 5 May formally defied the king. By now the original Northerners had been joined by the earls of Hereford, Norfolk and Essex, as well as the clever and charismatic Saer de Quency. John had made the latter earl of Winchester and a chief official at the exchequer, but had denied him the castle of Mountsorrel; de Quency was left an earl without a castle – almost as disastrous as a knight without a horse. Military leadership of the movement was assumed by Saer's brother-in-arms, Robert fitz Walter, under the grandiloquent title 'Marshal of the Army of God and Holy Church'.

The war which began on 5 May was transformed within twelve days. Despite John's charter early in the month giving them the right to have a mayor, on 17 May the Londoners let the rebels into the city. Its financial resources were now theirs; the security of its walls theirs also. (London remained the principal baronial base until the end of hostilities in 1217.) There was no way John could now bring the war to a speedy end, especially as he was also faced by the rebellion of large numbers of knights. In part that was because knightly tenants followed their lords, something very clear in the north where baronies were compact and the tie of tenure was reinforced by that of neighbourhood. But it was also because many knights were sympathetic to the rebel cause. Ralph of Coggeshall's statement that John's leading supporters were all deserted by their knights was an exaggeration (the loyalist earl of Derby was remarkably successful in keeping his tenants in line), but it indicates the flow of the tide. Some knights like Thomas of Moulton and Simon of Kyme, both ex-sheriffs of Lincolnshire, were as wealthy as many barons and clearly made their own decisions to rebel. So did those from areas without dominant lords, such as the counties of Northampton, Bedford, Cambridge and Huntingdon where at least seventy-eight knights were in the rebel camp. Many knights had griev-ances of their own; William fitz Ellis, for instance, alleged that his manor of Oakley in Buckinghamshire had been taken from him by King John 'by will, unjustly and without judgement'. (For the fitz Ellises, see below, p. 395.) The general administration of the shires and forests had been harsh, and was the harder to bear now that knights were increasingly staffing juries, holding office and developing the view (reflected in Magna Carta) that they should control local government themselves.

For all their support there was equally no way the barons on their part could win a quick victory, or not without the hazard of a battle which might go either way. John still held his castles throughout England, many commanded by ruthless military experts. Scraping together money, he had also recruited a considerable body of foreign mercenaries. He retained the allegiance of the earls of Chester, Derby, Warenne, Salisbury and Pembroke; the last, William Marshal, had been secured by a wise grant in January 1214 of the custody of Cardigan and Carmarthen. Marshal's adherence helped to secure the position in Ireland, and this meant that John could still draw supplies from the province. To make doubly sure, he had also patched up his quarrel with Walter de Lacy, in 1215 restoring him to Meath, a striking example of how English politics impacted on Ireland.

Stalemate produced negotiations, which took place from 27 May under cover of a truce. The baronial programme was rapidly developing. In one surviving draft, the Coronation Charter of Henry I was linked to twelve entirely fresh provisions (called by modern historians the 'Unknown Charter'). By 10 June, when John agreed 'The Articles of the Barons' as a basis for a settlement, the Coronation Charter had been forgotten and the new provisions numbered forty-nine. There followed five days of intense negotiations. Runnymede, the great meadow beside the Thames, where the baronial tents were pitched and the talks held with John who rode down from Windsor castle, is still redolent of those long summer days. Finally the negotiators reached agreement and John, seizing the initiative, went ahead at once and issued the Charter, later called Magna Carta, which embodied the terms. The date was 15 June. It was left to the baronial negotiators to sell the results to the assembled barons, many of whom (especially a group of Northerners) would have liked something much more radical. As a result, it was not until 19 June that the deal was accepted and peace proclaimed: a poor omen for the future.

*　　*　　*

The restrictions placed by Magna Carta on the workings of kingship were unprecedented and profound. In sixty-two interlocking chapters, the Great Charter sought to limit the king's 'money-making' operations, make his justice more equitable, reform the abuses of his local agents, and prevent him acting in an arbitrary fashion against individuals. 'No free man shall be taken or imprisoned or disseised or outlawed or exiled or in any way ruined . . . except by the lawful judgement of his peers or the law of the land,' ran chapter 39; 'To no one will we sell, to no one will we deny or delay right or justice,' ran chapter 40. Intended as fundamental bars to tyranny, these are the chapters of Magna Carta still on the Statute Book today. The Charter concluded with its 'security clause', setting up twenty-five barons whose task was to compel the king to keep its provisions. Henceforth he was to be subject to the law, the law Magna Carta itself laid down.

Yet the Charter's view of kingship was far from entirely negative. It accepted the new common law legal procedures of Henry II and sought to make them more readily available. Thus chapter 17 implied that the bench of justices was to sit permanently at Westminster to hear common pleas; under chapter 18, judges were to tour the counties four times a year to hear the petty assizes. So the king was not to be reduced to a mere feudal overlord. The huge expansion of royal justice begun by Henry II's procedures was to continue. In other areas, where the desire was to restrict kingship, the Charter was less radical than many hoped, largely because it was a negotiated document, not one dictated to John after military defeat. Whereas the 'Unknown Charter' had called for the reversal of the massive afforestations of Henry II, Magna Carta postponed the issue into some indefinite future. It did little about debts owed to the Jews, and apart from dismissing some foreign sheriffs and castellans, left John free to chose his local agents. Above all, John retained complete control of central government. The chancery still issued writs and charters on his sole orders. He could appoint whom he liked as his great ministers and, generally speaking, give patronage to whom he liked. These gaps in the Charter were to be the battleground of politics later in the thirteenth century.

The early clauses of the Charter benefited baronial families first and foremost since they were designed to limit the king's 'feudal' rights and revenues – those which derived from the tenurial relationship between him and his tenants-in-chief. Earls and barons were now to succeed to their estates on payment of a fixed £100 relief and the king was only to take 'reasonable issues' from wardships. Heirs of tenants-in-chief were to be married without disparagement, that is only to their social equals, and their widows were to enter their inheritances and dowers without payment. They were also not to be forced to re-marry, a clause which had a significant impact on the position of noblewomen in the thirteenth century (see below, p. 421.) The assembly which was to give consent to taxation was to be made up of lay and ecclesiastical tenants-in-chief. Yet the Charter was far from simply a baronial document. Chapter 1 guaranteed the liberty of the church and confirmed the earlier charter which had already granted free elections. Chapter 13 confirmed the liberties of all cities and boroughs, including London, whose mayor was one of the twenty-five barons. The baronial tenants-in-chief had to pass down the concessions they received to their own tenants, and were restricted in the number of 'aids' (that is taxes) they could take from them. The Charter gave special prominence to the knights. Twelve from each county, elected locally, were to investigate and abolish abuses by the king's local officials. Four knights, again locally elected, were to sit with the judges coming to the counties to hear the petty assizes: a striking testimony to both the expertise of the knights and their desire to control local government themselves. The Charter as a whole was granted 'to all freemen', a vast and diverse group of people, including many peasants. It was all freemen, not just barons, who were to enjoy the guarantees in chapter 39. Likewise it was all freemen who were to benefit from chapters 17 and 18, which sought to make the common law and the petty assizes more available. And then, under the terms of the security clause, everyone – apparently the free and unfree alike – would form 'the community of the land' bound by oath to help the twenty-five barons enforce the Charter.

Up to a point, though only up to a point, the Charter did indeed reach out to the unfree. The chapters regulating amercements (20–22) were explicit in covering all ranks in society, villeins as well as earls, barons, clerks and freemen. Chapter 23 was of exclusive benefit to the peasantry, laying down that 'no village or man' could be forced unlawfully to build bridges. In a more general way, everyone stood to gain from the clauses which limited the exactions of the sheriffs, notably chapter 25 which freed them from having to raise money above the 'ancient farms' of their shires. Again, everyone was included when John promised in chapter 40 that 'to *no one* will we deny right or justice'. There, however, was the rub. For it was the law itself which held the unfree in thrall, denying them access to the king's courts. Only freemen conspicuously benefited from the promises in chapter 39, and freemen, as we have seen, were the grantees of the Charter. The barons might speak of 'the common Charter of the realm' but it was far more common for some than it was for others.

The Charter had been created by the financial pressure of royal government both on the barons and wider sections of society. Some of the strains were of long standing. The Coronation Charter of Henry I had itself dealt with baronial grievances over relief, wardships and marriages. In that sense Magna Carta sought to resolve the tensions which stemmed from the feudal relationships established by the Conquest. Such pressures had been limited under Henry II but they had escalated rapidly under Richard and John, thanks to the growing burden of defending and recovering the Angevin empire. As for wider sections of society, here Henry II had created (or so it was thought) the extensive and oppressive jurisdiction of the royal forests; while Richard (in 1194) exacted money in excess of the ancient farms of the counties, a policy carried further by John and banned, as mentioned, by chapter 25 of the Charter. And it was Richard and John (Richard for his ransom, John in 1207) who for the first time since the Anglo-Saxon kings raised really large sums from taxation. No wonder the Charter insisted that such taxes needed consent. It did the same for scutages, a clear reaction to the large number John had levied. Ralph of Coggeshall affirmed that the rebellion of 1215 was against the abuses of Henry and Richard, and those which John had added. Yet John's additions were far more than a final straw. They were a large part of the burden. Under Richard the financial pips had squeaked, under John they had screamed.

Another important thrust of the Charter was to end the arbitrary way in which the king had treated individuals, his manipulation of inheritances, his denial and sale of justice, and his seizure of property 'by will' and without judgment: hence the importance for great men of chapters 39 and 40. Again, such grievances were often of long-standing: the Charter referred to the arbitrary disseisins of Henry II and Richard. Those of John 'without lawful judgement of peers' were to be redressed, if necessary by the twenty-five barons of the security clause; so were the fines and amercements which John had imposed 'unjustly and contrary to the law of the land'. In fact over fifty restorations were made at Runnymede or soon after, twelve to members of the twenty-five: Nicholas de Stuteville was now to recover Knaresborough, and the earl of Hereford, Trowbridge; at the knightly level William fitz Ellis was to get Oakley. Closely related to the king's behaviour in these areas was the issue of patronage. The stipulation that heirs should be married without disparagement was clearly an attack on marriages like that of the Tourangeau Peter de Maulay to the Doncaster heiress. Another clause dismissed from office the hated northern sheriff Philip Mark and his associates.

'Instead of law there was tyrannical will,' commented the Waverley abbey annalist on John's rule, reflecting another background to the

Charter's reforms. Views about government had been developing. John was far more hedged round by such ideas than Henry I had been a hundred years before. Of course, some of the key ideas in 1215 were already very old, notably the call for judgement by peers; that had been mentioned as correct procedure in Henry I's agreement with the count of Flanders back in 1101. Equally old was the idea that the king should govern lawfully and with the advice and consent of his great men. But around such basic concepts the Schoolmen of the twelfth century had created a far more elaborate system. Central to the thought of John of Salisbury in his influential *Policraticus* was the distinction derived from Gregory the Great and St Augustine between the just prince and the tyrant: the prince governs according to the laws for the good of his people; the tyrant tramples on the laws, oppresses his people and consults only his private will.

Such ideas became commonplace. In the 1200s they were interpolated into a compilation of older legal texts (the so-called 'Laws of Edward the Confessor') by a London author who quite possibly moved in the circle of the baronial leaders. 'Right and justice,' the tract opined, 'ought to reign in the kingdom more than depraved will.' The king should 'do all things rightfully in his kingdom by judgement of the magnates of his kingdom'. Archbishop Langton fed his own ideas into the heady mix. In his lectures on Deuteronomy at Paris he had criticized the avarice of 'modern kings' and urged them to study the law. He believed obedience was not obligatory if a king acted wilfully and without judgement. And his general view of the congregation of clergy and people, from whom temporal authority derived and in whose interests the king should rule, reflected the way the whole 'commune of the land' benefited from the Charter, or at least was assembled to support it.

John's opponents were also quite able to justify their rebellion. As we have seen, they simply issued a formal act of 'defiance' and renounced their homages to the king. This was a procedure that could be traced back at least to the reign of Stephen, and one which, whatever the king thought about it, allowed rebels to believe that their conduct was proper and legitimate. Nor was there any difficulty in contemplating the murder of the king, as in 1212. John of Salisbury in his *Policraticus* had reviewed the fate of evil rulers and stated, if in passing, that tyrannicide was justified. The idea of a charter, once murder was off the agenda, was easy to conceive. Urban communities had long been obtaining charters from the king conferring trading and governmental privileges. John himself had set a more general precedent when he issued in November 1214 the charter which conceded the church free elections. More crucial still was the Coronation Charter of Henry I. It formed the dissidents' first known programme and the foundation on which further demands were built. It dealt not with general principles, but with the kind of detailed issues with which Magna Carta was most concerned, and was also, if not in so many words, conceded to the whole realm. There was also, if attempts at restriction failed, no difficulty about deposing the king and choosing another, for the idea persisted that the royal office was elective. Later in 1215, after the rebels had offered the throne to Louis, eldest son of the king of France, his explanation for what had happened was succinct: the barons 'by the common counsel of the kingdom judging [John] unworthy, chose us as king and lord'.

Surrounded by a forest of such opinions, the Angevins made limited efforts to hack their way out. Henry, Richard and John, through ritual and display, sought to enhance the status of their kingship. They spent large sums on crowns, robes and great ceremonial feasts. Their language stressed the rights and dignity of the crown (see above, p. 196). Their royal seals, following the model since the Conquest, on one side showed them armed and galloping on horseback like any other noble, and sitting with orb and sceptre, crowned in majesty, on the other, utterly unique. Anointing at the coronation had poured into them the blessings of the Holy Spirit, and these gifts they sought constantly to renew and proclaim; hence Henry's penance at Becket's shrine and Richard's crusade; hence the customary round of alms-giving and pilgrimages. Spiritual gifts were not solicited simply for personal salvation. Henry II endowed religious houses for the souls of his family and also 'for the peace and stability of the kingdom of England'. But there were other factors, some of their own making, some not, which inevitably dulled these God-given qualities. Henry I's abandonment of lay investiture meant that kings could no longer claim priestly functions. Careful with his money, Henry also scaled down the triennial crown-wearing ceremonies, while Henry II, impatient and secure, abandoned them altogether. At times Henry II deliberately dressed down and cultivated informality. Charisma, in any case, rarely survives contact with real personality, and the Angevins had to be very real. In terms of genuine piety only Richard, shimmering in his royal robes, assiduous in his attendance at Mass and indeed conducting the choir, was the true embodiment, and even his death seemed (to Ralph of Coggeshall) a just judgement of God. Henry was Becket's murderer, and John's later rule, if it was divinely ordained, was surely just as punishment. Up to a point, the charisma of kingship was diminished by its routinization, something reflected in the very appearance of the writs which originated the common law assizes, scrappy little things in an everyday hand with the king's name and titles highly abbreviated and his seal, if applied at all, broken on opening. Yet these were the royal documents which people saw more often than any others.

The Angevins also did little to elevate their kingship by drawing on ideas from the revival of Roman law. The latter was certainly studied in England in the second half of the twelfth century first at Lincoln and then at Oxford. The maxims 'the prince is free from the laws' and 'the will of the prince has the force of law' were well known. However, when *The Dialogue of the Exchequer* observed that some of the king's revenues came not by process of law but by his 'arbitrary will', it seemed embarrassed about it. *Glanvill*, though written by one of the king's judges, referred to the will of the prince having the force of law, only then to observe that in England the prince was not the sole lawgiver since laws were settled 'on the advice of the magnates'. Roman law was itself contradictory, for some passages stressed that the prince *was* beneath the law, and that law derived its force from 'the will of the people'. A more solid defence of kingship was the stand on custom. Henry II constantly said he was restoring the customs of his grandfather. John often stressed he was acting in accordance with the law and custom of the realm and could fairly impugn the baronial demands of 1215 as 'novelties'. After all, the fixed £100 relief and the ban on revenue above the county farms contradicted rather than confirmed existing practice. John could also claim that some of the arbitrary disseisins of which he stood accused moved in grey areas where right was far from clear. The trouble, of course, was that however much John said he had acted lawfully, as in his dealing with the Braoses, many disbelieved him. And something could be customary without being right. The Coronation Charter of Henry I had specifically abolished 'evil customs' which had oppressed the realm. The church, moreover, was able to condemn such customs as contravening its own canon law. The secular barons were in a more difficult position. They could only appeal to the 'Laws of Edward the Confessor' (vague and apocryphal) and Henry's

Coronation Charter (of uncertain status). But in the end, however much they pretended otherwise, they were quite able to make new law in the Charter.

The Angevins thus fought in the same forest as their opponents, indeed they had done much to plant it. John proclaimed in 1199 that he had succeeded by hereditary right, 'divine mercy', *and* 'the unanimous assent and favour of clergy and people', thus precisely stressing the elective element later used against him. In 1205, faced with possible invasion, he had formed 'a commune throughout all the kingdom, which everyone from the greatest to the least from twelve years upwards should swear to observe', an anticipation of the commune of the land formed against him to defend the Charter. 'We do not wish that you should be treated henceforth save by law and judgement, nor that anyone shall take anything from you by will, nor that you be disseised of your free tenements unjustly and without judgement.' So spoke John himself, not under duress in 1215, but in his proclamation to Ireland in 1207. He was, of course, doing no more than enunciating the principles on which the petty assizes of Henry II turned. The year 1215 marked the moment when the realm demanded that the king obey his own rules.

Ideas were important in shaping the Charter. So was the balance of power in English society (discussed in chapter 13), hence essentially the way it was far more than simply a baronial document. The barons did not rule in lordly isolation. Indeed, if they resented the common law sapping the jurisdiction of their private courts, the power of knightly under-tenants, among that law's chief beneficiaries, meant they could do little about it. Conversely, it was the lack of power of the unfree which explained their exiguous entries in the Charter. Indeed, in some cases when they did appear it was potentially to the benefit of their lords who, as in the clause on amercements, might hope to preserve their men from oppression by the king so as to have more to take themselves. That the unfree featured at all, however, was not just due to baronial self-interest or idealism. It also reflected the real yet limited extent to which peasants too were part of the political community. The Charter was very much a commentary on the structure of power within England's political society. It was the immediate facts of power which determined its fate.

*   *   *

For John, Magna Carta was an end, for the barons a beginning. On that difference the agreement foundered. John hoped the Charter, having brought peace and a restoration of his authority, would become a toothless symbol. It was to that end that he had seized the initiative at Runnymede, issuing the Charter on 15 June before the twenty-five barons of the security clause had been chosen, thus keeping their names out of the document. The barons, on the other hand, expected the Charter to be rigorously enforced and to lead to further reform. The barons, in the short term, got their way. The reversal of John's arbitrary fines and disseisins commenced at once, as did the abolition of the evil practices of the local officials revealed by the twelve knightly investigators in each county. In the north it was soon open season on the royal forests. By the middle of July, John had had enough. He sent envoys to the pope asking for the condemnation of the Charter, and the resulting bull, issued on 24 August, arrived in England towards the end of September. There was little to prevent this outcome. Langton's mediatory role was at an end. He was eventually suspended by the pope for refusing to excommunicate the barons, and left England for the papal court. Since the Charter was unsustainable, the barons turned to other remedies. At a great assembly held sometime in September, they deposed John and offered the throne to Louis, the eldest son of the king of France. Louis had the vestiges of a hereditary claim (his wife was the granddaughter of Henry II). He was uxorious, pious, and chivalric, so different from John. Most crucial of all, which was why the barons did not look to King Alexander of Scotland, he could deploy the superabundant resources of the French monarchy. The Capetian prince would oust the Angevin tyrant.

At the start of the war, the rebels held London and were strong in the eastern counties and the north, where they set up their own local administrations. But the king's castellans held a spine of castles through the centre of England, protecting the chief bases of royal power to the west, where the barons of the Welsh March (apart from the Braoses) remained loyal. From there John could receive help from Ireland where the rebellion had no footing, thanks to William Marshal in Leinster and Walter de Lacy. There were also two royal castles of vital importance deep in rebel territory: Dover under Hubert de Burgh, and Lincoln held by the redoubtable widow Nicola de la Haye. (Her inheritance had included the castellanship of the castle.) Seizing the properties of the rebels within his reach, John built up his treasure and soon had around 800 knights in the field, many of them Flemish mercenaries. His aim was to win the war before Louis could intervene. From 13 October 1215, like a great cat hissing at some rival, he sat still besieging Rochester castle. Then, with the castle taken on 6 December, he was off in great bounds to the north to chase away not a cat, but a red fox, as John called him, King Alexander of Scotland.

Magna Carta was a British document. There were chapters, reflecting their co-operation with the barons, in favour of both Llywelyn and King Alexander, the latter having succeeded to the Scottish throne at the age of sixteen on the death of his father in December 1214. The twenty-five barons, nine of whom had Scottish connections, had also adjudged to Alexander possession of Carlisle and the three northern counties. Perhaps the moment had come for him to gain those long-coveted prizes, either as fiefs held from the English king or indeed, if opportunity offered, as part of Scottish realm. The ground seem favourable. In June 1215 an end had been put to a rising, again in Ross and Moray, led by Kenneth MacHeth and Donald MacWilliam, sons of the insurgents killed in 1186–7. Alexander was secure in Scotland. In England, the north was a major seat of the rebellion against King John, however firmly the latter retained many of his northern castles. Numerous cross-border ties of landholding and kinship, arguably more intense and influential than at any time since 1157, might also ease Alexander's take-over. He himself was lord of Tynedale, while the leading northern rebels, Eustace de Vesci and Robert de Ros, were his half-brothers, having married illegitimate daughters of William the Lion. Above all, Carlisle was already Alexander's, for John had unwisely made Ros constable of its castle in 1213, and had overtaxed its burgesses and alienated the canons of the cathedral by appointing a Serbian bishop. To Alexander himself, therefore, as to the sober councillors inherited from his father, it must have seemed like now or never. In October 1215, he laid siege to Norham on the Tweed border and received the homages of the barons of Northumberland. Early in the New Year some barons even from Yorkshire followed suit. But Alexander had miscalculated, because John was far from finished. With an army of around 450 knights, most of them foreign mercenaries, he marched north, recovered Carlisle, reached Berwick in mid January and went on to ravage Lothian. He then returned south via East Anglia, burning the lands of his enemies and taking their castles. But while he was triumphing in the north, his position had disintegrated in Wales.

Towards the end of 1215, with John bound for the north, Llywelyn took Carmarthen, 'for seventy years the centre of royal power in the valley of the Tywi' (as Sir John Lloyd put it), and then captured Cardigan, John's great gain early in his reign. William Marshal hung on to Pembroke. But with Glamorgan now with the rebel earl of Essex (son of Geoffrey fitz Peter) through his marriage to John's divorced wife, John's dominance of south Wales had been utterly destroyed. West of Hereford he had nothing.

On 21 May 1216 Louis landed in Kent. He brought several great French nobles and 1,200 knights, a formidable force that John feared to face. Louis took Rochester, entered a cheering London and then seized Winchester. John was deserted by a good number of his household knights, by the earl of Salisbury (his half-brother whose wife he had seduced), and by Hugh de Neville (whose wife had offered the 200 chickens). In August, Carlisle was surrendered to Alexander who then came south to do homage to Louis for the northern counties. The next month, with Louis besieging Dover, John marched north to relieve Lincoln, where he made Nicola de la Haye sheriff of the county in recognition both of her character and local prestige. Then, returning from King's Lynn by a short-cut across the Wellstream estuary, his baggage train was trapped by the tide, the so-called loss of his treasure in the Wash. By this time John was racked by dysentery. He reached Newark and died there during the night of 17–18 October as a great storm howled round the castle, whipping up from the flat empty valley of the Trent. Was this also the end for his dynasty?

10

The Minority of Henry III and its Sequel, 1216–34, Llywelyn the Great, 1194–1240, and Alexander II, 1214–49

No king of England came to the throne in a more desperate situation than Henry III. He was only nine and commanded less than half his kingdom. Louis, eldest son of the king of France, to whom the rebels had offered the throne, held London and the allegiance of nineteen of the twenty-seven greatest barons. Henry's coronation on 28 October took place perforce not at Westminster but at Gloucester, and there it was disturbed by news of a Welsh attack on Goodrich, less than eighteen miles away. Meanwhile in the north King Alexander had recovered Carlisle and done homage to Louis for the northern counties.

Nevertheless it was not all gloom. For fifteen weeks through the summer and autumn of 1216 Louis had personally directed the siege of Dover castle, and had been repulsed by its great castellan, Hubert de Burgh. The castle was indeed, as Hubert put it, 'the key to England'. Towering above and controlling Dover port, its possession meant the Angevins could still sweep the Channel and threaten Louis's communications with France. The next year Dover was to prove vital to victory. John's party of castellans and magnates also remained solid. The former, often parvenu foreigners, had nowhere else to go; the latter were often kept in place by private disputes with those on the other side. There was no point in Ranulf, earl of Chester, deserting when his rival for the earldom of Lincoln, Gilbert de Gant, was one of Louis's leading supporters. As for William Marshal, earl of Pembroke, his defection would give the green light to his enemies in Ireland. In any case, he had hedged his bets (and protected his lordship of Longueville in Normandy) by condoning or at least failing to prevent the rebellion of his eldest son. William's own explanation of his conduct was more inspiring and no less true. He would never desert the young king, he declared, even if it meant carrying the boy on his shoulders from country to country, begging for bread. 'No man will ever have earned such glory on earth,' cried William's faithful steward John of Earley, who provided much of the information behind *The Life of William Marshal*, the brilliant verse biography which the family commissioned in the 1220s.

The Marshal made his declaration when he had just been chosen 'ruler of the king and the kingdom', in effect regent, by Henry's supporters assembled for the coronation. His power – lord of Chepstow, Pembroke and Leinster – made him a natural choice. So did his overwhelming prestige. True, the Marshal was only a younger son of a middling Berkshire–Wiltshire magnate, the John Marshal who had been castellan of Marlborough in Stephen's reign. Yet his rise had been not through a series of acrimonious wheels and deals but a great marriage, to Richard fitz Gilbert's (Strongbow's) daughter. And that marriage, gift of King Richard, was a tribute not to his exactions as an administrator but to his staunchness as a councillor and his prowess as a knight – indeed, as victory in countless tournaments across France had shown, the 'greatest knight in the world'. Now nearly seventy, Marshal was still a *beau sabreur*, but he was also a calculating general and a canny politician: right at the start he delayed his election as regent until Ranulf, earl of Chester, his only possible rival, could arrive and agree to it. No one was better equipped to shoulder the young king's cause.

Above the Marshal was Guala, the papal legate. John had made England a papal fief and Pope Honorius III (who had succeeded Innocent III in 1216) now gave Guala the fullest powers. Although not involved in day-to-day government, or of course in the fighting, his ultimate supremacy was uncontested, a remarkable testimony to papal authority. Eye-catching in his red robes, astride his white horse, this Italian cardinal, whose foundation of a house of canons at Vercelli was closest to his heart, acted with extraordinary energy and commitment in England, excommunicating Louis and his supporters and in 1217 turning the war into a crusade. Louis might control Westminster Abbey, but deprived of significant ecclesiastical support, there was no one to crown him. This was a crucial factor in his failure.

John had demanded that all those submitting to him forswear the Charter. Now the regent and Guala, with no time to consult the pope, executed a momentous volte-face. In November 1216 they issued in the king's name, under their own seals (Henry's had yet to be introduced), a revised version of Magna Carta. This was the first step in its survival. The regent, like the rest of John's baronial supporters, had as much to gain from the Charter as the barons on the other side. The hope, of course, was that the latter, their cause conceded, would now return to the Angevin camp. That was slow to happen, both for reasons of honour and the private disputes which we have mentioned. The final arbitrament was by war. In the spring of 1217, King Alexander once again invaded the north. Louis split his army: he himself renewed the siege of Dover while sending the rest of his French forces to help his English allies who were inside Lincoln besieging the castle, gallantly defended by Nicola de la Haye. The regent, in the supreme decision of his career, exploited the division. Battles were rare events because they could be devastatingly decisive, as Bouvines had shown. Now he would fight one 'with all for all'. On 20 May, after a daring personal reconnaissance by Bishop Peter of Winchester had discovered a way through the walls, the Angevins charged into Lincoln (the regent himself so eager that he nearly forgot his helmet) and won a complete victory. The battle had been typically chivalric. Among the nobles, only the count of Perche, the French commander, died, the result of a chance thrust through the eye-piece of his helmet, about which everyone was sorry. Robert fitz Walter, William de Mowbray, Nicholas de Stuteville, Gilbert de Gant and the flower of the baronial party simply surrendered. Perhaps the issue of the Charter, the succession of an innocent boy and resentments against Louis's Frenchmen had indeed sapped their will. It remained for Hubert de Burgh to deliver the *coup de grâce*. On 24 August he sailed out of Dover (Louis having abandoned the siege on the news of Lincoln) and, in a great battle off Sandwich, destroyed the fleet bringing French reinforcements. The French captain, the fabled but non-noble Eustace the Monk, was captured and given one option: where on the ship was he to be beheaded? Chivalry was assuredly for the upper classes.

Louis was finished. Under the Treaty of Kingston-Lambeth in September he resigned his claims to the throne and returned to France, having secured good terms for his lay supporters. They were to be absolved from excommunication and recover their lands as held at the start of the war. The Charter was part of the package. In November 1217, as many former rebels renewed their homage to the king, another version of it was issued, again sealed by Guala and the regent, but this time with an entirely new charter alongside it regulating the bounds and administration of the royal forest. The name Magna Carta first appeared to distinguish it from its smaller forest brother.

The war was won, but the regent faced terrible problems. King Alexander soon resigned Carlisle, but Llywelyn was determined to retain his gains in Wales. Overseas, once the truce expired in 1220 King Philip might invade Poitou and Gascony, where in any case the king's seneschal was so impecunious that (as he complained) he was treated like a little boy. In England royal authority had collapsed, much as it had done during the civil war of Stephen's reign. The king's revenue between 1217 and 1219 averaged some £8,000 a year, only a third of John's in 1199, even without adjusting for inflation, and a mere bagatelle compared with his later takings. In November 1217 the king had only seven household knights, as opposed to John's hundred. There had been a huge transfer of power from the centre to the localities. During the war the loyalist castellans, some of them great barons like the earl of Chester, others foreign military experts, had necessarily spent the revenue from their sheriffdoms themselves rather than passing it to the exchequer. They had also, with or without John's consent, taken over royal lands. They saw no reason why things should change with the peace. Indeed they had (or so they said) taken an oath to King John not to surrender their offices until his son came of age, which – if baronial practice was followed – would not be until he was twenty-one in October 1228. Meanwhile there was another danger. Many of these local commissars refused to return possessions they had seized from rebels, a refusal which threatened to re-ignite hostilities. The loyalist castellans, having been the heroes of the war, became the villains of the peace.

At the start of his reign Henry II had quickly reasserted royal authority. For the minority government of his grandson it was a far more tortuous process. The regent looked after his own interests (especially in Wales) but also made a start on the king's behalf. In July 1218, with an army to which many former rebels were summoned, he turned Robert de Gaugi (John's Flemish knight) out of Newark castle and returned it to the bishop of Lincoln. Then in November 1218 a great council introduced a seal for the king and commissioned judges to tour the country, hearing all pleas both criminal and civil; this was the most comprehensive eyre since that of 1176. With a bench of justices at Westminster in session since early 1218, the Charter's demand for the king's justice to be more available and at a fixed place was thus fulfilled.

The regent resigned in April 1219 and died a month later, confident to the last in his values: 'The argument of the clerks must be false or no one could be saved,' he declared, reflecting that he could not now return a lifetime's winnings. The government was initially taken on by a triumvirate composed of Pandulf, the papal legate (who, equally determined in his methods, had replaced Guala), the justiciar Hubert de Burgh, and the king's tutor, Peter des Roches, bishop of Winchester. From these arrangements one person was absent: John's widow, Henry III's mother, Isabella of Angoulême. She had played no discernible part in politics under John, but in 1217, now in her late twenties, had pushed her way into the negotiations with Louis for the end of the war. Fiery and ambitious, she almost certainly aspired to a regency role like that soon to be played in France by Blanche of Castile, the mother of Louis IX. Its refusal may explain her decision, placing power above parenthood, to return to 1218 to Angoulême where her rights as countess were uncontested. There in 1220 she married the great Poitevin noble Hugh de Lusignan and produced a second family which later played a divisive role in English politics.

The future lay with Hubert de Burgh, who was to dominate English government and politics down to his fall in 1232. He was the younger son of a Norfolk knightly family which came from Burgh next Aylesham, near Norwich. Hubert's elder brother William had followed John to Ireland and founded the Irish de Burghs – a connection important throughout Hubert's career. Hubert himself had made his name as a heroic castellan, at Chinon (in 1205) and then at Dover. In 1215 John had made him justiciar in place of Bishop Peter, but it was only with the regent's resignation that he received the powers the office implied. Hubert could read and he was highly intelligent. He had clear objectives, yet moved stealthily towards them. His first aim was to oust Bishop Peter from central government: a case of kill or be killed, for Peter deeply resented Hubert's position as he himself had aspired to follow the regent. By the time of the king's fourteenth birthday in October 1221 when Peter ceased to be his tutor, this objective had largely been achieved. With Pandulf's withdrawal in the same year, Hubert ruled alone.

Hubert's second aim was to do his duty as justiciar and restore the authority of the crown. That meant recovering crown lands and dismissing the entrenched sheriffs and castellans, a programme which Pandulf and the papacy had been urging since 1219. It was a programme which chimed well with Hubert's own interests since it was Bishop Peter and his allies who held the largest share of local office. These included Ranulf, earl of Chester, and a whole group of foreigners: the Poitevin count of Aumale; the Norman Falkes de Bréauté; and Engelard de Cigogné, Philip Mark and Peter de Maulay, all, like Bishop Peter, from the Touraine or its borders. This foreign component was immensely significant for it meant the conflict could be regarded as one between a party of native magnates and ministers, led by Hubert de Burgh on the one hand, and irresponsible and oppressive foreigners on the other. That was not how the foreigners themselves saw it. 'All you native born men of England are traitors,' raged Falkes de Bréauté, an outburst relayed by his enemies to Hubert, which shows that these tensions were felt by the actors themselves and were not simply the invention of chroniclers. Although foreshadowed before 1216, the scale of the struggle between the English and the aliens was altogether new. It was to envenom politics throughout the reign of Henry III.

Hubert and his allies moved forward gradually. In 1220, after a brief siege, the count of Aumale vacated the royal castle of Rockingham. Early next year another siege turned Aumale out of Castle Bytham in Lincolnshire and it was restored to its lord, the former rebel William de Coleville. In June 1221, after trumped-up charges of treason, Peter de Maulay was prised from the royal castle of Corfe. A year later, following several false attempts, the government carried through a resumption of crown land.

The conflict reached a climax in 1223, sparked off by papal letters ordering the king to be given control of his seal, and the castles and sheriffdoms to be surrendered. Hubert now consolidated an alliance with William Marshal II, earl of Pembroke (1219–31), the regent's formidable son, by supporting his campaign against Llywelyn in south Wales. Then he came to terms with Archbishop Langton. Langton had returned to England in 1218. If he believed John a tyrant, he had nothing against kingship *per se*. On the contrary, it needed to be strong though subject to the law in order to fulfil its function: the protection of clergy and people. Langton was therefore a natural ally of Hubert, especially given the latter's positive attitude to Magna Carta. In December 1223 archbishop and justiciar combined to enforce the papal mandate. The king, nominally at least, took control of his seal and thus of central government, although the ban introduced in 1218 on grants made in perpetuity stayed. In practice Hubert remained in charge at the centre, although joined there by the Langtonian bishop of Salisbury. At the same time all the sheriffs and castellans were summoned to North-ampton where, intimidated by the size of the king's forces and Langton's threats, they surrendered their custodies, which soon ended up in the hands of Hubert's supporters.

These changes hit one man especially: Falkes de Bréauté. Of peasant stock, or so it was said, he had begun his meteoric career as one of John's serjeants-at-arms and called simply 'Falkes'. His name was said to derive from the scythe with which he had killed someone in Normandy. Falkes certainly stood out. He was little in stature, but clever, ruthless and valiant. Having been appointed during the war, he commanded until 1223 no less than six Midlands counties, together with their royal castles. He had married the widow of the earl of Devon and had been given custody of the earldom during the minority of the heir, becoming 'the equal of an earl'. Sharp of tongue, as we have seen, and embroiled in many private quarrels over land, he seemed to many the epitome of the jumped-up, disobedient, over-mighty foreigner, 'more than king in England', as the Tewkesbury annalist put it. Falkes had surrendered his custodies at the end of 1223, but the next year his brother William seized a royal judge and imprisoned him in Bedford castle, Falkes's chief base. From 20 June to 15 August 1224 the royal army lay siege to the castle, taking it bit by bit. Falkes, although he was not inside, tearfully submitted and died in exile. His brother and members of the garrison were hanged.

Royal authority had been affirmed in England, and in Ireland also. Early in 1224 Hugh de Lacy had entered the lordship, aiming to recover the earldom of Ulster which he had lost in 1210. He was allied with his half-brother, William de Lacy, who now intruded into Meath at the expense of the third and loyalist Lacy brother, Walter, restored by John in 1215. In May 1224 the government responded by sending to Ireland as justiciar William Marshal II, earl of Pembroke and lord of Leinster. Rewarded by marriage to the king's youngest sister, Eleanor, the appointment fitted perfectly with the Marshal's wider interests. In attacking the Lacys he was attacking their allies, namely Llywelyn and the earl of Chester, who were both his enemies. He was also indirectly attacking Falkes de Bréauté, 'that inconstant and mendacious man' as the Marshal put it, with whom Chester was closely linked. With the politics of Ireland, Wales and England so closely intertwined, this was then a very British crisis. In Ireland it ended with the Marshal driving William de Lacy from Meath (after a siege of Trim) and Hugh from

Ulster. Although the government eventually restored Hugh in 1226–7, it was only for the term of his life.

It was a different matter in France. In 1220 Philip Augustus had renewed the truce. In 1224 his son and successor Louis VIII (1223–6), the erstwhile invader of England, refused to do so. While Henry III laid siege to Bedford, Louis VIII conquered Poitou. Then Hugh de Lusignan, to whom Louis had granted Bordeaux, overran much of Gascony. This crisis on the continent led to the final establishment of Magna Carta in England.

A supreme effort was needed to save Gascony, and the government made it. In 1225 it dispatched an army under the earl of Salisbury and the king's younger brother, Richard, now sixteen and beginning his long political career. With Bordeaux and Bayonne remaining loyal, and Louis (content with Poitou) not helping Hugh de Lusignan, they expelled the latter's forces from Gascony. It remained in English hands until 1453. This success owed much to ample funds. In 1225 a great council agreed to levy a tax, a fifteenth on movables, which raised some £40,000. In return, in February 1225 the king issued new versions of Magna Carta and the Charter of the Forest, versions witnessed by those who had stood on opposite sides in the civil war, including eight of the twenty-five barons appointed to enforce the original Charter back in 1215. Here, then, was the final reconciliation. Although not very different from those of 1217, the Charters of 1225 were the first to be authenticated with the new king's seal. They became definitive; subsequent kings did not issue new versions, they simply confirmed those of 1225. Clauses of the 1225 Magna Carta remain on the Statute Book today. From that time on, the Charters were 'official'. This had not been achieved without controversy. In 1223 the rebarbative William Brewer with a career in Angevin service which stretched back to Henry II declared that the Charters, extorted by force, should not be confirmed. He was silenced by Archbishop Langton and certainly ecclesiastical and baronial opinion made the Charters inevitable. Hubert de Burgh appreciated as much. He had long enjoyed a reputation as a moderate. His appointment to succeed Bishop Peter at Runnymede was itself clearly a conciliatory gesture by King John. In the early 1220s his personal fortune was still to be made. He had every reason to tread carefully and court magnate favour.

The restrictions on kingship finalized in 1225 were both less and more stringent than those of 1215, reflecting the desire of ministers in the intervening period to maintain the rights of the crown on the one hand, and appease the country on the other. Alongside Magna Carta, there was now the Charter of the Forest (unchanged from 1217) which regulated for the first time the forest's bounds and administration. The 1225 Magna Carta itself had a large chapter (number 35), also introduced in 1217, which regulated the frequency of the shire courts and limited the exactions of the sheriffs at their annual check in the hundred court of the tithing groups (the 'view of frankpledge'). The clause reflected the size of the political community, for it dealt with grievances of both the gentry, for whom attendance at the county court could be a burden, and the peasantry, who had to pay the exactions at the view of frankpledge (see below, p. 413). Against this, however, John's promise of free ecclesiastical elections, dropped by Guala in 1216 (when it would only have meant freedom to elect Louis's supporters), was never restored, to Langton's disappointment. Also dropped for good in 1216 was the requirement for general consent to be given to taxation, although in practice, as in 1225, such consent remained a necessity. More significant was the continued exclusion of the chapter dropped in 1216, which forbade the exaction of revenue above the old farms of the counties, a gap which Henry vigorously exploited later, causing much discontent (see below, p. 350). There was a final excision, the most significant of all. The security clause of 1215, which empowered twenty-five barons to enforce the Charter, disappeared in 1216, and was never replaced. As a result, the Charter was left without constitutional means of enforcement.

So would the Charters be enforced? For baronial families, looking particularly to the regulations on relief, wardship, widows, marriages, amercements and arbitrary disseisin, the signs under Hubert's government were encouraging. If their great law cases were still subject to delay and manipulation, at least justice was not sold, the huge sums routinely offered before 1215 being things of the past; a highly significant change that both reduced royal revenue and the king's ability to control barons through their debts. The clauses of most concern to local society proved more controversial and county knights were particularly active in their exploitation and defence. In 1226 knights in Lincolnshire complained that the sheriff was breaching the new chapter on the holding of local courts. In the following year panels of knights, elected in each county, were instructed to bring to the king their complaints about contraventions of the Charter by the sheriffs. Most important of all was the struggle over the forest. Under chapter 2 of the 1217 Forest Charter, the areas made forest by Henry II were to be deforested. Since it was Henry who was generally blamed for the vast extent of the forest this was a major concession, and one which John had refused to make. How right he was, for in some counties the local knights now commissioned to establish Henry II's afforestations demanded almost total abolition of the forest. As a result, the regency government tried to stall, arguing that deforestation was only meant to apply to what Henry II had made forest *de novo*, not to what he had simply recovered after the losses of Stephen's reign. In Huntingdonshire the distinction made the difference between the whole county being deforested and no deforestation at all. It was not till the Forest Charter of 1225 that the government gave way on the issue, hoping to encourage payment of that year's tax, and major deforestation took place. When the king finally assumed full powers two years later, some of the concessions were reversed and the bitterness over these events lingered. None the less considerable deforestation did take place between 1225 and 1230. In effect, a compromise was achieved over the boundaries, which survived for the rest of Henry's reign. Meanwhile the Charters were becoming well known across society. The versions of 1217 and 1225 were sent to every county. Copies were made by monasteries and also by knightly families (like the Hotots, lords of Clopton in Northamptonshire). The Magna Carta of 1225 dispatched to Wiltshire was deposited for safekeeping in Lacock abbey by the county knights. There might be confusion between the different versions, but detailed clauses (like those on deforestation, judgement by peers, and the local courts) and the general principle that the king was subject to the law were widely known. In the minority of Henry III the Charters had taken root.

The minority was constitutionally important in another way because it reinforced the old view that the king should govern with the counsel and consent of his magnates. Great councils made decisions on a range of important issues; they made William Marshal regent in 1216 and Hubert de Burgh his effective successor three years later. Ideas about the powers of such assemblies were vociferously expressed, for example by the northern magnate Robert de Vipont, who affirmed that an order for the dismantling of a castle had no validity since it had been taken 'without the common counsel and consent of the magnates of England who are held to be of the chief council of the king'. The authority of such councils was to become the central political issue later in Henry's reign.

The great tax of 1225 had saved Gascony, and the young king hoped that would be just a start. In 1229 a royal letter cried out against 'the injustice with which the power and violence of our enemies has kept us disinherited and excluded from our rights'. The desire to recover his lost dominions dominated Henry's thinking into the 1240s. It would not be easy. By 1230 the royal revenues had recovered and stood at £22,300, but that was still three or four times smaller than that of the Capetians. 'The children of King John have neither as much money nor as much power to defend themselves as had their father,' Philip Augustus remarked with grim satisfaction. The logistical problems had been compounded by the loss of Poitou. The nearest port in Angevin hands was now as far south as Bordeaux. The acquiring of allies who would help the king 'recover all your lost land' (as an envoy put it in 1225) became the central aim of diplomacy, but such allies did not come cheap. 'The emperor thirsts for nothing save money and its accumulation,' the same envoy reported. In any case, from 1228 the emperor Frederick II was ruled out of contention by his crusade and quarrel with the papacy. But fortune's wheel could turn. In November 1226 Louis VIII suddenly died, leaving a twelve-year-old son, Louis IX (1226–70), under the regency of his Castilian mother, Queen Blanche. It was to exploit the opportunities that Henry, not yet twenty-one, assumed full power in January 1227, which meant he could now make grants in perpetuity. One man above all proved temptable. In 1229 Peter de Dreux, duke of Brittany (in right of his wife), did homage to Henry. Brittany, with frontiers contiguous with Normandy and Anjou, was indeed an ideal base for a campaign. In May 1230 Henry arrived there with an army. But he then avoided the battle with Louis IX which might have brought him victory, and instead of surging into Normandy tiptoed southwards to Bordeaux, giving pensions to many Poitevin nobles but failing to take the towns or recover the allegiance of his mother and Hugh de Lusignan, their price being the cession of Bordeaux. By the autumn of 1230 Henry was back in England.

Henry had shown no military drive and it was certainly not going to be supplied by the ministers and magnates (including nine earls) who dutifully went on the expedition. True, a Caen burgess in the 1220s believed that the prospect of recovering their lands in Normandy would galvanize the English nobility. But this expedition had not gone to

Normandy. In any case, was the burgess right in his analysis? The fact was that many magnates who had lost lands in the duchy had been compensated (like William de Warenne, who received Stamford and Grantham); the compensation was in the form of lands in England confiscated from Normans who had taken the French allegiance in 1204. Indeed, these 'lands of the Normans' were the great bank on which English kings drew for patronage throughout the thirteenth century. If Normandy was recovered, such lands in England were to be surrendered. Of course, the implication was that the grantees would then recover their Norman estates, but the mechanics of that were quite obscure. For many, a bird in the hand was worth two in the bush. Warenne did not go on the 1230 expedition at all. There were also many ministers (like de Burgh) who held 'lands of the Normans' without any land in Normandy to recover. Reunification thus threatened a tenurial maelstrom which many thought best avoided. The prospect was equally unappealing to the Normans. Re-conquest, for example, threatened Andrew de Vitré with losing the lands of the earl of Chester and the Mowbrays granted him by the king of France. And would he recover his estates in Cornwall? The experience of Fulk Paynel, the only important defector in 1230, was not encouraging.

Despite his setbacks in 1230, Henry III had not given up. He retained the allegiance of Duke Peter, and was determined to succour him and strike again once the truce which had closed the hostilities ended in 1234. That desire was to be one factor in the fall of Hubert de Burgh.

After Henry's assumption of full power in January 1227, Hubert de Burgh stuck like glue to his side, and continued in practice to control much of day-to-day government. 'The royal will waxed hot and fervent,' wrote one observer in 1230, only (he continued) to be soon deflected by Hubert's 'various stratagems'. The king's assumption of power in 1227 and with it the ability to issue charters and make grants in perpetuity meant that Hubert could now reap his rewards, all the more vital since his marriages had not led to the acquisition of wealth, however much the second (to the sister of King Alexander II) had enhanced his status. So now Hubert became earl of Kent; and then (arguably irresponsible alienations from the crown) received in hereditary right the royal castles and lordships of Montgomery, Cardigan and Carmarthen. Having already prised 'the Three Castles' of Grosmont, Skenfrith and White-castle in Monmouthshire from the Braoses, Hubert had become a great marcher baron. The time had also come to install his nephew, Richard de Burgh, in Connacht. Here the family claims dated back to John's grants to Richard's father William in the 1190s, and to Richard himself in 1215. But in practice these had never been implemented, and both John and the minority government accepted Cathal Crovderg O'Connor as king. In 1224 Cathal's son Aedh succeeded although without recognition of the hereditary right Cathal had been so desperate to obtain. Supreme in England, Hubert could now decisively change the government's policy, in the process beginning a major expansion in the area under English rule. In May 1227 Richard de Burgh received a royal charter granting him the 'land' of Connacht in hereditary right. Next year he became justiciar of Ireland as well. Exploiting divisions between various segments of the O'Connors, he gradually established himself in Connacht.

With his link through marriage to the Scottish court, Hubert's tentacles seemed everywhere, yet he was becoming 'isolated in his greatness', in the words of Sir Maurice Powicke. William Marshal had opposed Richard de Burgh's installation in Connacht, hence his own removal from the justiciarship. On the Marshal's death in 1231 Hubert quibbled over the succession of his brother, Richard Marshal, because he had been holding the family's Norman estates and was in the allegiance of the king of France. Hubert's relations with the king's younger brother Richard were also fractured. Richard had become count of Poitou in 1225 and earl of Cornwall in 1227, but it was not until 1231 that he was granted Cornwall, and the honours of Wallingford and Berkhamsted in hereditary right. In 1227 a large number of earls had rallied to Richard's support in a near violent quarrel with Henry and Hubert, and they had cleverly linked his cause to that of the county knights complaining about breaches of Magna Carta. Meanwhile Langton had died in 1228 and in 1232 the see of Canterbury was again vacant.

The stage was set for Peter des Roches, bishop of Winchester. In 1223 he had sworn 'if it cost him all he had' to pull the justiciar from power. In August 1231 he returned to England after four years' absence on crusade and seized his chance. He had left as a discredited former tutor and returned as an international statesman who had hobnobbed with emperor and pope. He now ascribed the failures in Brittany and Wales to the poverty of the crown, and with some justice. If by 1230 the revenue at some £22,000 was back to the level of 1199, thanks to inflation it was actually worth half as much. In March 1232 extraordi-

nary expedients were needed to scrape together £4,000 due the duke of
Brittany, by this means saving the Breton alliance. And was not all this,
Peter suggested, caused by the way the king had granted away his
lands, wardships and escheats, no beneficiary being more favoured than
Hubert himself? Half convinced, between June and July 1232 Henry
placed much of central and local government under the control of
Bishop Peter's kinsman, the clerk Peter de Rivallis. And then Bishop
Peter had one last trump card. He tarred Hubert with responsibility for
the riots sweeping parts of the country against Italian clerks appointed
by the pope to English livings. At the end of July Henry at last sent his
justiciar packing. In the next months the once all-powerful minister
was dragged from a chapel in which he had taken sanctuary, imprisoned
in the Tower of London and (rather than stand trial) forced to surrender
all he had gained from the crown.

Bishop Peter's government at first seemed well founded, with Richard
Marshal, earl of Pembroke, almost continuously at court. A great
council in September voted the tax (a fortieth on movables, raising
some £16,000) which it refused Hubert in March, the only time a tax
was granted without a *quid pro quo* in the whole of Henry's reign.
With the money, the new regime supported Duke Peter of Brittany and
the king's Poitevin allies. In one week in April 1233 they received
some £6,666 from the exchequer. Yet even here Bishop Peter was soon
thinking of simply renewing the truce. His vaunted financial reforms
proved almost entirely illusory. He made a start by reviving taxation
on the Jews, but did nothing to investigate the revenues from which the
sheriffs drew their county farms, the essential first step towards getting
them to answer for realistically larger sums. At the core of the regime
was a faction composed of the sheriffs, castellans and ministers whom
Hubert de Burgh had ousted in and before 1223, men such as Peter de
Maulay, Engelard de Cigogné and Brian de Lisle. Their essential aim
was to punish Hubert, gain power and make good their losses, hence
their drive to recover properties, usually 'lands of the Normans' which
they had received from King John and lost under Hubert. In February
1233 the king took the manor of Upavon in Wiltshire from Gilbert
Basset and returned it to Peter de Maulay. No one was closer to Bishop
Peter than Maulay; few families were closer to the Marshals than the
Bassets. Richard Marshal, with his spurs still to win, dared not desert
Gilbert. Nor would Bishop Peter desert Maulay. The result by the
autumn of 1233 was civil war.

Magna Carta itself seemed at stake. 'No freeman shall be acted against save by lawful judgement of his peers or the law of the land,' ran its most famous chapter. In 1233 both the Marshal and Gilbert Basset constantly demanded judgement by their peers, only (so they said) to be denied it. The clause was also designed to prevent arbitrary disseisin 'by will of the king' (*per voluntatem regis*), which was precisely what Gilbert Basset seemed to have suffered, for the dispossession of Upavon overturned a royal charter of 1229 granting him the manor in hereditary right. (Maulay's previous tenure had no such fortification.) Basset's case did not stand alone. Between November 1232 and February 1233 six others suffered disseisin *per voluntatem regis* as grants made in thirteen royal charters and letters patent were overthrown. One victim was the treasurer of the exchequer, Walter Mauclerc, bishop of Carlisle, who was replaced (under de Rivallis) by Robert Passelewe, a former clerk of Falkes and agent of the 1223 dissidents at Rome. All this seemed not merely tyranny, but worse, tyranny practised by foreigners, by 'Poitevins' as the St Albans abbey chronicler, Roger of Wendover, called them (although in fact Bishop Peter came not from Poitou but the adjoining Touraine). Of course, the regime had important English ministers, notably Hubert's successor as justiciar Stephen of Seagrave, but foreigners *were* close to its heart: Bishop Peter and Peter de Rivallis themselves, Peter de Maulay, Engelard de Cigogné, and two youngsters now starting their careers, Mathias Bezill (a kinsman of Engelard) and the Norman, John de Plessis. Given that Bishop Peter, Maulay and Engelard had been agents of King John and dissidents in 1223–4, it became easy to view the whole of English history since the 1200s as a struggle between the English and the aliens. In 1233–4 the demand was soon that Henry should dismiss the latter and 'adhere to the counsels of the native men of the kingdom', as the Margam annalist put it.

There was something incongruous about the Marshal championing this constitutional movement. Holding the family estates in Normandy and married to a Breton heiress, he was a last Anglo-Norman baron, not a first English patriot. He himself had profited from Henry's arbitrary disseisins, and only complained when they touched his man, Gilbert Basset. However, this did not make his stance any the less effective. 'He fought for the cause of justice, and the laws of the English race against the oppression of the Poitevins,' wrote Roger of Wendover. This impression was the easier to cultivate because of Bishop Peter's conduct.

Arrogant and assertive, irascible and impatient, the armour-plated prelate would teach Henry at last to be a king. He scoffed at the clause in Magna Carta promising judgement by peers and asserted that the king could try anyone through judges he himself had appointed. He justified arbitrary disseisins by referring to 'the plenitude of royal power', and scorned the idea that the king should govern through native subjects: on the contrary, he needed ministers (doubtless thinking of those like Falkes) who would punish the latter's pride and perfidy.

Characteristically, Bishop Peter sought a solution through war. In Ireland, the justiciar Maurice fitz Gerald and the Lacys soon overran the Marshal lordship of Leinster. In Wales it was different. Twice Henry led armies to destroy the Marshal's bastions in the south, only to abandon a siege of Usk in September 1233 and suffer humiliation in a skirmish at Grosmont in November. The Marshal meanwhile allied with Llywelyn (an extraordinary diplomatic *bouleversement*) and in October 1233 wrested Glamorgan from Peter de Rivallis, who had succeeded Hubert as custodian during the minority of Richard de Clare. If the great barons did not side with the Marshal, they were reluctant to fight against him. Gilbert Basset and another valorous Marshal knight, Richard Seward, plundered the properties of ministers and rescued Hubert de Burgh from Devizes. Had he too not saved England for the English? By early 1234 Henry had shot his bolt, and the end of the Breton truce was only months away.

It was at this point that a churchman very different from Bishop Peter took centre stage. At papal insistence, Edmund of Abingdon was elected archbishop of Canterbury in February 1234. An ascetic academic but with the common touch, he was determined like his mentor Langton to affirm the values of Magna Carta and bring peace to a troubled realm. That, as he made clear during a series of great councils, could only be achieved by the removal of the two Peters. Henry saw the light. On 15 April he began the process of dismissing Peter de Rivallis from his plethora of offices. Bishop Peter himself also left the court. Meanwhile there was trauma in Ireland. The Marshal had gone there in February and had been wounded in battle. He died on 16 April. There had been no murder plot (he was well on his way to recovery when gangrene set in) but it was easy to suspect otherwise. The ensuing scandal brought the downfall of Stephen of Seagrave, a 'flexible man', as Wendover put it, who might otherwise have survived. The final settlement took place in May at a great council held at Gloucester.

Henry received the rebels back into his allegiance and accepted Gilbert Marshal, Richard's younger brother, as successor to the family estates and earldom of Pembroke. Penitently he admitted denying magnates judgement by their peers and committing disseisins 'by will'. A decision of his court restored Upavon to Gilbert Basset. Bishop Peter's regime had tested the most fundamental principle of Magna Carta and proved its strength. The king was indeed now subject to the law, and could not arbitrarily deprive his subjects of their rights and property.

The events of 1232–4 were a terrible indictment of Henry's weakness and poor judgement, but as he wriggled free from the bishop's regime, chroniclers were full of praise for his humility when submitting to Archbishop Edmund and his sorrow when hearing of Richard Marshal's death. He was truly a 'most pious king'. That reputation at least would stand him in good stead in the years to come. It was of little help, however, in dealing with the immediate situation in Brittany, Wales and Ireland.

In Brittany, there was little Henry could do. With the truce expiring on 24 June, he sent out ninety household knights and a body of Welsh foot soldiers, but only a major expedition like that of 1230 could have stalled the French invasion. In November, Duke Peter submitted to King Louis. The whole basis of English policy since 1229 had collapsed. Between 1230 and 1234 Peter had drawn simply as a pension at least £13,333 from England. It had been spent in vain.

In Wales, the aftermath of the war left Henry virtually powerless. He granted Gilbert Marshal both Cardigan and Carmarthen in hereditary right until the family's Norman estates, now confiscated, were recovered, although in practice under a truce of June 1234 Cardigan remained with Llywelyn. Gilbert also received custody of Glamorgan during the Clare minority. Ruling most of the south from Chepstow to Pembroke, no Marshal had been more dominant. In Ireland, it seemed as though Henry might assert himself. There, after all, the Marshals had unequivocally lost the war. The fall of Hubert de Burgh had also impacted on the position of his nephew, Richard. He had lost the justiciarship and seen his castles in Connacht destroyed by Felim O'Connor, another of Cathal's sons. In 1234, soon after the death of the Marshal, a royal official in Dublin urged Henry to hasten to Ireland. He should keep Leinster for himself and, if he returned Connacht to Richard de Burgh, retain castles and cities throughout its length. His gains could now far outweigh his father's. But Henry never came, although the circumstances were comparable with those in 1171 and 1210 which had brought Henry II and John to Ireland. Henry remained content with drawing money and men from the lordship (several Anglo-Irish lords joined the Breton expedition of 1230). He also used it as a source of patronage. His failure to exploit the situation in 1234 was partly the result of his personality and lack of resources, but it also reflected two fundamentals about the relationship between England and Ireland in this period.

The first at the baronial level was the intimate connection between English and Irish politics, something already clear in the events of 1224 and the fortunes of Richard de Burgh. Now in 1234 it was the political situation in England which meant Henry had no alternative but to return Leinster to Gilbert Marshal. This interrelationship of politics was not surprising given that there remained many cross-Channel landholders both at the knightly and baronial levels. Indeed royal patronage could renew their numbers, hence the establishment in Ireland of the knightly family of Pitchford in the 1220s. Ultimately all those with ambitions in Ireland had to resort to the English court, because only the king could make the grants of title on which all the lordships ultimately depended. The events of 1234 also reflected a second fundamental, namely the power of the colonial lords themselves, which was why Henry hesitated to move against them. After the initial grants, they and their forebears had carved out their own lordships with little help from the English crown. The inscription on the grave of Meiler fitz Henry in 1220 described him as 'the indomitable dominator of all the people of Ireland'. In 1234 the colonial lords, led by Hugh de Lacy (doubtless remembering the events of 1224), had defeated Richard Marshal. One of their number was Richard de Burgh, who with deft footwork had ended up on the winning side. Henry was not prepared now to disown him and the other victors. In England the king turned on the enemies of the Marshals; in Ireland he thanked them and in October 1234 restored Connacht to Richard de Burgh. Next year, de Burgh recommenced its conquest from the O'Connors. This time it was to stick.

The whole period from the plot against John's life in 1212 to the death of Llywelyn the Great in 1240 was one in which English royal power was at a discount throughout the British Isles. In Ireland the colonial lords were able to fill the gap. It was very different in Wales.

*   *   *

In a career which lasted from 1194 to 1240 Llywelyn ab Iorwerth, Llywelyn the Great, gained far greater power than any previous ruler of Gwynedd and conceived a new vision of Wales's political unity, a vision of unity under his authority. Overcoming numerous shocks and setbacks, his staying power was remarkable. He was indeed the greatest ruler of medieval Wales.

Gwynedd was the most impregnable of the major Welsh regions. Powys had a long eastern border with Shropshire and its centre at Welshpool could easily be approached down the Severn valley from Shrewsbury, less than twenty miles away. Deheubarth was eaten up by the great marcher baronies of the south. Gwynedd was quite different. Its wealth derived from the flocks and herds on its hills and the corn grown on the lowlands of Llŷn and Anglesey. The wealth was well protected. At the heart of Gwynedd was the great Snowdon range which shielded Llŷn to the west. If both Llŷn and Anglesey were attacked from the sea, that would require a major operation. Landwards, Snowdonia was itself shielded by two ragged scythes of mountains, the outer sweeping round from the Dyfi to the Dee, the inner sprawling over the whole area between the summits of Ardudwy and the northern valleys of the Conwy and the Clwyd. The castles of Llywelyn and his successors were constructed as much to control Gwynedd as to defend it (see below, p. 499). Essentially, defence rested on the mountains and the rivers.

In terms of character, Llywelyn was superbly qualified to exploit Gwynedd's advantages. He was a flinty warrior, but also a sinuous politician. Again and again he knew when to fight the English crown and when to submit to it. He had a tremendous sense of his honour, destiny and personal integrity, yet the confidence and charisma to give way without losing face. Llywelyn had begun his career merely as one of several descendants of the great Owain Gwynedd (died 1170) who were struggling for power in the 1190s. In 1194 in the Conwy estuary he won a great victory over his rivals: 'Many were the foes of my lord,' sang the poet, 'but there fell of them in the fight seven times the number of stars.' By 1202 Llywelyn had gained control of all Gwynedd from the Dyfi to the Dee. He still faced internal dissent. The castle he built at Bere was partly designed to protect Meirionydd from the claims of his second cousins and his own illegitimate son. But from 1202 onwards he remained the sole ruler of Gwynedd. It was the foundation for his power, all the more significant for the disunity elsewhere in native Wales. Deheubarth remained hopelessly divided between the competing descendants of the Lord Rhys. Powys was divided north and south into Powys Fadog and Powys Gwenwynwyn, with two further branches of the ruling dynasty established in Mechain, and in Pennlyn and Edeirnion.

In 1205 Llywelyn took another step of decisive importance in his career. This was his marriage to Joan, King John's illegitimate daughter. The Welsh law texts of the late twelfth and the thirteenth centuries hardly suggest that the wives of Welsh rulers, though bearing the title of queen, played much part in politics and government. Indeed they say virtually nothing about their activities. They do, however, accord them an establishment of four officers, steward, priest, chambermaid and groom, and say that the king should give them a third of his 'goods from land and earth'. If kings actually did so, then queens were rich. They could also be important in helping to create political alliances. In that context, Dafydd ab Owain Gwynedd, Llywelyn's uncle, had already demonstrated the advantages of marrying an Angevin princess. Despite Joan's illegitimacy, which the pope corrected in 1226, she certainly conferred high status on Llywelyn's dynasty, something reflected in the coat of arms given to Gwynedd in thirteenth-century English sources, a differenced version of the royal arms of England. This status explains both Llywelyn's determination that he should be followed by his son by Joan, and his ability to marry his daughters by her to English barons. Above all, Joan gave Llywelyn a link with the English court which was central to his career. Joan herself was the reverse of a cipher. She was proud, passionate and highly political, playing an important part in negotiations with her father King John and her half-brother, King Henry. She betrayed Llywelyn twice, once in politics by revealing the 1212 plot to her father (or so it was said), and once, as we shall see, in love. Her role is reflected in the Gwynedd law texts of her time which double the queen's officials from four to eight. Since the new officials include a chamberlain and a cook they suggest that Joan was maintaining an establishment separate in some degree from that of Llywelyn – indeed that would have been very necessary for some of her activities. The best tribute to Joan's role is that paid by the implicit criticism of it in the law texts (which were not official productions). Although giving the queen more officials, they also stressed their subordination to the officials of the king, and implied that the queen's place was in her chamber, not the wider court.

Llywelyn's early success had depended very much on his co-operation with King John, sealed by his marriage to Joan. Relations had then broken down, however, and in 1211 John had invaded Gwynedd (see above, pp. 283–4). Even Joan's intercession had not saved Llywelyn from an exigent peace in which he lost the Four Cantrefs between the Conwy and the Dee. The year 1212 was the turning-point in Llywelyn's career. He brought the native rulers into a confederation, made an alliance with King Philip of France, joined the baronial plot against John's life, recovered the Four Cantrefs which he never afterwards lost and destroyed John's general hegemony in Wales. In December 1215, having married his daughter Gwladus to Reginald de Braose (now head of the house), Llywelyn was free, in alliance with the rulers of Deheubarth, to sweep through the south, taking the royal castles of Cardigan and Carmarthen, destroying the Marshal hold on Cilgerran and Emlyn in northern Dyfed, and throwing out the lesser marcher families from St Clears, Kidwelly and the surrounding area. Apart from Gower, held by his ally Reginald de Braose, the only English base – baronial or royal – in the south-west was the Marshal's Pembroke, where the great water-defended castle with its new ultra-modern circular keep resisted any attack. In 1216, Llywelyn presided over a great court at Aberdyfi where the spoils of the campaign were distributed between the fractious segments of the house of Deheubarth, though Llywelyn kept Cardigan for himself. Left out of this division was Llywelyn's old foe, Gwenwynwyn, which may have prompted the latter's desertion later in 1216 to King John, tempted in part by the grant of Montgomery. The response was devastating. Llywelyn summoned almost all the rulers of Wales to his army, drove Gwenwynwyn into English exile, and took southern Powys and Montgomery for himself. He held southern Powys for the rest of his life, greatly increasing his revenues. For the time being, Montgomery gave him a base at the very hinge of Wales. He could challenge the Mortimers and the Braoses (the latter uncertain allies) for possession of Ceri, Maelienydd and Elfael, the regions between the Wye valley and the Severn, which were the key to Gwynedd's power in the south.

Within Gwynedd, Llywelyn strove to increase his princely authority, especially by extending his jurisdiction over crime (discussed below, p. 497). His cash income was almost certainly increasing with the development of commerce and the commutation of renders in kind into money. He was able to raise formidable military forces, taking 1,600 foot soldiers on John's northern expedition of 1209. His vision of Gwynedd as a 'modern' state, fully integrated into the rest of Europe, was strikingly demonstrated by his religious patronage. He established the Knights Hospitallers at Dolgynwal, the Cistercians at Conwy, the Franciscans at Llan-faes, and the Augustinians on Bardsey Island, one of the holiest places in Wales, previously under the jurisdiction of the ancient *clas* church at Aberdaron.

In the triumphal years after 1215 Llywelyn was also staking out claims to status and authority. He was not obliged (so he said) to attend any conference outside the boundaries of Wales. He was 'of no less a liberty than the king of Scotland, who receives outlaws from England with impunity'. And above all he held a 'principality' within which the other native rulers were to do homage to him, and he alone was to do homage to the king of England. By this means the latter was excluded from any direct relationship with the native rulers. Books of Welsh law, edited in Gwynedd during Llywelyn's time, shared this vision of Wales. And they added that 'the word' of the ruler of Gwynedd, or the king of Aberffraw as they called him after his principal seat in Anglesey, 'prevails over that of all kings [of Wales] and the word of no [other king] prevails over his'. Llywelyn's vision was almost certainly a response to King John's practice, for John had much more formally than before demanded homage from the native rulers (see above, p. 283). The vital and distinctive element in the ceremony was that it involved a man swearing loyalty for the land he held from his lord. If the Welsh rulers held their territories formally from Llywelyn, if they 'received' them from him as the law books put it, that meant he would confirm – indeed perhaps determine – the descent of those territories and in particular how they were divided between family claimants. Given the prevalence of such divisions, the position of 'feudal' overlord gave far more potential power in Wales than it did England. The territories of the Welsh rulers would also, of course, be liable to forfeiture for any breach of the due loyalty and service. If, then, a principality could be constructed along these lines, its ruler would have formidable powers. Yet for Llywelyn this remained an ambition. Such a principality was ultimately created by his grandson. It was never created by Llywelyn himself.

The first obstacle lay with the king of England. In 1218 in the great settlement after the civil war Llywelyn was made to come to Worcester; he was therefore attending a meeting outside Wales. He acknowledged that he would receive no enemy of the king in Wales, and so he was 'of lesser liberty' than the king of Scotland. Above all, he promised that 'all the magnates of all Wales' should come to the king to do homage to him as their liege lord. In other words there was to be no Welsh principality in which Llywelyn alone did homage to the king and the other magnates of Wales did homage to Llywelyn. At Worcester, Llywelyn had preferred to bargain not for constitutional forms, however important, but territorial power. Under the treaty, he kept all his gains from the war. Southern Powys and Montgomery were granted to him in wardship until the majority – many years away – of Gwenwynwyn's heir. Although he formally surrendered Cardigan and Carmarthen he at once received them back as the king's bailiff until the king came of age, which might not be till 1228. Equally striking was the recognition of Llywelyn's practical authority over the other Welsh rulers. It was Llywelyn who was to prevent outlaws being received in Wales. He was also to ensure that 'the magnates of all Wales' did homage to the king, and surrender the lands they had seized in the war. In practice, he enforced no such restorations and permitted only one magnate to do homage.

The Treaty of Worcester made Llywelyn less the prince of Wales than Henry III's justiciar, much the position the Lord Rhys had held under Henry II. Llywelyn himself frequently posed thereafter as the king's loyal if sometimes disregarded councillor. His readiness to accept a position from the English crown is largely explained by his marriage to Joan, which always gave him an entrée to the English court, and by his early career, which had shown the dangers of challenging the king (as in 1211) and also the benefits of co-operating with him. Just like the Lord Rhys and other Welsh rulers he saw that a link with the crown would help him dominate the native rulers. It was the latter who presented the second obstacle to his wider ambitions.

In 1211 a good number of the Welsh rulers had fought for John against Llywelyn. In 1212, they had 'unanimously confederated' under Llywelyn against John. By 1215–16, when the *Chronica Wallia* described him as 'holding the monarchy and principality of nearly all Wales', Llywelyn had probably made them do him homage. Yet the fact that the homage of Gwenwynwyn had to be secured by hostages and ended in desertion shows that this formal supremacy was as likely to be challenged by the Welsh rulers as it was to be denied by the English crown. Gwynedd's law books, as we have seen, gave supremacy to the king of Aberffraw, but those drawn up in the south either gave the symbols of royalty to all rulers (see above, p. 228) or accorded equal supremacy to the kings of Aberffraw and Dinefwr, the latter the chief seat of the rulers of Deheubarth. In 1215 it was Maelgwn, according to the *Chronica Wallia*, who had been the 'head' of the princes of south Wales. He can only have resented Llywelyn's description of the castle of Dinefwr as 'once famous now ruinous, to which, as the head of south Wales, the dignities of all south Wales once belonged'.

In dealing with the native rulers, Llywelyn was as careful as he was with the English monarchy. Both indeed could be relatively relaxed about his use of titles. Llywelyn's grandfather had adopted the title 'prince of Wales' (see above, p. 215). Yet while Llywelyn certainly called himself prince (increasingly the only Welsh ruler to do so), he proclaimed himself prince only of 'north Wales', which might mean no more than Gwynedd. As his power grew, both Welsh and English chroniclers began to call him 'prince of Wales'. Llywelyn himself spoke of 'the state of Wales' as though he was its guardian. His wife styled herself 'lady of Wales'. However, Llywelyn himself when he changed his title (in or a little before 1230) called himself not 'prince of Wales' but 'prince of Aberffraw and lord of Snowdon'. 'Lord of Snowdon' impressed by the reference to its unconquerable mountains. 'Prince of Aberffraw', in Gwynedd circles, suggested a supremacy over all of Wales, but this was an assertion, as we have seen, which one could take or leave. It was 'left' by the English government who were perfectly happy with the new title. So apparently were the rulers of the south.

Llywelyn did not lose sight of his vision of a Welsh principality subject only to himself but, as he remarked in a different context, 'neither a skilled dicer nor yet a valiant knight may always win his heart's desire'. He was out for the reality of power and for that he needed to be flexible, hence his stipulation in his agreement with John in 1202 that he could choose whether his lawsuits were heard under Welsh or English law. His flexibility was evident, too, in his co-operation with English barons. The 'yoke of tyranny' he rebelled against in 1212 was that of the Angevin dynasty, not the English. Eventually he married all four of his daughters by Joan to English barons, two of them not once, but twice over. Co-operation with one baron above all was vital to Gwynedd's safety. In 1211 the support of Ranulf, earl of Chester, had made possible John's invasion. In 1218 Llywelyn reached a settlement with the earl, one affirmed in 1222 by the marriage of Ranulf's ward and eventual heir in Chester, John le Scot, to Helen,

Llywelyn's daughter. With the route of hostile armies blocked off, Gwynedd remained free from invasion for the rest of Llywelyn's life. Thus secure, in 1220 Llywelyn demonstrated his authority in the south against Welsh ruler and marcher baron alike. He forced the submission of Rhys Gryg (Maelgwn's brother), ravaged the lands of the earl of Pembroke (William Marshal II, son of the regent who had died in 1219), and took revenge on a former ally, Reginald de Braose, by installing his nephew and rival, John de Braose, in the old family lordship of Gower. Of course, Reginald had married one of Llywelyn's daughters – but then so had John.

Then came disaster. The old regent's great gain from the 1215–17 war had been Caerleon, which he had seized from its Welsh ruler Morgan, great-nephew of King Morgan of the 1140s. Yet the Marshals (once themselves royal bailiffs of Cardigan and Carmarthen) were grievously affected by Llywelyn's rise to power in the south, as the events of 1220 had shown. In April 1223 William Marshal II, having gathered a large army from his estates in Ireland, took his revenge. He descended on south Wales, and seized Cardigan and Carmarthen, where he was soon recognized once again as the king's deputy. The smaller marcher lords in the south-west at last recovered the lands they had lost in the 1215–17 war. William Marshal had replaced Llywelyn's supremacy with his own. There was also defeat further north where the minority government, led by Hubert de Burgh, recovered Montgomery for the crown, replacing the old castle down in the valley with a new one high up on the far tip of the Ceri hills. Faced with these blows Llywelyn submitted almost at once, without meeting his enemies in the field. This was nothing like 1211, for Gwynedd, protected by the alliance with the earl of Chester, remained unscathed. In practice, Llywelyn also retained southern Powys and the allegiance between Wye and Severn of the native rulers of Elfael at Maelienydd, something accepted by the rival claimant, Ralph Mortimer of Wigmore, when (in 1230) he married Llywelyn's daughter Gwladus, widow of Reginald de Braose.

Llywelyn's recovery was helped by the crown's lack of vigour. It was Hubert de Burgh, not the king, who asserted himself in the late 1220s, acquiring Cardigan, Carmarthen and Montgomery in hereditary right. In 1228 a perceived threat to Montgomery led Hubert and Henry to summon an army and commence building a castle in the Ceri hills. Characteristically placing substance over form, Llywelyn dutifully did homage to the king, as did the Welsh magnates who were with him. Henry and Hubert then abandoned their castle and went home, leaving William de Braose, captured in the fighting (he had succeeded his father Reginald in 1228), a prisoner in Llywelyn's hands. Under the arrangements for his release in 1229, William agreed that his daughter Eva should marry Dafydd, Llywelyn's son and heir, and have Builth as her marriage portion. Llywelyn had long coveted Builth. Astride the upper valley of the Wye, it put pressure on Elfael and controlled the great pass (followed by the present railway line) down the valleys of the Irfon and the Tywi into south-west Wales. Llywelyn held it for the rest of his life.

Llywelyn soon had a chance to break up the Braose patrimony (Radnor, Hay, Brecon and Abergavenny) altogether. In 1230, having found William de Braose, on a return visit, in his wife's bedchamber, he executed him with great publicity. This was the end of the senior line of the Braoses (the junior continued in Gower) because William had no son and his lordships passed to his four daughters, including Eva. For the moment, however, the lands were given by the king in wardship to William Marshal, whose bailiffs in Brecon were soon clashing with those of Llywelyn in Builth. The Marshal's sudden death in 1231 gave Llywelyn his chance. So did tensions in Glamorgan where the native rulers (notably Morgan Gam of Afan) resented the harsh lordship of Gilbert de Clare, earl of Gloucester and Hertford, and were now off the leash thanks to the earl's death. The descent of Glamorgan, usually linked with the earldom of Gloucester, illustrates the importance of heiresses; through them it had passed from Robert fitz Hamon to Robert, earl of Gloucester, illegitimate son of Henry I, thence to King John and (briefly) the earl of Essex, before ending up (from 1217) with the Clare earls of Hertford. In 1223, with the odds stacked against him, Llywelyn had wisely avoided fighting his enemies. Now in 1231 he led a great expedition through the south which burnt Radnor, Hay and Brecon, razed the castles of Neath and Kidwelly, and ended up with the seizure of Cardigan from Hubert de Burgh. Llywelyn had asserted his authority over a new generation of native rulers, and until his death he allowed Maelgwyn Fychan (son of Maelgwn ap Rhys, who had died earlier in the year) to hold Cardigan as his deputy.

Henry and Hubert made a static response to this lightning campaign. In the summer of 1231 they brought an army to Castle Matilda (Pains-castle) and rebuilt it with two lines of concentric walls and great dry moats. The aim was to secure Elfael, which Braose and Llywelyn satellites had disputed for so long, and block off Llywelyn's shortest route from Builth into the Herefordshire plain. But his was to inflict a wound in the flank, not at the heart. No attempt was made to recover Cardigan or attack Builth, let alone Gwynedd.

Two years later, in a remarkable turn-around, Llywelyn was in alliance with the Marshals – in alliance, that is, with William's brother and successor, Richard Marshal, in his war against King Henry. He helped Richard in his conquest of Glamorgan, and with the rulers of Deheubarth laid long though ultimately fruitless siege to Carmarthen. The war ended, as we have seen, with Richard's successor, Gilbert Marshal, dominant throughout south Wales, though in fact he did nothing to disturb Llywelyn's and Maelgwn's hold of Cardigan. Llywelyn also retained Builth and southern Powys. He had maintained a territorial power throughout Wales and had also kept alive the wider vision of his principality. This was inseparable from the whole question of the succession.

Llywelyn had long determined that his heir should be his son Dafydd, offspring of his marriage to the regal Joan. This was bound to cause friction within Gwynedd because it meant excluding his illegitimate eldest son, Gruffudd, and overturning what Llywelyn himself called (another sign of his Europeanization) 'the detestable' Welsh custom which placed legitimate and illegitimate children on the same footing. Another problem was whether Dafydd was to succeed simply to Llywelyn's territories or to some kind of wider principality embracing the other rulers. After 1218 Llywelyn's relationships with those rulers had taken various forms. In 1226 he extracted an oath of fealty to Dafydd 'from the great men of Wales'. They did not apparently do him homage. In 1228, during the brief Kerry campaign, he seems to have been head merely of a confederation of rulers, all of whom did homage (as we have seen) to King Henry. Yet in 1238 the English government believed that Llywelyn was trying to get 'the magnates of Wales' to do homage to Dafydd, though in the event what he secured (according to the Welsh chronicles) was simply fealty. Llywelyn's approach remained consistent. He kept alive the idea of a homage-based principality, but did not try to impose it.

Above all, Dafydd's succession depended on the English government. Whatever political entity he held, he would hold it from the king. In fact, King Henry was happy to accept Dafydd, after all his nephew, as the future ruler of Gwynedd, but he insisted that the homage of the other rulers belonged to the crown. There was to be no wider principality. Henry, however, continued to recognize that native Wales was in practice subject to Llywelyn. The yearly truces after 1234 were always with Llywelyn and his 'adherents'. Any attack by the earl of Pembroke on the castle of Morgan, erstwhile lord of Caerleon, was to be regarded as a transgression against Llywelyn himself.

Llywelyn died in 1240, three years after Joan. A visionary and a realist, a warrior and a diplomat, aspiring to rule the principality of Wales yet also masquerading as a loyal councillor of the king, this extraordinary man was called 'the Great' soon after his death by both English and Welsh chroniclers.

*   *   *

King Henry III's personality and lack of resources were equally important when it came to Anglo-Scottish relations, for they helped to create a long period of peace between the two kingdoms, the essential context for the policies of King Alexander II (1214–49). Alexander began his reign leading armies into England and attempting to make good ancient claims to the northern counties. He ended it on the island of Kerrera in the Firth of Lorn, leading an expedition to wrest the Western Isles and the Isle of Man from King Hakon of Norway. The contrast reflects a fundamental re-orientation of Scottish monarchy, though one long foreshadowed. Alexander's aim was to expand his kingdom north and west, not south into England. Appropriately it was King Hakon's Saga which described him 'a great chief and ambitious for this world's honours'. But Alexander was far more than simply a military leader. His legal innovations marked the birth of the Scottish common law.

The Treaty of Worcester in 1218 had allowed Llywelyn to keep his material gains from the war, not surprisingly for he had won them himself and was firmly entrenched. Alexander's situation was different. In the north-east he had gained no strongholds. In the north-west certainly he held Carlisle, where indeed the canons of the cathedral elected one of his clerks as their bishop. The leading barons of Cumberland and Westmorland, often with Scottish connections, had joined the rebellion, as had many knights. But once Louis had surrendered there was no way Alexander had the resources to keep these men on side, let alone continue by himself. In any case many northern rebels had been captured at the battle of Lincoln. Alexander's formal excommunication by the legate Guala in September 1217 made matters worse. So in December of that year Alexander, now nineteen, came to terms. He surrendered Carlisle and was allowed to keep Tynedale and the earldom of Huntingdon. His humiliation, aggravated by an Interdict briefly placed on his kingdom in 1218, was fundamental to the re-orientation of his kingship. He could never, he knew, have a better chance of southern expansion, yet he had failed utterly. Henceforth his policy was to live in peace with England. To the success of that policy Henry III's reluctance to raise the issue of England's overlordship over Scotland in any aggressive way was equally important. The mutual decision to live in peace was affirmed in June 1221 when Alexander married Henry III's eldest sister, Joan, the first of those marriages between the dynasties which did so much to harmonize relations in the thirteenth century. The chronicler Fordun saw this first union as the start of a peace 'which was to last time without end', and certainly Alexander's army of July 1217 was the last to fight across the border for nearly eighty years. Almost at once (as Joan assured her brother) Alexander refused to help Hugh de Lacy in his bid for Ulster (see above, p. 306).

Peace with England enabled Alexander to attend to dangers in the north of his kingdom. There royal Scotland, the Scotland of royal castles and sheriffdoms, effectively ended at Inverness and Dingwall, beyond which stretched Ross and Caithness (see above, p. 232). In 1215 Ross had been the centre of another MacHeth and MacWilliam rising, this one led by Donald and Kenneth, sons of the dead leaders of 1186–7. Both sons were killed. It was obviously a major aim of royal policy to prevent uprisings of this kind and one way was by establishing loyalist ministers in the north. So in 1212 the justiciar north of the Forth, William Comyn, became earl of Buchan through marriage, the first native earldom to pass to an incomer. Another preoccupation was to sustain the bishopric of Caithness (established around 1147–51) which had freed the region from the jurisdiction of the bishop of Orkney. In 1222, when the bishop was murdered, Alexander took an army into Caithness, briefly expelled the earl, John Haraldson (1206–31), and saw to the election of a new bishop from the loyalist Moray (Murry) family. A further challenge from the MacWilliams followed until in 1230 its leader, Gilleasbuig, was caught and killed. His infant daughter had her brains dashed out in Forfar market-place. The brutality (which contrasted with MacHeth's long imprisonment by King David) is a measure of the threat and also of the sense that it could be ended. This was indeed a decisive moment for the security of the dynasty, being the last MacWilliam challenge to the throne.

Earl John Haraldson died violently in 1231. In 1236 his successor attested a royal charter, the first earl of Caithness to do so. Meanwhile Alexander weakened the earldom by making a Murry earl of Sutherland in its south, and he secured Ross by appointing as earl, the first since Malcolm MacHeth's death in 1168, Farquhar MacTaggart, a native of the area who had put down the rising of 1215. Alexander also established the Comyns in the lordship of Badenoch, the mountainous but highly strategic part of Moray. There were still no royal castles or sheriffdoms in Caithness itself. As late as 1264–6 Dingwall was still the northernmost outpost of royal power and its bailiffs had no revenues worth speaking of. Nevertheless, Alexander had greatly enhanced his authority in the north.

Alexander was equally successful in the west, though here too he started from a fairly low base. Man and the Isles, like the Orkneys, were subject to the king of Norway. Alexander's overlordship was confined to the mainland where his direct authority was limited to the castle and sheriffdom at Ayr, created by William the Lion. For the most part, he relied on the great Anglo-Norman families established in the twelfth century, above all that of Stewart which, advancing from its original base in Renfrew, had secured Bute around 1200 and built a castle at Rothesay.

Between 1226 and 1231 great storms of conflict swept through the sea lanes of the west over control of Man and the Isles. At the eye of the storms was the rivalry between Reginald, king of Man (1188–1226), and his brother Olaf, who ruled in Lewis. Throwing in their lot on one side or the other were the MacSorleys, descendants of the great Somerled, who, divided into three often warring segments, were lords of Argyll, Kintyre, and several of the western islands. It was the MacSorleys who built the remarkable thirteenth-century castles which still ring the western coast. And then beside them, ranging with giant strides, was Alan, son of Roland, lord of Galloway. Roland, in accepting appointment as justiciar of Galloway, had apparently helped to tie the region to the centre. From one point of view Alan seemed to do the same. He had married a daughter of Earl David, King Alexander's uncle. He bore the title of Constable of Scotland, inherited from his Moreville mother.

He had raised armies for King John and been with him at Runnymede. He had married his daughters to Anglo-Scottish barons. However, this was the periphery of his activity. The core (which he had no particular desire to tie to anything) was the struggle to construct a great seaborne empire between Galloway and Ulster, the latter having been granted him by John in 1212 in a bid to keep out the Lacys. Able to raise a thousand foot soldiers and fleets of 200 ships, boasting that he could easily invade Norway, he was, in the words of Hakon's Saga, 'the greatest warrior . . . He plundered about the Hebrides and made great warfare widely throughout the western lands.'

Yet it was not Alan who emerged victorious from 'the great dispeace' between 1226 and 1231. He had to accept Hugh de Lacy's recovery of Ulster and failed to sustain his ally, Reginald, in Man. The real victor was the king of Norway. King Hakon, having seen off his domestic foes, became the first Norwegian king to intervene effectively in Scottish waters since Magnus Barelegs in 1098. It was he who punished the murderers of Earl John of Orkney and Caithness. It was his fleets which sacked Bute, established Olaf as king in Man, plundered Kintyre and Lewis, and generally (as his own Saga put it) 'won great honour for King Hakon in the west beyond the sea'.

Alexander himself (according to Fordun) led armies into Argyll against the MacSorleys in both 1221 and 1222. He may have established a castle at Tarbert on the narrow tongue between the mainland and Kintyre. But during the great dispeace he had virtually looked on while King Hakon triumphed. There was, moreover, a dangerous connection between disturbances in the north and west, for Gilleasbuig MacWilliam had drawn support from the Western Isles and timed his bid to coincide with the disorders there. Alexander's chance came with Alan of Galloway's death in 1234, because Galloway was then divided between the three Anglo-Scottish magnates who were married to Alan's daughters. There was no chance of *them* plundering about the Western Isles. Indeed there was now a vacuum which soon Alexander aspired to fill by taking Man and the Isles for himself. With Alan's demise he was able to develop his own position in Galloway. He turned Alan's chief seat at Kirkcudbright into a royal castle and probably set up a sheriffdom at Wigtown; an important expansion of royal power and a step towards achieving his wider ambitions.

The royal and baronial take-over of Galloway was eased by long-term changes which had already brought this great Celtic province into the

Anglo-Scottish world. Anglo-Scottish nobles, sometimes tenants of the crown elsewhere in Scotland, formed Alan of Galloway's immediate entourage, as they had that of his father. Alan's family had founded or helped to found two Cistercian abbeys (Dundrennan and Glenluce) and three Premonstratensian houses (one at Whithorn). Many houses from Scotland and Cumberland acquired property in the province, like Holmcultram's grange at Kirkgunzeon, north-east of Urr. But Galloway was also conquered, as the thick spread of mottes in the area testified. A thirteenth-century effigy of an abbot in Dundrennan's ruins shows him with a dagger in his breast but still managing to trample a semi-disembowelled kilted tribesman under foot. The Galwegians had initially supported as Alan's successor his illegitimate son Thomas who gained the support of Hugh de Lacy and native Irish chiefs. It took two substantial expeditions in 1235 and April 1236 and two battles before Alexander came out on top. Thomas surrendered and spent some sixty years in prison; two Irish chiefs were pulled apart by horses in Edinburgh and the land and churches of Galloway were ravaged with great violence and cruelty (so the contemporary annals of Dunstable and the later Fordun tell us). A further expedition was required in 1247 to restore Roger de Quency (earl of Winchester), married to one of Alan's daughters, after a revolt against his rule.

To be free to concentrate on Galloway, Alexander reached a final settlement with the king of England – already, of course, his brother-in-law. At York in September 1237 he surrendered all claims to the northern counties, and received in return £200-worth of land based on Tynedale, to be held from the English king with extensive liberties. A whole phase of Scottish royal history was thus at an end. The aim of securing the northern counties, which had provided the driving force of the kings of Scotland for centuries, was abandoned. Henry III spoke joyfully of a 'firm peace', and scaled down the costs of his northern castles. He too had shown statesmanship. The overlordship of the king of England, established by Henry II in 1174, had been formally abandoned by Richard in 1189. But John may well have revived the issue in 1209 and 1212, as presumably Henry did in 1221 when the pope refused Alexander a coronation on the grounds that 'the king is said to be subject to the king of England'. Henry had raised his claims again with the pope in 1235, drawing attention to the homages owed him by the earls and barons of Scotland, a recollection of the treaty of 1174; but when it came to it in 1237, Henry made no reference at all to his claims and the settlement was essentially one between two sovereign states. At this very time Henry was insisting, in his dealings with Llywelyn and Dafydd, that the homages of the Welsh barons were his. But that was practical politics. Overlordship over Scotland was not. Henry was opposed to a coronation which would clearly change the status of the Scottish kings, but he had no wish to pursue his claims if it meant disrupting a happy family peace between the kingdoms.

That family relationship was threatened in 1238 by Joan's death, although her influence had always been limited by her failure to produce an heir. In the following year Alexander married Marie de Coucy, daughter of a great French baron. But the family ties with England were soon renewed. In 1242, with King Henry anxious to secure the north during his campaign in Poitou, an agreement was reached for the marriage of Alexander's baby son to Henry's eldest daughter.

Alexander's success in defending and expanding his frontiers owed everything to his ability to mobilize armies: in 1221, 1222, 1228–30, 1235, 1236, and later in 1244 and 1249. The cavalry was presumably (for there is no evidence) composed of household forces and the contingents furnished by the barons, while the foot came from the quotas of the 'common army', mustered on the basis of so many men from units of land (ploughgates or ouncelands). In 1244 Matthew Paris, well informed about northern affairs, noted that the Scots did not have valuable horses from Spain or Italy, but he praised the size and discipline of their army, which he put at 1,000 horsemen (many probably sergeants) and – with some exaggeration – 100,000 foot. If Paris was impressed, how much more must have been the men of Caithness, Argyll and Galloway!

Such armies reflected Alexander's authority within his realm, an authority he was eager to enhance. The traditional inauguration ceremony of the Scottish kings at Scone differed from coronations elsewhere in Europe in that it lacked the crucial element of anointing. In 1221, as we have seen, Alexander sought papal sanction for a full coronation, which would put him on a par with the king of England. Papal refusal did not damage Alexander's hold over the church, which remained a mainstay of his rule, thanks above all to his influence over ecclesiastical elections. Both in Caithness and Galloway (in the bishopric of Whithorn) he placed his own men. His chancellor William de Bondington became bishop of Glasgow (1232) and his chamberlain David de Bernham, bishop of St Andrews (1239). Alexander also defended the church's independence and, with it, that of the realm. He was sticky about admitting papal legates, and doubtless helped to secure the bull of 1225 which allowed the Scottish church to govern itself through a national provincial council, confirming earlier rulings about its independence from York.

Little is known of Alexander's revenues although they were almost certainly expanding. Certainly expanding was the scope and authority of royal justice. Throughout the reign the justiciars of Lothian, and of Scotland north of the Forth, were probably travelling through the sheriffdoms twice a year to hear the royal pleas (murder, premeditated assault, robbery, rape, arson). There is no evidence for a justiciar of Galloway, though one may have existed. A provision in 1245 tightened up procedures, marking the beginning of process by 'dittay' or indictment, under which local juries (as had long been the case in England) revealed to the justiciars those whom they suspected of wrongdoing, the miscreants then being arrested and brought before the justiciars for trial. The chattels of those convicted of the serious crimes which constituted the royal pleas, the 1245 provision stressed, were to be forfeit to the crown – again as in England, and an indication of the financial motives for getting a tighter grip on justice.

The advances on the civil side were even more important. In 1230 a statute set up the action of novel dissasine, a remedy for anyone deprived of a tenement 'unjustly and without judgement'. Perhaps in the same year, or possibly somewhat later, a parallel action of 'mortancestry' was inaugurated, a remedy for anyone denied succession to their inheritance. The procedures were modelled on the English actions of novel disseisin and mort d'ancestor introduced by Henry II. They were initiated by a 'brieve' (a writ), which had to be obtained from the king or one of the justiciars, and ordered the truth to be recognized by a jury of 'good men of the country' before either the sheriff or the justiciar, probably the justiciar's eyre being the usual forum. In sharp contrast to England, there are virtually no surviving records of Scottish courts from this period, so it is impossible to trace the growing use of these procedures. By the 1290s, however, the brieves of novel dissasine and mortancestry, with some others, were described as brieves 'of course' (de cursu), which meant – as in England – that they were issued in standard form automatically and at small cost. The new procedures were thus readily available and offered access to a jury, replacing in the last resort the judicial duel. The new procedures might also transfer cases from courts of lords into the more impartial, or so it could be hoped, courts of the king. In protecting seisin and inheritance, they reduced the need for self-help and helped to maintain law and order. In bringing a whole new range of business into royal courts before the justiciar or the sheriffs, they increased the whole scope and authority of kingship.

Ecclesiastics like the prior of Coldingham made use of the new procedures to protect their properties. Women resorted to them to protect their right to inherit in the absence of brothers, in the face of much pressure in favour of collateral males. Another group to benefit may have been rent-paying tenants, quite low down on the social scale, who claimed their holdings were hereditable. This highlights another feature of the procedures, one of cardinal importance: they were open to those of Scottish, English, Norman and any other descent. There was to be no legal apartheid in Scotland, as there was in Ireland and in a different way in Wales, where English law was chiefly for the English. In that respect, in Scotland the new law really was 'common'. This was an important factor in the growth of national unity.

On the face of it the losers from the procedures were the lords. In the twelfth century the king had already been developing his appellate jurisdiction from their courts. Now the brieve of novel dissasine explicitly envisaged the plaintiff's lord as the disseisor (though not exclusively so). It was the lord, too, who was most likely to be guilty of obstructing the course of an inheritance and becoming the target in an action of mortancestry. The rule also evolved in the thirteenth century (again based on one in England) that no freeholder need answer for his lands save by action brought by the king's brieve. Lords, however, still wielded great jurisdictional power. In the first place the procedures operated primarily in royal Scotland, the Scotland of the sheriffdoms, because it was to the sheriffs that the writs were addressed. The justiciar's eyres likewise operated in the same areas and never went north of Dumbarton in the west or Inverness in the east. The procedures of civil (and criminal) justice therefore had a limited impact in the great provincial lordships and the 'outer rim' earldoms. They were probably unknown in Caithness and Argyll. Even within the core of the kingdom private courts continued to flourish alongside the new procedures, partly because they retained disciplinary jurisdiction over defaults of service and because they enjoyed other jurisdiction (often by royal grant), including at the most basic criminal level (as in England) the right to hang thieves taken red-handed. There was also a great deal of overlap between private courts and the courts of the justiciars and sheriffs. Laymen continued to take their property disputes to ecclesiastical courts, while the church complained vociferously about cases concerning ecclesiastical property going to secular courts (another sign of Alexander's control). The common law of Scotland in this period never paralleled the size and complexity of the law in England. There was no legal profession, and no equivalent to the bench at Westminster or the court of king's bench, both staffed by professional judges. The justiciars and many of the sheriffs were members of the nobility.

All this helps to explain the relative harmony of Scottish politics in Alexander's reign. The king was accused by the laity neither of financial oppressions, nor of arbitrary disseisins and denial of justice. 'A good man, just, pious and generous, beloved by all as well by the English as his own subjects and deservedly,' wrote Matthew Paris of Alexander II, though the Galwegians would have been less complimentary. When the last political crisis of Alexander's reign occurred in the 1240s it was essentially a factional struggle at court between new families who had risen in the service of the crown. Tension between nobles of Anglo-Norman and Scottish descent seemed a thing of the past. Indeed both groups had co-operated in putting down the MacWilliams

The most successful of the new families was that of Comyn. Coming to prominence under William the Lion, it remained at the centre of Scottish politics and government until brought down by Robert Bruce. There came to be two principal branches descended from the two marriages of William Comyn, one producing earls of Buchan, the other lords of Badenoch and (by the marriage of Walter Comyn around 1234) earls of Menteith. The fifteenth-century historian Walter Bower wrote freely of 'the Comyns', and certainly from the 1240s they often seemed to have acted as a cohesive family group. Yet their rise was remarkably uncontested by established families, perhaps because their marriage alliances had cast a wide net, with one of William Comyn's daughters marrying the earl of Mar and another the earl of Ross. (For further discussion of the family, see below, p. 423.)

The Comyns did sterling service for the king, although in the later writings of Fordun and Bower they often appear as archetypal over-powerful subjects – a judgement in which there was at least an element of truth. The crisis of 1242 centred on a conflict which had arisen with the Bissets, another family who had risen through royal service. After the latter had been accused of murdering Patrick of Atholl, nephew of Alan of Galloway, the young Alexander, earl of Buchan, and John the

Red of Badenoch, 'a keen fighter and most outstanding participant in all knightly encounters', pinned Walter Bisset down in his castle at Aboyne and ravaged his surrounding lands. King Alexander kept calm and told everyone not to mistake flies for eagles and mice for lions, but he had to call out the common army of Mar to conduct Walter to Forfar to stand trial. Ultimately the Bissets 'were outlawed from Scotland by judgement of all the nobles' in November 1242.

The forms of law had been observed, but only just. Alexander had come under humiliating pressure. What is impressive is the way in which he now reasserted his authority. He dismissed the twin justiciars of Scotland north of Forth for failing to act against the Comyns and replaced them with Alan Durward, an appointment which influenced Scottish politics into the 1260s. Durward, the name deriving from the post of usher or doorkeeper at court, represented another curial family very much on the make. From an original base at Lundie in Angus, the family had benefited from the northern expansion, for example in gaining the lordship of Urquhart on Loch Ness. Rivalries at court, in the north, and over claims to the earldoms of Mar and Angus, ensured that Alan Durward would stand up to the Comyns.

The crisis of 1242 had repercussions on relations with King Henry. Walter Bisset fled to the English court, and put it about that the Scots were negotiating with King Louis, that they were stirring up trouble in Ireland and building border castles. In August 1244 Henry took an army to Newcastle and Alexander marched to meet him, conspicuously declining to lay waste the country as he approached. A peaceful settlement quickly followed, and one that did little to detract from Scotland's independence. The affair was a storm in a teacup. The treaty of 1237 and the marriage agreement of 1242 were confirmed. Alexander acknowledged King Henry as his 'liege lord' and agreed not to enter alliances with his enemies unless oppressed 'unjustly', a qualification that rendered the pledge almost worthless. There was in any case no suggestion that Henry's overlordship operated for anything other than the estates Alexander held in England. Therefore Henry did not entertain Bisset's appeals for justice, and Alexander, as befitted his kingly status, did not swear in person to the treaty. True, a large number of Scottish magnates took oaths to uphold it, but that Henry saw these essentially as security for the agreement rather than as a prelude to the recovery of their homages was amply demonstrated by the events of the next decade.

Alexander was keen to settle with King Henry because he had more important things to do in the west. In 1244 he sent the first of many embassies to King Hakon offering to purchase the lordship of Man and the Isles. King Hakon was contemptuous. He had, he said, no need of such silver. Instead he continued to make his lordship of the west a reality: in 1248 King Harald of Man (son of Olaf) and a MacSorley, Ewen of Lorn, were both at his court, the former in order to marry his daughter and the latter to seek the title 'king of the Isles'. When Harald was drowned later in the year, Hakon sent Ewen to take charge of Man. This was too much for Alexander. He raised a great fleet and sailed into the Firth of Lorn. 'He made it plain to his men,' declared Hakon's Saga, 'that he intended not to turn back until he had acquired all the Norwegian king's dominion to the west of the Solunder sea.' Alas for such hopes. Alexander died suddenly in July 1249 during the expedition. It was King Hakon who settled the future of Man, eventually installing there Harald's brother, Magnus. Nevertheless, Alexander had redirected the Scottish monarchy and laid the foundations for the conquest of the west.

11

Britain During the Personal Rule of King Henry III, 1234–58

Until 1234 Henry III had been overshadowed by two great ministers inherited from his father, first Hubert de Burgh and then Peter des Roches. Much of the political agenda had been set by quarrels over power and property that had originated during the early minority. Now Henry could determine his own course. In some ways he did so with success. During the near quarter-century of his personal rule he gave England peace and at least for a while increased his revenues. Money and stability enabled him to play a far stronger hand than before in both Wales and Scotland. Overseas he eventually reached a statesmanlike settlement of the old quarrel with the Capetian kings of France. There was, however, another, less satisfactory side to Henry's rule. The settlement with the Capetians meant accepting the final loss of the Angevin empire. The attempt to offset this defeat by establishing the dynasty as a Mediterranean power was a fiasco. At home, Henry's policies created factional struggles at court, and widened rather than reduced the political chasm between monarch and nation which had opened under the Angevins. As a result, the most fundamental developments during his rule, the emergence of parliament, the widening of the political community and the growing sense of xenophobic national identity were shaped by opposition to royal policies. Ultimately in 1258 Henry's personal rule was ended by a political revolution far more radical than Magna Carta in 1215.

Henry's ideology and ability were central to both his successes and failures. 'A *simplex* and God-fearing man,' remarked the Osney abbey chronicler, picking up two of Henry's key characteristics. Henry's piety was intensely personal and also highly political. He strove to recover what the Angevins (Richard for a while aside) had seemed to lose: the image and the reality of a kingship protected and inspired by God. Henry multiplied the days on which his choirs chanted the ceremonial hymns invoking the aid of Christ for himself and his realm (the *Laudes Regiae*), attended Mass assiduously and fed 500 paupers daily; on special occasions the halls at Westminster were filled with thousands of them. There were no beggars in the Strand in Henry's day. At every place on his itinerary he made gifts to the local monasteries, friaries, hospitals and leper houses. Above all, from 1245 Henry rebuilt Westminster Abbey in honour of the saint who lay there, his patron saint Edward the Confessor, canonized in 1161. Entering by the great north door, the eyes of the worshipper were swept up to the statue of the Confessor high up in the south transept giving his ring to a pilgrim. The sequel was as well known, and so was the moral, for the pilgrim was St John the Evangelist, who would soon conduct the Confessor to heaven. The latter was a saint 'of mighty power' supporting the dynasty in this life and ready to lead Henry to the next.

Henry's status as a *rex piissimus* had already steered him out of the crisis of 1234, and helps explain how his personal rule lasted as long as it did. There was also nothing very objectionable about his wider political ideology, although that has sometimes been suggested by modern historians. True in 1250, in a conversation with Matthew Paris, Henry asked plaintively why he could not abrogate rashly granted charters just like the pope, certainly a highly threatening question. Later an opposition tract, *The Song of Lewes*, written in 1264, implied that Henry defended his right to choose his own ministers, the great battleground of the reign, by citing the Roman law maxim, 'the will of the prince has the force of law'. Henry's ideology, however, formed little part of the general case made against him in and after 1258. His stated position was that he wished to govern in accordance with the law and custom of the realm. It was on custom that he usually stood when he defended his right to choose his ministers, that and on a homely analogy between the king and his magnates. If they could choose their own servants, why could not the king? Henry confirmed Magna Carta both in 1237 and 1253 with every appearance of sincerity. Fundamentally, after the disasters of the des Roches regime, he was at one with the great law book *Bracton*, the work of his chief minister from 1234 to 1239, William Ralegh, which stressed that the king was subject to the law, and must not disseise freemen of property 'by will'. After all the Confessor himself, as Henry knew him from Matthew Paris's *Life*, had been wise, courteous, just and peaceable, giving ease to all. Henry was thus well aware of the need to stand at one with his subjects. The crown's rights needed to be secure, he declared, so that under its wings the rights of everyone else could flourish. 'I depend on you and you on me. If I am rich you are rich, if I am poor you are poor,' he told the assembled bishops.

Henry might seem an ideal king to tread carefully in the post-Magna Carta world, even more so because he had no martial talents and coveted the comfortable life. In place of John's hectic itinerary, Henry spent long periods at Westminster both for business and pleasure and then, as far as possible, toured his southern palaces and palace castles (Woodstock the most northern), commissioning glazed windows, paintings, tiled floors, and wainscoting. 'White bread, chambers and tapestries . . . to ride like a dean on a docile mount. The king likes better all that than to put on a coat of mail,' commented a Poitevin satirist.

What then went wrong? The answer lay in an unfortunate combination of armchair enthusiasm and naivety. Henry might not lead in war, but he still schemed to recover his lost empire and otherwise play a part on the European stage. His expansive, warm-hearted personality sought an outlet not merely in building and piety but in open-handed favours to those he liked and loved. Such impulses were dangerous in one described by the Osney annalist and many others as *simplex*. The word could be used as a compliment, meaning guileless and straightforward. It could also mean plain stupid. Where Henry was concerned, it mostly meant naive. Henry's long minority, surrounded by flattering ministers, had offered a poor political education. He found it very difficult to calculate what was practical, and see the likely consequences of his actions. As a result, the king who wished in his heart to stand with his nation ended by being separated from it. Whereas Louis IX, the great contemporary king of France, seized the initiative and carried through a series of domestic reforms in the 1240s and 1250s, in 1258 Henry III had reform forced upon him.

* * *

After 1234 Henry's court was of his own making. His first protégé was a noble much of his own age, Simon de Montfort. Montfort's rise was extraordinary, for he was simply the younger son of a great French noble, the Simon de Montfort who had led the Albigensian crusade. In 1230 he arrived in England seeking to make good a tenuous claim to the earldom of Leicester (his father, nephew of the last Beaumont earl, had briefly held the title under King John). Quick-witted and silver-tongued, Montfort carried all before him, gaining a share of the Leicester estates in 1231, the title earl in 1236, and in 1238 (by which time he was a leading councillor) the hand of Henry's sister Eleanor, the widow of William Marshal II. Henry had indeed been bowled over, yet he came to realize that Montfort was a man without 'give', quite different from himself, useful but demanding and dangerous.

Montfort's arrival was followed by Henry's marriage in 1236, a turning-point in the reign. His bride was Eleanor, daughter of the count of Provence. Her elder sister, Margaret, was already married to Louis IX of France. Her maternal uncles, from the ruling house of Savoy, had tentacles reaching throughout Europe: one, Thomas, became count of Flanders through marriage (1237–44) and then a count in Piedmont. Eleanor was therefore a wife of the highest status, yet she was only twelve on her marriage and brought no inheritance with her. She was vulnerable in other ways. In 1236 no queen consort had played a part in English government and politics since Eleanor of Aquitaine in the 1160s. Since then the framework in which queens operated had shifted to their disadvantage. The custom of giving queens substantial landed estates for their support had lapsed after 1154. Instead they simply received dower lands on the king's death. Arguably too the growing bureaucratization of government gave queens less scope than the informal structures of earlier ages. Certainly the loss of Normandy in 1204 had much reduced the opportunity for them to act as regents. If the increasing popularity in sculpture and painting of the coronation of the Virgin, with Mary depicted praying before Christ, gave by extension some added force to queenly intercession, it was force in a rather humble and subordinate role. Eleanor of Provence cut through all this, wielding more power than any of her post-Conquest predecessors.

Partly this was a matter of personality, for Eleanor grew up to be far tougher and more determined than her husband, while Henry, indulgent and admiring, gave her plenty of space in which to operate. Apart from some heated remarks during occasional quarrels, he felt they were very much a team. In the great hall at Dublin castle he ordered a painting of a king and queen sitting with their baronage; either side of the muniment room at Westminster Abbey (perhaps a throne room) were twin royal heads, large, confident and serene: Henry and Eleanor. Eleanor built up her own household (over a hundred strong), and soon ceased to be supported simply by Henry's financial advances, gaining control of queen's gold (a percentage levy on money offered the king for favours), and amassing and harshly exploiting a substantial landed estate derived from wardships. Eleanor's far-flung family naturally gave her a role in diplomacy. It also gave her a power base in England, something no English queen had possessed since the Confessor's Edith. Edith's family was indigenous. She was the daughter of the great Earl Godwin. Eleanor's was imported. All the kings since the Conquest had taken queens from outside the kingdom, but they had not taken their relations with them. Henry was different. Of Eleanor's uncles, Henry made William, bishop-elect of Valence, his chief councillor (until his death in 1239), Peter of Savoy in 1240 lord of the great honour of Richmond, and Boniface of Savoy in 1241 archbishop of Canterbury. Alongside these stars there were numerous satellites, including Peter d'Aigueblanche, bishop of Hereford (1240–68) and Imbert Pugeis who became steward of Henry's household. Eleanor also gained a major role through her children, who were brought up in her care at Windsor. She gave birth to the future Edward I in July 1239. Another son and three daughters followed. Eleanor's determination to advance her offspring and further the interests of her Savoyard kin both in England and overseas formed the core of her politics.

Neither the introduction of Simon de Montfort (after an initial spat over his marriage) nor that of the Savoyards proved initially too disruptive. Peter of Savoy behaved with caution and sensitivity. Boniface became a respected and reforming archbishop. Perhaps encouraged by this success, in the late 1240s Henry introduced another wave of foreigners. These were his half-brothers, the sons of his mother's second marriage to the great Poitevin noble, Hugh de Lusignan. In 1247 one of the brothers, William de Valence, married an heiress, gaining both Pembroke and lands in Ireland. (The last Marshal earl of Pembroke had died childless in 1245 and the inheritance had been split between the daughters of William I Marshal and their descendants, of whom Valence's wife was one). Supported as well by money fees worth £833 a year and Hertford castle, Valence took up almost permanent residence at court. In 1250 Aymer de Lusignan, youngest of the brothers, became bishop-elect of Winchester. Meanwhile Geoffrey and Guy de Lusignan were granted pensions and wardships and made frequent visits to England. By binding the family to him, Henry hoped to keep a foothold in Poitou and protect the northern frontiers of Gascony. He also established a trusted family in England. William and Aymer were young (hence the latter remained bishop-elect) and very much his creatures. Nevertheless Henry had no vision of a foreign court dominated by Lusignans and Savoyards, from which native magnates were excluded. In the 1250s the young and ambitious Richard de Clare, earl of Gloucester and lord of Glamorgan, became a leading councillor. So did Hugh Bigod, younger brother of the earl of Norfolk. Both Norfolk and the earl of Hereford were themselves frequently at court. Above all, Henry depended on the loyalty and loans of his canny and wealthy brother Richard, earl of Cornwall, who had taken as his second wife Sanchia, Queen Eleanor's younger sister. From the numerous marriages arranged between English families and Lusignans and Savoyards, in the latter case with urging from the queen, Henry hoped a harmonious court would emerge in which both native nobles and his foreign relations could flourish.

There were other ways in which Henry sought to appease his great nobles, native and foreign alike, to ensure peace and tranquillity. If lawsuits between magnates were still subject to manipulation and delay, there was no return to the disseisins 'by will of the king' which had defiled des Roches's period of power. Thus the revolution of 1258, unlike that of 1215, was not followed by the restoration of property to large numbers of individuals complaining of unjust dispossession by the king. Nor – again in contrast to 1215 – was 1258 a rebellion of the king's debtors. Henry rarely harried magnates to pay what they owed, and the level of their indebtedness was in any case reduced by Magna Carta's financial provisions. Here the minority had not proved a false dawn. 'Justice' was still not sold; baronial and comital reliefs remained at £100; widows were not charged nearly as much, and then infrequently, for permission to marry or stay single (see below, p. 421). Nor, with one or two exceptions, were they pressured into marriage.

In spite of these accommodating policies, Henry failed to create a harmonious court. For a start, the foreigners did not form a united front. On the contrary, by 1252 the conflict between the Lusignans, usually supported by the king, and the queen's party of Savoyards was acute. One reason was the competition over patronage. Henry formed queues, trying to bring some order to the chaos, but then jumped forward whoever was in favour, usually the Lusignans. Part of the problem was that Henry no longer had a large stock of crown land on which he could freely draw, so much of it having been given away by his predecessors. To safeguard what remained, after 1234 the doctrine that crown land was inalienable began to correspond with actual practice. Henry could still bestow money but it was land people really wanted, and for that he was dependent on the chancy flow into his hands of escheats, wardships and marriages. The immediate problem was that these were far less plentiful in the 1250s than they had been a decade earlier when the Savoyards were being established. As a result, only eight members of the Lusignan circle received land in England as opposed to twenty-eight Savoyards, but given the intensified competition, the favours to the former still created keen resentment. The Lusignans also had themselves to blame. Young and irresponsible, they fought out their quarrels with reckless abandon. It was one thing for legal actions brought against them by knights and lesser folk to be obstructed; quite another for the king to take their side in disputes over land and jurisdiction with the earls of Norfolk and Hereford, Archbishop Boniface, and Simon de Montfort who claimed Pembroke from William de Valence as his wife's dower. By 1258 there was a great deal of combustible material at court waiting to explode.

*   *   *

Another factor destabilizing Henry's government was the failure of his continental policies. By 1258 their condition seemed as farcical as they were infuriating.

The collapse of the Breton alliance in 1234 did not mean that Henry had given up hope of recovering his lost empire, but it was hard to see a way forward. Neither the marriage of his sister Isabella to the Emperor Frederick II in 1235, nor his own marriage in 1236, were of much practical help. Then in 1242 the chance seemed to come. Alienated by the establishment of Louis IX's brother in Poitou, Henry's mother and her husband, Hugh de Lusignan, at last looked for English help. Lusignan hostility had been fatal to Henry's expedition in 1230. Now the hour for which he had kept up pensions to the Poitevin barons had come. His letters about the campaign breathed a passionate commitment. Yet when in July 1242 Louis IX gallantly led his army across the Charente at Taillebourg, Henry, his funds already exhausted, beat a hasty and humiliating retreat to Bordeaux. The failure in 1242 ended any hope of recovering his lost empire. With Louis IX's brothers installed in Poitou, Toulouse and after 1246 in Provence itself, the Capetians seemed utterly dominant. In 1250 Henry transferred the rivalry to other fields when, inspired by Louis IX's crusade, he took the cross. To fund the expedition he amassed a treasure all in gold, gold being the currency in the east. In the event the treasure had to be spent in Gascony.

After 1224 Gascony, broadly the land running south and south-east between the Gironde and the Pyrenees, was all that remained of the Angevin continental empire. Since the eleventh century it had marched with Poitou to the north and had been subject to the same dynasty, forming together the duchy of Aquitaine. Its retention by the Angevins, however, was far from impractical because the province, with its great town of Bordeaux, was tied to England by the wine trade. 'How could our poor people subsist if they could not sell their wines or procure English merchandise?' demanded a fourteenth-century Bordelais. The problem was that ducal revenues in the 1230s were perhaps £1,500 a year, no more than those of a great English baron. Since the towns were largely self-governing and the nobility had much allodial land, the pattern of local power was like a patchwork quilt, with the patches of ducal authority few and scattered. An attempt to expand them was bound to cause dispute. Gascony was also under external threat, with the kings of Castile and Aragon both nursing claims to the duchy, thanks to their descent from Eleanor, daughter of Henry II. By 1248 the situation in the province was anarchic. Henry turned to Simon de Montfort, self-confident, militaristic, and with many connections in the area. But Montfort's abrasive rule soon set the duchy in flames, and prompted Alfonso X of Castile to assert his claims. So Henry sacked de Montfort and in August 1253 set sail for Gascony himself, leaving Queen Eleanor as regent (a striking vote of confidence), counselled by Richard of Cornwall. Henry's expedition was by far the most successful of his three overseas. Sieging castles on the one hand, showering concessions on the other, he recovered hold over the duchy. In November 1254 Edward, Henry's son and heir, married Alfonso X's half-sister, thus extinguishing the Castilian threat, Gascony forming part of Edward's appanage. Henceforth, it was stated, the duchy was to be inseparable from the English crown. It seemed the Angevins were now indeed an English dynasty with possessions overseas.

Even before Henry was free from his Gascon difficulties, entirely new vistas had opened up. Frederick II, king of Sicily and as emperor of the Romans titular ruler in both Germany and Italy, had died in 1250. The papacy looked for a candidate who would wrest the Sicilian kingdom (in its view a papal fief) from his Hohenstaufen successors. Henry was that candidate. In March 1254 he accepted the throne on behalf of Edmund, his second son. The kingdom, which included Naples and southern Italy, was wealthy. With no hope now of recovering the lost dominions in France, the dynasty would become instead a Mediterranean power. An extraordinary coup seemed to support such ideas. In January 1257, with the legitimate Hohenstaufen line now represented by a child, Henry's brother, Richard of Cornwall, scattering money on the electors, was chosen as king of Germany, or at least that was his popular title. Officially he was king of the Romans, and the next step for every king of the Romans was to try and secure papal coronation as emperor itself. Were the Angevins about to become the dominant power in Europe?

To concentrate on these new horizons, Henry finally settled the great conflict with the kings of France. The eventual Treaty of Paris was ratified in December 1259, after Henry had lost control of government, but negotiations were in train well before the 1258 revolution. Under the treaty's terms, Henry was to resign all claims to Normandy, Anjou and Poitou, and do liege homage for Gascony, retaining the title duke of Aquitaine. He thus had to abandon the titles duke of Normandy and count of Anjou, although on his new seal (to the pope's amusement) he compensated by sitting on a much grander throne than before. Later, when the vexatious consequences were apparent, lawyers argued that Henry had foolishly converted Gascony, hitherto an allod held in full sovereignty, into a fief held from the king of France. Yet there is no sign at the time that Henry was aware of this alleged allodial status. He saw the treaty as bringing security to Gascony and friendship with the king of France. He was right to abandon empty titles. Neither he nor King Louis looked at the settlement in neat accountancy terms. They had met for the first time in Paris in 1254 and made friends. Louis certainly was a far stronger character. But the kings were united both by their piety, though Louis's was more ascetic and intellectual, and their family life. Henry and Louis had married sisters. Relations between the courts were enlivened by teasing jokes at which Margaret, Louis's queen, was adept, and a shared sense of values: courtesy, generosity and good nature, essentially *débonnaireté* (see below, p. 429). Henry and Louis wanted peace between their peoples. The aspiration was both laudable and realistic. The Treaty of Paris was to keep the peace for twenty-five years.

But there was no happy ending to the Sicilian affair. By the summer of 1255 Manfred, Frederick II's illegitimate son, had secured the whole of the Sicilian kingdom and was threatening the papal states to the north. That April, Henry had already been required to lead or send an army to expel him. *Before* doing so, he was to pay the pope the £90,000 so far expended in the struggle. Thomas of Savoy, with his lordships in north Italy, had promoted the scheme, but in November 1255 he was captured by his enemies, and Savoyard money and diplomacy were thenceforth diverted to securing his release. Richard of Cornwall was occupied expanding his exiguous authority in Germany and never obtained papal coronation as emperor. In England, the church raised £40,000 towards the money demanded by the papacy, but it had little effect on Manfred's position, and seemed totally wasted. That the pope preferred Henry's cash to Henry's army (for it was pointed out he could have one but not both) showed how desperate he was and how little faith he had in English military intervention. Henry had looked at things differently. He could never forget, as he often said, how papal legates had helped save his throne at the start of the reign. His devotion to the pope was profound. Surely a gift from him was a gift from God, and God and the Confessor would find a way. Yet the hard fact was that Henry had returned from Gascony heavily in debt. His chances of securing money and military support from parliament, given the general unpopularity of his government, were non-existent. To be sure, the scheme blocked for some years any Capetian move on Sicily. Ultimately it was Louis IX's younger brother, Charles, who ousted Manfred. Yet such advantages were totally outweighed by the appalling damage done to Henry's reputation in England, illustrating all too clearly what Matthew Paris called his 'supine simplicity'.

*   *   *

The tensions at court and the fiasco over Sicily were central to the revolution of 1258. But it would never have taken the form it did had not Henry also alienated wide sections of local society, in the process expanding the size of the political community and strengthening its sense of national identity.

Initially Henry seemed to strike an acceptable balance between revenue on the one hand and good governance on the other. From 1234 a court headed by professional judges (the first was William Ralegh) travelled with him. Later called 'the court of king's bench', this gave the king greater expertise than before in both hearing great political cases and challenging encroachments on royal rights. In April 1236, urged on by William, bishop elect of Valence, who had arrived with his niece, the new queen, Henry formed a sworn council of twelve ministers, apparently the first time such a formal body had existed. They over-hauled the running of the sheriffdoms and concentrated the king's lands in the hands of two special custodians (hitherto they had been run by the sheriffs or dispersed in the hands of numerous individual keepers). These reforms increased the king's income by some £1,500 a year. This was also a period of remarkable legislative activity, shaped above all by William Ralegh. Striking a balance between the claims of the king and competing groups of his subjects, a series of statutes introduced new legal procedures, clarified the workings of courts, and restrained the abuses of local officials. This was all part of the long-term trend in which more and more people sought the king's justice both at the common bench at Westminster and before the general eyres. Indeed the eyres had such quantities of work that they now visited individual counties roughly once every seven years, the gap being filled by the appointment of judges – often county knights – with commissions to try criminals detained in gaols or to hear petty assizes. The demand of Magna Carta of 1215 (watered down in the subsequent versions), for assize judges to travel the counties four times a year and sit with four knights elected in the county court, a demand of great concern to local society, had not been fulfilled to the letter, but it had in spirit.

It was testimony to this co-operation that in January 1237 Henry once again confirmed Magna Carta and the Charter of the Forest (for the first time when of full age) and a great council conceded him a tax on movable property. But all this was an end, not a beginning. William Ralegh left court in 1239 to become bishop of Norwich and then, after a long conflict with Henry, bishop of Winchester. It was not till 1270, despite request after request, that Henry secured another tax on mov-ables, the result of increasing alienation from the political nation. None the less, for a while his revenues stood at a level considerably higher than earlier in the reign. Between 1241 and 1245 they averaged some £36,500 a year, against around £22,000 in 1230. Henry's court increased in size and splendour. Its food and drink cost an average £6 a day in the late 1220s and probably some £20 a day twenty years later. Henry was able to mount the 1242 expedition to Poitou, enforce his power in

Wales, and spend (after 1245) some £2,000 a year on Westminster Abbey. The trouble was that this money depended on exploiting sources of revenue which merely exacerbated the unpopularity which had prevented him securing taxation in the first place.

One result was that, for all his personal piety, Henry had alienated the institutional church long before the final denouement of the Sicilian affair. The revenues in the 1240s had owed a great deal to the ruthless way in which royal agents, in clear breach of Magna Carta, had exploited bishoprics while they were in the king's hands, as Winchester was for six years following des Roches's death in 1238. To be sure, Henry did not deliberately keep sees vacant (an important change) but the long disputes which followed his attempts to manipulate elections produced the same result. Another ecclesiastical grievance was the way the king's judges challenged the right claimed by many abbots and bishops to have the amercements levied on their tenants. In 1257 an ecclesiastical council drew up a long schedule of complaint covering these and other issues.

Another group which suffered from Henry's exactions were the Jews. In the early part of the reign, taxation on Jews had not been heavy, probably because their substance had been wasted by John's exactions and the 1215–17 civil war. All this changed between 1241 and 1255 with demands totalling some £66,000, probably amounting to half the total wealth of the community. In 1233 Henry had made clear that he only allowed to remain in the kingdom Jews who were of service to the crown. With their wealth now being broken by taxation, the general expulsion of 1290 moved a step closer. Religious attitudes were also sharpening. Henry was keen to convert Jews and founded a special house for such *conversi* in what is now Chancery Lane. But beyond that, his statutes in 1233 and 1253, influenced by the decrees of the Fourth Lateran Council, and measures in Capetian France, sought to prevent contact between Jews and Christians. In 1255 Henry put to death nineteen Jews from Lincoln on the grounds that they had kidnapped and crucified a small Christian boy ('little St Hugh'), the first time the government itself had sanctioned belief in such delusions. The Jews themselves had no political clout, but the king's exactions had a dire effect on those who owed them money – an increasing proportion were members of the gentry – from whom the taxation had ultimately to come. Aware of the source, the government was reluctant to intervene and concede such debtors lenient terms for their repayments. All this was part and parcel of a more general discontent with Henry's rule which spread through the shires of England.

Part of the problem centred on the activities of the sheriffs, who were made by the exchequer to answer for sums of increasing size (called 'increments') above the old farms of their counties: by 1258 the total demanded stood at £2,500, as opposed to £1,540 in 1242 and £750 in 1230. The result was that the sheriffs, with little left for their own upkeep, resorted to bribes, forced entertainment, and other illicit exactions. At the same time, upstanding county knights (like those appointed in the reforms of 1236) seemed to be replaced as sheriffs by knights from other shires or minor professional administrators, men unconstrained by local loyalties and more amenable to exchequer control. Burdensome too were the justices of the general eyre, at least on the crown pleas side. The nation-wide eyre of 1246–9 raised some £22,000, a year's annual revenue on the 1230 figures, and considerably more than the proceeds of the eyre of 1234–6. The forest eyres were likewise onerous, penalties totalling some £18,200 being imposed between 1244 and 1252; the demands were the highest since the reign of Henry II.

Alongside the unpopularity of the king's local officials, there was also a rising tide of complaint against the abuses of magnates and their bailiffs, the first time such grievances had reached the political agenda. One grievance concerned the way that great lords had forced men to attend their private courts where attendance before had not been customary, an issue ('suit of court') dealt with in great detail by legislation in 1259. Another allegation was that during Henry's personal rule lesser men found it impossible to obtain writs to begin legal actions against the king's foreign relations, and other magnates and ministers. If lawsuits were conmenced then the judges feared to give judgements against such men and were even in their pay. 'If I do wrong who is there to do you right?' taunted William de Bussey, estate steward of the Lusignans. The increasing use of professional administrators like Bussey helped the magnates spread their power in the shires. So did a change in the nature of the sheriff's office. In the past, kings had usually appointed a significant number of *curiales* as sheriffs. Often they were household knights. Their closeness to the king and the fact they were allowed to keep a good slice of the revenues from the farm meant they maintained a powerful royal presence in the localities. After 1236 the policy already mentioned of securing increasing revenue above the old farms of the shires meant the replacement of these curial sheriffs by county knights and minor administrators who were more amenable to paying in such additional sums. Although such sheriffs were perfectly able to enforce the king's rights against the general run of the population, they were much less able than their curial predecessors to do so against magnates and their officials. As a result great men were better able than before to usurp the king's rights and oppress their tenants and neighbours, this at the very moment when wider social changes made the latter better able to protest about such oppression (see below, p. 410).

In the shires the sufferings under Henry can scarcely have approached those under John, for royal revenue even at its height never rose to pre-1215 levels. But this was a fast-fading perspective, especially when Henry's exactions were no longer balanced, as they had been briefly after 1236, by much attempt to reform the realm. True, in 1250 Henry made a speech to the assembled sheriffs telling them to maintain his rights, cease their oppressions and monitor magnates' treatment of their men. That magnates should themselves observe Magna Carta was indeed one of his constant refrains. Yet Henry's pronouncements lacked teeth. 'Discuss with the king' minuted his justices when they discovered cases of local malpractice, but if the magnates were the culprits little came of such discussions. The fact was that the king's need for money, his desire to indulge and placate those important at court and his general lack of drive meant that he turned a blind eye to the abuses of both royal and magnate officials. His rule brought peace but it was peace with injustice.

The alienation of the localities was compounded by important changes in the structure of central government, one related to the crucial question of access to and processes at court. The small number of men who spent long periods of time with the king – the justiciar, the chancellor, the stewards, the leading household knights, the keepers of the chamber and wardrobe – had a tremendous opportunity to further people's affairs, and doubtless profit from so doing. 'Now is the time and place since the king is with a small household and few magnates are with him,' wrote one petitioner asking Ralph de Neville, Henry III's chancellor, to intercede for a favour. The justiciar and chancellor were particularly important because they controlled the use of the royal seal. Sometimes consulting the king, sometimes not, depending on their judgement, they had the power in response to petitions to issue writs to the exchequer, to judges, sheriffs and all other branches of the administration furthering people's affairs. Such writs were called 'writs of grace', thus stressing their discretionary nature and the distinction between them and standard 'writs of course' which initiated the common law legal procedures. Even the latter those in charge of the seal had the power to block, wrong though that was. One of the strengths of Henry III's early rule had been his great ministers. Ralph de Neville, bishop of Chichester, had held the seal for twenty years from 1218 to 1238. Judging from the encomia of Matthew Paris, he discharged his office in an open, independent and even-handed manner. So, up to a point, had the justiciar, Hubert de Burgh, between 1219 and 1232. Then everything changed. After Stephen of Seagrave's dismissal as justiciar in 1234, Henry did not appoint a successor. After Bishop Neville was deprived of the great seal in 1238, Henry gave it to minor officials rarely dignified with the title chancellor. The most trusted councillor in the 1240s and 1250s was the clerk John Mansel, who was conciliatory and courageous yet lacked official position or independent status. It was precisely the independence Henry wanted to be rid of.

The disappearance of the great officers of state did not matter for the nobles at court who always had access to the king. It was much more serious for those on the outside, minor magnates, knights, freemen and small ecclesiastical institutions in the shires. For them, defined and navigable channels of communication between the centre and the localities were closing down at the very moment when their grievances were mounting. Correspondingly the new structure was much easier for those on the inside to manipulate and corrupt, hence the complaint that it was impossible to obtain writs to begin legal actions against great men while the latter obtained whatever writs they wished. The formation of a small sworn council in 1236 did nothing to remedy the situation. It may well have remained in being down to 1258, but no attempt was made to proclaim its personnel or (before the drawing up of an elaborate oath in 1257) define its duties.

Henry had alienated the political nation and expanded its size, making groups outside the baronage more vocal than ever before. There was another quite different reflection of that, namely the appearance in Henry's reign of stories about Robin Hood. In 1261 an exchequer clerk, as some kind of joke, altered the name of a man called William, son of Robert Smith, to William Robehod. Clearly he thought the alias appropriate for Smith who was a fugitive criminal. Clearly too he was aware of tales about Robin Hood. The evidence for Robin Hood can indeed be found earlier still, as David Crook has shown. In 1225 the sheriff of Yorkshire seized the movable property of a fugitive called Robert Hood. In the same year he was ordered to hunt down and behead a notorious outlaw, Robert of Wetherby. Evidently he succeeded because he soon acquired a chain to hang up Wetherby's body. Was Robert Hood the alias of Robert of Wetherby? Was Wetherby the original historic Robin Hood? It is far from impossible. Robert and Robin were interchangeable in common speech. Barnsdale, Robin's haunt in the early stories (which only survive in written form from the fifteenth century) was in Yorkshire, the county in which Wetherby was hunted down. In those stories Robin's enemy was the sheriff of Nottingham and it was indeed as sheriff of Nottingham that the York-shire sheriff Eustace of Lowdham, who captured Wetherby, had made his name. The unpopularity of Henry III's sheriffs, justices and forest officials provided fertile ground for stories which transformed an outlaw into a hero. Robin himself belonged to the class of freemen between the gentry and the peasantry. The tales about him appealed across society to all those who felt oppressed by authority.

The unpopularity of Henry III's government had served to consoli-date that sense of community formed in opposition to the crown which had developed under the Angevin kings and been strikingly expressed in 'the community of the land' formed in 1215 to protect Magna Carta. Henry had also given to that community a new sense of its identity, its English identity, by pursuing policies which appeared to make the English a people under threat; this through the amount of favour he gave to his foreign relations and the objectionable way in which some of them behaved. There was a wider background here. The loss of Normandy in 1204 completed the long process by which all the king's subjects could regard themselves as English (see above, p. 8). Criticism of royal ministers as foreigners contemptuous of English customs can be traced from the 1190s. During Henry's minority such men had seemed to form a distinct and highly disruptive faction. Between 1232 and 1234 that faction had captured the king and imposed 'the Poitevin tyranny' on the English.

Once Henry's personal rule began he was well placed to close this gap between monarchy and people. He was far more English than any king since 1066. He lived almost exclusively in England and called it his homeland. His devotion to Edward the Confessor, after whom he named his eldest son, linked the dynasty to the Anglo-Saxon past. But in fact the gap widened rather than contracted. 'He loved aliens above all the English,' the Osney abbey chronicler dolefully remarked about Henry. In the 1240s and 1250s Matthew Paris ranted on and on about the king's favourites: how they fed on the wealth of England and oppressed its people so that the very race seemed in danger. Whether such views were exactly shared by the great English families around the court who had often intermarried with the king's foreign relatives is questionable. For the victorious faction in 1258 the revolution was aimed at one group of foreigners, the Lusignans, not foreigners as a whole. Indeed the Savoyards were actually part of the revolutionary party. More generally, the workings of commercial and ecclesiastical life depended absolutely on England being a full member of the community of Europe. Yet, for all these qualifications, there can be little doubt that Paris's views were widely shared, particularly outside the court. The great tides of xenophobia which swept England in the 1260s are incomprehensible on any other basis. The issue was particularly live at the frequent parliaments of the 1240s and 1250s, hence the constant demand there that the king should govern in concert with his 'natural', that is native-born, subjects. At such assemblies, composed as we shall see of far more than just a small number of great magnates, the king's foreign courtiers must have been very obvious. Stories of the marriages arranged for such men, the castles they held (including Gloucester and the Tower of London) and the oppressions of their local officials doubtless spread. If those officials were little worse, and certainly far less numerous, than those of the great English earls, their foreign connections gave an entirely different dimension to their misdeeds. Thus a Lincolnshire knight abusively described William de Bussey, chief local agent of the Lusignans, as a Poitevin although in fact he was English, a striking example of how the issue of foreigners played in local society. Not surprisingly therefore it is in a schedule of demands from 1258 which reflected the views of the wider community that the most striking expression of xenophobic national identity appears. In the view of the 'Petition of the Barons' (as it is misleadingly called), strategic castles should only be entrusted, and women only married, to men 'born of the English nation'. Otherwise the realm would be in danger and women 'disparaged'. Here what unified the English was their hostility to foreigners.

We have mentioned parliament as the focus of opposition to Henry III and its development was indeed the central constitutional fact of the reign. Up to a point when the name first appeared in an official record in 1237, to be used with increasing frequency thereafter, it was simply a new word for an ancient body, one called the 'witan' under the Anglo-Saxon kings and the 'council' or 'great council' under the Normans and Angevins. Yet a new name was apposite because under Henry III fundamental changes took place in the power of such assemblies, foreshadowing equally fundamental changes in their structure.

It was the king's novel need for taxation that gave parliament its new power. The background here was the financial weakness of the crown. Even at their height in the 1240s, Henry's revenues were still around £20,000 a year less than John's between 1207 and 1212, and probably half those of the Capetians. Valiant efforts to build up a reserve between 1250 and 1253 yielded a gold treasure worth some £20,000, a puny sum compared with the £133,000 John boasted in 1213. In peace, Henry could live within his means as the saving of his gold treasure showed, but he could scarcely accumulate the resources to fight a prolonged war. After 1255, moreover, Henry's annual revenue (thanks in part to the appanage created for Edward, his eldest son, the exhaustion of Jewish wealth, and the general bestowal of patronage) fell back to under £30,000, leading in part to his failure in Wales in 1257 and his inability to resist the revolution of 1258. Faced with this problem, what could the king do? John's general mulct of the kingdom, exploiting all available sources of revenue, required great energy and had provoked Magna Carta. An easier way out was simply to levy general taxation in the form of percentage levies on movable property. The tax of 1225 had raised £40,000 and saved Gascony. But in practice such taxes, however much the clause on consent had been left out of later versions of the Charter, could not be levied without the sanction of the realm. None of this had bothered the twelfth-century kings. They hardly needed such taxation, but the changing face of royal finance placed their successors in a very different position.

The great lever, refusal of supply, which was the source of all parliament's power against the king, had thus appeared. Between 1232 and 1257 Henry demanded taxation at fourteen or more assemblies, and only obtained it at two of them in 1232 and 1237. In the 1240s and 1250s he was refused supply at parliament after parliament save on conditions he deemed unacceptable. At the debates in these assemblies the tensions between the king and the political community came to a head. In the process parliament itself gained an altogether new sense of its identity and place in the constitution, one the reforms of 1258 sought to enshrine with the stipulation that parliament should meet three times a year to discuss the affairs of the kingdom. Parliament had indeed arrived.

Intimately related to the power of Henry's parliaments was the way they came increasingly to represent the wider realm, a development which foreshadows the establishment of the House of Commons. Magna Carta had stipulated that to gain common consent for taxation the greater barons were to be summoned individually by letter, and the lesser tenants-in-chief generally through the sheriffs. Despite the omission of the clause from subsequent versions of the Charter, this was almost certainly the way great assemblies were convened from the start of Henry's reign. Although not all the lesser tenants-in-chief attended, many probably did and they embraced a wide social spectrum, including many minor landholders of knightly or even less than knightly status. Henry's parliaments were therefore able to focus the debate between the king and the whole political community. Even so, there was a growing feeling that this informal and haphazard representation of the wider realm was not enough. In 1254 the county courts were ordered to elect two knights to come and grant taxation 'on behalf of everyone in the county'. This was the first known occasion when representatives of the shires were summoned to parliament. In 1225, 1232 and 1237 tenants-in-chief alone had given 'common consent' to taxation, just as envisaged in Magna Carta. Thereafter no tax was ever granted without the consent of knights from the shires. The need for such consent was the main factor in establishing the commons in parliament in the later part of the thirteenth century.

Ideas were important here, as was ecclesiastical example. The Roman law tag 'what touches all shall be approved by all' had been familiar in England since at least the 1220s. The same principle, when it came to taxation of the church, was enshrined in canon law. Bishops in resisting taxation by both the pope and the king made it plain (in 1226 and 1240) that they could not answer for the lower clergy (deans, priors, archdeacons and parish priests). The latter must be separately consulted. In 1254 representatives of the lower clergy were summoned to parliament together with the knights from the shires. If, however, theory was important, more important still were the simple facts of power (discussed in more detail below, pp. 395–410). One of the knights nominated to serve for Middlesex in 1254, Roger de la Dune, had only one principal manor, yet he served as a collector of the tax granted by the 1237 parliament and as a justice of assize. Some of his colleagues in other counties had soldiered in royal armies. Few had discernible connections with great magnates. These men could not be taken for granted. Dune himself refused to accept election in 1254, probably protesting against the proposed tax which indeed was never conceded, the conditions doubtless being unacceptable to the government.

Initially the demands made in return for taxation had been palatable enough for the king. In return for the tax of 1225 he conceded the definitive versions of Magna Carta and the Charter of the Forest; for the tax of 1237 (granted by the first parliament *eo nomine*), he issued the first confirmation of the Charters while of full age. Yet the belief was gaining ground that the Charters, although they had made a difference, were not enough. Even if they were enforceable, which they were not, they said nothing about who the sheriffs were to be and on what financial terms they were to hold office. Likewise they said nothing about the conduct of magnates and their officials. All these were important issues for those in the localities. Magna Carta was also silent about control of central government. The king remained free to choose ministers, bestow patronage and determine policy just as he liked. That freedom as Henry exercised it brought to a head longstanding problems over counsel and consent.

The Norman and Angevin kings often proclaimed that legislation had been issued and major decisions taken with the 'counsel and consent' of their lay and ecclesiastical magnates. It may be that such assemblies both before and after 1215 were usually summoned in the way laid down by Magna Carta, but they had no precise constitutional powers. If in practice both taxation and legislation required common consent, Henry had been quite able to sign up for Sicily without any consent at all, as was frequently pointed out. In any case kings rarely dealt with their magnates in a single body even during great councils. Nothing is more revealing of royal methods than the accounts, found in monastic chronicles, of Henry II, Richard I and John settling (or trying to settle) disputes on such occasions, now conferring with small groups ('You, you and you, the rest wait outside'), now with much larger ones, moving all the time according to the size of the meeting between chapel, chamber, chapter house and refectory, in a kind of ritual of the rooms. There was also a whole range of decisions, especially in the vital area of patronage, which kings routinely made outside great councils, taking advice as they wished from the ministers and magnates (often overlapping groups) who happened to be at court. In the hands of an able monarch, these structures could work well. It was a different matter if the king was malevolent or incompetent. And under Henry the king's incompetence was given a new framework both by the disappearance of the great offices of state and the formation of a small council, with the resulting question of its powers and personnel. There were no lack of ideas about how to deal with these difficulties. The twelfth and thirteenth centuries were a great age of constitution-making, in towns, universities, monasteries and the international religious orders of the Cistercians and the Friars. Everywhere there were elected officials and large and small councils or chapters, hence ultimately the king's small council in 1236. The idea that the great council in England should wield considerable authority had been sanctioned by practice during Richard's crusade and captivity. In 1215 Magna Carta laid down that it needed to consent to taxation. During Henry's minority the great council had chosen the king's ministers. Ralph de Neville indeed, appointed to keep the king's seal in 1218, had resisted dismissal by the king in 1236 on the grounds that only a great council could remove him. His reputation for fairness and independence seemed to demonstrate the value of ministers chosen in that way.

All this was the background to the so-called 'Paper Constitution' concocted at a parliament in 1244 ('Paper' because it was never implemented). The Constitution sought to deal with the problem of counsel at its two vital levels, that of the great council and the small. It thus stipulated that the great council or parliament should have sole authority to appoint and remove four of the king's small council, including the justiciar and chancellor, those offices thus being restored. These four were then to manage the king's treasure, hear everyone's complaints, and choose the justices of the common bench and the officials of the exchequer. In effect they were to control central government. The kind of scheme in the 'Paper Constitution' could certainly appeal to ministers and magnates at court who might feel that decisions over lawsuits, patronage and policy would be better taken if Henry had to listen to their advice. This indeed was the background to the councillor's oath drawn up in 1257, under which the councillors swore to refuse patronage offered by the king unless their fellows consented – a remarkable attempt to restrict the king from inside the regime itself. 'The 'Paper Constitution' had even more attractions for the lesser magnates, knights and freemen in the shires who had suffered most from the disappearance of the justiciarship and chancellorship, and were represented in parliament, as we have seen, by the minor tenants-in-chief. They had an additional incentive to be vocal: more than anyone else, they would have to pay the taxation which was to be offered in return for the Constitution's acceptance.

The kind of demands found in the 'Paper Constitution' were put, in various forms, at parliament after parliament after 1244 and were finally implemented in 1258. Their proponents did not find them hard to justify. *The Song of Lewes* was hardly treading new ground when it averred that since 'the government of the realm is the safety or ruin of all', the whole realm was rightfully concerned about who was set over it. Henry was thus drawing a false analogy when he sought the same freedom to choose his ministers as any earl or baron. There was equally a widespread view that if the king ruled badly it was the duty of the baronage, representing the community, to 'bridle' him. The baronage had in effect done just that at the Gloucester council of May 1234, an episode alluded to by *Bracton* and not with disapproval. In any case, since in form the revolution of 1258 was carried out with the king's consent and in his name, no elaborate justification proved necessary. It was indeed only later chroniclers, like Thomas Wykes, who grasped the revolutionary significance of what had occurred.

* * *

The crisis of 1258 was set off by the intensification of the struggles at court. By this time Edward, the heir to the throne, was nineteen, and already masterful and martial. After his marriage to Eleanor of Castile in 1254 he had received an appanage including Gascony, Bristol and the king's lands in Wales and Ireland. He was therefore badly affected by the resurgence of Welsh power in the 1250s, and in 1258 he turned to the Savoyards for help. When they could not supply it, stretched by their continental commitments, he got money instead from the Lusignans. Edward was already irked by restrictions imposed by his father on the running of his appanage, and bored by his rather staid entourage (including Peter of Savoy), mostly selected by his mother. He found the young William de Valence and his flashy circle far more congenial. Queen Eleanor was horrified. She seemed to be losing her son to her greatest enemies. She was quite ready to condone, perhaps encourage, the ensuing revolution.

In this tense atmosphere the touch paper was set alight. On 1 April 1258 at Shere in Surrey, during a dispute over the advowson, a posse sent by Aymer de Lusignan, bishop-elect of Winchester, attacked men of the magnate/courtier John fitz Geoffrey, killing one of them. A week later, a great parliament opened at Westminster. The harvest of 1257 having failed, it was a time of famine, with villagers flocking to London for food and vagrants dying everywhere of starvation. At the parliament fitz Geoffrey at once demanded justice from the king; Henry excused the bishop and refused it. John was incandescent. The whole episode seemed to sum up the arrogance of the half-brothers and how Henry's protection placed them pre-eminently above the law. Debates over Wales made matters worse. William de Valence (with his lordship of Pembroke attacked) accused both Montfort and the earl of Gloucester of conniving with the Welsh, while Montfort demanded justice against Valence, probably referring to his wife's claims to Pembroke. On 12 April Montfort, the earls of Gloucester and Norfolk, Hugh Bigod, Peter of Savoy, John fitz Geoffrey, and Peter de Montfort (no relation of Simon), all courtiers or close to the court, banded together. Savoy's presence reflected the blessing of the queen. They intended to deal with the Lusignans and reform the realm.

The Sicilian affair, the reason for the summoning of the parliament in the first place, produced the denouement. A papal envoy, Arlot, threatened the king with excommunication and the realm with Interdict if the money owed the pope was not forthcoming. Henry, having oppressed his subjects, failed in Wales, and denied justice to John fitz Geoffrey, now dutifully requested the necessary tax, a tax heavier than that of 1225. The answer came on 30 April. Unrestrained by Richard of Cornwall who was away in Germany, a group of magnates led by Roger Bigod, earl of Norfolk, marched in full armour into the king's hall at Westminster. Henry was a sitting target. His small treasure had been exhausted by the 1257 campaign in Wales, the number of his household knights had dwindled, and there was still a gap in the new walls of the Tower of London on which (after a scare in 1238) he had initially spent large sums of money. For a frightening moment he thought he was a prisoner. Instead he was made to accept a general reform of the realm. It was to be more than seven years before he fully and finally recovered power.

The crash of Henry's regime in 1258 should not obscure the fact that for nearly a quarter of a century it had brought peace to England.

Indeed, apart from the castle sieges of the minority, and the Marshal war in 1233–4 (largely confined to Wales and Ireland), there was peace in England from 1217 to 1263. It was that which made possible the proliferation of markets and fairs, the accelerating money supply (helped by Henry's re-coinage with a new style 'long-cross penny' in 1247), and the general economic recovery after the 1215–17 civil war. The stability of Henry's regime owed something to the resources of Ireland. It also enabled him to be far more assertive than before in Wales and Scotland.

*　　*　　*

For twenty years after 1234 Ireland provided Henry with valuable support. Treasure was constantly shipped across to England, between 1240 and 1245 averaging some £1,150 a year. Henry also turned to Ireland for the patronage he so desperately needed, the beneficiaries being Savoyards, Lusignans and native English courtiers. In the process there were significant changes in the political structure of the lordship. Henry was helped by a remarkable succession of deaths in the 1240s which brought a stream of wardships, widows and heiresses into royal hands. As in Wales, exercise of the king's 'feudal' rights in such circumstances could quickly transform patterns of local lordship. Henry made one gain himself: Ulster reverted to the crown on the death of Hugh de Lacy in 1242. The year before, on Walter de Lacy's death, Meath was divided between his two granddaughters, one of whom (in 1252) married the queen's lifelong friend Geoffrey de Joinville, Ireland thus becoming a mainstay of his extraordinary international career (see above, p. 25). Meanwhile Leinster, with the childless death of the last Marshal earl in 1245, was divided between the descendants of the old regent's daughters, with Wexford (as well as Pembroke) passing to the wife of William de Valence. Henry also resorted, much as John had done, to speculative grants of land in territory largely held by native rulers. In Thomond, beneficiaries were the queen's first household steward, Robert Mucegros, and John fitz Geoffrey, justiciar of Ireland (1245–54), later to play that key role in the crisis of 1258, another man very close to the queen. On the other hand, in the 'King's Cantreds' between Meath and Connacht, Henry granted land worth £500 to Geoffrey de Lusignan. If these grants could be implemented they would bring a considerable expansion in the territorial extent of the lordship.

In 1254 Ireland formed part of the appanage granted to Henry's son, the Lord Edward. As with Gascony, the grant stipulated that the lordship should never be separated from the English crown, ruling out the kind of concession to a younger son that Henry II had made to John. Ireland's future as a crown colony was assured.

*   *   *

The 1240s saw a transformation in the king's position in Wales. During the two previous decades Henry had made limited efforts to challenge the dominance of Llywelyn the Great, apart from trying to maintain the 1218 Treaty of Worcester's baseline by denying him the homages of the native rulers. One reason for inaction had been Llywelyn's alliance with successive earls of Chester, which effectively ruled out any invasion of Gwynedd. In 1237, however, the last earl had died without direct heirs. Previous kings had often held the earldom in wardship. Now Henry, wisely counselled, bought out the numerous co-heirs and acquired Cheshire for the crown, perhaps the best move of his career. He was to go on to replace Gwynedd's dominance in Wales with his own. Yet for all these advances, Henry's policy towards Wales still showed something of the lack of ambition characteristic of earlier years.

On the death of his father Llywelyn the Great in 1240, Dafydd did homage to King Henry for the whole of Gwynedd, including the Four Cantrefs; his elder brother Gruffudd was therefore excluded, the object for which Llywelyn had laboured for so long. If Dafydd was accorded no princely title in royal letters, he was knighted by Henry and at the same ceremony wore a coronet 'the insignia of the principality of North Wales', as the Tewkesbury annalist described it. Henry thus accepted Dafydd as a ruler of unique status while (in line with previous policy) making him repeat Llywelyn's acknowledgement of 1218 that the homages of the other native rulers belonged to the crown. Dafydd's real trouble lay less with the king than with the territorial ambitions of the marcher barons and Welsh rulers who claimed to have been disappropriated by his father, often in breach of the 1218 Treaty. In the south, on Llywelyn's death Gilbert Marshal had immediately seized Cardigan, at last possessing what the king had granted him in 1234. Between Wye and Severn, Ralph de Mortimer soon made good his claims to Maelienydd. Gruffudd ap Gwenwynwyn was equally determined to recover southern

Powys, for the tenure conceded to Llywelyn in 1218 had expired years ago with his majority.

It was Dafydd's resistance, courageous and resourceful, to these and other threatened losses (like that of Mold) which produced King Henry's invasion of August 1241. Like John in 1211, he enlisted native rulers from all over Wales, including Gruffudd ap Gwenwynwyn, and (from within Gwynedd itself) the long-excluded claimants to Meirionydd. He also envisaged partitioning Gwynedd between Dafydd and Gruffudd, giving dangerous currency to the belief that the division of princely inheritances was sanctioned by Welsh law. Henry penetrated as far as Rhuddlan, whereupon Dafydd submitted. Gruffudd ap Gwenwynwyn recovered his portion of Powys and Dafydd surrendered Builth, a grievous blow to his position in the south. He also agreed that should he rebel again or have no heirs by his wife then Gwynedd should be forfeit to the crown. Curtains! Yet in other ways the settlement was less severe than John's in 1211. Dafydd was deprived not of the Four Cantrefs but only the most eastern, Tegeingl, which Henry now held down by building a castle at Diserth, high above the valley of the Clwyd. For the rest, the rulers of Meirionydd were restored and did homage to Henry, but no major division of Gwynedd was implemented. Gruffudd simply swapped Dafydd's prison for the Tower of London.

In 1241 the king did not merely profit at the expense of Dafydd. When Gilbert Marshal died in a tournament in June, Henry accepted his brother Walter's succession to the earldom of Pembroke but secured his surrender of Cardigan and Carmarthen, although held by the royal grant of 1234 in hereditary right. Thus the two great royal bases in the south which John had lost to Llywelyn in 1216, and Henry had foolishly granted away to de Burgh and then to the Marshals, were recovered. In his triumph, the king's attitude to both Dafydd and the men of Tegeingl (who were to be treated according to Welsh law) was conciliatory, partly because his mind was now set on an expedition to Poitou. But his new officials both in the north and south were highly aggressive. Even the loyal Gruffudd ap Madog of northern Powys needed reassurance about their activities. Dafydd, of course, could never be reconciled to his losses and the death of his half-brother Gruffudd, killed in a fall while trying to escape from the Tower of London in March 1244, freed him from a rival and created grievances he could exploit. In 1241 the Welsh rulers had for the most part sided with King Henry. Now (apart from the two Gruffudds of Powys), having experienced the reality of

English rule, they did the reverse. Dafydd showed remarkable resource. He sent envoys to Louis IX, offered to hold 'his part of Wales' from the pope (thus declaring independence of King Henry) and, significantly, adopted the title 'prince of Wales'. That title had been used by his great-grandfather, Owain Gwynedd, but had been avoided by Llywelyn for fear it would provoke English king and Welsh ruler alike. It was now a symbol of Dafydd's leadership in a national cause.

Henry's response was sluggish. In August 1244, according to Matthew Paris he preferred 'the delight and rest' of Westminster to a campaign in Wales. The next year, however, with Felim O'Connor, native king of Connacht, enlisted to ravage Anglesey, Henry gathered an army comparable to Edward I's in 1276–7, only then (as in 1223, 1228, 1231 and 1241) to sit down and build another castle, this time on the rock at Deganwy above the Conwy estuary. Dafydd himself died in February 1246. By his own agreements, Gwynedd was now doubly forfeit because of his rebellion and his childlessness. Surely, with his new base at Deganwy, and with his captain Nicholas Molis having just marched up from Cardigan to maraud through the heart of Gwynedd, Henry would now move in and take possession. He had no continental or other distractions. He was in funds. And yet he did nothing. Under the Treaty of Woodstock (April 1247) Henry came to terms with Owain and Llywelyn, sons of the hapless Gruffudd, and thus grandsons of Llywelyn the Great. The brothers ceded the Four Cantrefs to the kings of England in perpetuity, but they kept the rest of Gwynedd undivided: Henry did not partition it between them or even retain the homage of the ruler of Llŷn, Gwynedd's westernmost cantref, which he had taken earlier in the year. If the brothers broke the agreement they would forfeit their lands for ever. But nothing, in contrast to 1211 and 1241, was said about Gwynedd escheating if they did not have heirs by their wives. Instead the grant was made more widely to them and their heirs, and the chances of escheat were thus much reduced.

If Gwynedd had been truncated, Henry had positively willed the survival of its heartland. He was similarly lenient in the south. He kept Maelgwn Fychan's lands around Aberystwyth (seized by Molis on his great march), but allowed him to recover commotes adjoining Cardigan. The rest of Ceredigion, apart of course from Cardigan itself, remained with Maredudd ab Owain and Maredudd ap Rhys, who had made an early submission in 1245 and accompanied Molis on his campaign. Henry's attitude was not simply the result of lack of ambition. He was also responding to wise advice from some of the marcher barons of the south, namely that the Welsh were controlled most effectively by men 'of their own tongue'. But once again this was only part of the story. The king's agents were frequently English, not Welsh, and their oppressions soon laid the foundations for another resurgence of Gwynedd.

The rise in royal power within ten years had been remarkable and was meant to be permanent. In 1247 the king announced that Chester and the Four Cantrefs were to remain annexed to the crown. In the south he held Builth, Cardigan, Carmarthen and northern Ceredigion. The division of both the Braose and Marshal baronies between co-heiresses (after 1230 and 1245) had enhanced his dominance. None the less, given his power, opportunities and rights (as he could have defined them), Henry's policies might have been far more aggressive. The fact was the actual conquest of Wales, unlike the recovery of the Angevin empire, was not something he was prepared to devote energy and resources to achieving.

The king's forward policies were also limited in another area, that of the privileges or 'liberties' claimed by the marcher barons. Here there was every reason for action. 'All wish to have nearly royal power and liberty,' wrote a royal agent in 1234 about the barons of Ireland. The same was true in Wales. The fitz Alans of Clun and Oswestry, the Corbets of Caus and the Mortimers of Wigmore were all determined to remove their lordships from the jurisdiction of the neighbouring sheriffs, and make them part of the March. The liberties of the March had originated in the powers wielded by Norman lords when they made and defended their original conquests. One of the most longstanding was thus the right of private war. In the thirteenth century the liberties were seen equally as a way of governing and exploiting the lordships more effectively. Magna Carta itself had distinguished the law of the March from that of Wales and England. The precise content of March law was never defined (it varied greatly) but its essential umbrella was the claim, made specifically in 1199 and 1221, that the marchers enjoyed all the king's rights ('regality'), and virtual autonomy within their lordships. The king's writ did not run, the lords controlling the whole process of criminal and civil justice. Faced with these problems, Henry did make some response. The court of king's bench became the forum for cases involving both marcher barons and Welsh rulers. In 1243 it summoned the earl of Gloucester (no less), as part of a general test case against the marchers, to show what rights he had over the bishopric of Llandaff during a vacancy. Then in 1247, the earl was made to acknowledge (after a complaint had been made against him by his tenant Richard Seward) that the king could review and correct judgements passed in his court of Glamorgan. Henry had made important points of principle, yet in the March, as in England, he did little in practice to follow them up. Indeed his pressure, such as it was, prompted the marchers to define their liberties all the more closely, the whole period being a watershed in that process of definition. In practice Richard de Clare succeeded in disappropriating Seward, retained control over the Llandaff's issues during a vacancy in the 1250s, and generally extended his authority within Glamorgan. While the Welsh within the great lordships often retained their own courts and law, for the English the marcher barons issued the same types of common law writs which ran in the king's name in England. In Henry's reign, even when his power was at its height, marcher kingdoms in miniature were developing.

* * *

Henry III's policies in Scotland showed a mixture of assertion and restraint similar to that seen in Wales. On his accession in July 1249 Alexander III (Alexander II's son by Marie de Coucy) was still two months short of his eighth birthday. The seal made for his minority bore the legend, 'Be you as prudent as a serpent and as pure as a dove', which when interpreted in its biblical context suggested the evil men from whom Alexander might be in danger. Certainly politics were soon factionalized into two rival camps, each appealing at different times to Henry III for help. Yet the period cemented rather than serrated the cordial relations between the two monarchies.

The government of the young king was a continuation of the old with Alan Durward, the justiciar of Scotland north of Forth, its leading figure. Marie de Coucy, perhaps denied a regency role like that played by Louis IX's mother Queen Blanche, soon returned to France where she re-married, an action which closely paralleled Isabella of Angoulême's desertion of Henry III. In July 1249 Alexander was inaugurated in the traditional ceremony at Scone, sitting on the famous stone kept reverently at the monastery. There were plans to enhance the king's dignity further when the pope was asked to sanction a full coronation ceremony with anointing. The king's seal indeed depicted him crowned, unlike those of his father and grandfather. The trouble was that all this seemed linked to the greater glory of Durward as much as to that of the king. The movement against Durward was led by Walter Comyn, earl of Menteith, and his kin. The Comyns had been out of royal favour in the last years of Alexander II, but had widespread support among magnates and clergy. King Henry became involved in their plot. At Christmas 1251, amid much joyful celebration, the marriage agreed in the 1240s between his daughter Margaret, now eleven, and Alexander took place at York. Immediately afterwards Durward and his allies were removed and replaced by a government dominated by the Comyns.

Before the coup Henry had protested, much as he had in 1221, at the plans for a Scottish coronation and anointing. At York he had gone further and asked Alexander to do homage for the kingdom of Scotland. When, however, the latter politely refused, Henry gracefully dropped the matter and never raised it again. Instead the relationship established was warmly paternal. Alexander now regarded Henry as 'his dearest father' and sought his counsel and protection. Accordingly Henry appointed two northern magnates, Robert de Ros and John de Balliol, to act as guardians of the young king and queen. It was Henry's anxieties as a father, not resentment at the limited role which Ros and Balliol actually played in Scottish government, which created the next crisis.

After his fall, Alan Durward went south to poison King Henry's mind. That was not difficult once Queen Margaret (in 1255) complained that Ros was preventing her sleeping with the king, and not allowing them out of Edinburgh castle. In September 1255 the royal couple were rescued from the fortress by the earl of Gloucester and John Mansel and brought to King Henry just across the border. Alexander dismissed his Comyn councillors and appointed a new ruling council (with fifteen members). This was the high point of Henry III's intervention in Scottish affairs. Under an agreement, his sanction was necessary for the dismissal of councillors and for the termination of the council's authority. Otherwise it was to last until September 1262, when Alexander would be twenty-one. Henry fiercely denied that he intended anything that would damage the 'liberties, rights and state of the kingdom of Scotland', which shows that such fears were current at the time. Yet his denials had the ring of truth. He promised that the new arrangements were not in any way to compromise the rights of the kingdom, which indeed, so he declared, his whole aim was to protect, 'bound as we are to King Alexander by the chain of paternal love'.

Alan Durward was back as one of the new councillors, but it was soon musical chairs all over again. The ousted Comyns petitioned Henry III for help, as they had in 1251. When this failed they resorted to the kind of *coup de main* which they had suffered in 1255, seizing the king at Kinross in October 1257. For much of the next year the kingdom stood on the brink of civil war, the Comyns making an alliance with Llywelyn under which neither was to aid the other's enemies. A month later, in April 1258, Henry III was removed from the scene by the political revolution in England, an event which perhaps helped the emergence of an eventual compromise in Scotland. In October 1258 a new council was created in which nominal headship was given to the king's mother, Marie de Coucy, and her new husband. Alan Durward again became a councillor, but for the rest both the higher and lower reaches of government (especially the sheriffdoms) were dominated by the Comyns and their allies.

It was in this uneasy situation that Alexander in the early 1260s assumed full control of government. The minority had been a traumatic time, with politics factionalized, the king twice seized, and the king of England in novel fashion involved in appointing and dismissing ministers. Henry, however, had treated Scotland quite differently from Wales. On Llywelyn's death he had at once asserted and enforced his rights to the homage of the native rulers. In Scotland, on the death of Alexander II, while he had registered old claims to overlordship he had done nothing to enforce them, although he must have known he would never have a better chance. The difference was that in Wales, Henry felt sure of his rights. They had been set out in the Treaty of Worcester in 1218. In Scotland the position was much less defined. Thus Alexander and Margaret remained part of an affectionate family circle, with Alexander enquiring solicitously in his letters about the health of Queen Eleanor, 'our beloved mother', and her children. 'Never did any of the English or British kings in any past time keep his pledges towards the Scots more faithfully than this Henry; for nearly all the whole time of his reign he was looked upon by the kings of Scotland, father and son, as their most faithful neighbour and adviser.' So said the Scottish chronicler Fordun, writing in the fourteenth century. These good relations fundamentally influenced Alexander's policies during the collapse of Henry's power in the years after 1258.

12

The Tribulations of Henry III, the Triumphs of Alexander III and Llywelyn, Prince of Wales, 1255–72

In the Westminster parliament at the end of April 1258, Henry III had agreed that the realm should be reformed by twenty-four men, half of them chosen by himself and half by the barons. Those close to him were in both camps because the court had split apart, but Henry's twelve were far less powerful and included only one English earl, John de Warenne of Surrey. The work of reformation was to begin in June at a parliament summoned to Oxford. It met in an atmosphere of great tension, for under the pretext of a proposed campaign in Wales both sides had summoned their military forces. It was therefore to prevent any royalist revanche that the reformers immediately stripped the king of physical power by putting their own men into the royal castles. They then took control of central government. A panel drawn from the twenty-four appointed a new council for the king with fifteen members, amongst whom the king's opponents (including Simon de Montfort and the earls of Gloucester and Norfolk) were in a large majority. The council was to choose the king's chief ministers and control the whole running of central government, the key stipulation being that the chancellor was not to seal charters and writs (other than those which were routine) without its permission. This was utterly revolutionary. Henry was in practice reduced to a cipher. The council was to rule. Yet it was to do so in co-operation with parliament which was to meet at least thrice annually to 'deal with the common business of the realm and of the king together'.

At Oxford the king's Lusignan half-brothers, William de Valence, Bishop-elect Aymer, Guy and Geoffrey, all of them on Henry's twelve, quickly realized they were marked men. Losing their nerve they fled to Winchester. The barons followed in hot pursuit and expelled them from the country. Some leaders of the regime may well have thought their main objectives were now achieved. But the Oxford parliament, crowded with knights, had already embarked on a much wider reform of the realm designed above all to deal with the local grievances which had arisen during Henry's rule. The totality of the reforms down to October 1259 were known loosely by contemporaries as 'the Provisions of Oxford' after the place where the movement had begun.

At Oxford Hugh Bigod, brother of the earl of Norfolk, had been made justiciar. The office was thus revived but with a new remit. Earlier justiciars had been in general charge of central government. Bigod's task was more specifically to hear complaints and dispense justice. He was to deal with grievances of great men; the first case he heard was that of John fitz Geoffrey (see above, p. 360). But he was also from the first expected to tour the country and give justice to all. Individuals could bring actions before him simply by verbal 'complaint' (*querela*), a deliberate attempt to make justice more readily available by removing the bother of obtaining writs. At the same time Bigod also heard complaints brought to light by the investigations of panels of four knights appointed in each county in August 1258. By July 1259 he had heard around 268 cases, determined most of them quickly and was lauded by the St Albans abbey chronicler for the impartiality of his justice. In November 1259 his efforts were supplemented by those of groups of judges whose eyres were designed to cover the whole country.

The reforms also dealt with grievances over sheriffs. At Oxford it was decided that they should hold office only for a year, that they should be major county knights and receive an annual salary or allowance. In practice the allowance proved unworkable, but the same result was achieved in 1259 by allowing the sheriffs to answer for smaller increments above the county farms than those in force in the 1250s, leaving more money for their upkeep. Then in October 1259 legislation, known to modern historians as 'the Provisions of Westminster', dealt (among other things) with the abuses of the justices in eyre. They were no longer to amerce villages because all males over the age of twelve had not attended coroners' inquests; nor were they to levy the *murdrum* fine in cases of death by misadventure – a reform prompted by the large numbers of unidentifiable vagrants left dead by the recent famine. Both these concessions were of particular value to the peasantry (see below, p. 413).

A striking feature of the reforms was that they were concerned as much with the malpractices of the barons as with those of the king, thus reflecting another problem which had grown during Henry's personal rule. The leading reformers in a proclamation of February/March 1259 promised not to obstruct complaints brought against themselves and their bailiffs, and Hugh Bigod and his colleagues did indeed hear many cases involving baronial officials. Likewise the Provisions of Westminster, in three long, detailed clauses right at the start, dealt with the issue of 'suit of court' (see above, p. 350). Tenants could no longer be forced to attend the courts of lords unless such attendance had been customary before 1230 or was a duty specifically mentioned in a charter of enfeoffment.

In stipulating that sheriffs were to be local knights, introducing the *querela*, remedying lordly as well as royal abuse, and above all in taking control at the centre, the measures of 1258–9 were far more radical and wide-ranging than those of Magna Carta. Richard de Clare for one was unhappy about how the local reforms impinged on his local power – not surprisingly, given the uniquely large network of courts and officials he controlled as earl of Gloucester and Hertford. Others may have felt the same way. But having coerced the king, the new regime needed support. Therefore the early reforms were explained in a proclamation of October 1258 issued, uniquely, in English as well as French and Latin, a striking indication of the desire to reach as wide an audience as possible. The regime also remained under pressure from below. Thus the Provisions of Westminster, with their regulations on private courts so unpalatable for Clare and his like, were only promulgated after a protest at parliament by 'the community of the bachelry of England', probably knights in magnate entourages, speaking here for powerful forces in the counties – the knights increasingly holding office in the shires and the substantial freemen running the hundreds.

Some of the reformers, for instance Roger de Mortimer who was seeking to recover the manor of Lechlade in Gloucestershire, were driven on by personal grievances. But the movement was also influenced by political ideas, ideas all the more precise and pervasive through being elaborated at a new base (Oxford university) and propagated by a new movement (the Friars). Franciscan teachers in Oxford, like John of Wales, following John of Salisbury, frequently compared the body politic to a human body in which the health of the whole was dependent on that of all its parts, an analogy used by the council of fifteen in a letter to the pope. It followed that reform should benefit everyone, hence in part at least the attention to peasant grievances. The embrace of the movement was summed up by a term used again and again in this period, the 'community of the realm'. It was this body which was said both to sanction reforms and profit from them. Admittedly, the 'community of the realm' spoken in one breath could sometimes become 'the community of the barons' in the next, showing where the leadership lay. But the term was also employed quite genuinely to mean everyone in the land. Indeed such a community had actually been formed at the start in 1258 by the oath taken by 'all faithful and loyal men' to support the reforms and treat opponents as mortal enemies.

Nowhere was the interaction between idealism and self-interest more blatant and more baffling than in the case of Simon de Montfort himself. He was the brother-in-law of the king, but from the outset the special force of his attachment to the Provisions was quite apparent. In 1259 he both upbraided Richard de Clare for dragging his feet over local reforms and made support for 'the common enterprise', as he called it later, a condition of his alliance with the heir to the throne, the Lord Edward. Again and again he pointed to the oath all had sworn to uphold the Provisions. He almost certainly came to see them as a crusading cause for which he would fight, and if needs be die, just as his father had died leading the crusade against the Albigensians. Montfort's attitudes had been shaped by Robert Grosseteste, bishop of Lincoln and former chancellor of Oxford, the greatest theologian of the age who died in 1253, and Grosseteste's friend Adam Marsh, professor of the Oxford Franciscans. Montfort had seen the tract in which Grosseteste (drawing on Aristotle's Nicomachean Ethics) had elaborated the distinction between just rule and tyranny: 'a tyrant devotes himself to his own interests; a king to those of his subjects'. And could anyone say Henry had done that? Grosseteste also ordered the malpractices of his estate officials to be investigated and redressed, just as Montfort in his will of February 1259 sought to compensate the 'poor people and cultivators of his land' whom he had harmed. But for all his concern for others, Montfort also thought the baronial enterprise should do justice to himself; it was easy therefore, especially for those on the inside, to think that he was driven on by private grievances and ambitions. Montfort certainly hoped that the 1258 regime would secure for Eleanor, his wife, the portion of the dower she had never received as the widow of William Marshal II. By 1259 the arrears, so the Montforts claimed, amounted to some £24,000! He also thought she should have a landed endowment fit for a king's sister, not just a money pension – all the more vital since Montfort's Leicester lands, all he held in hereditary right, were only worth £500 a year. He was thus left as one of the poorest earls with little to endow five sons (and also with far less to lose from local reforms than Clare). In 1259 the council indeed granted the Montforts at least temporary custody of royal manors worth £400 a year, thus in effect succumbing to blackmail, because Eleanor refused otherwise to make the renunciations required of her by the Treaty of Paris. And there was one other factor driving the steely Montfort on, namely his contempt for the waxen king. Henry had been too craven to settle the question of the dower (for it had to be prised from the Marshal heirs), too indulgent to others to afford Eleanor a proper settlement, and too fearful of the protests to back Montfort to the hilt in Gascony. 'You should be taken and locked up like Charles the Simple,' Montfort had burst out prophetically in 1242, comparing Henry to the ill-starred Carolingian king.

Not surprisingly, Montfort was at the centre of the crisis in 1260 which revealed the first serious cracks in the baronial regime. Henry, still in France after the ratification of the Treaty of Paris, and achieving a measure of independence, forbade the February parliament to meet in his absence. Montfort, in England, insisted it should go ahead, being one of the thrice-yearly meetings stipulated in the Provisions. He also threatened a hot reception to the king if he returned with foreign mercenaries, and warned the justiciar, Hugh Bigod, not to send him any money. What made this even more serious was that Richard de Clare stood by the king, while the Lord Edward, seeking to gain his own independence, was in alliance with Montfort. In the end violence was just avoided. Montfort and Clare patched up their differences and the council remained in control. At the October 1260 parliament Bigod (a broken reed in Montfort's eyes) was replaced as justiciar by Montfort's own man, Hugh Despencer, Clare's price being an ordinance which gave the magnates power to hear complaints against their bailiffs, the implication being that special eyres would no longer do so. Inevitably these events weakened the council and early in 1261 its authority collapsed. Henry recovered control over the chancery, once more issuing his own writs and charters. He then moved to the Tower of London, and launched a bid formally to destroy the Provisions of Oxford. He was aided by Richard of Cornwall, temporarily back in England, and by the queen, alarmed when Peter of Savoy left the council in 1260, and now reconciled to a recalled William de Valence (Aymer had died in exile). Henry also had money from Louis IX under the terms of the

Treaty of Paris, which he used to retain household knights and hire mercenaries. In June he published a papal bull, which he had contrived to obtain from Alexander IV, quashing the Provisions, and then dismissed the justiciar, Hugh Despencer, and the reform regime's sheriffs.

These moves provoked stiff resistance in the localities where rival sheriffs were set up in many shires. In Gloucestershire the local knight, William de Tracy, challenged the king's appointee Matthias Bezill, calling him a Frenchman set up in contravention of the Provisions. With Montfort and Clare standing together, resistance was partly orchestrated by the baronial leaders – Tracy indeed was in Gloucester's retinue. The king cleverly proclaimed that the reforms as a whole had simply been devices to increase baronial power, the 1258–60 sheriffs being their creatures. Nevertheless the strength of the resistance also reflected genuine support for the reforms among knights and those below them in local society. In the end it was the leadership which fell apart. Henry won over Richard de Clare, and by the end of 1261 Montfort was alone in refusing to accept the overthrow of the Provisions. Instead he withdrew to France, declaring that he would rather die landless than depart from the truth and be perjured.

Henry's recovery of power proved short-lived. His prestige was damaged by the failure to defeat Llywelyn in Wales. His support was reduced through antagonizing Gilbert de Clare, heir to the earldom of Gloucester, by preventing him succeeding while still under age on his father Richard's death in 1262. Even more important was the conduct of the Lord Edward. Aged nineteen in 1258, since the revolution he had aimed essentially to free himself from the restrictions imposed by the baronial regime. Now in 1262 he broke with own entourage, notably Roger of Leybourne and Roger of Clifford, accusing them of peculation. He was urged on by the queen. She had condoned the revolution of 1258 because it rid Edward of the Lusignans; now she turned on another group of undesirables, thereby inadvertently causing another revolution. In this crisis, Edward's disgraced friends, who included John de Warenne, earl of Surrey, and several marcher lords, held together. Needing an upheaval to restore their fortunes, they turned to Montfort to provide it, a man with a cause and the cutting edge to sustain it. Only Montfort had remained true to the Provisions. He alone had consistently urged that they should be defended by force. When he returned to England in April 1263 it was above all the return of a general. Montfort was joined by the ex-Edwardians, Gilbert de Clare, and his own affinity. The latter, including Peter de Montfort (no relation) and Hugh Despencer, was largely composed of knights and magnates from the midlands where the great Montfortian base was at Kenilworth castle. Also rallying to Montfort were several young magnates ('boys', as the chronicler Thomas Wykes contemptuously called them), like John fitz John (son of John fitz Geoffrey) and Henry de Hastings. As a whole, the party was a rag-bag, but Montfort's leadership was dynamic. Justified by the oath of 1258, he ravaged the estates of the royalists, secured the Channel ports, and then forced the surrender of the king, who was quailing in the Tower of London. The queen, made of sterner stuff, had tried to escape up the Thames but had been driven back by missiles pelted down on her from London Bridge. On 16 July 1263 the Provisions of Oxford were reimposed, which meant essentially that Henry was once more subjected to a council, which Montfort, of course, led.

Meanwhile, with consummate skill Montfort, short of major supporters, had transformed the nature of the reform movement. A foreigner himself, he had, as the Melrose chronicler put it, become 'the shield and defender of the English' against the terrible threat posed by foreigners. This period between 1263 and 1265 saw the apotheosis of all the xenophobia that had been gathering force during Henry's reign. Under Montfort's leadership such feelings gave 'the English' a new sense of cohesion and identity. For the baronial leaders the revolution of 1258 had been aimed at only one group of foreigners, the Lusignans. The queen's uncles, Peter and Boniface of Savoy, had actually been on the council of fifteen. But outside the court there was already, as we have seen (above, pp. 353–4), hostility to foreigners in general. After 1258 such sentiments had intensified. The queen was blamed for overthrowing the Provisions in 1261 and then for purging Edward's entourage in 1262. In 1263, for his abortive campaign in Wales, Edward had returned to England with large numbers of foreign knights. Might they not be used to oppress the king's native subjects? As early as 1260 Montfort had declared that Henry seemed to place his trust more in foreigners 'than in men of his own land'. Now, in 1263, he channelled the xenophobic tide to sweep him into power, beginning the war by arresting the Savoyard bishop of Hereford, Peter d'Aigueblanche, and then sanctioning attacks on the properties of the queen, on Italian clerks provided to English livings and on foreign money-lenders. When the king submitted on 16 July he was made to issue an extraordinary new 'statute', one which marked the high-water mark of antipathy to foreigners in medieval England. The statute confined office in England to native-born men, and, with certain qualifications, expelled foreigners altogether from the country 'never to return'.

Such a programme had wide appeal. It enabled Edward's ousted followers to punish the queen, and Gilbert de Clare to rid himself of rivals at court. It also enabled those in the localities from knights down to peasants to punish the Savoyards and Lusignans for their oppression and get the better of foreigners like Matthias Bezill. In 1261 he had dragged William de Tracy through the mud. Now it was his turn to be humiliated. Although the numbers who had actually suffered from the tyranny of the aliens and their agents was very small, stories of their activities were on every lip. The St Albans abbey chronicler caught the flavour of popular xenophobia in 1263 when he observed that 'whoever did not know the English tongue was despised by the masses and held in contempt'. Meanwhile churchmen resented the foreigners presented by the pope to English benefices and also entered fully into the more general xenophobia. *The Song of Lewes*, written in the aftermath of Montfort's great victory in 1264 by a learned friar in the entourage of the bishop of Chichester, opined that during Henry's personal rule 'certain men had aimed to blot out the name of the English'. Montfort stuck through thick and thin to the ban on aliens holding office. More than anything else the issue unified his movement and gave it meaning, so much so that chroniclers came to see the oppression by foreigners as the sole cause of the revolution of 1258. A common resistance to this purported threat sent for the first time since 1066 a sense of a shared membership of an English race resonating through all classes of society.

Montfort, however, still failed to hold on to power. The revolution of 1263, brought about by a noble faction, was quite different from that of 1258, which commanded wide noble support. Hugh Bigod, symbol as justiciar of the 1258 reforms, now sided with the king. So did his brother the earl of Norfolk, who had led the armed march that had begun the 1258 upheaval. Such men regarded Montfort as violent, power-hungry and extreme. To accept his leadership was anathema. Soon Montfort's own party began to break up. In August 1263 Edward, now full square behind his father, bribed back his former followers – probably what they had wanted all along. In October Henry himself shook himself free from Montfort's control and the realm divided into armed camps. All that could be agreed was to refer the quarrel to the arbitration of Louis IX. Hitherto Louis had been cautious about expressing his views, but the truth was, as he said later, he would rather break clods behind the plough than live under the Provisions. His verdict, the Mise of Amiens (January 1264) condemned them *in toto* and restored Henry to all his powers. This judgement Montfort and his followers refused to accept and the result was civil war.

Even with the adherence of Gilbert de Clare, Montfort had far less noble support than the king. His power centred on London and on his bases in the midlands, radiating out from Northampton, Leicester and Kenilworth. Henry and Edward placed themselves aggressively in between at Oxford and on 5 April by a surprise attack seized Northampton, taking many prisoners. Montfort's response to this disaster showed the measure of the man, for he now drove on the war with daring and judgement. First he mounted a brief siege of Rochester castle, bringing the king's army south as he had intended. Then on 6 May he marched out of London, determined to meet his enemies and fight 'with all for all'. On 14 May 1264, having led his army up onto the Sussex Downs during the night, he charged down the hill above Lewes and won a crushing victory, making Henry, Edward and Richard of Cornwall prisoners. The next month, in the spirit of the Provisions, a council of nine was imposed on the king, chosen by and responsible to three electors: Montfort himself, Gilbert de Clare and the bishop of Chichester. Although the three were to be responsible to the prelates and barons in parliament, in practice Montfort was dominant. He was the first noble in English history to seize power and rule the country in the king's name.

Montfort had now to stabilize his government, and it was not easy. Queen Eleanor, who had remained overseas after the Mise of Amiens, gathered an army in Flanders with Louis IX's support and threatened invasion. The papal legate, Guy de Foulquois, excommunicated Montfort and his supporters, although he was kept out of England. Meanwhile the great marcher baron, Roger de Mortimer, unwisely released by Montfort after Lewes despite a bitter private feud, refused to accept the regime's authority. Gilbert de Clare, now earl of Gloucester, was Montfort's only supporter from among the earls. The young earl of Derby, Robert de Ferrers, played a lone hand, obsessed by his claims for possession of the Peak, part of the Peverel inheritance which the Ferrers had long coveted.

Montfort's reaction was to base his regime on sections of society outside the great barons and he had good grounds for doing so. Even the unfriendly London alderman Arnold fitz Thedmar acknowledged in his chronicle that Louis IX's verdict had been rejected by 'the community of the middle people of the kingdom of England'. To the parliament of June 1264, which approved the new constitution, Montfort summoned four knights from each county, chosen by the county court to 'discuss the business of the realm'. To his parliament of 1265 he summoned burgesses from the towns as well, the first occasion they had been summoned. Here truly was the House of Commons in embryo. All this marked an important shift since 1258. Knights had certainly been present and influential at the parliaments of 1258–9, as the protest of the community of the bachelry showed. But the Provisions of Oxford had not called for any formal representation of the shires and boroughs, despite the precedent of 1254. Now Montfort took that momentous step.

Of all the cities, by far the most important for Montfort was London, which gave him massive support, providing a whole division at Lewes, just as it had supported the rebels in 1215. To be sure, the ruling elite of aldermen were tied to the court through supplying it with wine, cloth and precious metals. Yet some also resented Henry's attempt to tax the city at will and establish a fair for Westminster Abbey. In 1258, before the political revolution, Henry had purged his enemies on the city council and his supporters remained in power thereafter; London, therefore, was a safe base for the king's recovery of power in 1261. It was a political and social revolution in 1263 which changed the situation. This ousted the aldermanic regime and handed power to the folkmoot, the general assembly of the citizens, which elected a Montfortian mayor, Thomas fitz Thomas, a member of the old elite but with connections to those purged in 1258. Fitz Thomas permitted crafts, previously held down by the aldermen, to organize for the first time, and told the king to his face that the city's loyalty depended on his good behaviour.

Montfort also, as his summons to parliament shows, coveted the support of the knights, both for fighting and also for control over local government. (By this time there might be fifty or so knights active in a medium-sized county like Oxfordshire.) Montfort was not altogether successful. A large majority of the knights employed to investigate grievances in 1258 and as sheriffs in 1258–9 played no discernible part in subsequent events, doubtless keeping their heads down. On the other hand, of a sample of 123 knights drawn from Northamptonshire, Warwickshire, Cambridgeshire and Staffordshire, sixty-eight (or 55 per cent) opposed the king in some way or other, or at least were accused of so doing, between 1263 and 1265, this against only sixteen (though the evidence here is much less full) who were active royalists. The midlands were Montfort's heartland so the proportions were probably smaller elsewhere, but the figures are still impressive. Some knights had direct personal grievances against the king or members of his regime, like Gilbert of Elsfield (in Oxfordshire) who complained of disseisin by William de Valence. Many seem to have been situated in regional pockets surrounded by other contrariants, a pattern also seen in 1215 – Gilbert himself died at Evesham alongside his neighbour, Robert fitz Nigel of Iffley. Clearly neighbourhood was very important in determining political allegiances. So, within that context, was the power of lordship, with tenure, reward and coercion all coming into play. Given the paucity of earls in his party, Montfort relied increasingly on a group of minor barons. Some, like Ralph Basset of Drayton, he made keepers of the peace to act alongside the sheriffs after Lewes. Others, like Ralph de Camoys, he placed on the council of nine, a very different body from the earl-dominated council of fifteen in 1258. It was men of this stamp, in particular, whom Montfort helped by alleviating the debts they owed the Jews. They were also helped by a brutal attack on the London Jewry led by John fitz John. In some areas the political allegiances of such magnates depended more on the course of their local disputes than on the merits of the national cause. Thus in the west midlands Ralph Basset of Drayton, mixing litigation with violence, was struggling for regional dominance against the local royalists, Roger de Somery of Dudley and Philip Marmion of Tamworth. In that respect the conflict in the 1260s resembled those during the civil wars of Stephen and of John.

It was not merely knights and magnates who were politically active in this period. Many ordinary freemen and peasants took part in local raids, fought in the armies, and slaughtered the royalists fleeing from the battle of Lewes. When Montfort rallied the nation to resist the queen's threatened invasion in the summer of 1264 – invasion by 'a great multitude of aliens' – he summoned four to eight men from each village to Barham Down in Kent. The response was overwhelming and the atmosphere on the Downs perhaps rather like that in England in 1940. Equally impressive was the support of churchmen, despite the hostility of the pope. No less than five bishops were later suspended from office for supporting Montfort, including Walter de Cantilupe of Worcester, one of his oldest friends. Such prelates were inspired by Montfort's ascetic brand of personal piety and the connections they had all shared with the saintly Grosseteste. All would probably have shared the passionate commitment to reform which runs through the 968 mesmeric, throbbing lines of *The Song of Lewes*. The *Song* stands as an eternal warning against an explanation of Montfortian support simply in terms of local conflicts, personal grievances and the power of lordship. The churchmen who are known to have preached to the populace about the great earl must have spoken, like the *Song*, of how he stood for the community of the realm and was saving England for the English. In 1265 the peasants of Peatling Magna in Leicestershire attacked a royalist captain on the grounds that he was 'going against the community of the realm and the barons'. Even villagers, therefore, understood the concept, and believed they were members of the community of the realm.

For all his support, Montfort failed once again to stabilize his regime. He had to keep both the king and the Lord Edward as virtual prisoners. His decision to extract Cheshire from the latter in March 1265, to be held henceforth by the Montforts in hereditary right, shows that he thought reconciliation impossible. Faced with a choice between King Henry and King Simon, which was what *de facto* it boiled down to, most magnates preferred the former. Montfort's overweening power (a condition of survival, he would have said) led to the disastrous defection of Gilbert de Clare. In May 1265 Edward himself escaped, reaching Wigmore where he was welcomed by Matilda de Mortimer, Roger's wife, who was in command of the castle. Edward quickly struck an agreement with both Mortimer and Clare. Their army trapped Montfort's much smaller force at Evesham on the morning of 4 August 1265. Montfort, spurning suggestions that he should take refuge in the abbey ('churches are for chaplains; the field is for knights'), marched out of the town and up Green Hill where he was surrounded, killed and horribly mutilated, his head being sent to Lady Mortimer. Montfort's son Henry, Peter de Montfort, Hugh Despencer and over thirty other knights suffered with him.

'The murder of Evesham for battle was it none,' wrote the chronicler Robert of Gloucester. The slaughter was indeed unprecedented and reflected the fear and hatred Montfort had inspired. That bitterness also prevented any easy post-war settlement. London was punished by a fine of £13,333. The return of rebel lands which had closed the 1217 war was not repeated. Instead, the estates of the Montfortians were first pillaged by the victors 'in an irresistible wave spreading outwards from the battlefield' (Clive Knowles), and then, having been officially confiscated, were distributed by the king among his supporters in woefully haphazard fashion. Not surprisingly this led to a renewal of the war. One group of disinherited was defeated in a skirmish at Chesterfield in May 1266. Another, under the leadership of Henry de Hastings, set up their standard at Kenilworth castle, which the king in June 1266 began to besiege. Meanwhile wiser counsels prevailed, thanks in good part to the labours of the remarkable papal legate Ottobuono (later Pope Adrian V) who had now arrived in England. In October 1266 the Dictum of Kenilworth was issued, which allowed former rebels to redeem their lands at up to seven times their annual value, depending on the gravity of their offences. These were still harsh terms, however, and the Kenilworth siege continued till the garrison's provisions were exhausted in December, its length a remarkable tribute to Simon de Montfort's skill in developing the castle's water defences. Another group of rebels continued to hold out in the Isle of Ely, ravaging the surrounding area. In June 1267 Gilbert de Clare, with scant personal reward from rebel lands despite having led the initial pillage through his network of officials, intervened. He occupied London and forced an improvement in the Dictum's terms. Next month Edward extinguished the last resistance in the Isle of Ely and the war was over.

However, this was hardly peace. The earl of Derby, captured at Chesterfield, was saddled with a deliberately unpayable redemption fine of £50,000 and had to surrender his lands to Edmund, Henry's younger son, marking the end of the Ferrers earldom. Edward himself quarrelled acrimoniously with Gilbert de Clare. The king, pitifully short of money, formed patronage queues reminiscent of those of the 1250s, put stops on payments out of the exchequer, and then nullified the effect by coming up with all kinds of exceptions. Meanwhile the site of Montfort's death and his 'shrine' in Evesham abbey became places of miracle and pilgrimage. Yet there were more positive signs. The government soon after Evesham had looked after the wives and widows of the Montfortians, allowing them their inheritances and a proportion of their husband's lands (usually between a quarter and a third). Such provision was helped by family connections across the rebellion. For example the two daughters of one of the most respected loyalists, Philip Basset, were married to Hugh Despencer and John fitz John. Moreover, although the financial cost was high, the great majority of the Montfortians – magnates, knights and lesser men – did recover their lands, usually as soon as the redemption agreement was made. To some extent their cause was won. The king could not live with the central controls of 1258, but he could certainly accept the Provisions of Westminster, the legislation of October 1259, which aimed at controlling the abuses of sheriffs and justices, and limiting attendance at private courts. In January 1263, struggling for support, Henry had indeed reissued them. In November 1267 he did so again, definitively, in the Statute of Marlborough. Another lesson was learnt. Between 1268 and 1270 Henry sought taxation to support Edward's projected crusade. He negotiated with parliament after parliament, summoning to them knights and on at least one occasion burgesses as well. In the end he secured a tax, after imposing restrictions on the Jews and confirming Magna Carta. Legislation which conciliated the counties, the summoning of representatives to parliament and the granting of taxation: that was the way in which the monarchy could begin to close the gulf which had opened between it and the nation.

On 13 October 1269 Henry translated the body of Edward the Confessor to its shrine within the new church at Westminster. He had spent well over £40,000 on the works, a sum which could have built three or four of the castles with which his son later conquered Wales. But it was worth it. The new church was considered the finest in Christendom. The God-given nature of Henry's rule, which he had done so much to stress, had not saved him from revolution, but it may well have saved his throne. There was no attempt to depose Henry as there had been King John. Henry died in November 1272. Edward was still away on his crusade. Not the least of his problems was the transformation in the political shape of Britain produced by the collapse of English royal power.

*　　*　　*

In 1247 Llywelyn ap Gruffudd shared the rump of Gwynedd with his brother Owain. Twenty years later he was prince of Wales.

Welsh poets and chroniclers portrayed the movement Llywelyn led as one of national liberation against 'the grievous bondage of the

English', and with considerable truth. In the south, the rulers of Ystrad Tywi had long resented the jurisdictional claims of the king's bailiff at Carmarthen. In the north, the English administration of the Four Cantrefs was becoming increasingly harsh, especially after their conferral in 1254 on the Lord Edward, along with Chester and the other royal lands in Wales. The English chroniclers themselves wrote in terms of a tyrannical attack on Welsh law and custom. The boast in 1252 of Alan la Zouche, justiciar at Chester, that 'all Wales lies obediently and peacefully subject to English laws' reveals official attitudes all too clearly. Having stoked the fires, the English government was soon powerless to put them out. The long period of revolution, reform and civil war between 1258 and 1267 destroyed royal authority and absorbed baronial energy. It was not the king who brought down Llywelyn, but Llywelyn who twice brought down (or helped bring down) the king by his successes in 1257 and 1262–3.

There were Welsh rulers, however, who would have grimaced at Llywelyn's stance as a national hero, not least in Gwynedd itself where he had come to the top by eliminating his brothers. The decisive moment had been the great victory at Bryn Derwin in 1255, a battle fought 'for a kingdom' and won by a 'lion of the warband', as a court poet put it. The captured Owain was held prisoner for over twenty years, along with another brother Rhodri. Only Dafydd, Llywelyn's youngest brother, remained free, his disruptive career amply justifying the imprisonment of the others. On the back of this success, Llywelyn went on (in 1256) to wrest the Four Cantrefs from the Lord Edward (save the new castles at Deganwy and Diserth) and Meirionydd from his own kinsman, Llywelyn ap Maredudd. He was now master of all Gwynedd. He at once demonstrated his authority in the south by invading Ceredigion and seizing Edward's lands around Aberystwyth. This time, however (as the *Brut* noted), 'he took nothing for himself save the glory', preferring to reward his allies in Deheubarth. Next year (1257) he led a great plundering expedition which threatened the marcher lordships of Glamorgan, Gower and Pembroke.

The English establishment had every reason to respond to these events, yet it received scant leadership from the king, whose eyes were firmly set on Sicily. Henry talked big. He would seize Anglesey with a fleet from Ireland and keep it for the crown. But no fleet arrived. Henry reached Deganwy in August 1257, re-provisioned the castle, and then hurried back to Westminster in time for the feast of Edward the

Confessor. Llywelyn was free to expel the king's ally Gruffudd ap Gwenwynwyn from southern Powys.

After these triumphs, Llywelyn in 1258 assumed the title prince of Wales, which had been defiantly adopted by Dafydd towards the end of his career. Of course 'prince' implied a 'principality', and Llywelyn was clear about the kind he envisaged. As he later told the pope, 'the principality of Wales is such that all the Welsh barons of Wales hold their lands in chief from us and our heirs and do homage and fealty to us and our successors ... for which we and our successors are bound to do homage and fealty to the king and his successors'. This of course had been the vision of Llywelyn the Great, and in realizing it Llywelyn ap Gruffudd faced the same obstacles as his grandfather, obstacles which had persuaded the latter not to assume the title. One problem was the opposition of the English crown, which claimed the homages of the Welsh rulers for itself. Another was that the rulers themselves were hardly crying out for Gwynedd's overlordship. The unpleasant penalties for a breach of homage and fealty owed the prince were made plain in 1259 when Maredudd ap Rhys of Ystrad Tywi, an early Llywelyn ally, was imprisoned and deprived of his lands. If Welsh political unity was necessary to stand against English officialdom, such men might think it could be achieved as in the past through confederation, not Gwynedd's supremacy. Llywelyn's task was also impeded by the factional strife which divided the ruling families. A condition of Maredudd ap Rhys's return to Llywelyn's 'unity' in 1261 was that he should not have to ally with either his nephew and rival, Rhys Fychan, or Maredudd ab Owain of Ceredigion. Such conflicts overrode any 'patriotic' considerations. If one side was with Llywelyn, the other was as likely to be with the king. A major reason why Llywelyn needed recognition from the king was to deprive the native rulers of their English escape route.

In these treacherous waters, Llywelyn navigated at first as though piloted by his cautious grandfather. He was not merely a mighty warrior, as the bards at his court frequently proclaimed; he was also, at least early in his career, a sinuous politician. He adopted the title 'prince of Wales' in 1258, almost at once to abandon it. With the Welsh rulers, he continued at times to talk of mutual pacts and alliances. With the English government, under cover of a series of truces, he opened negotiations for a settlement. But the political revolution which had removed the crown as a threat had also deprived it of the ability to make decisions. So in 1260, as England hovered on the verge of hostilities, Llywelyn turned once again to war, depriving Edward of Builth, Dafydd's old strategic base in the upper valley of the Wye. At the same time, building on moves in 1256, Llywelyn established control over much of the area between Wye and Severn, while his chief rival, Roger de Mortimer, was distracted by his suit for the Gloucestershire manor of Lechlade and (from the end of 1263) by a personal feud with Simon de Montfort. From Builth, Llywelyn could move south and in 1262 he received homages from parts of Brecon, thus bringing his power to the northern fringes of Glamorgan. In all this he was aided again by the English conflict, for Humphrey de Bohun, eldest son of the earl of Hereford, the lord of Brecon, was fatally wounded at Evesham, after which there was a minority till 1271. As for Glamorgan, after the death of Richard de Clare in 1262, so long its astringent ruler, his son Gilbert first endured a period of wardship and then plunged into the English civil war. To the west, Pembroke was in the hands of Henry III's half-brother, William de Valence, who was expelled temporarily from England in 1258 and did not visit the lordship till 1265.

From the late summer of 1262, Llywelyn began once again to call himself prince of Wales, and this time he continued to do so. It was no empty title. In March 1263, from north, south and west Wales he mustered an army (so the English estimated) of some 10,000 foot. Edward's response in 1263 was a damp squib of a campaign, despite having tempted Dafydd into his camp. That August and September, while Edward and his father struggled to free themselves from Montfortian shackles, Llywelyn finally forced the surrender of Deganwy and Diserth, long lone outposts in the Four Cantrefs. At the end of the year Gruffudd ap Gwenwynwyn reluctantly did him homage. What Llywelyn still desperately needed, however, was recognition from the English government, just as Simon de Montfort desperately needed all the support he could get. Out of that mutual need emerged a treaty in June 1265. The puppet King Henry recognized Llywelyn's principality and his 'dominion' over all the native magnates of Wales. In return Montfort gained a large contingent of Welsh foot soldiers. They let out a blood-curdling shout before the battle of Evesham six weeks later, but for all their readiness for the fight they were unable to save Montfort from death at the hands of Roger de Mortimer.

Evesham destroyed Montfort, but did nothing to weaken Llywelyn. It was not till July 1267 that even a semblance of peace returned to

England. Edward wished now to fight, not in Wales but on crusade. The government was desperately short of money. So Llywelyn made an offer it could not refuse and in September 1267 the Treaty of Montgomery was concluded. Llywelyn was to pay £16,666 (25,000 marks), £3,333 at Christmas 1267, the rest at a rate of £2,000 a year. In return, Henry accepted the bulk of Llywelyn's conquests. He was to retain the Four Cantrefs, Cedewain and Ceri between Wye and Severn, together with Builth and his gains in Brecon. Even more significantly, he was given 'the principality of Wales' and was henceforth to be called 'prince of Wales' and have the homage of 'all the Welsh barons of Wales'. Only he as prince was to do homage to the king. All of this was conceded to Llywelyn and his heirs in perpetuity. He had established his principality. Would he sustain it?

*   *   *

When English royal power collapsed in the 1215–17 civil war, King Alexander II had allied with the baronial rebels and invaded England to reassert his claims to the northern counties. The conduct of his son, Alexander III, was very different. He sent a large Scottish force which fought for King Henry at the battle of Lewes and was about to dispatch another when news arrived of the battle of Evesham. His policy was therefore the exact opposite of Llywelyn's, who allied with the Montfortians. Indeed had Evesham been fought a few weeks later, it might have seen a confrontation between the Welsh and the Scots. Alexander's behaviour was a measure of the long period of peace between the two kingdoms and the family ties which now bound the English and Scottish courts together, cemented by his own marriage to Henry III's daughter. Alexander thus remained true to the reorientation of Scottish policy achieved by his father. During the period of English weakness, instead of moving south he moved west and secured control over the Isle of Man and the Western Isles, thereby achieving a major expansion of his kingdom. This is not to say Alexander did not profit from the English vacuum. A powerful English state might possibly have obstructed his conquest of Man whose kings, although they owed allegiance to Norway, had also sometimes been knighted at the English court.

If the fifteenth-century chronicler Walter Bower was basing himself on a reliable earlier source, then Alexander was tall and well-built, and very much a 'hands-on' ruler. With a picked retinue, and accompanied by the justiciar to dispense justice, he travelled the kingdom almost every year and was welcomed into each sheriffdom by a body of local knights who acted as escorts – quite the reverse of King Henry's sedentary rule. Alexander, at times masterful and at others conciliatory, quickly liquidated the factional struggles of his minority and never allowed them to revive. Those struggles had originated in the last years of his father with the conflict between the Comyns and Alan Durward. The compromise of 1259 had brought Durward back onto the council, but left the government very much in Comyn hands. The family remained prominent thereafter in the sheriffdoms and ecclesiastical office. At the centre Alexander Comyn, earl of Buchan, was justiciar of Scotland north of Forth for the whole period from 1258 until his death in 1289, and was more frequently at court than any other magnate. The tearaway of 1242, however, was now the sagacious councillor, with his daughters married to the earls of Dunbar, Strathearn and Angus and his son to the countess of Fife. That the Comyns formed no monolithic faction of which the king was the prisoner was shown by the events of 1261. On the death of Walter Comyn, earl of Menteith, three years before, the earldom had passed to his widow (in whose right he had held it) and her new husband John Russell, an English knight. This infuriated Walter's nephew, John Comyn of Badenoch, who seized the Russells and forced them to make the earldom over to himself, an act which recalled the Comyn violence back in 1242. But John was soon put in his place. The magnates decided against his claims and conferred the earldom on Walter, younger brother of Alexander Stewart.

Politically, Alexander was therefore well placed to renew his father's attempt to replace Norwegian lordship over Man and the Isles with his own. In 1261–2 he combined offers to buy out King Hakon with a violent assault on Skye, led by the earl of Ross. According to King Hakon's Saga, churches were burnt and men, women and children slaughtered. 'The Scottish king,' the Saga affirmed, 'intended to lay under his authority all the Hebrides.' King Hakon, aged though he was, was determined not to let him. He built a new ship entirely of oak with a long prow surmounted by a gilded dragon's head, and in July 1263 set sail from Bergen. His fleet, when joined with Hebridean forces, numbered between 100 and 200 vessels. If this was the Norwegian sunset, its rays were to be red and bloody.

Hakon made his first base in Orkney; its earl, Magnus Gilbertson, who was also earl of Caithness, had joined him in Bergen. King Magnus

Olafson, ruler of Man and Skye, and most of the MacSorleys (some of them threatened by the Stewart advance into Arran and Knapdale) likewise rallied to his cause. From Orkney, Hakon proceeded westwards through the Western Isles into the Firth of Clyde. He then sent the king of Man and the MacSorleys inland to ravage Walter Stewart's earldom of Menteith. King Alexander kept his nerve. His tactics were to hold his fortresses, defend the coastline and wait for Hakon to go away. Then he could assert his own dominance over the native rulers. In the north Alexander, earl of Buchan, and Alan Durward (a striking co-operation between two old rivals) were placed in command and they extracted hostages from Caithness and Skye. In the west Walter Stewart, earl of Menteith, commanded the king's main base at Ayr where ships were built and the castle held by 120 sergeants. On 4 October on the shore at Largs, under the looming Cunningham hills, there was a great fight between the two sides with the Scots, according to Hakon's Saga, commanding 500 horse. Certainly the accounts of Alexander's chamberlain in 1264 show £710 being spent on horses and saddles.

The campaign of 1263 had, in fact, ended in a draw. King Hakon had demonstrated Norwegian power in the west on a scale (as his Saga commented) unseen since Magnus Barelegs' expedition in 1098. Yet he had not dented Alexander's pretensions to the area and therefore he planned to winter in Orkney and renew the war in 1264. It was not to be. On 16 December the aged hero, consoled by readings from the Sagas of his predecessors (he had first listened to Latin books, doubtless of a devotional nature, but had not understood them), died in the bishop's palace on Orkney. Alexander at once saw his chance. He assembled a fleet and prepared to invade Skye, a move which brought Magnus of Man's submission and proffer of hostages. After that Alexander Buchan, Durward and the earl of Mar (who had 200 sergeants under his command) invaded the Western Isles where (according to Fordun) 'they slew the traitors who the year before had encouraged the king of Norway', and returned with much plunder.

Alexander now renewed his offers to buy out the Norwegians, and found Hakon's pacific son, King Magnus, ready to accept them. The result in 1266 was the Treaty of Perth, the first of the great thirteenth-century documents of conquest. Magnus retained Orkney and Shetland, but resigned Man and the other western islands to Alexander and his heirs. All the 'vassals' of the islands were to be 'subject to the laws and customs of the kingdom of Scotland'. However, the islanders were to be pardoned for injuries done in support of the king of Norway and could leave if they wished. In return for all this, Alexander paid £2,666 and promised Norway an annual fee of £66. For some of the native chiefs the Scottish conquest was a disaster, their fate foreshadowing that of the native rulers swept aside by the Edwardian conquest of Wales twenty years later. Dugald, lord of Garmoran refused to submit to Alexander; his son Eric threw in his lot entirely with the king of Norway. Murchaid of Knapdale (whose son was a hostage in 1264) fled to Ireland, where he was captured and imprisoned. Nothing more is heard of Rhodri, the MacSorley to whom Hakon had given Bute.

In Man, it was not just the ruling family who suffered. King Magnus had died in 1266 before the conclusion of the Treaty of Perth. The claims of Godfrey, his illegitimate son, to succeed were ignored and the island was governed by royal bailiffs. They may well (as permitted by the Treaty) have set about subjecting the islanders to the laws and customs of the Scottish kingdom, much as Alan la Zouche had subjected the Welsh of the Four Cantrefs to English law in the 1250s. The result was that when in 1275 Godfrey, son of Magnus, returned to Man he was accepted as king 'universally and unanimously'. Alexander gathered a large fleet and army from Galloway and the Isles and placed the Anglo-Scottish baron John de Vesci in command. A battle was fought in which (according to the local chronicle) 537 Manxmen perished. Godfrey and his wife escaped to Wales but it was the end of his ancient dynasty. The monastery of Rushen was sacked, the monks dispersed and the land was ravaged. Thus had King Alexander brought the west within his kingdom.

As so often, there was another side to the conquest, one of more peaceful integration. The Treaty of Perth was different from the 1284 Statute of Wales. The one was negotiated between equals; the other imposed after the defeat of a general rebellion. The Perth Treaty protected Norwegian supporters in the Isles from disinheritance, provided they were now faithful to the king of Scotland; the Statute of Wales followed an almost general forfeiture. Likewise, although the Treaty spoke of Scottish laws and customs, outside Man they were only gradually established: it was not until 1293 that Argyll and the Isles were finally divided into three sheriffdoms. One of the sheriffs, that of Lorn, was none other than Alexander, son of Ewen of Lorn, the MacSorley who in the 1240s had boasted the title 'king of the Isles'. From king to royal official: this might seem to sum up the decline of the MacSorleys. Nevertheless the western sheriffs were men of high status within the Scottish realm: Alexander's colleagues were the earl of Ross and the head of the Stewarts. Alexander of Lorn also retained wide independence within his own lordships. He was not alone in coming to terms with the Scottish crown. Another MacSorley, Alan of Garmoran, as well as Alexander, were involved in the final conquest of Man in 1275. The arrangements in 1284 for succession to the throne were witnessed by three MacSorleys (including Alexander), and the earl of Orkney, all described as 'barons of the realm of Scotland'. In their use of Latin charters, adoption of knighthood, marriages and naming patterns (*Alexander* married a daughter of John Comyn), these nobles were all coming within the Scottish realm and the wider European polity of which it was part. The expansion of the kingdom was achieved both by violence and accommodation.

*   *   *

The politics of England also helped set back the English position in Ireland, facilitating a recovery of the native rulers, just as happened in Wales. To some extent this would have occurred anyway with the demise of both the Lacys and the Marshals in the 1240s, and the de Burgh minority between the death of Richard in 1243 and the succession of his son Walter in 1250. A generation of self-confident conquerors had come to an end. The English situation made it difficult for successors to become established. The obstruction of Edward as the new Lord of Ireland effectively nullified the grant of land worth £500 to Geoffrey de Lusignan (see above, p. 361). Then John fitz John's Montfortianism meant that he could do nothing to consolidate the grant in Thomond made to his father, John fitz Geoffrey. The movement led by Brian O'Neill, 'king of the kings of Ireland', was ended by his defeat and death in 1260, but in the following year the MacCarthys killed John fitz Thomas, to whom Edward had granted the lordship of Desmond. Then from 1265 Aedh O'Connor, from his base in Roscommon, began to disturb the position of Walter de Burgh in Connacht.

By this time Edward's difficulties in England had led to a major restructuring in Ireland, Walter de Burgh being the beneficiary and the crown the loser. In 1263 Edward conceded Ulster, in royal hands since Hugh de Lacy's death in 1242, to Walter, thus joining Connacht and Ulster under de Burgh lordship. Like King John's restoration of Meath to Walter de Lacy in 1215, this concession was entirely due to the political situation in England. It took place on 15 July 1263, the day before Henry III surrendered to Simon de Montfort and became once more a cipher. At this moment of supreme crisis, Edward was enlisting de Burgh and his Irish resources for the continuation of the fight in England. He was not entirely disappointed. The immediate effect of de Burgh's installation was a violent conflict with the fitz Geralds who feared for their own position in Ulster, but with peace restored (by Geoffrey de Joinville), the main Irish barons crossed over to help Edward around the time of the battle of Evesham. The crisis in England had, however, destroyed the prospect of Ulster becoming a new royal base in Ireland.

If Edward wished to reassert royal authority in Britain and Ireland, he would have first, like Henry II, to reassert it within England itself. If the limbs were weak, the fundamental trouble concerned the heart.

13

Structures of Society

The upheavals in England in the 1260s had brought all sections of society into play: barons, knights, townsfolk, freemen and peasants. Significant roles had been taken by noble women; even peasant women were well informed about events. The growing production and survival of record sources enables English society in the twelfth and thirteenth centuries to be studied in ever greater detail. The rest of Britain is less well served. This chapter concentrates on England in these centuries before considering salient features of society in Scotland and in Wales. The wider economic framework has already been discussed in chapter 2.

* * *

The political importance of the towns, seen in the summons of burgesses to parliament, reflected their increasing wealth and the control they had achieved over their own affairs, usually by charter of the king – hence 'chartered borough'. Henry II (1154–89) granted nearly fifty municipal charters, building on the example of Henry I. There was considerable overlap in the terms of the various concessions (sometimes explicitly so), their effect being to confirm or establish the distinctiveness and independence of the townsmen by, for example, conceding them freedom from tolls throughout the kingdom and allowing them exemption from attending courts other than the borough's. The most important privilege and also the hardest to get was that of accounting directly to the exchequer for the town's farm, the annual payment due to the king, for this was nearly always linked to the right to choose the official who would do the accounting. In effect this emancipated the town from the authority of the sheriff and secured self-government under the king. Eight towns had this right by 1199, twenty-four by 1216 and forty-eight by the 1300s. To take one example: in 1200 the burgesses of Northampton were allowed to choose 'by common counsel of their vill' two 'provosts' to answer for the farm and four other men to keep the pleas of the crown and check that the provosts treated both rich and poor justly. Elections by common counsel, one group of officials monitoring another, justice to rich and poor, all these were pervasive themes between 1258 and 1265, and all long familiar at Northampton. That burgesses positively wished to elect representatives to parliament is clear at St Albans, where 'the community of the town' insisted that the abbot should allow them to do just that.

'Treat justly poor as well as rich.' Within town society the variations in wealth increasingly generated tension. The privileges of self-government did not come cheap and townsmen had banded together to buy them. Such associations had various names, and the great law book *Glanvill* (c. 1189) treated the two most usual, 'commune' and 'gild merchant', as virtually interchangeable. Some of the town charters were actually granted to the 'gild merchant', or gave the townsmen the right to form one. It was only the members of these associations, however described, who enjoyed the privileges conferred in the charters, and were technically burgesses. Their position was exclusive. 'Nobody not a member of the gild shall carry out their trade in the town,' ran Henry II's charter to Oxford. There was no room here for labourers, artisans (including in some towns weavers), and women. Moreover, although all householders probably qualified as burgesses, when it came to government a series of complex checks and balances usually kept control in the hands of a wealthy elite, something that becomes very clear from a study of the rulers of York and Newcastle upon Tyne in the thirteenth century. Not surprisingly this could create conflict. At Oxford in the 1250s, the 'burgesses of the lesser commune', as they called themselves, drew up a series of complaints against the thirty-two 'burgess magnates' who effectively monopolized the mayoral office and the advisory council of fifteen 'jurats'.

The chronicler Wykes averred that in 1263 'conjurations of ribalds' rose up against the great men of nearly all the towns, although only for London is there hard evidence. There, citizens and their families made up perhaps a third of the population, the rest being artisans, servants, labourers and paupers. Within the citizen body there was again a dominant elite who controlled the government in its own interests. London had always had its own sheriffs who were responsible for financial payments to the king, and under Henry I the citizens secured the right to choose them. Later in 1215 they also gained the right to choose their mayor, a man 'suitable for rule of the city', an office which had first appeared in the 1190s. The popular view was that the mayor should be elected in the traditional gathering of all the citizens, the folkmoot, but this was vigorously contested by the aldermen, who claimed the right belonged to them 'since they are as though the heads and the people are the limbs'. It was the aldermen for the most part who got their way.

The city was divided up into twenty-four wards each with an alderman as its executive and legal officer (he gave judgement in the ward courts), an arrangement which probably went back to long before 1100. Since the aldermen were elected for life, and in practice by the leading citizens of each ward, they naturally formed an elite. It was essentially to them, 'the barons of London', that John had conceded the right to elect the mayor in 1215. Seventy per cent of the aldermen who held office before 1263 belonged to sixteen interrelated families, most of them established in London since the early twelfth century. This was not, however, a closed oligarchy for new families if they had sufficient wealth were able to join its ranks, often gaining integration through marriage. The grandfather of the alderman Arnold fitz Thedmar, who wrote a detailed history of the city during the reign of Henry III, had come from Cologne.

The wealth of London's elite, like that of York and Newcastle upon Tyne, came from property, from trade, and from luxury crafts, notably goldsmithing. Fitz Thedmar himself had a great hall, shops, houses, rents, and a wharf all within All Hallows Haywharf parish. In York early in the thirteenth century the mayor, Hugh of Selby, exported wool to Flanders, and imported wine from France, sending some of it to the king. In London exporting wool and importing wine were likewise fundamental activities, together with supplying wine and luxury goods, cloth, gold and jewels to the court. The mayor, John de Gisors, who married fitz Thedmar's sister, provided the king in the 1250s with wine worth some £250 a year. This connection with the court was strengthened by London citizens holding both the chamberlainship of London, which gave them responsibility for buying the king's wine, and the keepership of the London mint and exchange.

Fitz Thedmar's chronicle of the city breathes the whole spirit of London's rulers, jealous of their privileges and hostile to the lower orders. The aldermen used and protected their position by preventing other 'mysteries' from organizing, arguing that the latter were only seeking their own benefit to the disadvantage of everyone else, both customers and workforce. Fitz Thedmar portrayed the uprising of the 1260s as one of the 'people', and many non-citizens may well have flooded into the meetings of the folkmoot. But the leaders headed the 'mysteries' which had been held down by the aldermen, and now briefly got their trade ordinances ratified. Of these, far and away the most important were the fishmongers and the cordwainers. The former bought from the ships at the wharves (trade with the Baltic in particular was expanding), while the latter made high-quality goods from leather imported from Cordoba in Spain. A master cordwainer might well have eight men working for him in his shed. These and other 'mysteries' saw their new charters nullified in 1274, but they could not be held down indefinitely and by the end of the century fishmongers were becoming aldermen.

The rulers of London, York and Newcastle upon Tyne were typical among urban elites in acquiring property in the country as well as the town. It was often from the country that they or their forebears had come. Around 1300 the rulers of Newcastle included both the younger son and the heir of local gentry families, the latter, Peter Graper, using his success in the town to re-establish his position in the country. Around this time leading citizens of York and Newcastle were being knighted by the king. In terms of outlook and way of life there was much which held the urban and rural elites together. All this helps to explain how town and country could co-operate politically, with the mayor of London being one of the twenty-five barons appointed to enforce Magna Carta in 1215, and later, of course, knights and burgesses joining together in parliament.

*   *   *

The political role of the country gentry in the 1260s, and especially of the knights who were its leaders, was as striking as that of London. Knights fought in the armies, held local office as sheriffs, and at the national level appeared as representatives of the shires in parliament. The records of the lawcourts and the chancery which appear from the start of the thirteenth century make it possible for the first time to trace the careers of such men in detail and to sense their importance. Take the example of William fitz Ellis, who flourished in the decades after

1190. His chief seat was the substantial manor of Waterperry in south Oxfordshire. He was also lord of nearby Oakley in Buckinghamshire, and held other property in Oxfordshire and Wiltshire. If his income was around £50 a year, it was less than the median income of the couple of hundred barons, which was around £115 a year according to one sample, and was dwarfed by that of the dozen or so earls, some of whom in the thirteenth century had annual revenues of several thousand pounds. None the less his income, if we are right in our estimate, was well above the minimum required to qualify for knighthood, which the government set from the 1220s at £15 or £20 a year. It made him a very substantial member of the knightly class. Fitz Ellis was a fighting knight and went to Ireland in John's army of 1210. The military might of the knights remained vital to their power. Equally important was their role in the administration of law and local government. Fitz Ellis attended the Oxfordshire county court and gave judgements there with his fellow knights. He also sat on numerous common law juries, and served the king on various local commissions: in Oxfordshire he assessed and collected the great tax of 1225 in return for which the final definitive version of Magna Carta was issued. In the Charter fitz Ellis had indeed a personal interest. Under its terms he had in 1215 secured the return of Oakley, which King John had taken from him 'by will, unjustly and without judgement'. Lordship or the lack of it was also important to fitz Ellis's career. The family's chief seat at Waterperry had originally been held from the d'Oillys, Oxfordshire's greatest baronial family, and in other circumstances this feudal link might have been highly significant. In fact, however, the bond had been weakened by a settlement in the 1180s which placed a tenant between the fitz Ellises and the d'Oillys, a tenant from whom Waterperry was thenceforth held. In any case Henry d'Oilly (c. 1180–1232), the last of the male line, was an incompetent nonentity. Fitz Ellis himself seems to have acted independently of any lord. Other d'Oilly tenants entered the service of a rival local magnate, Thomas Basset of Headington, who was Oxfordshire's sheriff in the 1200s.

The power of men like fitz Ellis, therefore, derived in varying degrees from their property, military prowess, and tenure of local office. They might be independent of great lords or profit from their service. Many such families sustained their power over generations. A hundred years after William fitz Ellis, his descendant, Robert fitz Ellis, was still lord of Waterperry and Oakley. He also acquired property through marriage, raised troops for the Scottish wars, served the great magnates Roger Mortimer and Hugh Despencer, worked for the king as Oxfordshire sheriff and escheator, and left a magnificent knightly effigy in Waterperry church by the same sculptor as that of the earl of Cornwall in Westminster Abbey. By this time family pride was displayed in a coat of arms which in its fleur de lys made punning reference to the fitz Ellis name.

Central to the survival and success of the fitz Ellises was the way their principal properties were kept intact down the generations. The structure of the family and the way it handled property were fundamental to the workings of society. We have already discussed the view that the Norman Conquest accelerated the transition from clan to lineage, from the extended to the dynastic family, so that property, instead of being divided widely on death, descended through primogeniture, that is to the eldest son (see above, p. 87). Certainly such was the case with the chief properties of large numbers of families in the twelfth and thirteenth centuries. The sense of lineage thus created was often emphasized by the use of the same selection of first names and the adoption of a surname either derived from an ancestor, as with the fitz Ellises, or from a place, usually of the family's principal property. Throughout the thirteenth century the lords of Rycote (in Great Haseley) in south Oxfordshire were called 'Fulk of Rycote'. When a son and heir was at last born to Fulk II on 16 November 1295, he gave a great pair of gloves to his steward and joyfully dispatched letters and messengers announcing the birth to his neighbours and relations: the line would continue.

The primacy of eldest sons did not mean that siblings were left without provision. A study of the gentry of Angevin Yorkshire by Hugh Thomas has shown how in practice a modified form of primogeniture was common, with the principal property descending to the eldest son while arrangements were made to give younger sons an endowment and daughters a marriage portion. Since by law as well as custom all property held on death descended by primogeniture, such arrangements had to be made during life. The property used could come from acquisitions but also, if necessary, from the inheritance. The amounts involved varied according to the wealth of the family. In minor gentry families, younger sons might have endowments of as little as fifty or sixty acres, which made them no more than substantial freemen. A family like the fitz Ellises could afford to be more generous. William fitz Ellis provided some hundred acres of land as a marriage portion for one daughter, and his descendants later parted with whole manors (Corton in Wiltshire and Tiddington in Oxfordshire) to set up a junior line.

In terms of the descent of property, family structure thus seems 'nuclear'. Parents provided for their children, not for their wider kin. Likewise when King John took hostages it was sons he wanted, not kinsmen. Yet kin continued to matter, and people knew all about it because the prospect of failure of direct heirs and of an inheritance passing to a collateral branch gave every incentive for the study of genealogy. There was also an assumption that the wider family might be relied on for support. Hence those related to litigants by blood (*de consanguinitate*) were removed from juries; hence the promise in the Coronation Charter of 1100 that children and their lands should be placed in the custody of their widowed mother 'or another of their relations'. At the high political level the Beaumont family, brothers, brothers-in-law and cousins, were an important faction in Stephen's reign. As administrators the Glanvills, brothers, cousins and relations through marriage, had their hands in many branches of Henry II's government. Great ministers like Ranulf Glanvill and Hubert de Burgh naturally sought to promote their relations, just as their relations looked to them for promotion. In such circumstances the kin could become, in the words of J. C. Holt, 'a mutual benefit society'.

There was, however, nothing necessarily cohesive about family units, whatever their form. In both the 1215–17 and 1263–7 civil wars fathers and sons sometimes took opposite sides, mirroring the conflict between Henry II and his sons which lay at the heart of the civil war of 1173–4. Moreover, in one significant area the law of inheritance gave rise to dispute, in part because it touched upon the very claim of the royal house to the throne. After Richard's death without children in 1199, John had become king at the expense of Arthur, the son of his elder brother, Geoffrey of Brittany, who died in 1186. In comparable circumstances, did the better claim to succeed lie with the child, like Arthur, of a deceased elder brother who had never inherited, or with the latter's younger brother? Rather than settling the matter, John's accession simply ensured that it was kept open. Between the Mandevilles and the Says, and within the families of Percy, Braose and Quency, there were disputes along equivalent lines, disputes whose course was determined more by politics than by law. Within the nuclear family itself the fact that all the children had some expectation of provision could also lead to friction, pitching sons, daughters and sons-in-law against each other. The closer the family relationships the more significant they were likely to be, but that might be significance as a source of conflict just as much as a source of co-operation.

The celebrations surrounding the birth of Fulk III of Rycote in 1295 reveal another aspect of local society, namely the tremendous importance of ties of neighbourhood. It was to the villages within a ten-mile radius of Rycote – Shabbington, Chalgrove, Ewelme – that the letters and messengers announcing the arrival went out. It was from men living in that area that Fulk II had drawn his steward, clerk and squire. And it was from the other gentry families in that area that Fulk had found both his wife and a husband for his daughter. In all this he was absolutely typical. Such local associations could also be carried into national politics, which accounts in part for the way rebels in the 1260s were so often concentrated in regional pockets (see above, p. 379).

In the twelfth and thirteenth centuries the basic structure of the family seems to have been remarkably stable. Ties of neighbourhood had always been important. But society in this period was also changing in significant ways. Families like the fitz Ellises and the Rycotes were part of what historians often call 'the gentry', that group of men found in each county who were lords of one or a few main properties and were active in local affairs. The thegns were the gentry of late Anglo-Saxon England and the county knights the gentry of the early thirteenth century. In the course of the thirteenth century, however, the nature of knighthood altered radically, laying the foundations for the gentry of the later Middle Ages, one stratified into knights, esquires and gentlemen. At the same time the gentry were becoming involved far more intensively than before in litigation and local government, and were also operating within changing frameworks of magnate power.

Central to the emergence of the late medieval gentry was the decline in the number of knights which took place in the thirteenth century. In the 1200s, according to the calculations of Kathryn Faulkner, there were roughly 4,500 knights throughout the counties of England, judging, that is, from the numbers of men who appeared as such on juries and in the performance of other legal and administrative tasks. A middle-sized county like Oxfordshire might have had something over a hundred knights, Lincolnshire three times as many. A hundred years later the number of knights had shrunk to as few as 1,250. The knights of the 1200s had varied greatly in their wealth. The most numerous were lords of single manors with incomes of between about £10 and £20 a year. Above this group were better-endowed families like the fitz Ellises, and below it knights who had only very small manors or parcels of land not in manorial form – some perhaps the descendants of the professional soldiers given small amounts of land after the Conquest. Essentially what happened in the course of the thirteenth century was that knighthood became confined to higher-echelon families like the fitz Ellises. Then in the following centuries the descendants and successors of the families who had given up the honour adopted status titles of their own, at the upper level that of esquire and at the lower that of gentleman.

Within the context of the thirteenth century, the decline in the number of knights was significant because it created a high-status elite of knights who acted as leaders of the gentry, considerably increasing the influence of the body as whole. The decline in numbers seems to have taken place fairly rapidly in the first half of the century. The growing number of juries, commissions and offices which (so the king said) needed to be staffed by knights made it increasingly important to define, at the local level, who exactly held the rank. Many of those who appeared as knights on juries in the 1200s were probably accepted as such because they vaguely looked the part. But increasingly that was not good enough. To be a knight it became necessary to go through a formal initiation ceremony which involved being girded with the sword of knighthood. But those conferring the honour, either the king himself or a great lord, were not prepared to admit anyone to a rank they had long considered highly honorific. They expected the candidates to have the right equipment (to take up knighthood was called 'to take military arms') and a fitting retinue. Not surprisingly, therefore, it was only the upper levels of the old knightly class of the 1200s who could still afford the rank. Even some of those who did have the wherewithal refused to assume the honour, hoping to avoid knighthood's military and administrative responsibilities.

One important hypothesis also links this decline in numbers with a much wider social and economic crisis which, it is argued, engulfed descendants of the knights in the thirteenth century. Such men ran into debt and were compelled to sell property, sometimes to the point of extinction, to religious houses and royal ministers. It was these difficulties, so the argument runs, which explain both the general pressure for local reform in 1258–9 and the Montfortianism of many individual knights. In 1255, for example, Stephen de Chenduit, lord of Cuxham in Oxfordshire and Cheddington and Ibstone in Buckinghamshire, owed £55 to the Jew Abraham of Berkhampstead. During the civil war, Chenduit deserted his lord, Richard of Cornwall, and threw in his lot with Montfort who obligingly pardoned the interest on his Jewish debts. Afterwards, having survived Evesham but with his finances worsened by the penalties of rebellion, he sold up to the king's chancellor, Walter of Merton, who used his lands to endow his new Oxford college. One cause of such crises, it is suggested, was the rising cost of knighthood. Thus the expense of assuming the honour was the stated cause of the debts of Nicholas of Whichford in 1233. Stephen de Chenduit himself may well have overspent in the flashy circle of Richard of Cornwall. Another cause was the inflation early in the century, for middling and smaller landholders, it is argued, were far less able to counter this than the great – less able, that is, to increase manorial rents, and to create large demesnes in order to sell more corn on the rising market.

There is no doubt that decaying knights like Stephen de Chenduit were familiar figures in the thirteenth century. Whether they were typical is less clear. A study of a large group of knights from the midlands involved in the 1260s rebellion has not revealed any pattern of pervasive debt. Studies of representative groups from Oxfordshire, Buckinghamshire and Warwickshire seem to show that families which began the century with at lest one manor of reasonable size usually came through (if the male line survived) with the bulk of their property intact and sometimes enlarged. Families in difficulties, like the Whichfords, often showed remarkable resilience and staying power. Around 1200 the fitz Ellises themselves lamented their great need, but the need was for money to finance litigation and this eventually considerably increased their properties. The costs of knighthood can scarcely have paralysed the whole group, because most simply declined the honour. If general economic conditions were more difficult than in the twelfth century, knightly lords were quite able to put up rents (like the Rycotes), and increase the size of their demesnes, as Stephen de Chenduit's father did at Cuxham. Many knightly manors had demesnes quite as large as those envisaged by the great expert on husbandry, Walter of Henley. Meanwhile the class was constantly being replenished by the successful lawyers and administrators who married into old families or bought up the properties of those on the way down. In short the general political importance of the gentry in the thirteenth century should be seen against a background of underlying economic strength rather than of weakness.

At the time in the early thirteenth century when the stratification of the gentry into ranks was beginning, it was also being transformed in another way, namely through its increasing involvement in litigation and local government. Of course, the gentry had always been involved in both. The cry 'Act like thegns' which went up before the thegns gave an important judgement in the Herefordshire county court in the time of King Cnut would have struck a chord with the knights who gave similar judgements in the thirteenth century. But now alongside their role in the county courts, which met much more frequently than in the Anglo-Saxon period, the gentry staffed the juries on which the new common law procedures depended, monopolized the old office of the sheriff, and filled the plethora of new offices called into being by royal government, acting as coroners, escheators, keepers of the peace, assessors and collectors of taxation, justices of assize and gaol delivery, and so on. The common law brought gentry litigation into the royal courts on an altogether novel scale: between the 1190s and the 1220s William fitz Ellis and his mother were involved in over fifteen separate actions before the justices in eyre and the common bench at Westminster. The whole framework of gentry life was being transformed.

At the centre of this activity there usually emerged a small group of knights, bearing the main burden. Nicknamed 'bigshots' (*buzones*) they appear constantly as jurors, commissioners, office-holders, and attenders at the county court. Robert Damory, Ralph fitz Robert, Gilbert of Finmere, Fulk I of Rycote, Richard Foliot of Rousham – these were some of William fitz Ellis's colleagues in Oxfordshire in the early thirteenth century. While such men all had ties to their immediate neighbourhood, they were also very much part of what contemporaries called 'the community of the shire'. Of course such communities could be the reverse of cohesive. When William fitz Ellis and a few colleagues gave a controversial judgement in the Oxfordshire county court in 1222, 'nearly all the knights of the shire' rose up as they did not wish to be involved. But the question of how the county was run and represented inevitably gave everyone in the shire a common and exclusive concern, for each county had its own local officials and its own MP; indeed the latter specifically represented 'the community of the shire'. MPs and coroners were both elected in the county court. Its regular monthly or six-weekly meetings brought together the gentry and the stewards of the great magnates (the two were often one and the same), who gave the judgements. Nor were its meetings without significance for it retained jurisdiction over minor cases of debt and detention of chattels, while a growing number of writs enabled other litigation to be initiated there. From such county concerns grew national political programmes. Essentially the gentry wanted the holders of local office to be chosen from and by itself, thus achieving congenial government 'by one of us'. When in the 1200s the Somerset knight Richard Revel spoke of 'native men and gentlemen of the country', he was precisely contrasting such men with the outsider sheriff. In calling in the gentry to staff local offices, the king was in part giving way to demand. Several counties in John's reign bought the right to have a sheriff chosen 'from themselves and wholly resident in the county' and it was essentially sheriffs of that type who were appointed under the reforms of 1258. It was in response to similar pressures that Magna Carta in 1215 had laid down that the king's judges touring the shires to hear civil assizes were to sit with four knights of the county chosen by the county court, a striking testimony to the ambition, expertise and self-confidence of the knights.

In general in the later Middle Ages the gentry achieved their ambition and largely monopolized local office. How far they had achieved 'self-government at the king's command', in the words of the historian A. B. White, depended on the local power of great lords. In some regions throughout the medieval period – regions which varied according to the rise and fall of families and the changing structures of great estates – that power was limited, and the gentry could make their own political decisions and create their own local order or chaos. Yet there were equally times and places where great lords were dominant. Alongside the ties of family and neighbourhood, the power of lordship was often fundamental to the workings of local society. Here too important changes were taking place affecting the way that power was exercised, a change sometimes described by historians as the transition from 'feudalism' to 'bastard feudalism'.

The feudal structures which the Normal Conquest introduced into England have already been described (see above, pp. 84–7). They turned on the relationship between the baron (as a major tenant-in-chief was called) and his tenants. This relationship was initiated by the ceremony of homage in which the tenant became the 'man' of his lord, and swore loyalty for the land he held from him. In return for the land, the baron was owed the service of a specified number of knights by each tenant, or a money payment, scutage, in its place. He could also profit from what historians have called 'the feudal incidents', exacting a payment (a 'fine' or 'relief') from a tenant to enter his inheritance, taking the revenues from tenanted estates during minorities, and controlling the marriages of widows and (when in wardship) those of heirs and heiresses. Tenants were also obliged to attend the lord's honourial court where, among other things, disputes over the possession of tenanted land and the services owed for it could be judged. The entity formed by the baron's tenants and demesne manors (the manors he kept in hand) is variously described by modern historians, with some contemporary warrant, as his 'fee', 'barony' or 'honour' (hence 'honourial court'). Since it was passed on to the baron's heir, it had some kind of continuous life.

There has been much debate among historians about the strength of these feudal structures in the period down to 1166 and the pace of their decline thereafter. This is not surprising because from the start barons could exploit their feudal rights in different ways and with different consequences. They might see them as a source of loyal service or simply of revenue. They might retain authority over some tenants but not others. And they might deal with tenants simply as individuals or as part of some kind of honourial community. Honours also had very different histories and structures. One should think less of a set of neat feudal pyramids than of a range of hills like that around Wastwater in Cumberland, hills of all shapes and sizes, merging into one another, some solid, others with their sides slipping into the lake. Honours might have just a handful or large numbers of tenants. The proportion between land held by tenants and that kept in demesne also varied widely. In the twelfth century between 150 and 200 baronial honours were in existence but it was only with the stipulation in the 1215 Magna Carta that a baron should pay a £100 relief for his 'barony' that any clear distinction emerged between estates which were baronies and which were not.

Within a large honour there was also a great diversity among the tenants themselves. In the Ferrers honour of Tutbury, for example, there was a group of around ten major tenant families, including the Shirleys and the Bacquepuits (see above, pp. 79–83), most with traceable origins in Normandy, who were established soon after the Conquest, each usually receiving several properties of substantial size. Such leading tenants, found on most large honours, were sometimes described by the lord in the early twelfth century as his 'barons', probably as a general recognition of their status rather than as an indication of any precise position. Below such major players there was a much larger and diverse group of tenants, some with very small holdings, others middling members of the gentry. All told in 1166 the Ferrers honour had forty-five tenants owing a notional service of around seventy-nine knights, the Shirley lord at the top of the scale owing nine knights, and many of the smaller tenants at the bottom only one. The honour was scattered across fourteen counties, but had a solid core in west Leicestershire, north Staffordshire, and Derbyshire, a core watched over by the great castle of Tutbury, rising on a cliff above the river Dove. Its jagged ruins still seem to dominate the southern Derbyshire plain.

Honours from the start were neither self-contained institutions, as we shall see, nor the sole bases for baronial power. From the first, barons sought jurisdictional privileges from the king (like private hundreds and wapentakes), and coveted the office of sheriff either for themselves or for one of their men. Until earldoms became largely titular under Henry II, they too might be an important source of local authority. In Stephen's reign the Ferrers appear as earls of both Nottingham and Derby (the latter was their title from 1199), while their steward was for a time sheriff of both counties. Their local power was also strengthened by the tenure of the Derbyshire wapentakes of Wirksworth and Appeltree, the first held initially under Henry I, the second finally acquired under King John.

When all the qualifications have been made, however, there can be little doubt that within the total mix of baronial power under both the Norman and Angevin kings feudal structures were very important. At the very least the feudal incidents provided the baron with a unique set of rights that were simply not present in any other type of relationship. There was also more to feudalism than simply making money. The ceremony of homage was solemn and significant. As *Glanvill* explained, it was supposed to create a 'bond of mutual trust' between lord and tenant, with the latter owing services and the former protecting the land from which they were due. The idea of the loyalty a tenant owed his lord and a lord his tenant was integral to the society of the twelfth and thirteenth centuries. Two factors helped turn theory into practice. One was that honours often mirrored that of Tutbury in having a solid geographical core. Feudal structures were always most effective when underpinned by ties of neighbourhood. The second was that honours often had a high proportion of tenants lacking substantial property held from other lords. A legal tract in the reign of Henry I, *The Leges Henrici Primi*, avowed that a man's chief loyalty was owed to the 'liege lord' from whom he held his principal property, and for many tenants in the twelfth century it was perfectly clear who that should be.

There is abundant evidence from the twelfth century of a close relationship between lords and their tenants. Both Earl William III de Warenne (died 1148) and Robert, earl of Gloucester (died 1147), are seen in the witness lists of their charters very much in the company of their leading men. It was from their tenants in the first half of the twelfth century and beyond that barons often drew their stewards and other officials. In cementing such relations, and in making the honour a real community, an important part could be played by mutual attachment to religious houses. A charter of Earl Robert de Ferrers (1101–39) making a grant to Darley abbey was addressed 'most especially to all the barons and men of my honour'. Darley, like the abbey at Tutbury, had been founded by the Ferrers, and together they served very much as honourial monasteries receiving benefactions from many of the tenants. Likewise, many tenants responded when their lord Gilbert fitz Richard (1090–1117) urged them to make gifts to the monastery he was founding at Clare. Evidence for the functioning of the honourial court is limited but Henry I stipulated that it should deal with land disputes between tenants of the same lord. In the first century after 1066 one should not underrate the utility of its justice and over-estimate that offered in the courts of the king. In the 1160s it was in the court of Earl Ferrers, not that of Henry II, that an important agreement was reached settling the future of the Shirley inheritance.

If Henry II's new legal procedures served to weaken baronial authority, the increasing incidence of scutage under Henry and his successors had the opposite effect, since barons had to control their tenants in order to collect it. The result was almost certainly to invigorate honourial administration. Viewed from many angles, England in the 1200s still seems very feudal. Magna Carta regulated the exploitation of the feudal incidents, and took for granted the existence of the honour and the loyalty of tenants to their lords. During the 1215–17 civil war, if there were many independent knights like William fitz Ellis, there were equally many barons who were followed by their tenants either in rebellion or, as in the case of William de Ferrers, earl of Derby, in loyalty to King John (see above, p. 288). The honour as a community can still be sensed in several agreements in the 1200s: the tenants of the Worcestershire Beauchamp honour, for example, offered King John £1,333 (2,000 marks) to have control of their lord and his lands during his minority.

This feudal theme can be pursued deep into the thirteenth century. Lords collected a scutage from their tenants with reasonable success in 1235, continued to exploit reliefs, marriages and wardships, protected such rights by striving to prevent the creation of intermediate or 'mesne' tenancies (like that at Waterperry), and insisted on the obligation to attend their private courts (hence the need for legislation on the subject in 1259). Before he finally forfeited everything for rebellion in 1266, Earl Robert de Ferrers, last of the line, is seen in his charters surrounded by tenants, many of whom now bore coats of arms which were derived from the Ferrers' own. It was entirely in feudal terms that the Ferrers knight Richard de Vernon justified his conduct between 1263 and 1266: 'In the time of the war he stood with his lord, Robert de Ferrers, earl of Derby, from whom he held his land and to whom he had done homage.'

By this time, however, such ideas of feudal loyalty were increasingly losing touch with reality. Vernon himself seems in fact to have left the service of Earl Ferrers for that of the Montforts. Although impossible to measure in any detail, the civil war of 1263–7 wears a distinctly less feudal aspect than that of 1215–17. While, moreover, great barons continued to exploit the feudal incidents, the number who exercised such rights over an extensive body of tenants was almost certainly diminishing. Honours like that of the Ferrers which continued to have some kind of communal life were probably exceptional. That was partly because the life of an honour had always been liable to disruption or termination. They could be forfeited for treason and then granted out again, in whole or in part, to entirely new lords. An honour might equally pass to a new family through the marriage of an heiress. If there were heiresses, then it was divided between them and ceased to exist as a single entity. No less than fifty-four of the 189 baronial honours existing in 1166 had passed into the female line at least once since 1086. The Ferrers were lucky indeed in continuing the male line all the way down to their forfeiture in 1266. Alongside barons from ancient families, there were always new men, often royal servants (like William Brewer), who were building up large estates, composed of demesne manors and a hotchpotch of feudal tenants, which were not baronies at all. As the number of such estates increased while that of undivided honours declined it became impossible to regard the great men of the realm simply as those who were baronial tenants-in-chief. Under the terms of Magna Carta in 1215 it had still been the latter who were to receive a personal summons to parliament, but in practice in the thirteenth century the king came to summon whoever was wealthy and important, irrespective of whether they enjoyed baronial status.

Even where honours remained intact, there were factors which helped tenants escape the control of disagreeable or ineffective lords. The greater tenancies seem to have been hereditary from an early stage. Lower down the scale, lords retained some power to chop and change (certainly this seems the case in the honour of Clare), but gradually in the twelfth century the lesser tenancies too became heritable. That tendency was reinforced by the new legal procedures of Henry II, which also diminished a baron's ability to discipline his men through seizing their lands. There were other ways too in which tenants might gain independence. Many lords were as ineffective as Henry d'Oilly in preventing the creation of mesne tenancies. *The Leges Henrici Primi* already considered the problems which could arise if tenants lived far from the baronial centre or held significant lands outside the honour from other lords. While such conflicts of loyalty often affected a minority of tenants, as we have said, that minority often included the wealthiest members of the honour. The honourial court itself was certainly no self-contained institution. Under Henry I cases were almost certainly transferred from it for default of justice to be heard by the county court or by the king himself. Under Henry II it no longer required default of justice to effect such transfers, for the new common law legal procedures opened up a range of ways in which tenants could litigate directly before royal judges. Likewise it was the under-tenants who staffed the juries required by the new procedures and came to hold the array of new local offices called into being by Angevin kingship.

As the structures of feudalism weakened, so in the twelfth and thirteenth centuries new forms of magnate power developed, forms of what historians have called bastard feudalism. Driving on this development, as Peter Coss has argued, was the threat posed to magnates by the direct relationship the king was forging with under-tenants. The relationship had always existed, but the Angevins, as we have seen, strengthened it many times over. In effect, bastard feudalism was the response. Here there were three interrelated strands. The first was that lords retained whoever they liked in their service, whether or not they were tenants. Clearly this was an absolutely necessary response to the king's own claim, enunciated in *The Dialogue of the Exchequer* in 1178, that he himself could employ any man in his service, no matter from whom that man held his land. Lords had to be able to do the same if they were not to be left behind. It was the competition for good service as well as good lordship which weakened the honour, breaking it up from above as well as from below. No ambitious lord could afford to be stuck with a circle of dud tenants, just as no ambitious tenant could afford to be stuck with a dud lord. In the second half of the twelfth century, therefore, retinues which owed little to tenurial connections begin to appear, as David Crouch has shown: William Marshal, earl of Chepstow and Pembroke (1190–1219), had no tenurial links with twelve of the eighteen knights closest to him. The second feature of bastard feudalism was the way in which great lords sought particularly to retain men whom the king appointed to local office, thus nullifying the threat to themselves implicit in such employment. In the 1220s the earl of Warwick seems to have been constructing a following very much of this kind. If great lords had long sought to control the office of sheriff, they now strove to bring a much wider range of officials within their orbit. In spinning such webs of local control, magnates were helped by changes in the structures of local government in the thirteenth century which arguably gave the king a less powerful presence in the shires (see below, p. 492). In the 1260s the complaint was that the sheriffs and bailiffs were the creatures of the magnates and the king's judges their 'tributaries', implying that they were retained with annual money payments or 'fees'.

Reference to such fees reflects the third feature of bastard feudalism, that rewards took the form of money rather than of land. 'Its quintessence was payment for service,' wrote K. B. McFarlane of bastard feudalism. The fact was that after the initial bonanza following the Norman Conquest, land was in increasingly short supply. The great majority of the tenancies revealed by the great survey of 1166 had been created before 1135, while those of later date were often small in size. Clearly lords were becoming cagey about parting with land, the most valuable of all commodities. Most of William Marshal's followers seem to have been rewarded not with land but with offices and other favours. They may also have received money 'fees', for whereas land was scarce, cash – with the huge expansion of the money supply (see above, p. 40)

– was abundant. Scott Waugh has demonstrated how lords in the thirteenth century increasingly rewarded their servants with such fees, beginning with their legal advisers and estate stewards, and then moving on to their knights as well. In this they were imitating the king. He had always used money to recruit mercenaries to fight in his armies. Now in the thirteenth century he began to use money fees on a regular basis as a reward for household knights, judges and other senior officials. That retention through money was becoming the norm was revealed in 1270 when the Lord Edward, at a cost of 22,500 marks, entered into formal contracts with eighteen English lords who were to supply him with 225 knights for his crusade. The implication was that the lords would use the cash to recruit their own retinues.

During the course of the twelfth and thirteenth centuries, at a pace uneven both chronologically and geographically, the structures of feudalism had waned and those of bastard feudalism had waxed. In managing the transition, great lords certainly preserved the essentials of their power but the new structures were more fluid and kaleidoscopic than the old, leaving the gentry correspondingly more independent. That after all was the view of the government. Under the terms of Magna Carta it was the barons and other lesser tenants-in-chief who were still to answer for the kingdom in matters of taxation. Taxes were indeed granted by such feudal assemblies in 1225, 1232 and 1237. But from the 1250s the crown felt it necessary to summon knights representing the counties to give their own assent. This surely reflected a major shift in how society was perceived. In 1215 the barons could still answer for the realm because it could still be seen, in certain lights, as composed of a series of honours in which each baron commanded the allegiance of a defined body of knightly tenants. Fifty years later this no longer seemed to be the case. The knights and through them the men of the shires must answer for themselves. The appearance of the knights in parliament is the best measure of the new society which was emerging in the thirteenth century.

*   *   *

Beneath the lords of the manors, but above the peasantry (because they did not labour themselves), were large numbers of freemen holding, at a rough estimate, between forty and a hundred or so acres of land. This group has been little studied by historians, yet it was immensely important for the functioning of local society. The group was fed from below by men rising from the ranks of the peasantry and from above, as we have seen, by the establishment of junior branches of minor gentry families. Some members were descendants of the soldiers established on small parcels of land after the Conquest, others of the kind of English families found on the hundred juries which had given evidence for the making of Domesday Book. These freeholders were essential to the running of the hundred, indeed were formed inevitably into a kind of community by so doing. At the three-weekly sessions of the hundred courts they gave judgements in cases of minor debt and disorder, and reviewed the more serious crimes which were passed up to the king's justices on their eyre visitations. At the eyres, they usually outnumbered lords of manors on the hundred juries which gave evidence to the judges. Of the jurors at the 1263 Surrey eyre, 70 per cent appeared again as jurors at other eyres. When such men litigated they generally did so for property within their hundred. These groups were therefore experienced, tightly-knit and local. They acted as a hinge between the peasantry and the gentry. In so far as there was a genuine community of the realm, they did much to forge it.

Peasant society itself has been studied far more intensively than that of the freemen just above it, though such studies mostly begin at the end of our period, being facilitated by the advent of manorial court rolls. At the peasant level the nuclear family of parents and children remained the central social institution. Indeed, if life expectancy was lower among the peasantry, then three-generational families were correspondingly less common than higher up the social scale. Zvi Razi's work on the manor of Halesowen in Shropshire suggested that tenants aged twenty could expect to live another twenty-five to twenty-eight years. Given that their normal age of marriage was around twenty, there was little time to enjoy grandchildren. On the other hand, some parents did live long enough to surrender their property to their sons. Formal maintenance agreements were exceptional. Children had an obligation to look after their aged parents.

Inheritance customs among the peasantry varied. In the south and east, especially in Kent and East Anglia, partible inheritance was prevalent with equal division among all the sons. Elsewhere the heir was more usually either the eldest son (primogeniture) or the youngest son (ultimogeniture). Under both systems daughters only inherited in default of sons. Even where inheritance was impartible, however, nuclear families felt a very strong obligation to provide for the non-inheriting children, thus enabling them to marry. Sometimes that might amount, as with one couple at Houghton-cum-Wyton (Huntingdonshire), to no more than a room in the house or a dwelling in the courtyard together with 'all the necessities of life'. But more often the aim was to endow younger sons and daughters with land in order to help them set up separate households. If necessary that land came from the inheritance, but it was clearly better if it could be acquired. The acquisition of small parcels of land in order to provide for younger sons and daughters was one of the main engines driving the village land market. How far the establishment of non-inheriting children created extended families as a significant force in village life depended very much on local economic conditions. At Brigstock in Northamptonshire, where the resources of the neighbouring forest relaxed pressure on the land, conjugal households appear (in Judith Bennett's study) as comparatively distinct and autonomous. At Halesowen, on the other hand, where land was at more of a premium, and a family's main house and holding might be surrounded by the cottages and smallholdings of its junior members, the extended family was a working unit. At the village level, of course, families quarrelled over the allotment of property just as they did higher up the social scale, but the imperative to co-operate was also much stronger − indeed co-operation could quite literally be a condition of survival.

Peasant society was stratified between smallholders with tenements of a few acres at the bottom of the scale and substantial families with thirty-acre holdings at the top. There were also individual peasants, often officials such as the reeve, who through the workings of the village land market succeeded in building up more substantial estates. If these were then broken up to provide for younger children, occasionally a family (like the Knivetons in Derbyshire) ascended over several generations into the knightly class. It was the poor smallholders who were most at risk from the economic conditions of the thirteenth century. At Halesowen, while the top and middling families seem to have kept their lands relatively intact from the 1270s down to 1348, only 35 per cent of the smaller families did so, sometimes selling out to their wealthier neighbours.

Within each manorial complex the peasant condition depended very much, of course, on the level of the lord's exactions. It depended too, if the peasants were villeins (that is, unfree), on how far the lord exploited his consequent rights, a much debated subject (see above, pp. 53–4). Even the half of the peasant population which was unfree, however, had a direct relationship with royal government, and was thus very much part of the wider realm. For a start, the king drew on all his subjects for defence of the realm; hence the 'Assize of Arms', which laid down the arms required by everyone according to their wealth, made no distinction according to status, and insisted that all who were able-bodied should at least have bows and arrows. Peasants were therefore armed by government decree. They were also very much embraced by the king's maintenance of the peace because serious crime was always the concern of the crown, even if committed by the most lowly peasant. At the most basic level of law enforcement the peasants were organized into 'tithings', groups of ten men who provided collective security for each other's good behaviour. It was on entering such groups at the age of twelve that peasants took their oath of fealty to the king. Some lords obtained or usurped the right to carry out themselves the annual check on whether the peasants were all arrayed in their tithings ('the view of frankpledge'), but if not this was done by the sheriff at the hundred court. If a tithing failed to arrest a delinquent member, then it was punishable by the king's judges. It was the village communities too which had to pay the *murdrum* fine to the king when they could not prove a dead body was that of an Englishman – in practice, this meant a peasant. The reeve and men from each village nearest to which bodies were found also had to attend coroners' inquests. It is striking testimony to the way local concerns reached the national level that both Magna Carta in 1217 and the Provisions of Westminster in 1259 alleviated peasant burdens in these areas, the former by limiting exactions by the sheriff at the checking of the tithing groups, and the latter by abolishing the *murdrum* fine in cases of misadventure, and preventing a judge amercing a village because all adult males had not attended an inquest. A combination of lordly self-interest and idealism contributed to such reforms; but peasants were also quite able to protest for themselves.

Manorial court rolls are full of fines for bad ploughing and default of reaping. At Little Ogborne (Wiltshire) the whole village was punished for not coming to wash the lord's sheep. Resistance could also be violent. The villeins of Brampton in 1242 chased the lord's bailiffs back to Huntingdon and rescued 'with axes and staves' the animals they had taken. The culprits could not be named individually since 'the greater part of the village' was there. There were also numerous lawsuits in which the peasants complained of increased burdens imposed on them by their lords. Unfree peasants, of course, were denied access to the king's courts in any matters concerned with their lands and rents, but such cases proceeded when the peasants claimed either to be free sokemen or the specially privileged class of peasants who lived on 'ancient demesne' manors, that is manors anciently in the king's hands. In the latter case the plaintiffs were perhaps imagining a mythical time when everyone had been directly subject to the king and had access to his courts. Since lords always responded to these claims by saying the peasants were actually villeins, the cases turned on the question of status. In one suit the peasants of Mears Ashby (Northamptonshire) litigated from 1249 to 1261 until at last they secured victory, appearing before the justices of the common bench, king's bench (this during the great revolutionary parliaments at Oxford and Winchester in 1258), and then before the justiciars of the reforming regime, Hugh Bigod and Hugh Despencer.

This movement at Ashby was led by substantial peasants, each with around thirty acres of land, who fought the case 'for themselves and the other men of Ashby in common'. The community of the village was the lowest rung of the communities in England created by the needs of government, in this case the need to govern the workings of the manor. Up to a point the peasants were forced to do that in the lords' interests, but they could also do it in their own, especially as they gave the judgements at the manorial court and assessed the amercements imposed by it. At Brightwalton (Berkshire) the villeins gave verdicts 'according to the custom of the manor' on complex disputes over inheritance, put up candidates to act as reeve and, as the 'whole community of the villeins of Brightwalton', reached an agreement with their lord (the abbot of Battle) over rights of common. Village society was stratified and competitive yet could co-operate for the common good. It also had wide horizons and plenty of political training, hence the role of the peasantry in the revolutionary period between 1258 and 1267. In 1265 'the community of the village' of Peatling Magna (Leicestershire) was able to see itself as very much part of the wider 'community of the realm'.

*   *   *

'Women differ from men in many respects for their position is inferior to that of man,' opined the great law book *Bracton*, put together in the 1220s. The reason, of course, was partly biblical, going back to Eve's role as Adam's serpentine temptress. Other female failings (in the view of the mid-thirteenth-century Oxford friar, John of Wales) were garrulity, sloth and ostentation, notably in dress and make-up. Walter Map, writing in the 1180s, declared that women led to only one thing: 'mischief'. How necessary then the injunction in Ephesians 5:22-23: 'Wives submit yourselves unto your own husbands, as unto the Lord. For the husband is the head of the wife, even as Christ is the head of the church.' Women also needed protection because they were frail. When Ughtred Smith of Botland pulled an arrow out of his head before going home it was 'so that my wife may not see it, for she would perhaps grieve over much.' Strong man. Weak woman.

In fact it was not always as simple as that. Women were not all weak. In May 1267 when the widow Desiderata met her friend William de Stangate coming along with a crossbow over his shoulder, she asked him in jest (clearly well informed about national events) whether he was one of those sent by the king to apprehend evildoers. Then, declaring she could overcome two or three like him, she grabbed his neck, crooked her leg and threw him to the ground. While it may be true that the status of women declined markedly in theological writings in the eleventh and twelfth centuries, many ecclesiastics remained remarkably free of such prejudices, especially when confronted with real women. St Anselm corresponded extensively with noblewomen, treating them as equals and individuals, respecting their abilities and stressing their influence as civilizers of their husbands and teachers of their children. Orderic Vitalis, in the first half of the twelfth century, portrayed noblewomen as co-operators with their husbands, and discriminated between their different personalities. He certainly criticized individual women, but never the sex as a whole. A hundred or so years later another great chronicler, Matthew Paris, viewed the many noblewomen of his acquaintance in a similarly balanced light.

It is true, of course, that the positive view of a wife's role in marriage found in writers like Anselm and later Thomas of Chobham reflected their subordination. If they exercised power it was through influencing their husbands. It is equally true that where women acted strongly on their own account they were often said to act like men, just as when men acted weakly they were said to act like women. Yet this too did not alter the admiration for women who did act manfully and on their own. Matthew Paris gave a long account of the way the widowed countess of Arundel, 'a woman but not acting in women's fashion', upbraided Henry III for his injustices. In the same way Orderic Vitalis wrote enthusiastically of Isabella de Conches, 'generous, daring and light-hearted ... who rode armed as a knight among the knights'. Indeed, women who fought were widely esteemed. In the mid thirteenth century the gentry family of Hotot still remembered their ancestress, Dionisia, who in the troubles of Stephen's reign, had charged a knight and unhorsed him with one blow from her lance.

The position of women, therefore, as Judith Bennett has remarked, was full of ambivalence and contradictions. In many ways they were subordinate, yet they could be real partners within marriage, and independent agents outside it, especially as widows. Moreover both the restraints and the opportunities were remarkably similar, with certain exceptions, at all levels of society.

The general inferiority of the female sex in male thinking and the more particular subordination of wives in marriage were certainly reflected in and reinforced by the exclusion of women from many areas of public life: private women, public men. Women did not serve on juries and did not act as judges, sheriffs and castellans save in the rare cases where they inherited a family position, like Nicola de la Haye (see above, pp. 252, 299). Within towns they could be members of gilds but they never held office. Within the village they never acted as reeves or ale-tasters and were not in tithings. A limited public role is also reflected in the way women were rarely either the victims or the perpetrators of crime. In a Lincolnshire sample of 322 people accused of homicide in 1202 and between 1281 and 1284, only 5.6 per cent were women, and many of these were acting with male accomplices. Only 13.6 per cent of the 286 victims were women, mostly as a result of domestic violence. As for other crimes, women were most likely to be involved in the non-violent activities of larceny and receiving, although even here the numbers were low: of 341 people accused of larceny between 1281 and 1284 only twenty-five were women.

Women were also more restricted than men when it came to bringing 'appeals' (that is, accusations) for personal injury. In law, as stated in *Glanvill*, they could only do this for rape and for the murder of their husbands provided they had witnessed the crime. Although in practice appeals for robbery, wounding and the death of sons and fathers were also allowed, increasingly in the thirteenth century the judges became more restrictive and applied the letter of the law. Success in rape actions was low. Not one of twenty-seven cases from Lincolnshire in 1202 resulted in a conviction. In twenty-two of them the victim failed to prosecute, perhaps forcing an out-of-court settlement, perhaps intimidated by having to detail the events. Not surprisingly, the number of actions fell markedly in the course of the century. It should be remembered, however, that nine out of ten men accused of rape are still acquitted today.

Women, especially once married, were also second-class citizens when it came to rights over property. Under feudal custom and the common law to which the law and custom in towns and manors often approximated, a daughter could inherit but only in default of sons (see above, p. 89). Within marriage the husband gained total control of both his wife's inheritance and her marriage portion (*maritagium*), the endowment given by her natal family. He could alienate them on his sole authority, as he could also alienate land to which his wife would be entitled after his death as dower. (Dower was supposed to amount to a third of the land the husband held on marriage, together with a third of any subsequent acquisitions unless another amount was stipulated.) 'Legally a woman is completely in the power of her husband,' wrote the law book *Glanvill*.

In some ways, however, the law also encouraged co-operation between husbands and wives. If wives could not prevent husbands alienating their possessions, they could as widows challenge such alienations. A wise husband secured the consent of his wife. Many of the grants made by twelfth-century earls of Chester were said to have been agreed by their countesses. The latter were also permitted to pursue policies of their own, notably in making endowments to favoured religious houses. In fact there were many areas in which wives worked closely with their husbands and not always as their civilizers. Early in the twelfth century within the town of Huntingdon, the parents of the future recluse Christina of Markyate were absolutely at one in trying to force her into marriage, and it was her mother who resorted to physical violence. Among the baronage, one can sense real political partnerships between couples like Matilda and William de Braose, Matilda and Roger de Mortimer and Simon and Eleanor de Montfort. These were very much the types of women admired by Orderic Vitalis and Matthew Paris. The household roll of Eleanor de Montfort in 1265 shows her moving around with her large establishment as it suited the needs of the Montfortian government, for a time taking command at Dover castle. In May and June 1265, she sent letters and messengers to the sheriff of Hampshire, the constables of Wallingford and Kenilworth, the prioress of Amesbury and the countesses of Devon and Lincoln, as well as to her husband and her son who was besieging Pevensey castle.

Within the home itself, a wife's role could be of central importance. Matilda de Braose was praised by Gerald of Wales for the economical way she ran her household. The association of women with household supervision is shown in the law book *Bracton* which opined that a woman, in some forms of tenure, would come of age (and thus be marriageable) when 'she knows how to order her house and do the things which belong to the arrangement and management of a house'. A wife might also be involved in educating her children, as Anselm envisaged: the baroness Denise de Montchensy, in the mid thirteenth century, taught her offspring French, the language of 'husbandry and management'. In this way wives forged close relationships with their children and naturally became involved in the politics of how they should be endowed and whom they should marry.

At the level of the village, the impression from coroners' reports on accidental death is that women were at home (or fetching water) and men were out at work. But that may simply reflect women's non-domestic work being less dangerous than men's – for example weeding, reaping and spinning, rather than ploughing. One striking fact to emerge from licensing fines is the number of women brewers. The capital involved in brewing meant such women were usually married (hence 'ale wives'), often to village officials and craftsmen like reeves and smiths. In villages like Brigstock and Langtoft (Lincolnshire) women dominated brewing, a core of professionals working on a regular basis and other women moving in and out of the business from year to year. Women were also active as brewers in towns. In Lincoln at different times in 1292–3 between twenty-nine and fifty-two women were involved, respectively 22 per cent and 44 per cent of the total number of brewers. Other female trades at this time included those of seamster, huckster, mustard-maker, midwife, salter, girdler, furmager (cheese-maker), ironmonger and taverner.

The marital status of these Lincoln women is often unclear. Many were wives but others were probably spinsters and widows, which brings us to the position of women outside marriage. As we have seen, the public invisibility of women was partly due to their supposed subordination to their husbands within the conjugal household. Yet there were also women, spinsters and widows, who had no husbands at all, and were sometimes heads of their own households. They did not thereby gain equality with men in the public arena – gender stereotypes were far too strong for that – but they did have more independence for good or ill than in the married state.

Spinsters with their own land were far more prevalent at the lower than the higher levels of society. Indeed among the nobility it is difficult to find examples of spinsters holding substantial acreages of land. The church certainly stressed that the free consent of both parties was necessary for valid marriage, but since women were allowed to give that consent at the age of twelve it did not amount to very much. Any woman who could expect a significant inheritance or endowment was likely to be married in her teens, as decided by king, lord or family, so the question of a period of independence as a landed spinster simply did not arise. Within the parental home an unmarried daughter might be given considerable responsibility. In Huntingdon, Christina of Markyate was not merely dressed finely, she was also given custody of her father's substantial treasure. But there was no question of her setting up on her own outside marriage, and it was only flight which enabled her to do so. On the other hand, the smaller the expectation of land and the less the local shortage of it, the more likely it was that a woman would marry late or not at all. In that case, if she had at least some property, she might well have her own household. On the 1240 Suffolk eyre a striking number of single women, apparently spinsters, are found fending for themselves, bringing actions of mort d'ancestor, novel disseisin and entry, often over just a few acres. Within the manor of Brigstock there is likewise evidence of landed spinsters, fathers endowing daughters with small amounts of land sometimes years before they married, land for which they answered themselves in the manorial court, and on which perhaps they lived. How far such women were truly autonomous, and how far, if they were, they enjoyed their autonomy, must have depended in part on the size of the provision. For some, without help from their families, independence was perhaps no more than independence to starve. Marriage, on the other hand, might bring security. The irony was that while a lack of resources made a husband necessary, it also diminished the prospect of finding one.

If spinsters, for good or ill, could have an independent role as landholders and litigators, it disappeared on marriage, only to reappear in widowhood. Under manorial custom widows recovered control of their inheritances and endowments and were also entitled to a dower, sometimes amounting to half of their late husband's lands. It was also common for women to have custody of the paternal inheritance when heirs were under age. All this explains why in many villages between 10 and 15 per cent of the holdings were in the hands of women. Widowhood could transform the lives of peasant women, replacing, in the words of Judith Bennett, 'public reticence with public assertion'. At Brigstock, for example, Alice Avice litigated in the manorial court far more frequently as a widow than as a married woman, and generally played a much fuller part in village life.

Higher up the social scale widows were in a similar position with respect to land. Feudal custom and the common law entitled them, on the death of their husbands, to control their inheritances, marriage portions and dowers. Magna Carta in 1215 tried to ensure that they entered into control of all three without difficulty. The growth of the common law too had helped widows, notably by providing them with two standard form legal actions. One of these enabled a widow to recover land which her husband, 'whom she could not contradict while living', had alienated from her inheritance or marriage portion; the other enabled her to recover her dower. There were parallel procedures in the towns. In fact, most widows gained their dowers without trouble, especially if the heir (from whose land it came) was a son. But problems arose when the husband had alienated the dower (often actions had to be brought against large numbers of his grantees) or where the inheritance had passed into other hands or into wardship. On the Surrey eyre of 1263 seventeen widows brought dower actions, the majority with success.

The wealthier the widow, of course, the greater the pressure to re-marry since the more valuable was the prize for a second husband (see above, pp. 89–90). In the case of widows of tenants-in-chief that pressure could come from the king, as it could come from a baron in the case of widows of under-tenants. Despite promises to the contrary in the Coronation Charter of 1100, the twelfth-century kings all forced widows into re-marriage or took large sums of money from them not to do so. In 1130 Lucy, countess of Chester, owed Henry I £333 for permission to stay single for just five years. The pressure on widows became particularly acute from the 1190s as the king's financial difficulties multiplied; Magna Carta therefore reiterated the Charter promise of 1100. This time it had real effect. While in John's sixteen-year reign 149 widows offered an average of 278 marks apiece to avoid compulsory re-marriage, the equivalent figures for the fifty-six-year reign of Henry III were forty-four widows and eighty-seven marks. Widows were freer to marry whom they wished and many perhaps were keen to do so. 'I re-married because as a weak and feeble woman I was not able and did not know how to control my dower, and my inheritance from my father, and my other rights and properties': this was how the friar Ralph Bocking imagined female thinking. After 1215, however, it was easier to take the option to remain single. Some noblewomen certainly had long widowhoods in the twelfth century, including several countesses of Chester, but the list is much longer in the thirteenth: Isabel de Forz, countess of Aumale and Devon (1260–93), Isabella, countess of Arundel (1243–82), Matilda, countess of Gloucester (1262–89), Alice, countess of Lincoln (1258–1311), Matilda de Mortimer (1282–1301) and Margaret de Lacy, countess of Lincoln and Pembroke (1245–66) are just a selection of its formidable widows.

The aim of Magna Carta in 1215 had not been to create a body of independent baronial widows. Rather, the point was to safeguard the interests of male heirs who had no wish to see their mothers' extensive lands taken away by second husbands. Yet some widows surely also enjoyed the power and freedom that came with widowhood. They administered their lands themselves and, though they often consulted their heirs, were entitled to make alienations from their inheritances and marriage portions on their own sole authority, often doing so to endow religious houses and create portions for younger children.

The career of Margaret de Lacy, studied by Louise Wilkinson, encapsulates the change between wife and widow. She was married at the age of twelve in 1221 to John de Lacy, lord of Pontefract, who was twenty-nine. The idea was for her to bring to Lacy the inheritance of her mother, Hawisia, a sister of the childless Ranulf, earl of Chester and Lincoln, an inheritance which was planned to include both the honour of Bolingbroke and the earldom of Lincoln itself. Lacy died in 1240, having indeed gained the earldom, and Margaret made a brief second marriage to Walter Marshal, earl of Pembroke, who died in 1245. After that, although holding dower thirds from two earldoms as well as her own honour of Bolingbroke, she remained unmarried until her death in 1266, when she chose to be buried not beside either of her husbands but beside her father, who had died in 1217. As a widow, with her son and heir Edmund de Lacy (born in 1230) married to one of the queen's Savoyard relations, Margaret became very close to the court. Her chief aim was to advance the interests of her family, and to do it herself. Instead of passing the honour of Bolingbroke to her son (as some widows did with their inheritances, although not legally obliged to do so), she kept it in hand and vigorously increased its lands for his ultimate benefit. She also headed the team which negotiated the marriage of her grandson Henry to the Longespee heiress, a marriage too good to be missed, despite the fact that both were children. On her son's early death in 1258, she and his widow Alice succeeded in buying the wardship of his lands from the king.

It is very much within such family contexts that the careers of noblewomen should be placed. As girl brides they were pawns, but as wives, and even more as widows, depending on age, personality and circumstance, they could play important roles in influencing and shaping family policies, exploiting the conventions of the day just as they had been exploited by them. The Coronation Charter of 1100 had given to widows (safeguarded against forced re-marriage) the custody of the lands and persons of their under-age children. It was not a promise which was kept, nor was it repeated in 1215. A century of royal exploitation meant that control over wardships was something no king would give up. If they were obtained by widows it was only occasionally and, as with the Lacys, at a price. Yet the aspiration of the 1100 Charter remains significant. There could be no better indication of the trust which was placed in women, trust in their competence to administer estates and their commitment to the future of the family.

In getting their way women made use of all possible contacts, male and female. But was there something distinctive – consciously so – in their contacts with fellow women, for example in those between Eleanor de Montfort, the prioress of Amesbury and the countesses of Devon and Lincoln? What is certain is that noblewomen were surrounded in their households by other women. When Margaret de Lacy was staying at court in September 1252, the queen gave brooches to four of her female attendants. The same was also true of wealthy townswomen. Both her servants and her wider female circle are reflected in the twenty women (double the number of men) to whom Avice de Crosseby, widow of a Lincoln citizen, made bequests in her will. In such ways women were able to shape a world of their own.

*　　*　　*

Some of the major themes emerging from discussion of the English nobility and gentry in the twelfth and thirteenth centuries are also relevant in Scotland. Scotland after all had comparable 'feudal' lordships with knightly tenants, and local government divisions (ultimately called shires) under sheriffs. When King Alexander III entered each sheriffdom on his tours of the kingdom, he was met by the sheriff and 'the chosen knights of the shire', according to Walter Bower, writing in the fifteenth century but perhaps using earlier evidence. It sounds very English. Within the feudal lordships inheritance practices were similar to those in England, as were the workings of both the nuclear and extended families. The position of noblewomen was also comparable with daughters inheriting jointly in default of sons and widows having the right to a dower third, with access to action by writ ('the brieve of terce') to obtain it. Lack of evidence, however, means there is no equivalent to the thousands of English baronial and knightly families whose histories can be worked out in detail. For that reason it is hard to chart how the relations between lords and followers changed over time. In significant ways, moreover, the framework was different from that in England. The Scottish earldoms and great provincial lordships, existing as they did outside the area of the sheriffdoms, the crown pleas and the common law, had no parallel in England. As a consequence the great Scottish lords may well have had a far tighter control of the lives of their tenants and subjects than was the case with the nobility south of the border. Equally, within the sheriffdoms there was neither the same proliferation of royal offices staffed by local men nor the same volume of common law litigation as there was in England, so the whole texture of local life was in that respect very different.

In the thirteenth century the Comyns (studied by Alan Young) provide a striking example of how an extended family group could work at the political level (see above, p. 335). The family also illustrates another important theme, one peculiar to Scotland, namely the increasing accommodation between old and new, between the old native nobility and the new nobility of Anglo-Norman descent. The Comyns originated in Normandy (though they did not come from a great noble house) and had risen in the service of the Scottish kings. In or soon after 1212 William Comyn, justiciar north of Forth, became earl of Buchan through his marriage to Marjorie, daughter of Earl Fergus. This was the first Scottish earldom to pass out of native hands, Comyn's installation being part of the king's policy to tie the north, home of challenges to the throne, more closely to the centre. To help establish his authority, Comyn founded a Cistercian abbey at Deer, an ancient monastic centre and very much within a Gaelic-speaking area, where he was buried. He and his descendants also built or re-built the castles (five ringed the earldom) from which their demesnes were administered. The surviving castles constructed by the Badenoch and Lochaber branch of the family at Lochindorb and Inverlochy show just how impressive these must have been.

However, in this new Comyn regime there was also substantial continuity with the past, in part because Buchan was already changing. Fergus, the last native earl, had himself made grants to his native followers in very much Anglo-Norman form, giving Fedderate and Ardendraught, for example, to John, son of Uhtred and his heirs, 'as any earl or lord in the Scottish realm may infeft any vassal'. Relief was to be paid, and the lord's court at Ellon to be attended three times a year – just the kind of attendance at private courts often required of knightly tenants in England. John son of Uhtred's descendants soon began to style themselves 'of Fedderate' like any linearly structured English knightly family. The witnesses to his charters shows that Fergus's entourage was composed both of native lords and knights of Anglo-Norman descent. The latter can likewise be found in the entourages of other native earls, who were certainly quite familiar with knight service and 'feudal' tenure. Thus King William the Lion granted Gilbert, son of the earl of Angus, land to be held in fee and heredity for the service of one knight 'as honourably as other knights hold their lands from me in the kingdom of Scotland'. The seals of the great native lords showed them galloping along in full armour. Their charters (like those issued by Alan of Galloway) might have come from the Scottish or English royal chanceries themselves.

If the Scottish nobility was changing, Comyn himself, in taking over the earldom, came halfway to meet it. His entourage included several men from Fergus's circle, notably the latter's illegitimate son, as well as John son of Uhtred, and Cospatric Macmedethyn. Comyn granted Cospatric land 'in fee and heredity', but such native landholders still remained 'different' from those of Anglo-Norman descent, for example in speaking Gaelic. In associating with them, Comyn in a sense was making a conscious effort to show he was 'Scots', something also reflected in the way he honoured his father-in-law by naming one son 'Fergus'. In the administration of the earldom, Comyn retained the old

Celtic judicial official of the *brithem*. He also accorded an important role to his wife. Marjorie both witnessed his charters and issued ones of her own, sometimes styling herself 'the daughter of Fergus once earl of Buchan' rather than Comyn's wife, thus stressing her independent status. It was such co-operation at the local level which underpinned the universal Scottishness emerging in the thirteenth century (discussed in chapter 1).

That Scottishness was, however, perfectly compatible with members of the nobility retaining an English identity as well, something exemplified in the history of the Comyns. At first sight they appear very much a family based in northern Scotland, but this is misleading. In 1264 the marriage of Alexander, second earl of Buchan, to one of the heiresses of the Quincy earls of Winchester and lords of Galloway brought properties throughout England to add to those in Tynedale which the family had held since the twelfth century. Alexander was reluctant to travel south, but the importance he attached to the English properties is shown by the way, long before his death, he granted some of the most valuable to his eldest son. All this was part of a wider pattern, and one very different from that in the twelfth century. Henry I had prevented cross-border landholding. Now it was extensive, and constantly renewed through intermarriage. In 1243 the Umfravilles of Prudhoe in Northumberland gained the Scottish earldom of Angus. The Bruces of Annandale likewise substantially increased their English estates. Indeed, according to one story, it was on the family manor of Writtle in Essex that the future king, Robert Bruce, was born. According to Keith Stringer's calculations, nine of Scotland's earldoms and half its provincial lordships were held at some time between 1200 and 1296 by lords who also held estates in England. Conversely, fourteen of the twenty-seven baronies in Northumberland and Cumberland were held in the same period by lords who held land in Scotland. In 1290, all told there were thirty lords and forty religious houses with significant holdings on either side of the border.

Facilitated by the meshing of the economies, these links were both cause and consequence of the political peace which illuminated Anglo-Scottish relations in the thirteenth century. There was no problem about a great Anglo-Scottish baron, John de Vesci, leading Alexander III's punitive expedition to Man in 1275 and commanding Edward I's forces in Anglesey two years later. At Alnwick, Vesci founded a hospital on the spot where his great-great-great-great-grandfather King

Malcolm of Scotland was killed in 1093. (Vesci's grandmother was an illegitimate daughter of King William the Lion.) He also preserved at Alnwick a silver reliquary containing the foot of Simon de Montfort, with whom he had fought at Evesham. With his great bases at Alnwick and Sprouston straddling the border, Vesci was very much a northerner, but his mother had also inherited Kildare in Ireland and Caerleon in Wales. He himself died in the service of Edward I in Gascony. His body was brought back for burial at Alnwick, while his heart eventually rested beside that of Edward I's Castilian queen at Blackfriars in London. Such nobles were genuinely Anglo-Scottish and were also part of a much wider world.

* * *

In Wales the great marcher baronies were not unlike the earldoms and provincial lordships of Scotland. Compact in size, beyond the remit of the sheriffs, and with the common law writs running (if they ran at all) in the name of the lord and initiating actions in his courts, the tenants of such lordships were certainly subject to much tighter control than anywhere in England, hence Richard de Clare's ability to deprive Richard Seward of his lands in Glamorgan, for all the latter's appeal to the king. Within native Wales, the cantref and commote, were comparable to administrative divisions in England and royal Scotland, but the structures of society were very different. There was no equivalent to the English and to some extent Scottish hierarchy of barons, knights, freemen and unfree peasants. Below the ruling families, the only distinction recognized by Welsh law books was that between the free and the unfree, all the former being noble. The free gave dues and renders to the ruler, including military service, and lived off the labour and renders of the unfree. Free land, moreover, was very much family land, partible among all the sons and grandsons, and inalienable, according to the Welsh law books, without consent of the kin. The reality of that was reflected in the way native grants to Margam abbey frequently mentioned such consent. The structure of the family was thus much more extended than in England. After the Conquest, Edward I accepted the continuation of partibility, and very different customs over inheritance were one reason why the marcher baronies, for legal purposes, became divided into Englishries and Welshries.

However, changes were taking place. Within Welsh society there was pressure to reduce the role of kin, especially when it came to liability for crime. The men of Ceri 'both great and small' asked Henry III to grant them the 'law of the king's lands' so that, in contrast to Welsh law, the kindred would no longer bear the responsibility if a member committed murder, theft or sedition. There was also a blurring of the distinction between free and unfree families as some of the former were reduced in wealth by the division of their lands between numerous heirs, and some of the latter elevated in status by the commutation into money rents of labour services. Llywelyn ap Gruffudd's insistence that both 'nobles' and 'rustics and *ignobiles*' work together in repairing his court buildings shows he thought them much on a par, although the protests reveal how cherished noble status was. Occasionally, as in England, the unfree were able to rise in the world. One Meirionydd bondman, Heylin ap Roger, paid for permission to leave his home in Tal-y-bont, and by 1292–3 was the wealthiest taxpayer in the village of Tywyn.

Most striking of all, at least in the upper levels of society, were the changes in the area of marriage. Here reforming ecclesiastics had long expressed horror at the Welsh situation. Instead of being solemnized and overseen by the church, marriage was an entirely secular affair, as the numerous provisions concerning it in the law books demonstrate. It was common within the prohibited degrees and, under Welsh law, could be ended for a whole variety of reasons, including adultery and bad breath. Failure to produce heirs was probably another accepted ground. When it came to inheritance, the law placed both legitimate and illegitimate offspring on the same footing, which reflected widespread concubinage and also the practice (referred to by Gerald of Wales) of marriage only once a woman had proved herself to be fertile.

In the twelfth century Owain Gwynedd and the Lord Rhys both married first cousins, the former braving Becket's resulting excommunication. The succession to Gwynedd after Owain's death in 1165 was disputed between his sons, both legitimate and illegitimate. Around the turn of the century, however, practices were beginning to change, in part thanks to Llywelyn the Great's desire to create and secure the future of his own dynasty. In 1203 he was careful to obtain papal sanction for a possible marriage to a daughter of the king of Man. In 1222 he got the pope to confirm his ordinance giving the succession to his legitimate son, notwithstanding the 'detestable' Welsh custom which put legitimate and illegitimate sons on the same footing. A growing number of high-status Anglo-Welsh marriages began to take place, which must presumably have been in ecclesiastically acceptable form. All the rulers of Gwynedd and southern Powys in the thirteenth century married royal or English baronial women. Llywelyn the Great married all four of his daughters to English barons, two of them twice over.

These developments were bound to have repercussions on the Welsh when marrying among themselves. When in 1273 Owain ap Maredudd of Ceredigion married Angharad from the ruling house of Cedewain it was the possibility of separation 'by the church' that he mentioned, although he then hedged his bets and added 'or by any other event'. The Welsh law books themselves reflected a state of flux. One passage defiantly rejected 'church law' and asserted the equality of legitimate and illegitimate offspring; another accepted that Llywelyn's ruling had altered the situation and that the law was now contradictory; yet another simply upheld the church view of marriage and inheritance. There were also signs of change in the position of women. Here Welsh law had allowed women to take the initiative in 'parting', but in contrast to the situation in England and Scotland there was no such thing as female inheritance. In default of sons, the patrimony was simply divided among the wider male kin. Therefore there were neither women heiresses nor the great widows so characteristic of thirteenth-century England. Women did not generally hold land at all. On marriage, provision both by their kin and their husbands took the form (with some exceptions) of goods, and it was a share of the goods which a woman would take away when widowed or separated. One passage in the law books, however, admittedly a solitary instance, spoke of female inheritance in default of a male heir; this was clearly influenced by English practice, and when Owain ap Maredudd married Angharad he granted her the commote of Anhuniog, effectively as dower. Such arrangements may well have been common at that level of society, although the practice of providing for wives and widows by the concession of movable goods was deep rooted, and was another reason for the division into Englishries and Welshries.

These changes in inheritance and marriage were part of a broader transformation in which the society, economy and politics of Wales were gaining more in common with those of England. In their handwriting and phraseology the charters of the minor Welsh rulers resembled those of English lesser magnates. The charters of the rulers of Gwynedd were similar to those of English earls and the king. There was also some equivalent in Wales to the English country gentry. In Meirionydd in 1292-3 there were about seventy to eighty substantial *uchelwyr*, that is important leaders of local society. They supplied the holders of local office and each had movable property assessed at £10 or more, being thus as wealthy as at least minor members of the English gentry. These men were not knights but then, given the decline in numbers, neither were their counterparts in England. Higher up the social scale the ethos of knighthood was important. Like the barons of England, it was as mounted knights that the Welsh rulers appeared on their seals. Indeed they had done so from the very first seal of a Welsh ruler to survive, that of King Cadell ap Gruffudd of Deheubarth of *c.* 1150. Within the marcher lordships of the south, the process by which some of the native ruling families, like that of Afan in Glamorgan, abandoned claims to independent status, took up knighthood, sported coats of arms and integrated themselves into the workings of the lordship had begun by the mid thirteenth century. Under the exigent rule of the Clares such transformations were probably a condition of survival, but that the native nobility enjoyed the world of chivalric culture is demonstrated by versions of Chrétien de Troyes's Arthurian romances appearing in that classic collection of Welsh epics known as *The Mabinogion*. And perhaps not all Welshmen needed translations, for some of the business letters of the Welsh rulers in the later thirteenth century (like such letters in England) begin to appear in French. Another reflection of chivalric attitudes amongst the elite lay in the field of political conduct. Murder and mutilation as a political weapon were largely replaced in the course of the twelfth century by imprisonment. After 1216, although hopelessly fragmented, not a single member of the Deheubarth dynasty was killed or mutilated by a rival; between 1071 and 1116 no less than seven had been. In this area, the Welsh were now just as 'civilized' as the English.

*   *   *

In October 1265 Queen Margaret of France, wife of Louis IX, wrote to King Henry III. She was, she said, hastening the arrival of her sister to England lest Henry, tired of waiting, should marry someone else, perhaps, she went on to hint, the countess of Gloucester. Margaret was, of course, joking. Her sister, Eleanor of Provence, had been married to Henry since 1236 and was now returning to England after her exile during the Montfortian war. The letter reveals the closeness of the family ties which linked the French and English courts. It also reflects the shared attitudes and values which made such 'in' jokes possible. Despite the loss of Normandy in 1204, despite some laughter at the way the English spoke French, a common culture bound the secular and religious elites of Britain, in varying degrees, to the rest of western Europe. The closeness of the connection with both France and Italy was epitomized in Britain's greatest church, the new abbey constructed by Henry III at Westminster between 1245 and 1269 in honour of his patron saint, Edward the Confessor. Built partly in stone from Caen in Normandy, the radiating chapels around the sanctuary, the censing angels, smiling and humane, in the south transept, and the forms of the lancet windows, from which the 'decorated' style of tracery spread throughout Britain, had their exemplars at Rheims, France's coronation cathedral. It was from there that Westminster's architect, Master Henry de Rheims, had come. The shrine of the Confessor, the tomb of Henry III and the great pavement before the High Altar were Italian, constructed from coloured porphyry stones taken from the buildings of antiquity by the Italian Cosmati family. The stones and craftsmen to make the pavement were brought to England by the abbot of Westminster, Richard Ware, after a visit to the papal court. The spread of papal government of the church and the wider development of ecclesiastical organization, discussed in the next chapter, were themselves important factors in homogenizing the different parts of Britain and integrating them with Europe.

14

Church, Religion, Literacy and Learning

In the two centuries after 1066 the face of Europe was transformed by the growing power of the papacy. Its supreme authority was clarified and proclaimed in the new study of theology and canon law. Its ability to govern the western church was established through new administrative structures. In the course of the twelfth century England, Scotland and Wales became fully integrated into this papal world. The consequences for secular politics and ecclesiastical life were profound.

It was to the papacy the rulers of Gwynedd appealed in the thirteenth century to settle the succession of the principality and complain about the oppressions of Edward I. Likewise it was to the pope that the kings of Scotland sent, if unavailingly, to ask permission for a full coronation. In the politics of England, in part because King John had made the kingdom a papal fief, the role played by the pope and his legates was as remarkable as it was usually constructive. After John's death the ultimate authority in temporal affairs of the legates, Guala and Pandulf (1216–21), was universally accepted by the king's party. Guala, with the regent William Marshal, sealed the new versions of Magna Carta in 1216 and 1217, while Pandulf, after the regent's death in 1219, issued the crucial order giving control of day-to-day government to the justiciar Hubert de Burgh. Henry III never forgot his debt to the papacy, hence in part his trusting and disastrous entanglement with the pope over the affairs of Sicily. During the subsequent period of reform and rebellion both sides constantly made their case at Rome, the papal bull quashing the Provisions of Oxford being central to Henry III's temporary recovery of power in 1261. Subsequently Gui Foulquois, legate in 1263–4 and later Pope Clement IV, fulminated against Montfort's regime, while his successor, Ottobuono, later Pope Adrian V, laboured wisely and indefatigably to restore peace to the country after Montfort's death. He also played a key role in negotiations between England and Wales, issuing the letter which proclaimed the Treaty of Montgomery in 1267.

The involvement of the papacy in British politics was in large measure a response to demand. That was equally true of the growing part played by the papacy in ecclesiastical government, especially when it came to the dispensation of justice. The background here was the acceptance that there were certain categories of plea which were the concern of the church, not the state. In England since before the Conquest that had been true of moral and spiritual causes concerning such things as marriage, adultery and wills. The settlement after the Becket dispute had likewise subjected criminous clerks to ecclesiastical jurisdiction (see above, p. 208). In the course of the twelfth century the division between church and state was also clarified when it came to disputes over property. Those over advowsons, the right to appoint parish priests, were to go to secular courts, and one of Henry II's assizes, that of 'darrein presentment', was introduced to hear them. Cases over the property (and there was a large amount of it) which the church held for secular services, that is for rents or knight service, were also the preserve of the state. On the other hand property granted 'in free alms' and held simply for spiritual services was the concern of church, as were questions of ecclesiastical jurisdiction and disputes over elections to abbacies and bishoprics.

A considerable body of these ecclesiastical cases could be settled in the court of the bishop, but the growing awareness of papal authority encouraged reference to Rome either in the first instance or on appeal. Cases of major importance, especially over elections, were heard at the curia itself, but in more routine cases the pope's response to appeals was to appoint local 'judges delegate' who would hear the cases back in Britain; one of the first know examples followed an appeal made by Bishop Urban of Llandaff in 1132. More than anything else in the twelfth and thirteenth centuries it was the growing flood of appeals to Rome and consequent appointment of judges delegate to hear them which (as Jane Sayers has put it) bound the provinces to Rome and Rome to the provinces. Many such cases were between ecclesiastics and involved conflicts over jurisdiction, and property. Important laymen resorted to the pope in disputes over marriages and wills, while knights and many smaller fry frequently appeared before judges delegate in cases over land, tithes and parochial jurisdiction. A large part of the life of the country was embraced by the apparatus of papal government.

If the papal role in the dispensation of justice, like the growth of the

English common law, was a reaction to local demand, that was not the case in two other areas where, from the late twelfth century, the pope became more directly involved in dealing with both the British and the wider European church: these areas were taxation and provisions. In asserting his right to tax the church the pope was able to reach a *modus vivendi* with the king of England because taxation was often – notably in the case of the Sicilian affair – for joint royal and papal purposes. That did not, however, make it other than deeply unpopular with the church. Even more unpopular was the way the pope asserted his right to provide, in effect to appoint, where necessary or convenient, candidates to ecclesiastical office. Here he could certainly come into conflict with kings, especially when he intervened in disputes over elections to bishoprics, the case of Canterbury under King John being the classic example. Later, both John of Cheam, bishop of Glasgow (1259–68), and John Pecham, archbishop of Canterbury (1279–92), were provided against royal wishes. But since the pope also allowed many royal candidates, both in England and Scotland, to reach the episcopal bench, here too accommodation was possible. The real unpopularity of provisions came lower down the scale, when the pope appointed his officials and relatives to parish churches and to cathedral and other canonries. Those provided were usually absentees, simply taking the revenues. If they did show up, as Italians they would not speak the language. In either case, they had prevented the patrons, bishops, abbots, abbesses, and lay lords (in the case of parish churches), from appointing their own candidates. Resentment was inevitably tinged with hostility to foreigners. In 1232 there were attacks led by the Yorkshire knight Robert Tweng, on the property and persons of Italian appointees in several parts of England. In 1245 complaints about provisions were loudly voiced by the English delegation at the papal council at Lyons. The general venality of the papal court made matters worse; 'oiling palms, not singing psalms' was often thought to be the way to make progress there. The papacy was well aware of the unpopularity of provisions and often tried to limit their number, yet it had to support its officials, as it also required money to defend its independence from the Hohenstaufens and other enemies in Italy. These were the necessary conditions for the fulfilment of its primary purpose, the purpose of the whole church: the cure or care of souls.

If that mission were to be fulfilled, all committed ecclesiastics agreed that the church needed reform. Equally, whatever the criticisms, no one could doubt that since the mid eleventh century the papacy itself had been reform's standard-bearer. To that end under both William the Conqueror and Henry I (in 1125) it had despatched legates to England who had presided over reforming councils. Similarly in the thirteenth century, councils were held by the legates Otto (1238–41) and Ottobuono (1265–8). The commissions of both covered the whole of Britain. Otto held a council in Scotland, while representatives from the Scottish church attended Ottobuono's great assembly in London in 1268.

Even more important for papal leadership of reform were the great central councils in which the pope brought together the whole of the Catholic church. These were the Third Lateran Council of 1179 and the Fourth of 1215, the latter attended by nine bishops from England, four from Scotland and two from Wales. In a modern English translation the seventy-one decrees of the Fourth Lateran Council run to thirty-three closely printed pages. The need for such legislation was intensified by changing ideas about the spiritual life of ordinary people, ideas which made the business of the cure of souls all the more difficult.

Part of the background here related to the concept of the afterlife. Both the Bible and the visions of holy men revealed how, on death, one's soul might either descend to the torments of Hell, like the rich man in the Dives and Lazarus parable, or (like Lazarus himself) be carried away by angels into Abraham's bosom, the state of bliss or Paradise enjoyed by the righteous. In either condition one awaited the reunion with the body and the ultimate agony or ecstasy brought by the Last Judgement. What though of the general run of men and women who deserved neither Paradise nor Hell? Here Paris theologians after 1170, following on from St Bernard, developed and popularized the idea of a definite place between the two, namely Purgatory. Certainly one was punished there, but the very idea of purgation implied hope. One might move up through the stations of Purgatory, and perhaps even escape altogether and reach Paradise. One English friar, Warin of Orwell, was said to have 'passed through Purgatory without delay and gone to the Lord Jesus Christ'. If such were the possibilities it became crucially important to consider how they could be realized, and one way at least of shortening the time in Purgatory was through proper confession and penance here on earth.

In regulations which opened up a new pastoral mission for the church and potentially transformed the life of the laity, the Fourth Lateran Council decreed that 'everyone of either sex' should confess all their sins at least once a year to their own priest and strive to perform the penance then enjoined. Penance before 1215 had often been imposed on a tariff basis with fixed penalties for various types of sin. Now the ideal was that it should be varied by the priest in accordance with the needs of each individual as discovered in the confessional. The priest was to be 'like a practised doctor pouring wine and oil on the wounds of the injured, diligently inquiring into both the circumstances of the sinner and the sin'.

The Fourth Lateran Council's injunction about confession and penance was immediately followed by the statement that all Christians were to receive 'with reverence' the sacrament of the eucharist at least every Easter. The stress here upon the eucharist reflected the way the notion of transubstantiation, as developed in the twelfth century, had, in the words of Miri Rubin, 'turned communion into an enormous event'. By attending the daily Mass every Christian could 'see his God on earth every day', see him at the moment when the bread was elevated by the priest and 'transubstantiated into the real body of Christ', to quote passages from English diocesan legislation of the 1220s and 1230s. When communion was actually taken, the body of God was not merely seen but actually tasted. This supreme experience was not to be assayed lightly and was closed to anyone in a state of sin, unlike attendance at Mass itself. Consequently, the decree of the Fourth Lateran Council directly linked communion with confession and indicated that for the laity both might perhaps take place only once a year.

The responsibilities all this placed on the priest were awesome. He alone could act as a confessor. He alone could perform the miracle of turning the bread and wine into the body and blood of Christ. As a confessor, he represented the church at its most personal and individual. As a celebrant of the communion he represented it at its most universal, the same ritual being performed every day throughout the parishes, abbeys and cathedrals of Catholic Europe. The basic structures governing the life of the local priest were comparable throughout Britain and Europe and had both strengths and weaknesses. During the twelfth century Scotland and Wales had followed England in gaining episcopal dioceses (ten and four respectively) with defined territorial limits and regular succession of bishops. The Scottish bishops had no metropolitan head and were accountable directly to the pope. In England, where there were fourteen dioceses, Durham and Carlisle (together with Galloway in Scotland) came under the metropolitan authority of York. The other English dioceses were subject to Canterbury, as were the dioceses in Wales, Llandaff and St Davids in the south and Bangor and St Asaphs in the north. By 1200 the English dioceses were divided into archdeaconries, rural deaneries and parishes. A similar structure was developing in Wales and Scotland. By 1300 St Andrews was fairly typical of a prosperous British diocese. It was composed of two archdeaconries and seven deaneries, and had 124 parishes.

In some ways this was an impressive structure which enabled the life of the parish to be monitored by a hierarchy of officials. Yet it had serious defects. Since it was often the local lord who had built and endowed the church around which the parish was formed, he naturally appointed the cleric, the rector, who ruled it. As a result the right of appointment (the advowson) was in diverse hands: king, baron, knight, bishop or monastery, the last because it was with advowsons that many monasteries were endowed. The rector derived his income from the land attached to the church (in England, the glebe) and also from the right to a tenth of the produce from the parish's land (the tithe). It was King David's order that tithe ('tiend') be paid in Scotland, which really initiated the parochial system there. Often these resources made rectors very wealthy, many (according to thirteenth-century valuations) having incomes of £15 a year and upwards, £15 being the minimum level at which a layman qualified for knighthood. It was this situation which produced the great evil which bedevilled the medieval church: the appointment to livings of men simply not interested in the cure of souls. Patrons frequently regarded the advowson as simply an item of property with which they could support clerical servants and relations, which was why disputes over advowsons were the business of the secular courts. In many cases such appointees drew the income and rarely went near the parish, hence the scandal of non-residence. Some indeed gathered a whole clutch of livings, hence the scandal of 'pluralism'; and there was yet another scandal, the failure of many rectors to take the trouble to become priests at all – hardly necessary if they had no intention of doing the job. Instead they remained in minor orders. Another variant was when monasteries 'appropriated' the churches of which they had been granted the advowsons and took over the entire revenues for themselves. In all these cases the parishes were run by a motley assortment of deputies, vicars and chaplains, living on pittances, often ill-educated, and not up to the job. Gerald of Wales laughed at priests who confused Barnabas and Barabbas and Judas and St Jude!

The value of livings could also have a rather different tendency, namely to encourage a married and hereditary priesthood, two further evils stigmatized by reformers, although such priests could sometimes be effective pastors.

It was these problems, Europe wide, which the Fourth Lateran Council faced up to, issuing a series of decrees designed to secure an educated, resident, remunerated, continent and committed priesthood; one which did not, as the decrees said, play dice, frequent mimes and taverns, and stay up at night gossiping and feasting. The efforts made by English bishops after 1215 to put these decrees into practice is one of the most impressive features of the thirteenth-century church. At first sight the extent of such activity might seem surprising, given the number of royal servants on the episcopal bench. Although in theory bishops were to be freely elected by the canons or monks attached to their cathedrals, in practice such electing bodies, willingly or unwillingly, often took full account of the wishes of the king. So, as we have said, did the pope if he intervened. As a result, between 1215 and 1272 twenty-two of the seventy-eight bishops appointed in England were royal officials associated with the wardrobe, chancery, exchequer or law courts. In fact, however, very few of these men were simply uninterested in reform. Many left royal service on their appointment, a striking indication of how powerful reforming ideas had become. Thanks in part to their training in government, they were often efficient diocesans. They also (though not always) helped to secure the co-operation between church and state on which such work depended. The king also acknowledged the need for bishops whose background was ecclesiastical. Eight of the seventy-eight bishops appointed between 1215 and 1272 were monks, while as many as forty had university degrees and some were celebrated scholars. The latter were particularly significant in linking the church to wider intellectual currents in Europe. Paris scholars included Richard le Poore, bishop of Salisbury and Durham (1217–28–37) and Thomas Cantilupe, bishop of Hereford (1275–83). Nicholas of Farnham, bishop of Durham (1241–9) had taught medicine at Bologna, Alexander Stavensby, bishop of Coventry (1224–38) theology at Toulouse, and John de Pontoise, bishop of Winchester (1282–1304) civil law at Modena. Pontoise was a Frenchman provided to Winchester by the pope. Throughout the thirteenth century a leaven of foreigners reached the English episcopal bench, in part thanks to Henry III's patronage of his wife's Savoyard kin. Boniface of Savoy, archbishop of Canterbury from 1245 to 1270, was no scholar but, by turns high-handed and honey-tongued, he vigorously defended ecclesiastical privileges, paid off his predecessor's debts and reached sensible compromises in disputes over archiepiscopal jurisdiction. His will made separate provision for his burial depending on whether he died in England, France or either side of the Alps.

In their efforts to carry through reform after 1215, the bishops were, of course, building on the work of their predecessors. When the Fourth Lateran Council urged proper examination of those chosen for the cure of souls it was essentially reinforcing existing practice. From at least the mid twelfth century English bishops had been asserting the right to institute those appointed to livings, which meant they could reject those unqualified. Some of Henry II's best bishops, notably Gilbert Foliot of London, Roger of Worcester and Bartholomew of Exeter, took their duty to find suitable priests extremely seriously. Bishops in the same period were also (again anticipating the decrees of the Council) beginning to set up 'vicarages' by stipulating that where a living had been appropriated by a monastic house, a 'perpetual' vicar was to be appointed to run the parish with a decent and fixed portion of its revenues. Archbishops were also beginning to hold synods for the whole of their provinces. Archbishop Richard of Canterbury's was the first in 1175, and it promulgated a whole series of reforming decrees. How far individual bishops were holding diocesan synods in the twelfth century is unclear, but they became characteristic features of the thirteenth century, when they were usually held annually. The decrees promulgated at his synod by Richard le Poore, bishop of Salisbury around 1219, based on those of the Third and Fourth Lateran Councils, were widely copied by other bishops. They had 114 clauses and encompass thirty-seven modern printed pages. The bishops were also far from issuing simply a series of 'dont's'. With the Statutes of the Coventry and Lichfield diocese was circulated a tract on confession and penance, part of a large body of literature to help the priest in this fundamental area.

The work of the bishops at their best was seen in the largest of all the English dioceses, that of Lincoln. Two of its bishops had extraordinary qualities. The first, Hugh of Avalon (1186–1200), was made a saint, and the second, Robert Grosseteste (1235–53) deserved to be. Both were outsiders. Hugh was a Burgundian whom Henry II in his pious final phase had plucked from the only Carthusian monastery in England, at Witham. Grosseteste was an Englishman from a lowly background who had studied at the provincial schools of Lincoln and Cambridge and perhaps also at Paris. He had then worked as a humble diocesan administrator before becoming a pre-eminent teacher of theology at Oxford. Both men were elderly on reaching the episcopate, yet were utterly fearless in putting the cure of souls before everything else. Both urged worldly ecclesiastics (like Hubert Walter and William Ralegh) to devote themselves to spiritual matters. Both showed deep respect for women. Both agonized over appointments and rejected candidates they thought unsuitable, infuriating the king. Few could have imitated Hugh's courage when he got hold of King Richard and shook him until his wrath subsided into laughter. Hugh also initiated the work which led to the complete rebuilding of his cathedral in the thirteenth century, golden in its oolitic limestone, inspirational on its ridge above the Lincolnshire plain.

Yet Hugh was more tolerant and less organized than Grosseteste, a reflection of their contrasting personalities and of the growth of administration and learning between the twelfth century and the thirteenth. 'Three things are needed for bodily health, food, sleep and a joke,' remarked Grosseteste, but it was Hugh who made the jokes. 'Well, I won't be the water for him to drink,' he laughed when reminded that Richard I thirsted for gold as a hydropsical man for water. The combination of righteous passion, threats, ingenuity and learning seen in Grosseteste's correspondence with William Ralegh over bastardy (so powerful that one has an almost physical sense of his presence on the page) was quite foreign to Hugh's humane and humorous nature. Hugh was much in demand as a judge delegate, but at heart disliked business, refusing to attend the hearing of his own accounts. Grosseteste, in contrast, composed a series of rules to guide the countess of Lincoln (Margaret de Lacy) in the administration of her household. He likewise innovated when it came to the visitation of his diocese.

Visitations of their dioceses to teach and inspect the local clergy became a key weapon in the thirteenth-century bishop's armoury. Yet when Grosseteste visited as bishop of Lincoln he was told he was innovating, his predecessors having simply inspected the religious houses in the diocese. In fact conscientious bishops in the twelfth and earlier centuries, like Wulfstan of Worcester (1062–95), had gone out to preach, confirm, and dedicate churches. Lanfranc himself, when based on his manors, had inspected the neighbouring clergy. What was new, and an important change, was the formality and organization of such visitations. In each rural deanery Grosseteste summoned before him the clergy and people. He himself preached to the former, while the friars preached to the latter, and heard confessions and enjoined penances. At these meetings in each deanery Grosseteste issued statutes governing the life of the clergy: they were to know and expound the ten commandments, seven sins, seven sacraments, and what was needed for the sacrament of true confession and penance. They were also to attend to prayer and the reading of the scriptures, visit the sick day and night, teach the people to bow at the elevation of the host and the boys (girls are not mentioned) the rudiments of the faith. They were also, of course, to be resident, in proper orders, strangers to taverns and dice, and both unmarried and without 'suspicious' women in their houses. Such injunctions were typical of diocesan legislation of the period. Hugh's own statutes were perfunctory in comparison.

Setting off these stars were other effective Lincoln bishops. Grosseteste's predecessor, Hugh of Wells (1209–35), was a former chancery clerk, yet he devoted himself to his diocese, and initiated what is the earliest surviving bishop's register, with one section devoted to his activity in setting up vicarages, another to instituting rectors and vicars. Such a record was clearly important as a safeguard against pluralism. It also shows Hugh rejecting appointees on grounds of insufficient learning or accepting them on condition they continued to study. A later bishop, Oliver Sutton (1280–99), gained the see by means of family connections, but was 'a man most just, most steadfast and most pure' (as his registrar put it), spending almost all his time in ceaseless visitations of his diocese. Below such visitations in Lincoln and elsewhere, an important role fell to the archdeacon who was supposed to make his own checks on the local clergy, holding general meetings in each deanery once every four weeks.

How effective these efforts were in improving the standing of the parish priest and by extension the spiritual life of his flock is impossible to measure. Records of visitations and of the procedures in decanal courts reveal a depressing round of whippings imposed on the laity for sexual misconduct, though only on the lower classes (it was 'not seemly for a knight to do public penance'). A married and hereditary priesthood does seem to have slowly disappeared from England in the course of the twelfth and thirteenth centuries, for what that was worth. Great strides were certainly made in setting up vicarages where livings had been appropriated by monasteries, but vicars employed by other rectors, together with the crowd of clerks and chaplains serving in many parishes, were less well provided for. Such clerks (not in priests' orders), moreover, were often married. Of the nearly 2,000 candidates for institution to benefices examined by Hugh of Wells, the majority do not seem to have been priests and thus cannot have functioned as such in their parishes, unless they subsequently took orders. When a visitation took place in part of Kent after Archbishop Pecham's death in 1292, only one of nineteen parishes passed muster completely. Six of the rectors were absentees (as were some of the vicars), four of them 'doing no good in the parish'. The fact was that, as all the legislation acknowledged, it was possible to get dispensation from the pope to be non-resident and also to hold livings in plurality. Despite Pecham's valiant efforts in the area it was impossible to insist that all rectors were priests. The idea that the income from parish churches should support clerks working for, or just connected with, pope, bishops, king and nobles was simply too deeply ingrained to be overthrown. Grosseteste, who did put the cure of souls before anything else, came into conflict over appointments with the pope and fellow bishops as well as with the king.

It may be wrong, however, to paint too gloomy a picture. Even if many of those he instituted to livings were non-resident, it is still significant that Hugh of Wells only rejected for lack of learning 100 of his nearly 2,000 candidates. Visitation records were themselves designed to criticize, not commend. Literary sources can sometimes give a very different picture. At Haselbury in Somerset around 1125 the priest Brictric spent days and nights praying and singing psalms in his church. His wife, Godida, made vestments for the services. After clerical marriage became impossible, some at least of the 'suspicious women' found by visitations in priests' houses may have been worthy successors of these good clergy wives. If their children could no longer follow in the living (as did the son of Brictric and Godida), perhaps they worked as chaplains within their fathers' parishes and as incumbents elsewhere. Chaucer's parson was poor, yet learned and charitable. He preached the gospel, visited the sick, and was generally 'rich in holy thought and work'. There may well have been many like him in the twelfth and thirteenth centuries.

Within the English church there was a positive desire to help with the work of reform elsewhere in Britain. In 1214 Lincoln cathedral prepared a digest of its customs for the Scottish church of Moray. The progress of reform in Scotland and Wales is, however, even harder to trace than in England. Certainly there were Scottish bishops active in the cause. David de Bernham, chamberlain of King Alexander II, followed the path of many English royal clerks by resigning to concentrate on diocesan affairs when he became a bishop. At St Andrews (1240–53) he issued statutes which showed the familiar concern to secure parishes run by incumbents who were celibate, resident and ordained. A provincial council in 1242 sought to endow vicarages with a fixed income (of ten marks), a particularly necessary measure in Scotland where possibly half the parishes were appropriated to religious institutions.

In Wales too there were particular problems, one being that livings were divided between large numbers of 'portionists', a consequence of the partibility of inheritances sanctioned by Welsh law. Not surprisingly, the general impression from Meirionydd's tax returns of the 1290s is that the local clergy were grindingly poor. The problem of hereditary succession to livings was also acute; priests were either married or had mistresses, it hardly mattered which because in Welsh law sons born in or out of wedlock were treated equally. Welsh law also made marriage a secular contract and one very easily ended by a form of divorce. Far from universally rebelling against all this, Welsh clerics were involved in producing the thirteenth-century law books which contained such uncanonical passages and were clearly in sympathy with their sentiments. And why not? If Gerald of Wales condemned the marriage practices of the Welsh, he also extolled their fervent piety. In the twelfth century, the religious community at Llanbadarn Fawr by Aberystwyth was a family enterprise, and notable both for its learning and pastoral concern. Attitudes, however, were changing. The way the ruling families in thirteenth-century Wales made their marriage practices more 'respectable' had already been noted (see above, p. 427). The Welsh law books themselves did not all sing to the same tune and some accepted the canon law ban on clerical marriage. Although we know little of their activities, there were bishops whose whole background must have made them committed reformers: Thomas Wallensis of St Davids (1248–55), for example, was a scholar of international repute who had been an archdeacon in the Lincoln diocese under Grosseteste. Admittedly, when Archbishop Pecham visited Wales after the Edwardian conquest he still lamented the portionary churches, and considered the clergy the most ignorant he had met. But then he was scarcely uncritical about the situation in England either.

Throughout Britain the struggle to reform the state of the local clergy was, therefore, hard and unending. It is when we turn attention instead to the monastic and religious orders that the picture appears brighter. Certainly the phenomenal spread of those orders between the eleventh and thirteenth centuries revolutionized the religious and social face of Britain, as it did that of the rest of western Europe.

In 1066 there were around forty-five Benedictine monasteries in Britain, none of them north of the Wash or west of the Severn. In Wales and Scotland there were *clas* and Culdee churches, but these were organized more like old English minsters than Benedictine monasteries (see above, pp. 115, 122). The immediate effect of the Conquest was to re-invigorate the English houses and massively enrich continental ones with English and Welsh resources. The new nobility also began at increasing pace to found houses in England and Wales, some independent, some daughter houses of individual continental monasteries, some (like the priory at Lewes) part of the great order of Cluny. In 1150 ninety-five Benedictine and Cluniac houses had been founded in Britain since 1066, nineteen of them in Wales. The movement had embraced the north of England and also been taken (by the royal family) in a small way into Scotland. The English and Welsh monasteries, initially at least, were very much houses of conquest, situated close to castles and proclaiming that the new nobility had come to stay. Like the priory founded by the Clares at Clare and later moved a short distance to Stoke to be less cheek by jowl with the castle, they often helped to foster a sense of community between lord and tenants.

There were also impelling spiritual reasons for such foundations, beyond, that is, merely giving thanks in a general way for the Conquest. Monks were very clear that life in the world was sinful, especially for knights habituated to violence. The way to be saved was by embracing the monastic profession. Confronted by these arguments, many knights became monks. The transition was eased by parallels between the professions because entrants exchanged 'the belt of knighthood in the secular world for the military service of a monk in a monastery', as the Selby abbey chronicler put it. Some did so in health, others when approaching death. They also placed their sons and daughters in monasteries as child oblates, hence the close relationship between many monasteries and the surrounding nobility and gentry. Becoming a monk was thus one solution. Another (and the two were not mutually exclusive) was actually to found or endow a monastery. This secured the services of monks offering prayers for the donor's soul and constituted a great act of alms-giving; 'alms extinguisheth sin as water does fire', remarked the monk bishop Herbert Losinga.

This spiritual dimension explains the phenomenal success of the Cistercians. Founded at Cîteaux in Burgundy in 1098 and energized by Bernard of Clairvaux (St Bernard), by the 1150s there were over 300 houses throughout Europe. The first English house was founded in 1128 at Waverley in Surrey, being followed in the early 1130s by Rievaulx and Fountains in Yorkshire. A period of dramatic growth then followed, the result being the establishment of some eighty-five houses in Britain, including nineteen from the order of Savigny which merged with the Cistercians in 1147. Of the total, thirteen were in Scotland and fifteen in Wales, the major expansion in England being over by 1152 and in Britain generally by 1201. The Cistercians were born of a burning desire to practise the Benedictine rule in all its intended austerity, solitude and simplicity, shorn of the comforts, worldliness and liturgical accretions found in many contemporary houses. As so often in the history of monks and friars, it seemed far easier to found a new order than to reform an old one. The Cistercians, however, hoped to preserve their purity through rules and organization. Each monastery was inspected annually by the house from which it had been founded. The governing body was the general chapter held every year at Cîteaux, which had to be attended by all the abbots. Cistercian churches were to be plain, without triforiums and elaborate sculptures, while the houses were to be founded preferably in regions wild and remote. Another unique feature enabled such wastes to be managed and the houses to be supported without recourse to the world, for each monastery had its own 'in-house' labour force composed of laymen, but laymen who were fully part of the order. Since many of these *conversi*, as they were called, were peasants, the order had a broad social appeal.

Cistercian monasteries could still of course be dynastic. Rievaulx's valley ran down from the castle at Helmsley, home of its founder Walter Espec, the great minister of Henry I. Requiring only tracts of uncultivated wasteland, and sometimes (as in the disorders of Stephen's reign) receiving land to which the donor's title was disputed, they could also be inexpensive to establish. The role of the order in Wales was particularly important. Unlike the earlier Benedictine and Cluniac foundations, its houses were not adjuncts of conquest. The lifestyle of the monks and the location of their houses matched Welsh temperament and terrain. Nine of the houses were either founded by the Welsh themselves or were in Welsh-ruled areas. Eleven received benefactions, sometimes substantial, from native donors. The Lord Rhys of Deheubarth embraced Strata Florida, while Strata Marcella was founded by Owain Cyfeiliog of southern Powys. Although Margam was established by Robert, earl of Gloucester, native donors considerably outnumbered Anglo-Norman. The compelling appeal of the early Cistercian movement is revealed in the Life of its greatest English abbot, Ailred of Rievaulx (1147–67), by his disciple Walter Daniel. In meditation 'the whole strength of Ailred's mind poured out like a flood upon God and his son'; in prayer he made himself 'light and easy for the leap to heaven'. This spiritual exaltation, far from turning Ailred proud, taught him tolerance and compassion towards others in their difficulties. Indeed, he considered those virtues to be Rievaulx's 'supreme glory'. He was never other than realistic about human weakness. No wonder that under such an abbot Rievaulx's numbers rose to 140 monks and 500 *conversi* and lay servants. The church on feast days, as Walter Daniel put it, was crowded with brethren 'like bees in a hive'.

There was another form of religious house which spread with remarkable speed in the twelfth century, namely that of the Augustinian or Black canons. These were houses not of monks but of priests who could go out into the world, though they lived together without personal possessions under the common rule outlined by St Augustine of Hippo. A variant later in the century was provided by the Premonstratensian canons who followed a more austere way of life influenced by the Cistercians. The pastoral role of such houses, with the priests supervising and sometimes serving the parish churches which often formed part of the endowment, was one of their main attractions, complementing as it did the enclosed activities of the monks. Old minster churches, for example at Launceston and Taunton, were often organized by bishops as Augustinian houses, as were the priests running hospitals and serving nunneries and cathedrals. The same thing happened to *clas* churches in Wales, and Culdee ones in Scotland. Since Augustinian houses were usually small and required limited endowment they could be founded by minor barons and knights, hence in part their popularity. But the initial drive behind the foundations in the early twelfth century came from the court of Henry I; it was associated with all but ten of the forty-three houses founded by 1135. It was King Alexander and King David who brought the movement to Scotland, establishing the Augustinians at Scone and St Andrews. In native Wales, where the Black and White canons fitted as well as the Cistercians, Llywelyn the Great brought the Premonstratensians to Gwynedd. By 1300 there were well over 200 Augustinian and Premonstratensian houses in Britain.

In the mid thirteenth century Henry III's brother, Richard of Cornwall, established a Cistercian abbey at Hailes in Gloucestershire, and his minister, John Mansel, the Augustinian house at Bilsington in Kent. But the great age of monastic, foundation and endowment was over by 1200. Existing houses continued to acquire property but through purchase (often to round off existing estates) rather than by pious gifts. Where nobles continued to be buried in monasteries, that reflected more family tradition than spiritual empathy with the house concerned. The fact was that even the Cistercians were losing the cutting edge of their spirituality. Gerald of Wales described how they had transformed their wildernesses into highly profitable terrain, often for sheep farming, and how they built fine churches and monastic buildings, and possessed 'all the wealth you can imagine'. The cost of building was probably the reason why so many Cistercian houses fell heavily into debt to the Jews. A great monastery like Furness, in a pleasant valley, with its kitchen, refectory, chapter house, dormitory, and infirmary all in warm red local stone, together with running water for drinking and drainage, offered a comfortable existence. That was even more the case with the old Benedictine houses. At Westminster Abbey, studied by Barbara Harvey, the monks in the later Middle Ages consumed in calorific terms considerably more than 'a rather heavy, moderately active' man does today. Alcohol contributed 19 per cent of the daily energy, as compared with 5 per cent in today's average diet. A great deal of monastic time was also devoted to administration and estate management. At Bury St Edmunds the hawk-eyed Abbot Samson (1182–1211) had far more praise for the monks involved in the abbey's administration than he did for those in the choir carrying out their conscientious and mellifluous round of services. According to his biographer and chaplain, Jocelin of Brakelond, Samson's own deeds 'worthy of immortal record and renown', were those by which he freed the abbey from debts, increased its income and defended its privileges.

The decline in monastic endowment brought into greater prominence and quite probably increased the scale of a different form of alms-giving; alms-giving for the support of the poor and distressed. Christ himself had made clear in his description of the Last Judgement (Matthew 25:31–35) that such acts of charity were absolutely necessary for salvation. The blessed were precisely those who had fed and clothed the poor and nursed the sick, in so doing, as Christ explained, feeding, clothing and nursing himself. Christ thus was present in the poor, just as he was present in the bread and wine of the eucharist. Such charity could take two forms. One was the support of the institutionalized poor who lived in 'hospitals', which were often in effect almshouses. The other was the giving of money or food directly to the 'naked poor' who 'beg from door to door'. There was a feeling that not all beggars were deserving. At Beaulieu abbey distributions were limited to the old, the young and the weak, the able-bodied by implication being excluded. The weak, however, would certainly have included those weak from hunger and in the thirteenth century there were plenty of such people about. It was common, in fact, for the wealthy to engage in both forms of alms-giving. King Henry III, in feeding hundreds of paupers at court every day and giving generously to the hospitals and leper houses he passed on his travels, was unique only in the scale of his activities. By his time it was far more common for a successful man to found a hospital than a religious house, and there was a network of such institutions across England. A related reason for such charity was to 'harvest the prayers' of paupers, especially for the souls of the dead. Henry III marked the anniversaries of dead relatives by ordering thousands of paupers to be fed – indeed in the case of his sister Isabella the number was over 100,000. In his will Archbishop Boniface gave money to numerous hospitals who were all to pray for the health of his soul.

Equally prominent in Boniface's will were his gifts to friaries both in England and on the continent. The spread of the friars throughout Europe was the most important religious phenomenon of the thirteenth century. It was they who filled the spiritual vacuum left by the monks. To support the friars, as we shall see, was to support the poor, and that was certainly a key to their success. Even more important, however, was the way in which the friars served the needs of a new and changing society, served, that is, an educated laity who through confession were moving towards a more personal religion, and through penance and other forms of piety were working out their own salvation in the world, unimpressed by the argument that it could only be found in the cloister.

The crusade, as we shall see, had taken away much of the stigma of knighthood; arms could be a holy calling. For this new audience preachers were essential and so were effective confessors. The Fourth Lateran Council, therefore, enjoined bishops to appoint men to travel their diocese to carry out 'the office of sacred preaching', and to place men in cathedral and conventual churches (usually in major towns) to hear confessions, impose penances and do 'everything else for the saving of souls'. The Council might well have been drawing up a job description for the friars.

The demand, especially in the towns, for a more personal and intellectual religion had already generated movements in France and Italy, notably the Waldensians, founded by Waldes, a merchant of Lyons, and the *Humiliati*, who became established in many cities in northern Italy. The friars shared certain characteristics with these movements and were also strictly orthodox doctrinally and in their acceptance of papal authority. Encouraged by Innocent III in the most inspired move of his pontificate, they canalized spiritual aspirations which might otherwise have run down less orthodox paths and were a major force in combating heresy in Europe and preventing its appearance in Britain.

St Dominic, a priest from Castile, had precisely conceived his movement as an order of preachers to battle against the Albigensian heretics in France. In 1217 he extended the mission world-wide and his followers were soon organized into territorial provinces with an elaborate system of elective officials. Dominic was inspired by a vision of 'the apostolic life', the life led by Christ and his apostles. This was even more the case with St Francis (1181–1226), the son of a cloth merchant from Assisi. A revelatory passage for him had been Matthew x:7–9 where Christ sent out his apostles, declaring,

As ye go, preach, saying the kingdom of heaven is at hand . . . provide neither gold, nor silver nor brass in your purses . . . neither two coats, neither shoes, nor yet staves for the workman is worthy of his meat.

Francis's movement was therefore based on preaching and poverty. As his Rule declared:

The brothers shall possess nothing, but as pilgrims and strangers in this world . . . they shall confidently seek alms and not be afraid . . . This is the highest degree of that sublime poverty, which has made you my dear beloved brethren, heirs and kings of the kingdom of heaven.

The brothers were not, however, to wander as individuals. Like the Dominicans, they were to live in a disciplined way as members of a family, usually in town houses for it was in towns that they could reach the largest audiences. Very soon an elaborate constitution for the government of the order was in place. By 1358 the Franciscans had 1,400 houses throughout Europe and the Dominicans 635.

The Dominicans arrived in England in 1221 and the Franciscans in 1224. No one could doubt their commitment, given their abject poverty. Nor was their message in any way simplistic, an important feature, given the audience. The preaching was not haphazard but was based on model sermons circulated from Paris. It was followed up by the hearing of confessions and the imposition of penances. The Dominicans were all priests (so they could hear confessions) and learned, designedly so. 'The purpose of study is preaching and of preaching the salvation of souls,' remarked Humbert of Romans, master general between 1254 and 1263. The Franciscans too, for the same reason, became increasingly a learned order, and one dominated by the priestly element. Indeed the Franciscan theological school in Oxford, established initially under Grosseteste, became one of the most famous in the university.

Townsmen, knights, academics and monks rushed to join the orders. The scholar Adam Marsh became a Franciscan 'for love of most high poverty'. Within twenty years of their arrival in England the Dominicans had established nineteen town houses and the Franciscans thirty-nine, the numbers by 1300 being respectively fifty-one and fifty-five. A large house might have as many as forty members. The property was usually given by the townsmen themselves. In London the Franciscans' chapel was built by the mayor, William Joyner, who also gave £200 towards other buildings. By 1260 there were also nine houses in Scotland and five in Wales, the Franciscans having been introduced to Gwynedd by Llywelyn the Great himself. The friars were not merely on a mission to towns and townsmen. They appealed equally to kings, princes and nobles, often acting in a highly personal capacity as confessors and spiritual counsellors. The Franciscan John of Darlington was confessor to Henry III, and Adam Marsh the counsellor of the queen and of Simon and Eleanor de Montfort. Above all, the friars were welcomed by the bishops, who saw them rightly as exactly the force of trained preachers and confessors the Fourth Lateran Council had demanded.

The success of the friars inevitably provoked hostility, some of it justified. Matthew Paris, monk of St Albans, complained that their buildings rivalled regal palaces in height. Parish priests were angered at losing money from confessions and burials to the friars, another area of mendicant activity. There were also tensions within the orders, especially among the Franciscans, where the needs of a properly based pastoral mission inevitably cut across Francis's original concept of Christ-like poverty as almost an end in itself. The order continued in its refusal to own property, but needing houses and churches got round the problem by having these held for it in trust. Some of the original leaders made desperate attempts to preserve the original ideals. The head of the English province, William of Nottingham, appeared at the provincial chapter in a torn habit made of the coarsest material and sat on the ground. 'I did not become a friar for the purpose of building walls,' he declared, and at Shrewsbury ordered the stone wall of the dormitory (built by the townsmen) to be pulled down and replaced by one of mud. But in the end, it was with a note of despair that he prayed God to send a new order to inspire and stimulate his own in the way of perfection.

For all their problems, the friars had a profound impact on the spiritual life of the country. In the twelfth century, as David d'Avray has remarked, a sermon by an educated preacher was an event; in the thirteenth it was a normal part of town and court life. The extent to which the friars had entered the fabric of society was reflected in wills, for example that of the clerical administrator William of Wendling (died 1270). Although the founder of a Premonstratensian house at Wendling in Norfolk, he made gifts to the Dominicans at Sudbury, to the Franciscans at Yarmouth and Ipswich, and to both orders at Norwich, King's Lynn, Dunwich and Cambridge. Joan, wife of Llywelyn the Great, was buried with the Franciscans at Llanfaes in Anglesey, and Beatrice, Henry III's daughter, with the Franciscans of London, where the heart of her mother, Queen Eleanor, was also laid to rest.

There had long been opportunities for noblewomen to lead lives dedicated to religion. One way of doing this was to become a recluse. Loretta, widowed countess of Leicester, lived as 'the recluse of Hackington' in Kent from 1211 until 1265, using her contacts to help the early friars. Another way was to enter a religious order. In 1066 there were ten nunneries in Britain, all south of the Wash. By 1300 there were over 150, many of them situated between the Wash and the Tees. There were ten in Scotland though none north of the Tay, and four in Wales. Male founders were diverse, partly because such houses were often small, and like houses of canons were affordable by minor barons and knights. However, it was the Lord Rhys who established the nunnery at Llanllŷr in Ceredigion, and Henry II, as part of his penance after Becket's murder, who re-founded Amesbury as a daughter house of Fontevraud. It was there that Henry III's queen, Eleanor of Provence, retired and was buried. The chief female order in England, however, was not that of Fontevrault but the native Gilbertines. This had its origins in a cell for a group of female religious established by Gilbert of Sempringham at Sempringham in Lincolnshire around 1131. By 1216 there were nineteen Gilbertine houses, although with two thirds of them in Lincolnshire and Yorkshire, this remained essentially a local order. Many had four elements: nuns, lay sisters, lay brothers living according to Cistercian rules, and male canons who lived according to the rule of St Augustine, the nuns and the canons together making these in effect 'double houses'.

Noblewomen, usually as widows, could also found nunneries for themselves, using their inheritances or marriage portions to do so. Godstow near Oxford was established in the 1130s by Edith, widow of William de Lancelene. Around a hundred years later, Lacock in Wiltshire was the creation of the widowed Ela, in her own right countess of Salisbury. During her long widowhood between 1243 and 1282 Isabella, countess of Arundel, founded Marham in Norfolk. Quite apart from upbraiding Henry III for his injustices (see above, p. 416), she also enjoyed close spiritual relationships with Edmund of Abingdon, archbishop of Canterbury, and Richard Wych, bishop of Chichester: Lives of both were dedicated to her. Edith de Lancelene and Countess Ela became abbesses of their foundations. Many female heads proved determined and effective rulers. Those of Wherwell abbey, near Salisbury, rebuilt the house after its destruction in the violence of Stephen's reign, secured forest privileges from Richard I and used all the tricks of the trade to resist papal provisions in the thirteenth century.

Female houses, however, remained 'inferior' to those of men, and not merely because they were fewer and generally poorer. The key difference was that women could not be priests, hence the need for the attached canons who could perform that function. Also young unmarried women, far more controlled by their families than young men, could find it much harder to follow a religious vocation. Christina of Markyate came from a wealthy family of old English stock based in Huntingdon, and enjoyed her father's trust, keeping the keys of his treasure chest. Yet to escape parental pressure to marry, having already survived attempted rape by the bishop of Durham, Ranulf Flambard, she had to flee disguised as a man, and then live in hiding with male recluses, enduring terrible privations in her tiny cell. Ultimately she made the same transition as the foundress of Godstow (also initially a recluse), and became the prioress of a community at Markyate. As her Life shows so well, to fulfil her overpowering sense of vocation and 'preserve her virginity for God' had taken quite extraordinary courage, ingenuity and hardiness. In pursuing that vocation she had been helped as well as harmed by men. In general, as we have seen, monastic writers remained open-minded about the women with whom they came into contact (see above, p. 415). Yet it is also true that as institutions in the twelfth century, male monasteries became increasingly uneasy about, and indeed sought to terminate, arrangements whereby they had taken nuns under their wing, either through the women living in close proximity or being formally part of a double house. Marton in Yorkshire, for example, into the reign of Henry II was a double monastery of nuns and Augustinian canons, but the nuns then moved to Moxby and set up on their own. Among the Gilbertines, hints of scandal eventually led to a far stricter separation between male and female elements. Of the new orders, the Cistercians were particularly unhelpful to women. Gilbert of Sempringham had asked for his order to be taken under the wing of the Cistercians, only to be told that they 'were not permitted authority over the religious life of others, least of all that of nuns'. Many of the nunneries founded in the twelfth century adopted a Cistercian way of life, though largely unofficially. In 1213 such houses were placed under neighbouring Cistercian foundations, but in 1228 further affiliations were forbidden and existing links diminished. The whole attitude – or so it seemed – was to wish the women would go away. The friars were equally unwelcoming. Both Dominic and Francis attracted female followers, and a female order of friars would have recruited heavily. Yet none was ever sanctioned. The sisterhood founded by Clare of Assisi, Francis's disciple, was enclosed; so were the women the Dominicans incorporated into their order. Having jumped the wall themselves, the friars made sure the women stayed behind it. William of Nottingham asserted that women were deceitful and malicious and by their blandishments turned the heads even of the devout. The ability of women to fulfil a religious vocation was always restricted by such attitudes.

Just occasionally with the laity in this period it is possible to penetrate a little behind the external forms of religion. Hubert de Burgh (died 1243), justiciar and earl of Kent, was a self-made man, yet he did not give thanks, as he would certainly have done a hundred years earlier, by founding a monastery. Instead he was a patron of the Dominicans and gave them his London house at Holborn. When they moved to what is now Blackfriars after he died, they took his body with them. Hubert was typical of the period in founding a hospital, that of St Mary Dover, a thank-offering for his sea victory against the French in 1217. He must also have added the exquisite early thirteenth-century chancels to the churches at three of his properties, Burgh itself, Grosmont in Wales, and Banstead in Surrey where he died. One aid to Hubert's devotions was his psalter: when a fugitive in 1233, 'he ruminated on the Psalms of David in the Psalter he had with him for comfort'. Earl Waltheof, executed by the Conqueror in 1076, was said to have learnt the Psalms by heart as a child. What was new was the growing number of lay men and women possessed of psalters and able to read them for themselves, a point we shall return to later.

As he read his psalter in 1233, Hubert implored the aid of the Virgin Mary, and immediately heard a voice saying, 'Do not fear, the Virgin will rescue you.' The words were repeated again and again until rescue came. The Virgin was naturally the focus of Hubert's prayers because her willingness to intercede with Christ and the intimate proximity which enabled her to do so were the subject of contemporary sculpture, stained glass and painting. The most pervasive image was of the Virgin praying before Christ as he crowned her; this depiction of the Coronation of the Virgin virtually replaced the earlier Triumph of the Virgin, in which she sat crowned beside the King of Heaven. Prayers might also, of course, be offered to the saints for they too stood around the throne of God. Herein lay the value of pilgrimages because the saints, it was believed, were all the more likely to exert their power when supplicants were in close proximity to their remains. Pilgrimages were also made to places with relics associated with Christ himself. Hubert de Burgh and Henry III frequently visited Bromholm priory in Norfolk where pieces of the Holy Cross were preserved. Later Henry III presented to Westminster Abbey in a great ceremony a phial containing drops of the Holy Blood, outdoing Louis IX who had built the Sainte-Chapelle in Paris to house the Crown of Thorns. Bodies, of course, were divisible and those of some saints were infinitely divided. The proliferation of relics made private collections possible. Collectors did not have to go to the saints, they had them permanently in their possession. Among the treasure of Hubert's wife, sister of the king of Scotland, was a silver cross, double gilt, in which were set rubies, emeralds and relics. Bishop Hugh of Lincoln built up a relic collection of fabled size and quality. He needed frisking on leaving any shrine for he was always trying to break bits off bodies, on one occasion biting a fragment out of Mary Magdalene's arm bone before slipping it to his chaplain in classic pickpocket mode. Henry III's collection was equally impressive. It included relics of numerous saints as well as of the golden gate of Jerusalem, the Holy Sepulchre, Calvary and the burning bush.

The importance of intercession to the Virgin and the saints was made all the more important by the doctrine of Purgatory, for they surely had the power to lessen one's term there. But – as in Hubert's case – they could intervene in this life too. This was a world in which the belief in prodigies, wonders and miracles was widespread; hence the space devoted to them by nearly all the chroniclers. While out on a ravaging expedition during the 1215 civil war, a figure of Christ crucified appeared to Hubert de Burgh in a dream, saying, 'When you next see my image, spare me', something he did the following day when a priest ran up to him carrying a crucifix, begging for his church to be preserved from plunder. Hubert was convinced this pious act was the reason why God restored him to the king's favour in 1234. As he had remarked earlier in a private letter to the chancellor, there was no hope of success in this life 'unless God gives aid, by whose grace all effective work is achieved, and without whom no one can triumph over his enemies'. Nothing is known of Hubert's attitude to the Mass, but it was central to the daily religious life of his master, King Henry III, who was very much in tune with contemporary views about the ceremony's importance. There was no question of Henry doing business during the service like Henry II, or hoping it would be over as quickly as possible like Henry I. Henry III's own records show that he regularly attended two Masses a day, and even three on great festivals. Like his bishops in their diocesan legislation he strove to ensure that the reserved host, the bread turned into the body of Christ kept permanently in every church, was decently housed, and on his journeys he constantly made gifts of precious cups for that purpose. When Louis IX, reflecting another strand in contemporary thought, reminded Henry that it was important to hear sermons as well as attend Masses, Henry replied that he preferred rather to 'see his friend' (at the elevation of the host) than hear about him.

Neither Hubert de Burgh nor Henry III ever went on crusade, but both took the cross and professed the intention of going. In the twelfth and thirteenth centuries the crusade was part of the air that everyone breathed.

The First Crusade was launched by Pope Urban II in 1095. It culminated in the taking of Jerusalem on 15 July 1099 and the setting-up of crusader states in the east. Of these by far the most important and long-lasting was the kingdom of Jerusalem, which survived the loss of the Holy City itself and was only terminated by the fall of Acre in 1291. The existence of this state was central to the crusades because it provided a base for operations and also – since the state was constantly under threat – the need for them. Deciding to crusade was a formal act which required the sanction of the church and was symbolized by the sewing of a cross to one's clothes. One became 'signed with the cross', *crucesignatus*, the word from which 'crusade' comes. It was perfectly possible for individuals to seek the church's sanction at any time, and groups of crusaders were constantly on the move to the east. There were also, however, a small number of great crusades, like the First, publicly proclaimed by the papacy and generally preached throughout the west usually in response to some great emergency.

Duke Robert of Normandy, the Conqueror's eldest son, was one of the leaders of the First Crusade, but participation by the great Anglo-Norman magnates was limited. Thereafter the pattern changed. A substantial contingent of Anglo-Norman nobles went on the Second Crusade, launched in 1146, including Waleran of Meulan, earl of Worcester, William de Warenne, earl of Surrey, and William Peverel, the last two dying on the expedition. When the Patriarch of Jerusalem begged Henry II to crusade in 1185 the king pleaded his home duties, but the refusal damaged his reputation despite the money he had been sending to the east, and was anyway unsustainable after the loss of Jerusalem in 1187. In the event, of course, it was Richard who led the Angevin contingent on the Third Crusade in 1190, taking with him a large group of England's lay and ecclesiastical elite. Later, magnates from either side in the civil war went on the Fifth Crusade of 1218–21 which was designed to capture Damietta. In 1240–41, contingents departed under Henry III's brother Richard of Cornwall and his brother-in-law Simon de Montfort, earl of Leicester. Henry's own response to Louis IX's crusade was to take the cross himself (in March 1250), and although he never set out, his commitment was genuine enough. Ultimately Henry's son, the future Edward I, unlike Henry II placed the cause of the crusade above domestic considerations. Despite the parlous condition of the kingdom after the Montfortian civil war, he led a large body of knights to join Louis IX's second crusade of 1270, continuing to the Holy Land even after Louis's death.

From what has been said so far the crusade seems essentially an enterprise involving Anglo-Norman and English magnates. But it was not quite like that. The Welsh chronicle the *Brut* took a close interest in the crusades and remarked on the passage of Welshmen to the Holy Land. Gerald of Wales's best-known work describes his tour of Wales in 1188 to preach the Third Crusade with Archbishop Baldwin, an enterprise, so he liked to think, which inspired some 3,000 people to take the cross. There is evidence that Scotsmen took part in all the main crusades, including the first, where they were distinguished more for their piety than their military equipment. Later Patrick II, earl of Dunbar, joined the crusade of Louis IX, dying at Marseilles in 1248. Adam, earl of Carrick, got further and died in 1270 at Acre. The crusade, it has been claimed, was one of the factors which helped to integrate Scotland into the fold of western Christendom.

Interest in the crusade was not confined to the baronial and clerical elite. There were county knights from Yorkshire on the Third Crusade, one group led by Ralph de Tilly heroically saving a siege engine from capture by the Moslem defenders of Acre. On the Second Crusade men from London, Southampton, Dover and Ipswich were all present at the siege of the Islamic city of Lisbon, which was attacked on the way to the Holy Land. Lists from the early thirteenth century of those from Cornwall and Lincolnshire who had failed to fulfil their crusading vows included tanners, blacksmiths, millers, cobblers, butchers, ditch-cutters and several women. In twenty Lincolnshire cases poverty was given as the reason for the failure to fulfil the vow.

Clearly, far from everyone who took the cross actually went to the Holy Land. Indeed, the church increasingly accepted money payments for the commutation of vows. It is easy to see why initial ardour might cool. The dangers of the crusade were great, many crusaders never returning, and the financial costs were high. Yet there were also compelling reasons for undertaking the expedition. Jerusalem itself was a magnet, the site of Christ's crucifixion and burial, the centre of the world in thirteenth-century *mappae mundi*. Pilgrimages to Jerusalem had not dried up with the Islamic conquest in the seventh century. They were frequently enjoined by the church as penance for sin, and could be regarded as the climax of a man's spiritual life. To go on crusade was frequently described as a *peregrinatio*, a pilgrimage. The crusade, of course, was a pilgrimage with a difference. The aim was not merely to visit but also to defend or recover Jerusalem. Here was the appeal for the warrior elite of the west, one which transformed the very nature of knighthood. Churchmen had long stressed the sinfulness of fighting, but now knights could fight in a war which was not sinful but holy. Instead of their martial activities necessitating penance, they were themselves acts of penance, at the very least cancelling out all previous punishments imposed by the church in the confessional. For those who died on the crusade, there was also the promise of remission of all sins and direct entry into Paradise. As Guibert of Nogent declared after the First Crusade, knights no longer had to abandon the world for the monastic life to achieve salvation. Instead they could attain God's grace while still pursuing their own careers. Behind that belief there lay another cardinal fact about the crusades, one which did more than anything else to certify their worth throughout Europe. The crusades were absolutely 'official', being made so by the highest of all authorities, the pope himself. It was the pope who had conceived and launched the First Crusade. It was his authority which sanctioned all subsequent crusading activity.

Crusaders could thus hope for reward in the next life. They might also gain name and fame in this. The exploits of Richard I in the Holy Land, depicted in tiles and paintings, later adorned the palaces of Henry III. Henry's own tutor, the knight Philip Daubeny who went to the Holy Land three times and died there, earned an obituary from Matthew Paris: 'a noble man, devoted to God and strenuous in arms'; in a crusader war and piety marched together.

Considerations of piety and reputation, as modern historians, notably Simon Lloyd and Christopher Tyerman, have stressed, functioned within existing political and social structures. Both Richard I and Henry III were sincere in taking the cross, but in doing so they were also continuing their competition with the Capetian kings of France. The great majority of those who travelled from England did so in retinues, the retinues of great lords, the king (in 1189) and the heir to the throne (in 1270). Such retinues were shaped by the same ties of tenure, money and neighbourhood which operated in society generally: in 1270 the Lord Edward built up a force of 225 knights by paying lords to bring them (see above, p. 410). Among those accompanying Edward there were also distinct regional groupings, with contingents from the north, East Anglia and the Welsh Marches. Ties of family were also important in bringing crusaders together. On the Fifth Crusade the earls of Chester and Derby were brothers-in-law, while John de Lacy was soon to marry Margaret, Chester's niece, a union probably arranged on the crusade itself.

Crusading did not merely reflect existing society and politics, it also impacted upon them. The raising of money to finance the expeditions of magnates, knights and lesser individuals brought significant amounts of land onto the property market. At the highest level, Duke Robert gained funds for the First Crusade by leasing Normandy to William Rufus, who levied a tax in England to raise the required amount. Later, Richard I's rush for money in 1189 destabilized government in England and enabled Scotland to recover its independence. In the early 1250s Henry III built up the treasure for his abortive expedition by selling numerous charters licensing new markets and fairs, with important effects on the economy. There were those who took the cross for entirely secular reasons with little intention of ever going. This was because from the moment of the vow a crusader, in church thinking, was entitled to various privileges, and to some extent this was accepted in English law. For example, taking the cross could be a way of delaying lawsuits and gaining a moratorium on debts. In Magna Carta John himself was conceded the 'crusader's respite', which lasted at least three years, for dealing with several controversial issues, including the royal forests. There was another way too in which the crusade entered English politics. The pope always had the power to confer the privileges of crusaders on those who undertook some equivalent mission, for instance fighting against heretics in what became known as the Albigensian crusade. After John's death Guala, the papal legate, had in effect done the same in England, promising those who supported the young King Henry remission of their sins and signing them with the cross 'as though they were fighting against pagans'. So ingrained was the link between the crusade and righteous warfare that in the 1260s Simon de Montfort, son of the Montfort who had led the Albigensian crusade, moved to exploit it. Before going into battle he and his followers confessed their sins and signed themselves with the cross.

No one could avoid the crusades. An elaborate apparatus was developed to preach them, of which Gerald's tour of Wales in 1188 was part. They also had in a sense a permanent presence in Britain, thanks to the crusading orders of the Knights Templars and Knights Hospitallers. These were founded in the first half of the twelfth century, the first to protect the roads approaching Jerusalem, the second to give succour to those who reached the east. Beyond that, both orders came to play very similar roles in providing expert military support for the crusading state. The recruits lived under a rule, that of the Templars being influenced by Cistercian practices and that of the Hospitallers by Augustinian. All this had an impact on the home front because the orders set up houses in the west both to administer the properties given in support of their activities and to act as recruiting centres. By the end of the thirteenth century there were eighty-four houses in Britain, fifty of them founded in the thirteenth century; clearly there had been no falling-off in crusading commitment. Although the great majority of the houses were in England, both orders were important in Scotland where King David (1124–53) established them with extensive privileges. His successor King Malcolm granted the Hospitallers, and probably the Templars too, one toft in each royal borough. Another Hospitaller patron was Fergus of Galloway (died 1161). Eventually both orders came to hold a string of tiny properties throughout much of Scotland as well as some more extensive baronies. The international links of the Templars meant they began to act as bankers, so that money deposited at the London Temple, where both king and magnates often stored treasure, could release money from the Paris Temple to pay a debt in France. The Temple church in London, like others of the order, was circular and was modelled on the church of the Holy Sepulchre in Jerusalem. There, under splendid knightly effigies, were buried William Marshal, the regent of England (died 1219), who had gone to the Holy Land in the 1180s, and two of his sons, a permanent reminder of the salvation and the status the aristocracy hoped to secure from the crusades.

*　　*　　*

Hubert de Burgh read his psalter for 'solace'. The desire to do that, and to understand the Latin Mass, was a major factor in driving forward lay literacy, both male and female. Indeed it was often for noblewomen that a new form of devotional book was produced from the mid thirteenth century, the Book of Hours (essentially a prayer book), perhaps invented by the Oxford illustrator William of Brailes. Hubert's ability to read was equally empowering in his role as the king's chief minister, enabling him to check a debt in the pipe rolls, or interpret the letters which poured in to him with their requests and complaints; the sixty or so from 1219 to 1221 which survive are a fraction of a much larger number. The way English society was transformed between 1066 and the early fourteenth century by the escalating use of documents for business and the resulting growth of 'pragmatic literacy', literacy that is for the practical purpose of using business documents, is the theme of Michael Clanchy's classic book *From Memory to Written Record*.

There may already have been a good deal of pragmatic literacy in England before 1066, and it continued to develop thereafter. From around 1090, as David Bates has shown, individuals increasingly recorded agreements in documents called 'chirographs' and 'conventions'. Since these often employed narrative and contextual detail to explain and affirm the agreements they recorded, they suggest a society working out and negotiating its own ways to memorize and understand transactions, achieving in the process a considerable degree of pragmatic literacy.

It was in this fertile ground that a huge increase took place in the output of documents by royal government. The way in which the need to master this output almost forced laymen into pragmatic literacy is a central argument of Clanchy's book. The number of writs and charters produced by the Norman kings may not have been that large. They do not seem to have influenced the forms of private chirographs and conventions which were derived rather from practice in France and Normandy. The decisive increase in the king's output probably took place with the formation of the common law in the reign of Henry II (1154–89), because every litigant required a writ from the chancery to initiate his action. It was also between 1154 and 1199 that the chancery gave set forms to the charters, writs patent and writs close which it issued, the three types of document developed from the Anglo-Saxon sealed writ. Then from 1199 it began to record its output (apart from the writs initiating the common law actions) on a series of annual rolls. In their modern often highly abbreviated printed form, the rolls down to 1307 fill forty-six volumes and contain some 23,000 pages. Around four scribes have been identified as working in the chancery around 1130. In the fourteenth century there were over a hundred. A series of rolls, apparently begun in the 1200s, recorded the receipts and issues of the king's chamber and the daily expenditure of his household on food, drink and the stables. From the late twelfth century the king's courts began to keep rolls recording the cases they heard, rolls which thereafter grew steadily in length. There were corresponding increases in the size of the pipe rolls and the other documents produced by the exchequer. (For further detail see below, pp. 474–5.)

The forms of royal output and its related habits of mind had a profound impact on the rest of society, something shown in the way private chirographs recording agreements were eclipsed by the more authoritative official versions provided from the 1190s by the king's judges: no less than 42,000 of the government's copies of such chirographs survive down to 1307. During the twelfth century the charters issued by great lay lords came to imitate very closely royal charters, just as the mounted warriors on their seals imitated the seal of the king. This was a trend which came to embrace the nobility of Wales and Scotland as well as of England (see above, pp. 425, 428–9). In the thirteenth century great lords, lay and ecclesiastical, started to imitate the king in their use of household records of daily expenditure on food and drink, in their pipe rolls (those of the bishop of Winchester began in the 1200s), in the plea rolls of their courts, and in their writs giving orders to local officials: within a short period in 1250 Richard de Clare, earl of Gloucester, fired off three to his bailiff at Cranborne. The use of writing was also filtering down through society. Members of the gentry kept numerous records relevant to the running of their estates and sometimes copied them into cartularies. Even peasants used charters to convey land to one another. A register compiled by Peterborough abbey contains over 450 of such documents.

In order to understand for themselves what the documents, so central to their lives, actually said rather than relying on clerks to tell them, people from all sections of society had the incentive to achieve a degree of literacy. Here reading was the important skill and one probably much more prevalent than writing. How common the ability to read was among the peasantry is impossible to know, but it seems to have been widespread among the freemen and gentry who staffed most juries: ten of thirteen men on a Norfolk jury in 1297 apparently could read. For members of the gentry who were having to deal with a deluge of royal writs both as litigants and holders of local office, reading skills must have been particularly valuable. Nearly all the documents which had to be read were, of course, in Latin, so the language had to be learnt as well as reading itself. At the lowest level, perhaps tuition was provided by parish priests. Within noble households there were formal textbooks, the 'Book which teaches us Clergie' (that is Latin), doubtless expounded by mothers and chaplains. At the highest level, Simon de Montfort sent his sons to be educated by Grosseteste, with the result that his eldest, Henry, who was killed at Evesham, was able in a fine clear hand to write his father's will.

Hubert de Burgh could read Latin but no contemporary described him as 'literate' (*literatus*). That was a term reserved for those with an altogether superior form of learning, usually achieved by formal study at an institution of higher education. Such institutions in the thirteenth century began to be called universities. Some of Henry III's household knights were literate in this sense, though usually when they had been educated as clerks and had become knights in later life. Essentially the only people who were 'literate' were clerks.

In England, clerks without higher education could always rise to the top in government through the chancery or the exchequer. Common lawyers, indeed, had no alternative other than to train through the courts, and were eventually not clerks at all (see below, p. 481). For many ambitious men, however, higher education seemed absolutely essential. From the late eleventh century the content of that education was being transformed by the rediscovery of lost works of Aristotle, the revived study of Roman law, the new collections of canon law, and the increasing interest in Arabic medicine and mathematics. In the basic arts degree, through lectures and disputations in large part on Aristotle, the student was schooled in logic, grammar and rhetoric, thus learning how to speak and write correctly and reason analytically. The skills achieved were transferable to all branches of government and administration. They also prepared one for yet higher studies in law, medicine and theology. The great expansion of ecclesiastical litigation placed a premium on canon lawyers. In the 1170s the abbot of Battle was upbraided for failing to send his relatives to the schools to study the law and the decretals, for they could then have defended him in lawsuits. For the most ambitious, intellectually and spiritually, study of theology had to be the goal. It was also, for the friars, a vocational requirement, effective preaching depending on knowledge of the Bible.

In the twelfth century the great centres of international learning were at Paris, Laon, Liège, Bologna and Salerno. It was at such schools that so many English clerics involved in the Becket dispute had studied, including Becket himself. In the 1200s the masters (that is, teachers) of the Paris School began to form themselves into a formal corporate body, which they called a 'university', and masters elsewhere soon followed their example. English schools in the twelfth century lacked international status, but several offered a perfectly good education. Grosseteste himself studied at the school of Lincoln. In the next century two centres came to eclipse all the others, forming the only English universities.

In 1231 Henry III issued letters in favour of both the 'universities' of Oxford and Cambridge. He had heard that there was a 'multitude' of students at both places who could not be disciplined by the chancellor and the masters. Henceforth no one was to be allowed to study who was not under a 'master of scholars'. At the same time Henry rejoiced at the multitude of clerks flocking to both universities, including those from overseas (there had been trouble at Paris), 'from which great advantage and honour comes to us and our kingdom'. To sustain this popularity, he ordered rents to be fixed 'according to the custom' of each university. Clearly both Oxford and Cambridge were very much going concerns, and were conceived as playing important roles in the life of the kingdom. The constitutions of both were heavily influenced by that developing in Paris. The corporate body, the university, was formed by the teaching masters, and as the letters of 1231 implied, no one could teach who had not been admitted to it. The chief officer of the corporation was the chancellor whose court (in Oxford) had disciplinary authority over the students. In Cambridge it was more a matter for the individual masters.

The letters of 1231 treat the two universities as equal but in fact Oxford was both older and more important. Although it never really recruited internationally in the same way as Paris, it was described by Matthew Paris in the 1250s as (after Paris) 'the second school of the church'. There had almost certainly been a school at Cambridge before the 1200s, but the real inception of the university came with an exodus there of Oxford scholars in 1209 after the first of the town–gown disputes. Oxford's history as a centre of learning is traceable (with gaps) back to Theobald of Étampes, who was teaching there in the early twelfth century. By the 1180s, Gerald of Wales, at least in his later recollection, was able to read his new book about Ireland to 'the doctors of the diverse faculties and their best pupils'. By the 1200s there were faculties of law, arts and theology, the last two being the ones for which Oxford later became most famous. The settlement after the 1209 exodus was followed by the appointment of the first chancellor in or soon after 1214.

The factors which explained Oxford's emergence included its central location which made it a frequent meeting-place for ecclesiastical councils, and its two large religious houses (Osney and St Frideswide's) whose constant litigation before judges appointed by the pope required the service of trained lawyers. Oxford, moreover, was not the seat of a bishopric which meant that (unlike Paris) it could grow up free from immediate episcopal supervision. Even so, the assertion by the bishop of Lincoln, in whose diocese Oxford lay, of his right to appoint the chancellor caused constant friction. Some of Oxford's advantages were shared by other towns, notably by Northampton where there was also an important school. But Oxford had one key advantage, namely the Thames, which made it a much more important centre of communications.

In the 1260s the position of Oxford and Cambridge was finally assured. Students had defected from Cambridge to Northampton with the intention of setting up a university there, this with the king's encouragement. But when Oxford students sought to join them, the bishops of the kingdom protested: harm to Oxford was harm to the English church. So the government closed the new university down and returned studies at Northampton to their previous levels. There was evidently a clear conception of the difference between a university and an ordinary school. Not long after this, the oath taken by Oxford masters forbade them to teach anywhere in England save at Oxford or Cambridge. There was to be a monopoly. This did not apply to Scotland or Wales, yet no universities were created there in this period. Up to a point Oxford and Cambridge served the whole of Britain. Thomas Wallensis taught the Franciscans there between spells as a professor in Paris and bishop of St Davids. William Wishart, bishop of St Andrews, and William de Bernham, nephew of David de Bernham, another St Andrews bishop, were both graduates. And it was an Anglo-Scottish magnate, John Balliol, and his wife Dervorguilla (daughter of Alan of Galloway), who founded one of the first Oxford colleges. But it was to England that the universities chiefly ministered. As a royal charter of 1355 put it, Oxford had produced 'most learned men by reason of which the kingdom, as well as its priesthood, has been adorned and strengthened in manifold ways'.

*   *   *

In 1275 Edward I ordered John de St Denis, 'custodian of our privileges', to 'transcribe and register our privileges, instruments and other documents as we have enjoined him'. He was clearly well aware of the importance of written records in the assertion of his authority. On reaching the throne he had much reassertion to do.

15

King Edward I: The Parliamentary State

When Henry III died in November 1272, Edward was in Sicily returning from his crusade. Instead of hurrying home, he went to Gascony to set the province in order. It was not until August 1274 that he reached England. His delay reflected his confidence in his ministers. The council left behind to look after his affairs had from the start played a major part in the government of the kingdom, designedly so since it controlled many sheriffdoms and royal castles. Now its members, led by Edward's clerk Robert Burnell, took over the reins at the centre. If they passed on problems, they also suggested solutions. The problems were formidable. With former rebels still saddled with heavy fines to recover their lands, and with widespread veneration for Simon de Montfort shown in pilgrimages to Evesham, there were constant fears of a renewal of civil war. The government had great difficulty prising Edward's brother Edmund from Chartley castle which he seized in April 1273. It struggled to contain the conflicts between Llywelyn and the earls of Gloucester and Hereford; it failed to enforce an embargo on wool exports to Flanders, making Edward (as he himself complained) a laughing stock; and in January 1273 it suspended the general eyres then in progress in the counties, an act of conciliation given the eyre's lucrative crown pleas business, which reflected the general unpopularity of the king's government in the shires. And over everything hung the financial weakness of the crown, a long-term problem exacerbated by the recent civil war. Essentially Edward needed to open up new sources of revenue, and forge a new relationship with the kingdom in order to do so. His achievement lay in establishing a new tax-based parliamentary state, and making the monarchy for the first time since 1066 at one rather than at odds with the Englishness of its people. Edward by these means gained the power to wage his wars against the Welsh and the Scots. There were also certain internal victims of his rule. The Jews were expelled from England in 1290. The burdens of his wars fell with disproportionate heaviness on the peasantry.

In 1274 Edward was thirty-five. Already a veteran in war and politics, he had learnt from his father's mistakes and his own early tribulations. Sketches and paintings show him with a straight nose and a massive rounded chin. When measured in 1774, his skeleton was six feet two inches in height; Edward stood literally head and shoulders above most contemporaries. He had the personality to go with the physique. Henry III had been a *rex pacificus*. Edward was a *rex bellicosus*. He had taken part in tournaments across France in his youth, won the battle of Evesham, and then gone on crusade. Both as a skilled strategist and a fighting knight (his personal duel with the rebel Adam Gurdun became the stuff of legend), he fulfilled all the expectations of the warrior king, expectations to be amply fulfilled by his victories in Wales and Scotland. Yet Edward also had a burning sense of the civilian duties of kingship – the preservation of the rights of the crown, the dispensation of justice and the maintenance of order. His father at heart had been soft and *simplex*. Edward by contrast was a man 'of tried prudence in affairs of state', as the chronicler Trevet put it. In his struggles after 1258 to free himself from baronial control, he had won over individual magnates by acts of patronage, and had seen how reform of the realm could conciliate local society. He was superbly equipped for kingship.

Edward's queen, Eleanor of Castile, played no role comparable with that of Eleanor of Provence. The elder Eleanor's exploits had received a mixed press from monastic chroniclers. On the one hand she had displayed 'the serpentine wiles of a woman' when persuading her husband to overthrow the Provisions of Oxford. On the other, she had been the 'most powerful *virago*' when raising an army to rescue her husband after his capture at Lewes. There was, however, no opportunity for the second Eleanor to be like the first. She had an important diplomatic role, thanks to her Castilian kin and her inheritance (she gained the county of Ponthieu following her mother's death in 1279). But unlike her mother-in-law she had no family party in England, for no Castilians were ever established there. Although she had six children who survived infancy, she died too soon (in 1290) to play a political role through promoting their careers. There is no reason to think that Eleanor resented her position, nor did it reduce her simply to a meek intercessor whose 'pity should surpass the pity of all men and women', as Archbishop Pecham put it. Eleanor certainly had a gentle and pious side. She protested at the early marriage of one of her daughters and was a great patron of the Dominican friars. When, however, she intervened for the earl of Cornwall in 1287, it was by arguing that the charges of incompetence brought against him were unjustified, not by playing the pity card. Indeed, Pecham himself lamented that Eleanor seemed more inclined to push Edward towards severity than mercy. She was a clever operator at court where Edward's lasting love (he was never unfaithful) gave her unique influence. Apart from when he was on campaign and she was in late pregnancy, the couple were rarely separated.

Eleanor's major objective, at Edward's urging, was to build up for herself a great landed estate, giving the same kind of landed base as the pre-1154 queens but without it having to come from the king (see above, pp. 192–3). In this she was doing better than her mother-in-law who also acquired land but largely on a temporary basis through wardships. Eleanor monitored the land market and pounced on those owing money to the Jews or otherwise in difficulties. By the time of her death she had acquired properties worth some £2,600 a year, including William of Leybourne's castle of Leeds in Kent. Careful about her good name at court, she seemed careless about her reputation in the country. 'The king would like to get our gold / The queen our manors fair to hold' ran one satire. Edward's grief on Eleanor's death in 1290 was profound. The great stone crosses, which marked the resting places of her body on its journey from Lincoln to Westminster Abbey where a beautiful gilt-bronze effigy was placed above her tomb, were intended to inspire prayers for her soul. With their graceful and imposing statues of the queen the crosses also summed up the resurgence of queenship which the two Eleanors had effected, in different ways, in the thirteenth century.

As soon as he returned to England in August 1274 Edward set about restoring the power and authority of the crown. In one area his determination was given striking physical manifestation. London had been the great seat of the Montfortian rebellion, so between 1275 and 1285 Edward spent some £21,000 building the Tower's present outer walls, moat and water gates. In 1285 he suspended the city's liberties, keeping the government in his own hands down to 1298. None of this would have been possible had Edward not restored the financial position of the crown. Here his task was formidable. At the start of the reign revenue was some £25,000 a year. Back in 1130 the revenue had been of similar size but since then the course of inflation, particularly in the early thirteenth century, had reduced the real value of money between two and three times over. The income which made Henry I rich left Edward poor. Nor was it easy to improve the situation. Henry III had been unable to sustain the higher revenues he generated for a while in the 1240s. John's far more spectacular efforts had provoked Magna Carta. The problem was compounded by the decline in the proportion of easy uncontentious income from land. In 1130 not far short of £10,000 of royal revenue had come from the king's own lands. If all of these had been retained, they might well have been worth in the thirteenth century upwards of £30,000 a year. The monarchy would still have been rich. In fact, however, so much land was given away for purposes of patronage after 1130 that even when exploited to the full in the 1240s what remained was only worth around £6,000 annually. There were also other sources of revenue which had become less lucrative. The heavy taxation between 1240 and 1260 had exhausted the wealth of the Jews; the money from general eyres was coming in more slowly as, swamped by business, they took longer and longer to complete; respect for the church meant that Edward, like his father, did not keep bishoprics deliberately vacant so as to take their revenues; and finally Magna Carta had made it more difficult to sell justice and charge hefty fines for succession to inheritances. What made all this worse was that while in real terms the wealth of the English kings had declined, that of the Capetian kings of France had spectacularly increased.

In this situation Edward developed a whole range of policies designed to increase his revenues, some more successful than others. Edward believed that during his father's lax rule privileges (or 'liberties') had leaked far too easily from the crown, with a commensurate loss of revenue. In the localities, for example, lay and ecclesiastical lords had set up private gallows, and usurped the jurisdiction of the hundred courts by preventing the attendance of their men. Edward's response came in 1278. When the general eyre was revived in that year it began to hear special *quo warranto* cases under which all who held lands and 'liberties' claimable by the crown had to show their warrant for them. Just how successful the campaign was is open to question. It certainly caused annoyance. According to one story John de Warenne, earl of Surrey, when he came before the judges flung down a rusty sword: his warrant was that his ancestors had conquered England with King William in 1066. The mighty Gilbert de Clare, earl of Gloucester, was forced to disgorge some of his father's gains, but many cases dragged on for years and never came to a conclusion. Often defendants were able to show that their lands and liberties had been conceded in royal charters, a warrant acceptable from the start. In 1290 Edward agreed to confirm all liberties enjoyed continuously since 1189, even if unsupported by written title. In 1294 with the suspension of the general eyres the whole campaign came to an end. It had asserted the principle that a warrant acceptable to the king was necessary, and may well have stopped fresh losses. But it had done little to increase royal revenues or impede developing patterns of magnate rule in the shires, to which we will return.

Edward's determination to preserve and increase the stock of royal lands was more successful. Henry III had stopped alienating royal demesnes, but had still given away (often in feckless fashion) escheats which had come into his hands, notably from 'the lands of the Normans'. Apart from gifts to his close family, Edward stopped alienations altogether. He also bent his energies to the acquisition of land, his wife's activities being part of a much wider enterprise. Henry III in an isolated act had bought out the heirs to the earldom of Chester. Under Edward procuring land, in large amounts and small, through purchase and pressure, became a matter of consistent, insistent policy. In 1293, in his most spectacular coup, he bought the Isle of Wight for £4,000 from the dying Isabella de Forz, countess of Devon. Edward also acquired two earldoms, the first (at the end of Henry's reign) by saddling the earl of Derby, Robert de Ferrers, with an unpayable £50,000 redemption fine, the second in 1302 by purchasing the reversion of the earldom of Norfolk from the childless Roger Bigod. Queen Eleanor's lands were kept to form the dower lands of Edward's second wife, while the earldoms of Derby and Norfolk were used to endow respectively his brother Edmund and his son by his second marriage. The original stock of crown lands thus remained intact.

However, the most important developments under Edward lay not in rebuilding old sources of revenue but in opening up new ones. This brings us to the customs, general taxation and Italian bankers. Experiments with customs under King John and again in 1266 had met with only mixed success. The real start came in 1275 when, after negotiations with merchants (whom Edward could threaten with punishment for breaching the recent embargo on wool exports), the April parliament conceded a customs duty of a third of a pound (6s. 8d.) to be levied on every exported sack of wool. Wool was England's greatest export, most of it going to support the Flemish cloth industry. Buoyant prices meant that it could easily support the new customs. From 1275 they were a permanent feature of English royal finance, bringing in around £10,000 a year with another £1,000 a year from Ireland.

Edward also had far more success than previous kings in levying general taxation. This involved the movable property, essentially the corn and the animals, of everyone being valued, and a percentage of that value being given to the king. The movables on the church's lands held for rents and knight service were also included in the levy. Only its spiritual property, essentially tithes and glebe land (which might be taxed separately) and the movables of the poor were exempt. The absolutely cardinal fact about taxation in this form was the enormous amounts it could raise. It had the power to transform the king's financial position. John's thirteenth of 1207 (that is a levy at the rate of 13 per cent) yielded some £60,000. The trouble was that for all practical purposes such taxation required the consent of parliament, consent which Henry III was consistently refused between 1237 and 1270. Edward changed all that. His taxation was new both in its scale and regularity.

Date	Rate of Tax	Assessment
1275	15th	£82,000
1283	30th	£48,000
1290	15th	£117,000

These taxes were collected with remarkable efficiency so that the yield was little short of the assessment.

Edward had opened up new sources of revenue. He also handled them in an entirely new way through the use of Italian bankers, the Riccardi of Lucca. The Riccardi were one of the great international banking firms produced by the commercial expansion of the thirteenth century. In England they were heavily engaged in the wool trade and also lent money. Henry III had done business with Luke of Lucca, head of the house in England, but on a small scale. Edward used the firm not for occasional loans but to fund over many years a large proportion of his expenditure. Above all the Riccardi supplied cash for the wardrobe, the great spending department travelling with the king, in some years furnishing nearly all its money usually in the form of a small number of large advances. The reason the Riccardi were able to make these advances was that Edward had entrusted them with the entire management and receipt of the customs revenues, and also with a good proportion of the issues from taxation. Since they could also use nearly £50,000 raised from the church, which they kept as bankers for Edward's second crusade whenever it should take place, they always had money on which to draw. All this was in striking contrast with wardrobe funding under Henry III when the money came in dribs and drabs from the exchequer and many other sources. Thus under Edward royal finance achieved a hitherto undreamt-of stability and smoothness.

Edward finally dismissed the Riccardi in 1294 when they failed to meet his sudden demands produced by wars in France and Wales. Thereafter wardrobe finance became much more hand-to-mouth. Yet the appalling strains of the period after 1294 (with the war with Scotland soon increasing the demands on revenues) revealed the strength of the Edwardian system. If the wardrobe by 1307 had run up debts of £200,000, that just showed how successful it had been in obtaining money and services on credit. The flexibility of the customs was shown by the way the duty between 1294 and 1297 was raised from a third of a pound to two pounds. Although the amounts raised by individual taxes declined, Edward was able to levy them at an unheard-of pace and they were still collected with great efficiency. Between 1294 and 1307 he raised six taxes with a total yield of £270,000, £191,200 coming between 1294 and 1297. Meanwhile taxation on the spiritual property of the church brought in some £224,600. Between 1294 and 1298 Edward was able to spend some £750,000 on war.

Some reflection of the gigantic difference in power between Edward and Henry III is provided by the figures for their wardrobe receipts (although these, of course, were only part of their revenues). Between 1234 and 1258 they averaged roughly £12,000 a year. Between 1274 and 1293 the figure was £38,000, and between 1294 and 1303 £75,000. Whether Edward was wealthier than King John is debatable, given the course of inflation and other difficulties of comparison. The real point is that a far higher proportion of Edward's revenues came from taxation: according to one calculation, the tax yield between 1290 and 1307 was some 120 to 200 per cent higher in real terms than it had been between 1199 and 1216. Edward tapped the wealth of all sections of society in a way not seen since the Conquest.

The power and authority of Edward's kingship was revealed both in its ideology and governmental apparatus. The God-given nature of his rule was as visible as his father's, but in a different way. He was equally punctilious in attending Mass, and making offerings to shrines and churches as he travelled the country. But he no longer fed paupers at court (giving money instead), lost interest in Edward the Confessor, stopped work at Westminster Abbey, and conjured up no 'St Henry' to rival St Louis (Louis IX was canonized in 1297). As a committed crusader – he took the cross again in 1287 – Edward had nothing more to prove. To gain God's favour for his first crusade and his war in Wales he founded a great Cistercian abbey at Vale Royal in Cheshire, here, as with the Eleanor crosses, imitating Capetian practice. Likewise in imitation of the Capetians he touched for the scrofula, on average nearly a thousand people coming before him every year. The face of Edward's monarchy was also martial, quite unlike that of his father. At the centre of the realm, in his great chamber at Westminster, he surrounded Henry III's painting of the Coronation of the Confessor with tiers of paintings depicting battle scenes from the life of the warrior king of the Old Testament, Judas Maccabeus. Edward's lawyers, buoyed up by his might, made higher claims for royal power than ever canvassed under John or Henry. The king was, they said (drawing here on Roman law), 'for the common utility, by his prerogative, in many cases above the laws and customs used in his kingdom'.

Alongside the Riccardi, the scope and power of Edward's kingship depended on the traditional institutions of central government: at Westminster the common bench and the exchequer; and travelling with the king, the chancery and the wardrobe. All these institutions worked through written documents and together generated a massive amount of them. The idea that orders were more likely to be effective when they were put in writing and recorded, that disputes were more likely to be settled if the courts made official records of the cases they heard, and, most deep-rooted of all, that records were vital for getting in the king's revenues and monitoring how they were spent, these ideas had long informed the workings of English government and encouraged the increasing reliance on documents (see above, p. 460). They were ideas which in a way reached fulfilment in the Edwardian state. Indeed, at the exchequer there was a belief that they had been fulfilled almost to excess.

The extraordinary expansion in the work of the common bench under Edward will be discussed later. For the exchequer, on the other hand, the early years of the reign saw its partial eclipse. The exchequer had always performed two main tasks. One was to collect, store and (as ordered) disburse the king's revenues, much of the disbursement taking the form of sending money to the king himself where it was paid into his chamber or (after 1216) his wardrobe. (In fact there was little difference between the two departments.) The second task was to audit annually the accounts of the sheriffs and all the other officials and individuals who owed money to the king, the result of the audit being recorded on the pipe roll. The first task had always been subject to one limitation, that imposed when the king ordered sheriffs and others owing him money to pay it direct to the chamber or wardrobe, thus bypassing the exchequer, something he was most likely to do when in urgent need of cash. This had happened to such an extent under Henry III that by 1258 there was a feeling among reformers and exchequer officials that financial affairs would be less chaotic if revenue was always paid initially into the exchequer. This was not, however, Edward's view. On the contrary, the assignments to the Riccardi reduced the proportion of revenue going through the hands of the exchequer to an altogether new low.

The exchequer none the less remained central to the workings of royal finance. Even where collectors of revenue and individual debtors paid their money direct to the wardrobe or the Riccardi, it still had to audit the transaction. Otherwise the money would continue to appear on the pipe roll as being owed to the king. The auditing functions of the exchequer thus remained unimpaired under Edward. Indeed they greatly expanded as it began to take cognizance of the king's new revenues, auditing accounts for the customs and the taxation on movables. It also heard the accounts of the Riccardi and, with an annual regularity never achieved before, the keepers of the wardrobe. All this activity was facilitated by moves to control the amount of documentation the exchequer had to produce. Since their first appearance in the twelfth century the pipe rolls had grown to unwieldy size. That for 1242 (the latest chronologically to be published) runs to 440 pages of modern print compared with the 161 pages of the roll of 1130. In part this was because a much larger number of people owed money to the crown. But it was also because the rolls were becoming clogged with a growing backlog of debts which there was no hope of recovering. Already in 1270 a reform had removed many of these 'desperate debts' from the pipe roll; in 1284 another measure excised further redundant sections. The exchequer was well prepared for the testing years after

1290. While its auditing functions ultimately fell into disarray, it came once again to play a major role in the collection and disbursement of royal revenue, in part thanks to the fall of the Riccardi. It was no longer a question of reducing the documentation: the memoranda rolls, which recorded a great deal of its business, tripled in size after 1290 from thirty to ninety membranes. That taxation continued to be collected so efficiently in this period owed a great deal to exchequer activity.

In 1274, on his return to England, Edward gave the chancellorship to his faithful clerk, Robert Burnell. Except for periods during military campaigns, the chancery largely followed the king until Burnell's death in 1292. A large part of the government of the realm depended on the concessions, proclamations and orders which it wrote and sealed for the king in the form of charters, letters patents and letters close (see above, p. 199). Much of this output, running to several thousand separate items each year, was recorded on the annual charter, patent, close, *liberate* and fine rolls which in 1291–2 took up some seventy membranes of parchment, many of them closely written on both sides. In fact the rolls had been much the same size at the start of Edward's reign. The real increase in chancery business after 1272 was in the production of the letters or writs close which initiated and processed the common law legal procedures, writs so numerous and standard form ('of course') that they were never enrolled. By the 1320s (when numbers can first be calculated) well over 20,000 of these writs were being issued annually. It was the volume of this business which led to the chancery in the fourteenth century ceasing to follow the court and taking up near permanent residence at Westminster.

Even in Burnell's day, the chancery with about a hundred clerks was essentially separate from the royal household. The wardrobe, on the other hand, was at the household's heart. For all the importance of the exchequer, it was the real nerve centre of royal finance, receiving and spending a large part of the revenues, as we have seen, and vastly expanding its activities in time of war. In the later years of the reign, with the decline of the Riccardi, wardrobe officials supplemented the flow of cash from the exchequer by actively seeking out for themselves money they could take into their coffers. When the chancery was separated from the king, the wardrobe also had the task of writing many of his letters, sealing them with the private or privy seal of which it was custodian. Ultimately in the fourteenth century, with the chancery having moved out of court, it was through such letters that the king most often expressed his wishes. Under Edward, the wardrobe was staffed by able and long-serving clerks like William of Louth and Walter Langton, several of whom went on to the treasurership of the exchequer and bishoprics, thus helping to bind together the royal administration as well as church and state.

The household also had a military wing headed by the king's stewards, usually one or two of whom were in office at any one time. Below the stewards were (around 1285) some eighty knights, a hundred esquires and thirty serjeants-at-arms, all retained with annual money fees. Around 1240 Henry III too had been giving money fees to about seventy knights, but Edward's household was far more militaristic, in part because it had a much higher number of knights actually 'staying with the king at court', as the wardrobe accounts put it. The household knights, many from families with a long tradition of service – Gorges, Leybourne, Seagrave – might not reap the landed rewards of their forebears under Henry (although they did gain marriages and wardships), but they had the honour of serving a famous king. Like household knights in the past, they were bound by a special oath to report anything spoken against the king, and were often sent out as castellans, investigators and diplomats, receiving, Edward decreed, the same wages as if they were actually present at court. In effect wherever they were, so was the king. Some of Edward's bannerets (a title now given to senior knights) were among the king's closest councillors and received personal summonses to parliament. Above all, the household forces, always quickly expandable, formed the nucleus of royal armies, contributing to the Welsh war of 1282–3 a third of the paid cavalry in the army.

The food, drink and horse fodder of the royal household cost around £12,000 a year in the 1280s, perhaps some £4,000 to £5,000 more than thirty years before. Around 570 members were in receipt of annual robes. The household's records in 1285–6 fill some 250 pages of modern print. Around the household was the wider court composed of the judges of the king's bench, who heard the cases of special concern to the king (see above, pp. 347–8), the other sworn councillors, and the regional magnates who came in and out as the king travelled the country. Such contact with local society was important, yet there is little sign that Edward, any more than his father, travelled for the purposes of routine government. If he was more itinerant, the purpose was for fighting or hunting. The Northamptonshire and New Forest hunting lodges came back into fashion. Apart from emergencies, Edward's remained a southern-based kingship. Fundamentally the realm came to him – above all, as we shall see, at the time of parliament.

The restoration of the resources and prestige of monarchy made Edward a powerful and sometimes oppressive ruler. Oppressive was certainly how he seemed after 1294 when he strained every nerve to raise men and revenue for wars in Wales, Scotland, Flanders and Gascony. In 1297 he ruthlessly crushed the church's resistance to taxation of its spiritual property by sequestrating its lands. In many ways Edward's rule after 1294 was comparable with John's after 1204: both kings were driving forward their governments in order to raise money for foreign war. Yet the political results were quite different. John's government ended in Magna Carta and civil war. Henry III's rather different misrule also culminated in a revolution. Nothing like this happened to Edward. He certainly faced serious unrest and in 1297 and 1300 confirmed Magna Carta, abolished the extra duty on wool, agreed that no taxation could be levied without consent, and accepted limitations on his right to take 'prise'. This was the ancient right of compulsory purchase to obtain goods for the royal household, which Edward had expanded to gain supplies for his armies as well. These were significant concessions but they were small beer compared with those of 1258. There was no attempt to impose a council on the king, take the control of government out of his hands, and carry through wide-ranging reforms in the localities. That was partly because of Edward's immense prestige as a war leader. But it was also because there was in his kingship elements that had been lacking under John and Henry III – a political balance and stability, fruit of his conciliation of interest groups and his reform of the realm.

Outside the great quarrel in the 1290s, Edward maintained a good working relationship with the church. He twice accepted Robert Burnell's failure to become archbishop of Canterbury, the pope appointing instead two distinguished churchmen in Robert Kilwardby (1273–8) and John Pecham (1279–92). In return there was always a spread of curial bishops including Burnell himself at Bath and Wells and John Kirkby at Ely, both of whom continued in royal service after their elevation to the bench. The pope, until his unavailing protest in 1297, permitted taxation of the church's spiritual property and even allowed Edward eventually to take the money supposedly reserved for his second crusade. (Its withdrawal from the Riccardi contributed to their fall.)

Edward could certainly treat his magnates in masterful fashion. He forced Roger Bigod, earl of Norfolk, to pay the debts he owed the crown; in 1290–91 he briefly imprisoned the earls of Gloucester and Hereford, and seized their lordships of Glamorgan and Brecon when they defied his orders and resorted to violence during a quarrel in the March. Although only partially successful, his *quo warranto* inquiries put far more pressure on the liberties of magnates than anything attempted by his father. This was, however, only part of the picture. Whatever was said by his judges, Edward's general conduct of business nearly always remained within the letter of the law. In acquiring property he resorted to sharp practice, but never arbitrary dispossession. On the whole he accepted the limits set by chapter 39 of the 1215 Charter. He also abided by the Great Charter's regulations on relief, the sale of justice and the treatment of widows. Edward quickly rehabilitated some former Montfortians, notably John de Vesci (see above, pp. 425–6), John fitz John, Nicholas of Seagrave, and Thomas Cantilupe who became bishop of Hereford. He was extremely close to several of his greatest barons, including Henry de Lacy, earl of Lincoln, John de Warenne, earl of Surrey (despite his rusty sword), and Roger de Mortimer, giving them extensive lands from the conquest of Wales. If his tightfistedness outside his Welsh conquests meant that he could not pose as the true Arthurian king (for whom largesse was a cardinal virtue), at least he avoided the factional struggles and scrambles for patronage which had plagued his open-handed father. If Edward was mean, he was at least mean to everyone.

Beneath the magnates, Edward, far more than any previous king, reached out and won the favour of the knights and those below them in local society, precisely the groups who had, through their representatives in parliament, to consent to the new taxation. Edward had been profoundly influenced by the Montfortian period between 1258 and 1267. He had seen how the realm could be reformed through the use of inquiries, eyres, legislation and parliament. He would do the same. In 1274–5 he staged a great inquiry into both the usurpation of royal rights and the malpractices of local officials. Many of the abuses brought to light were dealt with in the Statute of Westminster I (1275), legislation avowedly designed 'for the common good and the relief of those who are oppressed'.

Also important for that relief were changes at the centre. A major problem with Henry III's government, after the suspension of the justiciarship and the Bishop Neville type chancellorship, had been the lack of clear targets at the centre at which those in the localities could fire off their complaints. One solution in 1258 had been the revival of the justiciarship. Edward would not repeat that experiment, but he did have a chancellor very similar to Neville in Bishop Burnell. Scion of a knightly family from Acton Burnell in Shropshire (where he built a superb church and manor house), Burnell looked after his own interests but until his death in 1292 he ran the chancery in an accessible, even-handed manner, stressing repeatedly the duty of his officials to act justly. Edward's routine government seemed far more open and equitable than that of his father.

One man, however, could only do so much, and therefore Edward innovated, using parliament in a way never envisaged before, to hear petitions for justice and favour from his subjects. Until his departure for Gascony in 1286 at least two parliaments were held each year; they were able therefore to hear petitions on a regular basis. Before each meeting, proclamations were made calling for such petitions to be delivered by a certain date, and they were then heard, during the parliament, by the council or its committees. The response was sufficiently overwhelming to necessitate in 1280 the introduction of some filtering measures to prevent petitions swamping other business. For 'the people' for whom Edward so often expressed concern, the hearing of petitions was parliament's most important function.

Many of the petitions protested about the abuses by local officials and a main thrust of Edward's policies was indeed to make local government less oppressive. To that end he eschewed some of his father's unpopular policies: the sheriffs were never made to answer for increments above the county farms of pre-1258 levels; the forest eyres were never as lucrative as those held between 1246 and 1251; and in 1278 Edward dismissed most of the sheriffs and 'replaced them with knights from their own counties', as the annals of Dunstable put it. Thereafter for the most part it was county knights, serving in their own shires, who peopled the office. The long-standing demand of the counties for sheriffs to be such local worthies – a key feature of the reforms of 1258 – had thus been achieved.

Another important feature of the reforms of 1258–9 had been to send the justices round the shires to hear complaints or plaints (*querelae*), which could be brought by word of mouth or written 'bill'. That had been unpopular with some magnates who found their officials under attack, and the special eyres ended in 1260. Edward was more determined. When he restarted the general eyres in 1278, the judges were empowered to hear and determine *querelae* against all comers. Although on some eyres few plaints were heard (for reasons which are unclear), from now on they formed a separate section of the eyre's business.

Many plaints were of 'trespass', and it was essentially in Edward's reign that the action of trespass came to prominence. As a result a whole army of new business ultimately marched into the king's courts. Trespass became defined as an act by force of arms and in breach of the peace which was yet not serious enough to be a crown plea. By alleging trespass it was possible to bring a range of minor misdemeanours (assault, seizure of corn and animals, for example) into the king's courts, the preferred method ultimately becoming the civil writ of trespass. By the 1300s large numbers of cases were being heard by the common bench at Westminster. This was part and parcel of a general expansion of royal justice which had been continuing since the time of Henry II but now gathered quite extraordinary pace. Here Edward's legislation helped the process by making technical changes which maintained the popularity of old actions like novel disseisin and gave others an entirely new place in the limelight. Fifty replevin cases (in which plaintiffs sought the return of beasts seized by lords for arrears of service) came before the common bench between 1200 and 1267, and 1,500 between 1272 and 1307. Throughout the century there was also a steady growth in the forms of legal action. There were fifteen of these in 1189, sixty-five around 1270 and well over a hundred in 1307.

In order to cope with the increase of business, significant developments took place during Edward's reign in the structure of royal courts. After 1278 the general eyre remained in permanent session, with no interval between the completion of each nation-wide visitation. At the same time, in the long gaps between the eyres' appearance in individual counties circuit justices were commissioned more regularly than before to hear petty assizes and try those held in gaols. From about 1275 justices were also appointed, frequently in response to petitions in parliament, to hear and determine ('oyer and terminer') specific cases, often of trespass. And above all, largely because that was what litigants wanted, there was a vast increase in business done by common bench at Westminster, this being facilitated by widening the scope of the writs of *pone* and *recordari* which transferred business there. One reflection of the increase is the number of membranes of parchment the bench needed to record its business: forty-nine in 1200, 352 in 1275, and a colossal 1,520 in 1306. No wonder by that time there were twenty-three clerks writing the rolls!

In parallel with this increase in litigation and development in court structures, Edward's reign saw a transformation in the judiciary. For the first time it could be thought of as fully professional. Since the reign of Henry II there had been ministers who over many years had heard pleas both at the centre and in the localities. Increasingly in the thirteenth century such men came to specialize in legal work to the exclusion of anything else. Under Edward these long-serving professionals (like Ralph de Hengham and William of Bereford) were more numerous than ever before. It was also established for the first time that all the judges of the central courts (the common bench at Westminster and the king's bench travelling with the king) were entitled to salaries. An important change was likewise taking place in patterns of recruitment. Previously common bench justices had been drawn from clerks of former justices and from other branches of administration; by the end of Edward's reign, the judiciary was being recruited from the small group of serjeants ('barristers' in modern terminology) who pleaded in the central courts, particularly the common bench.

This reflected another important development in Edward's reign: the full emergence of a legal profession. In the 1260s there were around ten professional attorneys working at the common bench. By the early 1300s there were over 200 of them. These men represented their clients in court but did not actually plead. That was left to the serjeant barristers just mentioned, so already the division of the legal profession into barristers and solicitors was emerging. Serjeants formed the cream of the profession. They had to know both the standard form pleadings required by the numerous writs originating the actions, and the labyrinthine procedural rules governing the progress of each case. Hence, of course, the need for the profession in the first place. By the 1290s there were around thirty serjeants at the common bench, with entry being confined to apprentices trained by sitting in court and listening to the arguments. The monopoly the serjeants ultimately established over promotion to the judiciary meant that judges would be laymen (for clerks, prevented from pleading in court, could not be serjeants), members of a legal profession, and graduates of the courts, not the universities. They were for these reasons often unversed in either canon or Roman law; much of England's legal insularity can be attributed to this fact.

Under Edward, therefore, a law state had emerged as well as a tax state. Just as far more people than ever before paid taxes on a regular basis, so more than ever before they were involved in litigation through royal procedures in royal courts. In part this was simply due to the removal of cases from lower courts, especially the county courts. But it also represented a real increase in business, an increase which can only be explained by people positively wanting the kind of justice the king provided. The law state and the tax state were intimately related. It was because Edward dispensed justice and reformed the realm that his parliaments were ready to grant him taxes in a way those of Henry III had not. The Statute of Westminster I was promulgated 'with the counsel and assent of the community of the land' at a parliament attended by knights and burgesses. As the chronicler Wykes put it, such reforms served to 'join the hearts of the people to the king in the sincerity of inestimable love'.

The Statute of Westminster I was the first of the great Edwardian statutes. It was followed by the Statutes of Jewry (1275), Gloucester (1278), Mortmain (1279), Acton Burnell (1283), Westminster II, Merchants and Winchester (all 1285), and *Quo Warranto* and *Quia Emptores* (1290). In the years after 1234 Henry III had made some attempt to reform the realm through legislation, but Edward's efforts lasted much longer and were more detailed and wide-ranging. Westminster II itself runs to thirty pages of closely packed modern print. Not all the legislation was effective, but if there was a problem Edwardian government at least attempted a solution. The statutes dealt with a wide variety of issues including the workings of the common law, the maintenance of order, debts owed to merchants, and the difficulties created for lords by sub-enfeoffment. Taken as a whole they struck a balance between the claims of various interest groups, and in effect met the needs of 'the community of the realm'. They are a remarkable testimony to the grasp and hard thinking of royal officials and the sense of politics and responsibility of Edward himself.

One area where Edward's legislation seemed least effective was that of law and order, but it was also here that co-operation between king and community was in a sense at its most impressive. In his Statute of Winchester of 1285 Edward complained that there were more robberies and homicides than ever and that local juries refused to indict criminals when, as was often the case, they were local people. Edward's government was thus failing in its most basic task, the maintenance of the peace. The structures of law enforcement were, of course, very old. While lords in manorial and private hundred courts dealt with cases of minor disorder and sometimes had the right to hang petty thieves caught red-handed, all major crimes were included among the pleas of the crown, as they had been in effect since Anglo-Saxon times. In a knife-carrying society there was plenty of violence about. Even a small county like Berkshire had twenty homicides a year in the 1270s. Some of these deaths were the result of domestic violence; others, like many thefts and robberies, were the work of 'genuine criminals', often operating in gangs – criminals who largely came from and preyed upon the poorest sections of society. Edward's view that crime was increasing finds some support from statistics drawn from thirteenth-century eyre rolls. The rolls also reveal a chronic failure to arrest and convict criminals, not unlike the situation today. On the Surrey eyre of 1263 (not untypical), of the 232 persons accused of serious crime (including homicide), only 105 were brought before the judges and of these 73 were found not guilty, leaving only 32 who were actually convicted and hanged. Meanwhile 125 of the accused had absconded and had been outlawed – joining the ranks of the 'strangers' and 'unknown malefactors' increasingly blamed for crime. (They were responsible for 35 per cent of serious thefts reported in Lincolnshire legal records between 1281 and 1284.)

In his Statute of Winchester, Edward tried to address these problems by reinforcing earlier measures which had provided compensation for victims of robberies and set up a system of 'watch and ward', with watchmen in villages and constables in hundreds. Since Edward failed (other than intermittently) to appoint officials to enforce the statute, it is hardly surprising that by 1300 he acknowledged its failure. In Southwark the watchmen had gone off to the pub and then to bed. There is, however, a more positive side to all this. The hundred jurors, when they came before the justices in eyre, did at least identify large numbers of those outlawed as members of tithings, that is the units of ten men into which the peasant population was grouped for law-keeping purposes (see above, p. 62). In that respect the tithing system was working for thus placarded it must have been very difficult for outlaws to return to their local communities. Equally it may be that an accused's appearance before the judges and subsequent acquittal were often agreed beforehand within the local community, and were part of a process of settlement arranged by neighbours. The forms were royal but the justice communal, and perhaps all the better for that. The workings of law enforcement brought together all sections of society: the peasants in the tithing groups; the freemen on the hundred juries; the gentry holding office as sheriffs and coroners; the king's ministers appearing in the shires as justices in eyre; and the king himself in parliament overseeing the whole complex system.

Parliament was indeed the forum which held Edward's realm together. Its core was formed by the king's council, which included the justices of both the benches and the chief officials of the exchequer. One reason why parliaments met so regularly was to bring together the different parts of this expanding bureaucracy. Many of the great lay and ecclesiastical magnates were themselves on the council. Those who were not received an individual summons to parliament, the criteria often being wealth and status rather than baronial rank, the division of baronies and the rise of new men having rendered tenure by barony increasingly meaningless. The parliamentary peerage of the fourteenth century was beginning to develop. Meanwhile the House of Commons had actually arrived.

Before 1272 Henry III, both controlled by Simon de Montfort and as a free agent, had occasionally summoned knights and burgesses to parliament. Edward came to do so on a much more regular basis. One reason for this was that representatives could provide political support and spread the royal message in the localities. Edward's ministers had summoned knights and burgesses to the parliament of January 1273, where they swore allegiance to the new king and doubtless applauded the abandonment of the general eyre. In April 1275, the representatives went home to spread the glad news of the Statute of Westminster. In 1283 they came to Shrewsbury to witness Edward's triumph over Wales, the London burgesses taking back Prince Dafydd's head to be displayed on the Tower. There was also, however, another reason for the summoning of representatives, one which pre-eminently secured their place in parliament: no tax was obtainable without their consent (see above, pp. 355–6). Edward therefore had no alternative but to summon representatives to the parliaments of 1275, 1282 and 1290, parliaments where taxes were conceded. If the majority of Edward's early parliaments were still of the old-style magnate type, regular taxation, if it came, would be bound to change all that. So it did during the emergency caused by the French, Welsh and Scottish wars of the 1290s, with representatives attending four of the eight parliaments held between 1294 and 1297. One dramatic episode showed that from this there was no escape. In July 1297 Edward asserted that a tax had been granted 'by earls, barons, knights and laymen of all our kingdom', yet the magnates had not been properly summoned and the knights and burgesses had not been summoned at all. The earls of Hereford and Norfolk marched into the exchequer and said so. Edward was forced to back down and later in the year, in the 'Confirmation of the Charters', he accepted that taxation could only be levied 'with the common assent of all the realm'.

The attendance of representatives was now almost finally fixed. Between 1300 and 1307 they came to seven of the nine parliaments, even though taxation was only conceded at two of them. The Edwardian parliaments also saw the increasing appearance of the lower clergy (the deans and priors of the cathedral churches, the archdeacons and the delegates of the parish clergy), the reason again being to get their consent to taxation of their spiritualities. Edward's parliaments, with seventy-four knights (two from each shire), around eighty burgesses (two from each town, although the number of towns summoned varied) and no less than 148 members of the lower clergy, were fully representative of the realm in a way parliaments ceased to be later when clerical taxation was considered in a separate assembly, Convocation. Parliament had come a long way since Magna Carta, which had envisaged baronial and other tenants-in-chief alone providing 'common consent'. In contrast, a tract 'How to Hold a Parliament', written in the early fourteenth century, asserted that in all things 'which ought to be granted, done or refused in parliament', the knights from the shires carried more weight than the greatest earl. The magnates, it opined, spoke merely for themselves. It was the knights and burgesses who represented 'the whole community of England'. This parliamentary state necessitated, of course, a new kind of parliamentary monarch. There too Edward proved remarkably adept – not surprisingly perhaps since his experience stretched back to 1259 when the community of the bachelry of England had made its protest to him. In 1290 Edward restrained his temper, prolonged parliamentary sessions over many weeks, placated both knights and magnates with concessions, and in the end gained the largest tax of his reign.

In the late twelfth and thirteenth centuries a sense of community and national identity had been shaped in part by opposition to the crown.

Edward's achievement in the first twenty years of his reign was to close this gap between monarchy and nation. His reforms, as we have seen, 'joined the hearts of the people to the king'. His approach to patronage at last erased the idea that the king was rewarding foreign kinsmen and ministers at the expense of his native subjects. That Edward's most trusted councillor, Otto of Grandson, was a Savoyard caused hardly a ripple. Edward's uncle, William de Valence, so divisive a figure in the reign of Henry III, settled down as an unremarkable member of the regime. Matthias Bezille, reviled as a foreigner by the Gloucestershire gentry in 1261, produced descendants who themselves became members of the country gentry. Whereas Henry III was accused of bringing in foreigners to blot out the name of the English, in 1295 it was Edward who warned that a French invasion aimed to abolish 'the English tongue'. The eulogies poured forth on Edward's death in 1307 show that his reputation had survived the heavy burdens placed on the kingdom after 1294. Indeed no king since the Conquest had received such glowing tributes. One ballad written significantly in English and thus intended for a wide audience imagined Edward on his deathbed:

> 'Clerkes, knytes, barouns', he sayde,
> 'Y charge ou by oure sware [your oath]
> That the to Engelonde be trewe.'

At last the king himself was the leader of the English nation, not its enemy.

Edward deserves this fanfare, yet for some in the lower orders of society as also for the Jews it would have struck a discordant note. The king would certainly have regarded the peasants as part of the nation which he led. They were integral, as we have seen, to the system of law enforcement. They also reaped some benefit from reforms which restrained the abuses of local officials, and made litigation easier. A great many legal actions, as in the past, were between freemen of peasant condition over small amounts of land. Probably it was in such cases that royal justice was at its most effective. Peasant communities thought enough of the impartiality of the royal courts to bring actions in them against their lords, sometimes clubbing together to pay their serjeant barristers. They may also have gained indirectly from the common law, for it inspired record-keeping and comparable forms of action in manorial courts, both of which gave peasants greater security.

Yet while Edward might declare that 'we are all to obtain one reward in Christ, whether of servile or of free conditions', that 'one reward' was indeed in the next life, not in this. None of Edward's legislation altered the fact that the unfree half of the peasantry remained completely debarred from the king's courts.

> What can a serf do unless serve, and his son?
> He shall be a pure serf deprived of freedom.
> The law's judgement and the king's court prove this

ran the triumphal poem of Leicester abbey in 1276 after its villeins of Stoughton had failed to prove they were free sokemen. The peasantry also suffered particularly heavily in the latter part of the reign from the demands of the crown. It was largely their goods which were taken to supply royal armies under the right of prise. It was they who supplied the king with foot soldiers. The obligation on everyone to bear arms for the maintenance of the peace and defence of the realm was ancient, but it was one thing to send village contingents to resist foreign invasion as in 1264, and quite another to dispatch them (organized by new officials called 'commissioners of array') to Wales, Scotland and Gascony as in the 1290s. Although Edward normally offered pay after the muster, it was up to the villages to find the troops and their equipment. Launditch hundred in Norfolk in 1295 had to spend £52 raising 187 men for Gascony. Worse than either prise or military service was the burden of taxation, for it was both heavier (Launditch's bill in 1294 was £242) and general throughout the country. (Prise and military service bore most heavily on counties nearest to campaigns.) Admittedly a significant proportion of the English peasantry were too poor to be taxed, but that still left many who were liable. What made their sufferings disproportionately heavy was that they lacked the resources to bribe the tax collectors. There could be no equivalent of the entertainment of the assessors offered by Merton College, Oxford, which dramatically reduced its tax burden at Cuxham in the 1290s. So, as one lampoon put it, the rich man worth £40 is taxed at 12d., and so is the man with 'a heap of children' whom 'poverty hath brought to the ground'. In the 1260s Nicholas Franciscus, a peasant from Westerham in Kent, declared that the king's bailiffs deserved to be hanged because they never did good when they could do ill, a very Robin Hood type of utterance. Many in Edward's reign probably expressed similar sentiments about royal officials, if not perhaps of the king himself.

It was not, of course, merely royal officials who were oppressive.

Throughout Edward's reign peasant communities continued to resist their lords both by violence and litigation (see above, pp. 413–14). Meanwhile there was a large criminal underclass, swollen perhaps by over-population, 'the unknown malefactors' and 'vagrants' referred to so often in the eyre rolls. In the 1260s peasants had felt genuinely embraced by the great movement of 'baronial' reform. That is far less clear of the protests of the 1290s, for all their limitations on prise and taxation. By the end of the thirteenth century a general peasants' revolt may not have been very far away. The Ordinances of 1311 expressed concern that 'the people of the land will rise by reason of the prises and other oppressions made in these times'. Edward's power was always based on the exploitation by him and his lords of the great bulk of the population.

If the peasants, for all their burdens, were part of Edward's people, the Jews emphatically were not. In 1290 he expelled them from the country. There was one primary reason why Edward was prepared to take this step. The heavy taxation between 1240 and 1260 had destroyed the wealth of the Jews and thus their value to the crown. Concentrated in twenty-one towns with 'chests' in which were deposited the records of their business dealings, Jewish numbers had declined from between 3,000 and 5,000 in the 1240s to less than 2,000 forty years later. In most towns, as had always been the case, the bulk of the business was controlled by a handful of Jews (in Lincoln there were a dominant six, three of whom had London connections), but the scale of their transactions was small compared with those of the past. The total value of the debts owed to the Jews in 1290 was around £20,000 compared with nearly £80,000 in the 1240s. Whereas between 1241 and 1256 the crown gained not far short of £73,333 in Jewish taxation, between 1272 and 1290 it only made £9,300. Another £11,000 came from the seizure of property following coin-clipping allegations in 1278, but that only served to weaken the community further.

Edward could afford to be influenced by 'religious' considerations. A strand of church thought (mentioned by Edward himself in his Statute of Jewry in 1275) had always been that the Jews should be preserved and protected because they were reminders of Christ's passion, but during the thirteenth century other more hostile views were gaining ground. Legislation against usury reached a climax in the Council of Lyons in 1274. In 1286 Pope Honorius IV wrote to England fiercely criticizing the contacts permitted between Christians and Jews, and demanding more rigorous separation between the two. Edward himself had already moved in that direction by laying down the precise dimensions of the badge (the *tabula*) which Jews were to wear so that they could be shunned on sight. Another solution was through a policy of muscular conversion. Edward tried to force the Jews to attend the preaching of the friars, and to cope with the results he optimistically enlarged the House for Converted Jews founded by his father.

If, however, the Jews obstinately refused to convert, there was a growing belief that they should not be preserved but expelled – the dangers of contact, with horrific events like those at Lincoln fresh in people's minds (see above, p. 349), were just too great. During Henry's reign they were indeed expelled from a number of English towns (including Montfort's Leicester) and in 1275 Edward allowed his mother to remove them from her dower lands. In 1253 (while still on crusade) Louis IX had ordered all Jews to leave France save those who were traders and workers. Most significantly of all, Edward himself anticipated the expulsion of Jews from England by expelling them from Gascony when he was in the province in 1287. Making little money from the suppression, the king's motives were again 'religious': a thank-offering for his recovery from serious illness which also prompted his related (though abortive) decision once more to go on crusade.

There was one other continental precedent which revealed very real material benefits from Jewish expulsion. In December 1289 Charles of Salerno had expelled the Jews from his counties of Maine and Anjou quite specifically in return for a tax 'as some recompense for the profit we lose'. Edward was well informed about Charles, having secured his release from Aragonese captivity only the year before. His example tapped into an existing English background in which the king had for some time been imposing restrictions on the Jews in return for parliamentary taxation. The great tax of 1275 was related to the Statute of Jewry which abolished usury altogether, and instructed the Jews to live henceforth by lawful merchandise and labour. In this perspective, final expulsion in return for a tax must have seemed but a logical concluding step.

Getting the tax, of course, depended on expulsion being something which parliament wanted. Paradoxically, religious considerations aside, that may have been less true in 1290 than earlier in the century. The evaporation of Jewish wealth had reduced the numbers and status of their creditors. Great lay and ecclesiastical magnates had taken their overdrafts elsewhere: in 1281 it was to the Riccardi that the earl of Norfolk owed £1,133. Up to a point, moreover, the Jews after the 1275 Statute had adapted to a new non-usurious way of life. A large proportion of the bonds found in the chests in 1290 recorded debts owed not in money but in commodities, notably wool. That may simply have been a way of disguising usurious loans, about whose continuation Edward complained. But it is also likely that Jews were genuinely working as commodity traders, advancing money in return for wool and corn which they then sold on at a profit. The intense hostility to the Jews seen in Lincoln in the 1250s was not always typical. In Hereford in 1286 large numbers of Christians enjoyed the plays, sports and minstrelsy at a Jewish wedding, to the scandal of the bishop.

If, however, these developments had reduced hostility to the Jews, it had certainly not been eliminated. The Jews could not escape their history. In the 1275 Statute, Edward explained how he had seen 'the disinheriting of the good men of his land that has happened by the usuries which the Jews have made in the past'. Although their new clients were declining in importance, their old ones remained on the books until the debts were paid off. As late as 1264–5, when the Montfortian government made concessions over Jewish debts, the beneficiaries included many of magnate status. The legislation of 1269–70 prevented such debts being sold to Christians but only if they had no royal licence, which of course was often granted. So the queen and other courtiers bought them up and forced the victims to sell land in payment. The 1275 legislation likewise still allowed Jews to collect their old debts and indeed to seize land in the process. Although most of these magnate debts seem to have been liquidated in one way or another by 1290, they must have left a terrible residue of bitterness. For the knights it was not simply a question of residue, for they continued to contract debts. The Lincoln records of 1290 show that twenty-four of the 185 debtors (owing 25 per cent of the total outstanding) were knights or members of knightly families. A good many knights were also among the debtors of Aaron le Blund in Hereford. If some of these debts represented genuine commodity transactions, that is hardly likely to have been the case with all of them. So the knights in the 1290 parliament saw the expulsion of the Jews as having immediate financial benefits for themselves or their fellows.

*   *   *

By an unpleasant paradox the expulsion of the Jews showed Edward at his most ruthless and also his most conciliatory. Sacrificed on the parliamentary altar in return for taxation, they were victims of the consensus which underlay the might of the Edwardian state. In terms of the reach of the common law, that state was surely unique in its scope. In no previous period had so many people pursued and settled their disputes through royal procedures before royal justices. No one forced them to do so. The common law grew almost entirely in response to demand.

Whether, in terms of his English resources, Edward was uniquely powerful is more difficult to say, given the difficulties of making comparisons with earlier kings. Certainly the Edwardian state had more records and bureaucracy than ever before, but that is not the same thing. Already in 1230 the pipe roll was over twice the size of the roll for 1130, mentioning three times as many people and places, yet the revenue recorded was actually slightly less. It is at least debatable whether Edward's taxes raised any more money in real terms than the pre-Conquest gelds, although the latter required the barest fraction of the 25,000 pages of returns (if put into modern print) generated by a single Edwardian levy with everyone's corn and cattle listed and valued in remorseless detail. The fact was that a state which depended on tapping the wealth of large numbers of individuals needed far more bureaucracy and record-keeping than one where a large proportion of the revenue came from crown lands and a land tax.

The parliamentary tax-based state, with its bureaucracy and records, was therefore very much the consequence of declining revenue from land. It was also the product of weakness in other areas. Although impossible to measure in any precise way, Magna Carta had constituted a watershed between different styles of government, making it much harder for the king to treat individuals in an arbitrary manner, especially when it came to taking their money. The 1215 Charter itself pointed the way forward when it accepted the levying of general taxation if sanctioned by 'common counsel'.

The Edwardian state was also linked to changing structures of local power where again the balance was shifting in some ways against the king. True, during the twelfth and thirteenth centuries the king had prevented the localities falling under the control of competing magnates basing their power on castles, feudal honours and the tenure of liberties and local office. The king certainly allowed large numbers of hundreds to pass into private hands (over half the 628 hundreds in 1279 were privately held) but he had maintained his hold over the trial and punishment of serious crime, had reduced the earldoms to titular status, and had stopped the sheriffdoms becoming hereditary. He had also developed a direct relationship with his free subjects through the cascading procedures of the common law and had taxed everyone in the land. There were, however, other changes in the thirteenth century which served to diminish the king's local 'punch'. First, after 1236 there was the disappearance of the 'curial sheriffs', the sheriffs close to the king with the resources and court clout to uphold his will against the mightiest magnate (see above, pp. 350–51). And then came the end of the general eyre. It was suspended with the outbreak of war with France in 1294 and never properly revived. The eyres, weighed down with crown pleas, civil pleas, plaints and *quo warranto* cases were taking longer and longer to complete. The Suffolk eyre of 1240 already lasted about four weeks; that of 1286 took more than twice as long. A good deal of the eyre's work could be hived off to justices of gaol delivery, assize, and oyer and terminer, while the escheators could carry out its inquiries into royal rights. Justices of 'trailbaston', introduced in the 1300s, could target cases of serious disorder. By 1330, however, the king's judges themselves looked back nostalgically to the great age of the eyre in the thirteenth century, when it had maintained the peace and given justice to all without fear or favour. The single-purpose judicial commissions, even if headed by professional judges, could not replicate the eyre's overarching supervision of government and people in the shires. With the criminals, litigants, attorneys, local officials, assize juries, and juries for crown pleas from all the hundreds, over 5,000 people, it has been calculated, came before the judges when they visited Suffolk in 1240.

These changes were part of a general process in which the gentry came to staff local government office, monopolizing the old office of the sheriff, holding the new ones which royal government called into being, and helping to man the judicial commissions which replaced the eyre. In the fourteenth century, with the emergence of the justices of the peace, they obtained the primary responsibility for the trial and punishment of crime. This did not necessarily mean the gentry ruled the shires at the king's command. If that was the pattern in some areas, in others magnates strove to assert their own local rule by taking into their retinues and rewarding with money fees the gentry holders of local office, finding such men much easier to control than the curial sheriffs and justices in eyre of the past. They thus combated the threat implicit in the way the king had established a direct relationship with the gentry. Up to a point, therefore, the king had defeated one form of magnate power in the localities only to succumb to another, sometimes called by historians 'bastard feudalism'. Those on the losing side of the battles for local control complained increasingly at fourteenth century parliaments about magnates corrupting the entire workings of government. The king was now not too powerful but too weak. Things really had come full circle since 1215.

The basic fact was that these new local structures marched well with the developing tax-based parliamentary state. With Magna Carta restricting the financial burdens that could be placed on great magnates, the king had less need of great curial sheriffs to coerce them to pay their debts. Conversely, in order to get parliamentary consent to taxation, he had more need to conciliate local society, and one way of doing that was by allowing the gentry to staff the shire offices. The conciliation of local society itself had a long history, for Henry I had made concessions to under-tenants in his Coronation Charter of 1100. The political community had always been much larger than a few hundred lay and ecclesiastical barons. The difference was that the king was now dependent on taxation which only knights and burgesses gathered in parliament could grant. All this created an entirely new situation with which kings had to deal. When they did deal with it, they could obtain taxation and wield great power, like Edward I. In Edward's reign the rest of Britain bore the consequences.

There was another way too in which Edward's career marked a watershed, and again it was one where the consequences were first felt in Wales and Scotland. Politics were becoming more brutal. The chivalry introduced by the Conquest, in which the nobility were neither killed in battle nor executed for political crimes, was coming to an end. The first sign of that had been at Evesham where over thirty knights were deliberately killed in an unprecedented slaughter. Indeed Edward before the battle appointed a death-squad with no other task but to kill Montfort. In part this was because, with no precedent for political executions among the high nobility, murder on the battlefield was the only way to get rid of him. Yet under Edward executions also began. True, the victims were Welsh and Scots, but they were still men of the highest status: Dafydd, the self-styled prince of Wales, in 1283; the earl of Atholl in 1306. The Osney chronicler rightly described Dafydd's execution with its horrific ritual of drawing, hanging, beheading, eviscerating and quartering as 'unprecedented in past times'. In the next reign, that of Edward II, the English nobility too became engulfed in the blood-letting and a pattern was set for the rest of the Middle Ages. In battle the cry became 'Kill the nobles, spare the commons', the very reverse of what had happened in battles between 1106 and 1264.

These changes needed no new theory. The concept of treason, in the sense of breach of faith to one's lord, was very old, and it certainly could cover all cases of political revolt. Equally old was the idea that the penalty could be death. What happened under the Normans and Angevins was that kings decided not to impose the penalty. A major reason for that had been the structure of the Anglo-Norman polity (see above, pp. 126-7). With a nobility straddling England and Normandy, and with open frontiers into the rest of France, it was only too likely that an execution in England would set off a revolt somewhere in the overseas dominions. Although these basic conditions ended in 1204 with the loss of Normandy, for a while the amnesty continued. The long period without executions or killings in battle had created a virtuous cycle which the aristocracy was loath to break. John had wanted to execute the Rochester garrison in 1215 but was stopped when his own followers declared that if he did so it would be their turn next when they were captured. With its original props knocked away, however, the virtuous cycle came under increasing strain with each political crisis, and partially broke at Evesham. Once it had broken the waters were always likely to flow into an altogether different cycle – a vicious and far more enduring one of killings tit for tat. Ultimately it was the execution of Piers Gaveston, Edward II's earl of Cornwall, by the nobles themselves which set off Edward's own revenging executions. The clement centuries had given place to the centuries of blood.

The loss of Normandy had made English politics more enclosed and intense. It also meant that Edward could give far more attention than his predecessors to the matter of Britain.

16

Wales and Scotland: Conquest and Coexistence

When Edward came to the throne in 1272, he headed the least 'conquering' of British dynasties. Under the Treaty of Perth in 1266 King Alexander of Scotland had wrested Man and the Western Isles from the king of Norway. By the Treaty of Montgomery in 1267 Llywelyn ap Gruffudd of Gwynedd had gained dominion over the other native rulers and been recognized as prince of Wales (see above, p. 386). Meanwhile in England the king's power remained at a discount after a destructive civil war. Edward changed all this. His restoration of royal authority in England gave him the means to transform the political shape of Britain. Within five years of his accession, he had destroyed Llywelyn's principality. By 1284 he had eliminated nearly all the native rulers. Wales, unconquered by the Anglo-Saxons and the Normans, had finally succumbed to Edward I.

The ultimate disaster should not overshadow Llywelyn's years of triumph. When, at the height of his power in 1274, he came to inspect his new castle at Dolforwyn (built above the Severn in a vital strategic area just west of Montgomery), the visit sent shock waves through the district. Did he, wondered one correspondent, intend to go on into the forest of Clun to plan a new castle there? Had he summoned the great men of England to come and meet him? 'All the bailiffs of Wales' were forwarding supplies and Dolforwyn was stocked for a stay of three weeks. Here indeed was a mighty prince.

In considering the structures which supported Gwynedd's power in the thirteenth century, its three great rulers are best treated together: Llywelyn ab Iorwerth or Llywelyn the Great (died 1240), Dafydd (died 1246) and Llywelyn ap Gruffudd. If all three in terms of status were below the kings of Scotland and England, they were above everyone else in Britain, for they alone bore the title prince and wore a coronet to prove it. Dafydd's right to such an insignia as prince of North Wales had been recognized by Henry III. Perhaps Llywelyn ap Gruffudd adopted a grander version after he became prince of Wales. His coronet was made of gold and symbolic enough to be presented after his demise to the shrine of Edward the Confessor in Westminster Abbey. At Aberffraw on Anglesey, ancient seat of the dynasty, the hall of the 'palace', as it was later described, had an elaborate roof in which were set great stone bosses decorated with the heads of coroneted princes. The rulers made sure that no one forgot their elevated status.

The Welsh law books, whether edited in Gwynedd or elsewhere, always began with a section on the king and his court. Although it is difficult to know how far the rights and duties of the officials listed corresponded with reality, there is enough evidence from other sources to show Gwynedd's court was impressive, with some of the same kinds of ministers as found in England and in Scotland. It was headed by the steward (*distain*) who was also the prince's leading councillor and quite possibly the commander of his military forces (discussed later). Another of his duties was to act as 'justice' in the law cases before the prince, while an earlier official, the 'judge of the court' mentioned in the law texts, disappeared from view. As the principality expanded so did these legal responsibilities and on one occasion the steward was styled the 'justice of Wales'. By the early thirteenth century clerks at court almost certainly formed a writing office, its head being occasionally given the title chancellor or vice-chancellor. Passages in the law books suggest that this position was taken by the 'household priest', for he was to receive payment when charters or letters patent were sealed. The princes' charters were very similar in style and appearance to those of the two British kings, the use of the princely title and the plural 'we' making them quite distinct from those of the other Welsh rulers. The clerks must also have written the princes' administrative orders (now lost) and diplomatic correspondence. The latter was extensive: over twenty of Llywelyn ap Gruffudd's letters to Edward I survive.

At court it was the chamberlain who was responsible for receiving, storing and spending the king's money. Although (as in Scotland) there was nothing like a fixed exchequer, groups of ministers, including one of the prince's clerks, were sent to hear and record the accounts of local officials, if we may judge from this happening to the castellan of Dolforwyn. The effectiveness of government depended very much on a small ministerial elite drawn throughout the thirteenth century from around six curial families. Ednyfed Fychan, for example, steward of

Llywelyn ab Iorwerth and Dafydd, was followed in the same post by several of his sons. There is some anecdotal evidence that the size of the Gwynedd court was expanding. The abbot of Basingwerk complained that whereas he had entertained 300 men when Llywelyn ab Iorwerth and Dafydd came to hunt, under Llywelyn ap Gruffudd the number had risen to 500. Another complaint was that Llywelyn ap Gruffudd gave robes each year to 140 members of his household, the implication being that this was at everyone else's expense. In giving robes, Llywelyn's practice paralleled that of the kings of England. If the beneficiaries really did number 140 this did not compare with the 570 who were dressed by Edward I in the 1280s, but it still reveals a household of considerable size.

All the princes in the thirteenth century strove to increase their authority in Gwynedd. They insisted (here supported by the law books) that they should consent to alienations of land by free men, for example to religious houses, and that they (not the immediate lords) should have the chattels of those who died intestate. Llywelyn ap Gruffudd also demanded reliefs and control over wardships. Another area of advance was in that of dispute settlement. The basic practices here were deeply communal. Disputes over land were resolved by the judgement, or more often the arbitration, of 'law-worthy' local men, not necessarily in a court. An important role in decisions and settlements could be played by a semi-professional judge-jurist, the *ynad*. Yet this communal system was becoming embraced by regular sessions of commote and cantref courts presided over by the prince himself or (in his absence) his bailiff (the *rhaglaw*). While there was no equivalent to the standard-form pleading of the English and Scottish common law, the prince and his deputies were hearing a growing number of civil actions. Their situation was perhaps most akin to that of the justices in eyre under Henry I, who presided over the pleas but left judgement and procedure to be determined, according to varying local rules, by the suitors to the county court.

Even more striking was the way the princes were asserting jurisdiction in cases of theft and homicide, thus coming to play a much greater role in the maintenance of law and order. Statements in the law books and evidence of actual practice show that the rulers were beginning to fine thieves and killers and profit from their chattels. They were also executing thieves if the punishment was not a fine. All this cut into the rights of lords like the bishop of St Asaph and into the custom where homicide either led to feud or was settled by compensation payments (*gallanas* was the name given to both), without any necessary involvement of the ruler. The princes of Gwynedd were moving towards asserting a monopoly over the trial and punishment of serious crime like that exercised by the kings of England and Scotland.

Justice was clearly profitable, but the main resources of the princes derived from their own lands and bondmen, and from a set of renders (including hospitality for the court) given from free land controlled by kin groups and the church. Some of these resources came from the areas intermittently ruled by the princes (in Southern Powys, between Wye and Severn, and in Builth and Brecon) but the great bulk derived from Gwynedd itself, where the cattle of Snowdon and corn of Anglesey and Llŷn were especially important. With the increase in commerce and the money supply, the cash proportion of the revenue was increasing, in part through the commutation into cash of renders once made in kind. Such commutations were worth on one estimate around £400 annually in the 1270s. There was also a tax levied at 3*d*. a head on cattle. Whereas the tribute due under the 1211 treaty was entirely to be paid in animals, between 1267 and 1271, under the terms of the Treaty of Montgomery, Llywelyn paid the English crown certainly £9,166 and perhaps £12,500. Although little more than a guess from later evidence, Llywelyn's revenue from Gwynedd, at the height of his power after 1267, may have been around £4,000 a year, and there would have been some additional income from his other territories. He was probably just as wealthy as the greatest of the marcher barons, Gilbert de Clare, earl of Gloucester.

Central to Gwynedd's power in the thirteenth century was its military might. At times this was clearly formidable, reflecting changes which had transformed the forces of Welsh rulers since the advent of the Normans. At the heart of Welsh armies had always been the *teulu*, the ruler's warband of sworn followers. Llywelyn ap Gruffudd clearly had an equivalent body but it was now horsed, 'elegantly armoured' (in Matthew Paris's words), and supported less by plunder than by grants of land and perhaps also of money. The *teulu* does not appear *eo nomine* after 1215, and conceivably the name seemed inappropriate to a body now in some ways equivalent to the household knights of the English and Scottish kings. For all the costs of its elegant armour, Llywelyn could raise a cavalry force of respectable size. In 1263, with his own household troops supplemented by contingents from much of Wales, he was able to put about 180 armoured horses into the field, as well as others unarmoured, this according to a convincing estimate made in a letter by a knight on the spot. The princes of Gwynedd could also muster large numbers of foot soldiers, exploiting the obligation mentioned in the law books on all freemen to serve the ruler for six weeks a year outside 'the country', and probably also using pay. Llywelyn the Great, according to record evidence, took 1,600 foot on John's northern expedition of 1209. According to the 1263 letter, Llywelyn ap Gruffudd's infantry numbered more than 10,000. If that is an exaggeration, it at least suggests the force was several thousand strong.

The power of the rulers of Gwynedd also rested on the stone castles which they built in the thirteenth century. Apart from that at Dolforwyn, these were all in Gwynedd itself. Their positioning was clearly strategic in intent because, sometimes supported by the establishment of new cattle farms, they were on sites unrelated to existing courts and centres. Ewloe by the Dee estuary could monitor the main land route into Gwynedd from the north-east. Castell y Bere was in Meirionydd, the cantref which formed Gwynedd's south-western frontier. Two castles, at Dolbadarn and Dolwydellan, were placed within the heart of Snowdonia. The latter, with its square keep atop a rocky outcrop high in the hills, commanded the north–south route from Conwy through to Criccieth, where there was another castle. These buildings were certainly designed to bolster Gwynedd's formidable natural defences against invasion (see above, p. 318), but that was not perhaps their main purpose for they lacked the size to withstand major sieges. Rather, the point was to display the dynasty's power and enforce its rule within Gwynedd itself.

The princes' perambulations through Gwynedd were of vital importance in maintaining their authority. They could stay both in their new castles and also in the traditional court complexes which were at the centre of the commotes, the main administrative divisions in Anglesey and Gwynedd west of the Conwy. The sites of no less than twenty-one such courts have been identified, many rendered more impressive by being close to mottes, of which some had probably been built by Welsh rulers and others by the Normans during their brief hold of Gwynedd. At Rhosyr in Anglesey the court was impressive in another way: excavations have shown it had a walled enclosure, as well as a hall and chamber probably dating from the 1240s. The 'palace' nearby at Aberffraw we have already described.

With his string of new castles and web of old but refurbished courts, Llywelyn ap Gruffudd was therefore well placed to govern Gwynedd and assert his wider authority as prince of Wales. Yet he also faced grave problems. The intensity with which Gwynedd had to be exploited in order to pay the sums due under the Treaty of Montgomery created considerable resentment. Although the complaints drawn up after the prince's demise were designed to impress King Edward, they are too detailed and substantial to be dismissed. They show that Llywelyn had alienated both of Gwynedd's bishops, Anian of Bangor and Anian of St Asaph, in part by developing his jurisdiction over theft and homicide. He had also offended a considerable number of the leading freemen, the *uchelwyr* or 'nobles' on whom his rule depended. Equally serious were tensions with some of the leading ministerial families, in part perhaps because he now had so little patronage to give. In 1276–7 Rhys ap Gruffudd and his brother, the prior of Bangor, grandsons of Ednyfed Fychan, both conspired against him. And worst of all were the fissures within the house of Gwynedd itself, which climaxed in 1274 with a plot which was probably designed to eliminate Llywelyn and put his brother Dafydd in his place.

Llywelyn's problems were equally acute in his wider principality. Under the Treaty of Montgomery he had gained the homages of the other Welsh rulers, who now held their territories from him, not from the king. But Llywelyn still had to make a reality of the new relationships. He did not draw revenue or intervene directly within the domains of the other rulers, but they certainly owed him military service. He expected to confirm their land grants, and confirm too, if not control, the descent of the territories. Among the most striking indications of Llywelyn's authority are his confirmations of family settlements made by rulers in both Ceredigion and Northern Powys. Likewise, all the Welsh 'barons' were justiceable in Llywelyn's court and liable to forfeiture for disobedience.

Not everyone was happy with such a rule. The tensions apparent before 1267 (see above, p. 383) had not been banished by the Treaty. Indeed, Maredudd ap Rhys under its terms had gained exemption from Llywelyn's overlordship and remained a vassal of King Henry. The Welsh had a common law, language and history, but the difficulties of moving from those to a Gwynedd-dominated principality were as great now as they had been under Llywelyn's grandfather. While Llywelyn's court poet, Llygad Gŵr, celebrated the unity from north to south brought by Llywelyn's rule, 'the true king of Wales', he also indicated that it was unity through domination. It was in Llywelyn's nature to 'impose himself on other lands'. The fact was that Llywelyn's rule often seemed based on intimidation and coercion. The other rulers, now no more than 'barons', even in Welsh sources (*barwneit*), were expected to address him as 'serene', 'noble', 'most famous and honest'. Those no longer in his 'unity' were 'unfaithful', 'disobedient', 'rebellious', and very much in need of 'mercy'. Allegiance was ensured by the exaction of hostages, and threats of trial, fine, forfeiture and imprisonment. No wonder Gruffudd ap Gwenwynwyn, in one of his agreements with Llywelyn, sought to protect himself from trumped-up charges and excessive punishment. It was not merely great rivals like Gruffudd who were treated in this way. A similar regime seems to have enforced Llywelyn's rule among the *uchelwyr* between Wye and Severn, as well as further south in Brecon. Welshmen too might well have agreed with the English poet who described Llywelyn as 'a cruel leader, a plunderer of men'.

Yet initially Llywelyn triumphed over his difficulties. In October 1270 he beat off a challenge on the southern frontiers of his principality and destroyed the new castle Gilbert de Clare was building at Caerphilly in Glamorgan. When Llywelyn's brother Dafydd and Gruffudd ap Gwenwynwyn of Southern Powys plotted against him in 1274, Gruffudd was sentenced to forfeiture and had to beg mercy on his knees. When later in the year he fled to England (along with Dafydd), Llywelyn seized Southern Powys and ruled it directly, an awesome demonstration of his authority. It was not his internal difficulties which destroyed Llywelyn's principality. It was external attack.

The trail which ended in the war of 1277 began with disputes over the Treaty of Montgomery. It had given Llywelyn the homages 'of all the Welsh barons of Wales' without defining who they were. A conflict quickly arose over the allegiances of the native 'barons' of north Glamorgan, which Llywelyn claimed for his principality and Gilbert de Clare for his lordship. The Treaty had also allowed Llywelyn to keep his conquests in Brecon, but that left Humphrey de Bohun, earl of Hereford, retaining part of the district, and constantly encroaching on the prince's portion, or so the latter alleged. If then the marcher barons and the king would not observe the Treaty, Llywelyn decided he would not observe it either: after Christmas 1271 he made no further payments towards the £2,000 a year he owed under its terms. As a result the dispute escalated. In 1274 Edward gave shelter to Dafydd and Gruffudd ap Gwenwynwyn after their failed conspiracy. Consequently Llywelyn refused to do homage to Edward, even when (in August 1275) the king came to Chester to receive it. In the same year Llywelyn defiantly married by proxy none other than Eleanor, daughter of the late Simon de Montfort, only for Edward to capture her on her way to Wales early in 1276. Eventually, in November 1276, after several more demands for homage had been ignored, Edward decided to make war on Llywelyn as a 'rebel and disturber of the peace'.

In all this Llywelyn had seen the situation very clearly, or so he thought. As he told the pope in September 1275, he was faced with a king whose aim was to destroy the Treaty of Montgomery 'totally' (in totum). Nor did that seem surprising since it had deprived Edward himself of both the Four Cantrefs and the homages of the native rulers. If so, what was the point of conciliation? Better to make a stand now with power as yet unreduced. Nor did it seem entirely foolhardy to do so. Llywelyn could remember the disasters of the 1240s, but since then he had enjoyed unbroken success. He had defeated royal armies in 1257 and 1263; in 1274 he had scattered his domestic foes. Gilbert de Clare for one believed wholeheartedly in the prince's might, hence the mammoth scale on which he recommenced his castle at Caerphilly after its destruction in 1270. Llywelyn could hope a firm stand would persuade Edward to back down. If it did not, war was not necessarily a fatal opinion.

In the event, Llywelyn capitulated almost without a fight. There was nothing very novel about Edward's strategy, but it was implemented on a new scale and with a new thoroughness. Llywelyn's unpopularity and financial difficulties may well have reduced his forces way below the levels of the 1250s and 1260s. Soon he faced internal collapse. Edward established three separate commands. That in the north, operating from Chester with Dafydd one of the captains, provided cover, while Gruffudd ap Gwenwynwyn re-established himself in Southern Powys. The rulers of Northern Powys then quickly submitted. In the Middle March, Roger de Mortimer captured Dolforwyn in only a week (in April 1277), while the *uchelwr* Hywel ap Meurig (whose son Llywelyn had held hostage) led 2,700 Welsh foot soldiers from Brecon and Radnor into Edward's service. In the south, where the royal base was at Carmarthen, Rhys ap Maredudd, son of the Maredudd ap Rhys who had escaped homage to Llywelyn in 1267, entered Edward's service in April. His rival in Ystrad Tywi, Rhys Wyndod, submitted soon afterwards, as did the rulers of southern Ceredigion.

In these circumstances Llywelyn could do nothing to prevent Edward's southern force reaching Aberystwyth and then establishing control over northern Ceredigion. In Gwynedd itself he faced the defection of both the bishops and members of the ministerial elite. Edward's army reached Chester on 15 July. By the end of August, when numbers were at their height, he had some 15,640 foot soldiers in pay, of whom some 9,000 were Welsh. The army, its way cleared by 1,800 woodmen, advanced inexorably to Deganwy. Even more devastating was the fleet. A fleet to seize Anglesey had been envisaged in 1257 but had never materialized. This time, nearly twenty-six ships and eight tenders were assembled, manned by 726 sailors. Anglesey was occupied by 2,000 foot soldiers, and labourers were ferried across to reap the harvest. Gwynedd faced starvation.

In this desperate situation, Llywelyn came to terms. In November 1277, he surrendered the Four Cantrefs to the English crown, so Gwynedd was once again cut back to the Conwy. In return he recovered Anglesey, but for an annual payment of £333 until the sums owed under the 1267 treaty had been cleared. If he had no heirs of his body, then the island was to escheat to the king on his death. Llywelyn was allowed to keep his title prince of Wales, but little was left of his wider dominion. All his territorial possessions outside Gwynedd, in the area between Wye and Severn and in Builth and Brecon, were confiscated. All the homages of the native rulers, with a few insignificant exceptions, were returned to the king. The principality of Wales was at an end.

If Llywelyn believed he could sustain a war against Edward he had been grievously mistaken. Was he also mistaken about the threat he faced? Certainly even in 1277 Edward had no overwhelming desire to destroy Llywelyn and Gwynedd absolutely, otherwise he would have continued the war and done so. As it was, he did not implement an earlier plan to partition Gwynedd west of Conwy between himself and Dafydd. Instead he accommodated Dafydd at his own expense within the Four Cantrefs, stabilizing what remained of Llywelyn's state. The reduction of the payments from the £2,000 a year owed under the Treaty of Montgomery to £333 under the new treaty had the same effect. Nor is it clear that Edward had set out from the first to cut Llywelyn's principality down to size. In 1270 he actually made it more complete by selling Llywelyn the homage of Maredudd ap Rhys for

£3,333; this sale was to raise money for his crusade, a telling indication of his priorities. Later he humbled himself (as he complained) and came to Chester in the hope of receiving the prince's homage. If he also harboured Dafydd and Gruffudd ap Gwenwynwyn, and held Eleanor de Montfort captive, that was retaliation for Llywelyn's refusal both of homage and the Treaty payments. It is a striking fact that Edward neither challenged Llywelyn's right to treat Dafydd and Gwenwynwyn as he had, nor allowed them to appeal to him for justice. It would be hard to conclude that Edward had intended to provoke a war to destroy the Treaty.

If, however, Llywelyn was wrong in the short term, in a longer perspective was he not entirely right? Was there not a fundamental incompatibility between Llywelyn's claim that the 'rights of our principality are wholly separate from the rights of your kingdom, although we hold our principality under your royal power' and Edward's view of Llywelyn as 'one of the greatest amongst the magnates of our kingdom', 'doing and receiving right in the court of the king of England'? If Llywelyn had done homage, would not Edwardian law and officialdom soon have squeezed all life from the principality, just as they later made life intolerable for the Edwardian loyalist Rhys ap Maredudd, who was provoked into revolt in 1287 by the royal bailiffs of Carmarthen? Yet Llywelyn's territorial gains under the Treaty of Montgomery meant his situation was very different from that of Rhys, for he had pushed the king's bailiffs far away from Gwynedd's heart. Their activities had nothing to do with the stand which led to the war of 1277. The disputes with the earls of Hereford and Gloucester were themselves over land and allegiances in Brecon and north Glamorgan on the southern fringes of the principality. The fact was that under the Treaty, the opportunity for Edwardian officials to challenge Llywelyn was actually quite limited. There were none above all in the Four Cantrefs, where the risings of 1255 and of 1282 were set off by their tyrannies.

In the end, it is hard not to conclude that almost any course would have been better than the one Llywelyn took. It involved immediate execution. The other way might have brought a slow death, but the process had hardly begun and was far from certain. What was needed in the 1270s was the kind of flexibility shown by Llywelyn the Great, or earlier by the Lord Rhys: an awareness of when to concede and an ability to do so without losing face. That, however, was not so easy for someone who was now prince of Wales. Perhaps in 1267 Llywelyn should have followed the precedent of the Treaty of Worcester in 1218, making territorial gains but accepting a looser form of rule over the native rulers, thereby also escaping some of the financial burdens imposed by the Treaty of Montgomery. Perhaps too the pattern of a unified Wales sketched in the prologues to the law books, with Hywel the Good ruling in a spirit of consensus, suggested a better way forward than that adopted. Llywelyn would have treated such suggestions with contempt. The vision of Wales as a homage-based, Gwynedd-dominated principality had been Llywelyn the Great's. Given the intense particularism of the other rulers there was no way it could have been constructed through conferences and consensus. And with the collapse of English royal power in the 1260s, it was clearly now or never for bringing it about. Such a principality could have offered benefits to the native rulers. If it subjected them to the domination of Gwynedd, at least it protected them from potentially the far worse domination of English officialdom. The real misfortune was that Llywelyn's abrasive rule, however necessary given his objectives, prevented this vital point ever getting across.

The events of 1277 were a disaster for Llywelyn, yet he had been there before in the 1240s, and had subsequently pushed the king back. His grandfather had done the same after 1211. This time nothing like that happened. The next war, in 1282, was terminal. Llywelyn himself, however, did not set off the revolt that produced it, although he quickly joined in. After 1277 this proud man faced a series of petty humiliations: the king's officials at Chester impounded his horses and honey; those at Aberystwyth imprisoned his huntsmen. And then there was the legal action which Llywelyn brought in 1279 against Gruffudd ap Gwenwynwyn for the recovery of the cantref of Arwystli in Southern Powys. The 1277 treaty had allowed for such actions and had stipulated that they should be conducted according to 'the custom of the parts' where the land was situated. Llywelyn claimed that Arwystli was in Wales and that therefore Welsh law should apply, while Gruffudd, in possession and doing all he could to delay matters, said that the case should proceed by the common law of England. This and other issues meant that the case dragged on from year to year so that in February 1282 Llywelyn told Edward that he was 'altogether in despair', being more concerned 'about the disgrace to himself than about the profit he could ever derive from the land'. Yet Llywelyn with a pained dignity, as impressive in its own way as anything in the panoply of his power, persevered. He kept up the payments due under the 1277 treaty, and adopted a suitable tone in his letters to Edward: 'your devoted vassal'.

For all this there were some returns, which suggest – like the settlement of 1277 – that Edward had no wish to undermine Llywelyn further. In 1278 the prince achieved his marriage to Eleanor de Montfort. This union to the king's cousin was by far the most exalted marriage ever made by a Welsh ruler, a marriage fit for a prince. It outshone Llywelyn the Great's marriage to John's daughter, for she had been illegitimate. The marriage now showed deference to Edward rather than defiance, for the celebration took place under his auspices on St Edward's Day in Worcester cathedral. But Llywelyn could hope to profit from the new relationship with the king, to whom Eleanor was soon writing letters of petition. The prince was indeed slowly rebuilding his power: he recovered homages of native nobles in Brecon, re-established relations with the rulers of Deheubarth, and, most striking of all, reached an agreement in October 1281 with his old enemy Roger de Mortimer. It was not Llywelyn who was to begin the coming war, but his brother Dafydd.

Dafydd was a disappointed man. He had fought for Edward in 1277 and had been promised – or so he thought – a share of Anglesey and Snowdonia. He had ended up simply with the part of the Four Cantrefs Edward had granted him back in 1263, together with the lordship of Hope. And his title to the latter was now challenged by a marcher baron, William de Venables, in the county court of Chester. Dafydd had entered the court and cried aloud that the land was Welsh and that he should answer according to Welsh law. He was not alone in his anger. The Four Cantrefs, held down by a new royal castle at Rhuddlan, were now administered by the justiciar of Chester, Reginald de Grey, appointed in November 1281, who dismissed the popular Welsh bailiff Gronw ap Heilyn, and threatened the inhabitants with imprisonment and decapitation if they complained of their burdens. Dafydd's fear that Reginald was planning his arrest may well have been the immediate cause of the uprising.

This began on Palm Sunday, 22 March 1282, when Dafydd suddenly attacked Hawarden castle, seized its commander the oppressive Roger of Clifford, and slaughtered many of the garrison. Dafydd had plotted the uprising, not with his brother but with the rulers of Northern Powys and Deheubarth. On the same day as the attack, the former (the brothers Llywelyn and Gruffudd, sons of Gruffudd Maelor) had descended on

Oswestry. Both had been on Edward's side in 1277, and both (like many others) had been alienated by the exactions of the constables of Oswestry and Whitchurch. In the south the grievances were of much the same order. Its rulers (apart from Rhys ap Maredudd) had saved less than they hoped by their early submissions in 1277. Rhys Wyndod had not recovered his castle of Dinefwr, the traditional heart of Deheubarth. He had also (so he said) been forced to plead in legal cases not according to Welsh law at Carmarthen but according to common law before the king's judges. The sons of Maredudd ab Owain, clinging to commotes in southern Ceredigion and denied those in the north despite promises, complained that the king's judges at Cardigan had deprived them of their own courts over their men. So on 24 March, two days after the attacks on Hawarden and Oswestry, these southern rulers, in alliance with Rhys Ieuanc whom Edward had driven from northern Ceredigion in 1277, fell on the new royal castle at Aberystwyth.

Llywelyn hesitated, but only for a moment. If he stayed out he might save the rump of Gwynedd, but at the cost of seeing his brother becoming the true prince of Wales. For the war of 1282 was very different from that of 1277. The latter had in part been a Welsh revolt against Llywelyn. The former, with only Rhys ap Maredudd and Gruffudd ap Gwenwynwyn supporting the king, was a war of liberation against the English. Or certainly that was how it was presented to Archbishop Pecham during his attempt to broker a settlement, presented in schedules too numerous and too eloquent to be dismissed as simply the cloak for a few disappointed rulers: indeed the complaints included those from the 'men' of both the Four Cantrefs and commotes in Northern Powys.

At the heart of English oppression seemed the threat to Welsh law. Llywelyn himself, Dafydd, Rhys Wyndod and his brothers, and the sons of Maredudd ab Owain all complained about its denial. In part this was mistaken, or disingenuous. In the 1277 Treaty, Edward had actually agreed that disputes in Wales should be decided by Welsh law. True, he later added qualifications: he had a duty, he said, under his Coronation Oath, to root out evil customs and uphold the practices of his predecessors. Gruffudd ap Gwenwynwyn, in the course of the Arwystli case, converted this into the hopeful claim (as far as he was concerned) that Edward intended to abolish Welsh law altogether, but this the judges firmly denied. In fact Edward, placed in an impossible position between Llywelyn and Gruffudd, hesitated to make any decision in the case, and hoped the whole thing would go away. It is equally clear that the Welsh themselves were changing Welsh law and indeed setting it aside, often preferring that land disputes should be decided through the verdicts of sworn juries rather than the judgement of the *ynad* or *iudex*, the traditional judge-jurist learned in native law. One reason why Gronw ap Heilyn (before his dismissal by Reginald de Grey) had been so popular in the Four Cantrefs was that he allowed just that.

'Truth is worth more than law,' ran the Welsh proverb. So, one might add, was victory. Fundamentally both Welsh ruler and marcher baron appealed to whichever law they thought would bring it. But here was the rub; the Welsh seemed now always losers, not victors, and losers not merely in lawsuits but in suffering what seemed the general oppression and wrongdoing of Edwardian officialdom. Just as the war of the 1250s was provoked by the exactions of Geoffrey de Langley in the Four Cantrefs, so this one was described at the time as the war of Reginald de Grey. Before 1277 Llywelyn had pushed such men back. Now the game was played deep in the Welsh half. Royal officials were at Rhuddlan and in the Four Cantrefs, at Builth and Aberystwyth. Those at Cardigan and Carmarthen seemed far more intrusive than before. And with reason: whereas until 1277 the Welsh rulers did their homage to Llywelyn and were justiciable in his courts, now they did homage to Edward and were subject to royal courts and officials. The Welsh found too late that in swapping Llywelyn's principality for the Edwardian state, they had jumped from the frying-pan into the fire. They could appeal to Edward and make the long journey to London, but the best they found there was flannel and delay. As Llywelyn put it to Pecham:

For we and all the Welsh were oppressed, and trampled down and despoiled and reduced to servitude by royal judges and bailiffs against the form of peace and all justice, more than if we had been Saracens or Jews . . . and often we complained to the king and had no remedy. But always justices and bailiffs more ferocious and cruel were sent; and when they had been sated by their unjust exactions, others again were sent to excoriate the people, so much so that the people preferred to die rather than to live.

In this situation, the stand on Welsh law expressed a truth much greater than any argument over legal procedures, because the law seemed to define the Welsh as a people. 'Let the laws of Wales be immutable like the laws of other peoples,' Pecham was told. To attack the law was to attack the people's very existence, and against that one must fight to the end. As Dafydd put it, 'although it is hard to live one's life in war and ambushes, it is harder still for a Christian people to be destroyed and reduced to nothing, who seek nothing other than to preserve its rights.'

The Welsh were well aware of the odds in 1282. They themselves, in the discussions with Pecham, contrasted their sterile and uncultivated country with the fertile and abundant lands of England. They were, however, far more united than in 1277 and would a people perish who traced its descent back to the Trojans? The people indeed survived but not the ruling dynasties. These now faced a threat of altogether novel dimensions: a king both utterly determined to destroy them and absolutely capable of mobilizing the resources to do so. The war of 1282 was conceived from the start as a war of conquest.

Edward pursued the same three-pronged strategy which had worked so well in 1277, yet initially with less success. In June some of his forces in the south were ambushed in the Tywi valley and the eldest son of William de Valence, lord of Pembroke, was slain. In August and September Valence himself penetrated as far as Aberystwyth but was unable to hold it. The crucial events, however, were in the north. Here Reginald de Grey occupied Dafydd's castle at Hope and placed 2,600 archers there, blocking off any further Welsh activity in the Harwarden area. Edward himself advanced from Chester to Rhuddlan (where he was based from 8 July to 27 August), stationing 1,000 archers in the great new castle. Llywelyn, as we have seen, could perhaps field a few hundred cavalry and several thousand foot soldiers: a considerable army. But in 1282 Edward had in pay some 800 cavalry and 8,600 infantry, as well as other unpaid horse brought by his barons. Aided by a fleet, Edward had ample troops for what (as in 1277) was the key operation, namely the occupation of Anglesey. Moreover, this time the island was not be a bargaining counter in negotiations but quite literally a bridge to conquest. By the end of September, 200 carpenters, working flat out, had constructed a bridge of boats across to the mainland, opening up Snowdonia. Archbishop Pecham's attempted mediation in November only served to clarify the issue: Edward's best offer was to set Llywelyn up in an English earldom and pay for Dafydd's departure on crusade.

No need for that, the Welsh would have thought, when on 6 November they drove Luke de Tany, the commander in Anglesey, and sixteen knights off the bridge of boats into the sea. On the back of this success,

Llywelyn headed for his old stamping-grounds in the south. There on 11 December, in the valley of the Irfon near Builth, with 'the flower of his people killed', he was cornered while fleeing through woods and run through the body by a man at arms, Stephen of Frankton. His head was cut off and sent to Edward, who ordered it to be put up on the Tower of London, crowned with mocking ivy. It was a pathetic and tragic end to so glorious a career.

The death of Llywelyn did not end the war, for Dafydd at once assumed the title of prince of Wales which he had coveted for so long. But he was now faced by Edward's unprecedented decision to continue the war through the winter. In January 1283 William de Valence at last reoccupied Aberystwyth, ending resistance in Ceredigion. In the same month Edward, having mobilized over 400 cavalry and 5,000 foot, set off from Rhuddlan and soon occupied the princely castle of Dolwyddelan in the heart of Snowdonia. Dafydd fled to Castle y Bere in Meirionydd, where the stone statues of spearmen stood ironic guard over his diminished state. He could not stay, because William de Valence advanced from the south and laid siege to the castle with over 3,000 foot. So Dafydd fled back to Snowdonia and for a few last days in May held court at Dolbadarn, his final castle. With Edward swamping Snowdonia with 7,000 foot and dispatching search parties, he was soon on the run again. On 21 June he was captured and handed over by men of his own tongue.

Having won the war, Edward was in no mood to lose the peace. Of the major rulers all were swept away apart from the loyalists Gruffudd ap Gwenwynwyn of Southern Powys and Rhys ap Maredudd of Ystrad Tywi, the latter that is until his rebellion in 1287. To the extinction of 'the last survivor of the race of traitors', as he called Dafydd, Edward gave maximum publicity. At Shrewsbury in October 1283 he was ceremonially drawn, hanged, disembowelled and quartered, his head being sent to join Llywelyn's at the Tower. Eleanor de Montfort, meanwhile, had died (in June 1282) in giving birth to a daughter, who lived out her long life as a nun at Sempringham. The House of Gwynedd in its main line was at an end. With some exceptions, the rulers of Northern Powys were likewise disappropriated, as were those of Deheubarth: Rhys Wyndod, the sons of Maredudd ab Owain, and Rhys Ieuanc (who had been with Dafydd almost to the last) spent the rest of their days in prison, writing pathetic letters asking for more clothes and the regular payment of the few pence a day on which they lived.

With the native dynasties dispossessed, Edward could do with Wales as he wished. He gave out some rewards. In the north John de Warenne, earl of Surrey received Bromfield and Iâl in Northern Powys (shades of his ancestor's rewards after 1066); most of the Four Cantrefs were divided between Reginald de Grey and the earl of Lincoln. In the south, John Giffard gained most of Rhys Wyndod's lands in Cantref Bychan. But Edward kept the lion's share of Wales for himself. In 1284 the Statute of Wales, a document of breathtaking mastery and precision, set out the laws and governmental structures for his new territories. Wales was now a 'land annexed and united to the crown of England'. Its administration was to be on English lines. In Gwynedd west of the Conwy, Anglesey, Caernarfon and Meirionydd each became counties under English-type sheriffs and coroners, with the commotes treated much like hundreds. These officials were answerable not to the king and the London exchequer, but to a provincial governor, 'the justiciar of Snowdon', and to an exchequer based at Caernarfon. The same pattern was followed east of the Conwy, where the areas remaining to the king (which included the cantref of Tegeingl and the lands attached to Rhuddlan) were brought under the sheriff of Flint, who was answerable to the justiciar and exchequer at Chester. In the south (where the pattern had been developing since the 1240s) the 'shires' of Cardigan and Carmarthen were likewise to have sheriffs and coroners, the areas under their jurisdiction being greatly increased with the confiscation of Rhys ap Maredudd's lands in 1287. Here the local officials were answerable to the justiciar of west Wales and the exchequer at Carmarthen.

This colonial type of administration, similar in its autonomy to that in force in Gascony and Ireland, had a clear purpose: to establish governors with sufficient local power to hold down the conquered people. To that end, Edward retained them in office for long periods of time. Reginald de Grey, who had provoked the rebellion of 1282, was justiciar of Chester and Snowdon from 1281 to 1299. Robert Tibetot, who provoked the rebellion of Rhys ap Maredudd in 1287, was justiciar of west Wales from 1281 to 1298.

Behind his officials stood Edward's castles. These above all stamped down the conquest of Gwynedd: the war of 1277 brought Flint and Rhuddlan; that of 1282–3, Conwy, Caernarfon and Harlech; while after the rebellion of 1295 came Beaumaris on Anglesey. The great architect responsible for these works was Master James of St George whom Edward brought from Savoy. There was nothing particularly novel in either the individual features or the overall plans he adopted: Conwy bears a striking resemblance to Louis IX's castle at Angers. Yet it still took tremendous intellectual energy to plan six castles from scratch, all with features in common yet all quite different according to site, and all terribly formidable. Edward's contribution was as important. He doubtless made the fundamental decision to place all the castles down by the sea, having witnessed the starving-out of his hilltop fortresses of Deganwy and Diserth. He also supplied the drive and resources to get the castles built. To clear the site at Conwy he uprooted the Cistercian abbey (where Llywelyn the Great was buried) and moved it eight miles up the valley. To link Rhuddlan with the sea he built a canal two to three miles long. The castles were built at breathless speed, most being completed in their fundamentals within five years, so that during the summer a thousand or more labourers and several hundred masons drawn from all parts of England might be working on each one. The total cost between 1277 and 1304 was just under £80,000, roughly double what Henry III spent on Westminster Abbey. This was the most co-ordinated and impressive campaign of castle-building in medieval history.

In terms of their ground plan, none of the castles rivalled the area which, say, the Tower of London came to embrace in the thirteenth century. Rather they were like pocket battleships, packing immense power for their size. That power came principally from the number and strength of the great towers which flanked the walls (the eight at Conwy had stonework over ten feet thick), from the deadly precision of the details (like the arrow slits at Caernarfon from which fire could be directed in three different directions), and from the way all the castles were planned in conjunction with new towns which formed supportive English enclaves. There was also the arrogant panache with which the castles were finished, with watch turrets spiralling up above the four massive towers of the inner court at Conwy, and walls decorated by bands of different coloured stone at Caernarfon, a feature imitated from the Theodosian walls at Constantinople and thus a reference to the town's supposedly Roman past. In the late 1280s from Llywelyn's timber hall and chamber at Rhosyr on Anglesey one could gaze across the Menai Straits to Caernarfon rising in the distance. Rhosyr had been impressive in its way but the two structures reflected regimes in different leagues of power.

That there were only two risings against English rule after 1283 was a measure of the castles' strength and the reserve power of English government behind them. The revolt of Rhys ap Maredudd in 1287, denied Dinefwr despite his loyalty in the 1282–3 war and forced to plead according to English law in the county court of Carmarthen, was put down by the regency government (Edward was in Gascony). Rhys himself was finally captured and executed in 1292. The rising of 1294–5 was more formidable. Edward had eliminated the main line of the Gwynedd dynasty, but there remained a sprig of the Meirionydd branch, Madog ap Llywelyn, living on a small estate in Anglesey. In 1294 he proclaimed himself prince of Wales and led a revolt which drew on widespread resentments against the privileges of the new towns, the exactions of the sheriffs and the attempted levy (for the first time) of a general tax in Wales. Edward, with no less than £54,500 being sent from Westminster in the first year of the war, recruited the largest infantry forces ever seen in Wales, at their height some 31,000 men being in pay. Having based himself at Conwy through the winter, he put down the revolt by leading an army on a great march around the perimeters of native Wales, and then finished off by building the most symmetrical of all his castles, Beaumaris on Anglesey.

The Edwardian conquest was grim but there was another side to it, which helps to explain its success: there were attempts at rapprochement between the peoples. A lead here was taken by Archbishop Pecham, who toured Wales in the summer of 1284. His aim was partly to reassert Canterbury's authority and his attitude was patronizing. The Welsh, he said, should send their children to England for education. But he was genuinely shocked by the destruction of churches caused by the war and secured over £1,730 from Edward to repair the damage, the money going to over a hundred beneficiaries. Pecham urged the church to preach reconciliation between the English and the Welsh. The people should put their trust in Christ 'who in his blood made all races of men one'. There was also a measure of accommodation in the settlement Edward himself imposed. Under the Statute of Wales, the laws of England were certainly now to be used in criminal matters, abolishing (not always effectively) compensation payments for homicide, and making serious crime an offence against the state. This, however, was something the rulers of Gwynedd had themselves been trying to achieve. It was the Welsh themselves, so the Statute said, who petitioned for the truth in land cases to be inquired into by 'good and law-worthy men of the neighbourhood', and that may indeed have been the case, given the evidence already cited for the preference for juries. Balancing these changes, the Statute retained Welsh laws for disputes over movables, as it did the custom practised 'from time out of mind' by which inheritances were partible among all heirs male. Edward could fairly claim to have taken a careful and constructive look at Welsh laws, combining abolition with modification and retention. His attitude to the Welsh was not simply one of stern inflexibility. After the revolt of 1294 he mounted inquiries into the grievances which had produced it.

Rhys ap Maredudd's fate was not altogether typical of the Welsh rulers who tried to reach an accommodation with the crown. His own problems were compounded by quarrels with some of his leading native subjects who actually helped suppress his revolt. Of the lesser rulers, to the north of Rhys, in Ceredigion, Llywelyn ab Owain ap Maredudd retained the commote of Is Coed and half that of Gwinionydd. In Northern Powys, the descendants of Owain Brogyntyn held the commotes of Edeirnion and Dinmale, ruling them with minimal interference from the crown. Likewise the descendants of Gruffudd Maelor, despite involvement in 1282, retained Cynllaith and were the forebears of Owain Glyn Dŵr. And then, in Southern Powys, there was Gruffudd ap Gwenwynwyn. In the 1280s, married to a Lestrange and with his son married to a Corbet of Caus, with the sheriff of Shropshire his 'special friend' and with a direct line to the king's chief minister Robert Burnell, he might well reflect on the swing of fortune's wheel since the day he had grovelled at Llywelyn's feet after the unmasking of the 1274 conspiracy. Although Gruffudd ap Gwenwynwyn's male descendants died out in the early fourteenth century, Southern Powys survived as 'one of the most Royallest, greatest, lardgest and best seignories and Lordship Marcher of Wales', as it was put in the sixteenth century. Of course, it survived precisely as a marcher barony, not a Welsh princedom. Gruffudd had to fight his corner against both royal administrators and marcher barons, winning some cases, losing others (including one against Roger de Mortimer). It was precisely such struggles which his fellow rulers found intolerable. But Gruffudd's perspective was understandable. After all, a Welsh princedom was not on offer to the 'Welsh barons of Wales' (as they were called in the Treaty of Montgomery) in a Gwynedd-dominated principality either.

The real beneficiaries of the English conquest were the *uchelwyr*, the leading men below the level of the old ruling families, precisely those who had become disaffected with Rhys ap Maredudd's rule in Ystrad Tywi and with Llywelyn's in Gwynedd and further south. They now thrived in English administrative service, with which indeed many had long been connected. Although nearly all the early sheriffs and castellans were English, the bailiffs of the commotes remained Welsh. Later the Welsh reached more exalted positions. Goronwy Goch, Rhys ap Maredudd's constable at Drywslwyn, fought against him in 1287 and later became steward of Cantref Mawr. Gruffudd Llwyd, a descendant of Ednyfed Fychan, Llywelyn the Great's steward, entered royal service in 1283 and spent fifty years there, becoming sheriff of Caernarfon, Anglesey and Meirionydd and gaining a knighthood. The view of William Marshal II, earl of Pembroke (died 1231), that the Welsh were best controlled and subdued by men 'of their own race' had been forgotten with disastrous results in the 1250s and 1270s. Yet in the end it was that wisdom which ultimately prevailed after the Edwardian conquest. It was, of course, a wisdom precisely designed to facilitate the rule of conquerors.

The Edwardian conquest had required no new theory. Both John and Henry III had stressed that Gwynedd was liable to forfeiture if its rulers broke faith (just as it would also escheat if they failed of heirs). That was became its rulers had done homage to the king and held their land from him. After 1277 the other Welsh rulers were in the same position, hence Edward's statement in the 1284 Statute that Wales had become subject to him 'by feudal right'. The near universal rebellion meant a near universal forfeiture. It was as simple as that.

Or was it? For there was now something radically new, namely a king with the determination to put such theory into practice. In doing so, Edward knew very well what he was bringing about and positively willed it. There was nothing accidental about the conquest of Wales. In this Edward was quite different from his father who had allowed Gwynedd to survive in the 1240s although he had every 'right' to take it for himself. The contrast was not simply because of the different personalities of the two kings. It was also because of the different levels of provocation. In 1282 the Welsh declared war on Edward suddenly and brutally, through the seizure of Hawarden and the slaughter of its garrison. And the arch-insurgent was none other than Dafydd whom, as Edward raged, he had sheltered, enriched and trusted as one of his own. So it seemed better, as Edward announced in

November 1282, to endure labour and expense now so that 'the malice [of the Welsh] can be totally destroyed' than to suffer the fate of his ancestors and be continually crucified by their disturbances. The intention to conquer, its novelty and its reasons could not have been more clearly set out.

It was one thing to have the intention. Edward also had the ability to put it into effect. The knowledge that he could do so was an important reason for the decision in the first place. One critical factor here, and a new one, was his lack of continental distractions. The loss of Normandy in 1204 had destroyed the Angevin empire for good, but it was a long time before the dynasty recognized the fact. After the Treaty of Paris, the conquest of Wales. Certainly the first in 1259, under which Henry III at last accepted the loss of his continental possessions, made possible the second, for it initiated a quarter century of peace with the Capetians. In 1279 Edward had gone to Amiens and resolved disputes arising from the implementation of the Treaty, thus finally acquiring the Agenais. He also succeeded to the county of Ponthieu (the eventual inheritance of his wife) without difficulty, although the Capetians had blocked its acquisition by Henry III (through a marriage) in the 1230s. Edward was determined to retain and increase his authority in Gascony. He was there in 1272–4 and again in 1286–9. He played a major part in international diplomacy, going to endless trouble and expense to secure the release of Charles of Salerno. But the crucial and novel fact remained. Down to 1294 he was at peace with the Capetians. In 1174 a Welsh seer had prophesied correctly that Henry II's descent on Wales would be prevented by the king of France's siege of Rouen. There was no possibility of anything like that happening in 1282. Likewise there was no prospect of Llywelyn imitating his grandfather's alliance with the Capetians in 1212 or that of Owain Gwynedd in 1165. To conquer Wales, Gerald of Wales had affirmed, would need 'diligent and constant attention for a year at least'. It was that which Edward was able to give.

Edward was 'able' in another way. The conquest of Wales was facilitated by a military revolution. There was the masterful execution of radical strategies, some of them old like the occupation of Anglesey and the march round Wales (anticipated by Nicholas Molis in the 1240s), some new like the bridge of boats and the decision to fight on through the winter. Then there was the extraordinary campaign of castle-building, new in its scale, speed and concentration. And there was the size of the armies and how they were recruited. The changes were less marked on the cavalry side. If Edward had, say, 1,000 cavalry involved in the 1282–3 campaign, that was not much larger than the 800 John took with him to Ireland in 1210, nor were there significant differences in how they were recruited. Edward, like earlier kings, relied on his household forces (they provided a third of the cavalry in 1282–3), on 'feudal' contingents supplied by his barons, and on further bodies of paid knights. There was nothing new in a high proportion of the army being supported with royal cash, John in effect had done that through the 'loans' doled out to the knights in 1210. The Norman and Angevin kings had always employed large numbers of Flemish and Brabantine mercenaries. Where Edward did make a new departure was in the size of his infantry, culminating in a colossal 31,000 across the armies in 1294. These foot soldiers were supported by royal pay and many had been recruited in a new fashion, namely by the 'commissions of array' (in 1282 staffed by household knights) who were sent into selected counties to raise troops from the towns and villages, forcing the local communities to produce contingents and then to support them until they reached the muster. Admittedly numbers do not always make for efficiency and the high levels were not sustained for very long. But these may well have been the largest armies ever seen in Wales.

Behind Edward's military power lay one outstanding factor: money, money to build the castles and pay the troops. And his reform of the realm had given him this in abundance. Between 1276 and 1279 the Riccardi tripled their payments into the wardrobe and met nearly all the costs of the first Welsh war. For the second war between 1282 and 1284 Edward spent £120,000, including the initial costs of the castle-building. If that was the price of conquering Wales, it was beyond Henry III. Of the £120,000 (much of it channelled again through the Riccardi), £23,000 derived from the new customs duties agreed by parliament in 1275, and £37,500 came from a tax conceded by knights and burgesses in January 1283 during the actual course of the campaign. No wonder they were summoned later to Shrewsbury to witness Dafydd's execution. The new Edwardian state and the conquest of Wales were thus intimately connected. That was as true in the area of political stability as it was of financial resources. John, after all, had a treasure of around £130,000 at the time of the Welsh revolt in 1212. The reason he did not deploy it against Wales was only partly because it was destined for the continent. It was also because his hand was stayed by the baronial plot against his life, a plot in which Llywelyn was complicit. There was no chance of anything like that happening in 1277 or 1282.

* * *

As king, Edward's conduct in Ireland was very different from what it became in Wales. He wished to exploit the province but he did not drive forward a major expansion in the area under his direct control, an expansion from which the losers would have been the colonial lords and the native rulers. He certainly never dreamt of completing Ireland's conquest by eliminating the latter. Like his father, Edward never went to Ireland. Both his decision not to intervene and the general stability of English politics allowed the struggles between the native rulers and the colonial lords to follow their own patterns, as did the struggles within each camp, that between the de Burghs and the fitz Geralds continuing until a settlement in 1298. Edward had, of course, been lord of Ireland since 1254, since when his position had deteriorated badly. The crisis in England during the 1260s had forced him to concede Ulster to Walter de Burgh. There had also been a sharp decline in the revenues from the lordships. In 1271 the year's receipts at the Dublin exchequer were some £2,000, half those of twenty years earlier. The major achievement of Edward's governors in the first decade of the reign was to restore the situation so that in the 1280s the receipts recovered to between £5,000 and £6,000 a year. Eventually Ireland contributed some £30,000 towards the cost of Edward's castles in Wales, roughly 35 per cent of the total bill. The conquest of Wales and English rule in Ireland were thus intimately related.

* * *

In the 1270s and 1280s Edward's relations with Scotland were close and harmonious. Instead of exploiting the Manxmen's revolt in 1275, he helped King Alexander crush it. True, in 1278 when Alexander did homage for the lands he held in England, Edward reserved his claims to overlordship over the Scottish kingdom. Henry III had entered a similar reservation in 1251 and then forgotten all about it. Edward was tougher. He made an official record of his *démarche*, and omitted to mention Alexander's spirited response: 'Nobody but God himself has the right to the homage for my realm of Scotland.' Edward's conduct was part and parcel of his determination to preserve royal rights much more effectively than his father, but that did not mean he was planning to pursue them in an aggressive fashion. Up to a point both kings were going through the motions, neither really expecting the question of homage to come up and damage their cordial family relations.

Queen Margaret, Alexander's wife and Edward's sister, had died in 1275, leaving two sons and a daughter. By January 1284 all were dead. 'After the many kindnesses we have received from you,' Alexander wrote to Edward, 'you have now at this time of intolerable despair at the death of our dear son, your beloved nephew, offered much solace by saying that although death has borne away your kindred in these parts, we are united together perpetually, God willing, by the tie of indissoluble affection.' There was nothing the least bit false about these sentiments, and Alexander went on to imply that the union between the dynasties might still be maintained, this presumably through the marriage of his infant granddaughter and heir apparent (the daughter of the King of Norway) to Edward's son, the future Edward II. It would clearly be better, however, if Alexander could produce another son. To that end, in October 1285 Alexander married again, this time to Yolanda, the daughter of the count of Dreux. On a stormy night in March 1286, anxious to join his new queen, he left Edinburgh late in the evening, crossed the Forth by ferry, and then in the wind and rain became separated from his escort. Next day he was found dead on the seashore, having broken his neck in a fall from his horse.

The reign had been a great one for the monarchy both in terms of the conquest of the west and the political stability which made that possible. Behind both successes stood the resources of Alexander's kingship, resources which he enhanced in one important area. Following Edward's example in 1275, Alexander introduced exactly the same customs duty on wool exports as that in force in England, thereby raising perhaps £2,000 a year. There seems little doubt that Alexander's revenues were increasing more generally. His reign saw a stupendous expansion of the money supply, helped in part by his re-coinage in 1250, with a new 'long-cross penny' modelled on that introduced into England three years before (see above, p. 47). Apart from the substantial amounts of money coming direct from the burghs, the bulk of royal revenue (some of it still in kind) was collected by the sheriffs and derived from crown lands. Revenue from wardships was also important, although intermittent. Alexander kept the earldom of Fife (worth £500 a year) in hand from 1270 to 1284 to provide for his son and heir. In 1293 the revenue from the sheriffdoms was valued at £8,100 a year, and since this excluded the customs and other resources, Alexander's annual income was well over £10,000. In terms of resources, in the British league table he was roughly three times more wealthy than the princes of Gwynedd, even when their revenues were at their height, and three times less wealthy than kings of England, even before their income was expanded by general taxation.

The king's finances were essentially run from within the king's household by the chamber, the equivalent of Edward I's wardrobe. It was the chamberlain who received all the revenues collected by the sheriffs, apart from those the sheriffs themselves spent on royal orders. The chamberlain, the chancellor and other household officials audited the accounts of the sheriffs at various places as they travelled the country. There was no separate exchequer on the English model, although the board of audit was sometimes given the name. The board's accounts, which survive from the 1260s and 1280s in truncated seventeenth-century copies, prove that it was extremely proactive, ordering investigations, judging whether sheriffs should answer for particular debts, and commanding payments to be enforced by distraint. More than anything else, these fragments show that Scotland had a fully formed document-driven, record-based monarchy.

The chamberlain's own account, for an imprecise period but including the year 1264, provides a glimpse of the royal household, and its expenditure on horses, silks, spices, wine, gifts, messengers, wages of servants, fees of knights, expenses of the queen, and the king's gambling debts. The cost of what was probably the household's food and drink was £2,220, of which £590 was still owed 'the country', which suggests a right of prise (compulsory purchase) much as in England. If the £2,220 was for one year and not for longer it was much the same as Henry III's expenditure in the late 1220s, although Edward I's in the 1280s was to be five or six times as great. The chamberlain's total receipts were £5,300, roughly a third of the receipts of Edward's wardrobe for one year at the start of his reign, though later, of course, these too became much larger. A description of Scottish government written around 1292 describes in detail the role of the household officials – the steward, constable, marshal, almoner, and the clerks of liverance, provender, wardrobe and kitchen. Its discussion of the office of the chancellor suggests the same pressures of business as in England, hence its mention of routine writs 'of course', its acknowledgement that the chancellor might not always follow the king, and its observation that the king might issue orders to him through writs sealed with the privy seal.

Alexander's death brought to an end more than three centuries of royal success. The original core of the Scottish kingdom had been between the firths of Forth and Moray and the central Highlands. It was there that the great bulk of the king's lands lay, organized into thanages that were later subsumed into sheriffdoms. In some usages as late as the twelfth century it was this or indeed an even smaller area (thanks to the fissure with Moray) which was thought of as constituting Scotland (see above, p. 117). The essential achievement of the Scottish kings was to expand beyond this narrow base. In the tenth century they established their hold over Lothian. Thereafter persistent attempts down to 1217 to advance south of the Solway and the Tweed came to nothing. But instead the kingdom expanded north and west: north to recover hold over Moray and ultimately establish sheriffdoms at Cromarty and Dingwall; west with sheriffdoms at Lanark, Dumfries, Wigtown, Ayr, Dumbarton and (in 1293) in Argyll and the Western Isles (see Map 4). The financial accounts of the 1260s and 1280s show that there were twelve sheriffdoms south of the Forth, seven between the Forth and Kincardine and eight between Aberdeen and Cromarty and Dingwall, although the last had no revenues to speak of. This Scotland of the sheriffdoms was the area within which the kings had asserted, in the twelfth century, control over royal pleas (including cases of serious crime) and in the thirteenth had made available common law legal procedures similar to those in England. In Alexander's reign the three justiciars, of Lothian, Scotland north of Forth, and Galloway (the last reappears in the sources from 1258), were probably travelling their jurisdictions twice a year to hear both types of plea. The expansion of the kingdom was also reflected, if belatedly, in the spread of mints. The short-cross penny which ran between 1195 and 1250 was only struck at Berwick, Roxburgh, Edinburgh and Perth. The long-cross penny was minted (in its initial phase) in the north at Inverness and in the west at Dumfries, Ayr, Lanark, Glasgow and Renfrew. The burghs themselves, proliferating throughout the twelfth and thirteenth centuries, were dependent on the king for their privileges and supplied him with important cash revenues. They were potent instruments in the expansion and consolidation of royal power.

Beyond the Scotland of the sheriffdoms, the kings had tied the northern earldom of Caithness more firmly to the kingdom, in part through controlling its bishopric. Indeed with a proper diocesan structure coming into place, the control of episcopal appointments allowed the king to place his men in key positions throughout Scotland. The most essential method, however, of binding doubtful areas on the periphery to the realm's inner core was through the establishment of provincial lordships for the king's closest associates, most of them of Anglo-Norman descent. In the west the Bruces were placed in Annandale, the Morevilles in Cunningham, and the Stewarts in Kyle and Strathgryf and then in Bute, Cowal, Arran and Knapdale. The same pattern was repeated in the north with the Murrys in Sutherland and the Comyns in Badenoch and Lochaber. By 1286, five of the thirteen native earldoms had also passed to families of Anglo-Norman descent. The establishment of such families, fundamental to the 'Europeanization' of Scotland, had created tensions which spawned a series of political revolts, associated particularly with the MacWilliams and the MacHeths. The revolts were brutally suppressed, as were those in Galloway and Man, but the new edifice's stability depended as much on accommodation as on conquest. Native nobles continued to hold eight of the thirteen earldoms and also to rule in Argyll. They adopted much of the culture of the incoming nobility, while the latter, on its part, came to respect native history and traditions. Harmony between kings and nobles, whatever their background, was also helped by the basic structures of the kingdom, where there were significant contrasts as well as parallels with those south of the border. In England, while great nobles were often leading councillors of the king, they did not in the thirteenth century generally hold formal office either at the centre or in the localities. In Scotland they did both. Alexander Comyn was one of the Alexander III's justiciars and the earl of Mar his chamberlain. Nobles were equally appointed to sheriffdoms. Those who were unemployed were at least left alone. There remained a fundamental contrast between the Scotland of the sheriffs and the justiciars, on the one hand, and the Scotland of the 'outer ring' earldoms and provincial lordships on the other. How far crown pleas and the common law ran in these earldoms and lordships is unclear. Certainly their lords enjoyed very considerable independence. Their position was comparable to that of the Welsh marcher barons within the English realm, except that the territories they ruled were far more extensive. As James Campbell has observed, it is at least symbolic of the power of the Scottish nobility that the Gough Map of Britain in 1360 notes in Scotland not the administrative counties, as it sometimes does in England, but the territories of the earls.

Nobles were also less pressured than in England, even within the core of the kingdom. Private jurisdiction probably remained more important; certainly the common law bulked less large (see above, pp. 334–5). Royal revenue also came with far less strain, largely because so much of it derived from land. The surviving records of account lack the long lists of individual debts which are such a feature of the English pipe rolls. The customs introduced by Alexander were relatively painless. Painful general taxation was one area in which he did not imitate his brother-in-law. For that reason while Alexander frequently convoked great assemblies of the realm he had no need to summon local representatives to them in any formal way, as he did not need consent to taxation. Yet Alexander's kingship was still widely based. The 1,500 to 2,000 Scots, most middling freeholders, whose allegiance Edward took in 1296 may well have been the kind of men who were making increasing use of the new common law legal procedures. As in England, royal justice was in demand.

All this put Scottish kings in a very different political position from either the rulers of Gwynedd or the kings of England. There was no equivalent, after Alexander's death, to the long list of complaints made against Llywelyn. There was no need for a Scottish Magna Carta, Provisions of Oxford, or Edwardian-style reform of the realm. While the Scottish state was in some ways like the English state in miniature, in others it more closely resembled twelfth-century Capetian France, where revenue was 'easy' and political protest muted. As a result, in Scotland (as in France) a sense of national identity could centre upon the crown, indeed be created by it. If Wales was united in its language and people yet divided by its rulers, Scotland was divided in its language and people but united by its king. Indeed initially a common kingship was all that did unite it. The achievement of a universal Scottishness, against all the odds, is the supreme example of the power of 'regnal unity'. It was because the king was 'king of Scots' that all the diverse peoples in his realm came ultimately to regard themselves as just that. And as the kings pushed their authority outwards, the narrower usages of 'Scotland' were lost and 'Scotland' came universally to mean the whole land north of the Solway and the Tweed, essentially the area of modern Scotland. A lament for Alexander, written soon after his death, captured both his popularity and centrality to Scotland:

> When Alexander our king was dead
> That Scotland led in love and law
> Away was sons [abundance] of ale and bread
> Of wine and wax, of gaming and glee
> Our gold was changed into lead.

After Alexander's death, when the guardians put on their seal the motto 'St Andrew be the leader of the compatriot Scots', they expressed a common identity and also the need for help now that they had lost the leadership which had created it, the leadership of the king.

*   *   *

Where does one stop the clock in history? In 1272 the king of England seemed the least conquering of the British rulers. Twelve years later Edward had conquered Wales. In the 1290s he was virtually to conquer Scotland. The way there had been prepared by the death of Alexander III's granddaughter, 'the Maid of Norway', in September 1290, which ended plans for her marriage to Edward's heir. Edward had then insisted that his overlordship of Scotland be recognized – this before judging between the numerous candidates for the Scottish throne, all descendants of the sisters of Earl David of Huntingdon (died 1219), King William the Lion's younger brother. Edward thus enforced 'rights' which no Scottish king had acknowledged since Richard I had abandoned them in 1189. Edward's next forward move came after John Balliol had become king and done homage. Edward enforced his overlordship by demanding military service for his French war in 1294 and by hearing legal cases from Scotland on appeal. When this provoked resistance, Edward in 1296 invaded, forced Balliol's abdication and reduced Scotland to a 'land' annexed to the English crown, an awesome decision which simply extinguished a kingship which had existed for over four hundred years. Yet it was a decision exactly paralleled in the way he had enforced the forfeitures of the Welsh rulers in 1283–4. To defeat rebellion and hold down his conquest, Edward did not build castles, as in Wales, but his armies were of immense size. The

25,700 foot soldiers and at least 3,000 cavalry mustered for the Falkirk campaign in 1297 was certainly the largest single force raised in Britain since 1066 and one unsurpassed on a regular basis before the armies of the seventeenth century. Edward's gigantic revenues between 1294 and 1297 enabled him to fight wars in France as well as in Britain, something not required of him in 1277 and 1284. Yet he contained the resulting political protests in England. The conquest of Scotland, like that of Wales, was intimately linked to the stability of the Edwardian state. In 1305 Edward issued an Ordinance for the government of Scotland which paralleled in many ways the 1284 Statute of Wales. With his parliament in England hearing petitions from Wales, Scotland, and Ireland, with his exchequer inspecting accounts from subordinate exchequers at Caernarfon, Berwick and Dublin, the British Isles seemed, in the words of Robin Frame, to be 'in the grip of an irresistible organizing force'. In fact, of course, it did not work out like that. In 1306 Robert Bruce was crowned king at Scone and he went on to free Scotland from English rule.

That Wales succumbed and Scotland survived was not surprising, for the Scottish kings, as we have seen, had created a powerful and harmonious state whereas the Welsh rulers had not. Scotland was also far better protected geographically, with a single narrow frontier to England, no equivalent of the marcher baronies, and a much more extensive seaboard. Scotland, however, was also lucky in coming onto the agenda late in Edward's reign, when at times he was also fighting in Wales and France. Had the chronology been different, or had Edward not been followed by Edward II (1307–27), the most hopeless king to sit on the English throne, Scotland might well have gone under. Indeed, given the disparity in resources, there must have been many occasions after 1066 when kings of England could have conquered Wales and Scotland had they concentrated on doing so.

This is not to say such a conquest was necessarily inevitable. There was nothing uniform about English power. It collapsed under Stephen, and was weak, both in terms of direction and resources, for much of the time between 1212 and 1272. Nor did English kings have much concept of 'Britain' as an entity which should be united under their rule with the Welsh dynasties and the king of Scotland swept away. True, that vision was given powerful expression after Edward's victories, notably by Peter Langtoft (an Augustinian canon of Bridlington):

Now are the islanders all joined together
And Albany [Scotland] united to the royalties
of which King Edward is proclaimed lord.
Cornwall and Wales are in his power,
And Ireland the great at his will.
There is neither king nor prince of all the countries
Except King Edward who has thus united them.

Such unificatory rhetoric might seem to have had a long pedigree. Gerald of Wales after all had lauded Henry II for 'including by his powerful hand in one monarchy the whole island of Britain'. But in reality what Henry II actually sought, much like his grandfather Henry I, was overlordship over the other rulers, not unification through their elimination. In the first instance Edward sought exactly the same. His view of Britain was very much one of separate rulers owing allegiance to the king of England. In 1301, in a letter to the pope, he showed how the king of England's overlordship over the king of Scotland had arisen from the original division of Albion between the sons of Brutus and how that overlordship had subsequently been maintained. For Edward, the eventual reduction of Scotland to a 'land' annexed by the English crown was not the realization of some Langtoftian blueprint. It was simply the result, as Edward explained, of the king of Scotland having breached his oath of loyalty to his overlord. The forfeitures of the Welsh rulers, as we have seen, had worked in exactly the same way. In this perspective, the unification of Britain had been produced by the disloyalty of the subject rulers.

Kings had long been aware of the prospects of forfeiture (Welsh rulers had suffered it under Henry I) but they had hardly striven to create situations which might bring it about. Indeed the pressures they placed on Wales and Scotland were often relaxed rather than intensified. One reason for that, of course, lay in the activities of the Welsh and Scottish rulers themselves. But another, even more important, was simply that English kings had higher priorities elsewhere. Again and again, overseas necessities took Henry I and Henry II away when they might otherwise have campaigned in Wales. Even after 1204 the recovery of the continental empire and retention of its remnants had the highest priority, at least until the 1240s. Nor was that surprising given the relative value and prestige of Normandy, Anjou and Gascony, compared with Wales, Ireland and even Scotland.

In Wales the main advances of the Normans after 1066 had been the work of marcher barons rather than the king, but once these lost momentum the king showed little inclination to step in and finish the job. Both the marcher barons and the Welsh rulers could be allies or enemies depending on circumstances. Henry I condoned the growing power of Gruffudd ap Cynan in part as a counterweight to the earl of Chester, thereby helping to lay the foundations of a resurgent Gwynedd. Likewise Henry II made the Lord Rhys his lieutenant in the south, so gaining freedom to deal with Ireland. Later, Henry III in practice accepted the dominance of Llywelyn the Great for the whole period from 1216 to 1240. The next decade saw him pass up golden opportunities to conquer Gwynedd. In 1267, he and his son even surrendered longstanding royal claims to the homages of the Welsh rulers. Three years later, placing money for his crusade above recovery of power in Wales, Edward helped Llywelyn to consolidate his principality by selling him the homage of Maredudd ap Rhys. The crown's attitude to its own gains was scarcely desperately retentive. The Four Cantrefs in the north, and Pembroke, Cardigan and Carmarthen in the south, were allowed to pass back and forth between marcher baron, Welsh ruler and the king as it suited the needs of wider policy.

Over Scotland the nature of the overlordship asserted by the English kings fluctuated. William I had made King Malcolm his 'man'. Both Rufus and Henry I placed protégés on the Scottish throne and expected their obedience. Thereafter, however, the overlordship of Scotland (largely thanks to the enfeeblement of royal authority under Stephen) lapsed until Henry II renewed it in 1174, at the same time taking possession of several castles within the kingdom. Henry certainly sought to make a reality of his position, but that he saw the Scottish castles as a security measure designed to prevent invasions of England, rather than as a base for further advance, was amply shown by the way he resigned Edinburgh, the most important, once he was confident of King William's good behaviour. Henry's successor, Richard I, placed money for his crusade far above maintaining the overlordship over Scotland and achieved the one by sacrificing the other. Although later kings kept the idea of overlordship alive, in practice they accepted Scotland's independence. As a result, after 1217 relations became increasingly cordial. Henry III conspicuously refused to push claims to overlordship during Alexander III's minority. Edward I, more determined, formally registered his claims in 1278 but did nothing to prosecute them. In the

Treaty of Birgham of 1290, under which his son was to marry the Maid of Norway, he accepted that Scotland was to remain 'separate and free in itself without subjection'. It was only in the extraordinary circumstances produced by the failure of the direct Scottish line with the Maid of Norway's death that he revived his claims. Meanwhile kings of England put little effort into increasing their power in Ireland. After John's expedition of 1210 they never went there, regarding the lordship simply as a source of revenue and a place where they could find patronage for their supporters.

All this, therefore, left plenty of room for the expansive strategies of the Scottish kings and the Welsh rulers. The picture of Britain in 1272 is not a momentary illusion. It was often the reality. Indeed in the thirteenth century the English kings had far less clear-cut plans for mastery than either the king of Scots or the princes of Gwynedd, the former with a blueprint for taking over Man and the Western Isles, the latter with one for dominion over the other native rulers.

Edward's elimination of the Welsh rulers and termination of the Scottish kingdom was not, therefore, the culmination of a long and consistent drive by the English crown to intensify its overlordship over Britain, let alone unify it under a single ruler. This statement, however, while true, needs to be counterbalanced by another: if circumstances *did* arise in which English overlordship was exercised, then it was likely to be progressively more demanding and intrusive the later one moves in our period. The reason for this was the development of the English state. Written records, a common law and a professional judiciary made royal government increasingly detailed, uniform and all-embracing. Inevitably that had an impact on those in Wales and Scotland who came into contact with it. While Welsh and Scottish rulers from the Conqueror's time onwards may at times have done homage to the kings of England, thus acknowledging that they held their territories as fiefs which were liable to forfeiture, the written definition of such relationships by Henry II in his 1174 treaty with Scotland, and by John in the charters he granted to the Welsh rulers, gave those relationships a new sharpness. While the overlordship exercised by Henry I over the Welsh rulers was real enough, it was not a matter of law cases and legal records. In the next century the Welsh assize rolls, recording Welsh cases heard by English judges between 1277 and 1284, run to 350 modern printed pages. Merely an abbreviated English calendar of the special chancery rolls Edward opened in 1277 to record his Welsh letters runs to a 100 pages down to 1282. It was such law and bureaucracy which seemed to threaten Scotland after 1292. William the Lion had found Henry II's overlordship vexatious, especially the attendance at his courts, the loss of castles, and the interference in Galloway, but he put up with it. A hundred years later Edwardian overlordship, especially in the hearing of judicial appeals, threatened to be far more interventionist, and thus far more intolerable.

Of course, what made this worse were the equal pretensions of the rulers of Wales and Scotland. Llywelyn ap Gruffudd was himself trying to pin the Welsh rulers down to a precise set of rules, and was imbued with his status as prince of Wales. The kings of Scotland had created an English state in miniature, and were keen to round it off by getting papal sanction for a coronation. Faced by heavier demands with a lower level of toleration, it was highly likely that the result would be resistance, as indeed it was. Meeting resistance, a king like Edward, masterful and martial, was always likely to conclude that confiscation and conquest were the only solutions. The loss of Normandy, in confining the king largely to England, meant he could concentrate as never before on executing such a programme; and the new tax-based state Edward was creating gave him the resources to bring it about.

In thirteenth-century conditions, therefore, overlordship meant domination, domination led to resistance, and resistance was ended by conquest. But was it really as straightforward as that? The circumstances in which the full weight of English law and officialdom came to bear on both Wales and Scotland were surely avoidable, if in different ways. In Wales, if Llywelyn had maintained the 1267 settlement he and the other rulers would certainly have had far less English interference to cope with than they had after 1277. In Scotland, the events of the 1290s came like a bolt from a clear blue sky. In the long years of Anglo-Scottish peace, when Carlisle castle fell into disrepair, unfortified houses proliferated across the border, and a common currency united the realms, a union of the kingdoms by marriage seemed far more likely than one by conquest. Indeed had dynastic death stalked south of the border rather than north, a son of Alexander III (his mother the daughter of Henry III) could well have ended up as king of England; a single monarch for the two countries not after Elizabeth's death in 1603 but after Edward I's.

The transformation in their national identities and economies (discussed in earlier chapters) meant that the English, the Welsh and the

Scots never had more in common than when politics at the end of the thirteenth century cast them apart. If the coming together had been largely (though not entirely) on English and by extension western European terms, there was no reason why political hegemony should have come in its wake. Indeed, one result of the changes was that the English no longer regarded the Welsh and the Scots as inferior, barbaric races. Nor did the remodelling of national identities and the developing powers of the state destroy aristocratic nexuses which crossed political boundaries. Indeed, these were more pronounced than ever. Henry I had prevented cross-border landholding in the north on the grounds that one could not serve two masters. In the thirteenth century, with the masters living in peace, it was extensive. For the numerous Anglo-Scottish landholders the Edwardian wars were unexpected and unnatural disasters. In Wales, Matilda Longespee was the daughter of one marcher baron, and the wife of another. She was also a cousin of Llywelyn, for both were grandchildren of Llywelyn the Great. As soon as she heard of Llywelyn's death she begged Archbishop Pecham to absolve him from his sins. Such sympathies, founded on family and humanity, and transcending race, class and gender, gave hope for the future.

Genealogical Tables

1 The Rulers of England: The English Line

(Kings of England shown in capitals)

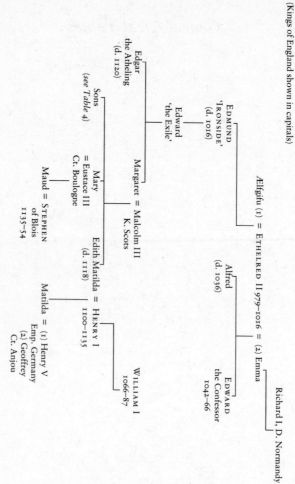

2 The Rulers of England: The Norman Line

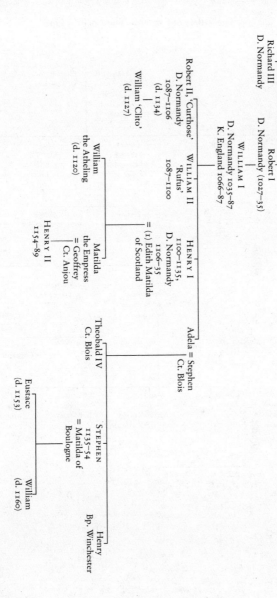

Richard III
D. Normandy
├── Robert I
│   D. Normandy (1027–35)
│   └── WILLIAM I
│   D. Normandy 1035–87
│   K. England 1066–87
│   ├── Robert II, 'Curthose'
│   │   D. Normandy
│   │   1087–1106
│   │   (d. 1134)
│   │   └── William 'Clito'
│   │   (d. 1127)
│   ├── WILLIAM II
│   │   'Rufus'
│   │   1087–1100
│   ├── HENRY I
│   │   1100–1135,
│   │   D. Normandy
│   │   1106–35
│   │   = (1) Edith Matilda
│   │   of Scotland
│   │   ├── William
│   │   │   the Atheling
│   │   │   (d. 1120)
│   │   └── Matilda
│   │   the Empress
│   │   = Geoffrey
│   │   Ct. Anjou
│   │   └── HENRY II
│   │   1154–89
│   └── Adela = Stephen
│   Ct. Blois
│   ├── Theobald IV
│   │   Ct. Blois
│   └── STEPHEN
│   1135–54
│   = Matilda of
│   Boulogne
│   ├── Eustace
│   │   (d. 1153)
│   ├── William
│   │   (d. 1160)
│   └── Henry
│   Bp. Winchester

3 The Rulers of England: The Angevin Line

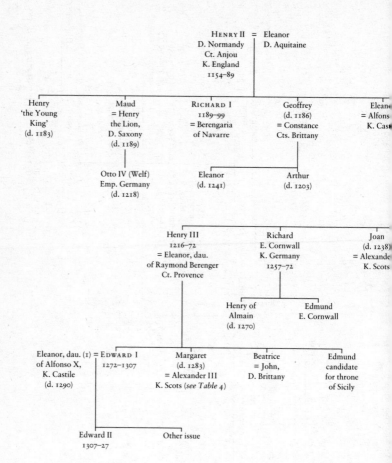

HENRY II = Eleanor
D. Normandy   D. Aquitaine
Ct. Anjou
K. England
1154–89

Henry
'the Young
King'
(d. 1183)

Maud
= Henry
the Lion,
D. Saxony
(d. 1189)

RICHARD I
1189–99
= Berengaria
of Navarre

Geoffrey
(d. 1186)
= Constance
Cts. Brittany

Eleanor
= Alfonso
K. Castile

Otto IV (Welf)
Emp. Germany
(d. 1218)

Eleanor
(d. 1241)

Arthur
(d. 1203)

Henry III
1216–72
= Eleanor, dau.
of Raymond Berenger
Ct. Provence

Richard
E. Cornwall
K. Germany
1257–72

Joan
(d. 1238)
= Alexander
K. Scots

Henry of
Almain
(d. 1270)

Edmund
E. Cornwall

Eleanor, dau. (1) = EDWARD I
of Alfonso X,   1272–1307
K. Castile
(d. 1290)

Margaret
(d. 1283)
= Alexander III
K. Scots (see Table 4)

Beatrice
= John,
D. Brittany

Edmund
candidate
for throne
of Sicily

Edward II
1307–27

Other issue

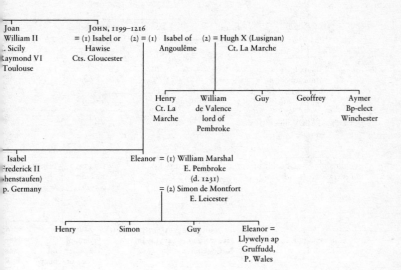

Joan
William II
. Sicily
Raymond VI
Toulouse

JOHN, 1199–1216
= (1) Isabel or   (2) = (1) Isabel of   (2) = Hugh X (Lusignan)
      Hawise   Angoulême   Ct. La Marche
      Cts. Gloucester

Henry   William   Guy   Geoffrey   Aymer
Ct. La   de Valence   Bp-elect
Marche   lord of   Winchester
               Pembroke

Isabel
Frederick II
henstaufen)
p. Germany

Eleanor = (1) William Marshal
              E. Pembroke
              (d. 1231)
        = (2) Simon de Montfort
              E. Leicester

Henry   Simon   Guy   Eleanor =
                                           Llywelyn ap
                                           Gruffudd,
                                           P. Wales

4 The Rulers of Scotland (*Kings of Scotland shown in capitals*)

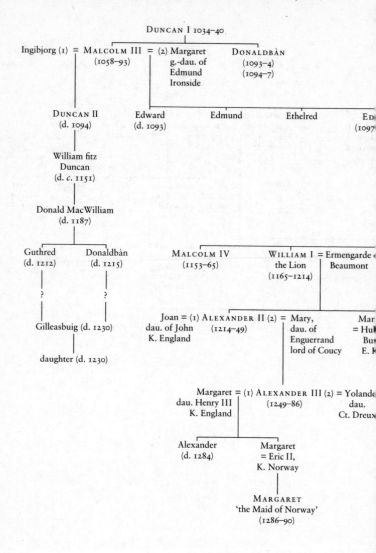

DUNCAN I 1034–40

Ingibjorg (1) = MALCOLM III = (2) Margaret   DONALDBÀN
(1058–93)   g.-dau. of   (1093–4)
   Edmund   (1094–7)
   Ironside

DUNCAN II   Edward   Edmund   Ethelred   ED
(d. 1094)   (d. 1093)   (1097

William fitz
Duncan
(d. *c.* 1151)

Donald MacWilliam
(d. 1187)

Guthred   Donaldbàn   MALCOLM IV   WILLIAM I = Ermengarde
(d. 1212)   (d. 1215)   (1153–65)   the Lion   Beaumont
     (1165–1214)

?   ?

Gilleasbuig (d. 1230)   Joan = (1) ALEXANDER II (2) = Mary,   Mar
   dau. of John   (1214–49)   dau. of   = Hu
   K. England   Enguerrand   Bu
daughter (d. 1230)   lord of Coucy   E. F

Margaret = (1) ALEXANDER III (2) = Yoland
dau. Henry III   (1249–86)   dau.
K. England   Ct. Dreux

Alexander   Margaret
(d. 1284)   = Eric II,
   K. Norway

MARGARET
'the Maid of Norway'
(1286–90)

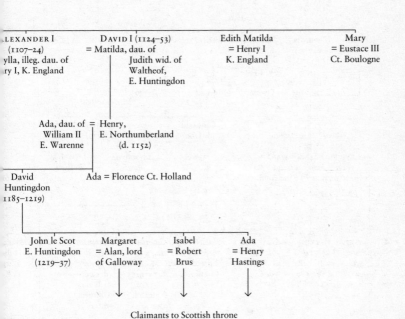

LEXANDER I   DAVID I (1124–53)   Edith Matilda   Mary
(1107–24)   = Matilda, dau. of   = Henry I   = Eustace III
ylla, illeg. dau. of   Judith wid. of   K. England   Ct. Boulogne
ry I, K. England   Waltheof,
      E. Huntingdon

Ada, dau. of = Henry,
William II   E. Northumberland
E. Warenne   (d. 1152)

David   Ada = Florence Ct. Holland
Huntingdon
1185–1219)

John le Scot   Margaret   Isabel   Ada
E. Huntingdon   = Alan, lord   = Robert   = Henry
(1219–37)   of Galloway   Brus   Hastings

Claimants to Scottish throne

5 The Dynasty of Gwynedd

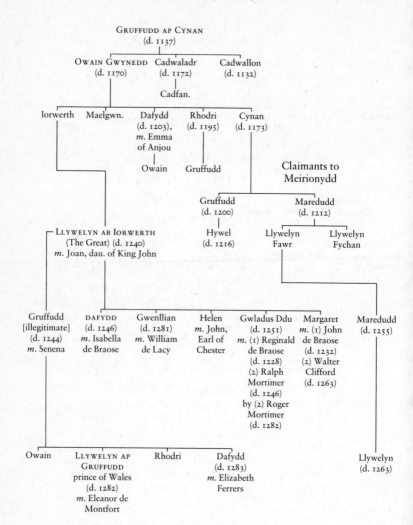

6 The Dynasty of Deheubarth

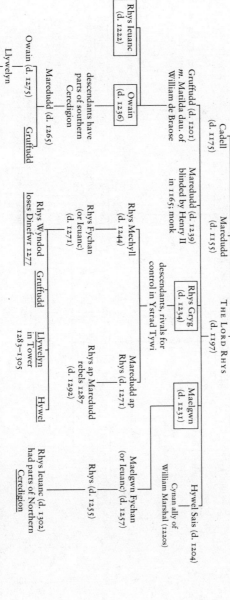

RHYS AP TEWDWR (d. 1093)

Nest, m. Gerald of Windsor

Gruffudd (d. 1201), m. Matilda dau. of William de Braose

Cadell (d. 1175)

Gruffudd (d. 1137)

Maredudd (d. 1155)

THE LORD RHYS (d. 1197)

Hywel Sais (d. 1204)

Maredudd (d. 1239) blinded by Henry II in 1165; monk

Rhys Ieuanc (d. 1222)

Owain (d. 1236)

Owain (d. 1275)

Llywelyn

line continues

Maredudd (d. 1265)

Gruffudd

descendants have parts of southern Ceredigion

Rhys Gryg (d. 1234)

Rhys Mechyll (d. 1244)

Rhys Fychan (or Ieuanc) (d. 1271)

Rhys Wyndod loses Dinefwr 1277

Gruffudd

descendants, rivals for control in Ystrad Tywi

Maredudd ap Rhys (d. 1271)

Rhys ap Maredudd rebels 1287 (d. 1292)

Llywelyn in Tower 1283–1305

Hywel

Maelgwn (d. 1231) Cynan ally of William Marshal (1220s)

Maelgwn Fychan (or Ieuanc) (d. 1257)

Rhys (d. 1255)

Rhys Ieuanc (d. 1302) had parts of Northern Ceredigion

☐ Descendants of the Lord Rhys among whom Deheubarth was partitioned.

— Involved in 1282 rising.

7 The Dynasty of Powys

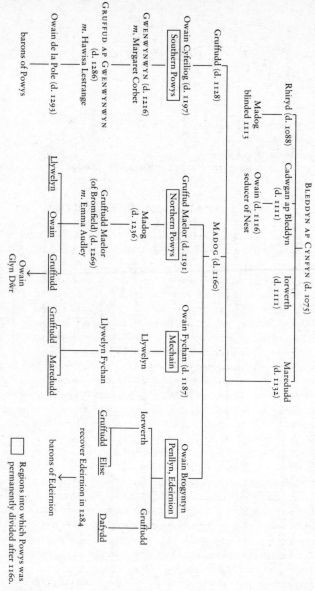

BLEDDYN AP CYNFYN (d. 1075)

Rhiryd (d. 1088)

Cadwgan ap Bleddyn (d. 1111)

Iorwerth (d. 1111)

Maredudd (d. 1132)

Madog blinded 1113

Owain (d. 1116) seducer of Nest

Gruffudd (d. 1128)

Owain Cyfeiliog (d. 1197) [Southern Powys]

GWENWYNWYN (d. 1216) m. Margaret Corbet

GRUFFUD AP GWENWYNWYN (d. 1286) m. Hawisa Lestrange

Owain de la Pole (d. 1293)

barons of Powys

MADOG (d. 1160)

Gruffud Maelor (d. 1191) [Northern Powys]

Madog (d. 1236)

Gruffudd Maelor (of Bromfield) (d. 1269) m. Emma Audley

Llywelyn

Owain

Gruffudd

Owain Glyn Dŵr

Owain Fychan (d. 1187) [Mechain]

Llywelyn

Llywelyn Fychan

Gruffudd

Maredudd

Owain Brogynyn [Penllyn, Ederinion]

Iorwerth

Gruffudd Elise

Gruffudd

Dafydd

recover Edeirnion in 1284

barons of Edeirnion

☐ Regions into which Powys was permanently divided after 1160.

— involved in 1282 rising.

Bibliography

Unless otherwise stated the place of publication is London.

PRINCIPAL PRIMARY SOURCES

A high proportion of the primary sources relevant to this book fall into two main groups. The first comprises the documents produced by the English and Scottish kings and the Welsh rulers together with other material about law and government. The second is formed by the writings of contemporaries about the period and individuals within it: histories, chronicles, biographies and saints' lives. In a third category are the records produced by ecclesiastics and ecclesiastical institutions, and in a fourth those produced by laymen. The very great bulk of this material is of English provenance, although English material can often shed light on events in Wales and Scotland.

An illuminating discussion of the proliferation of records in this period is found in M. T. Clanchy, *From Memory to Written Record. England 1066–1307*, 2nd edn. (Oxford, 1993). Those of the English kings were essentially generated by government inquiries and by the output of the chancery, the exchequer and the law courts. Contemporary writing about English history is fully described in Antonia Gransden's indispensable *Historical Writing in England c. 550 to c. 1307* (1974). The Latin texts of most of the works she discusses were published in the second half of the nineteenth century as part of the Rolls Series. Since the 1940s modern editions with scholarly introductions and translations have appeared first in Nelson's Medieval Texts series, and then in its successor, the invaluable and ongoing series of Oxford Medieval Texts. A wide variety of primary sources are translated in *English Historical Documents II 1042–1189*, ed. D. C. Douglas and G. W. Greenaway, 2nd edn. (1981), and *English Historical Documents III 1189–1327*, ed. H. Rothwell (1975). Henceforth these are cited as *EHD*.

Discussion of both historical writing in England and the output of English royal government falls naturally into three main periods, namely 1066–1154, 1154–1199, and the thirteenth century.

1066–1154

Before 1199 the royal chancery kept no record of the charters, writs and other documents which it issued. Those surviving in numerous archives either as originals or as copies have been brought together in *Regesta Regum Anglo-Normannorum: The Acta of William I 1066–1087*, ed. D. Bates (Oxford, 1998), and *Regesta Regum Anglo-Normannorum 1066–1154*, 4 vols., ed. H. W. C. Davis, C. Johnson, H. A. Cronne and R. H. C. Davis (Oxford, 1913–1969). The material in these volumes is absolutely central to the study of this period. The Coronation Charter of Henry I is translated as *EHD II*, no. 19.

The first surviving pipe roll of the exchequer, which recorded the annual audit of the money owed the crown, is that for the financial year 1129/30: *The Pipe Roll of 31 Henry I* (HMSO, 1929), a facsimile reproduction of the Record Commission's 1833 edition. *Dialogus de Scaccario*, ed. and tr. C. Johnson, F. E. L. Carter and D. Greenway (Oxford, 1983) contains a translation of the 'constitution of the king's household' drawn up soon after 1135. For the *Dialogus* itself, see the 1154–1189 section below.

The king's courts kept no official records in this period, or none which survive, but accounts of early law cases, drawn mostly from chronicle sources, are brought together in *English Lawsuits from William I to Richard I*, 2 vols., ed. and tr. R. C. Van Caenegem (Selden Society, 106–7 (1990–91)). *Leges Henrici Primi*, ed. and tr. L. J. Downer (Oxford, 1972), is an important work on legal procedure written in the reign of Henry I.

The full text of Domesday Book has now been published by Penguin: *Domesday Book: A Complete Translation*, ed. A. Williams and G. H. Martin (2002).

Key Norman accounts of the Conquest by William of Jumièges, a monk of the monastery there born about 1000, and by William of Poitiers, the Conqueror's chaplain, are now available in modern editions: *The Gesta Normannorum Ducum of William of Jumièges, Orderic Vitalis and Robert of Torigni*, 2 vols., ed. and tr. E. M. C. Van Houts (Oxford, 1992–5), and *The Gesta Guillelmi of William of Potiers*, ed. and tr. R. H. C. Davis and M. Chibnall (Oxford, 1998). The tapestry is reproduced in *The Bayeux Tapestry*, ed. D. M. Wilson (1985). The main English account of the Conquest is found in the Anglo-Saxon Chronicle, which survives in two versions: a northern one which ends in 1079 and one written at Peterborough abbey which continues as an important source down to 1154. There are translations in *EHD II* and *The Anglo-Saxon Chronicle*, ed. D. Whitelock (1961). Another version running to 1130 was used by the Worcester monk, John of Worcester, whose chronicle ends in 1140: *The Chronicle of John of Worcester*, iii (for 1067–1140), ed. and tr. P. McGurk (Oxford, 1998).

Bestriding the whole period from before the Conquest to the 1140s is the work of Orderic Vitalis. Orderic was born in Shropshire in 1175 of an English mother and a Norman father. At the age of ten he was moved to the monastery of St-Evroult in Normandy. There between 1114 and 1141 he wrote his *Ecclesiastical History*, a voluminous, discursive and highly anecdotal work which gives a brilliant picture of the Norman elite. This is now available as *The Ecclesiastical History of Orderic Vitalis*, 6 vols., ed. and tr. M. Chibnall (Oxford, 1969–90); and see Marjorie Chibnall, *The World of Orderic Vitalis* (Oxford, 1984). Also vital for this period are the works of William of Malmesbury, a monk of Malmesbury abbey of mixed English and Norman birth, who began writing in the 1120s and was one of the most intelligent and perceptive of all medieval historians. Modern editions of his works are *Gesta Regum Anglorum: The History of the English Kings*, 2 vols., ed. and tr. R. A. B. Mynors, R. M. Thomson and M. Winterbottom (Oxford, 1998–9), and (covering the first part of Stephen's reign) *The Historia Novella*, ed. and tr. E. King and K. R. Potter (Oxford, 1998). See also Rodney Thomson, *William of Malmesbury* (Woodbridge, 1987). Another historian of mixed birth and considerable ability was Henry, archdeacon of Huntingdon, whose history of the English to 1129, begun in or soon after 1123, was ultimately continued down to 1154. This is now available as *Henry, Archdeacon of Huntingdon*, Historia Anglorum *The History of the English People*, ed. and tr. D. Greenway (Oxford, 1996). His constant attendance on Anselm makes the works of the Canterbury monk Eadmer extraordinarily vivid and informative: *The Life of St Anselm by Eadmer*, ed. and tr. R. W. Southern (1962), and *Eadmer's History of Recent Events in England*, tr. G. Bosanquet (1964). Influenced by Eadmer, Hugh the Chanter of York wrote an equally informed account of the career of Archbishop Thurstan: *Hugh the Chanter: The History of the Church of York 1066–1127*, ed. and tr. C. Johnson, M. Brett, C. N. L. Brooke and M. Winterbottom (Oxford, 1990). *History of the Church of Abingdon*, 2 (for the years after 1066), ed. and tr. J. Hudson (Oxford 2002), now makes this major monastic history readily available.

The chief chronicle of Stephen's reign – *Gesta Stephani*, ed. and tr. K. R. Potter and R. H. C. Davis (Oxford, 1976) – was possibly written by Robert of Lewes, bishop of Bath from 1136 to 1166. A translation of William of Newburgh's later account of the period is found in *William of Newburgh: The History of English Affairs, Book I*, ed. P. G. Walsh and M. J. Kennedy (Warminster, 1988). *Scottish Annals from English Chroniclers 500–1286*, ed. A. O. Anderson (Stamford, 1991) is valuable for its translations of the Hexham chroniclers and of Ailred of Rievaulx's account of the battle of the Standard. Ailred's *Life of St Edward the Confessor* has been translated by Fr Jerome Bertram (Guildford, 1997). The spirit of the early Cistercians is captured in *The Life of Ailred of Rievaulx by Walter Daniel*, ed. and tr. F. M. Powicke (1950). Another remarkable life (written between 1155 and 1166) is *The Life of Christina of Markyate: A Twelfth Century Recluse*, ed. and tr. C. H. Talbot (Oxford, 1987). It is a pity there is no translation of *The Life of Wulfric of*

Haselbury by John Abbot of Ford, ed. Dom M. Bell (Somerset Record Society, 47 (1933)).

Geoffrey of Monmouth, *The History of the Kings of Britain*, translated by Lewis Thorpe, is readily available in a Penguins Classics edition of 1966. There is a translation of Gaimar in the second volume of *Lestorie des Engles solum la Translacion Maistre Geffrei Gaimar*, 2 vols., ed. T. D. Hardy and C. T. Martin (Rolls Series, 1888–9).

1154–1199

The surviving charters and writs issued by the chancery of Henry II will shortly be published under the editorship of J. C. Holt and N. C. Vincent, volumes which will transform study of the reign. Nicholas Vincent is also preparing an edition of the *acta* of Richard I. Meanwhile some guide is provided by *The Itinerary of Richard I*, ed. L. Landon (Pipe Roll Society, new series xiii (1935)).

The pipe rolls of the exchequer survive in continuous annual sequence from 1155 and have all been printed for this period by the Pipe Roll Society. The great account of the workings of the exchequer by the treasurer Richard fitz Nigel, written between 1177 and 1179, is published as *Dialogus de Scaccario*, ed. and tr. C. Johnson, F. E. L. Carter and D. Greenway (Oxford, 1983).

No official records of the royal courts from before the mid 1190s survive, so one is still dependent on Van Caenegem's *English Lawsuits from William I to Richard I*. *The Treatise on the Laws and Customs of England commonly called Glanvill*, ed. G. D. G. Hall (1965), produced late in the reign by the legal circle around Henry II's justiciar, Ranulf Glanvill, gives a remarkable analysis of the workings of the early common law.

EHD II prints the assizes of Henry II, and some returns both to the inquest of sheriffs and to the great inquiry of 1166 into knight service.

This period is illuminated by the work of some remarkable historians. As a royal clerk employed at court and on special missions, Roger of Howden was able to provide a unique insider's narrative of the period from 1170 to 1201 and one well informed about Scottish affairs: for his writings see David Corner's article in *Bulletin of the Institute of Historical Research*, 56 (1983). Howden's cautious and even tone contrasts with the outspoken and egotistical writings of another royal clerk, Gerald of Wales, archdeacon of Brecon, a man dogged, so he thought, by his mixed Welsh and Anglo-Norman descent. Totally different again is the humane and judicious William of Newburgh, an Augustinian canon who wrote his chronicle in the late 1190s. Another important historian and a great admirer of Henry II was the dean of St Paul's, Ralph of Diss. Diss is only available in the original Rolls Series edition, but nineteenth-century translations of Howden and Newburgh by H. T. Riley and J. Stevenson (in his *Church Historians of England*) have been recently reprinted by Llanerch Press (1996). Gerald of Wales comes alive in *The Autobiography of Giraldus Cambrensis*, ed. and tr. H. E. Butler (1937), and see Robert Bartlett's study, *Gerald of Wales 1146–1223* (Oxford, 1982). Gerald's works on Wales and Ireland are mentioned later. *Jordan of Fantosme's Chronicle*, ed. and tr. R. C. Johnston (Oxford, 1981), is essential and exciting for the 1173–4 civil war. *The Chronicle of Richard of Devizes*, ed. and tr. J. T. Appleby (1963), written by a Winchester monk, is valuable for Richard's reign, as are the work of Ralph of Coggeshall and the life of William Marshal, both discussed in the next section.

The Becket dispute inspired numerous lives of the archbishop and these are now available in *The Lives of Thomas Becket*, ed. and tr. M. Staunton (Manchester, 2001). The course of the dispute can be followed in *EHD II*, Part III (C), where the Constitutions of Clarendon are printed. *The Chronicle of Battle Abbey*, ed. and tr. E. Searle (Oxford, 1980) and *The Chronicle of Jocelin of Brakelond concerning the Acts of Samson abbot of the Monastery of St Edmund*, ed. and tr. H. E. Butler (1949) reveal the efforts of monastic institutions to defend their rights and properties. Jocelin's work, with its splendid picture of Samson, has become a classic. Both these chronicles provide glimpses of the Angevin kings at work. So does the life of Hugh of Avalon, bishop of Lincoln (1186–1200), by his chaplain Adam of Eynsham – *The Life of St Hugh of Lincoln*, 2 vols., ed. and tr. D. L. Douie and H. Farmer (1962); this magnificent biography gives a totally convincing picture of a good and great man. For the twelfth-century historians in general, see Nancy Partner, *Serious Entertainments: The Writing of History in Twelfth-Century England* (Chicago, 1977).

The Thirteenth Century

From the turn of the twelfth century the source material available to the historian is revolutionized by an explosion in the record-keeping of the English government. In 1199 the chancery began to record its output on a series of annual rolls so the historian is no longer dependent on the haphazard survival of originals or copies. Preserved in the Public Record Office, the resulting charter, patent, close, *liberate* and fine rolls for the thirteenth century have nearly all been printed either *in extenso* or in English calendar, beginning in the 1820s and 1830s under the auspices of the Record Commission and continuing from the 1890s under those of HMSO. An omission in the PRO calendars has been rectified by the publication of *The Royal Charter Witness Lists of Edward I*, ed. R. Huscroft and *The Royal Charter Witness Lists of Henry III*, 2 vols., ed. M. Morris (List and Index Society, 279, 291–2 (2000, 2002)). These provide key evidence for who was at court. A related publication is Robin Studd's *An Itinerary of Lord Edward* (List and Index Society, 284 (2000)).

Although they had probably been kept from a little earlier, records of the pleas heard by the king's courts survive from the mid 1190s. Down to 1245 the rolls kept by the central court at Westminster (the 'common bench') and the court travelling with the king (later called 'king's bench') have been printed in *Curia Regis Rolls*, 18 vols. (1922–99). Records ('eyre rolls') kept by the king's judges travelling in the localities, and surviving from the 1190s, have been printed by both the Selden Society and local records societies: see David Crook, *Records of the General Eyre* (1982). Local record societies have also published many feet of fines. *Bracton de Legibus et Consuetudinibus Angliae*, 4 vols., ed. G. E. Woodbine and S. E. Thorne (Cambridge, Mass., 1968–77) is the great work on English legal procedure written by the circle around the justice William Ralegh in the 1220s and 1230s. Paul Brand is editing the earliest English law reports, which survive from the 1260s, for the Selden Society. Extracts from the rolls of the justices of the forest are found in *Select Pleas of the Forest*, ed. G. J. Turner (Selden Society, 13 (1899)).

The pipe rolls of the exchequer are printed by the Pipe Roll Society down to 1222. The Society has also printed some exchequer memoranda rolls and receipt and issue rolls. The surviving plea rolls of the exchequer of the Jews have been published by the Jewish Historical Society. The great bulk of the financial material of the thirteenth century, like the legal material after 1245, has still to be printed.

Records of the royal household begin to appear in John's reign. They survive patchily in the reign of his son, and thereafter in abundance. Some are brought together in *Records of the Wardrobe and Household 1285–89*, 2 vols., ed. B. F. and C. R. Byerly (HMSO, 1977, 1986).

The returns to government inquiries of different kinds are printed in the *Calendar Inquisitions Miscellaneous*, 1 (1916), in the *Calendars of Inquisition Post Mortem* and in *Rotuli Hundredorum*, 2 vols. (1812, 1818). The second volume of the latter contains the great Hundred Roll inquiry of 1279, for which see also *The Warwickshire Hundred Rolls of 1279–80: Stoneleigh and Kineton Hundreds*, ed. T. John (Oxford, 1992). Inquiries and other material in *The Book of Fees*, 3 vols. (1920–31) provide important evidence for who held what land.

The key constitutional documents of the period – Magna Carta in its various versions, the Charter of the Forest, the Paper Constitution of 1244, the Provisions of Oxford and Westminster of 1258–9, and the concessions of 1297 and 1300 are all printed in *EHD III*, as are the principal statutes of Edward I. G. O. Sayles, *The Functions of the Medieval Parliament of England* (1988) provides translations of many of the early parliamentary texts.

While record sources become far more plentiful after 1199, the quality of contemporary writing declines. There are also very few modern editions of the works of thirteenth-century historians. Roger of Howden, William of Newburgh and Ralph of Diss all laid down their pens around 1200. The best chronicles for John's reign and the minority of Henry III are those by Ralph of Coggeshall (abbot of the Cistercian abbey in Essex), and the so-called 'Barnwell' chronicler, so called because the only surviving text of his work comes from Barnwell abbey in Cambridge. Both are printed in the Rolls Series, the latter in volume 2 of *Memoriale Walteri de Coventria*, 2 vols., ed. W. Stubbs (Rolls Series, 1872–3). The life of William Marshal, Henry III's regent, which was commissioned by his family in the 1220s, sheds graphic light on politics and chivalry in the Angevin period, and in terms of its quality is the secular equivalent of the life of St Hugh. *History of William Marshal*, ed. A. J. Holden and D. Crouch, tr. S. Gregory (Anglo-Norman Text Society, 2002), which covers the period to 1194, is the first of three volumes to appear. Meanwhile *EHD III*, no. 3, prints the last part of the life from 1216 to 1219.

St Albans abbey in the thirteenth century was the home of two celebrated chroniclers, Roger of Wendover and Matthew Paris. Wendover's chronicle is original from 1202 down to its termination in 1235. Its composition was probably begun in the 1220s, which explains why the later portions are the most valuable. The translation by J. A. Giles – *Roger of Wendover's Flowers of History*, 2 vols. (1849–50) – has been reprinted by Llanerch Press (1993, 1996). Paris's *Chronica Majora*, written within a few years of events, runs from 1235 to his death in 1259. It thus embraces the whole of Henry III's personal rule and is a major source for Welsh and Scottish as well as English history. Paris shared Wendover's hostility to the king's foreign favourites and ministers and was not an intelligent and perceptive historian like William of Malmesbury. However, he knew everyone, was interested in everything and wrote prolifically, often with a tolerable degree of accuracy. He was also a great artist. The only translation of the *Chronica Majora* is J. A. Giles, *Matthew Paris's English History*, 3 vols. (1852–4). For Paris see Richard Vaughan, *Matthew Paris* (Cambridge, 1958) and Suzanne Lewis, *The Art of Matthew Paris in the* Chronica Majora (Berkeley and Los Angeles, 1987).

Thomas of Eccleston's account of the early friars is available as *The Coming of the Franciscans: Thomas of Eccleston*, tr. L. P. Sherley-Price (1964). Although interesting, neither the life of Edmund of Abingdon, archbishop of Canterbury, by Matthew Paris, nor that of Richard of Wych, bishop of Chichester, by Ralph Bocking have the intimacy and insight of the life of St Hugh: *The Life of St Edmund by Matthew Paris*, ed. and tr. C. H. Lawrence (Stroud, 1996) and *St Richard of Chichester: The Sources of his Life*, ed. D. Jones (Sussex Record Society, 79 (1993)).

EHD III has translations of the annals of Dunstable and the London chronicle of Arnold fitz Thedmar for the 1260s and of Peter Langtoft for the 1290s. *The Chronicle of Bury St Edmunds*, ed. and tr. A. Gransden (1964) is centred on the reign of Edward I. The most intelligent historian in Edward's time was Thomas Wykes, a former servant of Richard of Cornwall who wrote in retirement at Osney abbey. A new edition of his work may be forthcoming in Oxford Medieval Texts.

In the thirteenth century political songs and tracts become an increasingly important source and many are found in *Political Songs of England from the*

Reign of John to Edward II, ed. and tr. T. Wright with a new introduction by P. R. Coss (Cambridge, 1996). The standard text of the Song of Lewes (also in *EHD III*) is *The Song of Lewes*, ed. and tr. C. L. Kingsford (Oxford, 1890). *Documents of the Baronial Movement 1258–1267*, ed. and tr. R. F. Treharne and I. J. Sanders, apart from containing the main constitutional documents, also prints important schedules of grievance prepared by both sides of the 1260s divide.

For Scotland there is no equivalent of the state records of English royal government. The Scottish chancery neither issued as many documents as its English counterpart nor kept a central record of them. The project to collect its output has so far produced *The Charters of King David I 1124–53 . . .*, (Woodbridge, 1999) and *Regesta Regum Scottorum: 1153–1214*, 2 vols. (Edinburgh, 1960, 1971), all edited by G. W. S. Barrow. For the earlier material see *Early Scottish Charters prior to AD 1153*, ed. A. C. Lawrie (Glasgow, 1905). Royal accounts, estimates of revenue and a description of the royal household, all from the second half of the thirteenth century, are printed in *The Exchequer Rolls of Scotland*, ed. J. Stuart and G. Burnett (Edinburgh, 1878), and 'The Scottish king's household and other fragments', ed. M. Bateson, in *Miscellany of the Scottish Historical Society*, ii (Edinburgh, 1904). The tangled question of the evidence for early Scottish law is unravelled in Hector L. MacQueen, *Common Law and Feudal Society in Medieval Scotland* (Edinburgh, 1993).

For much of the period covered by this book Argyll, Galloway, the Western Isles and the Isle of Man were, in varying degrees, outside the Scottish state and subject to independent rulers. Little survives of those rulers' documentary output but Keith Stringer has brought together evidence for some sixty-five documents, mostly charters, issued by the rulers of Galloway between *c.*1140 and 1230: 'Acts of Lordship: The records of the lords of Galloway to 1234', in *Freedom and Authority: Scotland c.1050–c.1650. Essays presented to Grant G. Simpson*, ed. T. Brotherstone and D. Ditchburn (East Linton, 2000).

Documents in English state records relevant to Scotland are calendared (not always trustworthily) in *Calendar of Documents relating to Scotland 1108–1272*, 2 vols., ed. J. Bain (1881, 1994). *Anglo-Scottish Relations 1174–1328*, ed. E. L. G. Stones (Oxford, 1965) is an invaluable collection.

The scanty chronicle and other narrative sources for Scottish history are found in *Early Sources for Scottish History 500–1286*, 2 vols., ed. and tr. A. O. Anderson (Edinburgh, 1922; Stamford, 1990), the life of Queen Margaret probably by Turgot, the Norse sagas, the Chronicle of Man, and the Melrose Chronicle being particularly valuable. There is a study of the last by A. A. M. Duncan in *Kings, Clerics and Chronicles in Scotland 500–1297: Essays in Honour of Marjorie O. Anderson*, ed. S. Taylor (Dublin, 2000). *Scottish Annals from English Chroniclers 500–1286*, ed. and tr. by A. O. Anderson (London, 1908; Stamford, 1991) is a much used collection. The fourteenth-century chronicle of John of Fordun contains earlier material not found elsewhere. For a translation see *John of Fordun's Chronicle of the Scottish Nation*, 2 vols., ed. W. F. Skene (Llanerch, 1993). The fifteenth-century chronicle of Walter Bower has similar value: *Scotichronicon by Walter Bower*, general editor D. E. R. Watt, especially volumes 3–6 (Edinburgh and Aberdeen, 1995, 1994, 1990).

Study of Welsh history will be greatly furthered by the publication of *The Acts of the Welsh Rulers, 1120–1283*, ed. H. Pryce with the assistance of C. Insley (Cardiff, forthcoming). For the Welsh law books see *The Law of Hywel Dda: Law Texts from Medieval Wales*, ed. and tr. D. Jenkins (Llandysul, 1986).

There are exemplary modern editions of the two versions of the principal Welsh chronicle of this period known as *The Brut* after Britain's eponymous and legendary founder Brutus: *Brut Y Tywysogyon or The Chronicle of the Princes Peniarth MS.20 Version*, ed. and tr. T. Jones (Cardiff, 1952), and *Brut Y Tywysogyon or The Chronicle of the Princes, Red Book of Hengest Version*, ed. and tr. T. Jones (Cardiff, 1955). Both versions are written in Welsh and are derived from a Latin chronicle compiled at the Cistercian monastery of Strata Florida towards the end of the thirteenth century. That chronicle was itself based on earlier chronicles kept at St Davids down to *c.*1100, at Llanbadan Fawr near Aberystwyth down to 1175 (being particularly detailed for the time of Henry I) and thereafter at Strata Florida. The full form of the Latin original is lost but a version of it survives in *Annales Cambriae*, ed. J. Williams ab Ithel (Rolls Series, 1860) and *Chronica de Wallia*, ed. T. Jones (Cardiff, 1946). Gruffudd ap Cynan's remarkable life, written in Gwynedd sometime between his death in 1137 and the 1160s, is published as *A Mediaeval Prince of Wales: The Life of Gruffudd ap Cynan*, ed. and tr. D. S. Evans (Llanerch Press, 1990). For a discussion of the work see Nerys Ann Jones's chapter in *Gruffudd ap Cynan: A Collaborative Biography*, ed. K. L. Maund (Woodbrige, 1996). Fundamental for Wales in this period are the works of Gerald of Wales, especially his 'Journey through Wales' (to preach the crusade in 1188) and his 'Description of Wales', both translated by Lewis Thorpe for Penguin Classics (1978). Also in Penguin Classics is *The Mabinogion*, ed. and tr. J. Gantz, the collection of Welsh chivalric epics written down in the thirteenth century.

For Wales in the thirteenth century important sources are the *Calendar of Ancient Correspondence concerning Wales*, ed. J. G. Edwards (Cardiff, 1935), a collection of letters written by English officials, magnates and Welsh rulers, mostly to the English government, which have survived in the PRO; *Littere Wallie*, ed. J. G. Edwards (Cardiff, 1940), a miscellaneous collection of letters issued by the Welsh rulers and their subjects which was put together by the English government at the end of the thirteenth century; *The Welsh Assize Roll, 1277–1284*, ed. J. Conway Davies (Cardiff, 1940); *Calendar of Various Chancery Rolls 1277–1326* (1912), which has Edward's letters concerning

Wales after 1277 and his inquiry into Welsh law; *Registrum Epistolarum Johannis Peckham*, 3 vols., ed. C. T. Martin (Rolls Series, 1882–4), ii, 435–92, which contains the Welsh complaints to the archbishop; Llinos B. Smith, 'The *gravamina* of the community of Gwynedd against Llywelyn ap Gruffyd', *Bulletin of the Board of Celtic Studies*, 31 (1984); and *The Merioneth Lay Subsidy Roll 1292–3*, ed. K. Williams-Jones (Cardiff, 1976). *EHD III*, no. 55, prints a translation of the 1284 Statute of Wales.

The contemporary works on the English arrival in Ireland are *Expugnatio Hibernica. The Conquest of Ireland by Giraldus Cambrensis*, ed. and tr. A. B. Scott and F. X. Martin (Dublin, 1978) and *The Song of Dermot and the Earl*, ed. and tr. G. H. Orpen (Oxford, 1892). Documents in English state records related to Ireland are brought together in *Calendar of Documents relating to Ireland 1171–1251*, ed. H. S. Sweetman (1875).

The records produced by ecclesiastics and ecclesiastical institutions fall into several categories. Synodal legislation is printed (but not translated) in *Councils and Synods with other Documents relating to the English Church: I part II 1066–1204*, ed. D. Whitelock, M. Brett and C. N. L. Brooke (Oxford, 1981) and *Councils and Synods and other Documents relating to the English Church 1205–1313*, 2 vols., ed. F. M. Powicke and C. R. Cheney (Oxford, 1964). The charters and other documents produced by English bishops are being steadily published in the British Academy's English episcopal *acta* series. For Wales see *Episcopal Acts and Cognate Documents relating to Welsh Dioceses 1066–1272*, 2 vols., ed. J. C. Davies (Historical Society of the Church in Wales, 1946–8). From the thirteenth century bishops' registers begin to appear, and many of these have been published by the Canterbury and York Society, often in conjunction with local record societies. The earliest is that of Hugh of Wells, bishop of Lincoln 1209–35: *Rotuli Hugonis de Welles*, 3 vols., ed. W. P. Phillimore and F. N. Davis (1907–9). See *Guide to Bishops' Registers of England and Wales*, ed. D. M. Smith (1981). The letter collections of Gilbert Foliot, Robert Grosseteste and Adam Marsh are only available in Latin editions, but for that of Lanfranc see *The Letters of Lanfranc Archbishop of Canterbury*, ed. H. Clover and M. Gibson (Oxford, 1979). The collections made of letters to and from Becket as archbishop have now been edited and translated by Anne Duggan: *The Correspondence of Thomas Becket Archbishop of Canterbury*, 2 vols. (Oxford, 2000). *Calendar of entries in the Papal Registers relating to Great Britain and Ireland 1198–1304*, ed. W. H. Bliss (1893) is central to the papacy's role in British affairs, and see *Selected Letters of Pope Innocent III concerning England 1198–1216*, ed. and tr. C. R. Cheney and W. H. Semple (1953). *EHD III* prints the decrees of the Fourth Lateran Council and Rule of St Francis (nos. 136–7).

Numerous charters granting property to religious institutions survive both in the original and in copies made in cartularies, for which see G. R. C. Davis, *Medieval Cartularies of Great Britain: A Short Catalogue* (1958). Many of these charters and cartularies have been published by local record societies. In the thirteenth century there is also a growing corpus of material, particularly in the form of surveys and account rolls, showing how ecclesiastical institutions ran their estates. A continuous series from the 1200s of annual pipe rolls for the estates of the bishop of Winchester have been particularly used by historians. See *The Pipe Roll of the Bishopric of Winchester 1210–11*, ed. N. R. Holt (Manchester, 1964).

Large numbers of charters issued by laymen are known in this period, many of them as copies in ecclesiastical cartularies. Those of some individual magnate families have been brought together and published, for example *Charters of the Honour of Mowbray 1107–1191*, ed. D. Greenway (Oxford, 1972). The collection *Early Yorkshire Charters*, 12 vols., ed. W. Farrer and C. T. Clay (Edinburgh and Yorkshire Archaeological Society, 1915–65) has been of the first importance for the study of society in the north. In the thirteenth century some noble and gentry families began to record charters, estate surveys and rentals in their own cartularies (these too are listed in *Medieval Cartularies of Great Britain*), an early gentry example being that of the Hotot family printed in *A Northamptonshire Miscellany*, ed. E. King (Northamptonshire Record Society, 32 (1983)). Some of the material in *Household Accounts from Medieval England*, 2 vols., ed. C. M. Woolgar (Oxford, 1992) belongs to the thirteenth century.

A wide variety of manorial surveys, account rolls and court records are usefully translated and discussed by Mark Bailey in *The English Manor 1200–1500* (Manchester, 2002).

Numerous charters survive relating to the financial business of the Jews, one important collection being *Starrs and Jewish Charters preserved in the British Museum*, 3 vols., ed. I. Abrahams, H. Stokes, and H. Loewe (1930–32).

A good idea of the art, architecture and artefacts (including coins) of the period can be gained from the splendid catalogues of two exhibitions: *English Romanesque Art 1066–1200* (Arts Council of Great Britain, 1984) and *Age of Chivalry: Art in Plantagenet England 1200–1400*, ed. J. Alexander and P. Binski (Royal Academy of Arts, 1987).

FURTHER READING

As explained in the Preface, I have set out a full version of the secondary sources on which this book is based under my name on the King's College London History Department web site: www.kcl.ac.uk/history. A good idea of the profusion and quality of recent research can be gained by looking through the volumes of three periodical publications: *Anglo-Norman Studies*, the proceedings of the annual conference established at Battle in 1978; the *Haskins Society Journal*, first published in 1989; and *Thirteenth Century England*, the proceedings of the conference held every two years from 1985, first at Newcastle upon Tyne and then at Durham. In what follows I make suggestions for further reading, concentrating on recent work and for the most part on books rather than articles.

General Works

Three seminal works opened up British history in 1980s and 1990s, demonstrating the value of comparing and contrasting the experiences of England, Wales, Scotland and Ireland, as opposed to simply writing about them in isolation. These were *The British Isles. Comparisons, Contrasts and Connections 1100–1500*, ed. R. R. Davies (Edinburgh, 1988); Robin Frame, *The Political Development of the British Isles 1100–1400* (1990); and R. R. Davies, *Domination and Conquest. The Experience of Ireland, Scotland and Wales 1100–1300* (Cambridge, 1990), which was followed by Davies's *The First English Empire* (Oxford, 2000). This comparative approach very much informs the chapters by seven leading scholars in *The New Oxford History of the British Isles: The Twelfth and Thirteenth Centuries*, ed. B. F. Harvey (Oxford, 2001).

Perhaps the most stimulating account of English history in this period is M. T. Clanchy, *England and its Rulers 1066–1272* (1983), 2nd edn., with an epilogue on Edward I (1998). Robert Bartlett, *England under the Norman and Angevin Kings 1075–1225* (Oxford, 2000) covers a shorter period but is a work of extraordinary range. The best account of the development of English law is found in John Hudson, *The Formation of the English Common Law: Law and Society in England from the Norman Conquest to Magna Carta* (1996). W. L. Warren, *The Governance of Norman and Angevin England 1086–1272* (1987) is clear and full of ideas. Studies of warfare include Matthew Strickland's highly original *War and Chivalry. The Conduct and Perception of War in England and Normandy 1066–1217* (Cambridge, 1996); Stephen Morillo, *Warfare under the Norman and Angevin Kings 1066–1135* (Woodbridge, 1994); and Michael Prestwich's comprehensive *Armies and Warfare in the Middle Ages: The English Experience* (New Haven, 1996).

A. A. M. Duncan, *Scotland: the Making of the Kingdom* (Edinburgh, 1975) remains an essential work of reference. G. W. S. Barrow, *Kingship and Unity: Scotland 1000–1306* (1981) is an excellent short survey. More recent and covering a longer period is A. D. M. Barrell, *Medieval Scotland* (Cambridge, 2000). Central to its field is Hector L. MacQueen, *Common Law and Feudal Society in Medieval Scotland* (Edinburgh, 1993). Important regional studies include R. Andrew McDonald, *The Kingdom of the Isles: Scotland's Western Seaboard c.1100–1336* (East Linton, 1997) and Richard Oram, *The Lordship of Galloway* (Edinburgh, 2000). See also John Roberts's general survey, *Lost Kingdoms: Celtic Scotland and the Middle Ages* (Edinburgh, 1997). Individual studies by Barrow are brought together in his *The Kingdom of the Scots: Government, Church and Society from the Eleventh to the Fourteenth Century* (1973). A great deal of recent work on Scotland has appeared in volumes of essays, notably *Essays on the Nobility of Medieval Scotland*, ed. K. J. Stringer (Edinburgh, 1985); *Medieval Scotland, Crown, Lordship and Community: Essays Presented to G. W. S. Barrow*, ed. A. Grant and K. J. Stringer (Edinburgh, 1993); *Alba: Celtic Scotland in the Middle Ages*, ed. E. J. Cowan and R. A. McDonald (East Linton, 2000). *Atlas of Scottish History to 1707*, ed. P. G. P. McNeill and H. L. MacQueen (Edinburgh, 1996) has many relevant maps.

John Edward Lloyd, *A History of Wales from the Earliest Times to the Edwardian Conquest*, 2 vols. (1911) provides a magnificent narrative. R. R. Davies, *Conquest, Coexistence and Change: Wales 1063–1415* (1987) has a wider range and is a literary as well as an historical *tour de force*. (The subsequent paperback edition was retitled *The Age of Conquest*.) A. D. Carr's concise *Medieval Wales* (1995) has a helpful first chapter on historiography. Valuable new work on Wales, as on Scotland, has appeared in collections of essays by various scholars, for example *Landscape and Settlement in Medieval Wales*, ed. N. Edwards (Oxford, 1997) and *The Welsh King and his Court*, ed. T. M. Charles-Edwards, M. E. Owen and P. Russell (Cardiff, 2000). *An Historical Atlas of Wales from Early to Modern Times*, 2nd edn. (1959) has detailed maps.

Standard works on Ireland are A. J. Otway-Ruthven, *A History of Medieval Ireland*, 2nd edn. (1980) and *A New History of Ireland*, vol. 2: *Medieval Ireland 1169–1534*, ed. A. Cosgrove (Oxford, 1987). Sean Duffy's *Ireland in the Middle Ages* (1997) is a short and perceptive survey. There are many relevant essays in *Britain and Ireland 900–1300: Insular Responses to Medieval European Change*, ed. B. Smith (Cambridge, 1999) and in Robin Frame's *Ireland and Britain 1170–1450: Collected Essays* (1998).

General works on the economy are mentioned under chapter 2 below and on the church under chapter 14.

1. The Peoples of Britain

The work of R. R. Davies and John Gillingham has pioneered discussion of national identity in this period. Davies's lectures as President of the Royal Historical Society on 'The Peoples of Britain and Ireland 1100–1400' appeared in *Transactions of the Royal Historical Society*, sixth series, 4–7 (1994–7).

Gillingham's essays on English identity, including ones on 'The beginnings of English imperialism', and on Geoffrey of Monmouth, Henry of Huntingdon, Gaimar and Roger of Howden, have been brought together in his *The English in the Twelfth Century. Imperialism, National Identity and Political Values* (Woodbridge, 2000). For wider consideration of national identity see Adrian Hastings, *The Construction of Nationhood: Ethnicity, Religion and Nationalism* (Cambridge, 1997) and Susan Reynolds, *Kingdoms and Communities in Western Europe 900–1300* (Oxford, 1984).

English identity before the Norman Conquest is the subject of a paper by Sarah Foot, 'The making of *Angelcynn*', *Transactions of the Royal Historical Society* (1996). For the changing identity of the Scots, the work of Dauvit Broun is fundamental. It includes 'Defining Scotland and the Scots before the Wars of Independence', in *Image and Identity: The Making and Remaking of Scotland through the Ages*, ed. D. Broun, R. J. Finlay and M. Lynch (Edinburgh, 1998). See also Broun's *The Irish Identity of the Kingdom of the Scots* (Woodbridge, 1999). Bruce Webster, *Medieval Scotland: The Making of an Identity* (1997) looks at identity in various forms.

2. The Economies of Britain

Christopher Dyer's *Making a Living in the Middle Ages: The People of Britain 850–1520* (New Haven and London, 2002) is a major new study and one of the few books to treat the British economy as a whole. The most comprehensive survey of the English economy is J. L. Bolton, *The Medieval English Economy 1150–1500*, 2nd edn. (1985). J. Z. Titow, *English Rural Society 1200–1350* (1969) provides a lively introduction to the question of the standard of living of the peasantry and the size of the population on which the latest word is contained in B. M. S. Campbell's *English Seigniorial Agriculture 1250–1450* (Cambridge, 2000). A careful estimate of the Domesday population is made by John Moore in *Anglo-Norman Studies*, 19 (1996). Christopher Dyer, *Standards of Living in the Later Middle Ages. Social Change in England 1200–1520* (1989) has been rightly acclaimed.

For towns and commerce see Susan Reynolds, *An Introduction to the History of English Medieval Towns* (Oxford, 1977), and Edward Miller and John Hatcher, *Medieval England. Towns, Commerce and Crafts 1086–1348* (1995), the companion volume to their earlier *Rural Society and Economic Change 1086–1348* (1978). R. H. Britnell's *The Commercialisation of English Society 1000–1500* (Cambridge, 1993) and *A Commercialising Economy. England 1086–1300*, ed. R. H. Britnell and B. M. S. Campbell (Manchester, 1995) are both very important. The latter includes a chapter by Robert Stacey on Jewish money-lending and one by Nicholas Mayhew which attempts to estimate England's money supply and gross domestic product. A significant new article on the inflation of the 1200s by Paul Latimer appears in *Past and Present* for 2001.

Two important works on the peasantry are Rosamond Faith, *The English Peasantry and the Growth of Lordship* (1997) and Paul Hyams, *King, Lords and Peasants in Medieval England: The Common Law of Villeinage in the Twelfth and Thirteenth Centuries* (Oxford, 1980), the latter essential for the origins of legal unfreedom. For slavery see David Pelteret, *Slavery in Early Mediaeval England* (Woodbridge, 1995). The many studies of individual manors and estates include Edward Miller, *The Abbey and Bishopric of Ely* (Cambridge, 1951); P. D. A. Harvey, *A Medieval Oxfordshire Village: Cuxham 1240 to 1400* (Oxford, 1965); and Edmund King, *Peterborough Abbey 1086–1310* (Cambridge, 1973). There is a chapter by Derek Keene on London in *The Cambridge Urban History of Britain I: 600–1340*, ed. D. M. Palliser (Cambridge, 2000), an important work with chapters by various scholars.

For Scotland and Wales, there are chapters in Duncan, *Scotland. The Making of the Kingdom* and Davies, *Conquest and Coexistence: Wales 1063–1415*. *Coinage in Medieval Scotland 1100–1600*, ed. D. M. Metcalf (British Archaeological Reports, 45 (1977)) is central to its subject. There are relevant studies in *The Scottish Medieval Town*, ed. M. Lynch, M. Spearman and G. Stell (Edinburgh, 1988). Wales is covered in *The Agrarian History of England and Wales II: 1042–1350*, ed. H. E. Hallam (Cambridge, 1988). *Landscape and Settlement in Medieval Wales*, ed. Edwards, contains the fruits of much new research, including chapters by Stephen Rippon on the Gwent levels and Jonathan Kissock on villages in Pembrokeshire.

Robert Bartlett's *The Making of Europe: Conquest, Colonization and Cultural Change 950–1350* (1993) paints the wider European developments of which Britain became part.

3. The Norman Conquest of England

The effects of the Norman Conquest on England have always been controversial, some historians stressing the continuities with Anglo-Saxon England, others the radical nature of the break. Debates new and old are discussed in Marjorie Chibnall's *The Debate on the Norman Conquest* (Manchester, 1999). Of general books, D. J. A. Matthew, *The Norman Conquest* (1966) and R. Allen Brown, *The Normans and the Norman Conquest* (1969) remain valuable, the latter a forthright restatement of the view that the Conquest introduced feudalism to England. David Bates, *William the Conqueror* (1989), a short biography, is a good introduction to the period in general. A full study of the Conqueror by Bates is forthcoming.

For Normandy, see David Bates, *Normandy before 1066* (1982). The 'maximum view' of the power of the late Anglo-Saxon state is expounded by James Campbell in papers brought together in his *Essays in Anglo-Saxon History* (1986) and *The Anglo-Saxon State* (2000). Patrick Wormald's papers, central to the same view on the legal side, are published in his *Legal Culture in the Early Medieval West; Law as Text, Image and Experience* (1999); see especially part IV.

For new ideas about Hastings, including the suggestion that the armies were much larger then previously imagined, see Ken Lawson's *The Battle of Hastings* (Stroud, 2002). *Anglo-Norman Castles*, ed. R. Liddiard (Woodbridge, 2002) brings together a series of studies, including one by Richard Eales, 'Royal power and castles in Norman England'. For the nobility before and after the Conquest see Peter Clarke, *The English Nobility under Edward the Confessor* (Oxford, 1994); Robin Fleming, *King and Lords in Conquest England* (Cambridge, 1991); and Ann Williams, *The English and the Norman Conquest* (Woodbridge, 1995) which gives the fullest account of the fortunes of the English nobility and gentry after 1066. For the north see W. E. Kapelle, *The Norman Conquest and the North: The Region and its Transformation* (1979) and Paul Dalton, *Conquest, Anarchy and Lordship: Yorkshire 1066–1154* (Cambridge, 1994). Two important articles are C. P. Lewis, 'The Domesday Jurors', *Haskins Society Journal*, 5 (1993) and J. J. N. Palmer, 'The wealth of the secular aristocracy in 1086', *Anglo-Norman Studies*, 22 (1999). I have brought together reading on feudal structures under chapter 13.

For the family the starting-point is chapter 9 of J. C. Holt's *Colonial England 1066–1215* (1997). The work of Pauline Stafford is vital both for queenship and the position of women: see her *Queen Emma and Queen Edith* (Oxford, 1997) and 'Women and the Norman Conquest', *Transactions of the Royal Historical Society*, sixth series, 4 (1994). For queenship more generally, see the essays in *Medieval Queenship*, ed. J. C. Parsons (Stroud, 1994).

Margaret Gibson's *Lanfranc of Bec* (Oxford, 1978) is a beautifully written study. Emma Cownie, *Religious Patronage in Anglo-Norman England 1066–1135* (Woodbridge, 1998) elucidates changing patterns of patronage.

Domesday Studies, ed. J. C. Holt (Woodbridge, 1987) brings together the work of various scholars. Challenging new ideas are advanced in David Roffe, *Domesday: The Inquest and the Book* (Oxford, 2000).

4. Wales, Scotland and the Normans

For North Wales and Gruffudd ap Cynan see *Gruffudd ap Cynan. A Collaborative Biography*, ed. K. L. Maund (Woodbridge, 1996). Helpful for military institutions is A. D. Carr's chapter on '*Teulu* and *Penteulu*' in *The Welsh King and his Court*, ed. Charles-Edwards, Owen and Russell. For Norman settlement and the formation of the marcher baronies, see C. P. Lewis on Herefordshire in *Anglo-Norman Studies*, 7 (1984) and Frederick Suppe, *Military Institutions on the Welsh Marches: Shropshire 1066–1300* (Woodbridge, 1994). David Crouch, 'The slow death of kingship in Glamorgan 1067–1158', *Morgannwg*, 29 (1985) reveals significant accommodation between the Welsh and the Normans.

Fundamental work on the structure of the early Scottish state has been done by Alexander Grant, for example in his chapter in *The Medieval State. Essays Presented to James Campbell*, ed. J. R. Maddicott and D. M. Palliser (2000). Alex Woolf, 'The "Moray Question" and the kingship of Alba in the Tenth and Eleventh Centuries', *Scottish Historical Review*, 79 (2000) is important. For a more positive view than the one I have taken of the royal hold over Moray, and indeed over Ross, the region to the north-west, see Grant's chapter on Ross in *Alba: Celtic Scotland*, ed. Cowan and McDonald. The definitive work on Carlisle is Henry Summerson's *Medieval Carlisle: The City and the Borders from the Late Eleventh to the Mid-Sixteenth Century*, 2 vols., Cumberland and Westmorland Archaeological Society, extra series, 25 (1993). Judith Green's chapter in *England and her Neighbours, 1066–1453: Essays in Honour of Pierre Chaplais*, ed. M. Jones and M. Vale (1989) covers Anglo-Scottish relations for the whole period between 1066 and 1174.

5. Britain and the Anglo-Norman Realm

The key work on the political structure of the Anglo-Norman realm is J. C. Holt's 'Politics and property in early medieval England', which appears as chapter 8 of his *Colonial England 1066–1215* (1997). David Bates, 'Normandy and England after 1066', *English Historical Review*, 104 (1989) criticizes the view found in John le Patourel, *The Norman Empire* (Oxford, 1976) that the kingdom and duchy formed a single political unit. The introduction of 'chivalry' is discussed by Strickland in his *War and Chivalry* and by Gillingham in *The English in the Twelfth Century*. Judith Green's *The Aristocracy of Norman England* (Cambridge, 1997) and her earlier *The Government of England under Henry I* (Cambridge, 1986) are both central to this period, as is Martin Brett's *The English Church under Henry I* (Oxford, 1975). J. O. Prestwich, 'War and finance in the Anglo-Norman state', in *Anglo-Norman Warfare*, ed. Strickland, first published in 1954, has proved a seminal paper. Frank Barlow, *William Rufus* (1983) is a highly readable biography. C. W. Hollister's biography, *Henry I* (2001), published posthumously, summed up many years of work on the reign by a great American scholar. For Queen Matilda, see Lois Huneycutt, 'The idea of a perfect princess: the Life of St Margaret in the reign of Matilda (1100–1118)', *Anglo-Norman Studies*, 12 (1989). Two celebrated studies are R. W. Southern's *St Anselm and his Biographer* (1963) and *Saint Anselm: A Portrait in a Landscape* (Cambridge, 1990). See also Sally Vaughn, *Anselm of*

Bec and Robert of Meulan: The Innocence of the Dove and the Wisdom of the Serpent (Berkeley and Los Angeles, 1987) and Donald Nicholl, *Thurstan Archbishop of York 1114–1140* (York, 1964). Henry I's relations with King David are discussed by Judith Green in *Scottish Historical Review*, 75 (1996).

6. Britain Remodelled

There has been much debate among historians about the causes of the troubles in Stephen's reign, and in particular how far they were due to the legacy of Henry I and how far to the king's own character and mistakes. Another area of debate concerns the extent to which the situation in England can be described as anarchic. The many excellent books on the period include R. H. C. Davis, *King Stephen*, 3rd edn. (1990); H. A. Cronne, *The Reign of Stephen: Anarchy in England 1135–1154* (1970); Keith J. Stringer, *The Reign of Stephen. Kingship, Warfare and Government in Twelfth-Century England* (1993); David Crouch, *The Reign of King Stephen, 1135–54* (2000); and Donald Matthew's *King Stephen* (2002). See also Crouch's *The Beaumont Twins* (Cambridge, 1986). *The Anarchy of King Stephen's Reign*, ed. E. King (Oxford, 1994) contains essays by leading scholars including one by Mark Blackburn on the coinage. Marjorie Chibnall, *The Empress Matilda: Queen Consort, Queen Mother and Lady of the English* (Oxford, 1991) is the standard biography.

Important studies of King David are G. W. S. Barrow's lecture, *David I of Scotland (1124–1153): The Balance of Old and New* (Reading, 1984); Stringer's chapter in *Government, Religion and Society in Northern England 1000–1700*, ed. J. C. Appleby and P. Dalton (Stroud, 1997); and Richard D. Oram's article (on David and Moray) in *Northern Scotland*, 19 (1999). G. W. S. Barrow, *The Anglo-Norman Era in Scottish History* (Oxford, 1980) deals with the new aristocracy. There is a chapter on the Scots in the north in Paul Dalton's *Conquest, Anarchy and Lordship: Yorkshire 1066–1154*. For Wales in this period see David Crouch's paper in *The Anarchy of King Stephen's Reign*, ed. King.

7. Henry II, Britain and Ireland

W. L. Warren, *Henry II* (1973) is a magisterial and finely written biography. A chapter by Jane Martindale in *Richard Coeur de Lion in History and Myth*, ed. J. L. Nelson (1992) gets closest to the thinking and policies of Eleanor of Aquitaine. The best introduction to the Angevin empire is John Gillingham, *The Angevin Empire*, 2nd edn. (2001). The chief study of Henry's recovery of royal authority in England is Emilie Amt's *The Accession of Henry II in England: Royal Government Restored 1149–1159* (1993), and see Graeme J.

White, *Restoration and Reform 1153–1165: Recovery from Civil War in England* (Cambridge, 2001).

The most enlightening overall account of the legal changes in Henry's reign is found in Hudson's *The Formation of the English Common Law*. There are important studies in Paul Brand's *Making of the Common Law* (1992), especially chapters 4 and 9, the latter a helpful critique of the ideas in S. F. C. Milsom, *The Legal Framework of English Feudalism* (Cambridge, 1976). A paper by Tom Keefe in *Albion*, 13 (1981) reveals the limited financial pressure Henry II placed on his earls.

The fullest biography of Becket is Frank Barlow's *Thomas Becket* (1986). A more sympathetic account is found in David Knowles, *Thomas Becket* (1970). For the other bishops see Knowles, *The Episcopal Colleagues of Thomas Becket* (1951). Papers by Charles Duggan are brought together in his *Canon Law in Medieval England: The Becket Dispute and Decretal Collections* (1982). For Becket's rival, see Adrian Morey and C. N. L. Brooke, *Gilbert Foliot and his Letters* (Cambridge, 1965). Beryl Smalley's brilliant book, *The Becket Conflict and the Schools* (Oxford, 1973) is indispensable for the wider European background.

Marie Therese Flanagan's *Irish Society, Anglo-Norman Settlers, Angevin Kingship* (Oxford, 1989) provides the fullest modern account of the arrival of the English. Brendan Smith, *Colonisation and Conquest in Medieval Ireland: The English in Louth, 1170–1330* is also important. The Cumbrian connections of John de Courcy are revealed in a paper by Sean Duffy in *Colony and Frontier in Medieval Ireland: Essays Presented to J. F. Lydon*, ed. T. B. Barry, R. Frame and K. Simms (1993).

The detailed introductions by G. W. S. Barrow to *Regesta Regum Scottorum*, volumes 1 and 2 (1960, 1971), cover all aspects of the reigns of Kings Malcolm and William the Lion. For Somerled and the west see Andrew McDonald, *The Kingdom of the Isles: Scotland's Western Seaboard*. Studies of Galloway include Keith Stringer's 'Reform Monasticism and Celtic Scotland: Galloway *c.*1140–*c.*1240', in *Alba: Celtic Scotland*, ed. Cowan and McDonald, and Richard D. Oram, 'A family business? Colonisation and settlement in twelfth- and thirteenth-century Galloway', *Scottish Historical Review*, 72 (1993). See also Oram's *The Lordship of Galloway* (Edinburgh, 2000), a comprehensive work which I wish I had come across earlier. For Caithness, Sutherland and Ross there are Barbara Crawford's chapter in *Essays on the Nobility of Medieval Scotland*, ed. Stringer, and Alexander Grant's chapter (on Ross) in *Alba: Celtic Scotland*.

Huw Pryce, 'Owain Gwynedd and Louis VII: the Franco-Welsh diplomacy of the first Prince of Wales', *Welsh History Review*, 19 (1998) is essential for Owain Gwynedd. For the Lord Rhys's policies towards the end of Henry's reign see Gillingham's 'Henry II, Richard I and the Lord Rhys', in his *The English in the Twelfth Century*.

8. Richard the Lionheart and William the Lion

In the last two decades John Gillingham has refashioned understanding of Richard's career, in part through seeing him as an able ruler with responsibilities for continental dominions as well as for England. His *Richard I* (1999) is a highly readable biography. Another recent work is Ralph Turner and Richard Heiser, *The Reign of Richard Lionheart* (2000). For the Jews see H. G. Richardson, *The English Jewry under Angevin Kings* (1960) and R. B. Dobson, *The Jews of Medieval York and the Massacre of March 1190* (York, 1974). C. R. Cheney, *Hubert Walter* (1967) is a concise and scholarly biography.

For William the Lion the reading mentioned under chapter 7 remains relevant. MacQueen's *Common Law and Feudal Society in Medieval Scotland* is important for the beginnings of legal change.

9. The Reign of King John

The works of J. C. Holt are fundamental to an understanding of this period, namely *The Northerners: A Study in the Reign of King John* (Oxford, 1961), *Magna Carta*, 2nd edn. (Cambridge, 1992), and (a volume of collected essays) *Magna Carta and Medieval Government* (1985). Biographies of the king include W. L. Warren, *King John* (1961), deservedly in print for over forty years, and Ralph Turner, *King John* (1994). There are papers by many scholars in *King John: New Interpretations*, ed. S. D. Church (Woodbridge, 1999), including V. D. Moss's on the revenues of Normandy and that of Daniel Power on the Norman aristocracy (essential for the loss of the duchy). The weakening connections with the duchy are explored by David Crouch in his chapter in *England and Normandy in the Middle Ages*, ed. D. Bates and A. Curry (Woodbridge, 1994). Nick Barratt's article in *English Historical Review*, 111 (1996) revealed for the first time the size of John's revenues from England. Angevin kingship's arbitrary face is laid bare in J. E. A. Jolliffe's *Angevin Kingship*, 2nd edn. (1963). For one foundation of the king's power see S. D. Church's revealing, *The Household Knights of King John* (Cambridge, 1999). For piety and ritual see Nicholas Vincent, 'The pilgrimages of the Angevin kings 1154–1272', in *Pilgrimage: The English Experience*, ed. C. Morris and P. Roberts (Cambridge, 2001). Two fine studies of major players in the reign are David Crouch's *William Marshal: Court, Career and Chivalry in the Angevin Empire 1147–1219* (1990) and Nicholas Vincent's *Peter des Roches: An Alien in English Politics 1205–1238* (Cambridge, 1996). Several royal ministers, including Geoffrey fitz Peter, are usefully studied in Ralph Turner's *Men Raised from the Dust: Administrative Service and Upward Mobility in Angevin England* (Philadelphia, 1988). *King John: New Interpretations* has papers by Sean Duffy, A. A. M. Duncan and Ifor Rowlands on Ireland, Scotland and Wales respectively. See also Brock Holden, 'King John, the Braoses and the Celtic fringe', *Albion*, 33 (2001). There is discussion of Stephen Langton's thought in J. W. Baldwin, *Masters, Princes and Merchants: The Social Views of Peter the Chanter and his Circle*, 2 vols. (Princeton, 1970).

10. The Minority of Henry III; Llywelyn the Great; and Alexander II

D. A. Carpenter, *The Minority of Henry III* (1990) covers the period in detail down to the mid 1220s. Vincent's *Peter des Roches* gives the fullest account of the tumultuous events between 1232 and 1234. D. J. A. Matthew, *The English and the Community of Europe in the Thirteenth Century* (Reading, 1997) sounds a cautionary note about the extent of hostility to foreigners. There are papers relevant to this chapter and the two following in *England and Europe in the Reign of Henry III*, ed. Björn K. Weiler with Ifor Rowlands (Aldershot, 2002), including one by Robin Studd on Gascony. Studies in Robin Frame's *Ireland and Britain 1170–1450: Collected Essays* (1998) explore the links between England and Ireland.

There is a striking account of Llywelyn the Great in Davies's *Conquest, Coexistence and Change*. For Welsh queenship in general and Joan in particular, see Robin C. Stacey, 'King, Queen and *Edling* in the laws of court', in *The Welsh King and his Court*, ed. Charles-Edwards, Owen and Russell. Titles are discussed in Charles Insley, 'From *Rex Wallie* to *Princeps Wallie*: charters and state formation in thirteenth-century Wales', in *The Medieval State* ed. Maddicott and Palliser.

Alexander II's role in the 1215–17 civil war is the subject of a chapter by Keith Stringer in *Scotland in the Reign of Alexander II*, ed. R. D. Oram (forthcoming). Also by Stringer is 'Periphery and core in thirteenth-century Scotland: Alan son of Roland, lord of Galloway and constable of Scotland', in *Medieval Scotland: Crown, Lordship and Community*, ed. Grant and Stringer. Oram's *The Lordship of Galloway* gives a full coverage of Alan's career and events after his death. MacQueen's *Common Law and Feudal Society in Medieval Scotland* is of cardinal importance for legal developments. For the Comyns, the definitive work is Alan Young's *Robert the Bruce's Rivals: The Comyns, 1212–1314* (East Linton, 1997).

11. Britain During the Personal Rule of Henry III

J. R. Maddicott, *Simon de Montfort* (1994) has the best modern account of Henry's personal rule and see the essays on various subjects in my own *Reign of Henry III* (1996), including one on parliament which gives references to other work on the subject. Robert C. Stacey, *Politics Policy and Finance under Henry III 1216–1245* (Oxford, 1987) breaks new ground, as does his crucial article on the Jews in *Historical Research*, 61 (1988). Margaret Howell, *Eleanor of Provence: Queenship in Thirteenth-Century England* (1998) shows for the first time the importance of Henry's queen and is a work of key importance for medieval queenship in general. For Westminster Abbey see Paul Binski, *Westminster Abbey and the Plantagenets: Kingship and the Representation of Power* (1995). In a series of articles, Huw Ridgeway has reinterpreted the role of Henry III's foreign relations in English politics and shown the importance of the struggle to control the Lord Edward in the crisis of 1258. See for example 'The Lord Edward and the Provisions of Oxford (1258)', *Thirteenth Century England*, 1 (1985) and 'Foreign favourites and Henry III's problems of patronage', *English Historical Review*, 103 (1989). A defence of the Sicilian project is mounted by Björn Weiler in *Historical Research*, 74 (2001). The difficulties of obtaining writs are explored in Andrew Hershey's 'Justice and bureaucracy: the English royal writ and "1258"', *English Historical Review*, 113 (1998). The early evidence for Robin Hood is set out by David Crook in a paper in *Thirteenth Century England*, 2 (1987).

For Wales, J. Beverley Smith's *Llywelyn ap Gruffudd, Prince of Wales* (Cardiff, 1998) now begins its magisterial course. For the minority of Alexander III see the paper by D. E. R. Watt in *Transactions of the Royal Historical Society*, fifth series, 21 (1971).

12. The Tribulations of King Henry; the Triumphs of King Alexander III and Llywelyn, Prince of Wales

For England, Maddicott's *Simon de Montfort* now holds centre stage while Howell's *Eleanor of Provence* continues to illuminate the crucial role of the queen. For the resettlement of England after the barons' wars the article by C. H. Knowles in *Transactions of the Royal Historical Society*, fifth series, 32 (1982) is of prime importance. There is a paper on 'Ireland and the Barons' Wars' in Robin Frame's *England and Ireland: Collected Essays*. The rise of Llywelyn ap Gruffudd is traced in detail in Beverley Smith's biography. For Alexander III the key book is *Scotland in the Reign of Alexander III 1249–1286*, ed. N. H. Reid (Edinburgh, 1990). It includes a chapter by Edward Cowan, 'Norwegian sunset – Scottish dawn: Hakon IV and Alexander III'.

The changing attitudes of the MacSorleys to the Scottish state are brought out in McDonald's *The Kingdom of the Isles: Scotland's Western Seaboard*.

13. Structures of Society

Gwyn A. Williams, *Medieval London: From Commune to Capital* (1963) provides a lively and learned account of London politics in the thirteenth century. The best introduction to the ethos and changing nature of knighthood is Peter Coss, *The Knight in Medieval England* (Stroud, 1993). Kathryn Faulkner, 'The transformation of knighthood in early thirteenth-century England', *English Historical Review*, 111 (1996) reveals the number of knights in the 1200s. Work on the gentry includes Coss's *Lordship and Locality: A Study of English Society c.1180–c.1280* (Cambridge, 1991) and Hugh M. Thomas, *Vassals, Heiresses, Crusaders and Thugs: The Gentry of Angevin Yorkshire 1154–1216* (Philadelphia, 1993). For the county court see Robert Palmer's *The County Courts of Medieval England 1150–1350* (Princeton, 1982). For the family see J. C. Holt's *Colonial England*, chapters 9–13.

Judith Green's *The Aristocracy of Norman England* is now a standard work. Also central to the early period is John Hudson, *Land, Law and Lordship in Anglo-Norman England* (Oxford, 1994). The classic study of the feudal structures of magnate power established after the Conquest is Sir Frank Stenton's *The First Century of English Feudalism 1066–1166*, 2nd edn. (Oxford, 1961). Recent work, however, has questioned how far the feudal honour was the cohesive and autonomous institution of Stenton's picture. See for example Paul Dalton, *Conquest, Anarchy and Lordship: Yorkshire 1066–1154*, chapter 7, and David Crouch, 'From Stenton to McFarlane: models of society of the twelfth and thirteenth centuries', *Transactions of the Royal Historical Society*, 6th series, 5 (1995). Crouch's article smoothes out the transition of feudalism to bastard feudalism, a transition debated by Coss, Crouch and myself in *Past and Present* for 1989, 1991 and 2000. See also Scott L. Waugh's important article 'Tenure to contract: lordship and clientage in thirteenth-century England', *English Historical Review*, 101 (1986). Studies of individual honours and nobles include Richard Mortimer on the honour of Clare in *Anglo-Norman Studies*, 3 and 8 (1980 and 1985); John Hunt, *Lordship and Landscape: A Documentary and Archaeological study of the Honour of Dudley 1066–1322* (Oxford, 1997); Crouch, *The Beaumont Twins* and his *William Marshal*; and K. J. Stringer, *Earl David of Huntingdon 1152–1219* (Edinburgh, 1985).

There is a chapter on peasants in politics in my *Reign of Henry III*. For the manorial court and its records see *Medieval Society and the Manor Court*, ed. Z. Razi and R. M. Smith (Oxford, 1996). R. H. Hilton's very readable *A Medieval Society: The West Midlands at the End of the Thirteenth Century* (1966) puts the peasants and the village community in their wider context.

Peter Coss, *The Lady in Medieval England 1000–1500* (Stroud, 1998) provides an introduction to the position of noblewomen. Jennifer Ward's *Women of the English Nobility and Gentry 1066–1500* (Manchester, 1995) brings together source material in translation. Matthew Paris's attitude to women is discussed by Rebecca Reader in *Thirteenth Century England*, 7 (1997). For peasant women see Judith Bennett's *Women in the Medieval English Countryside: Gender and Household in Brigstock before the Plague* (Oxford, 1987). Margaret de Lacy is studied by Louise Wilkinson in *Historical Research*, 73 (2000). Scott L. Waugh's *The Lordship of England: Royal Wardships and Marriages in English Society and Politics 1217–1327* (Princeton, 1988) reveals the changed situation for widows after 1215, and elucidates marriage strategies and how wardships were exploited by the king.

Important for the Scottish nobility are *Essays on the Nobility of Medieval Scotland*, ed. Stringer; MacQueen, *Common Law and Feudal Society in Medieval Scotland*; Young, *Robert Bruce's Rivals: The Comyns*; McDonald, *The Kingdom of the Isles*; and Oram, *The Lordship of Galloway*, where chapter 7 discusses 'acculturation'. For John de Vesci, see Stringer's 'Nobility and identity in medieval Britain and Ireland: the de Vescy family *c*.1120–1314', in *Britain and Ireland 900–1300*, ed. Smith. Stringer's work is vital for the cross-border nobility in the north, for example his 'Identities in thirteenth-century England: frontier society in the far north', in *Social and Political Identities in Western History*, ed. C. Bjørn, A. Grant and K. J. Stringer (Copenhagen, 1994).

T. Pierce Jones, *Medieval Welsh Society* (Cardiff, 1972) contains important essays including one on the growth of commutation in Gwynedd. The introduction to *The Merioneth Lay Subsidy Roll 1292–3*, ed. K. Williams-Jones, has a section on the structure of society. Changing attitudes to marriage and inheritance is a major theme in Huw Pryce's *Native Law and the Church in Medieval Wales* (Oxford, 1993).

For the common culture which in varying degrees came to embrace the whole of Britain, see David Crouch, *The Image of the Aristocracy in Britain 1100–1300* (1992). Written with his customary verve, this is the only book to treat the British nobility as a whole. The links with France are elucidated in Malcolm Vale, *The Angevin Legacy and the Hundred Years War 1250–1340* (Oxford, 1990).

14. Church, Religion, Literacy and Learning

For relations with the papacy, see the essays in *The English Church and the Papacy in the Middle Ages*, ed. C. H. Lawrence (1965), and Jane Sayers's two books, *Papal Judges Delegate in the Province of Canterbury 1198–1254* (Oxford, 1971) and *Papal Government and England during the Pontificate of*

Honorius III 1216–1227 (Cambridge, 1983). For the Mass see Miri Rubin, *Corpus Christi. The Eucharist in Late Medieval Culture* (Cambridge, 1991).

The history of the English church throughout this period can be followed in Frank Barlow's *The English Church 1000–1066*, 2nd edn. (1979) and his *The English Church 1066–1154* (1979); C. R. Cheney, *From Becket to Langton: English Church Government 1170–1213* (Manchester, 1956); and J. R. H. Moorman, *Church Life in England in the Thirteenth Century* (Cambridge, 1945). For episcopal efforts to enforce the decrees of the Fourth Lateran Council see M. Gibbs and J. Lang, *Bishops and Reform 1215–1272* (Oxford, 1934). Margaret Howell's *Regalian Right in Medieval England* (1962) gives a definitive account of the king's exploitation of ecclesiastical vacancies.

Studies of individual bishops include Emma Mason, *St Wulfstan of Worcester c.1008–1095* (Oxford, 1990); Mary G. Cheney, *Roger Bishop of Worcester 1164–79* (Oxford, 1980); C. H. Lawrence, *St Edmund of Abingdon* (Oxford, 1960); D. L. Douie, *Archbishop Pecham* (Oxford, 1952); and R. W. Southern, *Robert Grosseteste: The Growth of an English Mind in Medieval Europe*, 2nd edn. (Oxford, 1992).

For the Welsh church see Huw Pryce, *Native Law and the Church in Medieval Wales* which brings clarity to a complex subject, and also his 'Church and society in Wales, 1150–1250: an Irish perspective', in *The British Isles 1100–1500*, ed. Davies. There are studies of the Scottish church in Geoffrey Barrow's *The Kingdom of the Scots*. For the church in the time of Alexander III see the chapter by Marinell Ash in *Scotland in the Reign of Alexander III*, ed. Reid.

David Knowles, *The Monastic Order in England 940–1216*, 2nd edn. (Cambridge, 1963) and *The Religious Orders in England*, I (Cambridge, 1948) remain leisurely and humane classics. They cover Wales as well as England. Janet Burton, *Monastic and Religious Orders in Britain 1100–1300* is immensely helpful and is one of the few books to deal with the whole of Britain. It has excellent maps. Barbara Harvey's *Living and Dying in England 1100–1540: The Monastic Experience* (Oxford, 1993) is a vintage work based largely on the records of Westminster Abbey. For Westminster see also Emma Mason, *Westminster Abbey and its People c.1050–c.1216* (Woodbridge, 1996). For the friars see C. H. Lawrence, *The Friars: The Impact of the Early Mendicant Movement on Western Society* (1994), and D. L. d'Avray, *The Preaching of the Friars: Sermons diffused from Paris before 1300* (Oxford, 1985).

For women religious the starting-point is Sally P. Thompson, *Women Religious: The Founding of English Nunneries after the Norman Conquest* (Oxford, 1991). The few words I offer here on Gilbert of Sempringham do no justice to Brian Golding's great work, *Gilbert of Sempringham and the Gilbertine Order* (Oxford, 1995).

The piety of the Anglo-Norman nobility is discussed by Christopher Harper-Bill in *Anglo-Norman Studies*, 2 (1979). Nicholas Vincent, *The Holy Blood*.

King Henry III and the Westminster Blood Relic (Cambridge, 2001) is a fascinating study relevant to relics in general. For pilgrimage see Diana Webb, *Pilgrimage in Medieval England* (2000), and for an aspect of alms-giving Sally Dixon Smith, 'The image and reality of alms-giving in the great halls of Henry III', *Journal of the British Archaeological Association* (1999). For England and the crusade the chief works are Simon Lloyd, *English Society and the Crusade 1216–1307* (Oxford, 1987) and Christopher Tyerman, *England and the Crusades 1095–1588* (Chicago, 1988).

For the proliferation of records and the development of pragmatic literacy the central work is M. T. Clanchy's *From Memory to Written Record: England 1066–1307*, 2nd edn. (Oxford, 1993). See also David Bates's lecture, *Reordering the Past and Negotiating the Present in Stenton's First Century* (Reading, 1999). For Oxford University see *The History of the University of Oxford I: The Early Schools*, ed. J. I. Catto (Oxford, 1984).

15. King Edward I

Authoritative and judicious, Michael Prestwich's biography, *Edward I* (1988) covers all aspects of the reign. J. C. Parsons, *Eleanor of Castile: Queen and Society in Thirteenth-Century England* (1994) is a scholarly study which is important for queenship generally in the medieval period. J. R. Maddicott, 'Edward I and the lessons of baronial reform: local government 1258–1280', *Thirteenth Century England*, 1 (1985) is indispensable for Edward's reform of the realm. R. W. Kaeuper, *Bankers to the Crown: The Riccardi of Lucca and Edward I* (Princeton, 1973) unravels the firm's complex operations. For legal developments, see Paul Brand's original and definitive *The Origins of the English Legal Profession* (Oxford, 1992) and chapter 7 of his *The Making of the Common Law*. Henry Summerson's 'The structure of law enforcement in thirteenth-century England', *American Journal of Legal History*, 23 (1979) clarifies the whole subject, and see also his paper on the statute of Winchester in *Journal of Legal History*, 13 (1992). For the development of parliament see the chapters by J. R. Maddicott and J. H. Denton in *The English Parliament in the Middle Ages*, ed. R. G. Davies and J. H. Denton (Manchester, 1981). Paul Binski, *the Painted Chamber at Westminster* (1986) shows Edward's role in its decoration. Robert Stacey, 'Parliamentary negotiation and the expulsion of the Jews from England', *Thirteenth Century England*, 6 (1995) is crucial for the immediate circumstances of the expulsion, while Robin Mundill, *England's Jewish Solution: Experiment and Expulsion 1262–1290* (Cambridge, 1998) has the most detailed coverage of the last phase and argues that the Jews were finding a role as commodity traders. J. R. Maddicott, *The English Peasantry and the Demands of the Crown, Past and Present* supplement (1975) shows how the pressures of Edwardian government fell particularly on the peasantry.

16. Conquest and Coexistence

Beverley Smith's *Llywelyn ap Gruffudd Prince of Wales* is now the standard work. Sir Goronwy Edwards's introduction to *Littere Wallie* offers a well-known critique of Llywelyn's polices. David Stephenson, *The Governance of Gwynedd* (Cardiff, 1984) is a comprehensive coverage of its subject. For the growing claims of the prince in the area of justice see Pryce, *Native Law and the Church in Medieval Wales. Landscape and Settlement in Medieval Wales*, ed. N. Edwards (Oxford, 1997) has studies by David Longley and Neil Johnstone on the royal courts of Gwynedd. R. R. Davies's account of this period in his *Conquest and Co-existence* is compelling.

For Alexander III, the volume of essays edited by Norman Reid remains essential. The maps designed by Keith Stringer and Hector MacQueen in *Atlas of Scottish History*, ed. McNeill and MacQueen, illustrate the expansion of the Scottish kingdom. For Scottish national identity see Alexander Grant, 'Aspects of National Consciousness in medieval Scotland', in *Nations, Nationalism and Patriotism in the European Past*, ed. C. Bjørn, A. Grant and K. J. Stringer (Copenhagen, 1994) and his 'To the medieval foundations', *Scottish Historical Review*, 72 (1994). G. W. S. Barrow, *Robert Bruce and the Community of the Realm of Scotland*, 3rd edn. (Edinburgh, 1988) remains the chief work on the Scottish wars of independence. For discussion related to the concluding section of the chapter see R. R. Davies, *Domination and Conquest: The Experience of Ireland, Scotland and Wales 1100–1300* (Cambridge, 1990) and Keith Stringer, 'Scottish foundations: thirteenth-century perspectives', chapter 6 of *Uniting the Kingdom: The Making of British History*, ed. A. Grant and K. J. Stringer (1995).

Index

The majority of the items in the subject part of the index are grouped under England, Scotland and Wales in the following rough thematic sequence: economy, church, society, kingship and princedom, government, armies and military service.